PARAMETRIC AND
FEATURE-BASED CAD/CAM

PARAMETRIC AND FEATURE-BASED CAD/CAM

Concepts, Techniques, and Applications

Jami J. Shah

Department of Mechanical and Aerospace Engineering
Arizona State University, Tempe

Martti Mäntylä

Laboratory of Information Processing Science
Helsinki University of Technology, Espoo, Finland

A Wiley-Interscience Publication

JOHN WILEY & SONS, INC.

New York / Chichester / Brisbane / Toronto / Singapore

Library of Congress Cataloging-in-Publication Data
Shah, Jami J.
  Parametric and feature-based CAD/CAM : concepts, techniques, and
applications / Jami J. Shah, Martti Mäntylä.
    p.   cm.
  Includes index.
   ISBN 0-471-00214-3
   1. CAD/CAM systems.   I. Mäntylä, Martti, 1955-   . II. Title.
TS 155.6.S49   1995
670'.285—dc20   95-5673

10 9 8 7 6 5 4 3 2

Dedicated to Jami's parents Nasim and Maqsood Shah

and

to Martti's family Ritva, Teemu, Tiina, and Lauri Mäntylä

PREFACE

In the early part of this century, long before the advent of computers, it is re-ported* that Uffa Fox, a great designer of sailboats described a fantasy drawing board which he could use to design. The magic drawing board could understand what he wanted to do. By pressing buttons on this magic board, he could move lines around, and all other lines were adjusted automatically. Details were filled in and changes were propagated to the entire drawing effortlessly, always main-taining the integrity of the drawing.

Designers have long dreamed about such an intelligent device for producing their designs. It is now possible to go a long way toward realizing this dream with *parametric and feature-based CAD/CAM*. The initial design can be described with minimal input in terms of meaningful engineering concepts. Design changes can be made with just a few high level commands; the details are worked out by the system. Changes automatically propagate through the model, and all affected regions are changed so as to maintain predefined constraints and design rules. The benefits extend beyond design to engineering analysis, manufacturing, and inspection, which can all be automated and integrated with design to a higher degree than possible earlier.

Although research in features technology has been conducted for more than 15 years, features have only recently become available in commercial CAD/ CAM systems. Today designers in manufacturing companies across the globe need to find out what this technology can do for them. Engineering students must be educated about the characteristics and possibilities of features. CAD/ CAM vendors, engineering software developers, and researchers all need infor-mation on the range of techniques available in this area. At present, they must all search through hundreds of research papers and theses to locate comprehensive information on features.

The objective of this book is to make it easier to find, understand, and use the state-of-the-art techniques in parametric and feature-based CAD/CAM. There-

---

* In M. J. French, "Invention and Evolution," Cambridge University Press, 1988.

fore we provide comprehensive coverage of all topics related to features, from fundamental concepts to applications. Included are many specific techniques, algorithms, data structures, and even program code that implementers will find useful. The basic principles of conventional CAD/CAM are also reviewed; this includes curve, surface, and solid modeling.

This book is intended for an audience ranging from students and practicing engineers to system developers and researchers. Graduate students in mechanical and industrial engineering and also computer science can learn about basic feature concepts and techniques. Software developers will learn about various techniques required for designing and implementing feature based systems. Practicing engineers in companies will see how to evaluate feature based CAD/CAM applications with respect to feasibility of implementation and expected benefits, and how to begin the process of feature identification and formalization for their products and applications. Researchers in the field will discover the frontiers of this new and developing technology.

The book may be considered for use as a text for an intermediate level CAD class in engineering or computer science. For this use, review questions are presented at the end of every chapter. There is probably more material than what is possible to cover in one semester because the book is designed to be comprehensive. The students will find the book to be a useful future reference for topics not covered in the classroom.

To serve the different objectives of this book, we have organized the material into five parts, as follows:

I—Background	Puts feature modeling in the broader context of product modeling, reviews geometric modeling principles and the evolution of feature modeling techniques.
II—Fundamentals	Discusses the conceptual development of features as modeling entities, their properties, and relationship to other modeling entities. Classifies and overviews feature definition techniques.
III—Feature-Based Applications	Illustrates the use of features for a variety of applications in design and manufacturing. Presents systematic methods for identification, formalization, and validation of features in various domains. Also discusses issues related to viewpoint dependence of features and product data communication between different domains. Gives an overview of the current status of feature data exchange models contained in the ISO STEP standard. Directed at engineering managers and end users.
IV—Design and Implementation	Provides a systematic exposition of major architectural issues in specifying, designing, and implementing feature based systems. Describes a wide range of data structures and algorithms from which feature-based modeling systems

may be synthesized to fit a variety of functional requirements. Places special emphasis on applying features to process planning of machining operations. Directed at programmers and system designers.

V- Beyond Features Discusses the future development of product modeling methods beyond features.

The book deals with advanced topics in CAD/CAM. Readers are assumed to be familiar with computer programming, data structures, and computer graphics fundamentals. Previous knowledge of geometric modeling is helpful but not essential. We have included a background chapter on geometric modeling for those who may not have that knowledge. Those who only have a casual interest should read Chapter 1, Section 2.5, and Chapters 3 to 7. While every effort has been made to assure accuracy, the authors make no warranty, including suitability or fitness of products or systems derived from the use of concepts, algorithms, or code contained in this book.

Many people have helped us write, review, and improve this book. A very special thanks to my (Jami Shah's) longtime colleague, Mary Rogers, who provided valuable material and invaluable advice for the book. Thanks also to many of our graduate students, past and present, whose theses and dissertations at HUT and ASU provided fertile grounds for acquiring some of the techniques discussed here. We specially acknowledge the contributions of Timo Laakko, Mervi Ranta, Jussi Opas, Jukka Nieminen, Jukka Puhakka, Jukka Tuomi, Palat Sreevalsan, Viren Pherwani, Govind Balakrishnan, Darryl Syms, Yan Shen, David Hsiao, David Miller, Ahsan Ali, Anant Bhatnagar, Arvind Shirur, and Nadeem Khan.

We would also like to thank all the authors and publishers who granted us permission to include their material in our book. These contributions are acknowledged individually where the material appears in the book.

Jami Shah
Tempe

Martti Mäntylä
Espoo

July 1995

CONTENTS

PART II   FUNDAMENTALS

3   Feature Concepts

PART IV   DESIGN AND IMPLEMENTATION   257

8   Design-by-Features Techniques   259

PART V BEYOND FEATURES 545

12 Future CAD/CAM Technologies 547

BACKGROUND

Chapter 1 outlines the motivation, origin, and historical development of geometric and feature based CAD/CAM (computer-aided design and manufacturing) systems. Feature modelers are vital tools for realizing "agile manufacturing," where design and manufacturing activities are closely integrated to ensure rapid product realization. In particular, features can enhance the product model by enabling clustering of geometric entities and their attributes, which can be associated with engineering knowledge used in various applications. This has the potential for improving the design environment and enabling automation of various engineering tasks.

Conventional CAD/CAM systems are essentially surface or solid geometric modelers that do not support features. To understand feature-based CAD/CAM, one must first be familiar with the principles of curve, surface, and solid modeling schemes. Therefore Chapter 2 introduces various geometric modeling techniques such as computational geometry and solid modeling.

1

INTRODUCTION

Feature-based methods have emerged in response to vital industry needs in design and manufacturing, particularly the need to reduce product development time. This chapter discusses features in the larger context of product modeling and agile manufacturing, and outlines the historical development of CAD/CAM and features.

1.1 AGILE MANUFACTURING

The introduction of computer-controlled machine tools some 40 years ago created the need for a computer representation of the underlying product design and manufacturing information employed by companies. The introduction of later generations of advanced production technologies, such as DNC machines, flexible manufacturing systems (FMS), robots, automated warehouses, and part transport systems each increased the need for complete and accurate product information.

At the same time, social and economical changes in our societies and in international business have significantly changed the way in which production technologies are being used. Instead of the previously dominant functionally organized factories operating in nearly total insulation of the market situation, manufacturing systems have become more product oriented, aiming at decreased lead times, minimal work-in-process, just-in-time flow of material, and high efficiency and flexibility of manufacturing capacity utilization. The term *agile manufacturing* encompasses all these characteristics.

To implement agile manufacturing, product design and production engineering functions must become closely integrated with manufacturing, and all bottlenecks in the flow of product and engineering information from these functions to the manufacturing function must be eliminated. The close integration between design, planning, and manufacturing functions requires that sufficiently complete and accurate information of all aspects of products, production processes, and operations is available. Hence future design and planning systems will be closely aligned with manufacturing technology, and future manufacturing systems will need more complete and accurate product information than what is currently possible. Ideally this integration should lead to *concurrent life-cycle engineering*, where all design, manufacturing, maintenance, and eventual dismantling and reuse issues of the product can be considered simultaneously during its design.

For many companies, another sequence of functions that must become more closely integrated are those related to the *order delivery process*, the logistical chain consisting of mapping customer requirements to a product specification, engineering the required product configuration, sequencing production steps, and delivering the finished product to the customer. Again product and manufacturing information must be available in a useful form at all stages of the order delivery process to ensure rapid lead times and high quality. Effective *reuse* of existing engineering and manufacturing solutions is vital for achieving these goals.

The need for integration goes beyond the boundaries of a single company; there is an increase in companies working in cooperation and partnerships with other companies, vendors, and subcontractors creating what is commonly termed a *virtual enterprise*. Smooth operation of virtual enterprises will require accurate exchange of product and process information. Together with the characteristics of agile manufacturing, virtual enterprises form the basis of what several experts believe will be the next dominant manufacturing paradigm from year 2000 and beyond.

1.2 PRODUCT MODELS

At first glance the close integration between design, planning, and manufacturing functions conflicts with the objective of maintaining a healthy independence between the design of a product and the details of its manufacturing. A separation of concern is still important, since some products will live longer than the technology that is used for their realization. The independence of design and manufacturing provides additional degrees of freedom for manufacturing experts when they select optimal processes for a designed product. A product designer, who may not be knowledgeable about the possibilities and limitations of manufacturing technology should not unnecessarily diminish the manufacturing engineer's freedom of choice of the most appropriate approach for making the product. The separation of concern also supports the continual development of the manufacturing methods and practices of a company by leaving the door open for improving the manufacture of the product.

The logical solution to the dilemma between integration and separation of concern is to use sufficiently high-level *product models* to communicate design information of a product to production planning and manufacturing. While recording accurately and completely all essential properties of the product as created by the designer, a product model should not specify such details that are insignificant for the function of the product. That is, the principle of *least commitment* should be followed.

A product model, as vital as it is, is just one of the information resources needed to fully realize integrated operation of a manufacturing company. Indeed, we speculate that software systems for design, production engineering, and manufacturing in the future production paradigm will be based on four types of related models:

1. *Generic product knowledge*, that can record generic information of products and form a repository of basic engineering and performance information. The knowledge should be systematized—dependable, available, understandable, and verifiable.

2. *Product models*, that can represent all relevant aspects of a specific product to be manufactured while avoiding the harmful over specification of irrelevant details. In particular, it must be possible to represent incomplete or vague models when appropriate.

3. *Generic process models*, that can record the generic characteristics of manufacturing processes in a systematized form, including the resource needs, capability, cost, lead time, and capacity of the process. More generally, the full range of activities in the customer order delivery process should be covered in process models.

4. *Factory models,* that record a collection of particular instances of particular processes that constitute a particular factory. A factory model also represents the dynamic state of the manufacturing system. Similar to the above item, the full chain of processes constituting a complete customer order delivery process may be required in the model.

Among these models, the product model is assumed to be created in a process that includes product design and production engineering in an integrated form. The separation of the generic and specific models aims at achieving the separation of responsibilities between design, production planning, and manufacturing. The generic models will act as knowledge bases that will store relatively static information. This knowledge is used indirectly by means of the specific models that instantiate the entities stored in the generic models.

Figure 1.1 shows how these models might be used with some major software systems. As manufacturing systems become more complex and dynamic, the formal modeling and simulation of manufacturing systems (shown in the top block) will become a central component of engineering information systems. To maintain the independence between design and manufacturing without sacrificing efficiency and flexibility, design and production engineering functions (shown in the left block) are restructured as a sequence of phases where the design becomes increasingly bound with a particular factory represented in a factory model.

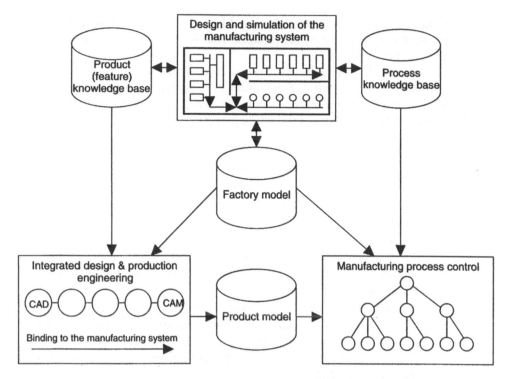

Figure 1.1 Hypothetical architecture of future engineering software systems (Mäntylä 1989)

Finally, the manufacturing-oriented product model is used as the source of information for the control of the manufacturing system (the right block). In the future several tasks currently in the domain of production engineering will be downloaded into the control of the actual manufacturing system.

1.3 PRODUCT MODELS IN DESIGN

To fully appreciate the issues relating to product models, let us briefly discuss the requirements placed by product design on product models. Design tasks undertaken in mechanical design vary widely, both in abstraction level and the type of information used (Dixon 1988). Therefore, it is unrealistic to expect any single kind of product model to fully satisfy the needs of all types of design activities. To illustrate this point, let us consider a few common types of designs:

- System/configuration design
- Assembly design
- Part geometry design

In system design one first synthesizes the system from components considering only function and input/output parameters that influence the system as a whole. What is going on inside each component is usually not a concern. Power, motion, flow, and force are usually the interaction variables considered. Components may be electro-mechanical, hydraulic, pneumatic, thermal, or mechanical. It is quite common to consider the values and variations of the above variables at only the interface between components when working at the system level. An essential element of system design is the selection and placement of components. This is preceded by the breaking up of the overall function into sub functions and finding components or subsystems that will accomplish the task. The configuration of the system is not fixed; one synthesizes the system by selecting, excluding, or modifying components iteratively.

There are three types of assembly design; the design process for each is different. First, there are *static assemblies* which, as the name indicates, do not contain parts that move relative to each other. For example, a heat exchanger, which involves welded structures and mechanically joined parts (bolted, riveted, screwed) is a static assembly. A second type of assembly is one that involves relative motion between constituent parts. The kinematics may be simple such as a shaft turning in a sleeve, the motion of a piston in an actuator, or an impeller in a pump. Such assemblies are called *dynamic assemblies*. When the kinematics is complex as with epicyclical gear trains, open or closed linkages, the kinematic synthesis problem must be solved first. In either case kinematic diagrams must be mapped into appropriate machine elements and the connections (joints) must also be "fleshed." Kinematic assemblies are hierarchical in that they can be decomposed successively into smaller assemblies containing fewer and fewer elements. They have certain degrees of freedom of motion; activating these degrees of freedom means changing the relative position and orientation of some elements or subassemblies to each other. Another important aspect is the space occupied by an element at a given time that cannot interfere with space for other elements at the same time.

In some cases it may be possible to decouple part design from assembly or system design. This is usually true in mechanism design where kinematicians reason in terms of "rigid links," "joints," "pitch circles," for example. At subsequent stages one must make sure that the links and other parts are structurally sound without violating any of the conditions from assembly or mechanism design. In such instances part design may be considered as the act of adding detail to the design. In cases where part and assembly design cannot be decoupled, one needs to be able to iterate between the two. Part design involves engineering analysis of various kinds, parametric studies, optimization, material selection, determination of shape, size, and tolerances allocation. At the part design level one works with the actual geometry, instead of abstract representations as in assembly, mechanism, or system design. All the details of the geometry may not be available (or important) at the early stages. Form and dimensions are partly fixed by earlier decisions at the system level and are partly determined from engineering analysis to meet some design objectives (minimum weight, etc.). Often one must select a standard part available off-the-shelf. In such cases, part design and analysis determines which standard part (type, size, etc.) comes nearest the performance required.

To address the requirements of different types of design tasks, many kinds of design software systems are available, or under development, based on a variety of product modeling methods such as solid models, surface models, feature models, parametric models, variational models, or knowledge-based expert system tools. Because design encompasses such a vast domain, no single type of design tool, environment, or product model can be expected to satisfy all needs. Many design systems put emphasis on detail design, and provide little support for the earlier stages. For example, solid modelers are useful when design involves geometric arrangement or layout of geometric objects, such as in electronic packaging and in certain kinds of assembly design. Unfortunately, solid modelers are of little use in system design.

1.4 FEATURE MODELS

In their full generality the various models of products and processes outlined above are topics for intensive research, and they are likely to remain so for many years. This book deals with a particular software technology for realizing advanced product models, an approach known as *feature modeling*. Unlike many other product modeling approaches currently investigated in academe, feature models are already in industrial use and their present applications provide the way for more general future product models.

By *features* we mean the generic shapes or characteristics of a product with which engineers can associate certain attributes and knowledge useful for reasoning about that product. Features encapsulate the engineering significance of portions of the product geometry and, as such, are applicable in product design, product definition, and reasoning about the product in a variety of applications such as manufacturing planning. In particular, features address the requirements of all four types of product and process models outlined in the previous section:

1. *Generic product knowledge.* Recurring characteristics of products can be modeled as *feature types* or *classes*, and used as a repository of reusable product knowledge that may be related to a particular shape or geometric pattern.

2. *Product models.* Specific products can be modeled through their constituent features, providing a more natural basis of interaction with the designer than mere geometric models. Generic knowledge may be accessed through the features recorded in the resulting product model.

3. *Generic process models.* Manufacturing knowledge can be associated with features, and accessed to determine the producibility of a designed object

or for planning its actual manufacture. More generally, information of the various steps of an order delivery process may be modeled for scheduling and sequencing.

4. *Factory models.* The capabilities of factories can be recorded on the basis of processes, which in turn are related to features. Features provide a natural separation between design and manufacturing domains.

These four important aspects of feature models will be discussed more fully in subsequent chapters. As we will see, feature-based computer-aided design (CAD) and manufacturing (CAM) systems have already demonstrated clear potential in creating attractive design environments and in facilitating geometric reasoning related to design function, performance evaluation, manufacturing process planning, NC programming, and other engineering tasks. Therefore, features are widely regarded as a key enabling technology for the implementation of concurrent engineering and CAD/CAM integration.

1.5 FEATURES AND GEOMETRY

Early versions of CAD/CAM systems were based on ordinary geometric modeling techniques. These techniques have found important use in documenting complete designs, geometric arrangement design and visualization, and as a front end to various engineering analysis tools such as the finite element method (FEM). Unfortunately, at the same time, geometric modeling techniques, including solid models, have proved deficient for many other design tasks as well as for many manufacturing applications such as process planning, group technology classification, coordinate measuring machine (CMM) path planning, and assembly planning.

There are three major reasons for the lack of utility and effectiveness of geometry-based CAD systems in the actual development of designs:

1. *The geometric construction methods provided are too low level for actual design.* Many design tasks are not related to geometry at all, but to other characteristics of the product. Some others can be based on idealized geometry that may still be radically changed. Instead of geometry, designers need to concentrate on the desired function and behavior of their design.

2. *Design changes are time-consuming* because the low-level model does not preserve the design intent of the designer. The resulting lack of associativity between the model entities means that a single conceptual change must be mapped to a set of changes of low-level model entities; changes in one entity cannot be automatically propagated through the model to other related entities because of lack of information.

3. *The database representing a finished design produced by traditional CAD systems does not contain all the information needed by downstream appli-*

cations, such as process planning, assembly planning, and inspection planning. In general, the reasoning used in such applications is based on part features, which are not available in a geometric model. Much of the initial work on features was motivated by a desire to devise methods to extract part information from geometric modelers in a form from which process plans, GT codes, and NC programs can be generated.

Clearly, a major advantage of features is that they can *provide an additional layer of information in advanced CAD systems to make them more useful for design and to integrate design with downstream applications.*

Conventional CAD/CAM systems are also lacking in other important functionalities. For instance, application of systematic quality management principles requires that complete tracking of product information from details back to the design rationale and customer requirements be performed. A mere geometric model is inconvenient as a basis for recording such information. Because of the higher semantic level of features, they can *provide a basis for recording a more complete product definition as required for such applications as life-cycle engineering and quality management.*

1.6 COGNITIVE FOUNDATIONS

At an abstract level, we can view features as modeling entities that allow commonly used shapes to be characterized and associated with a set of attributes relevant to an application. In this sense, features may be thought of as information clusters or "chunks."

"Chunking" is a natural way of storing and using knowledge. Human beings organize knowledge of other people, events, actions, and surroundings into connected structures. Cognitive psychologists believe that knowledge is clustered into "packets" in human reasoning, language, perception, and memory (Bartlett 1961; Kuhn 1970; Minsky 1981). These packets have factual and procedural contents that explain the apparent speed and power of mental activities. Packets allow knowledge to be organized, placed in a context, stored in memory, and retrieved rapidly. Once the mind finds the relevant packet, all relevant attributes and relationships become readily accessible (Sanford 1985).

It is believed that we reason by analogy, that we match stereotyped models to the situation at hand so that we may draw conclusions about that situation (*pattern matching*). Nowhere is it more evident than in human communications when we speak in compact elliptic form, making the assumption that the listener knows the various objects or actions, alluded to. For example, when the speaker uses the word "book," it is assumed that the listener knows what books generally look like, what they are for, that they have covers and pages, a title, authors, and text, pictures, and so on. The stereotypical "book" is a chunk, with certain general characteristics. Such chunks are likely to be central structures in our cognition.

We can think of the entities of a solid geometric model as providing a micro view of the characteristics of a part; these characteristics are localized and un-connected to the part's overall function and behavior. Features, on the other hand, provide a high level, or macro view. They may be thought of as packets of related facts and characteristics of a part. These facts and characteristics may be able to answer questions such as the following:

What does it look like?
Why is it there?
How big is it?
Where is it in relation to other features of the part?
How can it be incorporated into the part?
What will happen if it is moved or removed?

It follows that if a CAD system has knowledge structures similar to those presumably used in human cognition, it can be smarter. Designers will be able to converse with the system in shorthand because the system will know the general characteristics of features used in relevant applications (*design by features*). The system will be able to use pattern matching in its reasoning (*feature recognition*); it may be able to discover errors in design specifications (*feature validation*); it could take care of working out details when design changes are made (*change propagation*). Each of these aspects will be discussed in later chapters.

It should be noted, however, that theories based on cognitive schemata pre-sume the existence of predefined structures; there are no packets available for genuinely novel situations. Thus, too, *feature-based models must be limited within the well-bounded domain defined by available generic features.*

1.7 FEATURES IN ENGINEERING

Just as in any cognitive activity, engineers also use chunks of knowledge (fea-tures) in performing various engineering tasks. A subset of these features is those related to a part's geometry. These will be referred to as *geometric features*. The scope of this book is chiefly limited to geometric features.

There are various types of geometric features that are used in product defini-tion; some examples are the following:

- *Form features.* They describe portions of a part's nominal (or idealized) geometry
- *Tolerance features.* They describe geometry variation from the nominal form
- *Assembly features.* They describe relationships between parts in a mechani-cal assembly.

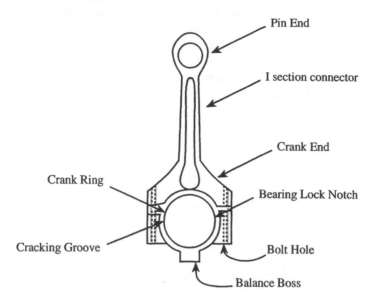

Figure 1.2 Design features of a conrod (courtesy Robert Mecoli, Ford Motor Company)

It is also common for a form feature to be classified according to the application in which it is used. For example, we commonly hear the terms design feature, manufacturing feature, inspection feature, fixturing feature, cost feature, etc., when talking about a product from a particular viewpoint. We will also adopt this usage here and in later chapters when discussing certain applications.

Let us look at the nature of features through two examples. First, consider the connecting rod shown in Figure 1.2. We can identify a number of form features on the part corresponding to various subfunctions that the part must serve. The three major design features are pin end, I-section connector, and crank end. The names of the features signify the design function. The overall shape of the part is synthesized from these features. The shape is "modified" or "detailed" with additional features shown: balance boss, used for dynamic balancing; the bearing lock notch and crank ring, for mating with the crank pin; and the cracking groove, for slicing the forging into two pieces so that the conrod can be mounted on the crankshaft. The fastening of the two halves is done by bolts, for which the bolt holes are provided. It can be seen that the designer designs with these stereotypical shapes, which facilitate encoding of knowledge structures used in the design process. It follows that they all are candidates for recurring *design features*.

Consider another artifact: a part produced by machining a casting, shown in Figure 1.3. The features shown in this case reflect the machining point of view. Machinists or process planners are not really concerned about the function of this part, nor are they concerned about surfaces of the casting that do not need to

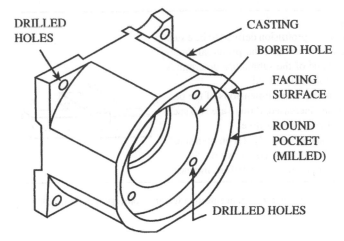

DRILLED
HOLES

CASTING

BORED HOLE

FACING
SURFACE

ROUND
POCKET
(MILLED)

DRILLED HOLES

Figure 1.3 Manufacturing features of a part produced by machining a casting

be machined. They only look at portions of the part that need to be created by machining, and the processes that are required to achieve that. So we can say that process planners look at parts in terms of shapes that can be produced by some stereotypical machining sequences—the chunks of knowledge that we call *manufacturing features.*

We can conclude from this discussion that *features are stereotypical knowledge structures embedded in cognitive processes in design, analysis, planning, and all other engineering activities,* and that *features are necessarily viewpoint and application dependent.*

1.8 FEATURE DESCRIPTION

Let us informally explore the contents of these clusters of knowledge that we call geometric features. Since features are stereotypes, they represent classes of objects, not specific objects. These classes have some properties and attributes that are useful in the reasoning process of one or more application. It therefore follows that a feature's description will be dependent on the intended application.

Figure 1.4 shows a feature that is needed in the determination of stress concentration factors. This feature description ignores attributes that are irrelevant to stress concentration. Another example is given in Figure 1.5. It shows a sheet metal feature, called a "crimp". The description contains the parametrized geometry and some geometric tolerances needed in planning the stamping operations. The design function is ignored in this description. Feature properties and attributes will be discussed in more detail in Part II.

Second Axis Protrusion

Description	Irregularity of a protrusion defined to be a step in a direction other than the principal direction. The shape of the subfeature determines the shape of the fillet blend.
Axis	Direction in which the dimensions of the parent section are increased. If there are two such directions, the axis is positive.
Number	1 if stepped on one side only, 2 if on both sides.
Major d	Total length of increased dimension.
Minor d	Dimension of parent section before increase.

Figure 1.4 Feature description example: Stress concentration feature (courtesy Ken Brown, University of Bristol)

1.9 BRIEF HISTORY OF GEOMETRIC MODELING

1.9.1 CAD/CAM Systems

The development of part modeling facilities for computer-aided design applications can be traced back into the late 1950s and early 1960s when the first CAD and CAM systems were developed. Of course CAD models are just tools intended to be used by some applications. Therefore the development of CAD models reflects the development of the underlying applications. Following (Requicha 1980), we can identify four areas that have influenced CAD modeling as we know it today:

1. *NC machines* were first introduced in the early 1950s at MIT. The existence of numerically controlled tools created a need for numerical part models that could be used to drive the NC machines.

2. Because the early NC machines were primarily used in aerospace and automobile industries, an interest in *sculptured surface modeling* was soon developed. This work culminated in the seminal works of Beziér, Coons, Gordon, and Ferguson in the first half of the 1960s. Companies such as Douglas, Lockheed, Boeing, McDonnell Aircraft, and General Motors in the United States, and Renault and Citroën in Europe, pioneered the development.

3. *Computer graphics* technology was also created in the early 1960s. Early interest was focussed on models consisting of polygonal planar surfaces. The first hidden line algorithm for such models was published in (Roberts 1963). A seminal work in modeling for computer graphics was Sutherland's Sketchpad system (Sutherland 1963). Techniques first presented in Sketchpad continue to be re-invented to date. In the application side, avail-

Crimp   Small bend configuration produced on a notch.

Applications: 1. Stiffening
Part Type: Sheet metal

Illustration   Feature Parameters

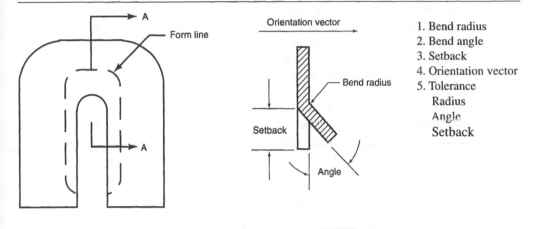

1. Bend radius
2. Bend angle
3. Setback
4. Orientation vector
5. Tolerance
   Radius
   Angle
   Setback

Figure 1.5 Feature description example: Sheet metal crimp

ability of computer graphics tools fueled the development of the first two-dimensional systems for drafting and detailing.

4. Another area where somewhat parallel development was taking place was engineering analysis based on the *finite element method* (FEM). Apart from the actual analysis code, application of FEM requires programs called pre- and post-processors. The former is used for defining the geometry, generating finite element meshes, and applying boundary conditions, while the latter is used for plotting the results of the analysis in various forms. In the 1970s interactive mesh generation became available commercially. Ever since, FEM software vendors have continually improved pre- and post-processing capabilities of their systems, which were eventually integrated with geometric modelers.

The early CAD systems were directed at drafting (engineering drawing), initially providing just 2D drawing functions. During the late 1960s and early 1970s, a desire to extend the early two-dimensional CAD systems to three dimensions emerged. This turned out to be far more complex than just adding the third coordinate in drawing representations. It was deemed desirable to have a central three-dimensional model that could be used to generate all required two-dimensional projections automatically.

Using techniques already developed for hidden line and surface removal, work toward realizing *solid modeling* systems began somewhere around 1970. Two "camps" soon developed. Ian Braid and his colleagues at University of Cambridge worked on *boundary representations*, models consisting of facets that were subsets of planar, quadric, or toroidal surfaces (Braid 1979). Voelcker and Requicha at University of Rochester introduced *CSG models*, consisting of a finite number of Boolean set operations applied to half-spaces defined by algebraic inequalities (Requicha 1977). Independently Okino et al. developed another type of a half-space based system (Okino 1973). The seminal groups in Cambridge and Rochester were soon followed by numerous others, and both lines of development eventually led to commercial application in the late 1970s and early 1980s.

The main advantage of solid modeling systems is that nonsense objects cannot be created. The designer has the option to work with solid volumes instead of lower-level geometric primitives such as point, lines, and arcs. Proponents of solid modeling technology (which, at one time, included the second author of this book) expected that, once perfected, solid models would rapidly replace drafting-oriented systems in design. Unfortunately, this turned out not to be the case: Even today most CAD applications are based on two-dimensional drafting. Instead of design development, solid modeling systems have found use in design documentation, packaging studies, robotics, and geometry definition for FE meshing and NC programming. We will return to the reasons for the failure of solid models for design in Chapter 3; the reader is also referred to the excellent analysis in (Liker 1992).

Over the years, the four original fields that contributed to the early progress of CAD models continued to influence the further development of CAD systems. During the 1980s, research addressed the problem of introducing sculptured surface facilities in boundary representation models, with the result that surface and solid modeling systems have by now been quite successfully merged. More lately, *implicitization techniques* have been introduced that may eventually make it practical to merge sculptured surfaces also in CSG models. Another significant development is the introduction of *nonuniform rational B-splines* (NURBS) to homogenize the various curve and surface representations used in CAD systems.

Computer graphics, notably modeling techniques for various phenomena involving non-rigid solids or non-solid objects (clouds, fluids, elastic objects, etc.), has continually provided ideas and methodologies that have eventually been applied also in CAD models. One example is *physics-based modeling* originally introduced for computer animation. Several recent studies have applied physics-based models in CAD, such as for design of sheet metal objects or for FEM mesh generation. *Volume-based models* originally introduced for visualization of medical data (e.g., CT scans) give another example of computer graphics work which has influenced CAD models.

1.9.2 Feature-Based Systems

The initial motivation for using features seems to have emerged from a desire to integrate computer-aided process planning (CAPP) with computer-aided design (CAD). Research on techniques for providing data on manufacturing features for NC programming dates back to the mid-1970s. Several researchers at Cambridge University's CAD Center worked on automatic feature recognition from 1975 to 1980. Grayer, in his Ph.D. dissertation in 1976, presented methods for automating NC programming for milling (Grayer 1976). Grayer's sectioning technique was applied to 2½ D milling, but it did not actually recognize features. Kyprianou appears to have been the first to introduce the idea of feature recognition by discovering topological and geometric patterns in CAD databases and comparing them to the characterizing features that needed to be found. The key idea was topological entity classification based on geometry (Kyprianou 1980). Almost all subsequent methods for feature recognition have used this idea in some form.

Independent of the work at Cambridge, Woo at Illinois developed the convex hull decomposition algorithm in 1980 (Woo 1982). His method was also directed at finding volumes to be removed by machining, without recognizing the features. Other significant early contributions to feature recognition were Choi and Barash's syntactic recognition (Choi 1984), Henderson's rule-based recognition (Henderson 1984), and CAM-I's volume decomposition algorithm (General Dynamics 1985). In the following years feature recognition appeared to be dividing into two camps: those investigating boundary-based methods and those looking at volume based methods. Attributed face adjacency graphs became the underlying structure for the former method, originally proposed by Ansaldi, De Floriani, and Falcidieno (Ansaldi 1985), and further developments by Joshi and Chang (Joshi 1988). Problems related to "entity growing" in feature extraction have been investigated by Sakurai and Gossard (Sakurai 1988) and Dong and Wozny (Dong 1988). Recognition from CSG models was investigated by Lee (Lee 1987). Subsequently research in feature recognition intensified considerably; we cannot cite them all here, but we plan to discuss all significant contributions in Chapter 9.

Around 1984 both the Process Planning and the Geometric Modeling Programs of CAM-I became interested in features. As a result of CAM-I sponsored projects, John Deere Company produced an elaborate report on feature taxonomies and feature parameters useful in manufacturing. In another CAM-I project, the concept of *design by features* was first proposed by Pratt and Wilson (Pratt 1987). Prototype feature-based modeling systems began appearing in the mid-1980s, mostly in university research labs. Among them were Miner and Gossard's system at MIT (Miner 1985), Dixon et al.'s system at University of Massachusetts (Cunningham 1988), Cutkosky's FIRST-CUT at Stanford (Cutkosky 1988), Turner and Anderson's QTC at Purdue (Turner 1988), Mäntylä et al.'s HUTCAPP at Helsinki University of Technology, Finland (Mäntylä et al. 1989), and Shah et al.'s ASU Features Testbed (Shah 1988).

Commercial implementations of feature-based modeling became available in the late 1980s. Some of the early ones were PRO-ENGINEER from Parametric Technologies and CIMPLEX from Cimplex Inc. (formerly owned by ATP). In the early 1990s we are seeing most major CAD vendors adopting feature-based modeling. SDRC, Unigraphics, Aries, Computervision, and Dassault have all released feature-based CAD systems. Many other CAD vendor companies are in the process of jumping on the bandwagon.

1.10 OUTLINE OF THE BOOK

To understand features, one must understand geometric modeling. For this reason, we review in the Chapter 2 the principal ideas of geometric modeling to conclude Part I.

In Part II we will establish the concept of features in more formal terms than what was presented here. Features need to be described by a set of properties and attributes. The selection of these generic properties and attributes is of critical importance. Once described, features may be classified into families to take advantage of common characteristics. When features are incorporated into a geometric model, the validity of the consequences needs to be checked. All these topics are discussed in Chapter 3.

Feature models can be built interactively, using a CAD system, or by automatic feature recognition from CAD databases. Some feature-based CAD systems are now also available for designing directly with features. The three methods for feature creation, mentioned above, are known respectively as *interactive feature definition, automatic feature recognition*, and *design by features*. Each of these methods has distinct advantages and disadvantages; sometimes it may be necessary to use them simultaneously to complement each other. Feature creation methods are surveyed in Chapter 4.

Feature-based systems (FBS) are being developed and used in a variety of applications, ranging from design and analysis to manufacturing and inspection planning. Part III of the book discusses feature-based applications in design and manufacturing from the user's perspective. The most time-consuming and strategically important step in the use of features is the identification and formalization of features in application domains of interest. A systematic methodology for feature identification will be presented in Chapter 5. The actual application of the identified features in mechanical design involves determining the nominal geometry of individual parts, their tolerance specification, and the relationships and constraints imposed by assembling the parts. The role of features in part design, variant design, assembly design, and tolerance specification is discussed in Chapter 5.

Chapter 6 focuses on applications of features in manufacturing, such as process planning, assembly planning, inspection planning, and design-for-manufacturing (DFM). Application of the feature identification methodology of Chapter 5 for identifying manufacturing features is discussed. Special issues related to representing manufacturing knowledge through features are also considered.

Since features are viewpoint dependent, it is necessary to transform them from one viewpoint to another to support concurrent engineering and information sharing. Although feature transformations can be classified into a number of generic classes, there are no general purpose mechanisms available for performing these transformations. Therefore feature mapping continues to be under investigation in the research community, and we discuss the major issues of the work in Chapter 7.

To support applications extending the boundaries of single CAD systems and companies, feature data exchange needs to be standardized. The Product Data Exchange Specification (PDES) was initiated in the United States and was later unified with the ISO effort STEP (Standard for Exchange of Product Data), at which stage PDES began to stand for "Product Data Exchange using STEP," The PDES/STEP schema contains many topical models that jointly define the geometry of a part. Chapter 7 will also give an overview of the portions of STEP that impact feature data exchange.

In Part IV of this book we will look at the design and implementation of feature-based systems from the system developer's perspective. Chapter 8 presents alternative approaches for design by feature (DBF) systems and compares their advantages and shortcomings. The chapter also investigates a number of algorithmic techniques useful for implementing a design by features system. Similarly Chapter 9 gives details of alternative methods used for feature recognition and compares them.

In Chapter 10 we present a number of "tools" on the basis of which the reader could build significant portions of a feature-based system. These include feature representation, geometry construction, constraint representation, and feature recognition. Because one of the most successful application areas of features has been in machining process planning, we have devoted Chapter 11 entirely to this subject. Finally, Chapter 12 will look at some of the most important development trends in product modeling that go beyond features.

The appendixes provide background material on mathematical preliminaries useful for feature modeling, such as set theory, graphs, and geometric transformations, and on solid modeling data structures.

REVIEW QUESTIONS

1.1 Describe how increased level of automation in manufacturing systems should be reflected in product definitions.

1.2 Study Figure 1.1. Describe the possible role of the various components of the architecture in various processes of an industrial company, such as

- new product development (innovative design)
- customized product design on the basis of existing modules (configuration design)
- design quality improvement
- process planning
- production management
- manufacturing process development
- quality management.

1.3   For each of the types of design problems outlined in Section 1.3, develop a list of functional requirements that a CAD system must support to be an effective tool for the designer. Also specify the relative importance of each requirement (essential, desirable, secondary). Now evaluate the CAD systems you are familiar with against these requirements.

1.4   Study a sample product you know well. Can you identify potential design features in it? Manufacturing features?

1.5   Try to write feature descriptions in the style of Figures 1.4 and 1.5 for the features identified in Question 1.4.

BIBLIOGRAPHY

Ansaldi, S., De Floriani, L., and Falcidieno, B., 1985, Geometric modeling of solid objects by using a face adjacency graph representation, Proc. of Siggraph '85, *Comp. Gr.* **19**(3):131–139.

Bartlett, F., 1961, *Remembering: A Study in Experimental and Social Psychology*, Cambridge University Press.

Braid, I. C., 1979, Notes on a geometric modeller, Computer Laboratory, University of Cambridge, CAD Group Document 101.

Choi, B. K., Barash, M. M., and Anderson, D. C., 1984, Automatic recognition of machined surfaces from a 3D solid model, *Computer-Aided Design* **16** (2): 81–86.

Cunningham, J., and Dixon, J. R., 1988, Designing with features: The origin of features, *ASME Computers in Engineering Conf.*, San Francisco, July 31–August 4, ASME Press, pp. 237–243.

Cutkosky, M., Tenenbaum, J. M., and Muller, D., 1988, Features in process based design, *ASME Computers in Engineering Conf.*, San Francisco, July 31–August 4, ASME Press, pp. 557–562.

Dixon, J. R., Duffey, R., Irani, R., Meunier, K., and Orelup, M., 1988, A proposed taxonomy of mechanical design problems, *ASME Computers in Engineering Conf.*, San Francisco, July 31–August 4, ASME Press.

Dong, X., and M. Wozny, 1988, FRAFES, A frame-based feature extraction system, *Proc. of Int. Conf. on Computer Integrated Manufacturing*, Rensselaer Polytechnic Institute, May 23–25, pp. 296–305.

General Dynamics Corporation, 1985, Volume decomposition algorithm—Final report, Technical Report R-82-ANC-01, CAM-I, Inc., Arlington, TX.

Grayer, A. R., 1976, A computer link between design and manufacture, Ph.D. dissertation, University of Cambridge.

Henderson, M. R., 1984, Extraction of feature information from three dimensional CAD data, Ph.D. dissertation, Purdue University.

Joshi, S., and Chang, T.-C. 1988, Graph-based heuristics for recognition of machined features from a 3-D solid model, *Computer-Aided Design* **20** (2): 58–66.

Kuhn, T., 1970, *The Structure of Scientific Revolutions*, 2nd ed., University of Chicago Press.

Kyprianou, L., 1980, Shape classification in computer aided design, Ph.D. dissertation, University of Cambridge.

Lee, Y. C., and Fu, K. S., 1987, Machine understanding of CSG: Extraction and unification of manufacturing features, *IEEE Comp. Gr. & Appl.* **7** (1): 20–32.

Liker, J. K., Fleischer, M., and Arnsdorf, D., 1992, Fulfilling the promises of CAD, *Sloan Manag. Rev.*, (Spring): 74–86.

Mäntylä, M., Opas, J., and Puhakka, J., 1989, Generative process planning of prismatic parts by feature relaxation, in B. Ravani, ed., *Proc. of 15th ASME Design Automation Conf.*, Montreal, September 17–21, ASME Press, pp. 49–60.

Miner, R. H., 1985, A method for the representation and manipulation of geometric features in a solid model, M.S. thesis, Mechanical Engineering Department, MIT.

Minsky, M., 1981, A framework for representing knowledge, in J. Haugeland, ed., *Mind Design*, MIT Press.

Okino, N., Kakazu, Y., and Kubo, H., 1973, TIPS-1: Technical information processing system for computer-aided design, drawing and manufacturing, in J. Hatvany, ed., *Computer Languages for Numerical Control*, North-Holland, pp. 141–150.

Pratt, M. J., and Wilson, P. R., 1987, Conceptual design of a feature-oriented solid modeler, Draft Document 3B, General Electric Corporate R&D.

Requicha, A. A. G., 1980, Representations of solid objects—Theory, methods, and systems, *ACM Computing Surveys* **12** (4): 437–464.

Requicha, A. A. G., and Voelcker, H. B., 1977, Constructive solid geometry, Tech. Memo. No. 25, Production Automation Project, University of Rochester.

Roberts, L. G., 1963, Machine perception of three-dimensional solids, Technical Report No. 315, Lincoln Laboratory, MIT.

Sakurai, H., and Gossard, D. C., 1988, Shape feature recognition from 3D solid models, *ASME Computers in Engineering Conf.*, San Francisco, July 31–August 4, 1988, ASME Press, pp. 515–519.

Sanford, A., 1985, *Cognition & Cognitive Psychology*, Basic Books, New York.

Shah, J. J., and Rogers, M. T., 1988, Expert form feature modeling shell, *Computer-Aided Design* **20** (9): 515–524.

Sutherland, I. E., 1963, Sketchpad: A man-machine graphical communication system, *Proc. of Spring Joint Computer Conference* **23**.

Turner, G., and Anderson, D. C., 1988, An object oriented approach to interactive, feature based design for quick turnaround manufacturing, *ASME Computers in Engineering Conf.*, San Francisco, July 31–August 4, ASME Press.

Woo, T., 1982, Feature extraction by volume decomposition, *Proc. of Conf. on CAD/CAM Technology in Mechanical Engineering,* MIT, Cambridge, MA, pp. 76–94.

2

GEOMETRIC MODELING

As we saw in the previous chapter, feature models were originally introduced as extensions of ordinary geometric models used in CAD, or more specifically, solid models. Nearly all feature modelers operate in more or less close association with a geometric modeler. Therefore the design of the interface with a geometric modeler is one of the major issues in the development of a feature-based system. To introduce features, we will first have to discuss geometric modeling technology to some depth.

We start by looking at the role of geometry in design and manufacturing and the consequent goals of geometric modeling. Then we review briefly *graphical models* used in computer-aided design and drafting (CADD) systems, and also *curve* and *surface models* used in computer-aided geometric design (CAGD) systems. This is followed by a more detailed discussion on solid modeling methods. Our somewhat disproportional emphasis on solid models is justifiable because nearly all feature-based systems are based on solid modeling techniques, and many algorithms for manipulating features are extensions of similar algorithms for solid models. We will also take a brief look at parametric and variational modeling techniques applied in geometric modeling; these techniques will be discussed further in connection with feature models later in this book.

2.1 GOALS OF GEOMETRIC MODELING

Shape and geometry have always played a special role in the creation of artifacts. However the need for an accurate record of the geometry of a product was greatly intensified by the advent of modern industrial mass production in the late nineteenth and early twentieth century. One of the key concepts introduced then was *interchangability of parts,* which required systematic attention to the geometry and tolerances of the individual components to ensure that any components intended to work together indeed can be assembled successfully. To record the needed geometric information, the various systematic geometry presentation methods and conventions that constitute engineering drafting methods were developed. Eventually these became the *lingua franca* of engineering: Every new generation of engineers was educated to communicate design and manufacturing information in terms of engineering drawings, and these drawing conventions ensured that drawings were produced and interpreted in a uniform and consistent manner.

As already noted in Chapter 1, the desire to represent and process product geometry information on a computer arose originally from several sources. To facilitate NC machining of complex surfaces needed for tool making in automobile and aircraft industries, methods for the representation of "sculptured surfaces" were developed starting in the early 1960s. To facilitate creation of drawings with the newly available computer graphics technologies, two-dimensional drafting systems were similarly and simultaneously developed. Later many other computer applications in various branches of engineering emerged, each posing additional requirements on geometry representations.

The recognition of geometric modeling as a worthwhile area of its own is deeply rooted in the special position that geometry has always had in engineering. It was a consequence of the desire to link the various applications in design, analysis, and manufacturing that utilize geometric information. Based on this view, we may characterize the objectives of geometric modeling as follows:

Geometric modeling studies computer-based representation of geometry and related information needed for supporting various computer-based applications in engineering design, analysis, and manufacturing, and other areas with similar requirements. This involves the study of data structures, algorithms, and file formats for creating, representing, communicating, and manipulating geometric information of physical parts and processes appearing in these applications, and also related numerical and symbolic technical information. Neutral representations that can support a variety of applications are of particular interest.

A *geometric modeling system* can be similarly characterized as an *application component responsible for creating, inspecting, analyzing, and distributing geometric models*. Observe that this also includes representation of geometry that may result from some computation performed by the geometric modeler on behalf of the application, say, an interference test involving two geometric objects. Hence the design of a geometric modeler involves also the design of the various model manipulation procedures that may be needed in the applications. Naturally a user interface for defining geometry is also a vital part of the modeler, as well as a secondary storage (file, database) interface. Some major components of a geometric modeler are outlined in Figure 2.1 (Requicha 1980).

Actual approaches to geometric modeling vary in the extent to which they are intended and capable of supporting the full range of geometric computations. In particular, some types of models are only intended to aid the production of human-interpreted geometric representations, whereas others are intended to support automatic applications that can work with limited or no human guidance.

In the following sections we will look more closely at three major types of geometric models:

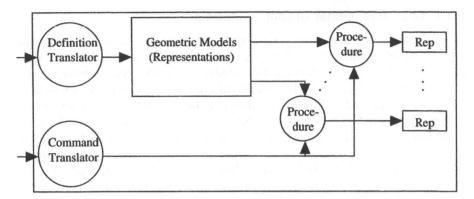

Figure 2.1 Components of a geometric modeling system (Requicha 1980)

1. *Graphical models* are mainly intended to support generation of engineering drawings and illustrations to be interpreted by humans.

2. *Surface models* are mainly intended for supporting the design and manufacture of complex sculptured surfaces. Since the techniques for representing complex curves and surfaces are closely related, we will discuss these together, even though curve representations might otherwise be better considered as graphical models.

3. *Solid models* are intended to capture "completely" the three-dimensional geometry of a solid physical object in order to support higher levels of functionality and automation than the other types of geometric models.

This list excludes some other types of related models such as *shape models* intended to represent raster images for image processing and other similar applications because they are of limited interest in CAD/CAM.

In actual CAD/CAM systems the originally distinct approaches to geometric modeling have continually converged. In fact feature models could be regarded as the most recent stage in this development, and they could be added as the fourth item in the above list. We have chosen to discuss the various approaches separately to be able to characterize their properties more clearly.

2.2 GRAPHICAL MODELS

As indicated in Chapter 1, early CAD systems were primarily drafting systems. For a long time "CAD" stood for "computer aided drafting", not "design". Even today it is debatable whether CAD, as commonly practiced, is much else than drafting, and drafting-oriented CAD systems based primarily on graphical models are still very commonly used in the industry.

2.2.1 Two-Dimensional Graphical Models

From the modeling viewpoint, drafting-type systems are based on *graphical models*, namely models consisting of *graphical primitives* such as lines, arcs, conics, text, symbols, and other notation needed to describe an engineering drawing. Each graphical primitive has *graphical attributes* that determine how it is displayed and plotted. For instance, lines may have a line thickness and a line style (solid, dashed, dash-dotted, etc.). Several graphical primitives may be combined into a *graphical symbol* that can have its own attributes such as a local origin and rotation around the origin. Application-specific information may be associated in symbols for tasks such as bill-of-materials computation. A complete drawing may be organized into several *layers* that can be displayed independently of each other; this facility is commonly used to separate basic geometry of a part from construction elements, dimension lines, and other supporting notation.

Graphical primitives are created using the *construction techniques* available in the drafting system. For instance, points may be created by using the graphical pointer, typing coordinates, or by selecting two intersecting lines. Lines may be generated between given points, starting from a point with a specified length into a specified direction, or in parallel with an existing line. Typically construction techniques require the generation of *construction elements* that are only used to describe the geometry; they do not form a part of the final design.

Some systems make a distinction between lines and line segments. Lines correspond to the mathematical notion of a line, extending to infinity, whereas segments are finite (or semi-infinite) subsets of lines. In these systems, lines might be created parallel to or at a given angle to an existing line (or segment), and *trimmed* to desired length using intersection points with other lines (or segments). Similar distinctions can be made between full circles and circular arcs.

Some drafting systems provide *associative graphical primitives*, a facility that supports parametric drafting. Associative primitives have two internal representations. A *canonical representation* stores information on the primitive in some convenient form for generating graphical output on screen; for instance, the canonical representation of a circular arc could consist of a reference to the underlying full circle (another graphical object) and the starting and ending points of the arc. The full circle in turn is represented canonically in terms of a reference to a center point (again another graphical object) and the radius (possibly the reference to a number object).

The *associative representation* stores a record of the construction technique used to create the primitive. In the case of the circular arc and the related entities (the full circle and the radius value), the associative representations could be as follows:

```
Arc:    Construction technique:  fillet-arc-between-
          straight-line-segments
        Point 1: intersection(Circle, Aux-line-1)
        Point 2: intersection(Circle, Aux-line-2)
```

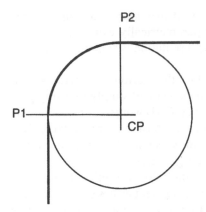

Figure 2.2 Geometric construction of a fillet arc

Circle: Construction technique: circle-touching-two-line-
            segments
          Radius: given-by-the-user
          Center point: (some computation involving the two
            lines)

The construction technique is represented here by the symbol fillet-arc-between-straight-line-segments, and each item of the canonical representation by a reference to a computable expression possibly referring to other model entities. The two auxiliary lines referred to in the representation of the arc are *internal entities* of the system, which are constructed by the filleting operation but not displayed. The graphical entities needed in this construction are shown in Figure 2.2.

The benefit of this type of representation is that the construction history can be fully captured and possibly re-executed later. In the case above, the designer may choose to change the value of the fillet radius, and re-evaluate the fillet. On the basis of the associative representation, the drafting system can re-execute the construction. As a result we have a *unidirectional parametric graphical model*.

Obviously a full-blown drafting system must include a great deal of other facilities as well, such as file and database management, graphical user interface techniques, a programming interface for application development, and neutral interfaces such as IGES or the "de facto standard" DXF used by AutoCAD*. Since our focus in this book is on modeling and model representation, we do not consider these additional facilities further, as important as they are for any practical system.

2.2.2 Three-Dimensional Graphical Models

Analogous to two-dimensional models, 3-dimensional graphical models consist of graphical primitives defined in the three-dimensional space. Lines just need a

---

*AutoCAD® and DXF® are registered trademarks of AutoDesk Corporation.

third coordinate; plane curves, arcs and conics need also information on the plane they reside on; space curves are represented parametrically using the facilities discussed in the next section. The resulting representation is sometimes referred to as the *wire frame* model.

The usefulness of wire frames lies in the fact that various projections typically needed in an engineering drawing may be generated simply by using geometric transformations on the graphical primitives. CAD workstations commonly can execute these in hardware, leading to a very responsive user interface. Geometric transformations are briefly introduced in Appendix A; for further information, consult any good textbook on computer graphics.

Unfortunately, construction of valid three-dimensional graphical models is quite difficult. Even experienced designers make frequent errors such as leaving out lines or inserting unnecessary elements. Moreover it is not easy to determine the occlusion status of the projected lines, as required in commonly used drafting notation. These problems have led to a situation where most three-dimensional drafting systems installed in the industry are exclusively used in two-dimensional mode.

As models of three-dimensional solids, graphical models are deficient. First, it is perfectly possible to create completely meaningless models from graphical primitives, such as the "Devil's fork" shown in Figure 2.3 on the left. Moreover even perfectly valid graphical models where all three-dimensional graphical entities are true edges of a solid object can have several interpretations; the standard example is shown on the right of the figure. This has the consequence that more advanced graphical visualization, such as hidden line removal, cannot be performed on the basis of a graphical model. The root of the difficulty of creating a valid graphical model resides precisely in this relative incompleteness: Dependable algorithms for checking the validity of a model are difficult to build.

From the viewpoint of the overall goals of geometric modeling as outlined in Section 2.1, graphical models are of limited utility. Their main purpose, after all, is to support the creation of drawings, and not to serve as generic models that can support several applications (even though useful applications working on the basis of graphical models can and have been built).

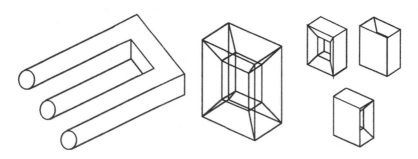

Figure 2.3 Problems of graphical models

2.3 SURFACE MODELS

Graphical models can capture simple geometric shapes that form the bulk of geometric information needed in engineering drawings. However, for some types of parts simple drawings cannot be used to represent the geometry of the shape. Notable examples are complex surfaces appearing in forgings and castings, turbine blades, automobile body sheet metal parts, aircraft, and ship hulls. To capture these geometries, various manual methods involving the representation of some main characteristic curves of the shape emerged in the above-mentioned industries. The first chapter of (Farin 1990) provides a nice overview of some of these methods.

With the advent of NC machining, a need to move from the existing curve and surface representation methods to a computer-based representation arose. As a result various schemes for the representation of parametric curves and surfaces were invented apparently simultaneously and independently by several well-known researchers, notably Bézier and de Casteljau. This section traces some of the main ideas of their geometric modeling methods; for more information, the reader is referred to more specialized texts, such as (Faux and Pratt 1979; Mortenson 1985; Farin 1990; Risler 1992).

2.3.1 Parametric Curves

Nonparametric and Parametric Forms   Familiar representations of some common planar curves include the following:

$$
\begin{array}{rl}
\text{Line:} & y = mx + c \\
\text{Circle:} & (x - a)^2 + (y - b)^2 = r^2 \\
\text{Parabola:} & y = bx^2 + C \\
\text{Ellipse:} & x^2/a^2 + y^2/b^2 = 1 \\
\text{Hyperbola:} & xy = k
\end{array}
$$

These equations are known as *analytical* or *nonparametric* representations of curves. For plane curves these equations take the form $f(x, y) = 0$ or $y = f(x)$, the first being known as the *implicit* and the second the *explicit* nonparametric form. Thus the equations of the line and the parabola listed above are explicit forms, while the others are implicit.

Although nonparametric forms of curve equations are used in some cases, they are not in general suitable for CAD because of the following reasons:

1. The equation is dependent on the choice of the coordinate system.
2. Unless additional constraints are provided, the curves are inherently unbounded.
3. The implicit form $f(x, y) = 0$ is inconvenient for computing points on the curve; values of x chosen may not lie on the curve, hence yielding no solution for y.

4. It is cumbersome to perform geometric transformations (rotations, translations, scaling) on the curve.

The *parametric* form of a curve equation overcomes these problems. In this form the equations are decoupled, in that there are separate equations for each of the coordinates expressed in terms of an additional variable u:

$$x = f(u), y = g(u), \text{ and for space curves } z = h(u) \tag{2.1}$$

where u, called the *parametric variable*, varies in a convenient range, typically from 0 to 1, and $f(u)$, $g(u)$, and $h(u)$ are all functions of u. Substituting a value of u in (2.1) gives the position of the point on the curve that corresponds to that value of u. For example, if the range of u is from 0 to 1, then substituting $u = 0$ gives the position coordinates of the start point and $u = 1$ gives the end point coordinates, and every value of u in between gives the coordinates of the interior points on the curve. The positive sense of the curve is the direction in which u increases. Since the pair (x, y) represents a position vector of a point, we can express the equation in vector form:

$$p(u) = \begin{bmatrix} x \\ y \end{bmatrix} = \begin{bmatrix} f(u) \\ g(u) \end{bmatrix} \tag{2.2}$$

where p is the position vector of points on the curve. If we were representing a curve in space, a third equation would be added for the z dimension:

$$p(u) = \begin{bmatrix} x \\ y \\ z \end{bmatrix} = \begin{bmatrix} f(u) \\ g(u) \\ h(u) \end{bmatrix} \tag{2.3}$$

Parametric Cubic Curves   To be useful for modeling purposes, the parametric functions $f(u)$, $g(u)$, and $h(u)$ should have a number of properties, such as being smooth enough, having good numerical properties, and supporting effective interaction. For these reasons polynomial functions are nearly always chosen as the basis of representing parametric curves.

For concreteness, let us study a particular family of parametric polynomial curves, the *parametric cubic curve* defined by the following equations:

$$\begin{aligned} x &= a_{31}u^3 + a_{21}u^2 + a_{11}u + a_{01} \\ y &= a_{32}u^3 + a_{22}u^2 + a_{12}u + a_{02} \\ z &= a_{33}u^3 + a_{23}u^2 + a_{13}u + a_{03} \end{aligned} \tag{2.4}$$

In Equations (2.4), u is a parametric variable that normally takes on values from 0 to 1 and a_{ij} are algebraic coefficients (scalars). Equations (2.4) can be written in matrix form as follows:

$$\underline{p}(u) = \begin{bmatrix} x \\ y \\ z \end{bmatrix} = [u^3 \ u^2 \ u \ 1] \begin{bmatrix} a_{31} & a_{32} & a_{33} \\ a_{21} & a_{22} & a_{23} \\ a_{11} & a_{12} & a_{13} \\ a_{01} & a_{02} & a_{03} \end{bmatrix} \qquad (2.5a)$$

or more compactly

$$\underline{p}(u) = [u^3 \ u^2 \ u \ 1] \ [A] \qquad (2.5b)$$

Since the coefficients a_{ij} in Equation (2.5a) are all independent, we say that the parametric cubic curve has 12 *degrees of freedom* (dof). This gives the designer considerable latitude in modeling various shapes; however, it is difficult to relate the values of the coefficients to the shape of the curve. Therefore this particular form of defining a cubic curve, known as the *algebraic form*, is not generally suited for geometric design.

To find a curve representation more attractive for curve design, it is easy to express Equation (2.5) in terms of geometric *boundary conditions*. One common choice of boundary conditions is to use the position vectors of the start and end points of the curve, $\underline{p}(u = 0)$, $\underline{p}(u = 1)$, and the tangent vectors at the start and end points, $\partial p/\partial u(u = 0)$, $\partial p/\partial u(u = 1)$. These are illustrated in Figure 2.4. On the basis of the boundary conditions, the shape of the curve can be controlled by the designer by manipulating the end points and the tangents, giving him better control over the shape.

Let us proceed by deriving a parametric form for a cubic curve in terms of the boundary conditions. To get the position of the point in terms of a_{ij}, substitute $u = 0$ in Equation (2.5b) for the start point, and $u = 1$ for the end point:

Start point, $\underline{p}(0) = [0 \quad 0 \quad 0 \quad 1] \ [A]$

End point, $\underline{p}(1) = [1 \quad 1 \quad 1 \quad 1] \ [A]$

To get the tangent at any point on the curve, we differentiate Equation (2.5b), then substitute the value of u at which the tangent is desired. Thus, tangent at u is found to be

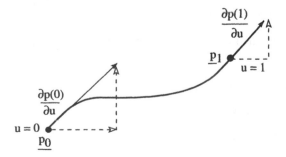

Figure 2.4 Boundary conditions

$$p''(u) = \frac{\partial p}{\partial u} = [3u^2 \quad 2u \quad 1 \quad 0] \, [A]$$

and the tangents at the start and end points are found by substituting $u = 0$ and $u = 1$:

$$p''(0) = [0 \quad 0 \quad 1 \quad 0] \, [A]$$

$$p''(1) = [3 \quad 2 \quad 1 \quad 0] \, [A]$$

Combining the above boundary conditions in matrix form, we get

$$\begin{bmatrix} p(0) \\ p(1) \\ p''(0) \\ p''(1) \end{bmatrix} = \begin{bmatrix} 0 & 0 & 0 & 1 \\ 1 & 1 & 1 & 1 \\ 0 & 0 & 1 & 0 \\ 3 & 2 & 1 & 0 \end{bmatrix} [A]$$

Multiplying both sides by the inverse of the coefficient matrix, we get

$$[A] = \begin{bmatrix} 0 & 0 & 0 & 1 \\ 1 & 1 & 1 & 1 \\ 0 & 0 & 1 & 0 \\ 3 & 2 & 1 & 0 \end{bmatrix}^{-1} \begin{bmatrix} p(0) \\ p(1) \\ p''(0) \\ p''(1) \end{bmatrix} = \begin{bmatrix} 2 & -2 & 1 & 1 \\ -3 & 3 & -2 & -1 \\ 0 & 0 & 1 & 0 \\ 1 & 0 & 0 & 0 \end{bmatrix} \begin{bmatrix} p(0) \\ p(1) \\ p''(0) \\ p''(1) \end{bmatrix}$$

Substituting the above result for [A] in equation (2.5b) we get

$$p(u) = [u^3 \ u^2 \ u \ 1] \begin{bmatrix} 2 & -2 & 1 & 1 \\ -3 & 3 & -2 & -1 \\ 0 & 0 & 1 & 0 \\ 1 & 0 & 0 & 0 \end{bmatrix} \begin{bmatrix} p(0) \\ p(1) \\ p''(0) \\ p''(1) \end{bmatrix} \tag{2.6a}$$

Expanding equation (2.6a), we get the desired result, the *geometric form* of the parametric cubic curve:

$$p(u) = (2u^3 - 3u^2 + 1)\, p(0) + (-2u^3 + 3u^2)p(1) + (u^3 - 2u^2 + u)p''(0) + (u^3 - u^2)p''(1) \tag{2.6b}$$

Suppose the polynomial expressions in (2.6b) are designated as F_1, F_2, F_3, F_4 respectively, then we can write:

$$F_1 = 2u^3 - 3u^2 + 1$$

$$F_2 = -2u^3 + 3u^2$$

$$F_3 = u^3 - 2u^2 + u$$

$$F_4 = u^3 - u^2$$

Using these functions, we may rewrite Equation (2.6a) in the even more condensed form:

$$p(u) = [F_1, F_2, F_3, F_4] \begin{bmatrix} p(0) \\ p(1) \\ p''(0) \\ p''(1) \end{bmatrix} \tag{2.7}$$

In Equation (2.7), F_1 are called the *blending functions*. Plots of the blending functions versus u are shown in Figure 2.5. Observe that $F_1 = 1 - F_2$ and that F_1 has the maximum influence on the curve shape near the start, F_2 near the end, and F_3, F_4 exert influence only in between the end points.

Recall that the algebraic form for cubic polynomials (Equation 2.5b) has 12 degrees of freedom. Therefore in the geometric form the four boundary conditions should also add up to 12 degrees of freedom. Indeed, the position vectors p_0, p_1 have 6 independent coordinates between them, that is, 6 degrees of freedom; the tangents p_0'', p_1'' have the other 6. Note that the tangent vectors are not unit vectors; they have a magnitude (1 degree of freedom each) and a direction that is a unit vector (2 degrees of freedom for each tangent).

Instead of using tangents as the boundary conditions, we could also use two additional points on the curve. Thus the boundary conditions are specified by four points on the curve. Four points also have a total of 12 degrees of freedom. These alternative boundary conditions are shown in Figure 2.6.

The parametric cubic equation can be expressed in terms of these boundary conditions as

$$p = \gamma_1 p_1 + \gamma_2 p_2 + \gamma_3 p_3 + \gamma_4 p_4 \tag{2.8}$$

In Equation (2.8) γ_i are new blending functions that can be determined in terms of the algebraic coefficients from (2.5) and (2.6). In general, various parametric

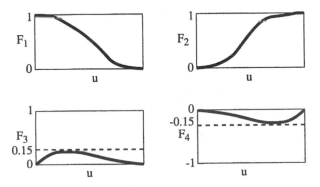

Figure 2.5 Plots of blending functions

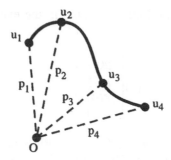

Figure 2.6 Alternative boundary conditions (four-point form)

forms of cubics can be derived in terms of various choices of blending functions. For further details refer to (Mortenson 1985).

Composite Curves   For geometric modeling it is often necessary to synthesize a curve from several separate segments. When two curves are joined, there are three possible *continuity conditions*, as shown in Figure 2.7. These conditions are defined below:

1. C^0 *continuity*, or *point continuity*, implies that two curves A and B are joined end to end with no restriction on end slopes or curvature (Figure 2.5a). This implies that

$$P_1^A = P_0^B$$

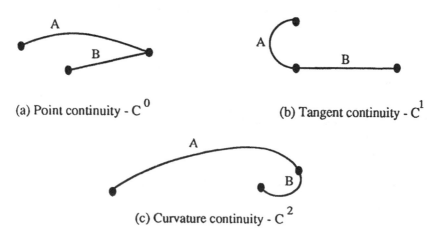

(a) Point continuity - C^0

(b) Tangent continuity - C^1

(c) Curvature continuity - C^2

Figure 2.7 Continuity conditions

2. *C¹ continuity*, or *tangent continuity* implies that two curves *A* and *B* are joined end to end and have the same slope at the common meeting point. This implies that

$$\underline{p}_1^A = \underline{p}_0^B$$

$$\underline{p}_1^{uA} = a\underline{p}_0^{uB}$$

Note that the magnitudes of the tangents are not necessarily the same, as indicated by the presence of the scalar *a* in the above.

3. *C² continuity*, or *curvature continuity*, implies that two curves *A*, *B* share not only a common end point and have the same slope at that point but also the same curvature at that point. That is,

$$\underline{p}_1^A = \underline{p}_0^B$$

$$\underline{p}_1^{uA} = a\underline{p}_0^{uB}$$

$$\underline{p}_1^{uuA} = b\underline{p}_0^{uuB}$$

Bézier Curves   Bézier curves were independently developed by P. Bézier for the car manufacturer Renault and by P. de Casteljau for Citroën. Both were investigating mathematical forms for shape design that could provide an intuitive feel to automotive body designers, which would allow them to design by pulling out curves in different directions to experiment with shapes. The use of tangents as boundary conditions did not fit these requirements. Instead, Bézier formulated an approach in which a curve would *approximately* pass through a set of points, as shown in Figure 2.8. Note that the curves pass only through the first and last points exactly. The position of the intermediate points affects the shape of the curve, as if each point was applying a pull on the curve towards itself. This type of curve is classified as an *approximated* curve, while a curve such as

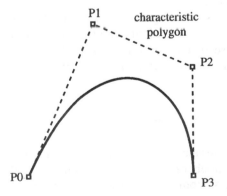

Figure 2.8 A Bézier curve defined by four points

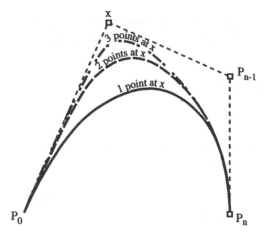

Figure 2.9 Increasing the "pull" with coincident points at x

a parametric cubic curve defined in terms of four points is called *interpolated* because it passes through all the points exactly.

The points used in the definition of the Bézier curve are called *control points*. The polygon joining all the control points is called the *characteristic polygon*. The curve is tangent to the line joining the first two points and the last two points. We can increase the influence (pull) of a control point by placing additional points coincident with it; this is illustrated in Figure 2.9 where we use 1, 2, and 3 coincident control points located at x to make the resulting curve pass increasingly close to it.

We can get a closed Bézier curve by specifying coincident first and last points as shown in Figure 2.10. If any of the control points is moved, it affects the shape of the entire curve. This can be seen in Figure 2.11 where one of the control points, P_2 is moved to a new position P'_2. This changes the shape of the entire curve, which sometimes creates frustration for designers because they are unable to make local changes in the shape easily.

Bézier used *Bernstien polynomials* as blending functions to get the desired properties. The degree of the polynomial is dependent upon the number of control points used to define the curve so that n control points yield an $(n - 1)$ degree polynomial. The mathematical formulation of Bézier curves is as follows:

$$\underline{p}(u) = \sum_{i=0}^{n} \underline{P}_i B_{i,n}(u) \quad 0 \le u \le 1 \tag{2.9a}$$

In this form, $\underline{p}(u)$ are points on the curve at a given value of the parameter u, $\underline{P}_i$ are the control points, n is the total number of control points minus 1, and the blending functions $B_{i,n}$ are Bernstein polynomials that are determined from

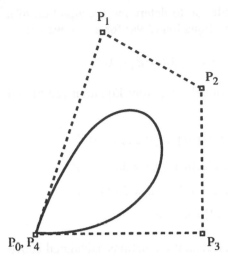

Figure 2.10 Closed Bézier curve

$$B_{i,n}(u) = C(n,i)u^i(1 - u)^{n-i} \tag{2.9b}$$

where the binomial coefficient is defined by the familiar expression

$$C(n,i) = \frac{n!}{i!(n - i)!} \tag{2.9c}$$

In evaluating these expressions, by convention, $0! = 1$ and $u^i = 1$ when u and i are 0; that is, $C(n, 0) = 1$ and $C(n, n) = 1$.

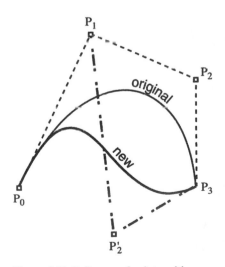

Figure 2.11 Influence of point position

Let us work through the above formulation to determine the equation of a Bézier curve defined by four points. From Equation (2.9a) for $n = 3$, we get

$$\underline{p}(u) = \underline{P}_0 B_{0,3}(u) + \underline{P}_1 B_{1,3}(u) + \underline{P}_2 B_{2,3}(u) + \underline{P}_3 B_{3,3}(u)$$

We determine the Bernstein cubic polynomials $B_{i,3}$ from Equation (2.9b) and (2.9c) as

$$B_{0,3} = C(3,0)u^0(1 - u)^3 = (3!/0!3!)(1 - u)^3 = (1 - u)^3$$

$$B_{1,3} = C(3,1)u(1 - u)^2 = (3!/1!2!)u(1 - u)^2 = 3u(1 - u)^2$$

$$B_{2,3} = C(3,2)u^2(1 - u) = (3!/2!1!)u^2(1 - u) = 3u^2(1 - u)$$

$$B_{3,3} = C(3,3)u^3(1 - u)^0 = (3!/3!0!)u^3 = u^3$$

If we now substitute the values of the four blending functions calculated above into Equation (2.9a), we get the desired equation of the four point Bézier curve:

$$\underline{p}(u) = (1 - u)^3 \underline{P}_0 + 3u(1 - u)^2 \underline{P}_1 + 3u^2(1 - u)\underline{P}_2 + u^3 \underline{P}_3 \qquad (2.10)$$

Note that the order of the polynomial is 3, which is one lower than the number of points.

These blending functions are plotted as functions of u in Figure 2.12. The plot gives an indication of the influence each point has on the curve's shape at different values of u. It can be seen that all points affect the curve shape for all values of u, except at the ends, where only B_0 and B_3 exert influence. The influ-

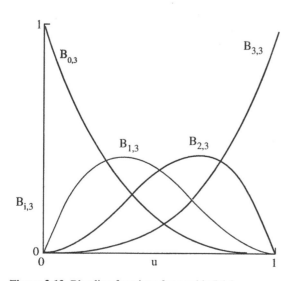

Figure 2.12 Blending functions for a cubic Bézier curve

ence of each function is largest in the vicinity of the point to which it corresponds. Also observe that the sum of blending functions is 1 at each value of u.

Instead of a single high-degree curve, a complex curve is typically defined as a composite of several lower-degree curves (typically, cubics) stitched together. The Bézier curve continuity conditions for this are analogous to those illustrated in Figure 2.7. Unfortunately, if a smooth composite curve is desired, the continuity conditions leave little freedom to the control of the individual components.

Bézier curves have a number of useful properties, generally shared by other parametric forms of curves and surfaces to be discussed later in this section. First, they are *invariant under affine transformations*; hence a Bézier curve is transformed simply by transforming its control points. Second, since the blending functions sum to 1, the resulting curve is contained within the convex hull of the control points (*convex hull property*), a fact useful for intersection computations and like. Another useful property is the *variation diminishing property*, indicating that the interpolating curve does not have more intersections with any plane than the original data. Hence we are assured that no artificial complex behavior can be present.

B-Splines B-splines can be regarded a generalization of Bézier curves. Similarities with Bézier curves are that B-splines are controlled by a set of points lying on an open polygon. They pass through the first and last points, and they are tangent to the first and last segments. Unlike Bézier curves, local changes to the curve are possible, and the degree of B-splines is largely independent of the number of control points. This also facilitates the control of composite curves. B-splines can be implemented either in approximated or interpolated form. For all of these reasons, B-splines are popular for geometry definition in CAD systems.

If the degree of the B-spline is $(k - 1)$ and the number of control points is $(n + 1)$, the equation of the curve is determined from

$$\underline{p}(u) = \sum_{j=0}^{n} \underline{P}_j N_{j,k}(u) \tag{2.11}$$

where $\underline{P}_j$ are the $(n + 1)$ control points, $N_{j,k}$ are the blending functions, and u is the parametric variable. It should be noted that the range of u in not 0 to 1, but it varies with the number of control points and the degree of the curve:

$$0 \leq u < ((n + 1) - (k - 1)) \tag{2.12}$$

Although the number of control points $(n + 1)$ and the degree $(k - 1)$ of the curve can be varied independently, the number of control points determines the maximum degree of a B-spline:

$$((n + 1) - (k - 1)) > 0 \tag{2.13}$$

Figure 2.13 shows the influence of k on the B-spline shape and the independence of the degree from the number of control points. Three B-splines are shown

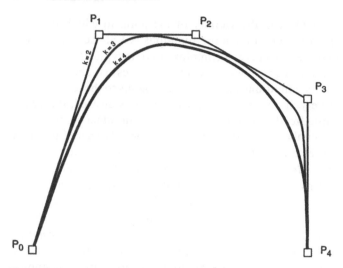

Figure 2.13 Linear, quadratic, and cubic B-splines

defined by the same control polygon but with different values of k. When $k = 2$, we get a linear "curve", which is coincident with the control polygon; that is, it connects the control points by straight line segments. When $k = 3$, we get a piecewise quadratic curve; it moves away from the intermediate control points and only passes through the end points. The curve is tangent to the first and last segments, P_0-P_1 and P_3-P_4. In addition to satisfying these conditions, the $k = 3$ curve also touches the mid-points of the intermediate segments. When k is increased to 4, the curve is smoother, and moves further away from the control points. The curve is piecewise cubic; it still passes through the end points and is tangent to the start and end segments. We can see that the lower the degree of the curve, the closer it resides to the control points.

The influence of adding or moving a control point can be seen in Figures 2.14(a) and (b), respectively. We can see that moving P_3 changes 2 segments for the linear B-spline ($k = 2$), 3 segments for the quadratic ($k = 3$), and 4 segments for the cubic ($k = 4$) curve; all other segments are unaffected. That is, each control point influences only k segments in its local area. This gives the designer an improved local control of the shape.

The local control property can be explained by examining the blending functions of B-splines. The functions are recursively defined as follows (Mortensen 1985):

$$N_{i,1} = \begin{cases} 1 & \text{if } t_i \leq u < t_{i+1} \\ 0 & \text{otherwise} \end{cases} \tag{2.15.a}$$

$$N_{i,k}(u) = \frac{(u - t_i)N_{i,k-1}}{t_{i+k-1} - t_i} + \frac{(t_{i+k} - u)N_{i+1,k-1}}{t_{i+k} - t_{i+1}} \tag{2.15.b}$$

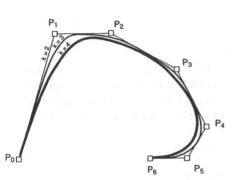

Figure 2.14 Influence of control point position

In Equations (2.15) t_i are called the *knot variables*, whose values are found as follows (uniform knots):

$$t_i = 0 \qquad\qquad \text{if } i < k \qquad\qquad (2.16.\text{a})$$

$$t_i = i - k + 1 \qquad\qquad \text{if } k \le i \le n \qquad\qquad (2.16.\text{b})$$

$$t_i = n - k + 2 \qquad\qquad \text{if } i > n \qquad\qquad (2.16.\text{c})$$

The range of i in Equations (2.16) is found from

$$0 \le i \le n + k \qquad\qquad (2.17)$$

In calculating $N_{i,k}$ from (2.15), the value of any expression which has division by 0 is taken to be 0.

To illustrate the representation of B-splines, let us determine the equation for a linear B-spline defined by four points. For this situation, $n = 3$ and $k = 2$. We substitute these values in (2.11) to get:

$$p(u) = P_0\, N_{0,2}(u) + P_1 N_{1,2}(u) + P_2 N_{2,2}(u) + P_3\, N_{3,2}(u) \qquad\qquad (2.18)$$

where P_0 to P_3 are the four control points and $N_{0,2}$ to $N_{3,2}$ are the corresponding blending functions. The steps in calculating the blending functions are as follows:

Determine the range of u from (2.12),

$$0 \le u < (3 + 1) - (2 - 1) \Rightarrow 0 \le u < 3$$

Determine the range of i from (2.17),

$$0 \le i \le 3 + 2 \Rightarrow 0 \le i \le 5$$

Determine the knots corresponding to all values of i from (2.16),

$$t_0 = 0 \qquad t_1 = 0 \qquad t_2 = 1 \qquad t_3 = 2 \qquad t_4 = 3 \qquad t_5 = 3$$

Determine the blending functions from (2.15).

Since the blending functions are defined recursively, we need to start by calculating $N_{i,1}$, then $N_{i,2}$, and so on, until we reach $N_{i,k}$. In the case of this example, $k = 2$, so we just need to find all the $N_{i,1}$ and $N_{i,2}$ for $i = 0$ to $n + 1$, which is 0 to 4.

Using the values of the knots found above, we calculate $N_{i,1}$ from (2.15a):

$$N_{0,1} = 0 \quad \text{for all u}$$

$$N_{1,1} = \begin{cases} 1 & 0 \le u < 1 \\ 0 & \text{otherwise} \end{cases}$$

$$N_{2,1} = \begin{cases} 1 & 1 \le u < 2 \\ 0 & \text{otherwise} \end{cases}$$

$$N_{3,1} = \begin{cases} 1 & 2 \le u < 3 \\ 0 & \text{otherwise} \end{cases}$$

$$N_{4,1} = 0 \quad \text{for all } u$$

The values of $N_{i,1}$ are then used to find $N_{i,2}$ from (2.15b):

For $i = 0$

$$N_{0,2} = \frac{(u - t_0)N_{0,1}(u)}{t_1 - t_0} + \frac{(t_2 - u)N_{1,1}(u)}{t_2 - t_1} = (1 - u)N_{1,1}(u)$$

For $i = 1$

$$N_{1,2} = \frac{(u - t_1)N_{1,1}(u)}{t_2 - t_1} + \frac{(t_3 - u)N_{2,1}(u)}{t_3 - t_2} = uN_{1,1}(u) + (2 - u)N_{2,1}(u)$$

For $i = 2$

$$N_{2,2} = \frac{(u - t_2)N_{2,1}(u)}{t_3 - t_2} + \frac{(t_4 - u)N_{3,1}(u)}{t_4 - t_3} = (u - 1)N_{2,1}(u) + (3 - u)N_{3,1}(u)$$

For $i = 3$

$$N_{3,2} = \frac{(u - t_3)N_{3,1}(u)}{t_4 - t_3} + \frac{(t_5 - u)N_{4,1}(u)}{t_5 - t_4} = (u - 2)N_{3,1}(u)$$

If these expressions are substituted in equation (2.18) we will get the desired equation for a linear B-spline defined by four points. In these calculations the

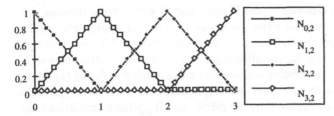

Figure 2.15 Blending functions for linear B-spline ranging over four points (k = 2)

value of 0/0 is taken as 0. The resulting blending functions are plotted in Figure 2.15. One can see that each blending function has influence only in a local region and that again they sum up to 1. Because the functions are piecewise linear, the final result is a curve with straight line segments. If the reader now repeats the above exercise for $k = 2$ but increases the number of control points to 5, it will be seen that the shape of the blending curves does not change.

Higher-degree blending functions are computed similarly. For instance, the quadratic blending functions ($k = 3$) ranging over five points are shown in Figure 2.16. Again observe that each function influences only some local region and that their sum is 1 for all values of u.

The influence of k is summarized below:

k	Degree of polynomial	Continuity
1	0	Disjointed points
2	1	C^0 (connected linear segments)
3	2	C^1 (tangent continuous)
4	3	C^2 (curvature continuous)

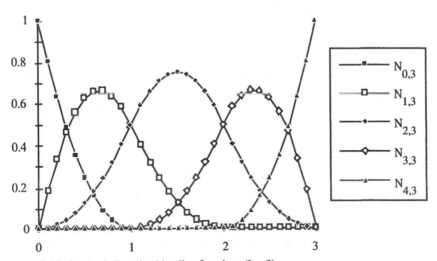

Figure 2.16 Quadratic B-spline blending functions (k = 3)

Rational Parametric Curves   The Beziér and B-spline formulations presented in the previous sections have the disadvantage that conics and circles cannot be represented precisely. This is inconvenient for a CAD system developer, who must provide special algorithms for intersection calculations involving both implicit forms (for circles and conics) and parametric forms (splines). A preferred approach is to use a uniform representation that can support the types of parametric curves captured by the Beziér and B-spline formulations and also circles and conics, exactly.

Such a canonical representation is possible using *rational parametric curves*. Rational curves are defined on the basis of *homogeneous coordinates* (see Appendix A). Homogeneous coordinates represent three-dimensional points in terms of a four-dimensional point with an additional coordinate axis w. If $P = (x\ y\ z)$ is a point in three-dimensional space, the corresponding point in the four-dimensional space is $P^h = (hx\ hy\ hz\ h)$, where the *homogeneous coordinate* $h > 0$. Conversely, a four-dimensional point is converted back to a three-dimensional one by dividing the three first coordinates by the fourth one.

Using homogeneous coordinates the equation (2.9a) defining the conventional Beziér curve becomes

$$\underline{p}^h(u) = \sum_{i=0}^{n} \underline{P}_i^h B_{i,n}(u) \qquad 0 \leq u \leq 1 \tag{2.19}$$

where $\underline{P}_i^h$ are now the control points in the homogeneous space. Hence the form defines a curve in the four-dimensional homogeneous space. The corresponding curve in the three-dimensional space is obtained by dividing the first three coordinates of each point by its homogeneous coordinate. Therefore the *rational Beziér curve* is given by

$$\underline{p}(u) = \frac{\sum_{i=0}^{n} h_i \underline{P}_i B_{i,n}(u)}{\sum_{i=0}^{n} h_i B_{i,n}(u)} \qquad 0 \leq u \leq 1 \tag{2.20}$$

Observe that conventional Beziér curves are included in (2.20). This can be demonstrated by setting all $h_i = 1$ and using the fact that the blending functions sum to unity.

The simplest form that can capture conics exactly is the *quadratic rational Beziér curve*. Substituting $i = 2$ and the Bernstein polynomials of Equation (2.9b) in (2.20), we get

$$\underline{p}(u) = \frac{(1-u)^2 h_0 P_0 + (1-u)u h_1 P_1 + u^2 h_2 P_2}{(1-u)^2 h_0 + (1-u)u h_1 + u^2 h_2} \tag{2.21}$$

Choosing $P_0 = (2\ 0\ 0\ 2)$, $P_1 = (1\ 1\ 0\ 1)$, $P_2 = (0\ 1\ 0\ 1)$, gives the first quadrant of the unit circle shown in Figure 2.17. The curve is plotted by using fixed steps of 0.05 for $0 \leq u \leq 1$.

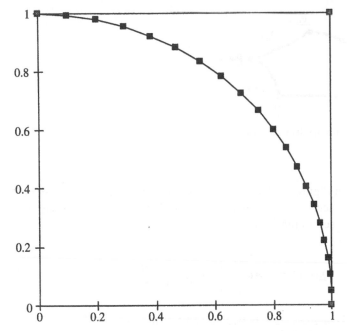

Figure 2.17 A circular arc represented as a rational quadratic Bézier curve

Similarly, it is also possible to modify Equation (2.11) to define *rational B-splines,* commonly known as NURBS (*non-uniform rational B-splines*). We get the form

$$p(u) = \frac{\sum_{j=0}^{n} h_j P_j N_{j,k}(u)}{\sum_{j=0}^{n} h_j N_{j,k}(u)}$$
(2.22)

This form can again capture both conventional B-splines and conic sections. The convenient properties of B-splines are also inherited, such as the local control property.

The increased expressiveness of rational forms is not free of cost, however. The homogeneous coordinates affect the parameterization of the curves and the magnitudes of the derivatives. It may be difficult to find parameterizations that provide useful properties such as approximate arc length preservation. For instance, the simple parameterization of the circle used above is not really attractive for curve plotting.

2.3.2 Parametric Surfaces

A major benefit of the parametric methods for representing curves is that they can be generalized to surface representations. Portions of surfaces, generally

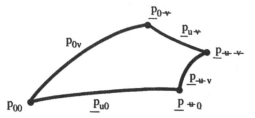

Figure 2.18 A surface patch and its boundaries

non-planar, such as in Figure 2.18, are referred to as *surface patches*. Parametric representation of surface patches involves two variables, u and v. The parametric equation is expressed in the form:

$$\underline{p}(u,v) = \begin{bmatrix} x(u,v) \\ y(u,v) \\ z(u,v) \end{bmatrix} \textit{ for } \begin{array}{l} 0 \le \underline{u} \le \textit{u} \\ 0 \le \underline{v} \le \textit{v} \end{array} \qquad (2.23)$$

In Equation (2.23), u and v vary between 0 and some upper limit, determined by the particular representation used. We will indicate this upper limit by the symbols $\textit{u}, \textit{v}$. When (2.23) is evaluated for any valid values of u, v, the position vector of the corresponding point p_{uv} is obtained. The four corner points of the patch can be found by substituting, in turn, the upper and lower limits of u and v. These are shown in Figure 2.18 as $\underline{p}_{00}, \underline{p}_{u0}, \underline{p}_{uv}, \underline{p}_{0v}$. The patch is bounded by four curves, whose equations can be found by substituting, in turn, the upper and lower limits of either u or v, and keeping the other as a variable. The figure shows the boundary curves as $\underline{p}_{u0}, \underline{p}_{uv}, \underline{p}_{uv}, \underline{p}_{0v}$. We will explore some specific types of surface patches: bicubic, Bézier, and B-spline. These are the same three formulations we reviewed for curves in Section 2.3.1.

Bicubic Surfaces   Bicubic surface patches are formulated in a way analogous to cubic curves. The algebraic form is a cubic polynomial in u and v:

$$x(u,v) = \sum_{i=0}^{3} \sum_{j=0}^{3} a_{ij}^{x} u^{i} v^{j} \qquad 0 \le (u,v) \le 1 \qquad (2.24a)$$

$$y(u,v) = \sum_{i=0}^{3} \sum_{j=0}^{3} a_{ij}^{y} u^{i} v^{j} \qquad 0 \le (u,v) \le 1 \qquad (2.24b)$$

$$z(u,v) = \sum_{i=0}^{3} \sum_{j=0}^{3} a_{ij}^{z} u^{i} v^{j} \qquad 0 \le (u,v) \le 1 \qquad (2.24c)$$

where a_{ij} are algebraic coefficients. Each equation above has 16 coefficients, giving a total of 48 coefficients for the surface patch. Thus, the bicubic patch has 48 degrees of freedom.

Since the upper limit of u and v is 1, we can replace u and v in Figure 2.18 with 1 to look at a bicubic patch in terms of its boundary conditions. As with curves, it is convenient to transform the algebraic form in (2.24) to the geometric form. The geometric form is defined in terms of geometric boundary conditions: four corner points ($\underline{p}_{00}, \underline{p}_{10}, \underline{p}_{11}, \underline{p}_{01}$), two tangent vectors ($\underline{p}^u = \partial \underline{p}/\partial u, \underline{p}^v = \partial \underline{p}/\partial v$) evaluated at each of the corners, and one *twist vector* ($\underline{p}^{uv} = \partial^2 \underline{p}/\partial u \partial v$) evaluated at each of the corners. The four corner points account for 12 degrees of freedom (3 coordinates each), the 8 tangents and their magnitudes account for 24 dof, and the twist vectors account for 12 degrees of freedom, adding up to a total of 48 degrees of freedom.

To convert the algebraic form to the geometric form, we can determine each of the boundary conditions from (2.24) in terms of the algebraic coefficients a_{ij}. For the corner points, simply substitute $u = 0, 1$ and $v = 0, 1$. For the two tangents, differentiate the equation with respect to u and v, in turn, and substitute the u, v values of the corner at which the tangent is desired. To get the twist vectors, differentiate $\underline{p}$ both with respect to u and v, and substitute (u, v) for the each of the corner points.

Following the above process, we will get 48 equations in terms of the boundary conditions and the algebraic coefficients. As demonstrated with curves, we can then use these relations to eliminate the algebraic coefficients from (2.24) to get

$$\underline{p}(u,v) = [(2u^3 - 3u^2 + 1)(-2u^3 + 3u^2)(u^3 - 2u^2 + u)(u^3 - u^2)] *$$

$$\begin{bmatrix} \underline{p}_{00} & \underline{p}_{01} & \underline{p}_{00}^v & \underline{p}_{01}^v \\ \underline{p}_{10} & \underline{p}_{11} & \underline{p}_{10}^v & \underline{p}_{11}^v \\ \underline{p}_{00}^u & \underline{p}_{01}^u & \underline{p}_{00}^{uv} & \underline{p}_{01}^{uv} \\ \underline{p}_{10}^u & \underline{p}_{11}^u & \underline{p}_{10}^{uv} & \underline{p}_{11}^{uv} \end{bmatrix} \begin{bmatrix} 2v^3 - 3v^2 + 1 \\ -2v^3 + 3v^2 \\ v^3 - 2v^2 + v \\ v^3 - v^2 \end{bmatrix} \quad (2.25)$$

The boundary conditions matrix in the middle is multiplied by the familiar blending functions that we saw for cubic curves. Thus bicubic surfaces are anologous to cubic curves, since the same blending functions are used for both. The four bounding curves of the bicubic patch are parametric cubic curves. The equivalent of the 4-point form of a cubic curve is a bicubic surface represented by 16 points. Alternatively, we could define the geometric form of a bicubic patch with 16 points, which avoids the difficulty of using tangent and twist vectors as boundary conditions; 16 points vectors also add up to 48 dof.

The normal to the bicubic patch at any point can be found by computing the cross-product $\underline{p}^u \times \underline{p}^v$. The direction of the normal vector depends upon the order in which the product is taken. A consistent order must be used, since surface normals are often used in performing many geometric modeling functions.

Composite surfaces can be formed by stitching together several surface patches analogously to parametric curves. The boundary conditions required for achieving various degrees of continuity involve equal partial derivatives of u and v analogously to the situation in Figure 2.7.

Bézier Surfaces   Bézier surfaces are defined by a network of points that forms the *characteristic* (or *control*) *polyhedron* shown in Figure 2.19. They have behavior analogous to curves; namely they approximately pass through their control points, except for the four corner points through which the surface passes exactly. The four bounding curves are Bézier curves and, as one would expect, they are also tangent to the start and end segments. We can get a closed Bézier patch by using coincident end points, as shown in Figure 2.20. It is possible to use more points in one direction than the other, as shown in the case of the Bézier patch defined by 5 x 4 array of points. As with curves, the Bézier patch can be pulled closer to its characteristic polyhedron by the use of coincident control points.

The general equation of Bézier patches can be obtained by extending the curve equation with another parametric variable, v, to yield a *tensor product surface* described in terms of two independent parameters:

$$\underline{p}(u,v) = \sum_{i=0}^{m} \sum_{j=0}^{n} \underline{P}_{ij} B_{i,m}(u) B_{j,n}(v) \qquad 0 \le (u,v) \le 1$$

In the equation, $\underline{P}_{ij}$ are the control points and m, n are the degrees of polynomials for the $(m + 1)$ x $(n + 1)$ control points. B are the same Bézier blending functions as those used for curves. It is not necessary for m to be equal to n. For example, for a 4 x 3 array Bézier patch the above equation expands to

$$\underline{p}(u,v) = [(1 - u)^3 \ 3u(1 - u)^2 \ 3u^2(1 - u) \ u^3] \begin{bmatrix} \underline{P}_{00} & \underline{P}_{01} & \underline{P}_{02} \\ \underline{P}_{10} & \underline{P}_{11} & \underline{P}_{12} \\ \underline{P}_{20} & \underline{P}_{21} & \underline{P}_{22} \\ \underline{P}_{30} & \underline{P}_{31} & \underline{P}_{32} \end{bmatrix} \begin{bmatrix} (1 - v)^2 \\ 2v(1 - v) \\ v^2 \end{bmatrix}$$

Observe that the above surface provides curvature continuity in one direction and tangent continuity in the other. Since the degree of the Bézier patch is determined by the number of control points, it is usually better to create a complex surface by combining several Bézier patches, using a small number of control points instead of defining it as a single patch.

As with Bézier curves, we can see that local changes are not possible; moving a control point causes the change to propagate throughout the surface. This makes the control of composite surfaces particularly tricky if continuity conditions across patches must be maintained. The various properties of Bézier curves carry over to surfaces. For instance, the surface is always contained in the convex hull of the control polyhedron, a fact that is useful in ray tracing and other intersection calculations.

B-Spline Surfaces   Analogously to B-spline curves, B-spline surface patches offer more local control than Bézier surfaces. B-spline patches can be expressed

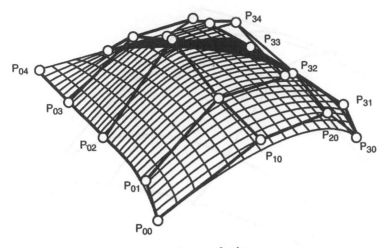

Figure 2.19 Bézier patch with 5 x 4 array of points

in both approximated and interpolated forms. Figure 2.21 shows an interpolated B-spline surface. The degree of a B-spline surface patch can be chosen independently of the number of control points. Therefore B-spline surface modeling capability is common in CAD systems.

The general equation of a B-spline surface patch is again formed by adding another parametric variable v:

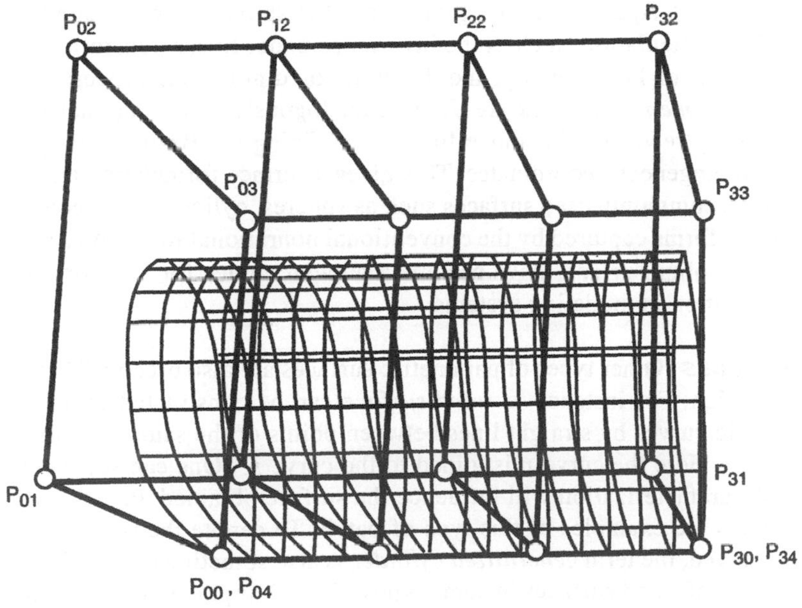

Figure 2.20 Closed Bézier patch

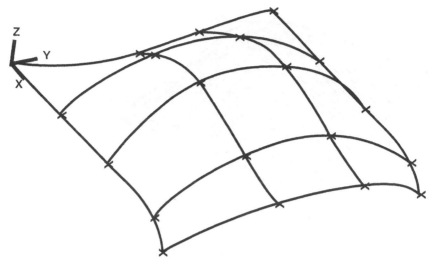

Figure 2.21 B-spline surface patch

$$p(u,v) = \sum_{i=0}^{m} \sum_{j=0}^{n} \underline{P}_{ij} N_{i,k}(u) N_{j,l}(v)$$

In the equation, $\underline{P}_{ij}$ are the $(m + 1)$ x $(n + 1)$ control points and N are the blending functions, which are calculated from Equations (2.15) already presented in the section on curves; k and l are the degrees of the blending functions polynomials in u and v, respectively. Note that k, l are independent of m, n as long as $m - k + 2 > 0$, $n - l + 2 > 0$. Again the useful properties of B-spline curves remain valid for the surface formulation, such as the invariance under linear transformations property, the convex hull property, and the variation diminishing property.

Rational parametric surfaces are defined analogously to the rational parametric curves by rewriting the above formulas defining the Bézier or B-spline surfaces in homogeneous coordinates. This gives a surface formulation that can record various commonly used surfaces such as spheres, cylinders, and cones in addition to the forms captured by the conventional nonrational forms. As a result the rational B-spline surfaces have become a popular choice for a uniform surface representation in modeling systems.

Ruled Surfaces Other types of parametric surfaces are also used in CAD and geometric design. For instance, a *ruled surface* can be constructed by joining two parametric curves by straight lines between points of the same u_i as shown in Figure 2.22. Here the curve $\underline{p}$ is joined to the curve $\underline{p}$'. One can see that the direction of parameterization will influence the surface obtained. Planes, cylinders and cones are examples of this type of patch. To denote the type of ruled surface displayed, the term *generalized cylinder* is also sometimes used. Despite the importance of ruled surfaces in some types of CAD applications, we choose

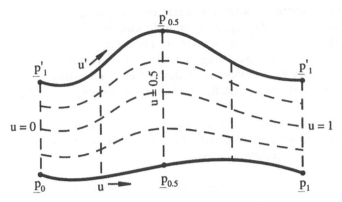

Figure 2.22 Ruled surface

not to investigate these forms further. Again, the reader should consult more specialized sources such as (Mortenson 1985) for more information.

2.4 SOLID MODELS

As we saw in Chapter 1, feature models can be regarded as an extension to solid modeling techniques. They are designed to overcome some of the deficiencies of solid modeling, and they provide increased functionality for various applications in CAD and CAM. Because of this relationship to the main subject of this book, we will discuss solid models to somewhat greater level of detail than the other types of geometric models. For more specialized texts, see (Mäntylä 1988); and (Hoffman 1989).

2.4.1 Goals of Solid Modeling

Solid models were originally developed to address the problems of graphical models, as outlined in Section 2.2. These problems are: lack of robustness, incompleteness, and limited applicability. Solid modeling may be characterized as a branch of geometric modeling that emphasizes the general applicability of models and strives to create only "complete" representations of solid objects that at least in theory are adequate for answering any geometric questions algorithmically (without the help of interaction with a human user). From the more practical viewpoint, solid modeling systems are aimed to support three-dimensional design better than systems based on graphical or surface modeling. In particular, they provide improved construction techniques that lend themselves to direct creation of three-dimensional geometry, and they can generate projected images automatically with hidden lines suppressed or displayed using suitable graphics attributes.

Two major issues in the design of a solid modeler are *integrity* and *complexity*. A solid modeler should have the capability of enforcing the correctness of the models created either on the basis of an integrity-checking algorithm or by providing only integrity-preserving modeling operations. Complexity is an issue in large models that may have hundreds of thousands of modeling primitives; to beat complexity, high-level modeling tools for the designer should be provided.

Many other characteristics of solid modeling techniques and systems are also of interest. In the following sections, we will characterize properties of solid modeling approaches using the following framework:

Expressive power	Characterizes a solid modeling approach by types of solids that can be represented, and determines whether the representation is accurate or approximate.
Validity	How is the validity of models enforced? Alternatives include model structure, validity preserving modeling operations, and validity checking.
Unambiguity and uniqueness	A solid model representation is unambiguous if every valid representation corresponds with just one solid; this property actually characterizes the "completeness" of solid models, and it should always be satisfied. Conversely, a representation is unique if each solid has just one possible representation.
Description languages	Characterizes the types of operations a representation can provide for the construction of solid models.
Conciseness	Characterizes the representation in terms of storage requirements.
Computational ease and applicability	Characterizes the representation from the application view point: What types of algorithms can be written on the basis of the representation? What are their demands on computer power?

Over the years, several main approaches to solid modeling have been developed and used in commercial and research systems. To characterize these, we may view solid objects as point sets of the Euclidean three-dimensional space satisfying restrictions that encapsulate our idea of "solidity." To such sets, solid models assign finite representations suitable for generating data for algorithms. In other words, a solid representation encodes the infinite point set in a finite amount of computer storage in a more generic fashion. On the basis of the point set representation view, solid models may be divided in three large classes as follows:

Decomposition models	Represent a point set as a collection of simple objects from a fixed collection of primitive object types, combined with a single "gluing" operation.

Constructive models   Represent a point set as a combination of primitive point sets. Each of the primitives is represented as an instance of a primitive solid type. Constructive models include more general construction operations than mere gluing, typically some form of set-theoretic operations (union, intersection, set difference).

Boundary models   Represent a point set in terms of its boundary. The boundary of a three-dimensional "solid" point set is a two-dimensional surface that is usually represented as a collection of faces. Faces are often represented in terms of their boundary being a one-dimensional curve. Hence boundary models may be viewed as a hierarchy of models where a higher-dimension object is represented through a collection of lower-dimensional objects. Many commercial systems have extensive facilities for modeling complex curves and surfaces using the various techniques described in Section 2.2.

These major approaches to solid modeling will be described in the following three sections. This is followed by a brief account of *nonmanifold models,* which may be regarded as a hybrid of decomposition models and boundary models. In each case we will discuss both the general principles of the representation and its algorithmic techniques to the extent that is required for introducing feature modeling techniques in later chapters of this book.

2.4.2 Decomposition Models

As the name implies, decomposition models represent solid objects through a collection of non-overlapping basic blocks of material that are "pasted" together. The various alternative schemes are further characterized by the types of blocks available and the way the collection of blocks constituting a solid is recorded:

Exhaustive enumeration   Represent a solid as a three-dimensional array of rectilinear, regular blocks ("voxels"). Each block either denotes solid material (possibly of several types) or empty space. This representation is primarily used in three-dimensional *volume visualization* and some special applications where the data are naturally generated in voxel form (e.g., medical modeling on the basis of NMR imaging).

Cellular decomposition   Represent a solid as a combination of irregular "cells" that are pasted together over common faces. *Finite element meshes* (FEM) used for engineering analysis are a prime example of this representation.

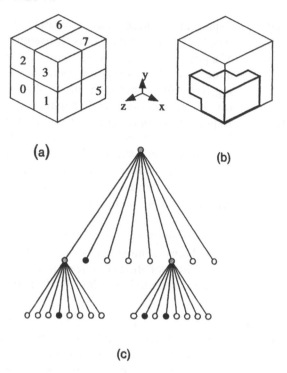

Figure 2.23 Octree concepts (Mäntylä 1988)

Space subdivision   Represent a solid as a recursive subdivision of a space
of interest, typically in rectangular blocks. Leaves of
the subdivision denote either material or void space.

Of the decomposition models, the space subdivision types serve best as general-purpose solid models. A good example of a model of this type is the *octree representation* (Jackings and Tanimoto 1980; Meagher 1982). Octrees use a recursive subdivision of the space into eight *octants* that are arranged into an 8-ary tree (hence the name). Figure 2.23 (Mäntylä 1988) depicts the octant subdivision. Usually the octree is located around the origin of its local *xyz*-coordinate system. The first-level octants correspond to the octants of the coordinate space, and in particular octant 3 is the positive octant *x, y, z* > 0. Hence the actual space of interest must be indicated separately in terms of an appropriate transformation.

Each node of an octree consists of a *code* and eight pointers. If *code = black*, the part of the space represented is all material and the pointers are empty; that is, the node is a leaf. If *code = white*, the part of the space is empty and the node is again a leaf. In the third case *code = gray*, the part of the space is partly material and partly empty, and the pointers refer to eight children that correspond to

```
struct octreeroot
{
    float xmin, ymin, zmin;      /* space of interest */
    float xmax, ymax, zmax;
    struct octree  *root;/* root of the tree */
};

struct octree
{
    char  code;                  /* BLACK, WHITE, GRAY */
    struct octree  *oct[8];      /* pointers to octants, present if GRAY */
};
```

Figure 2.24 Octree data structures

a octant subdivision of their parent node. For instance, the object of Figure 2.23 is represented by a two-level octree.

Figure 2.24 outlines a data structure for representing octrees. Here the space of interest is an orthogonal box of the xyz-space, represented by a special "root" node. It is easy to show that 7/8s of the nodes of an octree are leaves. Because of this, leaves are usually represented with another special node to avoid allocating storage for the eight nil pointers.

When applied to solid modeling, octrees are typically constructed from solid primitives such as blocks, cylinders, and spheres. For each primitive type a *classification procedure* between an instance of the primitive and an arbitrary node of the octree is needed. The procedure must be capable of distinguishing between the following cases:

- The node is completely in the exterior of the primitive.
- The node is completely in the interior of the primitive.
- The node is partially in the interior and partially in the exterior of the primitive.

The actual classification procedure works in a recursive fashion. Initially the whole space of interest is represented by one node with *code = white*, at which the algorithm is started. Each node is classified against the primitive with the classification procedure. If the first or the second case above applies, the node is marked *white* or *black*, and the recursion terminates. Otherwise, the algorithm proceeds by marking the node *gray*, subdividing it into eight octants and calling itself recursively for each octant. The subdivision is continued until a desired resolution has been reached, usually up to 6 to 12 levels.

Any primitives can be used for which a classification algorithm can be implemented. "Easy" cases include rectilinear blocks, half-spaces such as sphere, cylinder, and cone, and higher-order objects such as tori and objects bounded by so-called super quadrics (Barr 1981). In a practical implementation a "lazy classifier" using a quick and dirty intersection test is often preferable; the subdivision is continued if the quick classification test fails to determine the status of a node. Section 2.4.3 describes in more detail an algorithm for converting a constructive model to an octree.

The properties of octree representations can be summarized as follows:

Expressive power	Octrees are approximate representations. However, if a classification routine for a primitive can be written, arbitrarily accurate octrees for it can be generated at the cost of high storage use.
Validity	Octrees are always valid representations of some solid (or collection of solids). If connectivity is required, validity checking and enforcing are quite straightforward.
Unambiguity and uniqueness	Being approximate, an octree actually corresponds to a class of solids that shares the same approximation. Hence the model is not unambiguous. At a fixed resolution the representation is unique; however, an object has just one (compacted) octree representation with at most n levels.
Description languages	Octrees are usually formed by conversion from other representations, such as constructive models. In image processing, octrees can also be formed directly from rasterized image data.
Conciseness	At a fixed resolution the number of nodes in an octree of a solid object is proportional to the surface area of the object (Meagher 1982). Nevertheless, practically interesting octrees (eight levels of subdivision) are still large.
Computational ease and applicability	Most algorithms for octrees take the form of a tree traversal where a relatively simple operation is performed at each node of the tree. For further information, see (Mäntylä 1988).

For a comprehensive survey on various space subdivision schemes, see (Samet 1984b).

2.4.3 Constructive Models

Constructive models follow a set-theoretic approach to solid modeling where models are defined as combinations of primitive sets by Boolean operators (see Appendix A.2). Algorithms for the model work by inspecting the Boolean combination typically recorded in a tree-type data structure.

Half-Space Models A real-valued, analytic function $f(P)$, $P = (x, y, z)$, defined everywhere in the three-dimensional Euclidean space E^3, divides the space into two subsets: those for which $f(P) > 0$ and those for which $f(P) < 0$. (The restriction to analytic functions excludes certain "pathological" objects (Requicha 1977b).) These subsets are called *half-spaces*. For instance, functions

$$ax + by + cz + d > 0$$

$$x^2 + y^2 - r^2 < 0$$

define, respectively, the *planar half-space* that consists of all points in the positive side of the plane $ax + by + cz + d = 0$, and the *cylindrical half-space* that consists of all points inside an infinite cylinder whose axis is the z-axis and the radius is r.

Other half-spaces of interest include the remaining natural quadric surfaces such as spheres and cones, and certain higher-order surfaces such as tori. The collection includes both unbounded half-spaces (e.g., the infinite cylinder) and bounded half-spaces (e.g., the sphere $x^2 + y^2 + z^2 - r^2 < 0$). Observe that parametric surfaces cannot easily be included in the collection because the inclusion/exclusion test cannot be implemented.

On the basis of the half-space primitives, more complex objects are built with *Boolean set operations* union ($\cup$), intersection ($\cap$) and set difference ($-$). For instance, to describe a finite cylinder C of length h, we use one cylindrical half-space and two planar half-spaces, combined together with the set operation "$\cap$":

$$H_1:\quad x^2 + y^2 - r^2 < 0$$

$$H_2:\quad z > 0$$

$$H_3:\quad z - h < 0$$

$$C = \quad H_1 \cap H_2 \cap H_3$$

This construction is illustrated in Figure 2.25 (Mäntylä 1988).

Pure half-space models are not commonly used. Notable exception was the early TIPS system (Okino et al. 1978). TIPS used interesting algorithms for model evaluation on the basis of organizing representations in a sum-of-product form and using a cellular decomposition. Some of these techniques are still used in other types of constructive models.

CSG Models For human users it is easier to operate with bounded primitives instead of the unbounded half-spaces. This results in the *Constructive Solid Geometry* (CSG) approach (Voelcker and Requicha 1977). The user of a CSG modeler operates only on parameterized instances of *solid primitives* and Boolean set operations. Each primitive is internally defined as a combination of half-spaces just like the cylinder in Figure 2.25; the user has no direct access to them.

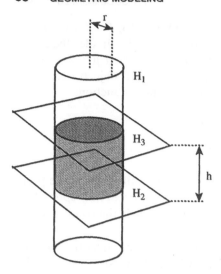

Figure 2.25 Half-space model of a finite cylinder (Mäntylä 1988)

CSG models are typically represented in a *CSG tree*. Primitives form the leaves of the tree, while interior nodes correspond to either a Boolean set operation or a rigid transformation (translation or rotation). Often several transformed copies of the same subtree may appear, in which case the tree actually becomes a *directed acyclic graph*. A sample CSG tree is shown in Figure 2.26 (Mäntylä 1988).

The primitives are chosen so as to define a bounded point set of E^3. Since the set operations available cannot destroy boundedness, CSG models are guaranteed to define bounded sets. While the ease of use of a CSG modeler depends on the collection of available primitives, the actual domain of the parts that can be represented by a CSG modeler only depends on the variety of half-spaces available in its primitives, on the available rigid motions, and on the available set operations.

Typically, the Boolean set operations in the CSG tree are regarded as being "regularized" that is, they are implemented in a way that only creates homogeneously three-dimensional models. In this case primitives are thought of as closed instead of open sets. See (Requicha 1980) for details.

Algorithms for CSG Models The CSG tree is a declarative, implicit description of the geometry of the solid. That is, it must be evaluated in order to create graphical output or perform computations on it. As suggested by the tree structure of the model, many algorithms for CSG can be formulated as a "divide-and-conquer" -type recursive traversal of the tree. In this approach the two subtrees of each internal node are processed recursively, and the partial solutions are joined to get the total solution. The recursion terminates at the leaves of the tree (primitives), which are handled with a specialized procedure for each primitive

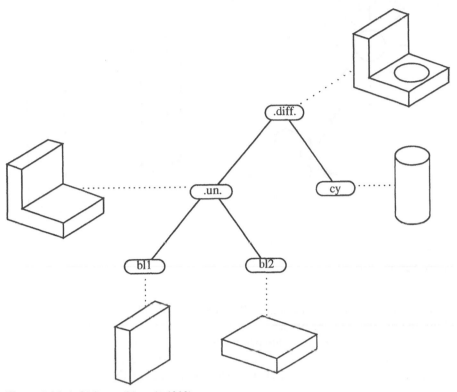

Figure 2.26 A CSG tree (Mäntylä 1988)

type. Another natural approach to CSG algorithms is based on treating the CSG tree as a Boolean expression and using Boolean logic to manipulate it. The following subsections give specific examples of both techniques.

Ray Casting The ray casting approach (Roth 1982) is a natural approach to deal with many problems on the basis of CSG models. The term arises from the problem of generating an image for a color raster scan display (see Figure 2.27). In ray casting, a "view ray" is sent from the location of the viewer through each pixel of the image. Based on the location where the ray first hits the object being viewed, the shade and the intensity of the pixel are calculated on the basis of a lighting model. By sending secondary rays from the hit location, special visual effects such as shadowing, transparency, and mirroring can be created. This process is termed *ray tracing*.

·Ray casting of CSG models can be implemented compactly on the basis of the divide-and-conquer approach outlined above. The basic idea is to *classify* each ray against the CSG tree, meaning that the ray is split into subsets residing inside and outside of the object modeled. As shown in the pseudo-code algorithm of Figure 2.28, the classification process can be performed recursively by processing left and right subtrees separately and combining the two partial solutions

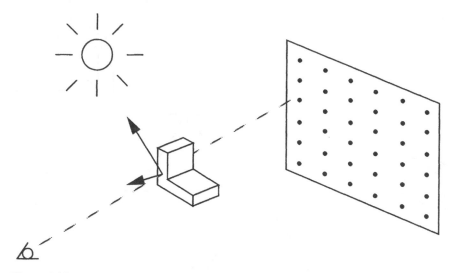

Figure 2.27 Ray casting

obtained. The image generation algorithm can now simply pick the first segment along the ray that hits the object.

The recursion terminates at the primitives. They are processed by finding the intersections between the ray and the primitive half-spaces, and subdividing the ray at the intersections found. For instance, in the case of Figure 2.29 (Mäntylä

```
Classification   RayCast(S, R)
CSGTree          *S;
Ray          *R;
{
    if(S->Op == <set operation>) {
        LeftClassification = RayCast(S->Left, R);
        RightClassification = RayCast(S->Right, R);
        return Combine(LeftClassification, RightClassification, S->Op);
    }
    else {
        switch(S->Op) {
            case "block": do 6 ray-plane intersection tests
            case "sphere": do 1 ray-quadratic intersection test
            case "cylinder": do 2 ray-plane and 1 ray-quadratic tests
            case "cone": do 1 ray-plane and 1 ray-quadratic test
            case "torus": do 1 ray-quartic intersection test
        }
        Classification = results of tests;
        return Classification;
    }
}
```

Figure 2.28 Ray classification algorithm

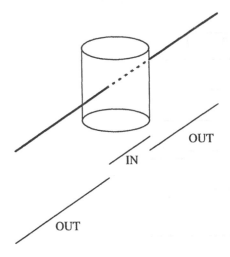

Figure 2.29 Ray classification with a primitive

1988) the result consists of two semi-infinite line segments, marked "OUT", and one finite line segment marked "IN". The required computation is straightforward. First, transform the ray so that the cylinder is of the form

$$x^2 + y^2 - r^2 \leq 0$$

and the ray of the parametric form

$$r(t) = p_1 + t(p_2 - p_1), \qquad p_i = (x_i, y_i, z_i)$$

where $t \geq 0$ is the parameter. This gives three equations

$$x^2 + y^2 = r^2$$
$$x = x_1 + t(x_2 - x_1)$$
$$y = y_1 + t(y_2 - y_1)$$

that can be solved for t.

If the system has no real solutions, the ray does not intersect the cylinder at all; if a double root occurs, the ray is tangent to the cylinder; otherwise, parameter values of two intersection points are given. The containment status of each segment found can be checked by computing its middle point and assigning the coordinates in the equation of the half-space.

In general, the result of the classification consists of a sequence of ray segments. By sorting the segments with respect to the ray parameter, the combina-

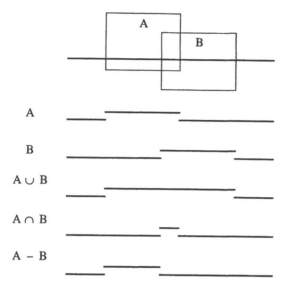

Figure 2.30 Combination of classifications

tion step is reduced to merging the sequences with a Boolean operator. Figure 2.30 (Mäntylä 1988) illustrates the nature of the required computation.

Ray casting is approximate: Instead of "evaluating" a CSG tree exactly, the tree is *sampled* along a finite number of lines, reducing the evaluation of three-dimensional set operations to one-dimensional ones. Within the limits of accuracy, ray casting is useful not only for image generation but also for calculating line drawings and integral properties of solids (Goldstein 1981).

The required computation may be large: To calculate an image at 1000 x 1000 resolution, a million ray classifications are needed. Each classification in itself can be a formidable task for realistically complex models having hundreds of primitives. Consequently various optimization schemes have been invented for speeding up the basic algorithm presented. One such optimization takes advantage of *ray coherence:* Two neighboring rays are expected to pass through the same half-spaces in the same order.

So-called *set membership classification* (Tilove 1980) algorithms are a general class of algorithms based on the divide and conquer approach. A set membership classification algorithm works on two point sets, namely the *candidate set C* and the *reference set R*. The algorithm is expected to *classify C* against *R* by forming three sets *CinR, ConR,* and *CoutR* representing the parts of *C* inside, on the boundary, and outside of *R* respectively.

Tree Manipulation Algorithms Another important family of algorithms for CSG models is based on some type of manipulation of the CSG tree on the basis of viewing it as a Boolean expression and using the elementary properties of Boolean logic (see Appendix I for basics of set theory and Boolean logic.) To give a flavor of these algorithms, we will review an algorithm for converting a CSG tree to an octree. In Chapter 9 we will see that a derivative of the algorithm is useful for machining region extraction on the basis of a CSG representation. Other uses include finite element mesh generation.

The crucial algorithm for the conversion is the *block-solid classifier* (Lee and Requicha 1982b):

Given a rectangular block and a CSG model, determine whether the block resides completely in the outside, completely in the inside, or intersects the boundary of the solid represented by the CSG model.

An ideal classifier would be expected to tell the exact answer in the case that the block intersects the solid. This is excessive, however, because the information is immediately discarded as the recursion proceeds, and the ideal classifier is too slow for practical purposes. Instead, a "lazy" classifier is used that returns one of the values IN, OUT, and ? denoting the cases that the block is definitely in the inside, in the outside, or that the (inexpensive) test used in the classifier is unable to determine the status of the block. This vagueness is not harmful because the conversion algorithm can subdivide the block in the last case so that the parts can be classified more easily.

Armed with a lazy block-solid classifier, the conversion can work recursively as shown in Figure 2.31. Initially the whole space of interest is classified against the CSG model. If the whole space is inside or outside the solid, we get a single-node octree and are done; otherwise, the space of interest is subdivided, and the parts are classified recursively. When the desired accuracy has been reached, a two-way classification can be used to determine whether the smallest voxel is inside or outside the solid. To deal with the case that after a subdivision, all parts turn out to reside in the inside or the outside, we add a "collapse" step that merges the octants into a single octree leaf node.

The preceding algorithm is generic in that it can be applied to any solid representation as far as the classifier procedure can be implemented. One way of specializing the algorithm for CSG models is based on Tilove's work on localization (Tilove 1980).

A *localization* of a CSG model S with respect to a block B is defined as another (simpler) CSG model S' such that the intersection of S and B is equal to the intersection of S' and B. That is, within B, S, and S' are identical but may differ outside B. This formulation leads to the identification of *redundant primitives* in a CSG expression. Tilove proves that if some CSG primitive P in the definition of S does not occur within B, a candidate S' can be generated by replacing P with the empty set $\varnothing$ in the expression of S. Similarly, if B is completely within P, P can be replaced by the universal set W. Generally this leads to a CSG expression that can be simplified (or in often-used parlance, *pruned*) using laws of Boolean algebra.

Localiz.tions can be computed with the *S-bounds* introduced by Cameron (1989); see Figure 2.32. Briefly, all primitives in the CSG expression are re-

```
CSG-to-octree(S, tree, depth)
solid     *S;     /* the CSG solid */
octree *tree; /* node of the octree, initially the root */
int    depth; /* initially max. depth of the recursion */
{
    switch (classify_block(B, S))
    {
        case IN:
            tree->code = BLACK;
            break;
        case OUT:
            tree->code = WHITE;
            break;
        case '?':
            if(depth == 0)
                tree->code = BLACK;
            else
            {
                tree->code = GRAY;
                subdivide(tree);
                for(i=0; i<8; i++)
                    CSG-to-octree(S, t->oct[i], depth-1);
                collapse(tree);        /* combine if all same color */
            }
    }
}
```

Figure 2.31 CSG-to-octree conversion

placed with their bounding boxes (b). These are used to compute the bounding boxes of all intermediate nodes of the tree (c), up to the root (d), by evaluating the Boolean set operations for the boxes. When this process is complete, the root box indicates the region where the actual solid resides; if some primitive is completely outside it, it is surely redundant. To find these, all bounding boxes replaced by their intersections with the root bounding box (e). In this case the result for the triangle is empty, indicating that it is redundant. If redundant primitives appear, the process can be repeated (e). The *active zones* of Rossignac and Voelcker (1989) are a similar concept.

Localization computation gives us the tool needed for implementing a block classifier for a block B against a CSG solid S along the following lines:

- For each primitive P of the CSG expression of S, check whether P is redundant within B, and perform the possible substitutions.
- Simplify the CSG expression.
- If the simplified expression is $\emptyset$, return OUT; else, if it is W, return IN, otherwise, return?.

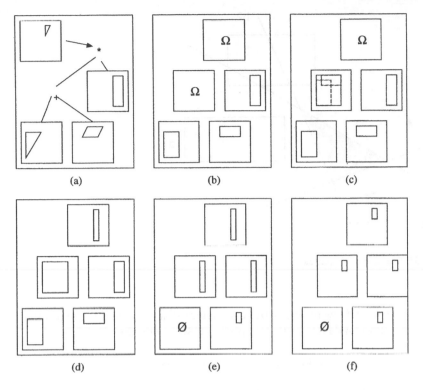

Figure 2.32 Redundancy testing with S-bounds (Cameron 1989)
+ = set addition; * = intersection; Ω = bound not yet computed

Some simplification rules applicable for set unions and intersections are as follows (see Appendix A.2):

$$\emptyset \cup A \Rightarrow A \qquad \emptyset \cap A \Rightarrow \emptyset$$
$$A \cup \emptyset \Rightarrow A \qquad A \cap \emptyset \Rightarrow \emptyset$$
$$W \cup A \Rightarrow W \qquad W \cap A \Rightarrow A$$
$$A \cup W \Rightarrow W \qquad A \cap W \Rightarrow A$$

To see a simplification of CSG expressions in action, consider the simple two-dimensional example of Figure 2.33. The CSG expression for the shaded triangle is

$$((h1 \cap h2) \cap h3)$$

For block $b1$, half-space $h3$ is $\emptyset$-redundant; hence inside $b1$ the valid local CSG expression is

$$((h1 \cap h2) \cap \emptyset),$$

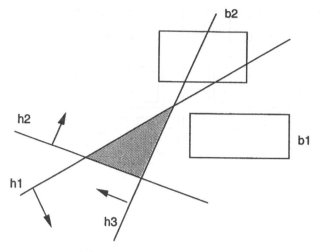

Figure 2.33 Example of simplification

which reduces to $\emptyset$. Now the classifier can deduce that $b1$ is outside the triangle. For $b2$, $h2$ is W-redundant, and the simplified CSG expression

$$((h1 \cap W) \cap h3) \Rightarrow h1 \cap h3$$

can be derived. No further pruning is possible; the block must be subdivided, and its parts reclassified with respect to the simplified expression.

Ultimately we will need a block-primitive classifier that can tell us whether a CSG primitive (or half-space) is wholly out of a block, completely contains the block or whether the surfaces of the block and the primitive intersect. Several methods for this are possible depending on the complexity of the underlying half-spaces of the CSG primitives. For instance, Samet and Tamminen (1985) solve the problem for linear half-spaces by keeping track of the minimum and maximum values of the defining function of the half-space within the block B:

- If the minimum is ≥ 0, B is IN.
- If the maximum is ≤ 0, B is OUT.
- Otherwise, a subdivision is still required to determine the status of B.

The problem that remains is the computation of the range of a half-space within a block. For this, Samet and Tamminen introduce a clever technique that maintains incrementally the information of the range during the subdivision process.

Other CSG Algorithms   The generation of images with hidden lines removed requires a much more complicated algorithm that calculates the "faces" of the solid modeled via the CSG tree. This process is termed the *boundary evaluation*. Ordinarily boundary evaluation is based on set membership classification between "primitive faces" (faces derived from CSG primitives) and CSG trees (Requicha and Voelcker 1985). In CSG modelers PADL-1 (Voelcker 1977; Requicha and Voelcker 1977a), PADL-2 (Brown 1982), and GMSOLID (Boyse and Gilchrist 1982) boundary evaluation is used to construct a complete boundary model based in the CSG tree. In particular, PADL-2 pursues *incremental boundary evaluation* (Tilove 1981, 1981b) that updates the boundary model according to incremental changes in the CSG tree. These and other CSG modelers that can construct a boundary model from a CSG model can, of course, utilize algorithms for boundary models whenever they seem more appropriate than the self-contained methods for CSG models.

Properties of CSG   The properties of CSG models can be summarized similarly as those of other models we have discussed.

Expressive power	Depends on the class of half-spaces available; typically includes planar, quadric, and toroidal half-spaces, sometimes also implicit blends of these. However, CSG cannot easily be extended to cover surface patches.
Validity	Every CSG tree is guaranteed to model a valid solid object, provided that the primitives are valid (bounded regular sets).
Unambiguity and uniqueness	Every CSG tree unambiguously models a solid. The trees are not unique, however.
Description languages	Usually textual descriptions. Nice graphical interfaces can also be provided.
Conciseness	CSG trees are very concise.
Computational ease and applicability	Divide-and-conquer and tree-manipulation methods for CSG are well understood. The simple algorithms presented above are slow; however, various optimizations are possible to make them quite interactive.

2.4.4 Boundary Models

Boundary models can be viewed as enhanced graphical models that add further graphical primitives for representing the "skin" of solid objects. Historically they emerged from polyhedral models used in computer graphics for representing objects and scenes for hidden line and surface removal. More recently various facilities for parametric surface modeling have been introduced into boundary models.

Boundary models represent a solid object by dividing its surface into a collection of *faces* in some convenient fashion. Usually the division is performed so that the shape of each face has a compact mathematical representation, for

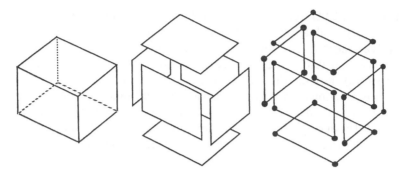

Figure 2.34 Basic constituents of boundary models

instance, so that it lies on a single planar, quadratic, toroidal, or parametric surface. The bounding curves of faces are represented through a division into *edges*. Analogously to faces, edges are chosen so as to have a convenient representation, say, a parametric form. The portion of the curve that forms the edge is chalked out in terms of two *vertices*. Figure 2.34 (Mäntylä 1988) illustrates these concepts.

Boundary Data Structures A boundary data structure must record the faces of the object modeled. Typically this is achieved by means of a hierarchical data structure where faces are represented in terms of their bounding edges, and these in terms of their bounding vertices. In addition to these basic types of objects and their relations, geometric information such as face and curve equations and vertex coordinates must be present. It is customary to bundle all information of the shape of the entities under the term *geometry*, and similarly information of their connections under the term *topology*.

Many data structures for encoding topology and geometry have been proposed for the representation of boundary models. Surveys and discussion of various alternatives can be found in (Baer et al. 1979, Weiler 1985). In this context, we will only look at some prime examples.

Polygon-Based Boundary Models A boundary model that has only planar faces is called a *polyhedral model*. Because all edges of a polyhedron are straight lines, a very compact representation for this special case can be designed. Typically each face is represented as a *polygon*, a sequence of coordinate triples. No other topological information (e.g., face-face neighborhood relationships) is present. This type of model is common as input to visualization packages. No surface information needs to be given because face equations can be computed on the basis of the vertex coordinates.

Vertex-Based Boundary Models In a polygon-based boundary model, vertex coordinates are repeated as often as the vertex appears in the faces. This waste-

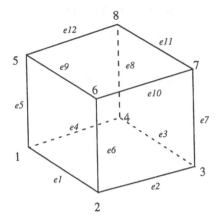

v1	x1	y1	z1	f1	v1	v2	v3 v4
v2	x2	y2	z2	f2	v6	v2	v1 v5
v3	x3	y3	z3	f3	v7	v3	v2 v6
v4	x4	y4	z4	f4	v8	v4	v3 v7
v5	x5	y5	z5	f5	v5	v1	v4 v8
v6	x6	y6	z6	f6	v8	v7	v6 v5
v7	x7	y7	z7				
v8	x8	y8	z8				

Figure 2.35 A vertex-based boundary model

fulness can be eliminated by introducing vertices as independent entities of the data structure, leading to various *vertex-based boundary models*. Availability of explicit vertices also makes it possible to derive topological relationships without expensive numeric comparison of the coordinates.

Figure 2.35 (Mäntylä 1988) gives a simple example of a vertex-based boundary model. Observe that the vertices around each face are listed in a *consistent order*, clockwise as seen from the outside of the cube. This is useful in many algorithms, such as hidden line or surface removal where it allows the elimination of *back faces* on the basis of face normal vectors ("back face culling").

Edge-Based Boundary Models If a boundary model also has faces other than planar, it becomes useful to include edge nodes explicitly in the data structure for storing information of curves. An *edge-based boundary model* represents faces by a closing sequence of edges, or *loops*. Each edge in turn has two vertices.

The inclusion of explicit nodes for each of the basic object types (face, edge, and vertex) opens the door for elaborating the model further. For instance, to aid algorithms such as hidden surface removal and shading, explicit face-face neighborhood information can be added. Of course, redundant information increases the risk of inconsistency.

The *winged-edge data structure* (Baumgart 1974, 1975) is a good example of a relatively complex boundary data structure with plenty of redundant information. The data structure is based on the observation that every edge has exactly one "next" edge and two "previous" edges in each of the two faces it appears in. These are recorded as the "wings" of the edge. Faces only need to record one of their edges; the rest of the loop can be traced by following the wings. Analogously, also the loop of edges around a vertex can be traced. See Figure 2.36 (Mäntylä 1988) for explanation. Appendix B describes in detail a particular data

eid	vstart	vend	fcw	fccw	ncw	pcw	nccw	pccw
e1	v1	v2	f1	f2	e2	e4	e5	e6
e2	v2	v3	f1	f3	e3	e1	e6	e7
e3	v3	v4	f1	f4	e4	e2	e7	e8
e4	v4	v1	f1	f5	e1	e3	e8	e5
...								...
e12	v8	v5	f5	f6	e5	e8	e11	e9

vid	estart	coords	fid	estart
v1	e1	x1 y1 z1	f1	e1
v2	e2	x2 y2 z2	f2	e9
...			...	
v8	e12	x8 y8 z8	f6	e9

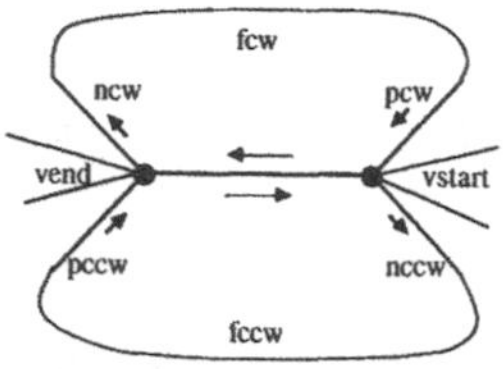

Figure 2.36 The winged-edge data structure

structure, the *half-edge data structure* which is a variant of the winged-edge representation.

Also *face-based* boundary data structures have been proposed. These concentrate on recording the face-face relationships of the object in a representation commonly termed the *face adjacency hypergraph* (FAH). In a FAH, faces act as the nodes of the graph, and links represent adjacency relations between the faces. This representation is of particular interest to feature modeling because face relationships are useful for automatic feature extraction. Chapters 4 and 9 will discuss the hypergraph representation further.

Validity of Boundary Models   A boundary model is *valid* if it defines the boundary of a "reasonable" solid object. This includes the following conditions (Mäntylä 1988):

1. Faces of the model do not intersect each other except at common vertices or edges.
2. The boundaries of faces are simple polygons that do not intersect themselves.
3. The set of faces of the boundary model "closes," that is, forms the complete "skin" of the solid with no missing parts.

The first and second conditions exclude self-intersecting objects. The third condition disallows "open" objects. The first condition can be enforced by demanding that each edge appears in exactly two faces; hence no edge can be the boundary of a missing part of the surface. Observe that the winged-edge data structure "automatically" satisfies this criterion because edges occurring in just one face cannot be represented. In mathematical terms, these conditions ensure that the surface forms a "2-manifold", that is, a surface where every point has a full two-dimensional neighborhood of other points of the surface (Mäntylä 1988).

Unfortunately, the *geometric integrity* of a boundary model defined by the second and third conditions requires using a computationally expensive test that involves a comparison of each pair of faces in the solid, or limiting the user's freedom by giving him only validity-enforcing solid description mechanisms.

Construction of Boundary Models   Being extensions of graphical models, boundary models are naturally suited for rich, drafting-type interfaces. The major problem that arises, however, is the integrity of the model.

One solution is to provide a CSG-based solid description language to the user and construct boundary models only through conversion from CSG. Unfortunately, Boolean set operations for boundary models are computationally expensive and sensitive to numerical problems. Moreover the 2-manifold condition may be broken. In this sense boundary models are usually *not* closed under set operations (regularized or not). Hence boundary model construction mechanisms based on CSG conversion or set operations are always vulnerable.

A more natural approach is to build boundary models incrementally, using various types of local manipulations. For instance, Figure 2.37 (Mäntylä 1988)

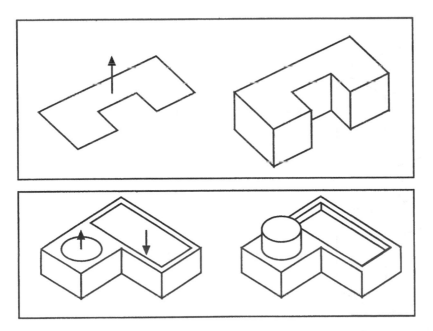

Figure 2.37 Solid construction by sweeping

gives examples of designs that can be created by "sweeping" operations. Unfortunately, these sweeping operations are not "safe" either. See (Braid 1979) for discussion on conditions under which sweeping and similar operations can be kept integrity preserving.

One popular approach for building various types of local manipulations of boundary models is based on the *Euler-Poincaré formula:* Let v, e, f, s, r, and h denote the numbers of vertices, edges, faces, shells (surfaces), interior loops in faces (rings), and through holes in a solid. Then

$$v - e + f = 2(s - h) + r$$

A collection of faces, edges, and vertices can be a valid boundary model only if the numbers of these elements satisfy the formula. Hence the equation can be considered a necessary integrity criterion for boundary models. Two sample objects with their Euler-Poincaré equations are shown in Figure 2.38 (Mäntylä 1988).

The main asset of the Euler-Poincaré formula is that it is possible to define a collection of model manipulation operators that add and remove faces, edges, and vertices to a boundary model in a way that maintains the validity of the formula. These are termed *Euler operators*. It can be shown that a collection of six operators (with their inverses) is sufficient for the creation of all objects of interest. A popular collection of Euler operators is shown in Figure 2.39 (Mäntylä 1988).

Objects constructed with Euler operators are always topologically valid. The power of Euler operators is captured by the following theorems (Mäntylä 1988):

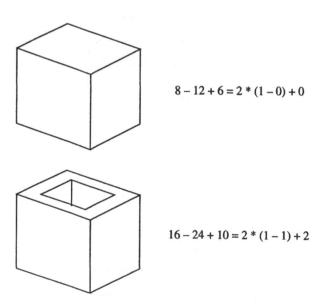

$$8 - 12 + 6 = 2 * (1 - 0) + 0$$

$$16 - 24 + 10 = 2 * (1 - 1) + 2$$

Figure 2.38 Two objects and their equations

Operator	Transition	Description
	v e f h s r	
mvfs	1 0 1 0 1 0	Make vertex, face, solid
mev	1 1 0 0 0 0	Make edge, vertex
mef	0 1 1 0 0 0	Make edge, face
kemr	0 -1 0 0 0 1	Kill edge, make ring
kfmrh	0 1 -1 1 0 0	Kill face, make ring, hole
kvfs	-1 0 -1 0 -1 0	Kill vertex, face, solid
kev	-1 -1 0 0 0 0	Kill edge, vertex
kef	0 -1 -1 0 0 0	Kill edge, face
mekr	0 1 0 0 0 -1	Make edge, kill ring
mfkrh	0 -1 1 -1 0 0	Make face, kill ring, hole

Figure 2.39 A collection of Euler operators

Theorem: Let S be a valid boundary data structure (i.e., S satisfies all topological integrity constraints). Then there exists a finite sequence of Euler operators that can completely remove S.

Corollary: All valid boundary data structures can be created with a finite sequence of Euler operators.

Theorem: Euler operators are *sound* in that they cannot create topologically invalid boundary data structures.

Algorithms for Boundary Models In comparison to CSG, boundary models are *explicit*: The available faces, edges, and vertices make the design of many algorithms straightforward. In particular, all "textbook" techniques for generating output from graphical models are applicable also to boundary models. Well-known techniques of hidden line and surface removal and shading can readily be applied. Advanced graphical display devices include hardware support for the rapid processing of polyhedral models, including shading and texturing computations. Two general techniques are available for the calculation of basic engineering properties based on boundary models, namely the method of *direct integration* and the use of the *divergence theorem* of calculus. See (Lee and Requicha 1982a, b) for details.

Properties of Boundary Models We can again summarize the properties of boundary models using our general framework:

Expressive power	The modeling space of boundary models depends on the types of surfaces that can be used. Parametric surfaces can be included relatively easily; hence boundary models can represent objects from a more general modeling space than CSG.
Validity	Validity of boundary models is difficult to establish. While it is possible to manage topological validity without large overhead, it is hard to enforce geometric correctness without penalizing interactive design.
Unambiguity and uniqueness	Valid boundary models are unambiguous. They are not unique. However, two different models of the same part can be compared much more easily than two CSG models.
Description languages	Boundary models can be created using graphical "drawing" and "sweeping" operations or on a CSG-like input on top of a boundary model. The large variety of construction methods is in fact a main asset of boundary models.
Conciseness	Boundary models of useful objects are large.
Computational ease and applicability	Boundary models readily include the data needed for driving a graphical display. Analysis algorithms based directly on boundary models are complex particularly if non-planar faces are present.

2.4.5 Non-manifold Models

Conventional boundary models can represent the surface geometry of a single part. This restriction can be problematic in some applications. Typical examples include the following:

- An application wants to compute heat transfer from one part touching another. The computation needs a representation of the two-dimensional region where the parts touch each other.
- An application wants to compute crack propagation within a part under a load. The computation needs a representation including one- and two-dimensional geometric elements within the part.
- An application needs to represent an object consisting of several materials. A representation of the internal structure of the part is again needed. Representing such a composite as a collection of parts, one for each connected piece of material, is unattractive, because high-level algorithms such as Boolean set operations cannot be supported easily.

So called *non-manifold* models have been introduced to deal with these issues. The term includes also other types of models than the 2-manifolds covered by conventional boundary models can be represented. It can be regarded an un-happy misnomer; in addition to that it is not very descriptive to say that some-thing is *not* a manifold, it appears that two different types of modelers are termed "non-manifold," although some systems seem to combine properties of both types.

First, several modeling systems recognize the usefulness of being able to in-clude lower dimensional entities than solids in a solid model data structure. Such entities can be used to represent, for instance, dimension lines and other nota-tion. The challenge is to support general geometric algorithms independent on the dimension. So, for instance, such a *mixed-dimensional* system is expected to be able to compute Boolean set operations involving, say, a solid and a two-dimensional region.

Another type of a system emphasizes the representation of composite objects. This leads to a *cellular model*, where objects consist of a collection of "cells" touching each other along two-dimensional regions (i.e., faces). This results in a scheme that is a strict generalization of the boundary representation scheme and shares similar validity criteria. For instance, in a cellular model every face should occur in exactly two cells (including the infinite "external" cell), and every edge must have a cycle of cells occurring around it. Furthermore the cells around each vertex must form a regular structure as follows: Imagine placing a small sphere at the vertex, and intersecting the cells with the sphere. The intersections define a graph on the surface of the sphere; the graph must be planar. This view sug-gests using similar modeling primitives as those used in boundary representa-tions; indeed several authors have proposed multi-dimensional extensions to Euler operators.

Basic Concepts of Non-Manifold Models   The term "non-manifold" is used because non-manifold models relax some of the topological correctness criteria for boundary representation models. Recall that ordinary boundary mod-els require that (1) all edges separate exactly two faces and (2) all vertices are surrounded by a single circuit of faces. This situation holds for the model in Figure 2.40(a); observe that all points belonging to the surface of the part are surrounded by a disk of surface. In a non-manifold model such as the one shown

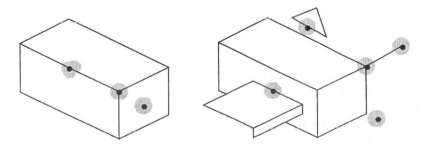

Figure 2.40 Manifold and non-manifold neighborhood configurations

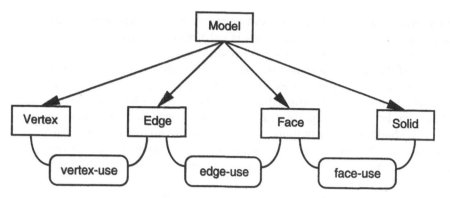

Figure 2.41 A basic non-manifold data structure

in (b), other types of point neighborhoods are also permissible. Observe that "dangling edges" and "dangling faces" are included. Moreover edges may have just one neighboring face, such as in the "dangling triangle" in the figure, or three faces, such as for the edges along which the L-plate is joined with the block.

By and large, non-manifold models are constructed from similar geometric elements as boundary representations. Typical basic elements include fundamental point elements of various dimensions, and connection elements linking the point set elements together. The point set elements of 0, 1, 2, and 3 dimensions match with the more common terms "vertex," "edge," "face," and "solid."

Connection elements generalize the notion of a "loop" of edges bounding a face of a boundary representation model (or, by dualism, a "cycle" of edges around a vertex). A "face-use" element denotes the appearance of a face in a solid; in a cellular model each face should have exactly two "face-use" elements. Similarly an "edge-use" denotes the appearance of an edge in a loop of edges around a face (Weiler 1986); as seen, an edge may have any number of "edge-uses." A basic data structure with these elements is depicted in the diagram of Figure 2.41.

Selective Geometric Complexes   To get a more concrete view of nonmanifold models and their properties, let us look at an important sample model in more detail. The _selective geometric complexes_ (SGC) model of Rossignac and O'Connor (1990) aims at providing a unified representation and manipulation approach for geometric models of various mixed dimensions. SGCs can represent nonmanifold and inhomogeneous point sets, non-closed point sets with incomplete boundaries, point sets with missing points or edges, and disjoint regions. This means that the representational power is sufficient for modeling such phenomena as cracks in material, finite element models, and open spaces with incomplete boundaries.

The basic entities of SGC are *cells* that are open subdivisions of n-dimensional manifolds; in other words, cells do not include their boundaries. With each cell is associated an *extent* that describes the geometry of the cell and *boundaries* that consist of lower-dimensional cells either bounding the cell or contained within it (in the case of internal cracks). The inverse relation from a cell to the higher-dimensional cells it is a boundary of is also stored; this is termed the *star* of the cell. A neighborhood indicator (left, right, full) is stored with each star link.

Each cell also contains a Boolean flag *active*. The point set represented by an SGC is the set union of the active cells represented in the data structure; hence, by changing the settings of the *active* flags, a given collection of cells can represent different point sets.

Let us introduce some terminology needed for discussing SGC algorithms. The *k-dimensional skeleton* of a complex A is defined as the union of A's cells of dimension k or less. Two complexes A and B are termed *equal* if they have the same cells. Two complexes A and B are *compatible* if for each cell $a \in A$ and $b \in B$, it holds that $a \cap b \neq \emptyset \Rightarrow a = b$. That is, if A and B overlap, they do it over the same cells. Last, a complex B is a *refinement* of A if every cell of A is the union of some cells of B.

Algorithms of SGC's are based on three main primitive operations:

Subdivision   The subdivision operation takes two SGCs, A and B, and makes them compatible by refining them, (by subdividing overlapping cells of A and B as needed). The result of the subdivision operation is two SGC's A' and B' such that A' is a refinement of A, B' is a refinement of B, and A and B are compatible.

Selection   The selection operation selects cells of one or several compatible SGC's, and sets their active flags according to some criterion.

Simplification   The simplification operation converts a given SGC A to a simpler SGC A' modeling the same point set by merging or deleting cells according to certain criteria.

The operations are specified in a completely dimension-independent fashion. For instance, the subdivision algorithm is implemented as described below.

The operation of the subdivision algorithm is illustrated in Figure 2.42 (Rossignac and O'Connor 1990). The two objects A (block) and B (circle) are made compatible by subdivision; for clarity, the top row shows the progress of the algorithm for A and the bottom row for B. In the first iteration ($k = 1$), a 0-cell of A is first used to subdivide the 1-cell of B; B has no 0-cells, so A is unchanged. Next A and B are subdivided at the intersections of their 1-cells. In the second iteration, subdividing the 2-cell of A with the 1-cells of B causes the 2-cell of A to be subdivided into three smaller 2-cells. Similarly B is refined with A's 1-cell.

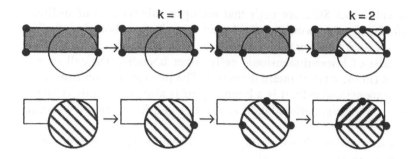

Figure 2.42 Making two objects compatible by subdivision (Rossignac and O'Connor 1990)

Boolean set operations of SGCs are trivially implemented on top of the subdivision algorithm followed by selection. For instance, the union of two SGC's A and B is obtained by first subdividing A and B and then selecting those cells that are active either in A or in B.

The simplification operation can work by applying three primitive operations exhaustively. The *drop* operation removes inactive cells whose stars are empty, namely those that do not bound any cells. The *join* operation merges two cells sharing a boundary. The *incorporate* operation removes an interior boundary cell. Again the definitions of the operations are dimension-independent. An example of simplification is shown in Figure 2.43.

2.5 PARAMETRIC AND VARIATIONAL MODELS

The construction of a complex model is not a straightforward task even when using the high-level and powerful operations of a solid modeler. The development of a large model may take days and weeks, representing a high investment. It is therefore important that a modeling environment supports reuse of existing

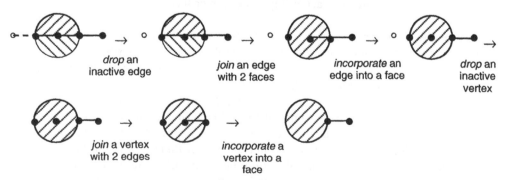

Figure 2.43 Simplification of an SGC (Rossignac and O'Connor 1990)

models. Indeed, it has been estimated that perhaps 80% of all design tasks are *variational* in that the goal of the design is to adapt an existing basic design to new requirements. Besides variational design, *reuse of existing designs* is also important to support standardized part and product families in innovative design.

2.5.1 Concepts

Parametric and *variational models* have been developed to address the above and other similar requirements. Terms "parametric" and "variational" have been used almost interchangeably in technical and particularly commercial contexts. From the viewpoint of the end user, the two types of systems are similar to the extent that it is not always straightforward to determine from the outside which type of a system one is using.

Indeed the overall design process supported by both parametric and variational systems is similar:

1. First, the user creates the nominal topology of the design by means of ordinary geometric modeling or solid modeling operations. The result is a model exhibiting the desired geometric elements and connectivity between the elements, but without the dimensions.
2. Next, the user describes the required properties between the model entities in terms of *geometric constraints*. The constraints specify desired mathematical relationships between the numerical variables of the model entities. Typical geometric constraints for two-dimensional designs are listed in Figure 2.44; the figure also indicates the mathematical relationships induced by the constraints.
3. The modeling system applies a general solution procedure to the constraints, resulting in an evaluated model where the declared constraints are satisfied, if possible. If the system of constraints cannot be satisfied, the system (hopefully) issues a warning message to the user, (hopefully) indicating the nature of the problem.
4. The user can create variants of the model by changing the values of the constrained variables. After each change, a new instance of the model is created by re-executing the constraint solution procedure. In more advanced cases the user can also add new constraints or remove existing constraints to model further variational designs.

A simple example of a parametric/variant design is shown in Figure 2.45. The model consists of five modeling entities, numbered from *1* to *5*. Declared constraints between the entities are indicated symbolically on the figure as follows:

- Line 1 is horizontal and of length *b*.
- Line 5 is perpendicular to 1 and of length *a*.

Constraint	Equation
Distance between two points 	$(x_1 - x_2)^2 + (y_1 - y_2)^2 - d^2 = 0$
Distance along a line at an angle 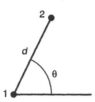	$(x_2 - x_1) - d \cos \theta = 0$ $(y_2 - y_1) - d \sin \theta = 0$
Distance along horizontal direction 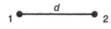	$(x_2 - x_1) - d = 0$ $y_2 - y_1 = 0$
Distance along vertical direction	$x_2 - x_1 = 0$ $(y_2 - y_1) - d = 0$

Figure 2.44 Examples of geometric constraints

- Line 3 is parallel to line 5.
- Line 2 is a circular arc, tangent to lines 1 and 3 on their respective sides.
- Line 4 is oriented at an angle α with respect to line 3.

Observe that the connectivity of the shape also can be interpreted as mathematical constraints; for instance, the end points of lines 1 and 5 must meet at the left top corner of the shape, leading to equality constraints between the end point coordinates.

2.5.2 Parametric/Variational Techniques

Even from the technical viewpoint, the line between parametric and variational models is blurred, because many systems employ a hybrid of both types of methods.

Rigid Constraint Satisfaction: Procedural Parametric Models The simplest type of a system providing support for variational design works along

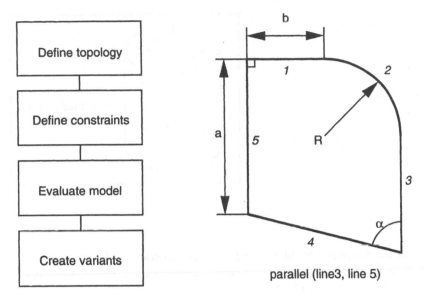

Figure 2.45 Sample parametric/variational definition

the lines of the drafting system example in Section 2.1. These systems store the construction sequence applied during the design of a part in the form of a procedure encoded in some suitable notation. Effectively this leads to representing the construction as a sequence of assignments to model variables, where each assignment in the sequence computes the value of a model variable as a function of the already computed variables or original *input parameters*. To create parametric variations, the construction sequence is re-evaluated after changing values of some of the input parameters (typically, dimension values). In some systems, the procedure can be directly edited and re-interpreted, or the procedures can be written from scratch by the user using a textual programming notation. Because the flow of computation is fixed by the procedural representation of the constraints, we will call these models *unidirectionally parametric,* or equivalently, *procedural.*

A procedural parametric model was included as a part of the PADL 1 CSG modeler. Solids in PADL-1 were described using the PADL language which included operations for defining parameters and instantiating solid objects using the defined parameters. A simple example of the syntax is given in Figure 2.46 (Requicha 1977). Relationships between primitives were described by using the same variables for their instantiation; for instance, another cylinder may be related to the one in the figure by the definition

```
&DX2 = &DX + 60.0 TOL .01
&DY2 = &DY + 85.0 TOL .01
&CY2 = &ZCYL(&RAD, &HGT) AT (&DX2, &DY2, 0.0)
```

```
&DX  = 100.0  TOL  .1
&DY  = 150.0  TOL  .1
&RAD = 20  TOL  .2
&HGT = 45  TOL  .05
&CY1 = &ZCYL(&RAD,  &HGT)
       AT  (&DX,  &DY,  0.0)
```

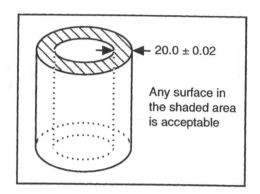

Figure 2.46 Parametric model of PADL-1

Observe that the language could be used to define tolerances; PADL-1 in fact had algorithms for computing *tolerance chains* over multiple relations and reasoning about the tolerances defined.

While being relatively straightforward to implement, procedural systems can only express a modest range of variations. The fixed sequence of assignments means that adding new types of dependencies between the variables is quite difficult. Hence reusing existing models as a basis of similar new ones is not generally possible. The procedural method also couples tightly the steps 1 and 2 of the parametric design process outlined in the previous section, leading to a rigid design environment not suited for exploration and "what-if" analysis.

Flexible Constraint Satisfaction   Recognizing these problems, more advanced parametric/variational models have been developed in which the fixed sequence of assignments is replaced by means of a general procedure that is not bound to the original sequence of modeling operations used in the original construction of the model. These systems employ some type of a declarative representation of the constraints, instead of a procedure; as discussed in more detail in Chapter 8, possible representations include constraint graphs and first-order predicate logic. To create variations of the model, the constraints are edited, and a general *constraint satisfaction algorithm* is executed to make the edited relationships satisfied.

A distinction between parametric and variational methods can be made according to the type of constraint satisfaction algorithm employed by these systems, as follows:

Parametric   Parametric systems solve constraints by applying sequentially assignments to model variables, where each assigned value is computed as a function of the previously assigned values. Unlike procedural systems, the order of the assignments is flexible, determined by a *constraint propagation algorithm*.

Variational   Variational systems solve constraints by constructing a system of equations representing the constraints, and solving all constraints of the system simultaneously on the basis of a numerical equation-solving procedure or some equivalent method.

To further highlight the distinction between parametric and variational systems, let us consider the two respective forms

$$x = \frac{-b \pm (b^2 - 4ac)^{1/2}}{2a} \qquad ax^2 + bx + c = 0$$

An *explicit equation* such as the first form can be used directly to compute the value of the variable x, given the parameters a, b, and c, and the sign of the square root. A parametric system can work by scanning the constraints and applying predefined solution methods such as the first form. In contrast, an *implicit equation* such as the second form needs to be "solved" for x. As in this case, multiple solutions are possible. On the other hand, the first equation is of little value if, say, a needs to be computed on the basis of the other variables, whereas the second form can be solved also for any of the "variables" a, b, and c.

Both methods have their advantages and problems. Being based on explicit sequential constraint satisfaction, parametric models can be evaluated rapidly. However, they cannot deal with general mutually coupled constraints. On the other hand, while variational models using implicit constraint satisfaction techniques can deal with coupled constraints, they are slower and more limited in their capability of handling incompletely specified models, and they may have difficulty in detecting inconsistent models.

This has led some researchers to look at hybrid techniques that try to decouple constraint equations in subsets that can be processed sequentially; see, for example, (Owen 1991, Verroust et al. 1992.) Another approach is to extend constraint propagation methods by a relaxation technique for handling coupled (cyclic) constraints. This method was pioneered by Sutherland in his Sketchpad system (1963); another well-known example is (Borning 1979).

Parametric and variational methods are discussed further in Chapter 8. Moreover Chapter 5 will discuss parametric and variational methods for inferring part positions in an assembly on the basis of declared assembly relationships.

Parametric Modeling in GEOMAP-III   To illustrate the distinction between procedural and parametric modeling further, let us give another example of influential work.

Figure 2.47 gives a simple example of a parametric model of the GEOMAP-III modeler (Kimura 1986). GEOMAP stores the relationships between geometric elements of a boundary representation model using a logic programming notation. The goal of parametric design is to compute locations (and tolerances) for all geometric entities of the model in a sequence starting from "fixed" enti-

```
X-Reference(F)
Y-Reference(G)
Z-Reference(I)
Distance(F, A, X)
Distance(F, D, Z)
Distance(E, G, Y)
Distance(E, B, W)
Distance(I. H. S)
```

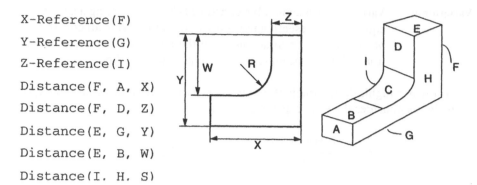

Figure 2.47 Parametric model of GEOMAP-III (Kimura 1986); reprinted by permission of Elsevier Science)

ties and working towards dependent entities. In logic notation, this process is expressed as the goal:

```
Fixed(A) and Fixed(B) and ... and Fixed(I)
```

To satisfy the goal, the following rules of inference are used:

```
X-Reference(X) -> Fixed(X)
Fixed(X) and Distance(X, Y, distance) -> Fixed(Y)
Fixed(Y) and Distance(X, Y, distance) -> Fixed(X)
Fixed(X) and Fixed(Y) and Round(X, Y, Z, Radius) ->
Fixed(Z)
```

By applying the rules, we get the following sequence of inferencing operations:

```
X-Reference(F)   -> Fixed(F)
Y-Reference(G)   -> Fixed(G)
Z-Reference(I)   -> Fixed(I)
Fixed(F) and Distance(F, A, X)   -> Fixed(A)
Fixed(F) and Distance(F, D, Z)   -> Fixed(D)
Fixed(G) and Distance(E, G, Y)   -> Fixed(E)
Fixed(E) and Distance(E, B, W)   -> Fixed(B)
Fixed(I) and Distance(I, H, S)   -> Fixed(H)
Fixed(B) and Fixed(D) and Round(C, D, B, R)  -> Fixed(C)
```

That is, the whole design becomes fixed, and the computation is finished successfully.

Observe that while the solution procedures (expressed by means of the rules of inference) are fixed, the order of their application is flexible, determined by the inferencing algorithm independently on the sequence in which the model was constructed by the user. Therefore we conclude that the model is parametric.

REVIEW QUESTIONS

2.1 Give examples of geometric computations in various applications in engineering. What types of answers are required?

2.2 Show that the Bernstein blending functions in Equation (2.10) sum to unity.

2.3 Derive the B-spline blending functions in Figure 2.16.

2.4 Why is the circle parametrization of Figure 2.17 unattractive?

2.5 What are the reasons for choosing parametric representations of curves and surfaces in CAD, instead of non-parametric representations.

2.6 Parametric cubic curves:

(a) have _____ degrees of freedom
(b) use _____ degree polynomial
(c) have _____ continuity

2.7 What is the difference between approximated and interpolated curves?

2.8 Why are B-splines more popular than Bézier curves? (Or, what are their advantages?)

2.9 For Bézier curves, n control points yield _____ degree polynomial; changing one control point affects _____ segments; u varies form _____ to _____.

2.10 For B-splines, n control points yield _____ degree polynomial; changing one control point affects _____ segments; u varies from _____ to _____.

2.11 Given the control polygons below, sketch (approximately) B-splines for $k = 2$ and $k = 3$.

 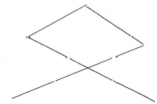

2.12 Why are rational polynomials used in curve/surface representations?

2.13 What conditions must be met in order to get tangent continuity between two Bézier curves? (A sketch will help.)

2.14 (a) Find the parametric cubic that best approximates the circular arc $x^2 + y^2 = 9$ in the positive quadrant. How close can you get?

(b) Repeat the above exercise for a bicubic patch to represent the sphere $x^2 + y^2 + z^2 = 9$.

2.15 Show that (asymptotically) $7/8$ of the nodes of an octree are leaves.

2.16 Outline an algorithm for computing the volume of an octree on the basis of the data representation of Figure 2.24.

2.17 Give definitions of (a) rectilinear block and (b) truncated cone CSG primitives in terms of half-spaces.

2.18 Explain how the edges of a loop can be traced by following the "wing" pointers of the winged-edge data structure of Figure 2.36. How about the edges around a vertex?

2.19 Test your understanding: Give the Euler-Poincaré equation for a disconnected boundary model consisting of (a) two rectilinear blocks and (b) a coffee cup.

2.20 (a) Topological validation is a necessary but not sufficient condition for solid model validation. Explain. (b) What are the different alternative methods for topological validation?

2.21 Outline an algorithm for approximating the volume of a CSG object on the basis of ray tracing.

2.22 What are the advantages and disadvantages of spatial solid models?

2.23 Distinguish between parametric and variational modeling.

BIBLIOGRAPHY

Baer, A., Eastman, C. M., and Henrion, M., 1979, Geometric modeling: A survey, *Computer Aided Design* **11** (5): 253–272.

Barr, A. H., 1981, Superquadrics and angle-preserving transformations, *IEEE Comp. Gr. and Appl.* **1** (1).

Baumgart, B., 1974, Geometric modeling for computer vision, Ph.D. dissertation, Department of Computer Science, Stanford University, also available as Tech. Rep. CS-463.

Baumgart, B., 1975, A polyhedron representation for computer vision, *National Computer Conf.*, AFIPS Conf. Proc. **44**: 589–596.

Borning, A., 1979, Thinglab—A constraint-oriented simulation laboratory, Technical Report SSL-79-3, XEROX Palo Alto Research Center, 3333 Coyote Hill Road, Palo Alto, CA 94304.

Boyse, J. W., and Gilchrist, J. E., 1982, GMSolid: Interactive modeling for design and analysis of solids, *IEEE Comp. Gr. and Appl.* **2** (2): 86–97.

Braid, I. C., 1979, Notes on a geometric modeller, Computer Laboratory, University of Cambridge, CAD Group Document 101.

Brown, C. M., 1982, PADL-2: A technical summary, *IEEE Comp. Gr. and Appl.* **2** (2): 69–84.

Cameron, S. A., 1989, Efficient intersection tests for objects defined constructively, *Int. J. of Rob. Res.* **8** (1).

Farin, G., 1990, *Curves and Surfaces in Computer-Aided Geometric Design: A Practical Guide*, second edition, Academic Press.

Faux, I. D., and Pratt, M. J., 1979, *Computational Geometry for Design and Manufacture*, Ellis Horwood.

Goldstein, R., 1981, Defining the bounding edges of a SynthaVision solid model, *Proc. of 18th ACM/IEEE Design Automation Conf.*

Hoffman, C., 1989, *Geometric & Solid Modelling*, Morgan Kaufmann.

Jackins, C. L., and Tanimoto, S. L., 1980, Octtrees and their use in representing three-dimensional objects, *Comp. Gr. and Image Proc.* **14**: 249–270.

Kimura, F., Suzuki, H., and Wingård, L., 1986, A uniform approach to dimensioning and tolerancing in product modelling, in K. B., L. Estensen, P. Falster, and E. A. Warman, eds., Computer Applications in Production and Engineering (CAPE '86), Elsevier Science, pp. 165–178.

Lee, Y. T., and Requicha, A. A. G., 1982a, Algorithms for computing the volume and other integral properties of solid objects. I. Known methods and open issues, *Comm. of the ACM* **25** (9): 635–641

Lee, Y. T., and Requicha, A. A. G., 1982b, Algorithms for computing the volume and other integral properties of solid objects. II. A family of algorithms based on representation conversion and cellular approximation, *Comm. of the ACM* **25** (9): 642–650.

Meagher, D., 1982, Geometric modeling using octree encoding, *Comp. Gr. and Image Proc.* **19**: 129–147.

Mortenson, M., 1985, *Geometric Modelling*, Wiley.

Mäntylä, M., 1988, *An Introduction to Solid Modelling*, Computer Science Press.

Okino, N., and Kubo, H., 1978, Technical information processing system TIPS-1, Institute of Precision Engineering, Hokkaido University.

Owen, J. C., 1991, Algebraic solution for geometry from dimensional constraints, in J. Rossignac and J. Turner, eds., *Proc. of First ACM Symp. on Solid Modelling Foundations and CAD/CAM Applications*, June 5-7, ACM Press, pp. 397–407.

Requicha, A. A. G., 1977, Mathematical models of rigid solids, Tech. Memo. No. 28, Production Automation Project, University of Rochester.

Requicha, A. A. G., 1980, Representations of solid objects—Theory, methods, and systems, *ACM Computing Surveys* **12** (4): 437–464.

Requicha, A. A. G., and Voelcker, H. B., 1977, Constructive solid geometry, Tech. Memo. No. 25, Production Automation Project, University of Rochester.

Requicha, A. A. G., and Voelcker, H. B., 1983, Boolean operations in solid modeling: Boundary evaluation and merging algorithms, *Proc. IEEE* **3** (7): 30–44.

Risler, J.-J., 1992, *Mathematical Methods for CAD*, Cambridge University Press.

Rossignac, J. R., and O'Connor, M., 1990, Selective geometric complex: a dimension-independent model for pointsets with internal structures and incomplete boundaries, in M. Wozny, J. U. Turner, and K. Preiss, eds., *Geometric Modeling for Product Engineering*, North-Holland.

Rossignac, J. R., and Voelcker, H. B., 1989, Active zones in CSG for accelerating boundary evaluation, redundancy elimination, interference detection, and shading algorithms, *ACM Trans. on Graphics* **8** (1): 51–87.

Roth, S. D., 1982, Ray casting for modeling solids, *Comp. Gr. and Image Proc.* **18** (2): 109–144.

Samet, H., 1984, The quadtree and related hierarchical data structures, *ACM Computing Surveys* **16** (2): 187–260.

Samet, H., and Tamminen, M., 1985, Bintrees, CSG trees, and time, Proc. of Siggraph '85, *Comp. Gr.* **19** (3): 121–130.

Sutherland, I. E., 1963, Sketchpad: A man-machine graphical communication system, *Proc. Spring Joint Computer Conf.* **23**.

Suzuki, H., Ando, H., and Kimura, F., 1990, Geometric constraints and reasoning for geometrical CAD systems, *Comp. & Gr.* **14** (2).

Tilove, R. B., 1980, Set membership classification: a unified approach to geometric intersection problems, *IEEE Trans. on Computers* **C-29** (10): 847–883.

Tilove, R. B., 1981a, Exploiting spatial and structural locality in geometric modeling, Tech. Memo. No. TM-38, Production Automation Project, University of Rochester.

Tilove, R. B., 1981b, Line/polygon classification: A study of the complexity of geometric computation, *IEEE Comp. Gr. and Appl.* **11** (2): 75–84.

Verroust, A., Schonek, F., and Roller, D., 1992, Rule-oriented method for parameterized computer aided design, *Computer-Aided Design* **24** (10): 531–540.

Voelcker, H. B., and Requicha, A. A. G., 1977, Geometric modeling of physical parts and processes, *IEEE Comp.* **10** (2): 48–57.

Weiler, K., 1985, Edge-based data structures for solid modeling in curved-surface environments, *IEEE Comp. Gr. and Appl.* **5** (1): 21–40.

Weiler, K., 1986, Topological data structures for geometric modeling, Ph. D. dissertation, Rensselaer Polytechnic Institute.

FUNDAMENTALS

Part II of the book introduces feature properties, classification schemes, and feature creation methods. Definitions and basic concepts are emphasized; architectural and implementational issues are postponed until later in the book.

From the user's perspective, features are product definition units, with a characteristic shape and certain intrinsic properties. Features also have geometric relations with other features on a part; additional properties characterize these relations. Designers and manufacturing engineers can also associate domain knowledge with each feature. Thus features are domain specific. Features may be classified into families on the basis of common attributes to facilitate knowledge re-use when extending the feature set. These basic concepts of features are the topic of Chapter 3.

There are many ways in which feature models can be created: Features could be extracted from solid models, either interactively by the designer or automatically by a feature recognition algorithm, or models could be created directly in terms of features. Chapter 4 provides an overview of feature creation methods; later parts of the book will investigate these in more detail.

3

FEATURE CONCEPTS

Features may be considered a natural next step in the development of product modeling techniques beyond the currently used geometric modeling methods. This chapter will first outline, from product modeling viewpoint, the deficiencies of geometric models that motivated the development of feature concepts. The remaining sections will introduce the main concepts related to feature modeling: feature types, feature properties, composite features, feature taxonomies, feature validation, and feature mapping. All these will be elaborated further in later chapters of the book.

3.1 MOTIVATION FOR FEATURES

As discussed in Chapter 2, geometry and geometric information have a special role in engineering. Indeed, technical drawings, mainly consisting of geometry, are traditionally the primary means of product documentation and communication amongst engineers. More recently technical drawings have been augmented by electronic documentation and communication on the basis of geometric modeling techniques.

As the sole means of documentation and communication, technical drawings are unsatisfactory in light of the requirements of agile production outlined in Chapter 1. In general, technical drawings require human interpretation, and hence are subject to errors and misinterpretations. They cannot record all aspects of a product that are needed during the various stages of its design and manufacture. The specification of a complex product is split into thousands of individual drawings, the consistency of which is difficult to maintain. The drawings cannot effectively be reused as a resource for the design and manufacture of similar new products.

The major motivation for the development of features is that conventional geometric modeling methods have similar deficiencies. This section will outline the problems of geometric modeling methods in light of requirements for product modeling, and will develop feature modeling concepts.

3.1.1 Role of Geometry in Design and Manufacturing

Design and manufacturing of a complex product can be a complicated process involving many kinds of expertise and decision making. During the early phases of the process, decisions about the desired characteristics and overall function of the product are made. In the later phases, the specifications are refined to ensure that the product indeed fulfills the specifications and it can be manufactured efficiently. Suitable resources are selected for the manufacture of the product, and control information for guiding the manufacturing process is generated. Finally the final product is realized and released to the customer.

Ideally product modeling facilities should be based on some degree of "understanding" of the design and manufacturing process, such as the nature of the decisions made during the various phases and the constraints that limit the designer's freedom during the phases. Modeling conventions and notations should also support sound engineering principles such as avoiding premature commitment to a certain design or manufacturing solution.

This leads us to consider the life cycle of a product as a process involving a number of phases. For instance, the life cycle of a mechanical product involves phases such as those listed below:

- Functional design of the product (specification in terms of customer-seen function)
- Conceptual design of the product (physical principles)
- Embodiment design of the product (system-level design, overall layout)
- Detail design of the product (module- and component-level design)
- Manufacturing process planning (choice of manufacturing methods, generation of process descriptions)
- Modular manufacturing of the product
- Final assembly of the product
- Installation, maintenance, and upgrading of the product
- Disassembly and reuse/recycling of the product

The product model information that would be required and generated in the various phases varies from symbolic, qualitative information to strictly numerical, quantitative information. Some parts of the information may be extracted from existing product models or databases relating to similar products. Some other parts of the information may be generated by designers and planners on the basis of heuristic methods or by algorithmic methods. Of course, design and manufacturing processes may sometimes include truly radical or innovative aspects that defy any formalization into computer representable forms.

3.1.2 Deficiencies of Geometric Models

Much of the information needed in the life cycle of a product, particularly its design and manufacturing process, evolves around the geometric shape of the product. Historically this led to the interest on geometric modeling and the current generation of CAD systems based on geometric modeling techniques that provide useful functionality for geometry drafting, detailing, visualization, and analysis.

In the larger context of the overall design and manufacturing process, geometric models are not as attractive. In particular, they do not consider the varying roles that geometry has during the design process. In general, functional design is only concerned with the key parts of the geometry necessary for establishing the interfaces of the product with its environment (other products or the human user). All other aspects of the geometry are insignificant and are best left unspecified or vague. Similarly conceptual design mainly deals with those essential geometric aspects of the product that are necessary for delivering its desired function, and embodiment design with geometry related to the interfaces between the major subsystems of the product. The detail geometry of the product is of interest only in the detail design phase, or even later during the manufacturing process planning phase. During all these stages geometric information is constantly changed, detailed, and augmented. Typically vital modules and components are detailed much earlier than the others, leading to the situation where the various design stages are actually interleaved. If concurrent engineering principles are followed, the interleaving includes all life cycle issues of the product.

In light of these characteristics and issues, geometric models have a number of deficiencies that seriously limit their usefulness to the extent that they are really attractive only for recording the detail design of the product. The following subsections characterize the deficiencies of conventional geometric modeling techniques in more detail.

Microscopic Data The data available in geometric models is at a low, microscopic level. For instance, boundary representation models are expressed in terms of edges, faces, curves, etc., and CSG in terms of solid primitives and set operators. Unfortunately, the decision-making and reasoning processes of most engineering tasks require macroscopic entities also.

Figure 3.1 compares the database of a boundary model [Mäntylä 88] to manufacturability rules that might be used in an expert system for manufacturing planning. It can be seen that vital entities needed for expressing the manufacturing rules such as "hole," "distance between holes," or "sheet thickness" are not explicitly available in the boundary model. Extraction of such high-level entities on the basis of boundary model is a non-trivial task.

In general, the many types of product information needed to support engineering decision making, analysis, and reasoning for the various life cycle stages cannot be conveniently or at all included in a model consisting of microscopic entities only. For instance, tolerancing information is fundamental for manufacturing process design; yet specification of tolerances requires elements of higher level than typical geometric model entities. We can summarize this problem by saying that using geometric models leads to *underspecification*.

(a) Boundary model database example

Edge	vstart	vend	fcw	fccw	ncw	pcw	nccw	pccw
e_1	v_1	v_2	f_1	f_2	e_2	e_4	e_5	e_6
e_2	v_2	v_3	f_1	f_3	e_3	e_1	e_6	e_7
e_3	v_3	v_4	f_1	f_4	e_4	e_2	e_7	e_8
e_4	v_4	v_1	f_1	f_5	e_1	e_3	e_8	e_5
e_5	v_1	v_5	f_2	f_5	e_9	e_1	e_4	e_{12}
e_6	v_2	v_6	f_3	f_2	e_{10}	e_2	e_1	e_9
e_7	v_3	v_7	f_4	f_3	e_{11}	e_3	e_2	e_{10}
e_8	v_4	v_8	f_5	f_4	e_{12}	e_4	e_3	e_{11}
e_9	v_5	v_6	f_2	f_6	e_6	e_5	e_{12}	e_{10}
e_{10}	v_6	v_7	f_3	f_6	e_7	e_6	e_9	e_{11}
e_{11}	v_7	v_8	f_4	f_6	e_8	e_7	e_{10}	e_{12}
e_{12}	v_8	v_5	f_5	f_6	e_5	e_8	e_{11}	e_9

Vertex	First Edge	Coordinates	Face	First Edge
v_1	e_1	$x_1 y_1 z_1$	f_1	e_1
v_2	e_2	$x_2 y_2 z_2$	f_2	e_9
v_3	e_3	$x_3 y_3 z_3$	f_3	e_6
v_4	e_4	$x_4 y_4 z_4$	f_4	e_7
v_5	e_9	$x_5 y_5 z_5$	f_5	e_{12}
v_6	e_{10}	$x_6 y_6 z_6$	f_6	e_9
v_7	e_{11}	$x_7 y_7 z_7$		
v_8	e_{12}	$x_8 y_8 z_8$		

(b) Manufacturability rules example
Minimum distance between punched holes should be greater than sheet thickness. Ribs in castings should have a height of 0.8 wall thickness.

Figure 3.1 Mismatch of abstraction level

Lack of Design Intent A related problem to microscopic data is that geometric models cannot make the distinction between the geometry which is there to satisfy interface constraints, or to satisfy functional requirements, or for other reasons, such as strength, conductivity, stiffness, and manufacturability. To capture this type of information, a *design rationale* representation is required, and that generally means using a higher-level model. We can summarize this lack of information by saying that geometric models *fail to capture the design intent of the designer*.

Without design intent information, a geometric modeler cannot provide much support for editing geometry. Typically, it means modifying, step-by-step, all

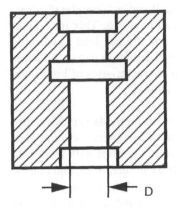

Figure 3.2 Rigid definition

affected parts of the model. Consider, for example, the part shown in Figure 3.2. If the hole diameter D needs to be reduced to $D' < D$, while the groove and recess depths are to remain the same, the designer must first fill the hole, the groove, and the recessed ends. Then he/she must re-create all the attached geometric elements. The problem can be alleviated if the modeler can capture and maintain relationships between the high-level constituents of the part, such as the hole and the elements attached to it. Instead of specifying microscopic entities with rigid dimensions, the model could be specified in terms of geometric constraints between various high-level entities. This allows the system to generate all the detailed elements on the basis of a single high level instruction, such as "change hole diameter."

Parametric and variational geometric modeling techniques are only a partial solution to this problem. To record the above design in terms of a parametric model, the designer must map the high-level specification of the desired behavior of the model in low-level constraints expressed in terms of the microscopic entities. This is not only inconvenient; it leads to a model that is difficult to understand and maintain. We will return to this and related problems of ordinary parametric and variational models in Section 3.8.

Single-Level Structure   Geometric models record the geometry at *a single level of abstraction* in terms of precisely dimensioned geometric entities. In other words, when ordinary geometric modeling methods are used, the exact geometry of the part being designed must be known in advance and defined using exact co-ordinates, orientations, geometric locations, and so on. For this reason geometric models are most appropriately used after the design is completed—for documentation, not for design itself.

If geometric modeling methods are used during design development, even if for only some geometric aspects of a product, a complete and formal geometric model that embodies them must be created. The inevitable result is *overspecification*: The designer is compelled to spell out a "complete" representation of the product even if there is yet no need to do so. This introduces problems in the later phases in interpreting the design and can lead to working under constraints that were not intended. A multilevel structure can avoid some of the problems. If details are handled as low-level characteristics of high-level entities, then they can be noted as missing or provisional.

Tedious Construction   The geometry construction methods typically supported in geometric modelers are not in line with how designers view the part. The primitives are very low level; locating and orienting entities with respect to each other must be done tediously by means of arbitrary points, lines, and planes.

Consider the example shown in Figure 3.3. Definition of the keyway requires the construction of two circles and relating their centers indirectly by locating them individually on the plane. Then the tangents to the small circle are constructed. The intersection points of the tangents to the large circle are then used to define the line segments needed in the profile. This makes it an inefficient and user-unfriendly process.

Model creation in terms of low-level entities not only is inefficient, but also does not support the desirability of reusing existing tested and trusted engineering solutions in design. Most engineering tasks can be characterized as variants of previous tasks where an existing basic design is modified. Indeed, reuse of existing constructions is a key prerequisite for a cost-effective result and diminished design lead time. If the adaptation of an existing model were to be done by manipulating large quantities of low-level entities, many designers opt to create a new model from scratch.

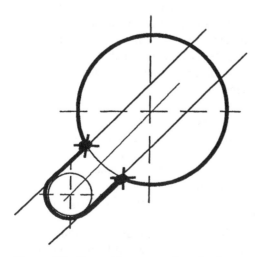

Figure 3.3 Geometric construction of a keyway profile

3.2 FEATURE MODELING

All problems of geometric models discussed in the previous section point in the same direction: Some *macroscopic entities* should be available in explicit form in the model. The high-level modeling entities can provide the hook needed by applications to store and retrieve information. They can also be used to associate geometric and other constraints with the model in terms of high-level characteristics of the part modeled, and to organize constraint propagation after a design change. The initial design can be synthesized quickly from the high-level entities and their relations. More generally, the high-level entities can provide a basis for linking the design rationale with the model, hence supporting reuse of information.

Feature modeling, in brief, is an approach where high-level modeling entities termed "features" are utilized to provide all the above improvements to ordinary geometric modeling techniques. This chapter will introduce the reader to the basic terms and concepts related to features. Later chapters will demonstrate the modeling techniques and their benefits in detail.

3.2.1 Definition of Feature

It is now time to give a more formal definition of a "feature." It is safe to say that a feature represents *the engineering meaning* or *significance of the geometry* of a part or assembly. Features can be thought of as building blocks for product definition or for geometric reasoning.

Hence features designate or are related to some physical, geometric aspects of a part or assembly. They are semantically significant and distinct entities in one or more engineering viewpoints. On this basis, we can characterize a "feature" as follows (Shah et al. 1988):

- A feature is a physical constituent of a part.
- A feature is mappable to a generic shape.
- A feature has engineering significance.
- A feature has predictable properties.

Several examples of features were given in Chapter 1 (Figures 1.2–1.5)

A *feature model* is a data structure that represents a part or an assembly mainly in terms of its constituent features. Each feature in the feature model is an identifiable entity that has some explicit representation. The *shape* of a feature may be expressed in terms of dimension parameters and enumeration of geometric and topological entities and relations, or in terms of construction steps needed to produce the geometry corresponding to the feature. The *engineering significance* may involve formalizing the function the feature serves, or how it can be produced, or what actions must be taken when performing engineering analysis or evaluation, or how the feature "behaves" in various situations.

We can immediately conclude that the number of genuinely different kinds of features cannot be limited *a priori*. The collection of features chosen to represent a part depends on the part type and the applications that the feature model is intended to support. New requirements are likely to lead to the introduction of new features. Nevertheless, within a chosen domain of applications, companies can choose a particular range of features that captures the geometry and the meaning of the geometry. It is precisely this customizability that makes features powerful.

3.2.2 Feature Attributes

While a *feature* is a physical entity that makes up some physical part, an *attribute (property)* is a characteristic or a quality of a thing. So one can say that attributes are characteristics or properties of features, features are constituents of parts, and parts are constituents of assemblies. Attributes can be used at any level from characterizing a feature, or a collection of features, to characterizing a whole part, or an assembly. Attributes may also record characteristics of relations among features or collections of features.

Assembly attributes may include (but are not limited to) such information as *mating surfaces*, *fits/clearances*, *depth of insertion*, or *relative orientation vectors*. Part attributes may include *material specifications*, *part number*, or *administrative data*. Feature attributes may be *position*, *orientation*, *dimensions*, *shape*, or *size tolerances*. Feature–feature relation attributes may have information about *relative positioning*, *geometric constraints*, or *compatibility*. Entity attributes for the individual entities making up a feature could include *surface finish* or *form tolerance*. Entity–entity relation examples are *adjacency* and *relative orientation* (parallel/perpendicular).

3.2.3 Types of Features

The term "feature" is used to denote modeling a wide variety of physical characteristics of parts. Therefore it is useful to distinguish between various types of features by using a sub-classification of features such as the following:

Form features	Portions of nominal geometry; recurring, stereotypical shapes.
Tolerance features	Deviations from nominal form/size/location.
Assembly features	Grouping of various feature types to define assembly relations, such as mating conditions, part relative position and orientation, various kinds of fits, and kinematic relations.
Functional features	Sets of features related to specific function; may include design intent, non-geometric parameters related to function, performance, etc.
Material features	Material composition, treatment, condition, etc.

Form features, tolerance features, and assembly features are all closely related to the geometry of parts, and are hence called collectively *geometric features*. Current feature-based CAD systems mainly address geometric features, in particular form features and some kinds of assembly features. This book deals largely with form features; tolerance and assembly features are briefly examined. Chapter 12 will look at some early work in functional features.

As mentioned in Chapter 1, geometric features can also be classified according to the intended application into groups such as design features, manufacturing features, and inspection features, etc. Observe that each of these may include form, tolerance, and assembly features. We will also adopt this language in later chapters while discussing the applications of features.

3.3 FEATURE PROPERTIES

A major function features serve is to create *associativity* between entities in a product definition. This association of entities makes it possible to encapsulate design or manufacturing constraints and to do geometric reasoning required in various applications. Thus the shape, behavior, and engineering significance of a feature need to be encoded in its representation.

The following exhaustive list of feature properties is a union of information supported by various modelers and indicates the range of information that may be included in a feature model:

- Generic shape (topology and/or geometry)
- Dimension parameters (independent parameters)
- Constrained parameters and constraint relations
- Default values for parameters
- Location/attachment method
- Location parameters
- Orientation method
- Orientation parameters
- Constraints relating dimensions, location, and orientation, possibly of several neighboring features
- Tolerances
- Construction procedure for geometric model
- Recognition algorithm
- Parameters computed on the basis of other features
- Inheritance rules or procedures
- Validation rules or procedures
- Non-geometric attributes (part number, function, etc.)

3.3.1 Generic and Specific Properties

A model may contain many instances of essentially the same kind of feature. For example, a part may have many holes This leads one to separate feature properties into two sets: *generic* and *specific*. All holes, for example, have certain generic properties regardless of their size and specific location. The generic properties, therefore, need only be formalized and archived once for each family of similar features, such as holes. Specific hole instances can then simply refer to the generic properties.

A hole as a general concept has generic properties such as a *characteristic topology* expressed in terms of entry, exit, and hole faces and their connectivity. It has a *generic geometry*: The entry and exit faces are planar, and hole face is cylindrical. We generally specify a hole in terms of high-level *generic dimensions* such as diameter and depth; these may have default values recorded in the feature definition. On the other hand, each hole instance in the model also has specific properties such as particular position, diameter and depth values, and references to geometric model entities (face numbers, etc.).

The distinction between generic and specific properties of features is fundamental from the viewpoint of the desired benefits of feature modeling. Generic properties record the engineering significance and generic shape of the feature; they also provide the basis for enforcing the predictable behavior of the feature in various applications. Specific properties record the details of a particular design.

Feature modelers usually provide a library of generic feature classes that have been pre-defined in terms of some of the properties listed above. A model can then be created by instancing such definitions, or by recognizing instances automatically, or by creating them interactively. The user needs to specify only the specific values for dimensions, location, etc. These specific data for each feature must somehow be associated with its generic definition in the library. To extract complete information of a feature, an application needs to combine its generic definition in the feature library with the feature's specific representation in the model.

Again, no *a priori* limits can be placed on the number of different feature classes. The number of classes reflects the range of parts and applications that must be covered, and new parts and applications often lead to the introduction of new feature classes. Some modelers allow users to define new generic classes; others restrict users to pre-defined generic classes, and hence limit the range of parts and applications. In some systems the level of support and functionality for pre-defined features may be much higher than for user-defined features, as discussed in Chapter 8.

The distinction of generic and specific properties is not always straightforward, and must depend on the intended application of features. Issues related to this distinction are discussed further in Chapter 5.

3.3.2 Intrinsic Properties

Some of the feature properties are *intrinsic* to the feature, while others are *extrinsic*. Intrinsic, or intra-feature, properties are those attributes that are independent of other features in the model. Some examples of intrinsic properties are the following:

- Geometric shape
- Parameter labels/names
- User-specified parameters and dimensions
- Dependent parameters and dimensions (when these depend only on user-specified parameters of a feature)
- Form and size tolerances
- Orientation tolerances (when both the target and the reference entities belong to a feature)

Geometric Shape Geometric shape is the most fundamental issue for features. As we will see in Chapter 8, geometry issues depend on the feature creation methods supported by the modeler:

- In the *design by features approach* the geometric model is created, modified, and extended through the feature model. In this scenario, features are defined directly by the user, and the appropriate geometric shape representation is generated either by pre-defined procedures or by solving a set of constraints. Such procedures and constraint declarations thus form a part of the definition of each feature class.
- When features need to be *recognized* from the geometry defined directly, recognition algorithms are specified in the feature class definitions.
- Alternatively, feature templates can be used for *interactive feature creation*. A template may contain prompts for helping the user pick the geometric entities on a graphic display, methods for checking the entity type picked, methods for determining geometric relationships between picked entities, and so on.

Parameter Labels A feature modeler needs to understand the terms used by designers so that the design environment is attractive to use. Familiar names or labels are commonly used for features, feature geometry, and feature dimensions. Some examples of feature names are: "T-slot," "UNC thread," and "flat bottomed hole"; examples of feature geometry names are "floor," "walls," "base surface"; examples of parameter names are "corner radius," "scallop height," and "wall thickness."

User-Defined Parameters and Dimension Each feature has certain parameters or dimensions that are specified at the time it is created. These are referred to as user-defined or unconstrained dimensions. The diameter of a hole or the width of a slot, for example, is usually independent of what else is on the model. Sometimes we also refer to these as dimensions that are *explicitly* defined.

Derived Parameters and Dimensions Some parameters or dimensions of a feature may derived from the user-defined parameters or dimensions according to some *derivation rules*. Such parameters may be needed for facilitating the creation of feature geometry, or for validating the feature. The derivation rules must be stored in the class definition of the feature. Derived parameters are intrinsic when all variables involved belong to the same feature. Derivation rules may be expressed as canned procedures or through a general purpose constraint specification language.

Intrinsic Tolerances Certain geometric tolerances are fully defined within the feature's definition, that is, no extrinsic entities or parameters are involved in their definition. These tolerances include size tolerance and form tolerance. Neither of these require reference entities outside the feature (i.e., a datum). Orientation and location tolerances may also be intrinsic if the datum and the toleranced entities belong to the same feature. For example, a perpendicularity tolerance between the bottom face and a side face of a slot would be intrinsic.

3.3.3 Extrinsic Properties

Extrinsic, or inter-feature, properties are attributes that involve two or more features. Examples of extrinsic properties are as follows:

- Derived feature parameters and dimensions
- Feature location
- Feature orientation
- Constraints on feature size, location, or orientation parameters
- Extrinsic tolerances

These properties are called extrinsic because they cannot be defined entirely within the feature itself. Instead, information about entities or parameters of other features is needed to complete the feature representation. These properties are explained below.

Derived Parameters and Dimensions When a new feature is added in a model, some of the parameters or dimensions of the new feature may be fixed by other features. These are termed *derived parameters* or *derived dimensions*. For example, a through hole in a block must have a length equal to the depth of the

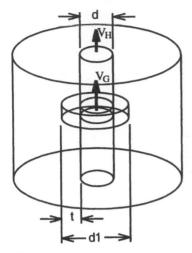

Figure 3.4 Example of simple parameter relations

block; similarly the diameter of a recess feature or chamfer feature will be fixed by the feature on which each is defined.

In simple cases, derived dimensions are simply copied (or referred to by pointers) from some other feature that limits or contains the new feature. In more complex cases, derived dimensions must be computed on the basis of values retrieved from several other features possibly involving arithmetic operations and even conditional statements. Special-purpose procedures or general-purpose constraint satisfaction methods may be used to define such derivation rules.

An example of simple parameter relations is shown in Figure 3.4. In the figure, the inner diameter of the torus corresponding to the internal-groove is equal to the diameter of the hole d. The outside diameter d_1 of the torus requires an indirect derivation rule defined as

$$d_1 = d + 2t$$

where t is the depth of the recess. As noted above, such a derivation rule may be represented through a special procedure associated with the feature definition, or by means of some general constraint specification scheme.

More complex parameter relations arise when geometric entities of a feature are constrained to lie on a specified face of two or more other features. For example, the hole shown in Figure 3.5 must start in face $f3$ of the boss feature and end in face $f1$ of the base feature. In this case the derivation rule of the length for the hole must clearly depend on parameters of both the boss feature and the base feature. Interactions with other features must be taken into account when such dependencies are maintained by the system.

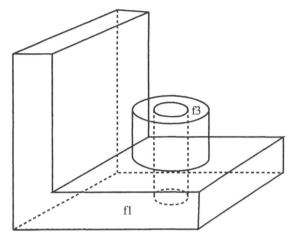

Figure 3.5 Complex parameter relations

Feature Position/orientation and Attachment In creating certain features, one needs to identify the entity on which the feature is to be placed and its location. For example, before a blind hole can be added to a block, the face through which it will pass and the position of the center line need to be identified. This can also be achieved by specifying the hole in the world coordinates used for the model.

Positioning by means of entities is more than just a convenient way to specify where to put the hole—it enables relationships to be recorded and thus reused in other applications. For example, in manufacturing planning one can then easily find all the features that lie on a certain face of a feature. In effect, the geometric entity used in positioning a feature becomes a property encapsulated in the definition of the feature.

To establish location/orientation on the basis of a given entity, some kind of a reference is needed for both the feature being positioned and the entity on which it is being positioned. Some systems use feature origins and feature coordinate systems that are predefined for every feature. Other systems allow users to pick reference entities for establishing a coordinate system. This makes the systems more flexible and also more convenient for defining position and orientation tolerances. A hybrid of these two methods is to provide a default coordinate system that is overridden when desired by the user.

The use of relative positioning methods offers the advantage of encapsulating geometric constraints on location. Therefore, when one feature is modified or deleted, the change can be propagated to adjacent and child features. For example, in a stepped shaft each step may be positioned with respect to the adjacent step, and their axes aligned; if the length of one of the steps is increased, all subsequent steps will be "pushed" outward by relative positioning.

Figure 3.4 serves also as an example of orientation and position constraints. The orientation vector (V_o) of the groove is specified to align with the orientation vector (V_H) of the hole. The position of the groove has only one degree of freedom; it can be located anywhere along the hole. For the purpose of locating the groove, we could pick the top face of the block and specify the distance from it to the center (or edge) of the groove. Of course we could also use the bottom face in a similar fashion to create a differently dimensioned model. To support possible later editing of the model, it is important to record the constraints specified; for instance, the modeling system should disallow any attempts to change the orientation of the groove.

Extrinsic Tolerances Many geometric tolerances require the specification of a system of reference (datum) entities from where measurements are controlled. These tolerance classes include position, orientation, and runout, when one or more of the datum entities belong to a different feature. Hence, these tolerances involve inter-feature relations.

3.3.4 Other Attributes

A major advantage of features is that they can also record other information that is not essential for feature geometry definition or for feature manipulation but useful for some applications. Examples of these are discussed in the following.

Non-geometric Attributes Many applications require auxiliary data to be associated with features or with one or more of its constituting entities. Such attributes may be numeric or textual, scalars or vectors, or other data types. Attributes can also be procedural, implemented as references to external subroutines or as expressions written in an interpretable language. To model any such data, one needs facilities to define the elements of the data type (similar to a C struct) and to link or embed them with the feature or its entities. Applications should be able to retrieve, modify, and delete such data and to perform computational or logical operations on the data elements. Application-specific relations and constraints may also be included.

An important subset of non-geometric attributes are *material attributes*:. These attributes may include the following:

- Material name
- Material composition code (standard or proprietary)
- Material properties (composition, physical, mechanical)
- Heat treatments
- Surface treatments, coatings, painting, etc.

Observe that some of these attributes relate to volumes and some to surfaces. Moreover the entire part may be made of the same material or it may be a composite part.

As an example of non-geometric data, consider process planning data for a hole feature. It may include items such as the following:

- Applicable machining operations (e.g., twist drilling, boring, reaming)
- Manufacturing cost information (e.g., a procedure for computing the cost)
- Tool and fixture information

An application-related intrinsic constraint might relate tool dimensions to hole diameter.

Symbolic or Skeletal Representations   Case studies in design and process planning show that engineering tasks are performed at many different levels of abstraction. One focuses on information relevant to the task at hand and filters out the rest. For example, in mechanism design one works with center lines of the rigid links and symbolic representation of the joints; in structural synthesis one works with centroidal axes of beam-columns, midplanes of plates or shells, and symbolic representations of supports and loads. In process planning, at the early stages, one considers global factors such as the part envelope and whether the part is generally rotational or prismatic. Later, when one is doing feature-by-feature process planning and NC generation, all the feature parameters and the detailed geometry need to be considered. Therefore sometimes features may be represented (or displayed) by:

- Centroidal axis
- Center point or centroid
- Cross section, midplane
- 2D profile
- 2D or 3D envelope (convex hull)
- Symbol or icon not corresponding to real geometry

It is also often useful that some features should not be displayed at all to avoid visual clutter and to speed up interactive work. Such features may include various types of *modifier features* such as fillets and blends, and *surface features* such as threads and gear teeth. If displayed at all, skeletal visualization is typically used to indicate the presence of threads and the like.

3.4 COMPOSITE FEATURES

Often it is desirable to treat a group of features as a single unit. Sometimes features of such a group may be related to the same function, and hence form a single entity from the design viewpoint; sometimes the features in the group may share manufacturing information; sometimes their geometric locations may be bound with shared constraints. For covering all these cases, *composite features* may be used.

It is difficult to distinguish between simple and composite features on an absolute basis. However it is safe to say that simple features are the lowest level features in a library in that they cannot be decomposed into other features present in the library, while *composite features* can be decomposed into two or more simple (or composite) features recognizable by the system as features in their own right. For example, a stepped hole can be decomposed into several hole features; therefore, a stepped hole is a composite feature if simple holes are available in the library.

The usefulness of the concept of composite features is related to manipulation of features at multiple levels. In using composite features, one is able to manipulate a related group of simple features as a unit, rather than operate on each individual feature. To support this, composite features should be represented as separate entities in the feature model, with their own properties and attributes. That is, the composite features are not just unstructured collections of individual features but have engineering significance at the collective level, coded through attributes archived at the group level. For instance, if all features in a group must have the same material attributes, it is simpler to assign the proper value once for the composite feature than individually for each simple feature. Another example is that of a composite pocket which is built from several simple pockets. It may be desirable in some application domain to permit the depth of the entire group of pockets to be changed by modifying the depth attribute of the whole group rather than the depth of the individual pockets.

Another function that composite features can serve is the ability to capture some constraint or relationship between a group of features. There are two possibilities: (1) *recurring relations* and (2) *non-recurring relations*. Examples of recurring type are shown in Figure 3.6(*a*); these commonly include bolt holes arranged in a circular or linear pattern, a row of slots, gear teeth, and splines treated as a single unit. Recurring composite features are often also referred to as *pattern features*. Examples of the second type are stepped holes and composite pockets built from simpler ones, as shown in Figure 3.6(*b*). This class will be referred to as *compound features*.

Constraints that may be needed to define composite features are expressed parametrically or through geometric relations such as adjacency and tangency. In Figure 3.6(a), the parameters θ and R for the bolt circle, and the location parameter a for the slot displacements are examples of attributes at the group level. The locations and positions of the individual features would be constrained on the basis of these group attributes, enabling one to modify, delete, or move features at the collective level as well as at individual level.

A nesting facility may also be useful for compounding of features. For example, composite features may be combined from other composite features, composite patterns from lower level patterns, and so on. From an object-oriented programming point of view, composite features are aggregation classes created from two or more classes, some of which may also be aggregation types.

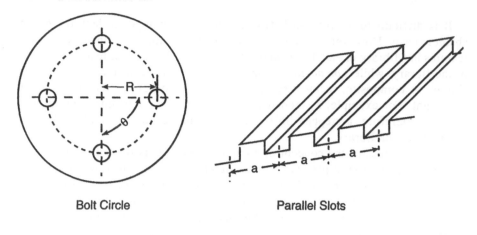

Bolt Circle

Parallel Slots

(*a*) Pattern features

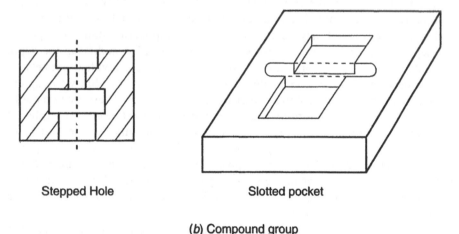

Stepped Hole

Slotted pocket

(*b*) Compound group

Figure 3.6 Examples of composite features

3.5 FEATURE TAXONOMIES

Although the number of possible features and feature classes is not finite, it may be possible to categorize feature classes into families that are relatively independent of the intended application domain of the features. Such classification may be useful in the several ways. First, if feature classes can be sorted into families with identified properties, then generalized mechanisms can be designed to support each family in place of specialized methods for each feature class separately. Second, feature families could lead to the use of common terminology across applications that could eventaully evolve into to a more universal interface to a modeling system and facilitate extensions to the set of available feature classes. Third, universal families could be useful in developing product data exchange standards. These considerations lead one to consider developing a universal *feature taxonomy* where feature classes are grouped in a single "family tree" according to some shared or similar characteristics such as geometry, properties, or intended use.

In such a family hierarchy one could make features *inherit* common properties from features higher up in the tree. Hierarchical arrangement in families and inheritance can reduce the number of properties that have to be independently specified for each new feature. The properties inherited might include parameters as well as procedures. Each property is treated separately in inheritance. For example, the property "symbolic representation" may be the same for "internal-groove" and its descendants "internal-v-groove" and "internal-u-groove." However, the geometric representation property may be different for each of these features. If an inherited property is altered, the change propagates to all lower-level features. If necessary, children can override an inherited definition with a local definition. Also procedural properties can be inherited. For instance, the method for locating and orienting the above types of groove features might be shared.

These considerations lead to the notion of using *object-oriented programming* as a basis for organizing the feature taxonomy. This approach is commonly followed by implementors of feature-based systems. The principles of object-oriented programming will be briefly reviewed in Chapter 10 in the discussion of software tools for feature modeling.

As mentioned above, there are a many ways in which features can be classified. Feature taxonomies could be based on product categories, intended applications of features, or feature shapes, as indicated in Table 3.1.

At the present time there are no universally accepted, or widely used, feature taxonomies. Several taxonomy schemes have been proposed for classification entirely by shape rather than by application. For instance, Part 48 of STEP (*Standard for Exchange of Product Data*) considers features as consisting of three basic types: *volume, transition,* and *pattern* features (Dunn 1992). Volume features are further classified into six basic types:

Table 3.1 Typical criteria for classifying shape features

Product Type	Applications	Shape
Sheet metal features	Design	Prismatic
Composite panel feature	Finite Element Analysis	Rotational
Machined features	Process Planning	Flat
Injection molding features	Inspection	Uniform Cross section

Passages	Subtracted volumes that intersect the pre-existing shape at both ends
Depressions	Subtracted volumes that intersect the pre-existing shape at one end
Voids	Subtracted volumes completely enclosed by material
Protrusions	Added volumes that intersect the pre-existing shape at one end
Connector	Added volume joining two previously defined pieces
Stand-alone	Added volume not connected to other pieces of the model.

The STEP feature models are discussed further in Chapter 7.

A very elaborate feature classification scheme was developed by John Deere for CAM-I (Butterfield et al. 1985). This scheme was developed for process planning, as evidenced by classification criteria like "corner access," and "internal/external." At the highest level in this taxonomy, form features are classified into rotational, non-rotational, and sheet categories. Portions of that taxonomy for non-rotational form features are shown in Figure 3.7. Features are either volumetric (depressions/protrusions) or surfaces. Volumetric features are classified further on the basis of volume addition or subtraction, which results in depressions or protrusions.

Feature taxonomies covering a limited range of shapes can also be identified. An example sheet metal classification scheme is shown in Figure 3.8 (Shah and Bhatnagar 1986). In the scheme features are first classified by two major categories, *flat shapes* and *transverse shapes*, representing a manufacturing viewpoint. At the next level flat shapes are classified according to whether they are located on the boundary or the interior. Transverse shapes are classified by major sheet deformation operations: bending, drawing, deep drawing/spinning, or roll forming. Further examples of feature taxonomies are given in Chapters 8 and 11.

3.6 FEATURE VALIDATION

When features are created, modified, or deleted one needs to determine if the operation and the result are valid. This should not be confused with geometric or topological validity, which are based on mathematical laws. Features are invalid if any of the conditions declared in the generic definitions are violated. Such conditions may be based on size limits, shape, location, or orientation Therefore it is possible that some operations may result in valid (physically realizable) solids but still produce invalid features.

Unlike the case of geometric models, there are no mathematically elegant ways of validating feature models. Feature models carry design intent, function, and meaning of the geometry. All these aspects may be important for feature validation. Nevertheless, one can identify certain generic types of validity checks:

- Attachment validation
- Dimension limits

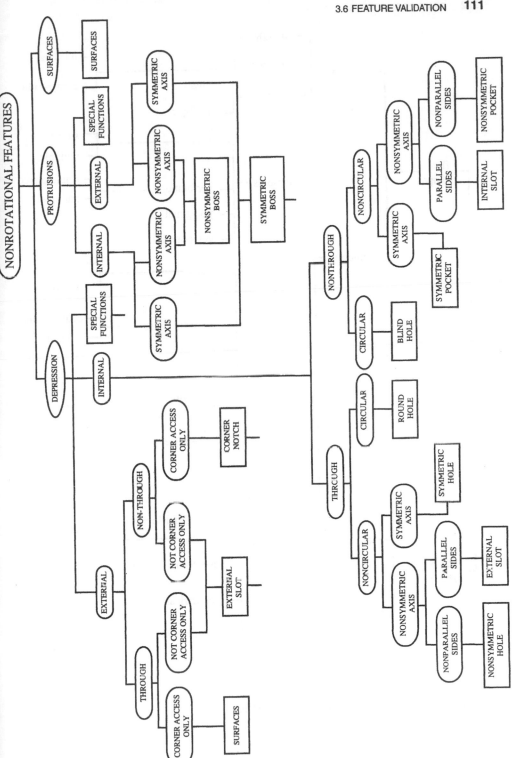

Figure 3.7 Partial view of the CAM-I/John Deere feature taxonomy

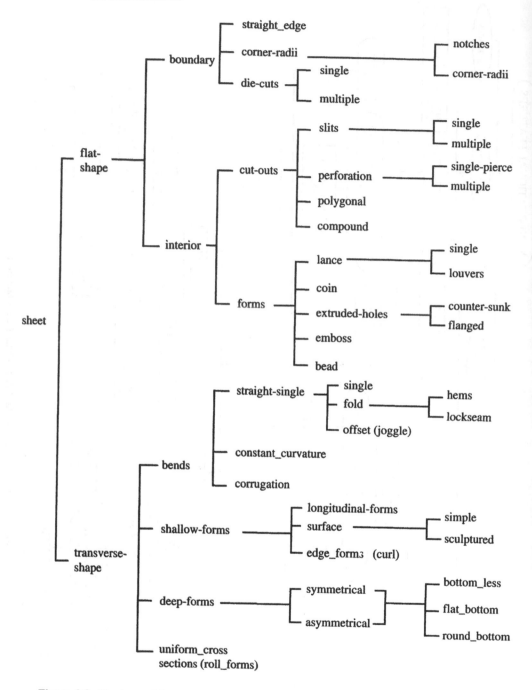

Figure 3.8 Sheet metal features classification scheme

- Location limits
- Interaction validation

Attachment validation involves the determination of the compatibility of adjacent features, compatibility of neighbors, and compatibility of geometric entity type on which a feature is defined. For example, one cannot attach a recess feature to the outside face of a block. Similarly a step feature cannot be attached to a corner of a prismatic feature. When a feature is deleted or modified it may create problems for its neighbors, and validation is required. Some applications may need to validate features on the basis of information regarding the surroundings of a feature (e.g., free space in tool approach direction in machining).

Dimension limits are restrictions on size parameters of a feature specified in order to maintain certain engineering meaning. For example, a hole cannot be larger than the body it is being put in. More specific validation rules may be posed by application viewpoints; for instance, long and thin holes may be regarded invalid if no machining methods are available for their manufacture.

Location limits are restrictions on the position and orientation parameters of features. For example, a hole should not be so close to a boundary that it breaks through it. Again, more specific criteria may be posed by applications; for instance, manufacturability concerns dictate that holes should be oriented orthogonally to their starting planar surface.

Feature interactions are intersections of feature boundaries with those of other features such that either the shape or the semantics of a feature are altered from the standard or generic definition. Note that interaction may not necessarily be invalid—it may even be a useful relation.

Several types of interactions have been identified (Shah 1991b). These are shown in Figure 3.9. In (*a*) the hole is too close to the outside surface, so it breaks through. The passage created no longer qualifies as a hole—its topology is not that of a hole, and it may not be able to serve the function of a hole. As a manufacturing feature it may also be invalid if machining methods for a hole are inapplicable for this arrangement. In both of the examples shown in (*b*), two legitimate generic features intersect and produce a new shape. In (*i*), a non-documented, non-generic shape is produced whose topology and engineering meaning are non-standard. In (*ii*), a generic shape is created whose function is different than that of either of the original features. In (*c*), the creation of the pocket has eliminated the original entry face of the hole, consequently changing the depth of the hole, even though the user did not modify explicitly the hole parameters. In (*d*) two slots intersect, thus creating new topological entities. In (*e*) a new feature has completely deleted an older, smaller feature from the geometric model. In (*f*) a new feature has closed off a feature that was originally open. In (*g*) a groove placed on a tube is deep enough to make the part disjoint. In (*h*) the addition of a new volume fills in a cavity.

Validity of interacting features depends on the particular context and application. The situations in examples (*c*) to (*e*) may generally be acceptable, pro-

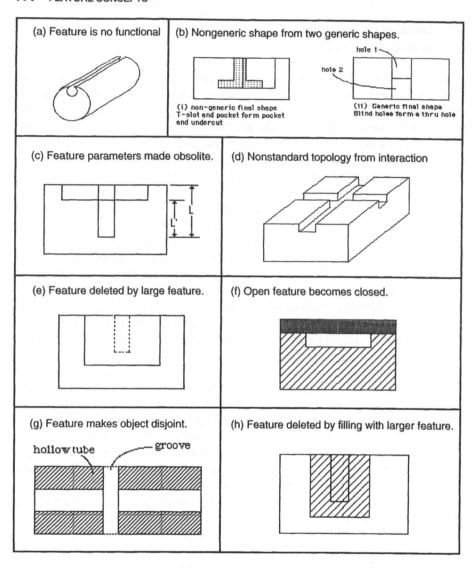

Figure 3.9 Feature interactions (Reprinted by permission of Springer-Verlag)

vided the feature database is updated as follows: Delete the obsolete features in (*e*) and (*h*); modify the depth and entry face in (*c*). The situations in (*a*), (*f*), and (*g*) will not be permitted generally, but it could be left up to the person setting up the feature library to allow or disallow this.

In general, validation by visual checking is unreliable and inefficient. Also visual checking assumes an interactive use of a program, whereas many systems provide both command (program file) and interactive modes of operation. Therefore it is necessary to detect the existence of feature interaction conditions in order decide on acceptability of an operation, and determine if any corrective action is required. If non-documented (ad-hoc) features are permitted, certain applications may not be able to process the model properly, and there may even be problems in manipulating the model that contains such features.

3.7 FEATURE MAPPING

How a part is viewed in terms of features varies from application to application: Features are in the eye of beholder. Figure 3.10 shows a housing used in some AlliedSignal products (Hummel 1989); in Figure 3.11 this part is decomposed into features from four viewpoints: design, machining, inspection, and deburring. The *design*, or more appropriately, the *product definition view*, represents the geometry construction units in terms of which it is convenient to define the part shown; the *process planning view* shows features as volumes to be removed by separate machining operations; the *inspection view* shows the paths that are to be traversed by a CMM probe and the dimensions to be gauged; the *deburring view* shows the edges that need to be finished by deburring operations. Therefore the same part could be viewed as having different features, depending upon

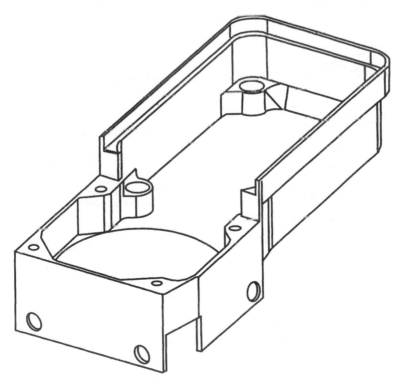

Figure 3.10 Housing example (Hummel [1989]; by permission of ASME)

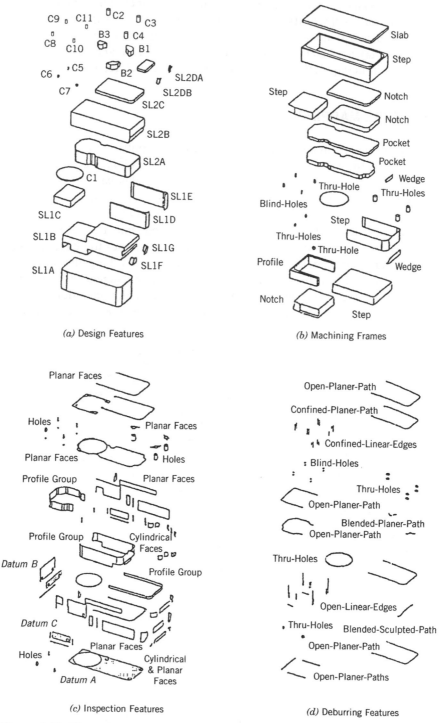

(a) Design Features

(b) Machining Frames

(c) Inspection Features

(d) Deburring Features

Figure 3.11 Viewpoint dependence of part features (Hummel [1989]; by permission of ASME)

the engineering task being undertaken. The derivation of a task-specific feature model from another feature model is referred to as feature *mapping*, feature *transformation*, or feature *transmutation*.

Feature mapping is a "catchall" phrase. It covers many different types of transformations between feature models; there is no standard process for mapping because the relationship of one feature model to another varies. The following are some general observations to support the preceding statement:

- Feature models may differ in the level of abstraction/detail; for example, the same object may be treated as a three-dimensional model in design but a two-dimensional model in finite elements.
- Some feature models do not contain the complete definition of the part geometry; they cover only some selected portions of the geometry. For example, the inspection features shown in Figure 3.11 cannot be used to generate the entire geometry of the part shown.
- The same feature may be parametrized in different ways in different applications in order to conform to the application view.
- Often features of one application are obtained from features of another by regrouping the geometric model entities.
- One application may look at the *solid* portions of a part as features, while another looks at the *voids* as the features. Examples are design features versus injection molding features of a part; and structural features versus machining features.
- Many features have application-specific attributes that are of no relevance in other applications; for instance, geometric tolerances are relevant to design and manufacturing but not to stress analysis.
- Some feature models use more than one geometric model: Process planning requires a part model, a stock model, and several fixture and tooling models.

It can be seen from the above observations that feature mapping represents a wide range of problems. The *automated* derivation of one feature model from another is clearly very desirable. However, very little work has been done in this area; at the present time some experimental systems are available for design-to-finite element and design-to-machining feature transformation. We will return to this subject in Chapter 7.

3.8 FEATURES VERSUS GEOMETRY

Now that we have reviewed the fundamental concept of features, we turn briefly to the contribution that features make in solving the problems of ordinary geometric modeling discussed in Section 3.1:

- Microscopic data
- Lack of design intent
- Single level structure
- Tedious construction

Microscopic Data Perhaps the main advantage of features is that a product model can be described using high-level primitives, defined as generic abstractions of recurring shapes. The open-ended nature of features makes it possible to include exactly those primitives that are natural for some application domain; composite features may be used to describe further recurring macroscopic shapes. All these entities can have properties that characterize them at a macroscopic level; relations among the entities characterize parameter constraints and provide a basis for change propagation.

Lack of Design Intent By letting a design to be described in terms application-oriented entities, feature models clearly provide a better record of the intent of the designer than mere geometric models. Hence, in principle, they can also support higher-level model manipulations. Of course, geometric features are only good for recording the geometric aspects of the design; functions, physical principles, design rules used, for example, require modeling concepts beyond the capability of geometric features. Some other approaches are briefly reviewed in Chapter 12.

Single Level Structure Feature modeling typically results in a multilevel structure where distinctions can be made between a few gross features modeling the overall shape of the part, several detail features modeling the more detailed shapes, and the detail geometry recorded in a geometric model. Parameter relations in such a model often result in a situation where a few overall parameters of the gross features determine (completely or partially) parameters of the detail features, and these in turn the geometric model. This quite naturally leads to a decomposition of the parameters in "abstract" and "detail" ones. Default values for missing data can be introduced to support the case where incompletely specified interim models need to be supported during design.

Tedious Construction Another major benefit of features is that they lead to a much improved user interface for manipulating geometric designs. To change the diameter of a hole, the user of a geometric modeler must first delete or "plug" the old hole, and then create a new one. As a side effect, all attributes possibly attached to the hole are lost, and must be reentered. The user of a feature-based system simply picks the hole and changes a parameter; affected attributes are recomputed and the rest remain unchanged. Feature modelers can also do a much better job in validating the changed model on the basis of feature-specific validation rules.

Some of the above benefits are partially realized also by parametric and variational techniques. The main distinction between feature-based modeling and ordinary parametric variational modeling is in the level of detail and abstraction. In parametric techniques working on the basis of geometric models, geometric constraints must be defined on microscopic level, namely on the basis of parameters of entities such as edges, vertices, and faces. In feature models constraints can be defined also at the macroscopic level of feature parameters. Moreover features lead to the distinction of intrinsic and extrinsic constraints; in particular, intrinsic constraints can be encoded in feature definitions and inserted "automatically" in feature instances, hence facilitating the creation of a parametric model.

As an example of intrinsic constraints, consider the rectangular slot feature shown in Figure 3.12(*a*). In the figure, the intrinsic geometric constraints can be specified as follows:

```
f1 perpendicular f3
f1 parallel f2
slot_depth = d1 = d2 (also equal to d6, d7)
slot_width = d3 = d4
```

When the feature is placed in a model, all these constraints can be added automatically. For example, in Figure 3.12(*b*) the slot feature (a group of three faces) is positioned on the block feature (a group of six faces); the placement of each face of the slot is completely defined on the basis of the position, orientation, and dimensions of the slot.

Features facilitate also the specification of the remaining constraints. Some placement constraints for the slot can be deduced directly from feature relations, without any further input from the user. In this case the slot is defined to reside on a planar face of the block, leaving only three degrees of freedom for placement of the slot on the face to be specified with further constraints. The specification of these is simplified by the available macroscopic parameters, such as

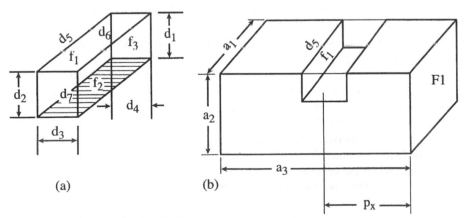

(a)   (b)

Figure 3.12 Positioning of a slot feature

the position and orientation of the two features. In the case of Figure 3.12(*b*), the orientation of the slot can be specified to agree with one of the local coordinate axes of the block.

In parametric or variational geometric modelers there is no clustering of entities to form features, such as the slot or the block in the example. Hence macroscopic entities (features) and their parameters are not available during the design process, for specifying positioning, orientation, or other constraints, nor are they available to applications downstream of design.

Features also lead to improvements of more technical nature over ordinary parametric and variational models. For instance, feature relations of a feature model can be used to guide constraint satisfaction, potentially leading to much faster solution of the constraints. Feature models enhance greatly the capability and convenience of parametric and variational techniques and can in fact be considered a superset of these.

REVIEW QUESTIONS

3.1 Study some part of a product you know well. What aspects of its geometry are essential to its function? What aspects of its geometry are significant for its manufacture? What is the significance of the rest of the geometry?

3.2 Discuss the features shown in Figure 3.4 in terms of the definition of a "feature". What is the engineering significance of each feature? Can you outline the "predictable properties" of each, for instance, in editing the model? Can a "generic shape" for each be defined?

3.3 Outline the possible attributes for some of the features in Figure 3.6. Can you give examples of feature relationship attributes?

3.4 Give a derivation rule (formula) for the length of the hole in Figure 3.5. (Invent a convenient parametrization for the base and boss features.)

3.5 Give further examples of composite features besides the ones discussed in Section 3.4. What attributes can you identify for your examples?

3.6 Analyze sample parts and their features (e.g., the parts in Figures 1.2, 1.3, or 3.6). Can you place the features in some of the taxonomies discussed in Section 3.5?

3.7 Give (informally) validation rules for sample features of the part in Figure 3.4. Label each rule as intrinsic or extrinsic.

3.8 Consider the example in Figure 3.12. What intrinsic constraints can be specified for the block? Which further constraints need to be specified to specify the location and orientation of the slot? (Invent a convenient parametrization for the block feature.)

3.9 Distinguish between two types of parameter inheritance, one encountered in feature hierarchies and the other between interdependent features instanced on the same part.

3.10 What are the advantages of supporting composite features in a system?

3.11 What is the difference between feature-based systems and parametric systems? What are the advantages/disadvantages of each approach?

BIBLIOGRAPHY

Butterfield, W., Green, M., Scott, D., and Stoker, W., 1985, Part features for process planning, Technical Report R-85-PPP-03, CAM-I, Inc., Arlington, Texas.

Chung, J., and Schussel, M., 1990, Technical evaluation of variational and parametric design, *ASME Computers in Engineering Conf.*, Boston, August 5–9, ASME Press.

Dunn, M., ed., 1992, *Industrial Automation Systems and Integration—Product Data Representation and Exchange—Part 48: Integrated Generic Resources: Form Features*, second edition, ISO/WD 10303-48.

Hillyard, R. C., and Braid, I. C., 1978, Analysis of dimensions and tolerances in computer-aided mechanical design, *Computer-Aided Design* **10** (3): 161–166.

Hummel, K, Brown C., 1989, The role of features in the implementation of concurrent product and process design, Symposium on Concurrent Product and Process Design, ASME Winter Annual meeting, San Fransisco, CA, pp 1–8.

Light, R., and Gossard, D., 1982, Modification of geometric models through variational geometry, *Computer-Aided Design* **14** (4): 209–214.

Luby, S., Dixon, J. R., and Simmons, M. K., 1986, Creating and using feature databases, *Comp. in Mech. Eng.* **5** (3): 25–33.

Mäntylä, M., An Introduction to Solid Modeling, Computer Science Press, 1988.

Pratt, M. J., and Wilson, P. R., 1986, Requirements for support of form features in a solid modeling system, final report, Technical Report R-86-ASPP-01, CAM-I, Inc., Arlington, TX.

Requicha, A. A. G., and Vandenbrande, J., 1989, Form features for mechanical design and manufacturing, *ASME Computers in Engineering Conf.*, Anaheim, ASME Press.

Shah, J. J., 1991, Assessment of features technology, *Computer-Aided Design* **23** (5): 58–66.

Shah, J. J., 1991b, Conceptual development of form features and feature modelers, *Res. in Eng. Design* **2**: 93–108.

Shah, J. J., and Bhatnagar, A., 1986, GT coding scheme for sheet metal features, Tech. Report, Department of Mechanical Engineering, Arizona State University, Tempe, AZ.

Shah, J. J., Rogers, M., Sreevalsan, P., and Mathew, A., 1989, Functional requirements for feature based modeling systems, Technical Report R-89-GM-01, CAM-I, Inc., Arlington, TX.

Shah, J. J., Sreevalsan, P., Rogers, M., Billo, R., and Mathew, A., 1988, Current status of features technology, report for task 0, Technical Report R-88-GM-04.4, CAM-I, Inc., Arlington, TX.

Turner, G., and Anderson, D. C., 1988, An object oriented approach to interactive, feature based design for quick turnaround manufacturing, *ASME Computers in Engineering Conf.*, San Francisco, July 31–August 4, ASME Press.

Zhang, K., and ElMaraghy, H., 1993, Validity check for a function oriented modeler, in B. Ravani, ed., *Proc. of 19th ASME Design Automation Conf.*, Albuquerque, ASME Press.

4

FEATURE CREATION TECHNIQUES

A feature modeling system must include facilities for creating feature models. The power and usability of these facilities have a large impact on the overall usefulness of a feature-based system. This chapter provides a classification and an overview of feature creation methods; detailed information on selected methods will be given in later chapters.

4.1 OVERVIEW

It is convenient to look at the total feature-based model as consisting of two interrelated components, namely a feature model and a geometric model. Even if there is no physical separation between the two models, we can view the data conceptually as being of two types, as shown in Figure 4.1. The geometric model contains a boundary representation, CSG, or other geometric representation of the object. The feature model contains the clustering information, feature properties, relationships of interest, and other higher level data.

Many alternative techniques have been devised for creating feature-based models. We can divide them into two main categories based on whether features

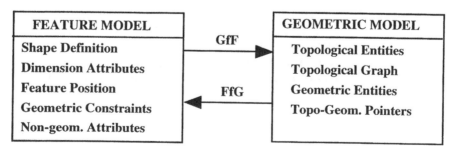

Figure 4.1 Relationship between features and geometry

are extracted from geometry (FfG), or on whether geometry is created from the features (GfF). Traditionally the FfG methods are called *feature recognition*, while GfF methods are called *design by features*. FfG may be automated by means of computer algorithms, or it may be necessary for the user to perform the task. The former is labeled *automatic feature recognition*, while the latter is called *human-assisted* (or *interactive*) *feature recognition* (Shah, 1988).

The procedure followed in creating feature models, in each of the above cases, can be described as follows:

1. *Interactive feature recognition.* A geometric model is created first, then features are created by human users, such as by picking entities in an image of the part (Figure 4.2*a*). User1 and User2 may be the same person.
2. *Automatic feature recognition.* A geometric model is created first, then a computer program processes the resulting model to automatically find features (Figure 4.2*b*).

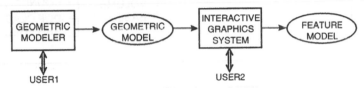

(a) Interactive Feature Definition (FfG)

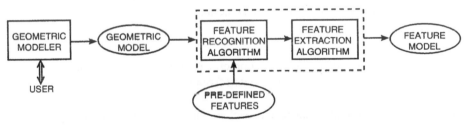

(b) Automatic feature recognition (FfG)

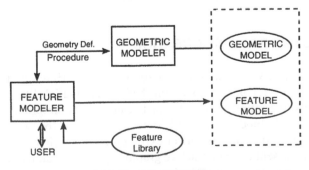

(c) Design by features (GfF)

Figure 4.2   Schematics of feature creation approaches

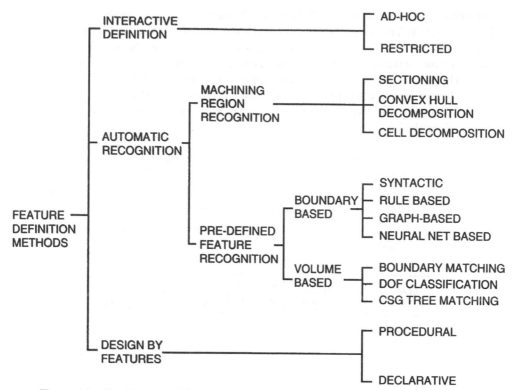

Figure 4.3 Classification of feature creation methods

3. *Design by features.* The part geometry is created directly in terms of features; geometric models are created from the features (Figure 4.2c).

Within each of these three basic approaches, there are several sub-categories, as shown in Figure 4.3. The major characteristics of each of these categories and their sub-categories are briefly discussed in the following sections.

4.2 INTERACTIVE FEATURE CREATION

Although the interactive feature creation approach was originally developed to provide feature data for process planning before the availability of design by features systems, it continues to find uses because of its simplicity. In this approach the geometric model is created first, using a solid (or two-dimensional drafting-type) geometric modeler. After exiting the geometric modeler, the geometric model file is sent to an interactive graphics program that renders an image of the part in order to let a user view the geometry and create features on it. The user can interactively pick entities (vertices, edges, faces) needed to create a feature. This information is sometimes augmented with attributes such as tolerances, finish, or high-level nominal parameters (e.g., hole diameter).

In its simplest form, interactive feature creation can be just adhoc grouping of geometric entities by the user, with some user-specified data added; the resulting model is aimed specifically for use by some application program. It is entirely the user's responsibility to ensure that the feature model is valid and complete. All that is needed to implement such a system is to record pointers to the entities picked and associate them with a feature name and other data, specified by the user. Such representation may be specially geared to a specific application program.

Interactive feature creation is sometimes implemented in conjunction with feature libraries containing generic definitions of feature classes. The library definition of feature classes may contain some of the properties listed in the previous chapter. This may include, for example, a list of faces that is needed to create a feature, and the geometric relationships between them. Such pre-definition of feature classes can aid the user creating features interactively, and also facilitate downstream applications. The job of the interactive user can be made easier if the system prompts him or her for proper type of input in order to pick entities needed for the desired feature. Also the system may be able to check if geometric conditions between the picked entities are satisfied. For example, if the user chooses to identify a flat-bottom hole, then the system prompts that he or she must pick a cylindrical face and a planar face. When entities are picked, the system will check if the entities are of the appropriate type, if the axis of the cylinder is perpendicular to the bottom face, and if the two faces are adjacent. Further support can be provided by procedures for calculating selected dimensions once a feature has been interactively created.

The advantage of ad hoc features over pre-defined library features is that the user is free to create features "on the fly"; this is particularly useful when special one-of-a-kind features are often encountered in the domain of interest. It is convenient for, say, an NC programmer to specify the ride plane, cutting plane, and closed profile from which to generate tool paths, without caring about the particular shape of the feature. The disadvantage of adhoc features is that the user is responsible for validation, and the semantic level of information is low. These difficulties are overcome by restricting users to a pre-defined set of features at the cost of flexibility.

4.3 AUTOMATIC FEATURE RECOGNITION

Various techniques have been developed to provide, without any human intervention, the product data input needed by applications such as process planning, NC part programming, and inspection planning. This is popularly referred to as *feature recognition*, although the output of some techniques is not in the form of features but rather as machining volumes. These latter methods typically assume that all machining will be done by milling, so it is not necessary to know the specifics of a feature other than its boundaries corresponding to final machined surfaces. For example, it does not matter if a machining volume is a rectangular pocket or an L-shaped slot because tool paths can be generated without this distinction. For this reason we classify these methods into two groups: *machining region recognition* and *pre-defined feature recognition.*

4.3.1 Machining Region Recognition

Machining region recognition methods were devised for generating NC tool paths directly from CAD databases. The objective of these algorithms is to determine volumes that need to be removed by machining, usually by end milling. There is no comparison made to pre-defined shapes. Machining region recognition techniques may be classified into three categories:

- Sectioning
- Convex hull decomposition
- Cell decomposition

Sectioning is typically used to generate feature boundaries corresponding to material removal regions at each z-level in 2½ D milling. The part is oriented such that its principal feature directions coincide with the three milling axes. The part volume is sliced with planes parallel to x-y plane at fixed Δz values, representing a series of tool positions. This results in one or more intersection profiles, representing the part's boundaries (Grayer 1977, Corney 1993). These profiles are classified as "material" or "void," and offset curves are generated to form the basis for generating NC tool paths.

Convex hull decomposition is used to decompose a volume into convex machining volumes. The part is first subtracted from its convex hull, and the process is repeated until each volume is equal to its own convex hull. (A convex hull of an object is the minimal convex volume that can completely enclose the object.) The original algorithm (Woo 1982) had the problem of nonconvergence in many cases and often resulted in volumes that did not bear resemblance to common manufacturing features. Recent developments have overcome these problems by partitioning of nonextremal faces (Kim 1994).

Cell decomposition techniques may be thought of, in some respect, as spatial equivalents of sectioning methods. The sectioning is done along three sets of parallel planes, x-y, y-z, z-x, where x, y, z represent the machining axes of a three-axis milling machine. The x, y, z range corresponds to stock dimensions, from which the desired part is to be manufactured. The partitioning produces a lattice of cubes (Armstrong 1982). The intersection of these cubes with the finished part is computed. Cells are then classified as "stock cells" or "part" cells, depending on whether the intersection is closer to 0 or 1, respectively. Thus one gets a spatial decomposition model of the part; of course this step is trivial if the geometric modeler already produces such a model. Stock cells correspond to regions that need to be removed. Adjacent stock cells can be concatenated to determine tool paths. The cell sizes can be chosen to correspond to feed amounts.

4.3.2 Pre-defined Feature Recognition

Feature recognition differs from machining-region recognition in that portions of the geometric model are compared to pre-defined generic features in order to identify instances that match the pre-defined ones. Specific tasks in feature recognition may include the following:

- Searching the geometric model to match topological and geometric patterns
- Extracting recognized features from the geometric model (i.e., removing the portion of the model associated with the recognized feature).
- Determining feature parameters (hole diameter, pocket depth, etc.).
- Completing the feature geometry (edge/face growing, closure, etc.).
- Combining simple features to get higher-level features.

Both *volume-based* methods and *boundary-based* methods have been devised. Boundary-based methods find sets of faces that satisfy a set of conditions for each feature. The face sets may bound a closed volume, or they may be open; the faces may be contiguous or not. Volume-based methods deal only with closed volumes; all features are complete (closed), contiguous volumes. There are many alternative methods for implementing boundary- or volume-based recognition. These are briefly discussed below.

Common to boundary-based methods is that they operate primarily on boundary models and use geometric and topological relations between boundary entities to find a match for pre-defined features. For each feature, the geometric and topological conditions that need to be satisfied are identified. To find features in a solid model, the model is searched to see if the conditions corresponding to each feature are present. Boundary-based methods can be classified into rule-based, graph-based, or syntactic methods. Neural net-based systems are a special case of rule-based systems that allow probabilistic recognition of partial features that often result from feature interactions.

Topological criteria for feature recognition include the number of topological entities that the feature must contain, and their adjacencies. Topological conditions alone are usually insufficient to recognize features to a satisfactory degree. For instance, consider the highlighted features on the part cross-sections shown in Figure 4.4. All features consist of three faces, with one face that is adjacent (shares an edge) to the other two. However, (*a*) is a slot and (*b*) is a rectangular boss, while (*c*) is a domed boss; the three features will be regarded as quite different in most applications. If we want the system to discriminate between them, we need to make use of material and geometric conditions as well.

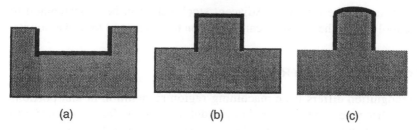

Figure 4.4 Different features with the same topology

By *material condition*, we imply distinguishing between solid and void "sides" of a feature. For example, in Figure 4.4, (*a*) represents a void, and (*b*) and (*c*) are solid. The distinction can be made by a clever edge classification scheme devised originally by Kyprianou (Kyprianou 1980) that measures the solid angles between adjacent faces. The solid angles between the middle and each of the side faces in (*a*) are greater than 180 degrees, while the opposite is true for (*b*) and (*c*). The edges that are at inter-face angles greater than 180 are called *concave*, while the others are *convex*. Using this material condition, we can distinguish depressions from protrusions, (*a*) from (*b*) and (*c*). We can distinguish further between (*b*) and (*c*) by looking at geometric conditions.

Geometric conditions can be face types (planar, cylindrical, etc.) or relative face orientations (perpendicular, parallel, etc.). For instance, a rectangular boss must have three planar faces, while the domed boss has two planar side faces and a cylindrical middle face. Even if we apply topological, material, and face type conditions, the level of resolution may not be sufficient for the desired application. Consider the two part cross-sections in Figure 4.5. Both features have two faces, mutually adjacent, a concave edge (labeled by *V*) between them, and convex edges (labeled *X*) with the adjacent part faces. From a design or manufacturing point of view, one feature is a step and the other a V-slot. To resolve this situation further, we need to look at the magnitude of angles between the faces.

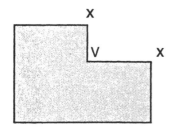
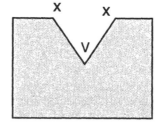

Figure 4.5 Insufficient resolution

The actual mechanics of representing and matching geometric and topological relations may vary considerably. A popular method is *rule-based recognition* in which features are formalized by production rules of the form:

```
IF (topological conditions &
    material conditions &
    geometric conditions)
THEN (shape is feature_x)
```

For each feature to be recognized, one needs to define a set of such rules. Each of the conditions in each of the rules has to be tested separately by means of procedures specified in the system; all conditions have to be satisfied in order for the feature to be discovered. It is only through trial and error that one can determine if the set of rules are necessary and sufficient (complete) for recognizing a given feature. Rule-based systems have to do exhaustive searches of the model database in order to find the features of interest. Therefore the search time can be prohibitive for large models and complex rules.

Graph-based methods match subgraphs in the solid model to graphs representing the features to be recognized. It is usually better to build a separate data structure, such as a *face adjacency graph* (FAG), to facilitate the search. In a FAG the nodes represent part faces (PF) and the arcs represent adjacencies,. If two faces meet at an edge, then there is an arc joining the nodes that represent those two faces; otherwise the nodes are unconnected. Geometry information is also added to a FAG by putting attributes on the arcs. The attribute serves as a flag that indicates when two faces meet at a convex or concave edge. Figure 4.6 shows a part and its attributed FAG. Figure 4.7 shows the sub-graphs for thru-slot and blind-step features. These sub-graphs are present in the graph of the part shown in Figure 4.6. It is obvious that the attributed graph will be the same for the two features shown in Figure 4.5; more complex arc attributes are needed to resolve the features further. Alternatively, one might use a graph-based algorithm to find general features and rules to recognize more specialized features.

Another technique that has been used in matching portions of boundary models to topologic and geometric conditions is *syntactic pattern recognition*. Adapted from vision systems, these systems use geometric patterns typically described by a series of straight, circular, or more complex curved line segments (Choi 1984). Simple patterns can be concatenated to give compound patterns. Languages have been developed for describing these sequences algebraically and manipulating them with operators that form a grammar. Features can be recognized by parsing the feature against the object's description in the grammar.

Despite their popularity, boundary-based feature recognition methods have suffered from the lack of robust algorithms, particularly when feature interactions are present. This is because feature interactions alter the topology, which forms the basis for rules, graphs, and algebraic expressions used in these methods. The match between the specialized feature rules, sub-graphs, or expressions

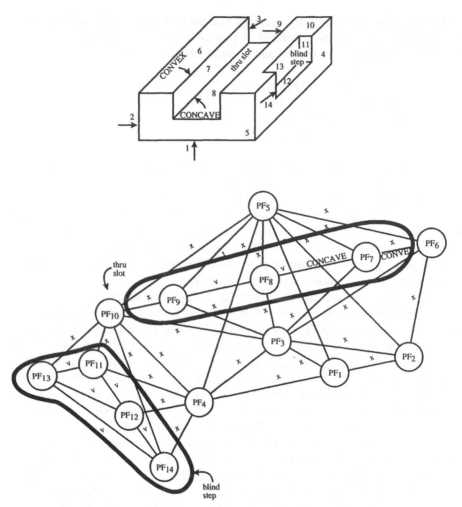

Figure 4.6 A part and its attributed FAG (adapted from [Joshi 1988]; by permission of Butterworth-Heinemann journals, Elsevier Science Ltd.)

and the conditions found in the model needs to be exact. Feature interactions remove portions of features involved in the intersection, and these traditional methods are unable to recognize partial or incomplete features. Consider what happens to the FAG when the steps is so deep that it penetrates the slot. Face F13 will disappear, and F9 will be split into two faces, if the vertical depth of the slot and the pocket are the same. Now we will be unable to find a match for either the slot or the step sub-graphs in the new FAG.

Probabilistic methods, based on neural networks, have been developed to overcome this problem. By using weights for each of the conditions, rule-based methods can be modified to yield the probability that a certain feature exists, instead of a simple yes/no answer. Further details of boundary-based feature recognition methods are given in Chapter 9.

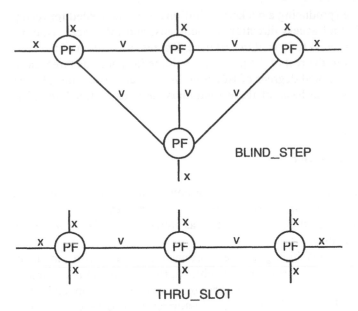

Figure 4.7 Sub-graphs for thru-slot and blind-step features

Volume-based recognition either operates directly on constructive solid models, such as CSG trees, or they produce and classify volume features from boundary models. CSG tree based recognition involves manipulation of trees to cast them in some canonical form, from which features can be recognized by matching sub-trees. CSG trees are non-unique in that we can have many CSG tree representations of the same part, corresponding to alternative construction histories. This is why it is necessary to restructure the tree in some "standard" (canonical) form. Because of this problem, CSG-based recognition methods have not progressed to a mature state.

Like cellular and convex decomposition methods for machining feature recognition, volume decomposition based feature recognition is used to identify the material to be removed from a base stock and to decompose this volume into *delta volumes,* which are units corresponding to distinct machining operations (General Dynamics 1985). These volumes may be determined either by Boolean differences between the stock and the part or by surface extensions to produce closed volumes. Feature recognition, unlike machining region recognition, involves the additional step of classifying and matching decomposed delta volumes to pre-defined volumes such as pockets and slots.

After the delta volumes have been obtained, they may be classified by rule based recognition applied to their topology and geometry. Alternatively, the volumes may be classified on the basis of their "degrees of freedom," which correspond to cutting tool motion needed to produce the volume. For example, the degree of freedom is 1 for plunging (producing a hole), 2 for plunging and linear sweeping (producing a through-slot), and 2.5 for plunging and sweeping along a planar curve (producing a pocket). Additional criteria needed for recognition may include tool access direction, dimensions, and tolerances. Another way to classify volumes is to look at the relative degrees of freedom of the delta volume with respect to the rest of the part. Any volume in space has three translational and three rotational degrees of freedom. Volume classification schemes have been devised on the basis of these imaginary degrees of freedom (Shah 1994).

4.4 DESIGN BY FEATURES

Two methodologies for design by features are commonly used: *destruction by machining features* and *synthesis by design features*. The destructive approach goes by various names in the literature, such as *destructive solid geometry* or *deforming solid geometry*.

In the destruction by machining features approach, one starts with a model of the raw stock from which a part is to be machined; the part model is created by subtracting from the stock, features corresponding to material removed by machining operations. This facilitates a manufacturing plan to be concurrently developed. Prototype systems using this approach have been demonstrated (Arbab 1982, Cutkosky 1988, Turner 1988). Some commercial systems also support this approach. All these systems use a set of pre-defined features that are subtracted from the base solid.

The synthesis by design features approach differs from the above in that models can be built both by adding and subtracting features; it is not neccessary to start with the model of the base stock. Many research and commercial systems belong to this category; for example, systems described in (Miner 1985, Luby 1986, Shah 1988,) etc. follow this approach.

In all of the design by features approaches, parts are created directly using features and the geometric model is generated from the features. This requires that the design system have generic feature definitions placed in a *feature library* from which features can be instanced by specifying dimension and location parameters, the feature/face/edge on which it is to be located, and various other attributes, constraints, and relationships. How constraints are handled varies from system to system. This includes the determination of constrained feature dimensions from independent variables. We can classify constraint management in design by feature systems into two generic approaches: *procedural* and *declarative*. We define these approaches as follows: In the procedural approach, features are sets of procedures, while in the declarative approach, features are sets of constraints. The procedural approach is similar to parametric modeling approach, and the declarative approach is similar to variational modeling.

To understand the difference between procedural and declarative approaches, consider the example discussed in Section 3.8 (Figure 3.12). In that example a slot feature was described by a set of constraints. In the procedural approach these feature constraints may be buried inside the procedures. However, declarative modeling separates feature definition ("declaration") from implementation for a particular geometric modeler; the declaration is in a neutral format, that is, independent of construction history. *This distinction between procedural and declarative approaches is being made not because we can clearly classify feature-based systems into these two categories but because we want to study the inherent properties of these "pure" approaches. Many implemented systems are neither purely procedural, nor purely declarative.*

4.4.1 Procedural Design by Features

In the procedural approach generic features are pre-defined in terms of rules and procedures. Procedures may include methods for instancing, modifying, copying, and deleting features, generating solid models, deriving certain parameters, and validating feature operations. For instance, in a typical modeler, information associated with procedural features available in the library includes:

- List of parameters (organized into dependent and independent variables)
- Inheritance (deviation) rules
- Validation rules

The derived parameters are determined using procedures based on "rules" that are sometimes referred to as *inheritance rules*. These rules trigger pre-defined mathematical procedures for finding the values of constrained variables from the independent ones. One can also incorporate validation rules that trigger procedures to enforce size, location, orientation constraints. Features can also have a solid representation associated with them in the form of a procedure. This may be done by including geometric construction procedures, using common techniques, such as primitive instancing, sweeping, and Boolean operators. The position and orientation of features in appropriate coordinate system may be specified in the feature producing volume. The first feature is typically located in global coordinates, and all other features are then, directly or indirectly, located with respect to this starting feature by default coordinate systems associated with features and their faces. Some systems allow a user to define coordinate systems at instance time (Turner 1988), while others hard code it in a feature's generic definition stored in the library. While positioning features, the user must select an adjacent feature, a face on that feature, a face on itself, and then a local position and orientation on the face.

All of these functions are performed by pre-defined procedures. The methodology can be made quite general, and users can define their own generic features or assemblies without making changes to the code. Some characteristics of the procedural approach are:

- The defined inheritance rules/procedures create a unidirectional chain for change propagation and for initial derivation of derived parameters; the constraints are already decoupled and one sided. There is a *reference-to-target* entity precedence: If the reference is moved, the target moves to maintain the constraint, but not the other way around.

- Conflicts in parameter values are avoided by using a parameter hierarchy.
- Special purpose rules are needed to specify how features or parts need to be attached or assembled to other features or parts. This leads to a combinatorial problem.

We will study the reasons for these properties in Chapter 8.

4.4.2 Declarative Design by Features

The declarative approach involves defining feature classes by explicitly stating the spatial relationships that must exist between geometric entities that constitute the feature, either in terms of relationships between primitive volumes or in terms of relationships between boundary based modeling entities like faces and edges. The main capabilities needed for declarative modeling are

- Constraint definition
- Constraint representation
- Constraint solution and validation
- Dynamic interfacing with geometric modeler

Further discussion of declarative systems is postponed until Chapter 8 and 10. For now we will only make some high level remarks about these two design by feature approaches.

In the procedural approach one must define special rules or procedures for every situation in which the feature will be used. For example, consider putting a through hole in a block rather than through a sphere. The determination of hole location, hole depth, and size or position limits will be in the form of special rules, one version for each type of parent feature. However, the declarative constraints are general, so just one feature definition can cover different contexts. One can argue that procedures can be made more general, but it is not always possible.

The procedures in the procedural method actually establish a unidirectional chain for change propagation. For example, if a through-hole derives its length from the block, there is a one-way relationship. In other words, if the block's depth is changed the hole will follow, and not the other way around. The order in which procedures are used is pre-determined. Also changes made to the location of a feature are propagated by using the face and coordinate system attachments defined while instancing the feature. On attaching a feature to a face, the transformation matrix associated with the face gets attached to that of the feature. Subsequently each time a change is made, change propagation is achieved by re-evaluating the transformation matrices associated with each of the features. On the other hand, if the declarative approach is adopted, each time a change is made to the position or orientation of a geometric entity, all the constraints are checked to see if they have been violated. Change propagation takes place only if all the violated constraints are satisfied once again. This means that the entire set of constraint equations has to be solved. This is not a trivial task, and the overheads involved are significant. As we will see in Chapter 8 it is sometimes possible to group constraints into sets that can be solved independently of other constraints.

4.5 COMPARISON OF FEATURE CREATION TECHNIQUES

From the discussion in the previous sections it can be seen that each of the three basic feature creation methods, namely interactive creation, automatic recognition, and design by features, has some strong points and some drawbacks.

The interactive creation method is easy to implement. Only the features needed for an application (e.g., process planning) are identified; the entire model does not need to be featurized. For models containing a large number of features that need to be interactively created, this method can be time-consuming. The user is responsible for feature validation, unless generic feature definitions are pre-defined to guide the user and to validate the entities picked. Interactive creation may be used to supplement automatic recognition when reliable algorithms cannot be found, or features cannot be fully formalized.

Automatic feature recognition is the oldest branch of features technology, and it now appears to be on the verge of commercial implementation (Ames 1991, Tech-Ex 1994). Rule-based and graph-based methods appear to be more developed than other recognition techniques. Exhaustive searches of large geometric databases and failure of recognition algorithms in the presence of feature interactions have created the biggest bottlenecks for these methods, but recent developments in variants of these methods offer much promise. These developments are discussed in Chapter 9. Surface-based recognition, instead of face-based, reduces the search time, since it considers faces sharing the same surface as a single unit. Use of fuzzy logic, neural nets, and incremental recognition have all shown that partial features can be recognized when there are interactions. Use of silhouette models reduces the size of the geometric model that needs to be searched. There are also many new developments in volume decomposition schemes that have lead to prototype applications in industry. Specifically, decomposed volumes may be matched to meaningful shapes, such as those produced by machining operations.

CSG-based recognition and convex hull decomposition techniques are not yet mature enough to be used in practical applications. Sectioning techniques suffer from many inherent problems but are nevertheless successful with simple 2.5 D parts that do not have any undercuts. The presence of undercuts, inclined surfaces, and non-planar surfaces creates complications. When many features occur in the same plane, each feature is machined before moving to the next plane. This yields non-optimal tool paths.

Interactive and automatic recognition both offer the advantage that recognition can be made application-specific, allowing each application program to have its own recognition method. However, features are created after the geometry and designers do not have these features available, so this makes their job harder. Feature recognition has been referred to as "redundant effort" by some people because designers know the features of the part; these features are then "lost" because a geometric modeler is unable to archive them. On the other side, people have argued that design features do not necessarily correspond to features used in other applications, so a system is needed to recognize the application features, anyway.

Design-by-feature systems are already available commercially; their capabilities are rapidly growing. Design by features has the advantage that it allows designers to transfer to the model not only the features important to the part function but also their dimensioning and tolerancing scheme, which encodes, to some extent, also the design intent. It further allows designers to create the part faster and more conveniently, and to make changes rapidly by taking advantage of associativity information. This richer and higher level model is available for use by downstream applications. One needs to determine how many features should be contained in the feature library, the level of abstraction or granularity. The provision of specialized features can result in feature library explosion. Since features are application-specific the need for feature recognition by applications does not go away when one designs by features. Finally, interactions between features can result in non-generic shapes that do not exist in the database, or they can make invalid some generic dimension values.

Many variations of design-by-feature systems are available; some restrict users to a set of pre-defined, hard-coded features, while others allow users to define their own features. Some of these systems do not afford the same level of functionality to user-defined features as those of the vendor-defined features. In some systems features are just construction macros (procedures), while they are variational geometry in others.

4.6 UNIFICATION OF FEATURE CREATION TECHNIQUES

In light of the advantages and disadvantages discussed in Section 4.5, it is logical to consider if interactive creation, automatic recognition, and design by feature approaches can be combined in some way to yield a system that is more powerful than any one of them used alone. A unified system would combine the positive aspects of all the methods. The weaknesses of one option would be offset by the corresponding strengths of the others. The user would be free to choose what he or she feels to be the most convenient of the methods and would also have the freedom of mixing and matching. For example, if a company wants to create feature models of parts that were previously created in traditional CAD (with no features), it would need feature recognition. The new model would then be easier to modify by working directly with features.

One of the disadvantages of human-assisted creation is that it can be very cumbersome to create complex features. For example, gear teeth or splines require enumeration of many faces of complex geometry. The job could be made easier by using automatic feature recognition. Once a part is created users should be able to modify, copy, delete, all features in some uniform way.

Feature recognition or interactive creation can identify the entities in the geometric model that correspond to a feature. In some cases it is also possible to extract the dimensional parameters of the features and their values, such as the diameter of a hole, or the depth of a slot. Thus recognition amounts to making explicit what is implicit in the model. However, features created by the design by feature approach usually contain richer information that is not even implicitly represented in the geometric model. All of the additional information associated with features that is not available from the geometric model has to be incorporated somehow, if there is to be no difference between features created by different modes. This may include the feature hierarchy, constraint system for feature location and orientation, tolerances, surface finish, and material properties. Unified systems are discussed at the end of Chapter 9.

REVIEW QUESTIONS

4.1 Draw a subgraph for a rectangular pocket feature following the style of Figure 4.7.

4.2 Can you give an example where the subgraph constructed in Question 4.1 erroneously matches a pattern due to insufficient resolution?

4.3 Give informal rule-based procedures for recognizing (a) a straight through hole (b) a conical bottom hole, and (c) a countersunk hole.

4.4 Devise a control strategy for using the rule-based procedures constructed in Question 4.3 to recognize correctly a part that has all three types of holes.

4.5 What are the delta volumes of the part in Figure 4.6? What are the degrees of freedom of each delta volume?

4.6 (a) What is the motivation for developing unified feature creation systems? (b) What are the difficulties in realizing such a unified system?

4.7 At a conceptual level, compare boundary-based and volume-based recognition systems, with respect to computational complexity, size of domain, and reliability.

4.8 Define a T-slot (to be placed on a brick) by (a) a set of procedures that can be executed by a solid modeler and (b) a set of constraints that is independent of construction procedure.

BIBLIOGRAPHY

Ames, A. L., 1991, Production ready feature recognition based automatic group technology part coding, in J. Rossignac and J. Turner, eds., *Proc. of First ACM Symp. on Solid Modelling Foundations and CAD/CAM Applications,* June 5–7, ACM Press, pp. 161–169.

Ansaldi, S., De Floriani, L., and Falcidieno, B., 1985, Geometric modeling of solid objects by using a face adjacency graph representation, Proc. of Siggraph '85, *Comp. Gr.* **19** (3): 131–139.

Arbab, F., 1982, Requirements and architecture of CAM oriented CAD systems for design and manufacture of mechanical parts, Ph.D. dissertation, University of California, Los Angeles.

Armstrong, G. T., 1982, A study of automatic generation of non-invasive N.C. machine paths from geometric models, Ph.D. dissertation, Department of Mechanical Engineering, University of Leeds.

Armstrong, G. T., Carey, G. C., and de Pennington, A., 1984, Numerical code generation from a geometric modeling system, in M. S. Pickett and J. W. Boyse, eds., *Solid Modeling by Computers: from Theory to Applications,* Plenum Press, pp. 139–157.

Bunce, P. G., Pratt, M. J., Pavey, S., and Pinte, J., 1986, Features extraction and process planning—Specific study, Technical Report R-86-GM/PP-01, CAM-I, Inc., Arlington, Texas.

Burchard, R., 1987, Feature based geometric constraints applied to CSG, M.S. thesis, Purdue University.

Chang, T.-C., 1982, TIPPS—A totally integrated process planning system, Ph.D. dissertation, Virginia Polytechnic Institute.

Choi, B. K., Barash, M. M., and Anderson, D. C., 1984, Automatic recognition of machined surfaces from a 3D solid model, *Computer-Aided Design* **16** (2): 81–86.

Corney, J., and Clark, D. E. R., 1993, Face-based feature recognition: generalizing special cases, *Computer Integrated Manufacturing* **6** (1 and 2): 39–50.

Cunningham, J., and Dixon, J. R., 1988, Designing with features: The origin of features, *ASME Computers in Engineering Conf.,* San Francisco, July 31–August 4, ASME Press, pp. 237–243.

Cutkosky, M., Tenenbaum, J. M., and Muller, D., 1988, Features in process based design, *ASME Computers in Engineering Conf.,* San Francisco, July 31–August 4, ASME Press, pp. 557–562.

Dong, X., and M. Wozny, 1988, FRAFES, A frame-based feature extraction system, *Proc. of Int. Conf. on Computer Integrated Manufacturing*, Rensselaer Polytechnic Institute, May 23–25, pp. 296–305.

Falcidieno, B., and Giannini, F., 1987, Extraction and organization of form features into a structured boundary model, in G. Maréchal, ed., *Proc. of Eurographics '87,* North-Holland, pp. 249–259.

General Dynamics Corporation, 1985, Volume decomposition algorithm—Final report, Technical Report R-82-ANC-01, CAM-I, Inc., Arlington, TX.

Gossard, D. C., Zuffante, R. P., and Sakurai, H., 1988, Representing dimensions, tolerances, and features in MCAE systems, *IEEE Comp. Gr. and Appl.* **8** (2): 51–59.

Grayer, A. R., 1976, A computer link between design and manufacture, Ph.D. dissertation, University of Cambridge.

Grayer, A. R., 1977, The automatic production of machined components starting from a stored geometric description, in D. McPherson, ed., *Advances in Computer Aided Manufacture,* North Holland, pp. 137–150.

Gupta, S. K., Nau, D. S., Regli, W. C., and Zhang, G., 1994, A methodology for systematic creation and evaluation of alternative operation plans, in J. J. Shah, M. Mäntylä, and D. Nau, eds., *Advances in Feature Based Manufacturing,* Elsevier Science Publishers, pp. 161–184.

Henderson, M. R., 1984, Extraction of feature information from three dimensional CAD data, Ph.D. dissertation, Purdue University.

Hummel, K. E., and Brooks, S. L., 1986, Symbolic representation of manufacturing features for an automated process planning system, *ASME Winter Annual Meeting,* Anaheim, ASME Press, pp. 233–243.

Jakubowski, R., 1982, Syntactic characterization of machine parts shapes, *Cybernetics and Systems: An Int. J.* **3** (1): 1–24.

Jared, G. E. M., 1984, Shape features in geometric modelling, in M. S. Pickett and J. W. Boyse, eds., *Solid Modelling by Computers: From Theory to Applications,* Plenum Press, pp. 121–137.

Joshi, S., and Chang, T.-C., 1988, Graph-based heuristics for recognition of machined features from a 3-D solid model, *Computer-Aided Design* **20** (2): 58–66.

Kim, Y. S., 1994, Volumetric feature recognition using convex decomposition, in Shah, J., Mäntylä, M., and Nau, D., eds., *Advances in Feature Based Manufacturing,* Elsevier Science Publishers, pp. 39–63.

Kyprianou, L., 1980, Shape classification in computer aided design, Ph.D. dissertation, University of Cambridge.

Laakko, T., 1993, Incremental feature modelling: methodology for integrating features and solid models, Dr. Tech. dissertation, Helsinki University of Technology, Laboratory of Information Processing Science.

Lee, Y. C., and Jea, K.-F. J., 1988, A new CSG tree reconstruction algorithm for feature representation, *ASME Computers in Engineering Conf.,* San Fransisco, July 31–August 4, ASME Press, pp. 521–528.

Luby, S., Dixon, J. R., and Simmons, M. K., 1986, Creating and using feature databases, *Comp. in Mech. Eng.* **5** (3): 25–33.

Miner, R. H., 1985, A method for the representation and manipulation of geometric features in a solid model, M.S. thesis, Mechanical Engineering Department, MIT.

Parks, R. D., and Chase, T. R., 1989, Representing mechanical parts using feature specifications and positional constraints: A contrast with PDES, *ASME Computers in Engineering. Conf.,* Anaheim, ASME Press.

Pratt, M. J., 1988, Synthesis of an optimal approach to form feature modeling, *ASME Computers in Engineering Conf.,* San Francisco, July 31–August 4, ASME Press, pp. 263–274.

Pratt, M. J., and Wilson, P. R., 1986, Requirements for support of form features in a solid modeling system, final report, Technical Report R-86-ASPP-01, CAM-I, Inc., Arlington, TX.

Requicha, A. A. G., and Vandenbrande, J., 1989, Form features for mechanical design and manufacturing, *ASME Computers in Engineering Conf.*, Anaheim, ASME Press.

Sakurai, H., and Chin, C., W. 1994, Definition and recognition of volume features for process planning, in J. J. Shah, M. Mäntylä, and D. Nau, eds., *Advances in Feature Based Manufacturing*, Elsevier Science Publishers, pp. 65–80.

Shah, J. J., and Rogers, M. T., 1988, Expert form feature modeling shell, *Computer-Aided Design* **20** (9): 515–524.

Shah, J. J., Rogers, M., Sreevalsan, P., Hsiao, D., Mathew, A., Bhatnagar, A., Liou, B., and Miller, D., 1990, The ASU features testbed: An overview, *ASME Computers in Engineering Conf.*, Vol. 1, Boston, ASME Press, pp. 233–242.

Shah, J. J., Shen, Y., and Shirur, A., 1994, Determination of machining volumes from extensible sets of design features, in J. J. Shah, M. Mäntylä, and D. Nau, *Advances in Feature Based Manufacturing*, Elsevier Science Publishers, pp. 129–157.

Shah, J. J., Sreevalsan, P., Rogers, M., Billo, R., and Mathew, A., 1988, Current status of features technology, Report for task 0, Technical Report R-88-GM-04.4, CAM-I, Inc., Arlington, TX.

Staley, S. M., Henderson, M. R., and Anderson, D. C., 1983, Using syntactic pattern recognition to extract feature information from a solid geometric data base, *Comp. in Mech. Eng.* **2** (2): 61–66.

Tech-Ex, 1994, Boyce & Goodrej demonstration at the ACIS Users Conference and Exposition, Spatial Technologies, Ft. Lauderadale, FL.

Turner, G., and Anderson, D. C., 1988, An object oriented approach to interactive, feature based design for quick turnaround manufacturing, *ASME Computers in Engineering Conf.*, San Francisco, July 31–August 4, ASME Press.

Vandenbrande, J. H., and Requicha, A. A. G., 1993, Spatial reasoning for the automatic recognition of machinable features in solid models, *IEEE Trans. on Pattern Analysis and Machine Intelligence* **15** (12): 1269–1285.

Wang, E., 1992, Using automatic feature recognition to interface CAD and CAPP, *ASME Computers in Engineering Conf.*, San Fransisco, ASME Press, pp. 215–231.

Woo, T., 1982, Feature extraction by volume decomposition, *Proc. of Conf. on CAD/CAM Technology in Mechanical Engineering*, MIT, Cambridge, MA, pp. 76–94.

Woodwark, J. R., 1988, Some speculations on feature recognition, *Computer-Aided Design* **20** (4): 189–196.

APPLICATION OF
FEATURES

Features have found use in a wide range of applications: part and assembly design, design for manufacturing, process planning, inspection planning, finite element mesh generation, and many other areas. The first two chapters of this part examine these applications.

There is no such thing as a universal set of features. For each application, one needs to identify, formalize, and archive generic features required for performing the necessary tasks of that application. CAD vendors cannot be expected to provide turnkey feature-based systems; product and process specific features must be defined by the user organizations themselves. Therefore we will discuss methodologies for identifying and formalizing features for various design and manufacturing applications in Chapters 5 and 6.

As discussed in Part I, a key objective for product modeling is to share product data across various applications. For this to happen, there are two problems that must be solved: Feature data exchange and feature mapping between applications. Several STEP models are important in feature-based product data exchange. These models are in varying stages of development, maturity, and stability. Feature mapping is a difficult problem; few general purpose methods exist. Feature mapping and data exchange are discussed in Chapter 7.

III

APPLICATION OF FEATURES

5

FEATURES IN DESIGN

Features are useful in many design tasks such as part geometry creation, tolerance specification, and assembly design. Not only can features enhance the design environment of a CAD system, they can also make it possible to analyze the design concurrently using numerical or knowledge-based systems. Examples of such analysis methods are stress analysis using finite elements, manufacturability evaluation using rule-based systems, tolerance sensitivity analysis using numerical methods, and cost estimation. These applications can only be automated if a feature-based product description is available. The designer can make more informed decisions when provided feedback from these applications, thus reducing product development time and avoiding problems during manufacture or service. Some of these applications are discussed in the next chapter; this chapter will focus on design.

5.1 FEATURE-BASED PART CREATION

In this section we will demonstrate, by means of a simulated walk-through, the following two benefits of using features in creating the geometry of a part:

1. Ease and speed of geometry creation
2. Propagation of design changes

The first benefit is possible because features are collections of entities with predefined attributes, the user simply needs to instance a feature as one unit and fill in a few blanks. The designer does not need to create everything from scratch; the generic characteristics are already captured in the feature class definitions available in a feature library. The second benefit is made possible because geometric constraints are stored in the form of intrinsic or extrinsic feature relations, the system can automatically propagate the changes by maintaining any defined constraints.

143

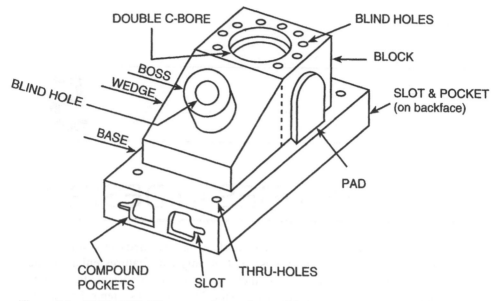

Figure 5.1 CAMI–ANC 101 test part (somewhat modified)

The part chosen for the demonstration is shown in Figure 5.1. It is the well-known ANC-101 test part. This test part is not a real part with any real functions; it was designed by the Advanced Numerical Control (ANC) program of CAM-I, Inc., to test geometric modeling capabilities. We will first describe the generic library feature classes needed to create this part and then simulate a session that creates the part geometry by instancing these pre-defined features.

Design-by-features systems support generic feature archival in one or more feature libraries. A feature library contains the generic definitions of features needed in an application. Depending on the nature of the product(s) that a company designs, it might make sense to organize features into many separate libraries, each for product specific types. For example, an automotive company might decide to have separate feature libraries for pistons, conrods, crankshafts, camshafts, etc. The common features, of these could either have identical definitions in each library or be placed in a common general-use library.

Since the ANC-101 part is a hypothetical design, we cannot determine its features based on the design process. Instead, the features we have chosen for modeling this part are based only on geometry creation, not design or manufacture. The feature types needed for creating the demo part are shown in Figure 5.2(a) through (c). Each feature is defined by its generic shape, shown by a parametrized sketch. The parameters are organized into three groups: independent dimensions, derived (constrained) dimensions, and parameters needed in positioning the feature with respect to other features. Obviously these features could have been parametrized differently, depending upon user preferences.

Feature and Sketch	Independent Dimensions	Derived Dimensions	Positioning
BLOCK	Length width, height	None	World coordinates or on the face of another block
WEDGE	Length, width, height 1, height 2	None (optional; length and width derived from parent block)	World coordinates or on face of another block
THRU-HOLE	Diameter	Depth (distance between entry and exit faces)	On entry face; specify *x, y* distance from reference edges on entry face:
BLIND HOLE	Diameter depth, radius	None	Same as thru-hole
DOUBLE C-BORE HOLE	Dial, dia2, dia, len1, len2	Length (optional: fixed ratios for dial/dia and dia2/dia)	Same as thru-hole

Figure 5.2(a) Generic feature library

Feature	Dimensions	Derived/Other	Positioning
BASE 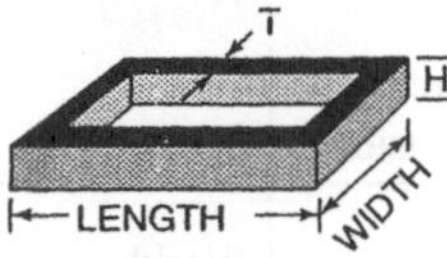	Height, width, length, T		Positioned in *WCS*
BLIND SLOT 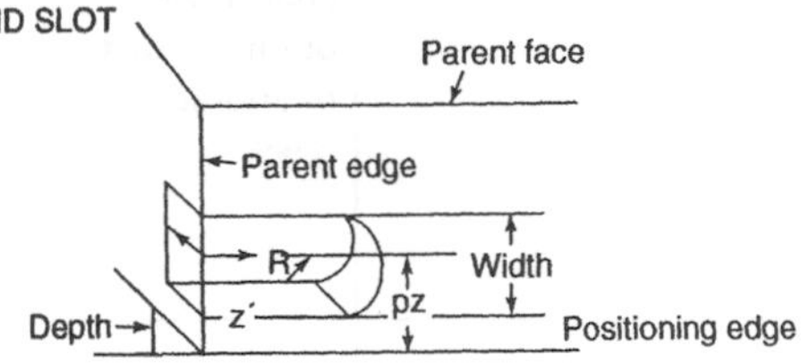	Depth, width, length	$\text{Radius} = \dfrac{\text{width}}{2}$	On planar face: along an edge: specify distance from the reference vertex
TAPER POCKET (THRU) 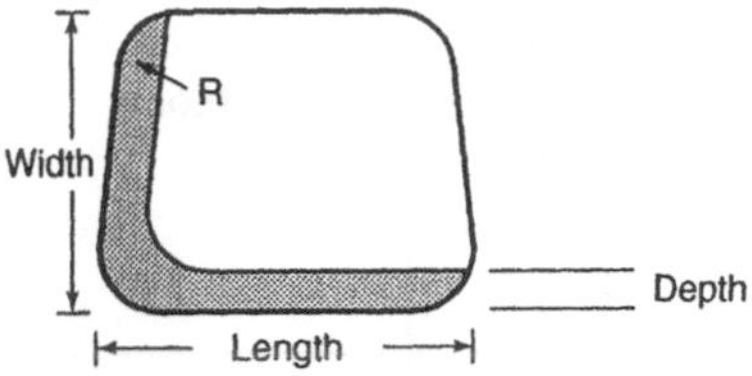	Length, width, R, taper_angle	Depoth (determined) by distance between entry & exit faces)	On planar face: specify x, y position of center point/ axes wrt edges (optional: specify orientation)
BOSS 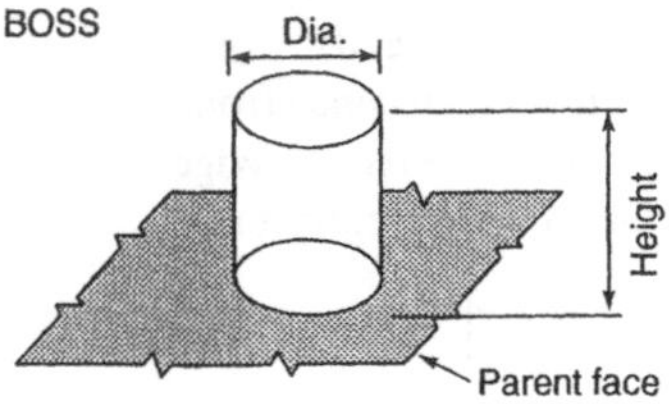	Dia, height		On planar face: specify x, y position of centerpoint wrt edges
RECESS 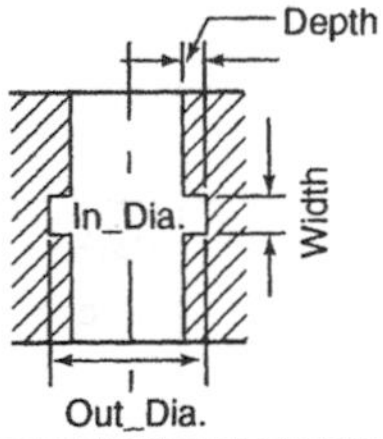	Depth, width	in_dia (= hole _dia) out_dia (= in_ dia + 2* depth) where DIA is the diameter of the hole	Distance from entry face of hole
RIB 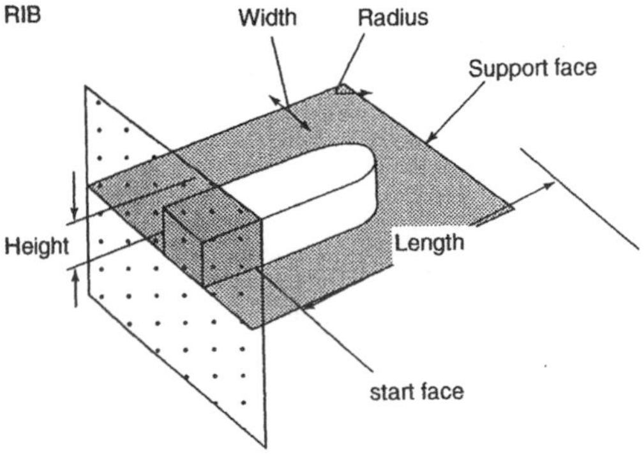	Height, length width	Radius (= 0.5 width)	On support face and start face as shown specify distance from reference edge

Figure 5.2(b) Generic feature library (continued)

CIRCULAR HOLE PATTERN

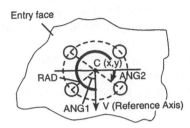

Compound parameters

C = pattern center position
RAD = pattern radius
V = reference axis
ANG1 = position of first hole
ANG2 = position of last hole
NUM = number of holes

RECTANGULAR HOLE PATTERN

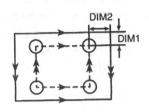

Rectangular pattern aligned with edges
of reference rectangle (as shown)   es
DIM1, DIM2 = distance from ends

SYMMETRIC POCKETS

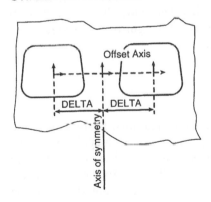

Axis of symmetry; offset axis
DELTA = offset distance

Figure 5.2(c) Generic pattern library

In our decomposition we see this part as consisting of 25 instance features
that can be characterized by 11 generic feature classes. We consider the double-
cbore-hole as a single composite feature, but this represents our preference. The
two obround-pockets and blind-slots in the front face of the base can also be
combined into composite features, but in this example we have shown them as
separate features.

We also notice that this part has several feature patterns: a circular pattern of blind holes and a rectangular pattern of through-holes. The slotted-pockets can also be seen as reflected features across a plane of symmetry. These patterns are described in Figure 5.2(c). The pattern descriptions are generic in that the patterns can be applied to different hole types or pocket types.

By capturing constraints and by relative positioning of features, the system requires only the input of independent parameters from the user, Also, when changes are made, the dependent dimensions can be automatically re-calculated, and features re-positioned when their parent entity is moved or otherwise modified.

The test part can be created in 13 steps, 10 of which are illustrated in Figure 5.3. The operations on the backfaces, and some minor features, are not shown. The reason that a fairly complex part can be created in such a small number of steps is that some of the required information is already captured in the feature library. Obviously, for the feature based paradigm to pay off, it is necessary that more or less the same set of features be needed for creating families of parts that are frequently designed. This ensures that the investment in identifying, formalizing, and archiving features saves time in later design projects.This is discussed further in the next section.

After creating the part, suppose that we want to move feature2 (block) with respect to the base. The change will propagate to all features that were positioned on feature2; this includes the boss, the pad, the double-cbore, and so on. It creates a chain reaction: All features that were positioned with respect to the boss, the cbore, etc., will also be re-positioned. For example, the circular hole pattern (positioned with respect to the cbore) and the blind-hole (positioned on the boss) will all move with their parent entities. The same change mechanism applies to dimension changes. For example, if the height of the wedge is reduced, the cbore's depth will also be reduced.

5.2 FEATURE IDENTIFICATION

Each product type has its own characteristic set of features. Features are also dependent on the process used to engineer a product. For each application, one needs to identify, formalize, and archive generic feature classes required for performing the necessary tasks of that application. By *identify* we mean determining which portions of the part can be considered to be a stereotypical shape that is treated as a single unit in the user's mind. By *formalize* we mean the articulation of the properties of a feature class that are needed in a given application. And by *archive* we mean storing formalized definitions of features in a feature library of the feature-based modeling system. CAD vendors can only be expected to provide a few general feature classes, but not features specific to a company's products and processes. These tasks must be undertaken by user organizations themselves.

The identification and formalization of features can be very time-consuming. It should be regarded as an investment that must be made before an organization

1 - INSTANCE BASE IN WCS

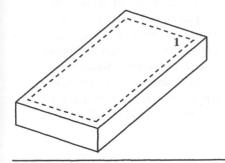

2 - PLACE BLOCK ON TOP FACE OF BASE

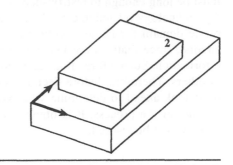

3 - PLACE BLOCk & WEDGE ON TOP
    FACE OF SMALL BLOCK

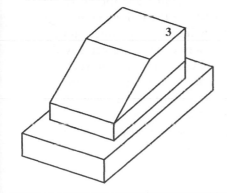

4 - POSITION BOSS ON WEDGE FACE
5 - POSITION PAD ON BASE & BLOCK

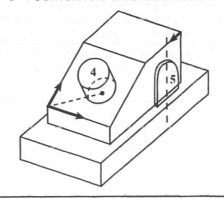

6 - PUT DOUBLE C-BORE ON TOP FACE
    OF BLOCK
7 - PUT BLIND HOLE CENTERD ON BOSS

8 - INSTANCE CIRCULAR HOLE PATTERN
    AROUND C-BORE
9 - INSTANCE COMPOUND POCKETS &
    POSITION W.R.T FACE CENTER
10 - CREATE RECTANGULAR HOLE
     PATTERN ON BASE

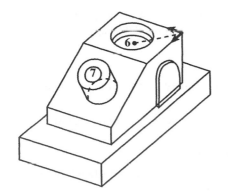

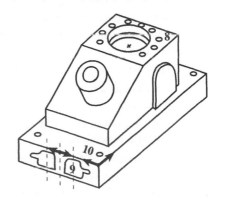

Figure 5.3 Geometry creation walk-through

can benefit from features technology. The implication is that the product's life must be long enough to justify such an investment. If the design or manufacturing technology related to a product is rapidly changing, it may not be an appropriate domain for feature applications. This should not come as a surprise to anyone, since features are vehicles for the re-use of design or manufacturing information. Such information can become obsolete faster in some domains than in others. Therefore, before deciding to use features in any given domain, one must look ahead to determine what kind of changes are on the horizon for a product or the process. It is obviously not worthwhile to archive information that will not be re-used.

5.2.1 Featurizing a Part

Featurizing a part refers to the process by which we identify and formalize features of a part for use in some application. Let us use the following analogy: Imagine that we are developing a language for engineering a product, through various stages, from conceptual design to manufacture. Then we can say that features are the nouns in that language and feature operations are the verbs. To develop this feature language, we need to consider both the process and the product. The two are closely coupled; however, it might make it easier to initially examine the attributes of the product and the process separately and then to relate them. Here a systematic methodology is suggested for part featurizing for design; similar procedures can be devised for other applications.

Product

1. Examine part drawings or CAD models of the component class that needs to be featurized. Look at representative versions and several generations of the same part.
2. Identify regions of interest for a designer.
3. Identify macro shapes on the basis of different functional regions (mating region, containment region, reinforcement, etc.).
4. Decompose each region into the lowest level units that a designer would treat as single units; call these units "simple features." These units must satisfy these four requirements:
   - They serve a design function.
   - They act as a recurring shape seen in several versions of the part being featurized.
   - They are parametrizable, or describable by a set of geometric relations and/or a procedure.
   - They belong to the designers vocabulary.
5. Draw a generic sketch for each simple feature identified and label all its dimensions using the designer's terminology.

6. Determine if there are any "composite features," such as simple features arranged in a geometric pattern, or features with fixed inter-relationships. Draw sketches of these composites and label their inter-relationship parameters.

By examining the finished part drawings, we only see the final result of the design process. There is no record of the evolution of the design. We do not know how the feature is related to the rest of the part, how it is located, when it is created, how its attributes are determined, and so on. Therefore we need to study also the design process.

Process The design evolves through a number of "design states"; each design action changes the design state. Design states are snapshots taken during design; they tell us what information is available at each stage and help us study how the transformation between them took place. There are a number of tools available for giving a structured description of processes. For example, IDEF0 is a popular language for studying engineering processes (Colquhoun et al. 1993). Each step is described in a uniform format by input, output and control parameters. Process decomposition can be done at various levels of abstraction.

Geometric form features usually do not come about until embodiment or detailed design; functional and conceptual design uses more abstract and incomplete product representations. Therefore our discussion here is aimed only at stages of the design where physical embodiment of the design begins to evolve.

1. Identify the base or reference feature; it is the shape, surface, or outline from which the designer begins his design. This is the initial state of the design. The reference feature could be the footprint of a mating part, the boundary of the housing where the part needs to go, the inverse of a part (e.g., forging or molding die design starts out as the inverse of the part to be forged or molded as the base-line shape)

2. Divide the design process into major sub-processes; establish the process structure and sequence.

3. Define the input and output from each sub-process.

4. Determine the reasoning or computation that transforms the input to the output. This can be done recursively at more and more detailed levels.

5. Use the information from step 4 to determine what is a single feature, based on whether it materializes as a unit.

6. Determine how the feature parameters are derived: whether they are based on other features or are independent. See if default values can be given for some of the parameters.

7. Determine how the feature is located on the part; what is the reference coordinate system used and how the position and orientation parameters are determined.

Reconciliation   The information from both of the above studies (product and process) will next need to be consolidated and reconciled. Finally, using a uniform format, describe each feature in terms of the following:

- Generic shape (sketch)
- Dimension parameters
- Positioning reference entity (entities)
- Positioning method and positioning/orientation parameters
- Geometric constraints (intrinsic and extrinsic)
- Adjacency relationships that need to be captured between neighboring features

The attributes may be organized into intrinsic and extrinsic, as discussed in Chapter 3. In some applications it might be useful to associate a function (or several functions) with each feature. It is also useful to include validation rules for the feature. One might think about situations in which a feature would not have its intended meaning, or some other undesirable characteristics. This can lead to the documentation of rules for detecting such situations or constraints that will prevent the feature from becoming invalid.

In addition one could define "composite features"; these are combinations of simple features that may be created, referenced, and manipulated together (see Chapter 3). Composite features allow users to operate on them at multiple levels while maintaining geometric and topological relationships. If there are a large number of features, one might consider some further logical organization, such as the development of a feature taxonomy based on common feature attributes. Refer to Section 3.5 for classification methods.

The above list of steps provides a systematic framework for a first-cut identification of features and formalization of their properties. Because we consider the design process, only features that are useful in product creation are identified. These features must be further refined and validated, as discussed later.

Trade-offs   Two questions often arise when featurizing a part:

- Should the entire part be featurized, or just certain selected regions?
- How general or specific should the features be?

To answer the first question, consider the definition and utility of features. Features are about re-use of product definition data; they must recur often enough to justify the investment in formalizing and archiving them. There must be a stereotypical pattern to be identified and parametrized. If the variations from version to version are large, or if it is difficult to find a generic parametric definition, then features for design are not worthwhile. One might as well design in terms of geometry directly. There are also cases where geometry construction techniques can create a part more rapidly than the feature techniques. Therefore one might consider designing partly with features and partly with geometry. However, one must also consider the information needed by downstream applications. If portions of the model are not featurized, some of the parameters needed by downstream applications may not be easily extractable.

The second question is answered by observing that the level of information associated with a feature is inversely proportional to the flexibility in using the feature. The more specific it is, the less information needs to be added when the feature is instanced. Specific features enable a part to be created rapidly; however, a large number of features are needed. For example, we could have specific features such as perpendicular-through-hole, angular-through-hole, flat-bottomed-perpendicular-blind-hole, etc. The number of instance parameters that need to be specified by the user at the create time is rather small, but the user will need many different hole features. Instead, if there is a general-hole feature, it can be used anywhere. The user will need to specify at the time of creation whether the hole is through or blind, its orientation with respect to the entrance face, the bottom type for blind holes, and so on.

5.2.2 Validation of Candidate Feature Sets

The identified feature set needs to be examined with respect to the following characteristics:

- Completeness
- Unambiguity
- Simplicity
- Duplication

Completeness implies that the identified set of features can be used to create all part designs in the class of designs for which the system is intended. We could look at additional part drawings and see if those parts can be described completely by the identified feature set.

Unambiguity implies that all the parameters that are needed to fully define a feature have been included in its list of properties. It should be possible, for example, to create a geometric model of each feature. Additionally we need to examine constraints to determine if there are any conflicts.

Simplicity implies that feature properties include only those that are of use in some application. Also features are defined at a level that is no higher than what is used by targeted application.

Duplication occurs when two features have almost identical properties. Since feature libraries can get large and unmanageable very quickly, it is desirable to reconcile and remove such minor distinctions between features.

Once the project team is satisfied with the feature set it has identified, design sessions should be simulated to create "skeleton" parts using paper and pencil in order to get feedback from designers. It might seem that it would be better to involve designers earlier, but our experience indicates that this is not productive until there are some tangible results to show the designer.

5.2.3 Case Study: Automotive Body Panel

The featurization of automotive body panels was investigated by Syms at ASU (Syms 1993). We give here a simplified version of one of the case studies undertaken.

Design features of a window regulator back plate were identified by analyzing the design process. The back plate provides support for the components of a gear operated scissors mechanism, shown in Figure 5.4. Since the back plate mounts to the door inner panel, the work surface is extracted from the panel geometry (assume it to be planar for the purpose of this discussion). The key reference for all the features on the back plate is the position of the main pivot, which is determined from the mechanism dimensions and the window position. The beads (shown by the center lines in Figure 5.5) and rivet holes are needed to

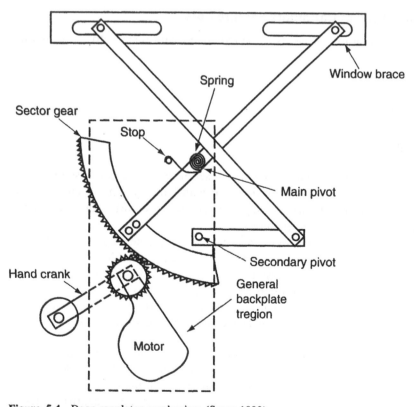

Figure 5.4   Door regulator mechanism (Syms 1993)

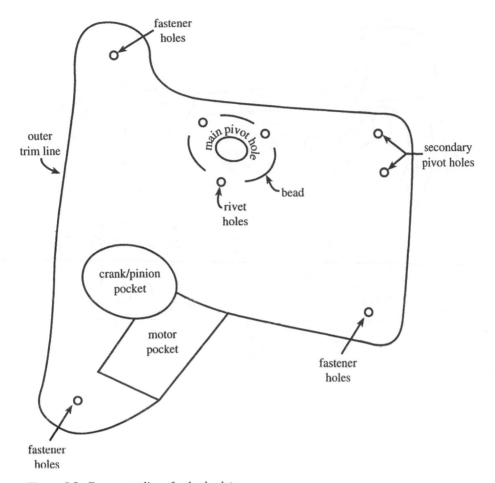

Figure 5.5 Feature outlines for back plate

mount the mechanism. This group of features (main pivot hole, rivet holes, beads) may be considered a composite feature because they form a stereotypical geometric pattern. The position of the secondary pivot holes is determined with respect to the main pivot, using the mechanism's dimensions and orientation.

Next the outer profiles and the bottom planes of the crank/pinion pocket and motor clearance pocket are determined. The former is essentially a circular pocket, and the latter a rectangular pocket. The dimensions of these pockets are based on the selected components. The crank pocket is positioned with respect to the main pivot; the motor pocket is positioned with respect to the pinion pocket.

The back plate is mounted to the door inner panel by means of fasteners, whose position is specified by the designer. The preliminary design of the back plate is then completed by creating the trim line encompassing all the features created so far. The geometry at this phase of the design is shown in Figure 5.5.

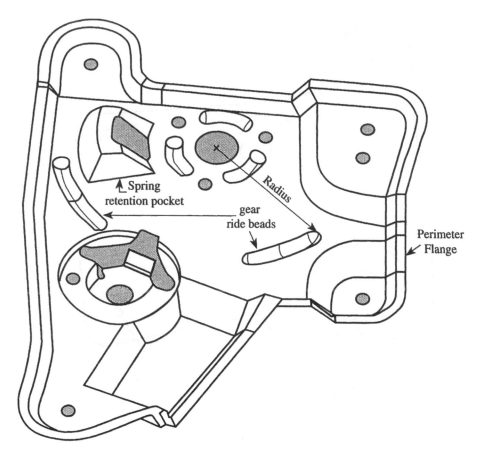

Figure 5.6 Refined creation of back plate features

More features are now added and existing features are detailed/refined. Beads are created for the sector gear to ride on, with reference to the main pivot, as shown in Figure 5.6. For all the beads, the cross-sections need to be created. The spring retention pocket is a composite feature comprising a four-sided pocket with a rectangular hole, as shown. Further refinements are made to the crank pocket and the outer trim region; details of these steps have been omitted here. Refer to (Syms 1993) for further information.

From the case study, the following feature classes were identified as ones needed by designers: (the dimensions are shown in parenthesis)

Simple Features

Circular hole (diameter, center position)
Rectangular hole (length, width, orientation, position, corner radius)

Bead (cross-section, radius, center, arc length)

Rectangular pocket (rectangle dimensions, corner radius, position, orientation, depth)

Circular pocket (diameter, center position, depth)

Perimeter flange (height, width, parent edge)

Pattern Features

Main pivot pattern (pivot hole, rivet holes, beads)

Gear ride beads (common radius and center position)

Compound Features

Spring retention pocket (pocket + hole)

Crank pocket (many features combined)

The next step might be to define these features in a library and get feedback from designers after they attempt to design back plates with these features. Of course these features can be generalized so that they can be used in designing other types of body panels. But, as discussed in the previous section, the trade-off is flexibility versus ease of use and depth of information.

5.3 DESIGN BY FEATURES

The actual industrial design processes have considerable variation. We make a distinction between two main types: *innovative design*, where a new product is designed, and *routine design*, where a new variation of an existing basic design is created. For truly innovative design, entirely new features may be required, and they may limit the utility of features. In routine design, however, we expect that all features required are already defined and can be reused. To illustrate this, we will study two cases of routine design by features. Chapter 8 will investigate an approach for supporting feature-based innovative design.

5.3.1 Part Creation by Features

Let us "simulate" a design-by-features session supported by a "typical" graphical user interface. The part that will be used for this simulation is a simplified version of connecting rods found in internal combustion engines. The conrod converts and transmits motion from the piston to the crankshaft. It is not a single part, but an assembly of two parts, fastened by two bolts. However, the conrod is manufactured as a single forging, which is also machined as a single piece. It is then cut along the notches to yield two matching pieces. The conrod is a typical example of a design where there is reusable design knowledge available which can be formalized in terms of features.

In a typical design session the designer will select the appropriate feature library and preview the available features, shown in Figure 5.7. The primary features in the library are pin-end, crank-ring, and I-rod. Other features are ribs, bolt-holes, counterweight, notch (not shown), and blends. The main stages in the design process are shown in Figure 5.8. The designer knows the piston and crank pin diameters, d and D, and the distance between their centers, L (Step 1). The pin-end and crank-ring are defined in Step 2. The profile parameters of the I-rod are determined from stress analysis. The I-rod dimensions may be directly defined or obtained by running a design procedure which can calculate the dimensions based on design rules (Step 3).

The ribs for mounting the fasteners are created next. Again rules of thumb or stress analysis might be used. The designer then places the counterweight feature in place and blends the ribs to the I-rod. Notches are placed on opposite sides of the crank-ring to mark the position at which the cut will be made for separating the conrod into two parts.

5.3.2 Variant Design with Part Families

In the previous section the part was designed on the basis of features. Alternatively, we can treat the entire part as one feature to support variant design of standard parts. The design then amounts to pure instancing of the part by specifying all the attributes in its definition. At this level of granularity, we lose the flexibility of creating different part designs with the same set of features. However, this disadvantage may be offset by the speed with which specific parts can be designed.

For instance, let us consider variant design of a bearing housing. The part in question belongs to a paper manufacturing machine, where its function is to provide a bearing for a paper roll. A complete paper machine has easily 80 variations of essentially the same part in different sizes and configurations. To speed up the design of such parts, parametric variant design techniques are attractive.

There are two possible ways in which variant design may be approached:

1. Instance an old (similar) design and edit the model.
2. Specify the values of all parameters which are the input to a procedure which produces the geometric model.

The parametrization of the bearing housing and other components in the same assembly are listed in Figure 5.9. The most essential parameter is da, the diameter of the paper roll shaft. The parameters are of course not independent but have various constraints in place. Manufacturing considerations dictate that as much as possible predefined parameter assignments should be used. Parametric modeling is made possible by procedures that take a list of parameters defined as input and generate a model as a result.

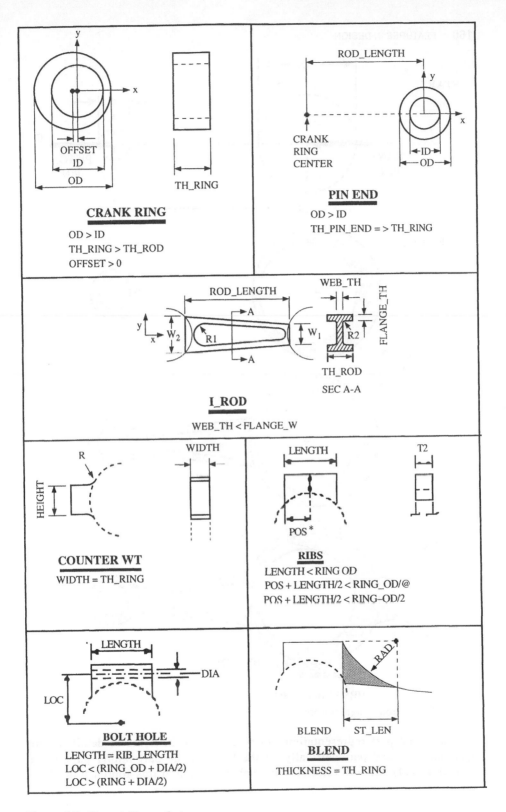

Figure 5.7 Conrod library features

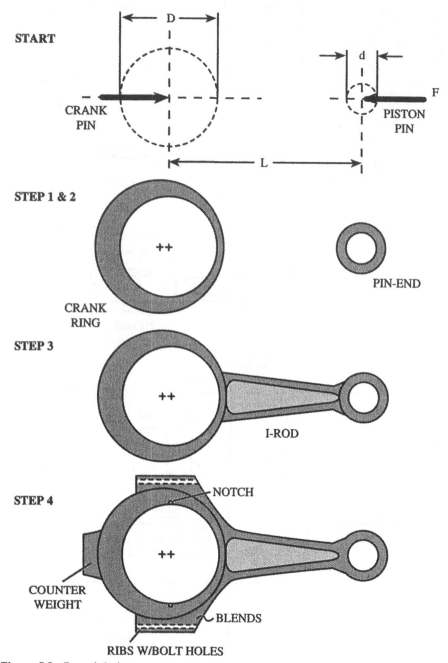

Figure 5.8 Conrod design process

The actual part representation can be expressed in terms of detail feature instances, created parametrically on the basis of the part family parameters (Laakko 1994). We will return to the implementation of this approach in Chapter 8.

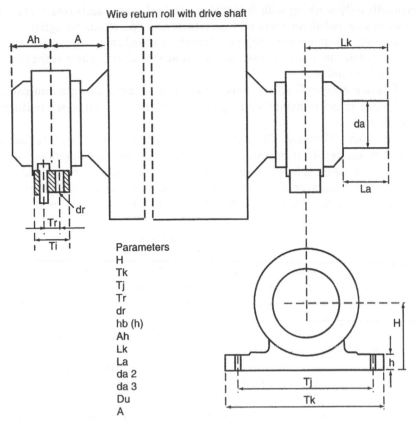

Figure 5.9   Parameters of the bearing housing assembly

5.4 TOLERANCE SPECIFICATION

Under production conditions, real manufacturing processes cannot make identical parts; the allowed variations in size and shape are termed *geometric tolerances*. From a designer's point of view, the specification of tolerances serve the following purposes:

- They ensure that parts will function properly.
- They ensure that mass produced parts will be interchangeable.
- They ensure that parts are manufacturable (at reasonable cost) and assemblable.
- They ensure that the design is robust (critical dimensions have minimum sensitivity to expected variations).

In design, the allocation and analysis of tolerances is usually done at the detailed design stages. In conceptual and embodiment design, the designer is typically only working with the ideal or *nominal* shapes and sizes, that is, deviations in size and shape from real manufacturing operations are ignored.

Tolerance problems in design fall into three broad categories: *tolerance specification*, *tolerance allocation*, and *tolerance analysis*. Their respective tasks are outlined below.

Tolerance specification. This serves the purpose of communicating the designer's intent to manufacturing in a format that is interpreted uniformly by both sides.

Tolerance allocation. The dimension, or *clearance*, that impacts function or performance, results from a stack-up of all dimensions and tolerances with which it forms a dimension loop (D-loop). An example of a one-dimensional dimension loop for the clearance c between the two plates is shown in Figure 5.10. The value of c is determined by the dimensions and tolerances of a, b, d, and f.

$$a + b + c + d + f = 0$$

A 2D dimension-loop will also account for orientation and form deviations between the mating parts. The designer is concerned with controlling c within some limits; the tolerance on c is distributed (allocated) between a, b, d, and f on which c is dependent.

Tolerance analysis. Once the designer chooses a set of dimensions and tolerances, he or she needs to analyze the consequences; the tolerance analysis is the opposite of tolerance allocation. There are many software packages available commercially to do such analyses, but their level of integration with CAD systems is rather low. The geometry must be input manually. A few systems allow analysis on 2D sketches, but there is little support for standard tolerance classes, other than size and orientation. These systems help the designer determine if the critical dimensions are within desired tolerance, given the specified allocation

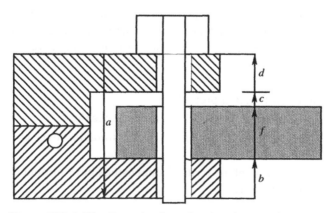

Figure 5.10 A 1D dimension loop for pinned connection

scheme. This may be based on worst-case or statistical (e.g., ±3σ) methods. The designer can also study sensitivity to change from all D-loop dimensions, for the purpose of robust design.

There are both ISO and ANSI standards for geometric tolerances. These two standards are slowly reconciling their differences, but there are still some remaining. Both standards were designed for use with engineering drawings, not CAD models. Consequently the intention of the standards is to create a common language, by use of symbols, conventions, and rules so that the person interpreting the tolerance on an engineering drawing will follow the intentions of the designer.

Since the standards were designed for human use and interpretation, it was not necessary to base them on a formal theory. Instead, the standards are based on design practice. Difficulties in modeling computer understandable tolerance specifications and mathematical validation of tolerances has provided the motivation for finding a theory of tolerances, on which future standards can be based. The Tolerance Mathematization Committe working on behalf of ANSI has prepared a draft proposal for a revised standard. In the discussion below, we somewhat follow the main concepts common in the current ISO/ANSI standards, but details such as "material conditions" and "diameter modifiers," etc., are not considered.

This section demonstrates the need for features when specifying geometric tolerances, but it is not our intent to discuss subjects such as tolerance allocation or statistical analysis here. We will focus only on what information is needed by a designer to specify geometric tolerances (Section 5.4.1) and how it can be incorporated into feature-based models (Section 5.4.2).

5.4.1 Review of Tolerance Specifications

The ANSI Y14.5M tolerance standard uses some definitions that conflict with terms used in this book. Therefore we would like to introduce the user to the terms *feature, feature of size, datum,* and *datum reference frame*, as defined in the tolerance standard. A feature is a face or edge of the part; it is what we have been referring to in this book as a geometric entity. A feature of size may be a cylindrical surface (e.g., a hole or boss surface), a set of parallel planes (e.g., opposite faces of pockets or slots), or a spherical surface. We can say that a feature of size is a shape defined by a set of faces and size dimensions. Therefore, to some extent, what we call a feature in this book, the Y14.5M standard calls a feature of size.

A datum is a reference for controlling the location or orientation of a feature of size on a part. Up to three data might be required to control all the relevant degrees of freedom; such a set of data is called a *datum reference frame*. A datum may be either a feature or a feature of size.

Tolerance Classes The shape and size of part features can vary in several possible ways. These variations are classified into standard tolerance classes,

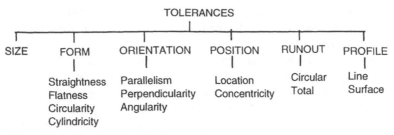

Figure 5.11 Classification of tolerance types

shown in Figure 5.11. Size tolerances are plus/minus variations applied to dimensions of volumetric features (blocks, holes, slots), referred to as "features of size" by tolerance standards; there are no data necessary. Tolerance values specify the size of the tolerance zone within which the toleranced feature must lie. Figure 5.12 shows how the tolerance zone is generated for each class. Form tolerances are applied to geometric entities and are self-referencing, in that no datum is needed. Orientation tolerances can be applied to edges, faces, or features of size. When used for the latter, the center line, or center plane, of the feature is used for controlling the orientation. When a part feature is used as a datum it means that the gauge or machine table from which measurement is taking place will be placed such that three points are in contact with the datum feature.

Position tolerances require the specification of as many as three data. Each datum entity has a precedence: primary, secondary, and tertiary. The secondary datum must be orthogonal to the primary, and the tertiary orthogonal to the other two. If one wants to specify an axis or center plane as a datum, the corresponding feature of size is labeled as the datum.

5.4.2 Integrating Features, Tolerances, and Geometry

In today's CAD systems the support for tolerances is superficial to nonexistent. To capture tolerance semantics, the CAD system must do more than just store tolerance data; proper structure must be available to associate tolerances with appropriate features and data. Datum precedence and datum type must also be recorded. This allows the designer's tolerance specifications to be validated. For example, the system must be able to answer the following types of questions:

1. Does the selected geometric entity satisfy the conditions to be a datum; for example, is it planar or cylindrical, an edge or a face?
2. Are datum features mutually orthogonal, for position tolerance?
3. Is the entity a feature or feature of size?

When several types of tolerances are specified on the same feature (size, position, form), the combination may even be meaningless. If the semantics of the tolerances are captured, the system can catch such problems and issue warnings

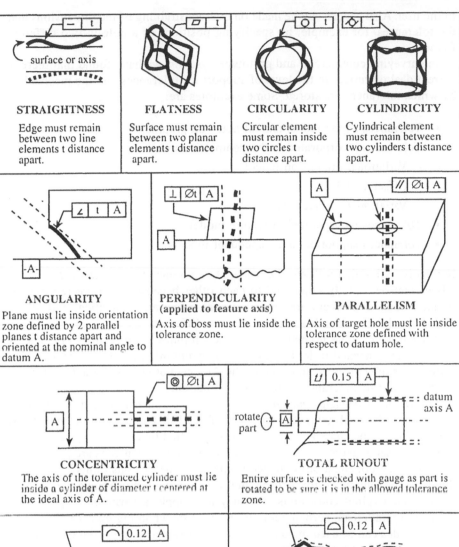

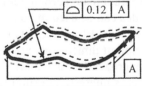

Figure 5.12 Tolerance zones and datum specification (Adapted from Miller 1989)

to the user. Also checks can be made on overconstraining of the dimensions and the tolerances, for example, by specifying positions of a hole in two different frames.

In surveying commercial and prototype systems, we have found that there is a great deal of variety in the level of support for tolerances and the mechanism by which tolerances are stored. Some examples are:

- Tolerances supported as textual notes on graphics
- Tolerances incorporated in the geometric model:
  - Variational dimension model
  - Offset model
  - Variational surface model
- Tolerances incorporated in feature model
- Tolerances supported as independent models.

In the discussion that follows, the reader should remember that the above methods cannot be directly compared to each other because some are representational models and others are computational, some are syntactical and others semantic; also the intended applications are different.

Textual Notes. The textual notes method mimics engineering drawings. A human user is needed to look at the graphics and interpret the tolerances. The support for tolerances is superficial. The data cannot be used in automated applications nor for tolerance analysis or validation.

Variational Dimension model. The variational dimension model (VDM) is based on variational geometry approach. Recall that in variational geometry, the nominal shape and size of an object is specified by a set of explicit dimensions and a set of geometric constraints. The implicit dimensions are determined by solving a set of equations obtained from the geometric constraints and explicit dimensions. Tolerances are incorporated by allowing a plus/minus variation in each of the explicit constraints. We may also apply a variation to geometric relations (parallelism, perpendicularly, etc.), as shown in Figure 5.13. Of course the same idea can be used in conjunction with parametric (procedural) modelers as well. The only difference between parametric and variational approaches is in how the implicit dimensions are determined, as discussed in Chapter 2.

VDM approach is particularly suited to tolerance sensitivity analysis, since the designer is interested in finding out how sensitive a dimension is to changes in other dimensions on which it is dependent. This type of analysis requires one to express the dependent dimension, say X, in terms of independent dimensions n_i, as

$$X = f(n_1, n_2 \ldots n_n) \tag{5.1}$$

where f signifies "some function of." This function may be non-linear. Suppose that a linearized version of the above function is an acceptable approximation, and suppose that dimensions $n_1, n_2 \ldots n_n$ are independent. The linearized expression for X is

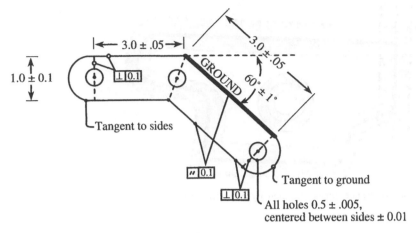

Figure 5.13 Variational dimension model

$$\Delta X = \frac{\partial f}{\partial n_1} \Delta n_1 + \frac{\partial f}{\partial n_2} \Delta n_2 + \dots \frac{\partial f}{\partial n_n} \Delta n_n \qquad (5.2)$$

In Equation (5.2,) Δn_i can be interpreted as the tolerance range. If we assume normal distribution, then from statistics formulas the variance in X is found as

$$\sigma_x^2 = \left(\frac{\partial f}{\partial n_1}\right)^2 \sigma_1^2 + \left(\frac{\partial f}{\partial n_2}\right)^2 \sigma_2^2 + \dots \left(\frac{\partial f}{\partial n_n}\right)^2 \sigma_n^2 \qquad (5.3)$$

where σ_i are standard deviation of dimension n_i. The contribution to changes in X from each dimension n_i is:

$$\text{Contribution} = 100 \frac{(\partial f / \partial n_i)^2 \sigma_i^2}{\sigma_x^2}$$

The designer needs to consider these contributions when allocating tolerances. This analysis requires relations in the form of Equation (5.1) which can be obtained from the VDM approach.

The VDM approach has been typically used with two-dimensional sketches. Despite recent advances in applying it in three dimensions, the method is limited to polyhedral models because the equations are written and solved for vertex positions. Thus form tolerances cannot be supported. Also orientation and position tolerances cannot be supported, since there is no method for distinguishing target from datum entities (i.e., all geometric constraints are mutual). This is not suitable for dimensioning and tolerancing, where datum and targets need to be clearly specified. Also, there are no mechanisms for specifying the datum reference frames, (i.e., encoding the primary-secondary-tertiary datum

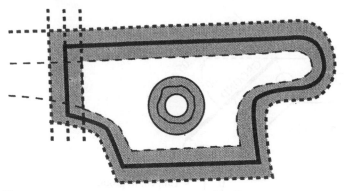

Figure 5.14 Tolerance zones obtained by offsetting boundaries

order) that are required for position tolerances. Many tolerance classes are applied to features, not geometry, so these cannot be supported.

Offset Zone Model. The tolerance zone is defined as the region within which the object's boundaries must lie. The tolerance zone is created by the Boolean set difference between the maximal and minimal object volumes. The maximal and minimal object volumes are obtained by offsetting the object by equal amounts on either side of the nominal, as shown in Figure 5.14. An object's boundaries can lie anywhere in the tolerance region for it to be acceptable; therefore the boundaries are not required to have "perfect" shape, as required by the VDM approach.

We see in the figure that instead of treating different types of variation (size, form, orientation, etc.) separately, a composite zone is used for the combined effect of all tolerances. This is in conflict with current tolerancing practice. For example, when both a size and form tolerance are specified as shown in Figure 5.15(a), the form tolerance is used as a refinement of the size tolerance. The form tolerance zone is self-referencing, that is, it floats within the size tolerance zone and can be in any orientation. If a size tolerance and an orientation tolerance are applied together as shown in Figure 5.15(b), then the orientation is a refinement of the size. Also the orientation zone, like the form zone, can float inside the size zone, but unlike the size zone, its orientation is fixed with respect to the datum. If we use a composite zone for all tolerances, it amounts to making the form and orientation tolerances equal to the size tolerance! In engineering practice this is the default; that is. the form and orientation tolerances are assumed equal to the size if *only* a size tolerance is specified.

Another problem with offset tolerance zones is that position tolerances set-up a tolerance zone for the *resolved entity,* not the boundary of the feature. A resolved entity is the axis of a hole, the mid-plane of a slot, and so on; a resolved entity is used as a reference for positioning a feature. The interpretation of position tolerances depends upon whether or not a modifier is used that specifies whether the tolerance zone applies to the resolved entity or to the feature bound-

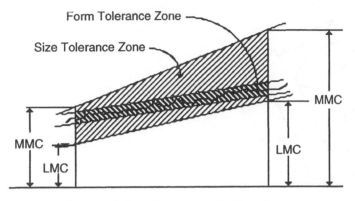

(*a*) Form and size tolerance applied together

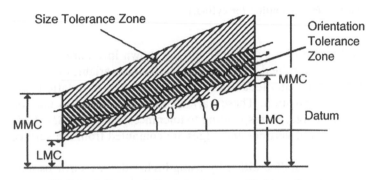

(*b*) Orientation and size tolerance applied together

Figure 5.15   Comparison of tolerance zones (Shah 1990)

aries. In the absence of a modifier a tolerance zone for feature boundaries cannot be constructed. Also, if a feature of size is used as a datum with material modifiers, both the size and position of the tolerance zone are variable. Once again, the tolerance zone cannot be constructed.

Variational Surfaces. The VDM approach cannot work with non-polygonal/ polyhedral models, and it cannot represent all types of tolerances; the offset zone method does not preserve tolerancing practice. To overcome these problems, a surface-based approach to variational modeling (VSM) has been proposed (Martinsen 1993). If all vertices are allowed to vary independently, the surface geometry may become undefined. For example, if a planar face is defined by four vertices, and all of them vary independently, it might not be possible to find a plane passing through all four points. Therefore, in the VSM approach, each surface is varied independently by changing the values of model variables from which surface coefficients are calculated.

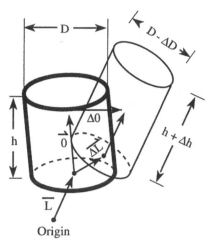

Origin

Figure 5.16 Variational surface definition for cylinder

For example, in the case of a cylindrical surface shown in Figure 5.16, the surface coefficients are determined from the nominal model variables D (diameter), h (height), $\mathbf{L}$ (bottom center location vector), and $\mathbf{O}$ (axis orientation vector) in the exact size and position. These variables can be relaxed to take on values in some specified range, corresponding to tolerances, namely $\pm \Delta D$, $\pm \Delta h$, $\pm \Delta \mathbf{L}$, and $\pm \Delta \mathbf{O}$. Positions of vertices and edges are computed from the surface variations.

Form tolerances can be handled either by using higher-degree surfaces than the nominal surface or by surface triangulation. In the latter case the model variables are the three triangle vertices and three other control points that vary independently.

VSM leads to some topological problems, namely maintenance of tangency and incidence conditions without a change in topology. Gupta and Turner (Gupta 1991) have solved these problems by replacing vertices/edges with virtual faces. The individual faces then vary independently, and the virtual face is used for trimming the object faces, sometimes resulting in new topology.

Tolerances as Feature Attributes. Tolerances may be considered to be a type of attribute. They could be attributes of dimension parameters (size tolerances), attributes of edges or surfaces (straightness, flatness), or attributes of feature relationships (position, orientation). With the development of feature modeling, it has become possible to associate tolerances with features. For example, in Figure 1.5 (Chapter 1) the feature definition of a sheet metal crimp contains not only the dimension parameters (bend radius, angle, setback) but also the tolerance parameters on each of these dimensions. The radius and angle tolerances are size tolerances, namely there are no data. However, the angle tolerance belongs to the orientation class, so it requires an explicitly specified datum. Although in this example the datum may be obvious (the top, undeformed sheet surface), it is not always the case. Consider a rectangular machined slot (Figure

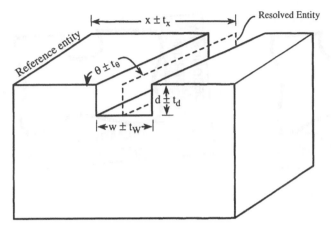

Figure 5.17   Slot tolerances

5.17) defined by nominal dimensions *depth* and *width*. The slot is positioned by relating one of its side faces (or mid-plane) with respect to a reference face. Some tolerances that might be relevant are:

Size tolerances: depth, width (t_d, t_w)

Form tolerances: bottom face, side faces

Perpendicularity: bottom face with each of the side faces

Parallelism: side faces (only when both perpendicularity tolerances are not specified)

Location tolerance on the slot resolved entity (t_x)

Orientation tolerance on the slot resolved entity (t_θ)

If each of the above parameters was supported by creating an attribute slot in the feature property list, the tolerance specification will be ambiguous and incomplete. For example, we do not know whether the bottom face is the datum, or the side face, for the perpendicularity tolerance. We have the same problem with the parallelism tolerance. The location tolerance of the slot applies to the resolved entity (mid-plane); it determines the location of the mid-plane with respect to the reference system. When we are dealing with perfect geometry, it is sufficient to specify the reference face and the dimension $x \pm t_x$; however, for an imperfect (real) part a location tolerance requires three data, with a specification of precedence. Figure 5.18 demonstrates how the measurement varies by swapping the primary and secondary data. Another problem is that the method of attaching a ± variation to the angle is not in conformance with engineering standards. Also supporting feature position and orientation tolerances as variations of feature position and location dimensions implies that the same datum must be used in tolerancing as that in geometry construction. Unfortunately,

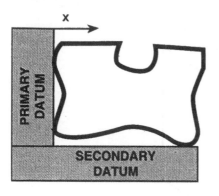 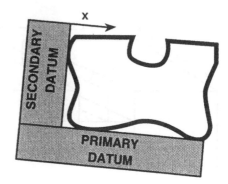

Figure 5.18 Significance of datum precedence

positioning and orienting methods convenient for geometry creation are quite different from what is needed for controlling dimensions in manufacturing.

Designers do not specify tolerances of all types for all entities; it is only done for those dimensions that are critical to some function. All unspecified tolerances default to values documented in drafting standards, or an organization's own codes. It is not known in advance which tolerances will be specified by the designer and which ones will be left to default values. For the simple slot there are ten possible tolerances that a designer might wish to specify. If tolerances are supported as feature attributes, one needs to create attribute slots for every one of the possible tolerances for each feature. This is not very efficient.

Tolerance structures. The above-mentioned problems provide the motivation for developing independent tolerance structures that capture the semantics of each of the tolerance classes. For each of the tolerance classes Table 5.1 shows the entity to which the tolerance is applied (target) and the entity (entities) used as references (datum). Also against each target or datum entity shown in the table we note, in parenthesis, whether it resides in the feature modeler (FM) or the geometric modeler (GM).

From Table 5.1 we see that the target and datum combination result in five groups:

- Geometry intrinsic (form)
- Feature intrinsic (size, straightness applied to axis)
- Inter-geometry (orientation, profile)
- Feature-feature (position, concentricity, orientation, runout)
- Feature-geometry (orientation, position, profile, runout)

The distinction between the last two groups is superficial. Whether we use geometry or features as data, they can be handled in the same way. It seems logical to associate tolerances with the target entities, where the modeler data

Table 5.1 Morphology of tolerance classes

Tolerance Class	Target Entity	Datum Entity (Entities)
Size	Dimension attribute (FM)	None
Straightness	Face-in one view (GM)	None
	Feature axis/plane (FM)	None
Circularity	Face-in one view (GM)	None
Flatness	Face (GM)	None
Cylindricity	Face (GM)	None
Orientation	Face (GM)	Planar face (GM) or
	Feature (FM)	Feature axis (FM)
Position	Feature (FM)	Up to three ordered data consisting of mutually orthogonal features (FM) or faces (GM)
Concentricity	Feature (FM)	Feature (FM)
Line Profile	Face-2D control (GM)	Face (GM)
	Feature profile (FM)	
Circular Profile	Face (GM) or	Face (GM)
	Feature (FM)	
Circular or Total Runout	Feature (FM)	Feature axis (FM), or two coaxial features (FM) or a face (GM) and a feature (FM) that are orthogonal

structure permits. Geometry intrinsic tolerances may be supported simply as face tags, since no references are needed. Feature intrinsic tolerances can be treated as feature attributes, as discussed in the previous section. Inter-geometry and feature extrinsic (inter-feature) tolerances require datum reference frames, which must be separate structures. Based on the above philosophy, tolerance class structures could be used for supporting all types of tolerances. The advantage of this approach is that we do not have to enumerate all possible classes of tolerances when defining a generic feature in the library. By associating the tolerances with target entities, the tolerances automatically become part of the feature through the feature's constituting entities. Object-oriented tolerance class definitions can be found in Chapter 10.

5.5 DESIGN OF ASSEMBLIES

Most mechanical products are not single piece parts but assemblies of several components. This is necessitated not only by the function needed or mechanical power transmission requirement but also for products that consist of different materials, and parts with varying sizes and shapes that are best produced separately. Moreover the production and maintenance of complex-shaped parts becomes easier when they are made by assembling simple components. The assembly process is used for producing finished products in almost all industries.

Some of the considerations on which assembly design is based are:

- Kinematics
- Interchangeability of parts
- Geometric arrangement of components to produce compact packages
- Assemblability and disassemblability
- Collisions and interference
- Tolerance allocation to produce the proper quality function

Assemblies can be classified by the mobility of the components, by the type of construction, or by the manufacturing process. By mobility, assemblies fall into three categories: *static/rigid*, *rotational*, and *articulated*. By the construction method, assemblies fall into three groups: *chassis-mounted* (all parts mounted on the same base or frame), *modular* (many combinations are possible from the same set of modules), and *stacked* (components assembled one on the top another). The design process is different for each type of assembly.

The assembly (manufacturing) process can often be simplified by redesigning the product. Reducing the number of different components to a minimum without affecting the functionality of design eases the process of manufacturing. It is also possible to simplify the product by employing new processes that produce complex parts. It is necessary in an automatic assembly to have a base part on which the assembly can be built. The base part should have features compatible for quick and accurate placement of the part on a work carrier.

Just as in component design, the use of non-feature based geometric modelers for assembly design causes several problems:

Low level of abstraction. Assembly design using Boolean operations and transformation primitives on solid models produces a database that is unattractive for many downstream applications, such as assembly process planning. In performing assemblies in real life situations, the assemblability is analyzed in terms of feature associations pertinent to the constituent parts and their mating conditions; such information is missing in non-feature based modelers.

Unfavorable design environment. Most of the modelers do not facilitate convenient creation of assemblies, and design change propagation. Design is an iterative process that requires many modifications and alterations before it is finalized. For instance, after modeling a piston-cylinder assembly in an internal combustion engine, if the designer changes the cylinder size, the modeler should be able to validate, determine, and propagate the rest of the changes needed to make the assembly still valid. Hence provisions for manipulating and modifying the assembly design at any stage of operation are essential in an assembly modeler.

Incompatible design paradigm. The *bottom-up design approach* is widely used in the commercial modelers. This requires detailed design of all the constituent parts and sub-assemblies before laying out the design for the assembly. However, the more natural way is to design assemblies by the *top-down approach* where the designer begins with an abstract concept and recursively divides it into logical sub-assemblies until the level of parts is reached. Hence, this method is best suited for the conceptual design of assemblies. Figure 5.19 compares the bottom-up and top-down approaches. The example in Figure 5.19(*a*) shows the top-down procedure; a conceptual assembly of the gear pair is designed first, determining pitch diameters, number of teeth, and rpms. This is then decomposed into subassemblies and parts, whose detailed geometry is designed within the constraints set by top-level design. In (*b*) the opposite procedure is shown for packaging of a number of interconnected components of a thermal system.

Significant research is being carried out to overcome these deficiencies and build efficient and intelligent modeling systems that aid the designer in the design and analysis of mechanical assemblies. The major aspects of assembly modeling are discussed in the next sections.

5.5.1 Assembly Modeling

The information that needs to be captured and represented at the assembly level by an assembly modeler includes the following:

- Hierarchical relations (components, sub-assemblies, assemblies, etc.)
- Mating conditions (geometric constraints, fits, contact, etc.)
- Component/sub-assembly positions (global or relative)
- Degrees of freedom (possible relative motions of parts or sub-assemblies)

The assembly model is needed to drive some of the following analyses and applications:

- Interference detection between parts
- Motion simulation
- Constraint satisfaction
- Assemblability evaluation
- Assembly manufacturing planning

An assembly model could be constructed at various levels of abstraction. Three possibilities are shown in Figure 5.20. They are, in decreasing order of abstraction, *component-level*, *feature-level*, and *geometry-level assembly models*.

All these models are stored as graph structures. The component level model (Figure 5.20a) shows the assembly hierarchy in terms of components and sub-

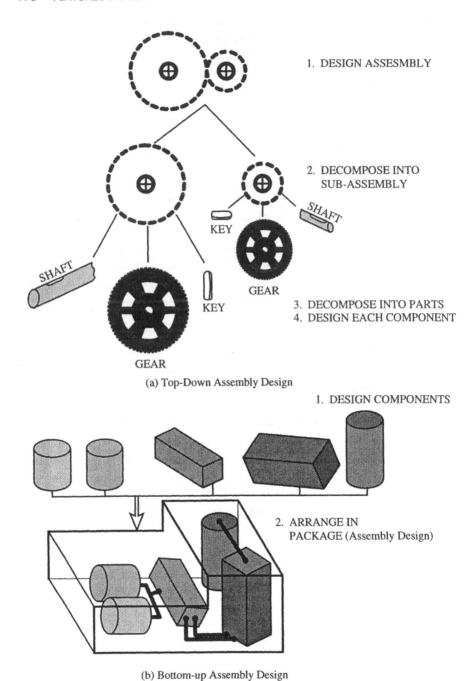

1. DESIGN ASSESMBLY

2. DECOMPOSE INTO
   SUB-ASSEMBLY

KEY

SHAFT

GEAR

3. DECOMPOSE INTO PARTS
4. DESIGN EACH COMPONENT

SHAFT

KEY

GEAR

(a) Top-Down Assembly Design

1. DESIGN COMPONENTS

2. ARRANGE IN
   PACKAGE (Assembly Design)

(b) Bottom-up Assembly Design

Figure 5.19 Comparison of assembly design paradigms

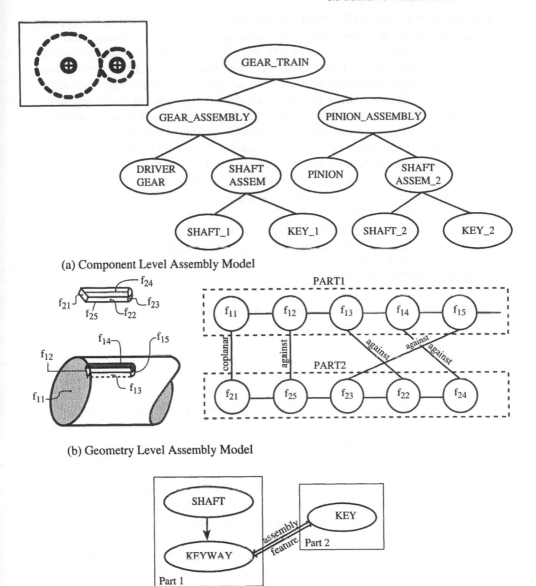

(a) Component Level Assembly Model

(b) Geometry Level Assembly Model

(c) Feature Level Assembly Model

Figure 5.20 Assembly models at three abstraction levels

assemblies. The leaf nodes are components, the interior nodes are sub-assemblies, and the root node represents the entire assembly. The arcs represent "part-of" relations. The definition of a sub-assembly may be related to kinematics or to the assembly order. The former applies only to dynamic or articulated assemblies, while the latter applies to all assemblies. In dynamic assemblies a group of components constitutes an assembly when the group has some common motions with respect to the other groups of parts. For all assemblies, a sub-assembly is a set of components that are assembled together into a unit and then assembled with other components/sub-assemblies. As an option one might associate each node with the corresponding geometric model and the arcs of the component graph with geometric transformations needed to position each component/sub-assembly with respect to its parent sub-assembly. This requires that there be a co-ordinate system attached to each component/sub-assembly; the geometric transformations then need to be specified and applied at the component/ sub-assembly level. This is not the most convenient (natural) way to define assemblies. Also, when changes are made to component geometries (size, shape, position), the geometric transformations cannot be automatically updated.

Geometry level assembly models specify and model assemblies in terms of "mating conditions," which are commonly treated as relationships between geometric entities belonging to different parts/sub-assemblies. Some examples of such relations are:

Against: Two faces against each other, normals pointing in opposite directions
Align coplanar: Two faces aligned to lie in the same surface
Co-axial: Two axes aligned to lie in the same straight line
Coincident: Two points constrained to be coincident.

Figure 5.20(b) shows the assembly model created at the geometry level. The nodes are faces, edges, vertices, or axes, and the arcs are mating conditions. We make the following observations about assembly graphs. First, a constraint solver is needed to determine if all the mating conditions can be simultaneously satisfied. Second, the geometric transformation matrices of the component level model need to derived from solving the constraints. Third, the geometric entities used in describing the constraints are not all present in typical manifold models (e.g., axes). Fourth, specifying geometric constraints at the geometric level may be very tedious is some cases.

A compromise between the two extremes (component level and geometry level) is to use features in defining assemblies, shown conceptually in Figure 5.20(c). Features have the advantage of capturing higher level mating conditions from which geometry level conditions can be derived, thus relieving the designer of microscopic details. At the same time the capturing of mating conditions allows design changes to be propagated even after part models have been assembled. The concept of assembly features is discussed in the next section.

5.5.2 Assembly Features

We define an *assembly feature* as an association of two form features that are on different parts. When expressed in some standard canonical form, this associa-

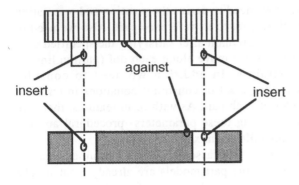

Figure 5.21   Examples of assembly features

tion becomes a generic assembly feature class which can be stored in a library. Figure 5.21 shows examples of assembly features, such as the two pin/hole insertion features.

Assembly features provide a structure for encoding mutual constraints on shape, dimensions, position, and orientation of mating features. This can provide the following benefits:

1. Assembly features allow assembly creation at a higher level by storing all of the constraints between the mating features as a single unit.

2. Assembly features allow constraints to be expressed in terms of feature dimensions rather than face relations.

3. Assembly features allow design changes to a part propagate to other parts in an assembly.

These benefits show that assembly features are an extension of the idea of form features. One can see the significance of the first benefit from the key/keyway example of Figure 5.20 (c). The five geometric constraints in (b) are replaced by a single assembly feature in (c), which encodes all the details of the assembly. The second benefit can be seen by the pin/hole insertion example; we can express the constraint in terms of hole and pin diameters, length, and position.

Assembly features can be formalized in the same way as form features. We can enumerate all the size, shape, and position constraints needed to satisfy an assembly between two features, such as pin/hole insertion, and key/keyway insertion. The information that defines an assembly feature consists of both directly specified attributes and derived parameters. Derived parameters are those that are constrained by something already in the model, while independent parameters are user choices at the time of assembly. For example, the position and orientation of a pin is constrained by the hole in which it is to be inserted, while the depth of insertion is user specified.

From constraint specifications we need to derive the position and orientation of the part being assembled with respect to its reference part. Also we need to find the degrees of freedom (dof) that remain after satisfying the specified constraints, the extent to which the part can move along each dof (motion limits), and implicit size/shape constraints. In addition we need to consider assemblability. This involves solving a set of constraint equations in terms of position and orientation variables of each part. As with form features, there are two "pure" approaches for determining these parameters- procedural and declarative—although many systems follow a mixture of the two.

In applying the procedural approach to assemblies, it is assumed that the assembly is done bottom up, that is, the part models are already created. The parts are assumed to be obtained from a collaborative form feature modeler, which provides feature dimensions, shape creation, feature-face associations, tolerances and other relevant parametric relations. Of course both part and assembly modeling could be performed by the same modeler. Assembly features can be archived in assembly feature libraries, and instances of assemblies stored in a new data structure. Like form features, assembly feature classes can also be defined as lists of properties. In the procedural approach pre-defined procedures are used for determining a unit's position based on mating conditions relevant to the assembly features. Degrees of freedom and motion limits are also determined from pre-defined procedures.

For modeling an assembly, the data of the individual parts needs to obtained from the form feature modeler. When the mating form features of the proposed assembly are selected from each of the two parts, the modeler needs to check for the existence of an assembly definition between this pair of form features in the library of assembly features. The constrained parameters are derived as specified by the generic definition of the assembly feature. The assembly is checked for dimensional and shape compatibility, and for other geometric constraints, as specified in the assembly generic definition. If the assembly is valid, the transformation matrices required to assemble the features and database alterations are automatically generated by using a procedure pre-defined for that purpose.

In declarative assembly modeling only the constraints between the parts are specified. A general purpose constraint solver then determines the position of each part (and its features) if the constraints represent a complete and nonconflicting set. Kramer developed a degree of freedom approach for solving assembly constraints (Kramer 1991). We will return to this subject in Chapter 8.

Once created, the instances of assembly features can be modified by selecting the form features in an assembled part. Since the assembly features store the relationships between the form features involved, modification of these features results in re-evaluation of the validity of the assembly. The same constraints, initially used to model the assembly are checked again for assembly compatibility. The modeler re-evaluates and updates the assembly model. As in part modeling we can use either the procedural or the declarative approach for constraint satisfaction. These approaches will be discussed in Chapter 8.

REVIEW QUESTIONS

5.1   Draw a diagram indicating the dependencies between the features and their parameters created in steps 1–5 of Figure 5.3.

5.2   Using the diagram constructed in Question 5.1, explain what should happen if the width of the base feature is diminished. Outline informally rules for propagating the change.

5.3   Apply the featurization process of Section 5.2 to a product you know well. (This exercise should preferably be done in a group.)

5.4   Outline a feature definition for the slot in Figure 5.17. Include as feature parameters the types of tolerances listed. Discuss the feasibility of this approach.

5.5   Repeat Question 5.4, but define informally separate entities for modeling the tolerances. Compare the result to Question 5.4.

5.6   Discuss the top-down and bottom-up approaches to assembly design illustrated in Figure 5.19. Can you recognize types of design projects where one of the approaches is attractive but not the other?

5.7   Outline a definition for the pin-hole assembly feature in Figure 5.21 in terms of constraints on the dimensions, positions, and orientations of the part features. Restrict your analysis to just one pin-hole combination.

5.8   Figure 5.21 actually contains two pin/hole assembly features. Discuss how this could be captured in an assembly feature model by applying the concept of *composite assembly features* in analogy to composite features introduced in Chapter 3.

BIBLIOGRAPHY

Design by Features

Burchard, R., 1987, Feature based geometric constraints applied to CSG, M.S. thesis, Purdue University.

Colquhoun, G. J., Baines, R. W., and Crossley, R., 1993, A state of the art review of IDEF0, *Int. J. of Computer Integrated Manufacturing* **6** (4): 252–264.

Cunningham, J., and Dixon, J. R., 1988, Designing with features: The origin of features, *ASME Computers in Engineering Conf.*, San Francisco, July 31–August 4, ASME Press, pp. 237–243.

Grabowski, H., and Rude, S., 1988, Intelligent CAD-systems based on technical associative modeling, *Theory and Practice of Geometric Modeling*, Heinrich Fabri Institut Blaubeuren, October 3–7, 1988.

Luby, S., Dixon, J. R., and Simmons, M. K., 1986, Creating and using feature databases, *Comp. in Mech. Eng.* **5** (3): 25–33.

Magleby, S., 1988, Design by functional feature for aircraft structure, Ph.D. dissertation, University of Wisconsin–Madison.

Pratt, M. J., 1988, Synthesis of an optimal approach to form feature modeling, *ASME Computers in Engineering Conf.,* San Francisco, July 31–August 4, ASME Press, pp. 263–274.

Pratt, M. J., and Wilson, P. R., 1986, Requirements for support of form features in a solid modeling system, final report, Technical Report R-86-ASPP-01, CAM-I, Inc., Arlington, TX.

Shah, J. J., and Rogers, M. T., 1988, Expert form feature modeling shell, *Computer-Aided Design* **20** (9): 515–524.

Shah, J. J., et al., 1990, Conceptual design of feature based modeling system, Technical Report, CAM-I, Inc., Arlington, TX.

Shah, J. J., Rogers, M., Sreevalsan, P., Hsiao, D., Mathew, A., Bhatnagar, A., Liou, B., and Miller, D., 1990, The ASU features testbed: An overview, *ASME Computers in Engineering Conf.,* Vol. 1, Boston, ASME Press, pp. 233–242.

Syms, D., 1993, Feature based design of automotive sheet metal parts, M.S. thesis, Department of Mechanical Engineering, Arizona State University.

Turner, G., and Anderson, D. C., 1988, An object oriented approach to interactive, feature based design for quick turnaround manufacturing, *ASME Computers in Engineering Conf.,* San Francisco, July 31–August 4, ASME Press.

Zhang, K., and ElMaraghy, H., 1993, Validity check for a function oriented modeler, in B. Ravani, ed., *Proc. of 19th ASME Design Automation Conf.,* Albuquerque, ASME Press.

Product Families

Laakko, T., and Mäntylä, M., 1994, Feature-based modeling of product families, in K. Ishii et al., eds., *ASME Computers in Engineering Conf.,* Vol. 1, Minneapolis, September 11–14, ASME Press, pp. 45–54.

Tolerance Modeling

Aldefeld, B., 1986, Rule based approach to variational geometry, *Knowledge Engineering and Computer Modeling in CAD. Proc. of CAD: Seventh Int. Conf. on the Computer as a Design Tool,* Butterworths, pp. 59–67.

Aldefeld, B., 1988, Variation of geometries based on a geometric reasoning method, *Computer-Aided Design* **20** (3): 117–126.

ASME, 1982, *Dimensions and Tolerancing,* American Society of Mechanical Engineers, New York.

Bernstein, N., and Preiss, K., 1989, Representation of tolerance information in solid models, DE-Vol. 19–1, *Proc. of 15th ASME Design Automation Conf.,* Montreal, September 17–21, ASME Press, pp. 37–48.

Bjorke, O., 1989, *Computer Aided Tolerancing,* second edition, ASME Press.

Cognition, Inc., 1989, *Mechanical Advantage Reference Manual,* Cognition, Inc., Billerica, MA.

Dong, Z., 1992, Automation of tolerance analysis and synthesis in conventional and feature-based CAD environments, *Int. J. of Systems Automation: Research and Applications (SARA)* **2**: 151–166.

Faux, I. D., 1986, Reconciliation of design and manufacturing requirements for product description data using functional primitive part features, Technical Report R-86-ANC/GM/PP-01.1, CAM-I, Inc., Arlington, TX.

Giacometti, F., and Chang, T.-C., 1990, A framework to model parts, assemblies, and tolerances, in ASME PED-Vol. 47, *Advances in Integrated Product Design and Manufacturing*, Dallas, November 25–30, ASME Press, pp. 117–125.

Gopin, A. M., and Gossard, D. C., 1979, Symbolic dimensioning, *Computer Graphics in CAD/CAM Systems*, pp. 268–281.

Gossard, D. C., Zuffante, R. P. and Sakurai, H., 1988, Representing dimensions, tolerances, and features in MCAE systems, *IEEE Comp. Gr. and Appl.* **8** (2): 51–59.

Guilford, J., and Turner, J. U., 1992, Representing geometric tolerances in solid models, *ASME Computers in Engineering Conf.*, Vol. 1, San Francisco, ASME Press.

Gupta, S., and Turner, J., 1991, Variational solid modeling for tolerance analysis, *ASME Computers in Engineering Conf.*, Vol. 1, pp. 487–494.

Hillyard, R. C., and Braid, I. C., 1978, Analysis of dimensions and tolerances in computer-aided mechanical design, *Computer-Aided Design* **10** (3): 161–166.

Hillyard, R. C., and Braid, I. C., 1978, Characterizing non-ideal shapes in terms of dimensions and tolerances, Proc. of Siggraph '78, *Comp. Gr.* **12** (3): 234–238.

Jacobsohn, J. F., Radack, G. M., and Merat, F. L., 1990, Incorporating knowledge of geometric dimensioning and tolerancing into a feature-based CAD system, *Proc. of Second Rensselaer Int. Conf. on CIM*, Troy, NY, May 21–23, IEEE Press, pp. 152–159.

Johnson, R., 1985, Dimensioning and tolerancing—Final report, Technical Report R84-GM-02-2, CAM-I, Inc., Arlington, TX.

Kimura, F., Suzuki, H., and Ando, H., 1987, Variational geometry based on logical constraints and its applications to product modeling, *Ann. of CIRP* **36** (1): 65–68.

Krulikowski, A., 1989, *Fundamentals of Geometric Dimensioning and Tolerancing*, second ed., Effective Training, Inc., Westland, MI.

Light, R. A., 1982, Variational geometry: Modification of part geometry by changing dimensional values, *Proc. of Conf. on CAD/CAM Technology in Mechanical Engineering*, MIT, Cambridge, MA, pp. 64–75

Light, R. A., and Gossard, D. C., 1982, Modification of geometric models through variational geometry, *Computer-Aided Design* **14** (4): 209–214.

Lin, V. C., Gossard, D. C., and Light, R. A., 1981, Variational geometry in computer-aided design, Proc. of Siggraph '81, *Comp. Gr.* **15** (3): 171–177.

Martino, P. M., 1988, Tolerance design in CAD systems, Ph.D. dissertation, Rensselaer Polytechnic Institute.

Martino, P. M., and Gabriele, G. A., 1989, Application of variational geometry to the analysis of mechanical tolerances, in B. Ravani, ed., *Proc. of 15th ASME Design Automation Conf.*, Montreal, September 17–21, ASME Press, pp. 19–27.

Martinsen, K., 1993, Vectorial tolerancing for all types of surfaces, *Proc. of 19th ASME Design Automation Conf.*, Albuquerque, Vol. 2, ASME Press.

Miller, D., 1989, A structure for supporting tolerances in feature based geometric models, MS thesis, Arizona State University.

Parametric Technology, 1989, *Pro/ENGINEER User Guide*, Parametric Technology Corp., Waltham, MA.

Ranyak, P. S., and Fridshal, R., 1988, Features for tolerancing a solid model, *ASME Computers in Engineering Conf.*, San Francisco, CA, July 31–August 4, ASME Press, pp. 275–280.

Requicha, A. A. G, 1983, Toward a theory of geometric tolerances, *Int. J. of Robotics Research* **2** (4): 45–60.

Requicha, A. A. G., and Chan, S. C., 1986, Representation of geometric features, tolerances, and attributes in solid modelers based on constructive geometry, *IEEE J. of Robotics and Automation* **RA-2** (3): 156–166.

Roy, U., and Liu, C. R., 1988, Feature-based representational scheme of a solid modeler for providing dimensioning and tolerancing information, *Robotics and Computer-Integrated Manufacturing* **4** (314): 333–345.

Shah, J. J., and Miller, D. W., 1990, A structure for supporting geometric tolerances in product definition systems for CIM, *Manufacturing Review* **3** (1): 23–31.

Shah, J. J., and Zhang, B., 1992, Attributed graph model for geometric tolerancing, *Proc. of 18th ASME Design Automation Conf.*, Scottsdale, ASME Press, pp. 133–139.

Treacy, P., Ochs, J. B., Ozsoy, T. M., and Wang, N., 1991, Automated tolerance analysis for mechanical assemblies modeled with geometric features and relational data structure, *Computer-Aided Design* **23** (6): 444–453.

Turner, J. U., 1987, Tolerances in computer-aided geometric design, Ph.D. dissertation, Rensselaer Polytechnic Institute.

Turner, J. U., 1990, Exploiting solid models for tolerance computations, in M. J Wozny, J. U. Turner, and K. Preiss, eds., *Geometric Modeling for Product Engineering*, North-Holland, pp. 237–258.

Turner, J. U., 1990, Relative positioning of parts in assemblies using mathematical programming, *Computer-Aided Design* **22** (7): 304–400.

Turner, J. U., and Gangoiti B., 1991, Commercial software for tolerance analysis, *ASME Computers in Engineering Conf.*, Vol. 1, ASME Press.

Turner, J. U., and Wozny, M. J., 1990, The M-space theory of tolerances, in B. Ravani, ed., *Proc. of 16th ASME Design Automation Conf.*, ASME Press, pp. 217–225.

Wang, N., and Ozsoy, T. M., 1991, A scheme to represent features, dimensions, and tolerances in geometric modeling, *J. of Manufacturing Systems* **10** (3): 233–240.

Zhang, G., and Porchet, M., 1993, Some new developments in tolerance design in CAD, in B. Ravani, ed., *Proc. of 19th ASME Design Automation Conf.*, Albuquerque, ASME Press.

Assembly Modeling

Anantha, R., Crawford, R., and Kramer, G., 1992, An architecture to represent over, under, and fully constrained assemblies, *ASME Winter Annual Meeting.*, ASME Press.

Balakrishnan, G., 1993, Constraint based approach to product modeling, M.S. thesis, Department of Mechanical Engineering, Arizona State University.

Boothroyd, G., 1994, Product design for manufacture and assembly, *Computer-Aided Design* **26** (7): 505–520.

Crawford, R., and Srikantappa, A., 1992, Intermediate geometry and inter-feature relationships for automatic group technology part coding, *ASME Computers in Engineering Conf.*, San Fransisco, ASME Press.

Eastman, C. M., 1981, The design of assemblies, SAE technical paper No. 810197.

Freeman, P., and Newell, A., 1971, A model for functional reasoning in design, *Proc. of Second IJCAI*, Los Altos, CA, pp. 621–633.

Kim, S., and Lee, K., 1989, An assembly modeling system for dynamic and kinematic analysis, *Computer-Aided Design* **21** (1): 2–12.

Ko, H., and Lee, K., 1987, Automatic assembling procedure generation from mating conditions, *Computer-Aided Design* **19** (1): 2–10.

Kramer, G. A., 1991, Using degrees of freedom analysis to solve geometric constraint systems, in J. Rossignac and J. Turner, eds., *Proc. of First ACM Symp. on Solid Modelling Foundations and CAD/CAM Applications,* June 5–7, ACM Press, pp. 371–378.

Lee, K., and Andrews, G., 1985, Inference of positions of components in an assembly: Part 2, *Computer-Aided Design* **17** (1): 20–24.

Lee, K., and Gossard, D. C., 1985, A hierarchical data structure for representing assemblies: Part 1, *Computer-Aided Design* **17** (1): 15–19.

Libardi, E. C., Dixon, J. R., and Simmons, M. K., 1988, Computer environments for the design of mechanical assemblies: A research review, *Engineering with Computers* **3**: 121–136.

Mäntylä, M., 1989, A modeling environment for top-down design of assembled products, IBM Research Report RC 15250 (No. 68063), T. J. Watson Research Center, Modeling Science Project.

Mäntylä, M., 1990, The Design Browser—A hierarchical part-of graph browser, IBM Research Report, T. J. Watson Research Center, Modeling Science Project.

Popplestone, R. J., 1987, The Edinburgh designer system as a framework for robotics, *Proc. of 1987 IEEE Int. Conf. on Robotics and Automation,* pp. 1972–1977.

Popplestone, R. J., Ambler, A. P., and Bellows, I., 1980, An interpreter for language for describing assemblies, *Artificial Intelligence* **14** (1): 79–107.

Press, W. H., Flannery, B. P., Teukolsky, S. A., and Vetterling, W. T., 1992, *Numerical Recipes in C,* 2d edition, Cambridge University Press.

Requicha, A. A. G., 1977, Part and assembly description languages, Tech. Memo. No. 19, Production Automation Project, University of Rochester.

Rocheleau, D., and Lee, K., 1985, System for interactive assembly modeling, *Computer-Aided Design,* **19** (2): 65–72.

Schubert, L. K., 1979, Problems with parts, *Proc. of Sixth IJCAI,* Tokyo, pp. 778–784.

Schubert, L. K., 1979, *Representing and Using Knowledge about Parts,* Computing Science Technical Note, University of Alberta, Edmonton.

Shah, J. J., 1991, Assessment of features technology, *Computer-Aided Design* **23** (5): 58–66.

Shah, J. J., and Rogers, M. T., 1994, Assembly modeling as an extension of feature based design, *Research In Eng. Design,* March.

Shah, J. J., and Tadepalli, R., 1992, Feature based assembly modeling, *ASME Computers in Engineering Conf.,* San Fransisco, ASME Press.

Shah, J. J., Balakrishnan, G., Rogers, M., and Urban, S., 1994, Comparative study of procedural and declarative feature based geometric modeling, *IFIP WG 5.2 Conf. on Feature Modeling and Recognition,* Valenciennes, France, May 1994.

Tadepalli, R., 1991, Feature based assembly modeling of mechanical components, M.S. thesis, Department of Mechanical Engineering, Arizona State University.

Tsai, J-C., 1992, Issues in incremental analysis of assemblies for concurrent design, *AI in Design,* Kluwer.

Veltkamp, R., 1992, Geometric constraint management with Quanta, in D. Brown, M. Waldron, and H. Yoshikawa, eds., *Intelligent Computer Aided Design*, Elsevier Science Publishers.

Wesley, M. A., Lozano-Perez, T., Lieberman, L. I., Lavin, M. A., and Grossman, D. D., 1980, A geometric modeling system for automated mechanical assembly, *IBM J. of Res. and Dev.* **24** (1): 64–74.

Wilson, R., and Rit, J.-F., 1990, Maintaining geometric dependencies in an assembly planner, *Proc. of 1990 IEEE Conf. on Robotics and Automation*.

6

FEATURES IN MANUFACTURING

The historical origins of computer-aided design and manufacturing are quite separate from each other. Early CAD systems were influenced by the emerging computer graphics technology, leading to emphasis on 2D drafting and surface design. The origin of CAM is rooted in programming numerically controlled machine tools and the subsequent introduction of the APT language. For a long time CAD and CAM were distinct technologies; data transfer between them took place by paper drawings which were interpreted by human users. This situation still exists in many industrial companies.

It was soon realized that a closer integration of CAD and CAM could bring about many advantages. Elimination of human reinterpretation of design information for manufacturing would reduce errors and save time. Feedback from manufacturing to design would lead to products that were easier to manufacture, avoiding costly rework. Shortening of the overall lead time from design to manufacturing would allow more design and manufacturing alternatives to be investigated within a given time, leading to a superior product. Unfortunately, on the basis of the low-level CAD models expressed in terms of geometric elements, it proved difficult to create sufficiently general and/or powerful manufacturing applications.

Much of the initial impetus of developing feature-based systems stems from this background. Indeed, one of the primary advantages of features is that they make it possible to link design and manufacturing information in a fashion that supports the use of manufacturing information during product design, and conversely design information during manufacturing planning and actual manufacture. It is therefore not surprising that the application of features in manufacturing is more advanced than that in design. Most of the existing work in feature-based manufacturing has taken place for machining processes. More recently, however, the attention of research has turned to other types of processes, such as sheet metal forming, casting, injection molding, and most recently, various emerging rapid prototyping technologies. To satisfy the requirements of modern manufacturing environments, where several types of manufacturing processes are integrated into autonomously operating production cells and lines, inspection planning and assembly planning must also be regarded as important application areas for features in manufacturing.

This chapter provides a review of the basic concepts, methods, and issues related to manufacturing applications of features. Chapter 11 will focus specifically on the details of techniques for machining process planning. For an overview of features in manufacturing, including applications in nonmachining processes, see the collection of papers in (Shah et al. 1994).

6.1 MANUFACTURING FEATURES

Features can be defined from different viewpoints, such as design, analysis, assembly, and function. For manufacturing applications, features must be defined in a form that supports the planning and execution of various types of *manufacturing processes* on the modeled product.

A *manufacturing feature* is typically defined as a collection of related geometric elements which as a whole correspond to a particular manufacturing method or process or can be used to reason about the suitable manufacturing methods or processes for creating the geometry. In single-part machining applications, typical manufacturing features would include holes, slots, and pockets; in sheet metal products, cutouts, bends, and welds; in assembly planning, mechanical joints such as bearings. In each case the presence of a manufacturing feature in a product gives us the capability of deducing what types of manufacturing operations must be performed, and also determining information required for the (automated or manual) execution of these operations.

A prismatic mechanical part and its typical manufacturing features are shown in Figure 6.1. In the case shown, the feature-based representation of the part is organized in a tree-type data structure where the root represents the rough stock (in this case, a rectangular block of material), and the other nodes are machinable feature instances. The representation also encodes some geometric relationships between the features; for instance, that the pattern of holes is considered to be located on the bottom surface of the relief feature R1 is represented by arranging the node PTRN1 to be a child of R1 in the tree. Such information is useful for determining the sequence in which the corresponding machining operations are performed.

As discussed in Chapter 3, we can make the distinction between *manufacturing feature instances*, used to record information about particular features appearing in a part, and *manufacturing feature classes*, used to record generic information shared by all instances of the class, and stored in a feature library consisting of feature class definitions. Apart from the definitions of feature attributes and geometry, the shared information of manufacturing features includes various types of manufacturing knowledge.

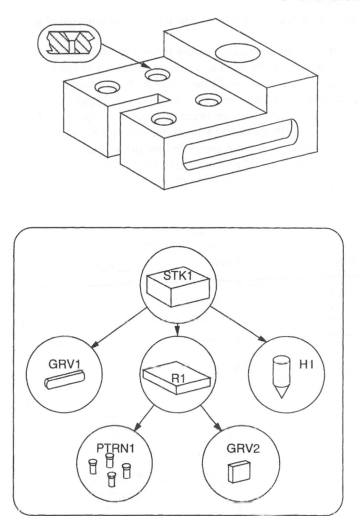

Figure 6.1 A part and its manufacturing features

The link between manufacturing features and manufacturing information is typically realized in terms of *manufacturing process models*. For the typical case of machining, process models can be organized into a taxonomy containing elementary processes such as milling, drilling, facing, and turning. Process models are expressed in terms of the *manufacturing resources* which can be used to realize the process (machines, tools, fixtures, auxiliary materials), *process parameters* related to the use of the resources (for machining, feed and speed), and *attribute information* guiding the choice of a particular process (e.g., time and cost). Often also *procedural knowledge* is included, such as procedures for computing the process parameters on the basis of feature attribute information. An important aspect of a process model for machining is representation of the *tool kinematics*, such as tool access direction, and possible technological constraints.

To implement the linkage, manufacturing feature types refer to a collection of possible process models which can be used to generate instances of the feature type. Thus, for instance, a hole feature might be linked with alternative process models related to drilling and milling processes as shown in Figure 6.2. The concept of "method" is used to denote a sequence of processes capable of producing a feature; as shown, methods contain planning knowledge such as the (relative) cost. The actual processes are represented by further data structures not shown. They describe the required process parameters and refer to the required resources. Examples of the representation of process information will be given in Chapter 11.

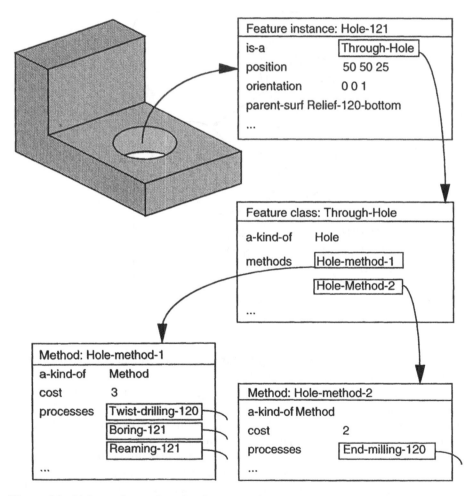

Figure 6.2 Linkage of manufacturing features and process models

On the basis of the above, it is clear that the identification and formalization of manufacturing features is intrinsically bound to the identification and formalization of the underlying manufacturing processes. Hence the task of "featurizing" a product from the viewpoint of manufacturing must start by cataloging the manufacturing steps and processes of interest. This suggests a feature identification process with the following outline:

1. Select the scope of the manufacturing processes to be covered. For instance, the scope may be restricted to pure machining steps only, or it might also include inspection and assembly. The widest scope would consider the whole material flow from suppliers to the customer. The importance of the properly chosen scope cannot be overemphasized; as will be discussed in later sections, the application scope has significant impact on the issues that must be resolved during the featurization process.

2. Identify the individual process steps within the chosen scope. Existing process plans, process sheets, and so on, as well as part drawings, NC programs, and manufacturing orders, are useful sources of information. Company standards for production should also be analyzed.

3. Formalize the process steps as recurring process elements; identify process parameters and relationships between processes.

4. Identify recurring process sequences related to the production of a certain type of geometry; formalize the relation between the geometry created by the process sequence and the process parameters of the individual steps of the sequence.

5. Call the resulting geometric shapes "manufacturing features"; draw a generic sketch for each manufacturing feature identified, and label all its parameters using terminology from the manufacturing viewpoint.

6. Validate the candidate manufacturing features by similar lines as discussed in Section 5.2.2 in the context of design features.

Obviously the process outlined above is far from simple. Unless the scope is very limited, or the production methods of the target company are on a very high level of standardization and documentation, several person-months or even person-years of effort must be allocated to creating a library of manufacturing features suited for a chosen application. On the other hand, at some level of abstraction, the basic manufacturing processes used by all companies are similar. After all, the range of processes that can be executed by a CNC milling center is roughly similar from one company to the next, even though the details of the processes will vary according to the products, materials, tools, and auxiliary materials used. This means that published feature sets may be used as a basis for development of a tailored feature library.

In the experience of the authors, a prototyping approach is recommended. The initial scope should be selected as relatively narrow, perhaps only covering a single machining cell in the case of machining applications, and only a few chosen product types. The process of featurizing the pilot case should be carefully monitored and documented to gain a realistic view of the complexity of enlarging the scope of the first pilot.

6.2 ISSUES AND ALTERNATIVE APPROACHES

There are several issues related to the definition of manufacturing features that have significant consequences as to how a manufacturing feature-based system is constructed. Ultimately the resolution of the issues should depend on the type of manufacturing environment and application being considered. Some of these issues will be revisited and elaborated in Chapter 11.

6.2.1 Level of Abstraction

Several fundamental issues deal with the relationship of manufacturing features and process models. The *level of abstraction* of manufacturing features can vary. At the low end of the abstraction spectrum (rough granularity), manufacturing features could correspond directly with manufacturing processes. In this case a countersunk hole could be seen as a compound of several low-level features (e.g., a "free-hole," a "bore," and a "sink"). At the high end of the spectrum (fine granularity), manufacturing features may represent a considerable variation of shapes and processes; for example, a large variety of stepped holes could be regarded as simply "holes."

A simple example of levels of abstraction is given in Figure 6.3 depicting hole features. In case (*a*) the feature is represented as three elementary features related one-to-one with manufacturing processes. In (*b*) a higher-level feature is used; in this case the feature would be related to a sequence of processes. At a next possible level of abstraction, the feature would simply be called "hole," and geometric reasoning would be used to distinguish between various types of holes as required by applications. In practice, the level of abstraction may vary between different types of processes; for example, milling features might be modeled at a lower level than turning features to take advantage of the fact that the geometric reasoning needed for process planning of turning operations is simpler than that required for general milling operations.

Obviously low-level features give greater control of the manufacturing process to the developer of the feature model, while leaving little freedom of choice to planning applications choosing manufacturing processes. High-level features postpone many of the details of manufacturing processes to applications working on the features. Therefore the choice of the level of abstraction may reflect the stage of product development being considered. During the initial development of a new product, high-level manufacturing features may be preferred to provide a wide choice of optional manufacturing processes, whereas during the operative application of features for everyday manufacturing operations of an

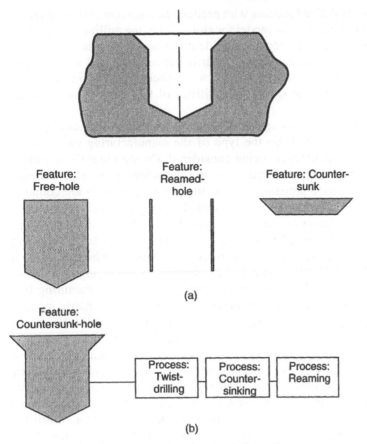

Figure 6.3 Hole features at various levels of abstraction

already designed standard product, low-level features may be preferred. The best solution may be to leave the choice of granularity to the system administrator, and to provide him or her with the facilities for including feature types of the desired level of abstraction. For instance, for standard shapes, the system administrator might create rough granularity features linked with standard process sequences. Nonstandard shapes would be represented by means of finer granularity features.

6.2.2 Level of Specialization

Related to the abstraction level is the issue of the *level of specialization*. In the low end of the spectrum, the processes related to a manufacturing feature are expressed in generic terms, and the process parameters and resources are not precisely determined (except by means of generic rules and procedures related to the feature type). In the highly specialized case a manufacturing feature corresponds to a precisely defined process with predefined resources and parameters. For instance, in a generic process model for slot milling, the milling cutter might be specified only in terms of a tool family identifier and constraints on the tool dimension. In a very specialized model a particular machine tool and physical tool instance would be specified, augmented with specialized machining knowledge taking into account the special capabilities of the machine tool and its control.

The trade-off in this issue is again between generality and user control, and the choice ultimately depends on the type of the manufacturing environment and the stage of product lifecycle being considered. During the early life-cycle stages generic features might be used to specify the processes in generic terms. Later, in actual production preparation time, the generic processes are bound to actual physical resources, and the result is coded in a highly specialized model. To facilitate such evolution of the feature model, some feature-based systems support several levels of specialization, which in some cases has led to replacing the simple type-instance scheme by a more complex scheme where features at several levels of specialization can act as prototypes for instancing.

Variable level of specialization may also be required if manufacturing features are created through feature recognition on the basis of geometric models, or by feature mapping from design features to manufacturing features. Neither of these approaches can be expected to create very specialized features. It follows that a feature-based manufacturing system should support changing the level of abstraction or specialization of a manufacturing feature originally created by feature recognition or mapping. For instance, a feature recognizer may be capable of locating "through-hole" features on the basis of the geometry. Once a manufacturing process has been selected for a recognized hole (e.g., a drilling process on a certain machine with a certain tool and certain process parameters), it may be preferable to replace the feature with a more specialized "through-hole-½"-inch-diam" feature that records the selected process for operative use of the model.

To see how this might be implemented, consider the example of a hypothetical feature library illustrated in Figure 6.4. To support generic manufacturing analysis, where the emphasis is on determining the process requirements and routing, the system provides a generic feature `Counter-sunk-hole`, which is linked with a generic process sequence consisting of `twist-drilling`, `reaming`, and `countersinking`. None of these entities are specified in detail; the dimensions of the feature are unspecified, as are the details of the processes such as tooling and process parameters. A product model for generic analysis would therefore be specified in terms of instances of such generic features.

To support detailed analysis, the system also provides a more precisely specified variant feature `Counter-sunk-hole-d45`. Observe that the dimensions of the variant feature are predetermined. Correspondingly the processes are more precisely predetermined by including information of the tool type as indicated with the expanded process specification names. A product model for detailed

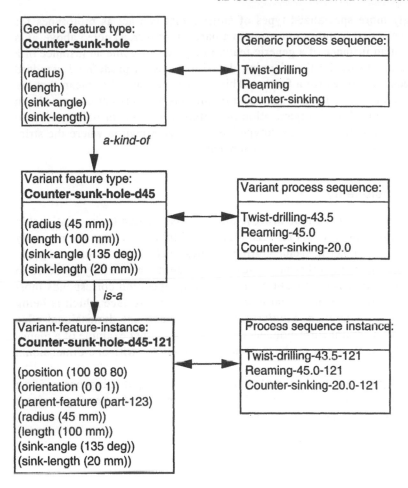

Figure 6.4 Generic, variant, and instantiated features

analysis might consist of variant feature instances such as the one shown at the bottom of the figure.

For some applications it might become necessary to identify further levels of detail. During the actual manufacture, features will be actually realized by applying the specified processes in proper sequence. Fixture planning needs precise knowledge of the state of the features, which might be modeled by further distinction of "planned" versus "realized" features. Inspection planning might require the notion of "measured" versus "unmeasured" features. Of course some of these distinctions could be modeled by attribute information instead of feature types.

From the point of view of feature classification and object-oriented implementation of feature libraries, these different levels of detail can all be viewed as increasingly more specialized types of entities that can act as prototypes for instantiating actual features appearing in a part. Moreover, as noted above, it is possible that an instance of a generic feature may later become an instance of a variant feature to model the planning decision to use a predefined standard process sequence to realize a feature. This can be interpreted to mean that the strict division between feature types and feature instances is not necessarily an appropriate model for the organization of features. In terms of object-oriented programming, this leads to a prototype-based characterization where the strict distinction of classes and instances disappears.

6.2.3 Dimensionality

The *dimensionality of manufacturing features* is also related to the relationship between features and process models. Many machining processes are naturally associated with volumetric manufacturing features, such as holes, slots, and pockets. Nevertheless, many other processes seem to be more naturally modeled in terms of lower-dimensional features. Face milling operation corresponds most naturally to a surface feature that models (a part of) a surface which is being machined by the operation. Similarly arc welding and one-dimensional edge features are in a natural correspondence. Turning is another example of a manufacturing process that seems to be most naturally modeled with one-dimensional features.

Figure 6.5 gives a typical example of a complex casting that is processed in a machining center. Both volume (the holes) and surface (the bearing surface) features seem to be required to capture the processes.

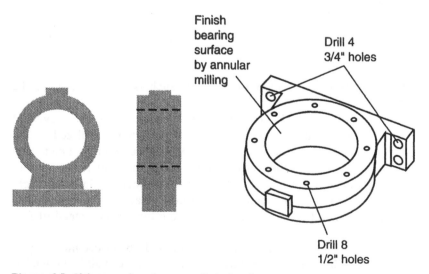

Figure 6.5 Volume and surface manufacturing features

6.2.4 Completeness of Feature Model

Still another issue is the *completeness of the feature model*, namely whether all the geometry of a part belongs to a feature. Some applications of manufacturing features can work even if only the part of geometry of direct interest to the application is modeled. Consider, for instance, the machining of complex castings. A detailed model of the casting may not be required for some applications; surfaces that can be left unmachined need not appear in any features. Such would be the case of the part in Figure 6.5 where many surfaces of the casting are left unmachined and do not need to be absolutely modeled as features.

Some other applications require detailed geometric information on the whole part, such as fixture planning, and may need to consider also unmachined surfaces. The issue is related to the feature creation method used. Typically design-by-features systems correspond to complete feature descriptions, while recognition systems can deliver partial models.

6.2.5 Feature Relationships

Feature-based manufacturing applications require the capability to perform geometric reasoning on the geometric relationships of the features of a product. For instance, process planning requires geometric reasoning to determine the setup requirements of a part (Which machining directions are required? Which features are machined from each chosen direction?) and the sequencing of the individual processes of each setup. To implement such reasoning, information on the geometric relationships of the features appearing in a part is required. An important subset of this information is the dimensioning and tolerancing relations between the features.

A fairly complete taxonomy of feature relationships for geometric reasoning is presented by (Srikantappa and Crawford 1994). Their representation uses a vocabulary of *structural primitives,* denoting important partial areas of features, and *geometric primitives,* denoting various spatial configurations of structural primitives or symmetry axes of features. The structural primitives include bot-tom, side, top, and end. Their definition is illustrated through examples in Figure 6.6; observe that the definition of the primitives depends on whether the feature is subtractive or additive. Also observe that some primitives denote *real* faces of the object, while others are *virtual* faces not actually appearing in the final object. Another type of structural primitive is the *feature axis,* the axis of symmetry of the feature. For subtractive features, the feature axis gives the access direction of the feature for machining. For instance, for the slot feature on the left side of Figure 6.6, the feature axis is the line connecting the middle points of the two opposite end faces.

Structural primitives are used to specify feature interference. So, for instance, the end of the slot of Figure 6.6 interacts with the side of the block feature because the entry face of the slot resides on the side of the block. The geometric primitives represent further spatial relations of structural primitives. These include:

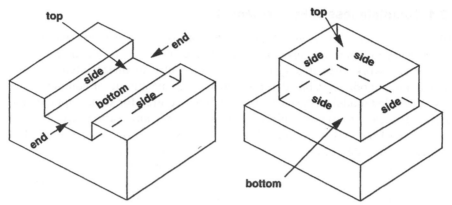

Figure 6.6 Structural primitives (Srikantappa and Crawford 1994; reprinted by permission of Elsevier Science)

- *Planar* (two features touch each other along a two-dimensional region)
- *Coplanar* (two features reside on the same surface, but are not planar)
- *Offset* (two features include parallel surfaces whose normals are oriented in the same direction)
- *Parallel* (the feature axes of two features are parallel)
- *Orthogonal* (the feature axes of two features are perpendicular)
- *Collinear* (the feature axes of two features are on the same line)
- *Angular* (the feature axes make an angle other than 0 or 90 degrees)

Figure 6.7 (Srikantappa and Crawford 1994) shows an example part and its intermediate geometry stored as a semantic net.

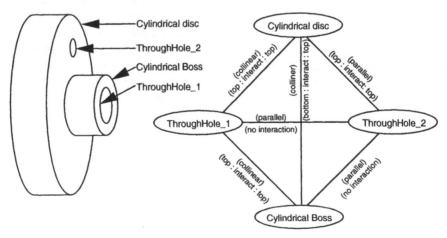

Figure 6.7 Intermediate geometry example (Srikantappa and Crawford 1994; reprinted by permission of Elsevier Science)

Some tasks in feature-based manufacturing require further information on the geometric and structural relationships of features. For instance, the position tolerance between two features may be needed to determine whether the features must be machined in the same setup. The sequencing of the setups themselves is also generally determined on the basis of tolerancing relations; see Chapter 11 for further discussion of this.

6.2.6 Temporal Ordering

An issue that is unique to the application of features in manufacturing is the *temporal ordering of features*. In discrete parts manufacturing the processes related to the manufacturing features of a part are executed in some order. Therefore the features themselves are created on an initial rough part in some order, or possibly partly in parallel; for instance, the roughing cuts of a group of similar features are normally executed before the finishing cuts to optimize tool changes. For a product consisting of several independent subassemblies, truly parallel execution of the processes is normal. Many applications, such as fixture planning or inspection planning, need information of this temporal ordering to operate properly. A further complication is that features may appear in a part temporarily (e.g., for fixturing), only to disappear from the final product.

The general concept behind the issue of temporal ordering is the representation of *precedence relations* amongst the processes related to the manufacturing features. The simplest type of precedence relation between two processes a and b is the end-start relation $a \rightarrow b$, denoting that process a must be executed before process b can be started. For instance, the temporal ordering of the three processes in Figure 6.3(*b*) must obey this relation. Note, however, that this does not preclude the execution of some other processes between the three. Other precedence relations of potential interest include the start-start relation, indicating that the processes must start simultaneously, and the immediate end-start relation, indicating that the two processes must be executed one after another with no other processes interleaved in between.

The temporal order of features can to some extent be captured in a data representation that includes feature relationships. Precedence information can also be deduced from dimensioning and tolerancing relationships between the features. Consider, for instance, the model shown in Figure 6.1. Clearly, the parent-child relations can be interpreted as precedence relations between the features, so that the relief R1 is made before the hole pattern PTRN1. On the other hand, the representation should not commit a process planning application prematurely to a certain order of producing the features.

6.2.7 Product Families

Much of the information for manufacturing applications is best related to a whole part or even a collection of parts produced simultaneously, for example, fixtured on the same pallet of a FMS system. The concept of variant features

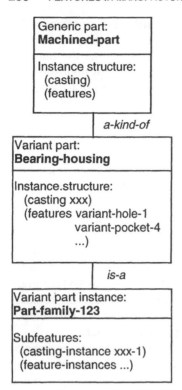

Generic part:
Machined-part

Instance structure:
  (casting)
  (features)

a-kind-of

Variant part:
Bearing-housing

Instance.structure:
  (casting xxx)
  (features variant-hole-1
          variant-pocket-4
          ...)

is-a

Variant part instance:
Part-family-123

Subfeatures:
  (casting-instance xxx-1)
  (feature-instances ...)

Figure 6.8 Generic and variant parts

introduced above can be extended also to these entities. Consider, for instance, the hypothetical situation shown in Figure 6.8. At the top the generic feature machined-part models the general concept of a part that is made of a casting to which some detail features are machined. To the generic entity, fairly generic manufacturing knowledge would be associated.

The second level is a variant feature of machined-part, a bearing-housing. A bearing-housing feature models a more or less strictly defined *product family*, a collection of parts similar enough to each other to have similar manufacturing requirements. As indicated, the feature structure of a bearing-housing part would be specified to some detail, such as the casting type and the (main) features contained. Somewhat more precise manufacturing knowledge might be associated with such a model, such as a description of the part routing or a part family fixturing plan. The third level is an actual part instance that conforms to the part family specification and inherits its manufacturing knowledge.

6.3 GENERATION OF MANUFACTURING FEATURES

Manufacturing features are convenient product representations for manufacturing process planning and related tasks such as NC code generation and fixturing analysis. Unfortunately, before these advantages can be exploited, product representations in terms of manufacturing features must first be generated. Several approaches to the generation of product models consisting of manufacturing features can be identified. They are outlined in the following subsections.

6.3.1 Interactive Feature Identification

In interactive feature identification method, manufacturing features are identified interactively by picking geometric elements of a geometric model displayed on computer screen. This method is still assumed by many manufacturing applications due to the present relatively immature state of the other approaches described below. For instance, surface features such as those required in for the part in Figure 6.5 cannot generally be recognized using standard feature recognition facilities.

6.3.2 Design by Manufacturing Features

In the existing prototype systems, the design by manufacturing features approach is perhaps the most common choice. For instance, the First-Cut system by (Cutkosky and Tenenbaum 1990) implemented concurrent part design and process planning by assuming that the designer creates the part model directly in terms of its manufacturing features. Hence no conversion, mapping, or extraction of manufacturing features was required.

The problem of the design by manufacturing features approach is that it forces the designer to think in terms of manufacturing operations, which often is not natural for him or her. Moreover, because manufacturing features are idealizations of certain manufacturing processes, creating a product model consisting of manufacturing features requires ample knowledge of the underlying manufacturing processes. In effect, the designer is forced to assume the role of a process planner. The danger of suboptimal models from the manufacturing point of view is clearly present.[1]

The HutCAPP system by (Mäntylä et al. 1989) was also based on the design with manufacturing features approach. However, the system provided a facility for changing the feature specification of the part by means of *feature relaxation*. Essentially the system treated functionally similar features as interchangeable and used the possibility of modifying the given features to optimize the manufacture of the part. This eliminated to some extent the problem of inexpert part formulation in terms of manufacturing features. However, because the system had no capability of judging whether a change in a feature shape was functionally acceptable, a human user was needed to accept the proposed changes. HutCAPP's method is discussed in more detail in Chapter 11.

---

[1] In a concurrent engineering environment where manufacturing experts are available in a multifunctional team performing the design and manufacturing planning simultaneously, the problem may not appear. However, in most engineering environments such close teamwork is not practical.

One of the problems of the design with manufacturing features approach from the viewpoint of the designer is that only negative features are available. Because of this, the approach has also been called *destructive solid geometry*—one way to represent the part is in terms of a CSG tree with only subtraction operators. Most designers would prefer to have also protrusion features available for creating pins, stiffeners, and ribs, for example, in the part. Unfortunately, the positive protrusion features have no direct counterparts in machining operations; therefore they must be mapped to equivalent material removal features. Algorithms for this are discussed in Chapters 7 and 9.

6.3.3 Design to Manufacturing Feature Mapping

Ideally designers should be given the freedom to design in terms of features most convenient for their use. These design features must then be mapped to manufacturing features. Like feature recognition, feature mapping may be done interactively or automatically. In some cases it may be possible to do the mapping at the feature level, that is to get manufacturing features directly from design features. Generally, it is also necessary to use the underlying geometric model in conjunction with features to do the mapping. However, the most common approach today is to use only the geometric model to find the manufacturing features, which amounts to manufacturing feature recognition, discussed in the next section. Feature mapping is not a mature methodology today; the state-of-the art is reviewed in Chapter 7.

6.3.4 Manufacturing Feature Recognition

A diametrically opposite approach to design with manufacturing features is to rely completely on feature recognition. The problem of this approach is that little information from the design stage can be transferred to manufacturing planning. For instance, dimensioning and tolerances are lost. The benefit, however, is that a complete separation of concern between design and manufacturing is achieved. The designer is free to design the part in terms of whatever features he or she finds convenient. Similarly the manufacturing features extractor is free to represent the part in terms of any features that are appropriate for the manufacturing environment and its processes in question.

A difficulty related to feature recognition is that some apparent features may turn out not to be features at all from the viewpoint of the range of processes being considered. For instance, a precision-cast rough part may include a hole that is not to be machined; therefore the hole is not a manufacturing feature from the perspective of machining planning application. For instance, the large hole appearing in the part shown in Figure 6.4 (the bearing surface) is not a hole from the viewpoint of process planning for machining because the rough shape appears already in the casting. In general, recognition of machining features requires *a priori* determination of the initial shape of the part. That is, feature recognition of manufacturing features should always be done with respect to a

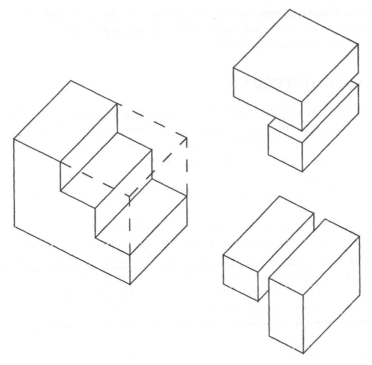

Figure 6.9 Two interpretations of a part in terms of manufacturing features

given blank shape, or the blank must be determined at an initial stage of the recognition process.

An important benefit of the recognition approach is that the recognizer can create several alternative models of the part. To appreciate the utility of generating alternative feature models of a part for process planning, consider Figure 6.9 which shows a simple staircase part on the left and two possible breakdowns of the material to be removed off a rectangular workpiece for making the part. The processes to be considered by a process planner for the two alternatives would be different as well. The two interpretations will most likely have different characteristics in terms of machining cost and resulting surface characteristics; moreover the information needed to choose the better interpretation generally requires in-depth knowledge of the available manufacturing processes and their characteristics. This information is best available to a process planner but not to the feature recognizer. Therefore both interpretations should be made available in the process planning application to give the planner maximal freedom of choosing the best plan for the part. Also observe that if design by manufacturing features is used, only a single interpretation is available to the process planner. Therefore a suboptimal plan will be generated if in fact the missing interpretation would have provided a superior manufacturing process.

Recently various feature recognition methods that can generate alternative feature models for a given stock and part have been developed. Some of the major examples are reviewed in Chapter 9.

6.4 GROUP TECHNOLOGY CODING

Group technology (GT) is a system that exploits similarities among parts by using common characteristics to classify parts into part families. Each family is identified by a multiple digit alphanumeric code that signifies those characteristics of the family that influence the application for which the GT scheme was developed. Thus a GT code is an abstraction of part specification; the detailed part data is replaced by a code representing only a few high-level aspects of the part.

GT is being increasingly applied to manufacturing-related activities such as variant process planning, design retrieval, and scheduling for cellular manufacturing. Studies indicate that GT can effect considerable cost savings by eliminating design and process plan duplication, automating part data retrieval, reducing the cost of introducing new parts, and reducing the number of changeovers in tooling and fixturing by scheduling similar parts together (Hyde 1981). These characteristics have made GT code generation an important and popular manufacturing-related application of features.

GT schemes are developed for specific applications, such as for design retrieval or manufacturing planning. It is the application that dictates the level of information that must be encapsulated in the GT code. GT schemes also differ in the range of parts that are coded. To implement GT, an organization must pick or develop a GT scheme, customize it, then classify all existing parts on the basis of the selected scheme. When new parts are introduced they must be classified too.

GT coding is basically a case analysis of possible part shapes. That is, part classification is done by comparing part characteristics to the rules used by the GT scheme. Figure 6.10 shows an example of part coding according to the Opitz coding system (Opitz 1970). The roughest level of the analysis determines the first digit of the code on the basis of the general shape of the part, for instance, if the part is rotational, prismatic, or sheetlike. The following digits are determined from characteristics of the part, such as its overall size, ratio of its main dimensions, and the presence or lack of certain important characteristics. In the case of Figure 6.10, the code digits are formed as follows:

Digit	Meaning	Code
1	Rotational part, L/D ratio > 0.5	1
2	Step to one end	1
3	Internal bore without shape element	1
4	No external plane surface	0
5	Gear teeth	6

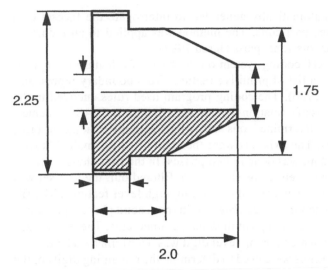

2.25

1.75

2.0

Figure 6.10 Sample part for GT coding (Chang 1990; reprinted by permission of Addison-Wesley Publishing Co.)

Hence the code of the sample part is "11106." This code can be used to access manufacturing information of the part such as a rough process plan; observe, for instance, that all parts sharing this code are likely to have the same fixturing characteristics.

GT schemes are usually partly or fully hierarchical; thus a decision tree can be used to represent these schemes. Computer programs have been written (e.g., DCLASS [Allen 1979]) to traverse the decision tree, prompt users to answer questions interactively, and to keep track of user responses. Users of such programs need a paper engineering drawing of the part being classified. This method has two major disadvantages:

1. Parts can be classified differently by different people because of the way a person responds to a question. For example, the question "Is the part rotational?" is rather subjective and can be interpreted many different ways.

2. The process is not automated: it requires human intervention, even though a CAD database of the product's definition may be available somewhere in the organization.

The application of features for GT coding aims to solve the above problems by supporting automatic GT coding on the basis of a feature-based model and a description of the coding scheme. GT coding is a historically important application of features technology; in fact, the earliest work in using features for GT was done by (Kyprianou 1980). He proposed a method for recognizing features based on classification of edges and faces and building a face-set data structure; a shape grammar was also devised for finding features by pattern matching. He created a meta language for describing GT classification schemes from which an interface program was automatically generated to interrogate the faceset data structure to determine the part code. The method was applied to an industrial classification scheme for rotational parts (Jared 1984).

Henderson devised a GT coding system on the basis of a feature recognizer program which produced a list of primitive features from boundary representation models (Henderson 1986). The coding program used rules encoded in the PROLOG language to classify rotational parts according to DCLASS schemes. The coding program first determined axis sets, which are lists of adjacent faces all sharing the same axis. The axis sets were then classified as "main," "external," and "internal." Coding was done in two phases. In the first phase, features that did not change the basic envelope shape were filtered out, the axis set was modified, and a feature list was created containing high level features. The filtered features were collected into a separate list. In the second phase, "phantom" features were introduced to cover up cavities such as undercuts. The basic shape was then classified (from which the top level digit was determined). The filtered features and phantom features were used to determine the remaining digits of the code.

Shah and Bhatnagar (1989) have developed a GT coder on the basis of a feature mapping approach. In their system a feature model was first converted to an intermediate form by a generic feature mapping shell; the intermediate form was used for actual GT classification. In the intermediate form, features are mapped to a six-digit taxonomy code that conveys the essential characteristics of the feature from GT coding viewpoint as shown in Figure 6.11. For instance, a form feature Straight-Cylinder has a taxonomy code of 111 101 because it is a rotational, primary, and external feature; the generic class to which Straight-Cylinder belongs is 10, and it is the first member of this class.

The actual geometric reasoning was implemented on the basis of the taxonomy codes and feature information. For instance, to determine the overall shape (rotational or nonrotational) of the part, the questions that need to be answered are:

1. Are all of the primary features (i.e., those that influence the external shape envelope of a part) axisymmetric individually?
2. If the part has nonaxisymmetric features, how does the size of the biggest cross-sectional axisymmetric feature compare with the nonsymmetric features present?

DIGIT 1	DIGIT 2	DIGIT 3	DIGIT 4	DIGIT 5	DIGIT 6
Rotational (1) / Non-rotational (0)	Primary (1)/ Sub-feature(0)	External (1)/ Internal feature(0)	Generic class		Sub-class of generic type

Figure 6.11   Feature taxonomy code for GT

3. What are the relative orientations of the centroidal axes of major primary features with respect to each other (collinear, parallel, or intersecting)?

These tasks were simplified because of the information available in a feature-based modeling system. The feature taxonomy code was used to determine if a feature could be regarded as primary and axisymmetric. The centroidal axes orientations and the parameters needed for calculation of cross-sections were extracted from the detailed feature information.

A powerful GT coder is described by (Ames 1991). Its method is based on a feature recognition algorithm specialized for group technology classification. Similar to the taxonomy coding idea above, the algorithm concentrates on locating such properties of features that are deemed essential for GT coding. Srikantappa and Crawford (1994) perform GT code generation on the basis of an intermediate-level part representation using the geometric relationships discussed in Section 6.2.5.

6.5 FEATURE-BASED PROCESS PLANNING

The term *process planning* stands for a family of planning tasks that must be completed before a designed product can be manufactured. These include tasks such as the following:

- Selection of manufacturing technologies to be used for the manufacture (machining, turning, casting, injection molding, welding, etc.)
- Determination of the sequence in which these technologies are to be used (the *routing* of the product)
- Selection of the actual processes (milling, drilling, facing, etc.) for creating the individual features of the product
- Determination of the proper sequence in which these processes must be executed (*process sequencing*)
- Determination of various types of resources needed for the realization of the processes (human labor, machines, tools, fixtures and jigs, cutting fluid, etc.)
- Selection of the process parameters for specifying the processes (for machining, feed and speed)
- Detailed task planning of the processes (e.g., NC code generation)

In its most general setting, process planning is a difficult and demanding task that requires thorough understanding of both the design requirements of the product and of the available manufacturing processes and their capabilities. Consequently computer-aided process planning has been an active area of research for more than 20 years.

The development of a fully automatic process planner is a very demanding—perhaps impossible—task. Algorithmic approaches are dwarfed by the fact that process planning is a "wicked problem" that does not break into a sequence of subproblems whose solutions can be combined to yield the total solution. For instance, for machining, tool selection is not possible before the processes have been selected. Process selection requires knowledge of the *setups* of the part—the orientations in which the part will be fixtured in a machine tool. Finally, fixturing design requires knowledge of the processes to determine which types of cutting forces must be contained by the fixture, hence completing the cycle where everything depends on everything else.

At present, there are two primary approaches to process planning—*variant* and *generative*. In variant process planning, the process engineer typically uses a group technology (GT) coding scheme to map a proposed new design into an alphanumeric code. This code serves as an index in a database to retrieve a process plan typical of the family of parts into which the new design is classified. The process planner then modifies this process plan manually to produce a customized plan for the new design. Several variant process planning systems are commercially available and have provided significant increases in productivity, but they also have drawbacks. For example, if there are problems with the family process plan (e.g., if it uses out-of-date processes on old machines), these same problems may also occur in the variant of the plan unless the process engineer makes a point of correcting them. For variant process planning, the primary use of features is in the GT coding schemes that are used to map products (which are usually machinable parts) into codes based on various characteristics of the product that are deemed relevant for manufacturing.

In generative process planning, the computer system attempts to synthesize the process plan directly. For machined parts, the typical approach is to consider the part as a collection of machinable features and to do the planning on a feature-by-feature basis. A number of experimental generative systems have been developed that deal with various pieces of this problem, such as process selection, process sequencing, and fixturing. Unfortunately, few generative systems are capable enough to have achieved significant industrial use, primarily because of the extreme difficulty of devising computer systems that can deal well with the subtle interactions that can arise when trying to integrate these pieces. The application of features in process planning is discussed in detail in Chapter 11.

6.6 FEATURE-BASED ASSEMBLY PLANNING

Most products are assemblies of discrete components. Therefore a key stage in their manufacture is the physical assembly of the components. In light of this obvious fact, it is odd that assembly modeling and assembly planning have received far less research attention than discrete part manufacturing.

Assembly planning can be roughly divided into the following phases:

1. *Selection of assembly method,* where the purpose is to recognize the most suitable assembly method for the product, taking into account the type of the assembly system which will be used.
2. *Assembly sequence planning (routing),* where the purpose is to recognize a sequence of assembly operations that can be implemented with the chosen overall assembly method.
3. *Assembly operations planning,* where the emphasis is on the details of the individual assembly steps, such as access directions, mating movements, and application of fasteners.

At the present time, it is generally recognized that assembly process problems such as poor quality, poor efficiency, or high cost (which are all interrelated) are most effectively handled at conceptual design stage. This has resulted in the *design-for-assembly* approach where the most economical production process is already selected during the design stage, and the design is adapted to the characteristics of the chosen method.

A well-known approach to design-for-assembly has been developed by (Boothroyd 1994). The method has also been commercialized as a computerized analysis procedure. The chief objective of the method is to reduce the number of parts in the assembly, which almost universally will lead to diminished assembly costs and also reduced material costs in handling, storing, and so on. To determine whether a part should be included in a design, the method examines it against the following three criteria:

1. Does the part move with respect to other already assembled parts during the operation of the product?
2. Must the part be of different material than other parts already assembled?
3. Must the part be separate from all other parts because assembly or disassembly of some other part would otherwise be impossible?

Unless one of the above criteria applies, a part is considered to be nonessential, and a candidate for merging with other parts. Its existence must be specifically justified by the designers. See (Boothroyd 1994) for an overview of this and other similar methods.

Features can be applied for the data retrieval and geometric reasoning tasks required for the design-for-assembly approach. For instance, product design guidelines for automatic assembly include the following items:

- Reduce the number of different components to a minimum without affecting the functionality of design.
- Simplify the product by replacing a sub-assembly of the product by a more complex single component.
- Replace some of the assembly operations by fewer alternate procedures such as adhesion or welding.

- Introduce guides and tapers to improve the ease of assembly.
- Provide a base part on which the assembly can be built. The base part should have features compatible for quick and accurate placement of the part on a work carrier.
- Projections, holes, or slots that will cause tangling with identical parts should be avoided. This may be achieved by making the holes or slots smaller than projections.
- Parts should be made symmetrical whenever possible to avoid the need for extra effort to orient them correctly.
- If symmetry cannot be achieved, asymmetrical features should be exaggerated to facilitate orientation of parts. This means corresponding asymmetrical features should be provided on the part that can be used to orient other parts.

Many of these analysis rules can be expressed in terms of the assembly features of the product.

The assembly sequence planning and assembly operations planning stages remain problems related to the production engineering phase of a typical product design process. Assembly sequence planning is closely related to the path planning problems of robotics and inspection planning; its task can be defined as "to generate a sequence of assembly operations (placing an individual component in its final position in the assembly) that can be used to implement an assembly task in a given assembly system." The same applies to assembly operations planning, where the objective is to generate detailed information on given assembly operations. For robotic assembly this involves the design of a valid sequence of rigid motions (translations and rotations) that will bring a component into its final position in the assembly. Various tools for assembly must also be designed, such as grippers, jigs, fixtures, pallets, and component feeders. Assembly cells must be laid out while the physical restrictions of robot's motions are being observed.

Again features are regarded as an attractive approach in solving the numerous issues related to assembly planning. Obviously the actual physical arrangement of components in an assembly, as well as attribute information on the physical fit between linked components, is fundamental for recognizing what assembly operations are needed for the assembly and their sequencing. For instance, for rough assembly path planning, the possible *access directions* for positioning the component must first be extracted. Then a *geometric search* for free space in the access direction can be performed.

The access direction can be defined as the final tangent along the path of the component as it is moved in its final location in the assembly. Obviously the access directions depend on the local geometry of the mating assembly features. Some examples of access directions are given in Figure 6.12. In the figure arrows indicate the possible axes of the directions. The directions can be modeled as attributes associated with the assembly features; alternatively, they can be com-

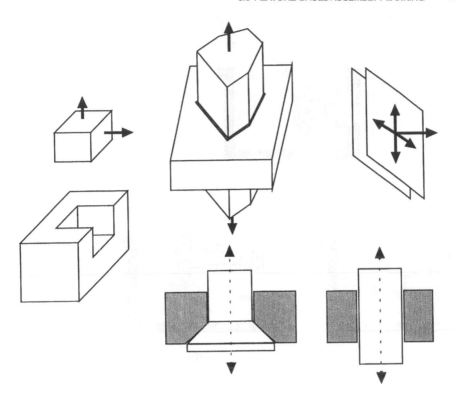

Figure 6.12 Examples of assembly access directions

puted from the primitive joints included. To see how, observe that the set of
access directions for a joint is the intersection of the sets of access directions of
the corresponding geometric primitives. For instance, the compound joint on
the left in Figure 6.12 can be regarded as a combination of three instances of the
plane-plane primitive joints shown in the top right part of the figure. It is easy to
see that the intersection of the three sets indeed resolves into the set shown for
the compound. Three other examples are shown in the figure.

To implement the geometric search for free space, a popular method for translational path planning is the *obstacle polygon* method. The basic idea is to
transform the problem of moving a (two-dimensional) solid to a problem of
moving just a point by growing the obstacles along the route appropriately. For
instance, consider the case in Figure 6.13, where the goal is to translate the
subassembly from location *s* to location *e*. In the figure the shaded areas represent the obstacle polygon for the reference point A. This means that if A is

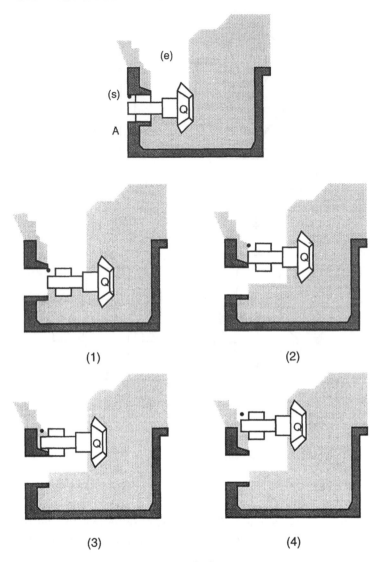

Figure 6.13 Obstacle polygon method

translated into the area of the obstacle polygon, an overlap would occur. The obstacle polygon can be efficiently computed by means of so-called Minkowski sums.

With the obstacle polygon, the path planning problem is reduced to finding a free path for point A from s to e. Any path within the allowable area is valid. Finding the shortest path can be achieved by a greedy technique, often known as Dijkstra's algorithm on a directed graph. In this case the path marked (1) to (4) is found; generally, the best path will trace the edges of the obstacle polygon.

6.7 FEATURE-BASED INSPECTION PLANNING

One of the strong current trends in manufacturing is the goal for error-free "six-sigma" manufacturing, where defective parts are hardly ever produced. Manufactured part inspection is vital to achieve this, not only to discard defective parts but more important, to provide a closed loop control on the quality of parts being produced. This, and other similar trends, mean that *inspection planning* must be treated as an integral part of manufacturing planning. Consequently software support for inspection planning is becoming a key issue.

There are several unresolved problems under investigation in inspection planning. Of course one should concentrate on the characteristics of products that have the biggest influence on its correct function in relation with other parts and avoid the cost of inspecting characteristics that are of little significance. This means that inspection planning is deeply coupled to product modeling issues such as the representation of dimensions and tolerances, assembly relationships, and, ultimately, functions and behaviors of physical shapes.

Inspection planning is also related to process planning. Once characteristics to be inspected have been selected, the inspection processes themselves must be organized in efficient sequences. This involves, say, the determination of accessibility of geometric details to be inspected, sequencing of accessible details, and actual path planning of the motion of the measuring device to the region of space being measured. The last problem is analogous to path planning in robotics. Quite obviously, features can play a big role in all these tasks.

6.8 FEATURE-BASED MANUFACTURABILITY EVALUATION

Reducing the cost and complexity of manufacturing a product is essential for competitiveness and agility of a company. These desirable characteristics are mainly determined by decisions made by the product designer, while a process planner or a manufacturing engineer can directly affect perhaps only 10% of the cost. Therefore early analysis and detection of possible manufacturing problems is essential. Problems encountered at prototype manufacturing stage or even later at production ramp-up stage usually lead to costly process and tooling changes and delayed product introduction to market. One approach to achieve this is to employ integrated product design teams that include manufacturing experts, aiming to generate error-free and production-friendly designs at the first iteration. Nevertheless, this organization also carries a relatively high cost, and it is not attractive for small batch or one-of-a-kind product design unless special producibility analysis tools can be used during design.

The above considerations form the motivation for various *design-for-manufacturing (DFM)* applications that can evaluate the production-friendliness of a design at early stages of product development by means of manufacturing knowledge encoded in a knowledge base. This section will discuss briefly some issues and basic approaches of DFM applications from the viewpoint of features.

The major problem in manufacturability analysis is how to enable a designer who is not (nor needs to be) deeply knowledgeable about manufacturing to access and utilize expert information for judging his or her design. Clearly this requires that manufacturability analysis knowledge must be stored separately from information on the designed object itself. This leads one to consider a feature-based approach, where the designed object is represented by means of its manufacturing features and the manufacturing features are used to access a knowledge base that represents manufacturability analysis procedures. Unfortunately, manufacturing features are not the preferred way of describing a product from designer's point of view. Therefore, in systems that organize manufacturability analysis information on the basis of manufacturing features, mapping the information originally entered by the designer to the form required by the analyzer is required. Observe that a two-way map is needed: The analysis results must be mapped back to the entities originally manipulated by the user in order to provide relevant feedback. The problems, issues, and methods of feature mapping are the subject of the next chapter.

Another problem is that design for manufacturing analysis rules depend not only on the designed object itself, but also on the manufacturing technology contemplated for the production of the object. Manufacturability rules of a casting are completely different from those of a machined object. To access the manufacturing context, at least some amount of process planning must be performed. Qualitative manufacturability feedback can be generated simply on the basis of the knowledge of the manufacturing technologies to be needed. More detailed feedback requires knowledge of machines, tools, and fixtures. Rough quantitative cost models need a rough process plan that contains the sequence of processes to be applied (casting, turning, three-axis machining, surface finishing, painting, etc.) for the designed object. Detailed analysis requires deep models and knowledge of the individual machining processes all the way to chip formation, vibration, and heat transfer. The desired level of feedback must of course be balanced to the level of commitment that the designer has to the details of the product: It is not reasonable to generate detailed analysis information on the basis of a rough idea. Therefore it should be possible to control the level of detail of the manufacturability analysis.

To gain further insight into the issues of feature-based manufacturability analysis, let us consider *qualitative manufacturability analysis* which is concerned with the following kinds of questions:

- Which manufacturing processes are required for the manufacture of the designed object?
- Are all resources required for the processes (materials, machines, tools, fixtures, auxiliary materials) available?
- Is it physically possible to implement all required manufacturing processes?
- Are the feature parameters in conformance with good practice?

Answers to these questions are either binary (yes/no) or not numerically comparable. A part can be regarded as "bad" or as "good," but the goodness of two parts cannot clearly be compared.

Qualitative analysis can be carried out by means of *manufacturability rules*. Typically if-then rules are used where the if-part determines the feature or the pattern of features to which the rule applies, and the then-part contains the corresponding action for reporting the problem to the user. In the simplest case the rules relate to a single manufacturing process and a single manufacturing feature. For example, the rule

```
IF   feature ?x is a slot
     the depth of ?x is larger than producible by any cutter
     available
THEN  ?x is not manufacturable
```

determines the manufacturability of a slot against a known selection of tools. The rule is applicable if slot milling is required for the manufacture of the part. Depending on the manufacturing context, the selection of tools being considered can be limited to the tools physically present in a tool palette or include all tools that can be obtained.

Besides the binary yes/no scale, manufacturability rules can apply other qualitative scales as well, as exemplified by the following example:

```
IF   ?x is a hole on face ?z of part ?p
     ?y is a hole on face ?z of part ?p
     diameter of ?x is not equal to diameter of ?y
THEN  manufacturability of ?p is marginal
     generate-feedback "Consider making diameters of ?x and
     ?y equal"
```

The rule judges qualitatively the manufacturability into the scale "good"–"marginal"–"bad." Observe that the rule also includes an action of generating feedback to the designer.

We may observe that to express the rules, a fairly detailed interface to feature information is required. In the examples, pattern matching for features and their attributes is being used. Besides exact matching, some arithmetic capabilities and inequalities may be required. As indicated by the second example, a rule can also relate to several features.

Most published work in design for manufacturing applications on the basis of features is related to machining processes. More recently, however, results of work on other processes has started to appear. For instance, (Wozny, Pratt, and Poli 1994) discuss using features for manufacturability evaluation of injection molded or die cast parts using features. They address the early design stage, where the exact dimensioned shape of the part is not yet known. Consequently their manufacturing features become quite different in nature, say, from features in machining applications.

6.9 OTHER MANUFACTURING APPLICATIONS

Before the manufacturing operations for a product are started, usually a scheduling step is needed where the various processes are allocated to certain machines in a certain sequence. Scheduling is closely linked with process planning to the extent that sometimes the two tasks cannot be separated. For instance, if several routings in the factory are possible for a given part, the process planner should postpone the choice of the routing to the scheduler, which can make the optimal choice on the basis of dynamic capacity utilization information of the machines. In the most complex situation a new rush production order may change the schedules of less critical orders, causing the need for rescheduling. Rescheduling may also be necessary to recover from production hardware problems. Features can contribute to the solution of these and similar problems by giving the process planner or scheduler extra degrees of freedom compared to the more conventional process plans or routing charts. A manufacturing feature may be associated with several alternative process sequences; if one of them becomes unavailable due to a dynamic bottleneck or hardware failure, the planner/scheduler may choose another feasible process.

Apart from the operative applications discussed above, manufacturing features should prove useful for addressing a number of deeper issues in production engineering. One of them is the problem of designing and maintaining the manufacturing processes of a manufacturing facility. The capability of a manufacturing facility to make parts and products is determined by the range of manufacturing processes available in the facility, and their operational characteristics (range of part and feature sizes that can be manufactured, achievable tolerances, setups, cycle and change times, etc.). To support a full range of factory design and production engineering applications, these data should be presented in a *factory model* of the production facility.

A factory model is of course not a static entity. It evolves in time as the factory and its processes are changed to accommodate new processes or products. Manufacturing features can serve a big role in this process. In the factory model a manufacturing feature is seen as a commitment of the factory to produce a certain shape specified in the feature definition. A sequence of processes related to the feature can be regarded as a plan on how this commitment can be fulfilled. Obviously, from time to time, new production facilities will make it possible to improve over the existing plans, in which case the new processes should be introduced to the manufacturing of all relevant products. If the production requirements of products are expressed in terms of manufacturing features, this task can be facilitated.

Sometimes a new production facility (factory, production line, production cell) must be designed from scratch for a given product (or range of products).

Again, if the production requirements of the product(s) are represented in terms of features, and if past knowledge of feature-process mappings is available, the initial synthesis of feasible factory structures can be greatly simplified on the basis of features.

REVIEW QUESTIONS

6.1 Apply the featurization process to identify manufacturing features of a simple mechanical product you know well. For best results this exercise should be performed in a team.

6.2 For the part of Question 6.1, compare the design features to the manufacturing features. Determine if each of the manufacturing features can be determined (a) only from the design features (b) only from the geometric model (c) from both features and geometric models.

6.3 What kind of problems might be encountered if one tries to fully automate GT coding?

6.4 What are the similarities and differences between GT codes and feature models?

6.5 In identifying manufacturing features, what are the advantages/disadvantages of making features (a) general versus specific (b) abstract versus detailed?

6.6 Compare variational and generative process planning methods. Which one represents the cognitive process of human process planners better?

6.7 Discuss the various criteria for automatic assembly presented in Section 6.6 that can be inspected on the basis of assembly features. What types of geometric reasoning operations are needed?

6.8 Outline an algorithm for computing the access directions for an assembly component on the basis of the primitive surface contacts (see Figure 6.12).

6.9 Enumerate a set of manufacturability rules for holes to be made by drilling. Which rules can be checked on the basis of high-level feature information? Which rules require geometric reasoning on the solid model level?

BIBLIOGRAPHY

Allen, D. K., 1979, *Generative Process Planning Using the DCLASS Information System*, Monograph no. 14, CAM Software Research Laboratory, Brigham Young University, Provo.

Ames, A. L., 1991, Production ready feature recognition based automatic group technology part coding, in J. Rossignac and J. Turner, eds., *Proc. First Symposium on Solid Modelling Foundations and CAD/CAM Applications,* June 5–7, ACM Press, pp. 161–169.

Boothroyd, G., 1994, Product design for manufacture and assembly, *Computer-Aided Design* **26** (7): 505–520.

Chang, T.-C., 1990, *Expert Process Planning for Manufacturing*, Addison-Wesley, Reading, MA.

Cutkosky, M., and Tenenbaum, J. M., 1990, A methodology and computational framework for concurrent product and process design, *Mechanism and Machine Theory* **25** (3): 365–381.

Henderson, M. R., 1986, Automated group technology part coding from a 3-dimensional CAD database, *ASME Winter Annual Meeting*, Anaheim, ASME Press, New York.

Hyde, W., 1981, *Improving Productivity by Classification, Coding, and Database Standardization*, Dekker.

Jared, G. E. M., 1984, Shape features in geometric modelling, in M. S. Pickett and J. W. Boyse, eds., *Solid Modelling by Computers: From Theory to Applications*, Plenum Press, pp. 121–137.

Kyprianou, L., 1980, Shape classification in computer aided design, Ph.D. dissertation, University of Cambridge.

Mäntylä, M., Opas, J., and Puhakka, J., 1989, Generative process planning of prismatic parts by feature relaxation, in B. Ravani, ed., *Proc. 15th ASME Design Automation Conference*, ASME, New York, pp. 49–60.

Opitz, H., 1970, *A Classification System to Describe Workpieces*, Pergamon Press, Oxford.

Shah, J. J., and Bhatnagar, A., 1989, Group technology classification from feature based geometric models, *Manufacturing Rev.* **2** (3).

Shah, J. J., Hsiao, D., Robinson, R. 1990, A framework for manufacturability evaluation in a feature based CAD system, NSF Grantees Conference, Arizona State, January.

Shah, J. J., Mäntylä, M., and Nau, D., eds., 1994, *Advances in Feature Based Manufacturing*, Elsevier Science Publishers.

Srikantappa, A. B., and Crawford, R. H., 1994, Automatic part coding based on interfeature relationships, in J. Shah, M. Mäntylä, and D. Nau, eds., *Advances in Feature Based Manufacturing*, Elsevier Science Publishers, pp. 215–237.

Wozny, M., Pratt, M., and Poli, C., 1994, Topics in feature-based design and manufacturing, in J. Shah, M. Mäntylä, and D. Nau, eds., *Advances in Feature Based Manufacturing*, Elsevier Science Publishers, pp. 481–510.

7

FEATURE MAPPING AND DATA EXCHANGE

In developing a product, many types of design, analysis, planning, and decision-making tools and software are used. Traditionally these tasks are done sequentially. In recent years there has been increasing interest to perform these tasks concurrently in order to cut down the product development time. Regardless of the design process organization, sequential or concurrent, there is a need to share product data between various applications used during the process. A number of standards have been developed for transferring product data, such as IGES and PDES/STEP. These standards specify the format and contents of physical files that are used in exchanging product data. When dealing with features, there is a further complication: viewpoint dependence of features. This implies that feature data needs to be transformed from one viewpoint to another when exchanging product data between two dissimilar applications, such as design and manufacturing. In this chapter we will discuss these two subjects: *feature mapping* and *feature data exchange*.

7.1 FEATURE MAPPING

Feature models are domain dependent: When a part is designed by features, the resulting model is usually not in a form convenient for other applications, such as manufacturing process planning. Indeed, design features are stereotypical shapes related to a part's function, its design intent, or the model construction methodology, whereas manufacturing features are stereotypical shapes that can be made by typical manufacturing operations. These two families of features are genuinely different. To transfer product information from a design-oriented feature model to a manufacturing-oriented model, it is necessary to transform the model from one viewpoint to another. As we saw in Section 3.7, this process is termed *feature mapping*. Now we will examine this subject in a little more depth.

The major difference between feature recognition and feature mapping is in the initial state of the model from which features are derived. In feature recognition, application-specific features must be extracted directly from a geometric model. In feature mapping, application-specific features are recognized from another set of features. In theory, at least, we can say that feature mapping takes place at a higher level because it can take advantage of features that already exist in the original feature model.

The following discussion (Shah 1989) creates a theoretical framework for understanding feature mapping, borrowing concepts of vector spaces from linear algebra. Since features depend upon product type, application, and level of abstraction, we define a *feature space* to be a domain specified by these three attributes. A feature space can be thought of as an *n*-dimensional vector space where *n* is the maximum number of independent vectors in that space which measures its "informational complexity". Individual features can be considered analogous to vectors defined as linear combinations of the basis vectors. Suppose that the totality of information related to every kind of product, in all its aspects, over its entire life cycle, and for all conceivable applications defines a domain called a *feature hyperspace*. Then actual feature spaces for a given product or application are subsets of this high-dimensional hyperspace. These subsets are lower in dimension in that they contain less information. Various kinds of relationships can exist between two subspaces of the same or different dimensions.

Feature spaces of the same dimension may be partially or wholly overlapping or be completely *disjoint*. Overlapping *(conjoint)* regions correspond to features with identical semantics; for example, a through hole has the same meaning on a machined part as on a sheet metal part and can be regarded as a conjoint feature. In regions that do not overlap features are meaningful in only one domain. For example, a blind-hole can be machined, but it has no meaning for a sheet metal product. On the other hand, a joggle can only be formed on thin sheets, but it has no equivalent for machined parts.

Another type of relationship between feature spaces exists when the spaces are of unequal dimensions. In particular, information from a higher-dimensional domain may be selectively abstracted to suit a lower-dimensional domain. This may be referred to as a *projection transformation* from n to $(n - m)$ space. The mapping from n to $(n - m)$ space is unique but the inverse is not. For example, for an electronics designer, a printed circuit board can be a 2D layout drawing, whereas for the packaging designer it is a 3D composite object. A unique mapping from the packaging view to the layout view is possible, and not vice versa.

Yet another relationship is that between *conjugate spaces,* which are those subspaces that contain features composed of different variations of the same elements. These are created when model elements are grouped in different ways to obtain different form features depending upon the user's point of view. For example, the designer may place three rib features on a workpiece, but together these result in two slot features that can be milled or shaped out from a workpiece:

The ribs and slots are therefore complementary features because they are different groupings of the same set of underlying geometric elements. *Adjoint spaces* are created by associating elements in one subspace to certain elements in another subspace. For example, "load" in structural analysis space can be associated with "boundaries" in geometric space.

When two subspaces are fully disjoint there is no transformation available. For conjoint regions of overlapping spaces an identity transformation is used for the subspace formed by intersection. Conjugate transformations require geometric reasoning. Projection transformations are achieved by selective discarding of information (abstraction). Inverse projection transformations are generally not unique.

7.1.1 Mapping Classes

Feature mapping is still a research topic. The types of transformation mechanisms have been identified as discussed above, but methods for implementing general purpose transformations have not yet been found. Therefore the remainder of the treatment of feature mapping in this book is restricted to mapping between spaces of the same dimensionality. Several common situations that arise in transforming feature models between conjugate spaces have been recognized and defined as *mapping classes*. These are enumerated below:

One-to-one mapping. Features such as holes, pockets, slots, and ribs may be similarly defined in two systems, even though the names given might be different. In such cases the feature transformation between the two systems is trivial.

Variant reparametrization. The typical case of this mapping class arises when design features that map directly into process planning features have been parametrized in different ways and positioned using different reference systems than those convenient for process planning. Since design features encode feature shape, size, and position unambiguously, one just needs to write expressions for computing process planning feature parameters from design feature parameters.

Specialization mapping. This case occurs when the levels of specialization of two sets of features are different. For instance, a through-hole design feature may be mapped to several alternative manufacturing features, depending on the diameter and the length of the hole. Hence this is a $1 \rightarrow n$ mapping. The geometry and parametrization of all these may be the same; they only differ in the manufacturing knowledge associated.

Generalization mapping. This case is the inverse of specialization mapping outlined above. That is, several semantically different features are all mapped to a single more abstract entity, by ignoring the differing attribute information. In this sense this is projection mapping.

Discrete aggregation: In this situation m features ($m > 1$) are combined into a single feature. A slotted pocket (see Figure 7.1a) is an example of a feature commonly considered a single feature in process planning, but typically it is represented as several interdependent features in the design model. The examples

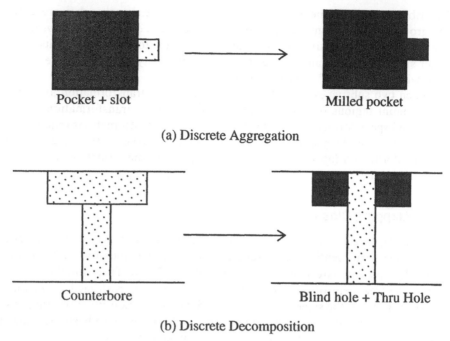

Pocket + slot   Milled pocket

(a) Discrete Aggregation

Counterbore   Blind hole + Thru Hole

(b) Discrete Decomposition

Figure 7.1 Examples of mapping classes

we have looked at indicate that such compounding takes place when there are children features of children features (recess is a child of the hole and slot of the pocket). A universal rule to this effect may be included in the mapping program or in rules that operate on selected feature sets. Once such features are found to exist, it is no problem to combine the features into one because it involves computations similar to that for reparametrization. However, whether such a feature is considered a single unit or not is a process planning decision. For instance, the decision of performing the aggregation of Figure 7.1(*a*) may depend on the dimension of the slot (i.e., it must be large enough for pocket mills).

Discrete decomposition. In this class, one feature is decomposed into *m* features (*m* > 1). In the example of Figure 7.1(*b*) the counter-bored hole is to be manufactured by a sequence of operations for producing the hole, and another sequence of operations to enlarge the bore at the top. Again this type of transformation is dependent on the process planner's decisions.

Conjugate mapping. In this type of mapping, features are broken down into their constituting faces, and the faces are regrouped in such a way that new features are formed from portions of several different features. This is *m* → *n* mapping, that is *m* features produce *n* features, where *m*, *n* > 1. This is the most complex of all mapping classes.

Because the design model is usually built in a different way from how the part is physically manufactured, some of the features needed in manufacturing are missing. Material corresponding to these features needs to be removed from the stock. These features depend upon stock shape, stock size, manufacturing method, and sequence of manufacturing operations. There is nothing inherent in the design model from which such information can be extracted—the process planning decision model (or process planner) must determine these features.

7.1.2 Mapping Techniques

The most commonly encountered problem is the transformation of design features to manufacturing features. Various methods have been proposed for avoiding the mapping problem as mentioned in Chapter 6. For example, one method is to use Destructive Solid Geometry (DSG), where the designer is required to define a part by first instancing the machining stock from which he or she needs to subtract features corresponding to machining operations. Since the part is defined directly in terms of the stock and machining features, there is no mapping required for automated process planning. However, machining features are not suitable for design, nor is the stock shape usually known to the designer before the part is designed. Another way to avoid the mapping problem is to use only the geometric model as the communication between various applications, and to use domain-dependent feature recognition. Unfortunately, geometric models alone cannot support many critical pieces of information, such as tolerances, material attributes, and surface finish. Hence much of the data that could be available in the design features cannot be shared between applications if a geometric model is used as the mediator.

General-purpose methods for feature mapping have not yet matured. In the following sections we review some lines of development that are currently evolving: heuristic methods, mapping with intermediate structures, mapping by cellular decomposition, and graph based methods. These techniques should be viewed as experimental and not prescriptive.

Heuristic Methods A simplistic method to map features between two specific applications is to use pre-specified transformation rules. For example, we could define how the features shown in Figures 7.1(*a*) and (*b*) are to be combined or decomposed, respectively. Unfortunately, such rules are difficult to enumerate *a priori*; they are narrow in scope, they result in combinatorial explosion, and they cannot process user-defined (undocumented) features because of their shallow knowledge.

In the case that a part description in terms of both negative and positive features is available, a feature mapping approach that handles the negative and positive features differently is possible and preferable. For instance, Chamberlain et al. (1993) propose an approach where the designer can express the part model both in terms of negative depression features and positive protrusion features. Those depression features that can be directly mapped to manufacturing features are first identified and handled separately from the rest of the part. The remaining features are converted to a B-rep, which is then used as the input of a special feature recognizer. The recognizer "grows" the B-rep until a workpiece shape (block) is achieved (Wang et al. 1993); this part of the method is heuristic. The resulting workpiece and information on the growing steps needed to create it are used to identify manufacturing features that must be removed from the workpiece. These features are mapped to machining features, and the complete model is created by adding also the non-interacting depressions.

Hsiao investigated the feasibility of design to machining feature mapping for an extensible feature system, which can produce both documented and undocumented features (Hsiao 1990). Documented features are defined as those design features that are known to the application program, while undocumented features are design features of which the application program does not have knowledge. A machining process is represented by its elementary machinable volume, the limitations of tool motions, and size/tolerance limitations. The faces of the elementary volume are classified into the entry face, the exit face, the bottom machining face, and the side machining face. Undocumented features are represented in terms of constraint face sets and a bounding box. The constraint face sets describe the machining faces and any neighboring faces that restrict the accessibility of cutting tools. The bounding box is an indication of the size of the feature to be removed. Each constraint face set of the undocumented feature is evaluated to see if it can satisfy the constraints implied by the elementary machinable volume and the limitations of tool motions of a machining process. The machining process tree is derived from applicable machining processes and precedence relationship between them.

Intermediate-Level Structures Feature mapping, like feature recognition, requires geometric reasoning to find features of interest to a given application. Features in any domain are used to "package" certain topological and geometric relationships and entities that reflect that domain's point of view. When we go from one domain to another, the groupings of entities and the geometric relationships of interest change. The reason that mapping poses a problem is that the relationships of interest in application A are not all available in a model created by application B. For example, consider a fuel tank casing that is created by subtracting a small block from a larger (offset) block. Suppose that we are interested in the thickness of the fuel tank and that this dimension does not exist in the model; that is, the distance between the inner and outer walls of the tank is not explicitly stored. Then, if an application was interested in such a relationship, it would have to derive it by geometric reasoning and/or computations.

Theoretically one can solve the problem by storing the superset of relationships from which all viewpoint models can be derived by selectively extracting and grouping the relationships and entities of interest. Obviously such a super model will be very large and may contain relationships that are not useful in any domain. Instead of embedding all data needed by all applications, we might consider the option of each application inferring all needed relations from a minimal model (geometric model).

Srikantappa and Crawford (1992) have proposed a compromise between these two extremes by use of what was termed "intermediate geometry," a level of

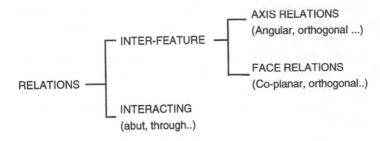

Figure 7.2 Intermediate structures

abstraction that lies between geometry and features, shown in Figure 7.2. Intermediate geometry consists of abstract geometric relationships between feature faces and axes. Although these concepts were developed for mapping design features to GT (group technology) features, the methodology is general purpose. It is assumed that a part is first designed with features; then a processor determines the intermediate geometry, which is passed on to the application, making it easier for the application to find features of interest to it. The existence of features provides a basis for determining the intermediate geometry. First, feature faces (real and virtual) are tagged as bottom, top, and side based on predefined topological conditions. Next, two types of feature relations are determined: inter-feature and interacting. The former are relations between axes and the latter are relations between faces. Feature axes are also determined from predefined geometric conditions, such as an axis is a line joining two opposite end faces of a feature. Interacting relations store the type of intersection between the feature volumes.

A different type of intermediate structure is proposed by (Gadh 1994), who describes a feature modeling environment where the designer can work on the basis of elementary features termed "C-loops," defined as concave or convex loops of edges. C-loops can be used to characterize typical features such as depressions and protrusions. On the basis of a grammar, the geometry created is mapped to a higher-level set of features. An immediately subsequent feature recognition step can reveal further application-specific features. The method is discussed further in Chapter 9.

For some applications, feature mapping can be facilitated by using taxonomical coding scheme as an intermediate structure. This scheme can be interpreted as a kind of projection mapping: Some essential characteristics of the feature are mapped onto the taxonomy code, while the rest of the characteristics are ignored. An example of this method is the feature mapping shell by (Shah et al. 1988); its use for group technology coding was outlined in Chapter 6.

Cell-Based Mapping The general idea behind cellular schemes for mapping is that in conjugate mapping, volumes are combined into different groups to yield features for different applications. Therefore a model that consists of a cellular decomposition, where the cells are solids or voids, can facilitate feature mapping. Cellular decompositions may come directly from the original model or be obtained by various partitioning algorithms.

Cellular or volume decomposition has also been used in feature recognition. There is a fine line that differentiates volume decomposition for feature mapping from that for feature recognition. For one thing, mapping must take advantage of features in the original model. (Current work does not appear to show much evidence in this regard, however.) Another difference is that in feature recognition we need to match portions of the input geometric model to pre-defined features. However, feature mapping in some domains, like machining, can be done without matching to pre-defined shapes. We need only determine which machining operation can remove a given volume; such volumes may have very different geometries and topologies but similar manufacturing characteristics. Volume decomposition methods for feature recognition are reviewed in Chapter 9. Since some proposed algorithms can be used both for feature mapping and for feature recognition, we will outline them here from mapping viewpoint and in Chapter 9 from recognition viewpoint.

Several methods based on volumetric cell decomposition have been proposed for extracting machining features from design features. All these methods involve four major phases:

1. Determine volume to be removed by machining as the raw stock minus the finished part (the unshaded area in Figure 7.3a).
2. Partition each material removal volume into some "elementary" sub-volumes. (In the example of Figure 7.3(b) there are six sub-volumes: 1, 2, and 3 are cylindrical; 4 and 5 are annular; and 6 is a block with a hole.)
3. Combine the elementary volumes into "machinable" features (five sets of combinations are shown in Figure 7.3c).
4. Match machinable features to machining operations on the basis of the above classification.

Step 2 is designed to yield a unique volume decomposition, while step 3 generally results in many alternative sets of machinable features, and this reflects the fact that there usually are many ways of machining a part. The classification of volumes is based on tool accessibility and directions in which the tool is free to move in order to remove the material. Often depression features that can be mapped directly are filtered out from the model before step 1.

Different researchers have proposed different versions of the above four steps. For example, Vandenbrande and Requicha's method (Vandenbrande and Requicha 1993, 1994) is based on the generation and use of "hints" for simple mappings. This method is effective in dealing with the feature interaction problem, namely feature intersections that remove portions of the boundaries of a feature. If a minimal trace of a feature is found, then the faces found are extended into a number of directions to get the largest possible nonintrusive machinable

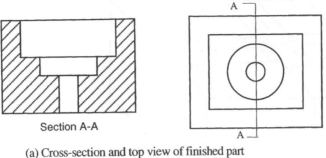

(a) Cross-section and top view of finished part

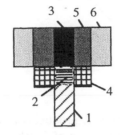

(b) Removal volume decomposed into six sub-volumes

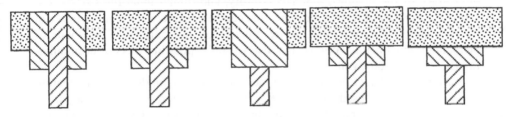

(c) Alternative cell compositions from sub-volumes

Figure 7.3 Example of mapping by volumetric cell decomposition (Shen 1994; reprinted by permission of the author)

volume corresponding to the hint. The portions of the feature that are disconnected due to feature interactions are thus reconnected. Each volume is partitioned into "required" and "optional" components; the latter component is the region shared between several features. The implication of this is that the optional component can be removed by combining it with the volume of other features. Figure 7.4 shows the optional volume for the interacting slots; in this case the optional volume for both features is the same (the shaded region).

Since this method was developed for 2.5-dimensional milling features, volumes were classified into three groups, based on degrees of freedom of the tool:

dof = 1 for plunging

dof = 2 for plunging and sweeping along a trajectory

dof = 2.5 for plunging and multiple sweeping to clear an area

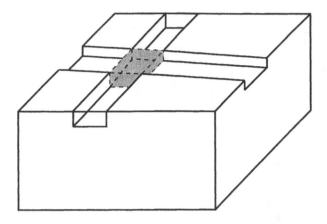

Figure 7.4   Optional volume for interacting features

The feasibility of a machining operation for producing a certain volume is based on four conditions: nonintrusion (no gouging of finished part), presence (minimum trace of the feature), tool accessibility, and dimensional rules (e.g., tool size). The number of feature elements that can be considered as feature hints can be very large. Moreover, the feature hints result not only from the shape of elementary machinable volumes but also from the possible ways of accumulating these elementary volumes.

Karinthi and Nau (1992) approach the same problem on the basis of a feature algebra that can be used to map one feature-based representation of a part to another. They concentrate on feature interactions and formalize operations such as feature truncation and semi-infinite extension on the basis of feature patches, which essentially is a cellular decomposition of interacting features.

Consider, for instance, the part shown in Figure 7.5 defined in terms of subtracting a hole feature $h1$ and two slot features $s1$, $s2$, in that order, from a rectangular solid block of material. Because of the interaction between the hole and the slots, alternative hole features can also be formed, each corresponding to a particular machining sequence of the features. The other interpretations of the hole feature can be formed on the basis of the algebra; in this case, $h2$ is $h1 -^* s1$, where $-^*$ stands for regularized set difference operation of the algebra.

In a further development of this method, Gupta and Nau considered all the part surfaces that needed to be created, and identified manufacturing feature instances capable of creating those surfaces (Gupta et al. 1994). Further they maximized the identified feature (i.e., enlarged the feature, similar to "extending" of features used by Vandenbrande and Requicha) such that the feature volume did not intersect the part. The method can handle a variety of holes and pocket features with accessibility constraints on the features. In our opinion, a limitation common to both of the feature extraction methods described above is that only a predefined set of stereotypical machining features are considered,

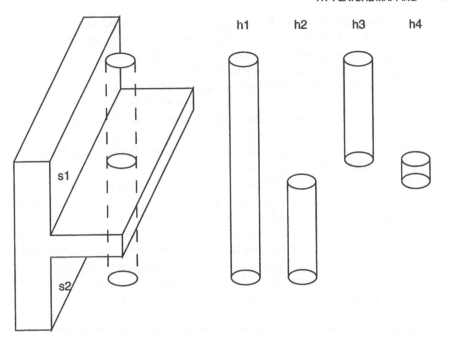

Figure 7.5 Cells corresponding to a hole (Karinthi and Nau 1992; © IEEE, reprinted by permission)

making them unsuitable for dealing with feature modelers that have extensible feature libraries.

Shah et al. (1994) also address the problem of mapping from design features to manufacturing features. In particular, their objective is to generate all possible interpretations of the object in terms of manufacturing features. The chosen approach is to perform manufacturing feature search on the basis of a convex cellular decomposition. This is followed by a geometric reasoning technique essentially based on dimensional reduction along the main axes of cells, computed with the help of a kinematic model of the machine tool.

Since the first step in all volume decomposition methods involves decomposing a part into sub-volumes, or cells, it might occur to the reader that perhaps a cell based design model (e.g., using a cellular nonmanifold solid representation) might provide a better medium for feature mapping. Bidarra and Teixeira (1993) did just that; in their design model cells are present from the very beginning.

Each volumetric feature class is associated with a collection of topological entities (a set of characteristic faces) on its boundary called definitional entities set. Definitional entities have a status attribute that is either positive or negative. Positive definitional entities are part of the model's boundary, whereas negative ones do not belong to that boundary. For example, a slot must have a positive floor and a negative roof in the model. Definitional entities can be disjoint provided that they are all coplanar. A set of semantic constraints are imposed on each definitional entities set. When all constrained definitional entities of a particular feature are non-empty, the feature is semantically complete and therefore valid. Otherwise, it is invalid.

Feature interaction is detected based on feature definitional entities. For example, if a positive wall of a pocket is changed to negative by feature interaction, it is known that the feature interaction transmutes the pocket into a slot. Feature models are represented in a cellular scheme which is a combination of CSG and boundary representation (Gomes and Teixeria 1991). Each feature is represented by either a positive cell or a negative one. Whenever two features interact, the respective cells are further decomposed. Parts of the resulting cells belonging to both features represent the interaction extent, while the remaining cells belong to either feature and carry some morphology of the original features. Because each set of definitional entities and semantic constraints are determined *a priori* for each pre-defined feature, this scheme is unable to handle those feature interactions that result in new features that are not pre-defined. The primary goal of their system is to assist feature editing and feature validation checking under the circumstances of feature interaction and not feature mapping, although the possibility of doing this might be interesting to investigate.

The volume decomposition methods discussed in this section so far do not take much advantage of feature level information. The method for finding complementary features uses feature level information (construction history) to find complementary features. Virtual faces of a feature are faces that have been "lost" as result of Boolean operations. Also included are faces not on the part and faces that are coincident with other feature faces. Feature definitions are used for finding all faces before the Boolean operation. To find the complementary features, virtual faces are first added, redundant faces are discarded, stock faces are then added, and again redundant faces are discarded. The surviving workpiece faces are used to produce complementary features for regions that are not already enclosed by features. In some cases these complementary features need to be decomposed.

An example of the application of this method is shown in Figure 7.6. In (*a*) we see a part's real faces only; it is assumed that the part was built by putting the block $R2$ on top of $R1$, subtracting the pocket $C3$ and the hole from $R2$, and subtracting the bottom pocket from $R1$. In (*b*) we show four virtual faces added: entry and exit faces of the hole, top of the pocket $C3$, and top of the pocket in $R1$. The outer most shell (C) in Figure 7.6(*c*) represents a complementary feature, which may be made in several separate operations; it will then need to be decomposed (discrete decomposition). Also note that in Figure 7.6 the dark shaded area on the left $C2$ (machined step) is a complementary feature, but the dotted area on the right, $C3$ (pocket) is not a complementary feature. Thus complementary features depend not only on the relative volumes of the part and workpiece materials but also on the construction history of the part. If the part had been built by subtracting the step feature $C2$ from a larger block, the step would not be a complementary feature, either. It would, instead, materialize when virtual feature faces are added to the part.

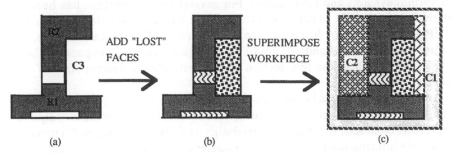

Figure 7.6 Complementary features via virtual faces

Graph-Based Mapping In graph-based geometric models, features are sub-graphs that are isomorphic to stereotypical sub-graphs. These stereotypes are different in different applications. Thus feature mapping on a graph based model involves abandoning one partitioning of a graph in favor of another (or transforming one to the other).

A direct graph transformation approach to feature mapping is presented by Falcidieno et al. (1992). In their method an application-independent neutral feature-oriented model forms the common basis of possibly several different application-dependent models. The primary representation is a hierarchical graph structure called *Shape Feature Object Graph (SFOG)*. The root node of the SFOG corresponds with the main shape of the object, while other nodes represent depressions and protrusions. Arcs between the nodes represent face-face relationships. Each node is linked with a boundary representation in the form of a *Face Adjacency Hypergraph* (FAH).

In the secondary representations, several shapes of the primary representation may be merged together. A T-slot feature is an example of a composite feature with explicit geometric relationship of the constituent objects. Other types include patterns and coaxial holes. A complex object is defined in a structure called "macro-component" that may have its own boundary representation. Components of no particular interest in a secondary representation may be merged with the root object. No explicit algorithms for converting between the primary and the secondary representation have yet been developed; moreover the assumption that the representations share the same exact geometry seems restrictive.

The transformations of the graph required for feature mapping can also be formalized on the basis of graph grammars (Fu et al. 1993). This approach will be discussed in more detail in Chapter 9.

7.2 FEATURE DATA EXCHANGE

Feature-based systems are required to work with other systems and application programs. Therefore it is necessary to be able to exchange feature data between the various systems and applications. For several years now there has been an international effort in developing product data exchange standards under the STEP program. Feature data exchange is included in STEP. Once complete, the feature data exchange standards are likely to have a significant impact on CAD/CAM systems. Therefore this section will investigate the current state of relevant STEP models.

As far as feature data is concerned, there are two distinct purposes the exchange standard could serve: (1) to enable exchange of data between two equivalent feature modelers, for example, two design by feature systems, or (2) to transfer feature information from a feature modeler to a different application. If the purpose is data transfer from design to process planning, then a "snapshot" of the model may suffice. However, exchange between two equivalent modelers must also address how information on the feature behavior, functionality, validation, and so on, is to be exchanged. This will ensure that when a model is transferred from one system to another one, users can continue to modify or add to the model in the second system. The features must have the same meaning in both systems.

We have seen that features consist of parametrized geometry, attributes, and geometric constraints. For data to be exchanged between two systems, there must be considerable similarity between them. In particular, the systems must support the same level of information, same entities, and same semantics; only the representation and implementation can be different. If these conditions are not met, what is meaningful to one system may not mean the same thing or anything at all to another system. Therefore feature-based systems must satisfy the above requirements, or there will be only a partial exchange of data.

7.2.1 Introduction to STEP

STEP (STandard for Exchange of Product data) is a set of evolving international standards, designated as ISO 10303 (ISO is the International Organization for Standardization). STEP includes representation of product data and the mechanisms necessary for the exchange of product data. PDES (Product Data Exchange using STEP) is the U.S. effort, administered through IGES/PDES Organization (IPO), in support of the development and deployment of STEP. Thus PDES and STEP are synonymous.

Each part of the STEP standard needs to go through three major development phases: Draft (CD), Draft International Standard (DIS), and International Standard (IS). STEP consists of many parts, each of which is at different levels of development (CD, DIS, or IS). At the time of writing this book, feature standards were still at the draft level.

In the long run, four levels of data exchange (modes) are envisaged:

1. Physical file transfer
2. Shared memory access exchange

3. Shared database access exchange
4. Knowledge-based data exchange

The first implementation mode involves the use of sequential files of an agreed upon format; this is the only mode currently well developed in STEP and goes by the name of Part 21, the purpose of which is "a clear text encoding of the exchange structure". The difference between modes 2 and 3 is that mode 2 does not have data persistence. Mode 2 is being addressed by SDAI (STEP Data Access Interface), which goes by the designation of Part 22. Mode 1 represents "static" or "snapshot" data exchange, while modes 2 to 4 are dynamic data exchange. The latter are independent of data storage technology.

STEP consists of a set of fundamental principles that apply to all parts, a definition language (EXPRESS), a set of Integrated Resources (IR), and Application Protocols (AP). APs define industry or product-specific data exchange standards, for example, sheet metal die planning and design, design and analysis of composite structures, and electronic printed circuit assembly. Integrated resource models provide the entities needed to service the APs. Examples of IRs are geometry, finite elements, drafting resources, and configuration management. The resource models are not just a collection of independent models; they are formally and structurally integrated. The AIM (Application Interpreted Model) is the implementable portion of an AP. It uses specializations and aggregations of entities in resource models. The same resource entity may be used in very different ways in two APs. For example, a line resource may be used for defining the axis of a feature in one AP, while a line may be used for defining pipes in another AP. APs cannot make extensions to integrated resources; they may, however, add constraints.

EXPRESS is a product description language defined by ISO standard 10303-11. It is in a computer sensible lexical form, but it is not a programming language. Its purpose is to support precise definition of STEP information models. EXPRESS has an object-oriented flavor. It supports definition of schemas, data types, entities, rules, functions, and procedures. It supports multiple inheritance and partial binding of methods to entities. For further information on EXPRESS refer to STEP Part 11 documents and literature (Spiby 1991, Owen 1993, Schenck and Wilson 1994, Sanford 1994). At the time of writing this book, various STEP documents were available electronically using the STEP On-Line Information Service (SOLIS) maintained by NIST. The documents could be fetched by anonymous FTP from the Internet address solis.cme.nist.gov (129.6.32.54), directory /pub/step. Login as anonymous, and give your Internet e-mail address as the password.

STEP documents are organized into parts, referred to as ISO 10303-x, where x is the part number. The coding scheme for part numbers is as follows:

Series 1   Overview of STEP
Series 10   EXPRESS documents (11-EXPRESS, 12-EXPRESS-I)

Series 20   Implementation documents (21-Physical file; 22-SDAI)

Series 30   Conformance documents

Series 40   Generic Integrated Resources documents (42-Geometry and Topology, 47-Tolerances, 48-Form Features, etc.)

Series 100   Application Integrated Resources documents (101-Drafting, 104-FEM, etc.)

Series 200   Application Protocols (207-Sheet metal dies, 210-Electronic PCBs, 224-Features for process planning, etc.)

APs are built using series 40 and series 100 integrated resource models; the difference between generic (series 40) and specific (series 100) integrated resources appears to be arbitrary.

A somewhat parallel effort to STEP is P-LIB, a standard for exchange of parts library data. The standard is given the code ISO 13584; it is also divided into several parts. At the time of writing this book, P-LIB exists only as a rough draft.

It is not possible, nor appropriate, to discuss STEP and EXPRESS in much detail here. We gave a very brief overview above. We will now proceed to discuss the portions of STEP that are relevant to the main subject of this book namely features. At present there are two STEP models, Part 48 and Part 224, that are directly related to features. Part 48 (Dunn 1988, 1992) provides a general purpose form feature data model, while Part 224 (Slovensky 1994) provides form features specific to computer-aided process planning. Part 48 appears to be no longer an "official" part of STEP, while Part 224 is. We give overviews of these two parts of STEP in the following sections.

7.3 ISO10303-48: FORM FEATURES

At the time of writing of this book, Part 48 existed only as a draft (Dunn 1992). It is not clear if and when Part 48 will become an accepted standard. There is also currently an informal initiative to extend STEP to cover parametric and variational geometry. The AP for process planning features (Part 224) overlaps, and even conflicts, with Part 48. It is unclear what impact this will have on feature data exchange standards of the future. Official status notwithstanding, it is worthwhile examining the contents of Part 48 draft proposal because it gives an insight into feature data exchange issues. For further discussion, see (Shah and Mathew 1991).

Part 48 defines a form feature to be a *shape aspect* that conforms to some preconceived pattern or stereotype. A *shape aspect* is defined as a shape or a distinguishable portion of a shape. The specification of a feature consists of a feature name, one or more parameters, and an optional descriptive label. Part 48 deals with feature information at two levels, listed below:

Form feature schema. Consists of generic shape properties, with no application connotations and no specification of representation.

Form feature representation schema. Consists of a variety of representations to model shape properties for use in geometric modeling.

For example, a "depression" and "rectangular cross-section" are the generic shape properties of a rectangular pocket at the form feature schema level. One representation of such a feature is a "rectangular profile" and a "linear sweep." The two schemas can be used independent of each other, even though the representation schema is designed to support the feature schema.

Part 48 is limited to nominal geometry only. Tolerances are addressed in Part 47. Part 48 does not provide a generic model for characterizing a feature, which precludes the ability to model user-defined features. Features are characterized only by form, not by size.

7.3.1 Form Feature Schema

The schema defines *feature types, feature elements, cross-sections,* and miscellaneous other types of information, such as parameter types. Selected parts of the schema are discussed briefly in the following sections.

Feature Types   Part 48 schema supports three types of features: *volume features, transition features,* and *feature patterns,* each of which has several subtypes, as shown in Figure 7.7. A volume feature is an increment or decrement to the volume of a shape, such as a hole or a boss. Attributes of a volume feature are an associated volume and cross-section type (optional). A transition feature separates or blends surfaces, such as fillets or chamfers. A feature pattern is a set of similar features in some regular geometric arrangement.

Volume features, transitions, and patterns are each classified into sub-types, as shown in the Figure 7.7. Below, we give a short description of each of the sub-classes of form features supported in STEP.

Volume Features   Examples of the six sub-types of volume features are shown in Figure 7.8. The formal definitions of the sub-types are:

Protrusion	An additive volume that protrudes from the part and terminates in space rather than on the part
Connector	An additive volume that joins the part in two distinct locations; a connector may join two disconnected volumes or already connected volumes
Stand-alone volume	An additive volume that does not connect previously defined volumes of the part
Passage	A subtractive volume that creates two distinct openings in the part
Depression	A subtractive volume that creates only one opening in the existing volume

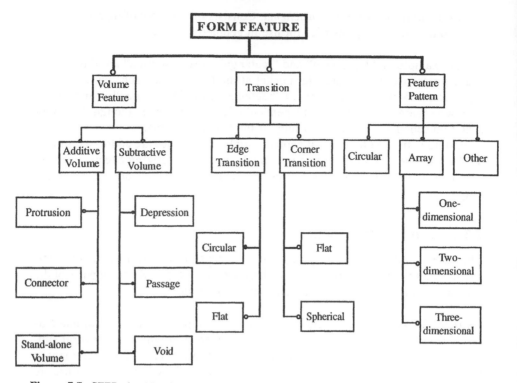

Figure 7.7 STEP classification of form features

Void	A subtractive volume completely enclosed by pre-existing volume

Transitions Examples of the four sub-types of transition features are shown in Figure 7.9. The formal definitions are:

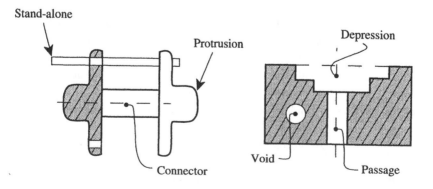

Figure 7.8 Sub-classes of volume features

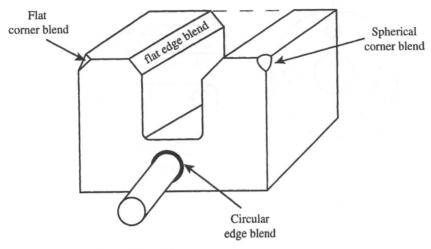

Figure 7.9 Sub-classes of transitions

Circular edge blend	A transition whose surface elements are circular in planes normal to the replaced edge. An optional attribute is the number of non-smooth intersections between this feature and the two surfaces it blends.
Flat edge blend	A transition whose surface consists of elements that are linear in planes normal to the replaced edge.
Flat corner blend	A transition feature that replaces a corner with a flat surface to blend three or more surfaces.
Spherical corner blend	A transition feature that replaces a corner with a spherical surface to blend three or more surfaces.

Patterns   Three examples of feature patterns are shown in Figure 7.10. The formal definitions of the pattern sub-types are:

Circular pattern	A set of features arranged in a circular pattern, such as bolt holes or spline teeth.
Array pattern	A set of features arranged in a one, two, or three-dimensional array.

Feature Elements   *Form feature element* is a volume, face, area, edge, or corner, that is a constituent of a form feature and plays some role related to that feature. In other words, it associates a shape aspect, a form feature, and a textual label specifying the role played by the element with respect to the form feature. For example, a face can be a "bottom" or an "entry" face, etc. *Volume-feature elements, transition-feature elements*, or *feature-pattern elements* are feature elements of volume- and transition-features and feature patterns, respectively.

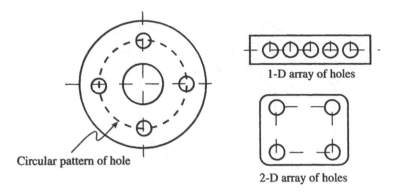

1-D array of holes

2-D array of holes

Circular pattern of hole

Figure 7.10 Feature patterns

Feature elements for feature patterns are its constituent features, referred to as *feature-pattern elements*. Volume- and transition-feature elements are divided into several sub-types, with the hierarchy going multiple levels.

Figure 7.11 shows examples of feature elements. *Volume-feature elements* can be either regions on the pre-existing volume, or those created by the addition/removal of the feature volume from the pre-existing volume. The "end-body-surface" belongs to the former category, while "side," "top," "bottom," and "corner" are in the latter category. Similarly we may have "intermediate-

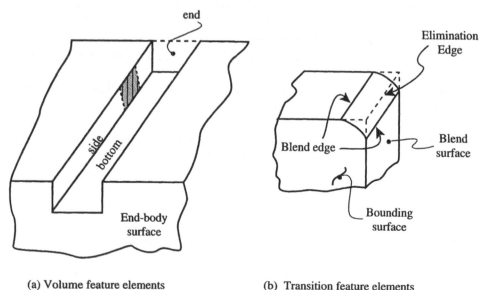

(a) Volume feature elements   (b) Transition feature elements

Figure 7.11 Feature elements

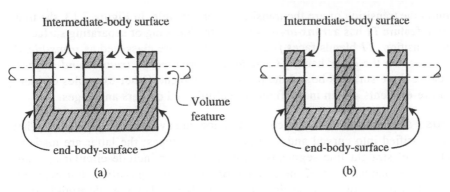

Intermediate-body surface

Volume feature

end-body-surface

(a)

Intermediate-body surface

end-body-surface

(b)

Figure 7.12 Effect of feature bounds

body-surface" to define feature boundaries between the end-body-surfaces. Figure 7.12 shows how end-body-surfaces and intermediate-body-surfaces can be used to control the feature bounds. As can be seen, intersections are performed on the new and pre-existing volume only between the intermediate- or end-body-surfaces. Therefore in (*b*) no intersection is performed with the middle prong because no body-surfaces are specified on it. The end-body-surfaces establish the outer limits of a feature.

Similarly *transition-feature elements* are entities that have certain significance for transition features. Examples of these are shown in Figure 7.13. These elements are further classified by dimensionality (2, 1, 0), and by whether they

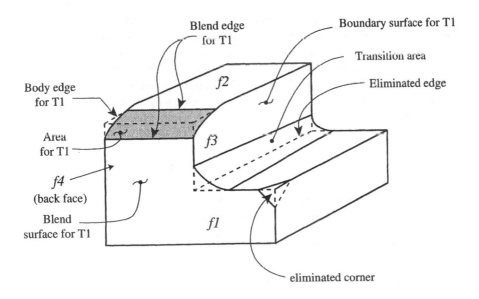

Blend edge for T1

Boundary surface for T1

Transition area

Eliminated edge

Body edge for T1

f2

f3

Area for T1

f4 (back face)

Blend surface for T1

f1

eliminated corner

Figure 7.13 Examples of transition-feature elements

bound the transition or are the transition. For example, in Figure 7.13, the transition feature *T1* has a *trans-area*, which is the blending or separating surface of the transition. *T1* blends faces *f1* and *f2*, so these are classified as *trans-blend-surfaces*. On the other hand, *f3* and *f4* are classified as *trans-bound-surfaces* because these surfaces bound the trans-area element. Other examples of trans-feature-elements shown in the figure are eliminated corners and edges.

Cross-sections A variety of common shapes are available in the schema. They are classified into curved and straight-sided sub-types; the latter are made up entirely of straight line segments, while the former include circular arcs and straight segments. Each of these categories is further classified. For example, curved cross-sections include circular, racetrack, and dome, while straight sided include equilateral triangular, isosceles triangular, square, trapezoidal.

Other Contents of Schema Miscellaneous other types defined in the form feature schema are various parameter types (length and angle measure), parameter value, number of edges in a cross-section, and form feature type name (to identify the type of form feature, e.g., "blind hole"). Another type of interest is *opening-or-join*, which indicates the intersection between volume features and a surface bounding that volume feature. This has, obviously, two sub-types, as shown in Figure 7.14.

7.3.2 Representation Schema

The representation schema supports several representations used in geometric modeling to model shape properties, for specific shape situations. The feature model, which consists entirely of form feature representations, is largely independent of the particular type of geometric modeler used, such as wire frame, boundary representation, or CSG. In fact it is not even necessary to use the form feature model in conjunction with a geometric model at all; there are many applications, such as process planning, where the application program can work directly off of the feature data. When used without a geometric model, the form feature model is an independent shape model; otherwise, it augments the geometric model.

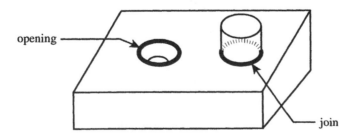

Figure 7.14 Opening or join type

A *form feature representation* is any means of establishing the shape, size, and location of an aspect of the modeled shape. Part 48 representations may be considered to be special purpose, being applicable to a limited class of shape configurations. Some entities from other parts of STEP (Parts 41 and 42 of ISO 10303) are also utilized by Part 48. These include:

Geometric_shape_schema	`solid_model, union, difference`
Topology-schema	`edge, edge_loop, path`
Geometry-schema	`axis_placement, axis1_placement,`
	`axis2_placement, curve, direction,`
	`line, point-on-surface, vector`
Specific_measure_schema	`length_measure, plane_angle_`
	`measure, value_in_degrees`

Figure 7.15 shows the classification of representations used in Part 48. Two basic types of representations are supported: *enumerative* and *implicit*. Enu-

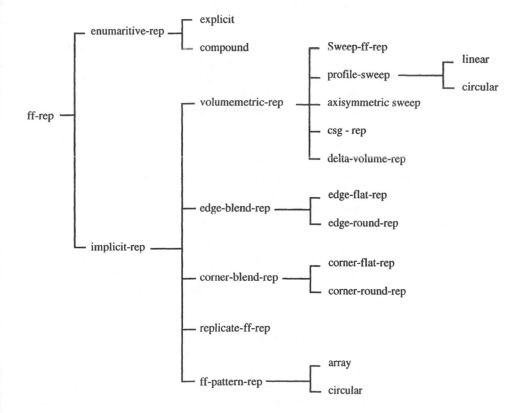

Figure 7.15 Classification of form feature representations

merative representations are lists of constituent elements. They are of two sub-types: *explicit* and *compound*. Explicit representation is a list of geometric entities belonging to the feature. For example, a blind hole may be represented as a list of two faces—a cylindrical face, and a planar face forming the bottom of the hole. Compound representation is a list of constituent features.

Implicit form features model shape information parametrically rather than geometrically. An implicit representation contains sufficient information to allow the evaluation (in boundary representation terminology) of the feature geometry. It is considered to be applied to some pre-existing shape. For example, a hole can be defined as the axisymmetric sweep of a straight line about a specified axis. It is important to note that it is not necessary to do the evaluation in order to use the implicit representation. Implicit representation has five subtypes: *volumetric, edge-blend, corner-blend, replicate-ff,* and *ff-pattern*. We will cover these in the next section.

A feature may have both an explicit representation and an implicit representation. It may also have a number of concurrent implicit representations. The information for supporting explicit features is treated very generally, while implicit features are specific types, divided into several classes according to the effect of the feature on the pre-existing shape.

Implicit Representation An implicit representation consists of the feature's intrinsic shape and its location and orientation with respect to the pre-existing shape. The location of the feature can be defined in several ways. The most versatile way of representing volume-based features is by using a local coordinate system for the feature and positioning it in a known axis system, which is generally the world coordinate system. In some cases a geometric entity can be used to locate the feature. For example, a bend-line can be used to represent the bend deformation feature. Other features such as transition features and area features can be easily located by reference to pre-existing shape elements. For example, a fillet may be located by the surfaces it blends.

Usually there are many alternative ways for parametrizing an implicit feature. The standard supports a maximal, rather than minimal, set of parameters for each feature, that is, all useful dimensional parameters are set as a feature's attributes. Both full measures (like diameter) and half measures (like radius) may be used. Rules are then included in the feature's definition to specify the number of parameters that must be present to prevent under- and over-dimensioning.

Because implicit features are applied to a pre-existing shape, it is necessary to specify, directly or indirectly, the sequence in which evaluation should take place. For example, if we want to put a hole in a block by subtracting a cylinder, the block must exist first. If we want to chamfer a pocket, the pocket must be evaluated before the chamfer can be applied. The precedence can be established indirectly because of references to geometry or features that are specified in the definitions (as bounds, or for locating, etc.). If this is not the case, the standard provides the capability for direct definition of precedence.

Since implicit features are not evaluated, it is not possible to refer to their constituent geometry elements directly. However, the standard provides mechanisms by which one can reference the geometry elements indirectly. For example, the sweep profile used in volumetric definition can be referenced indirectly.

Volumetric Representation   Volumetric representation is a sub-type of implicit feature representation. Volumes may be represented as CSG trees, or stand alone delta volumes, or various kinds of sweeps, as shown in Figure 7.15. *CSG representation* is annotation of Boolean operators of a CSG tree to identify the feature created at that node. An example of a CSG representation is shown in Figure 7.16. Note the annotations "boss" and "hole" at the nodes that contain the operators that result in the creation of the respective features. *Delta volume* representation contains three components: a solid model, axis placement, and Boolean operation.

Volumes represented as sweeps may be of three alternative types: *sweep-ffrep* (planar curve sweeping along a curve), *profile-sweep* (planar profile swept along a curve), and *axisymmetric-sweep* (a planar curve swept 360 degrees about a coplanar axis).

A profile-sweep can be linear or circular, depending on whether the sweep path is a straight line or a circular arc. Additionally a profile-sweep can be an *along-sweep* or *in-out-sweep*. The former has a sweep path roughly along the pre-existing shape, while the latter has a sweep path that either plunges into or protrudes out of a pre-existing shape. Examples of along-sweeps are gears, splines, and threads; examples of in-out-sweeps are pockets, bosses, and holes. Yet another characteristic of profile-sweep that is supported is the variation of the profile along the swept path: straight (constant profile), tapered (uniform scaling), or contoured (non-uniform scaling). For circular sweeps we also need to encode whether it is complete (full circle) or partial. For partial circular profile-sweeps and linear sweeps, we also need to specify the end condition: flat or rounded. Also profile-sweeps can have optional initial, intermediate, and terminal bounds.

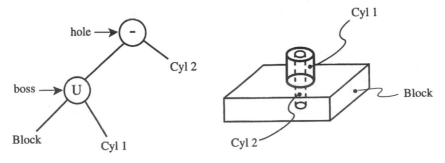

Figure 7.16   CSG representation

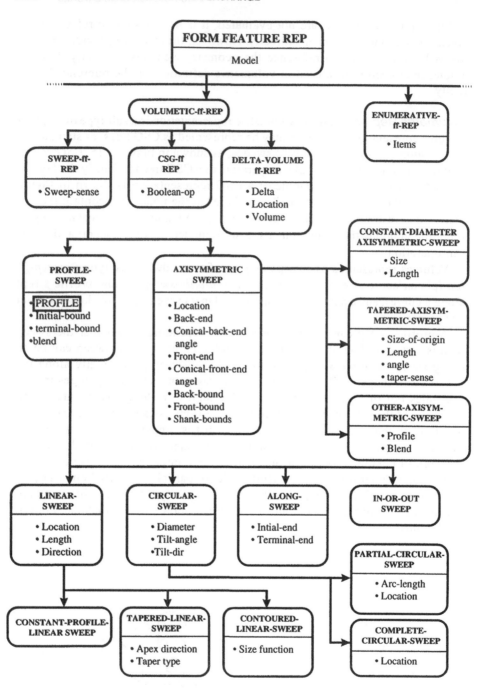

Figure 7.17 Specification of swept volumes (courtesy of M. Rogers)

To specify a profile-sweep, we need to specify:

1. *Sweep-profile*. The geometry of the profile to be swept (the standard provides a large variety of closed and open profiles, e.g., square, vee, and tee).
2. *Sweep-profile-blends*. A modification of profiles to provide flat or rounded blending at the corners.
3. *Sweep path*. The many alternative ways shown in Figure 7.18.
4. Optional attributes, such as end conditions and feature bounds.

Axisymmetric-sweeps are straight if the generating curve is parallel to the axis, and tapered if it is inclined. Figure 7.17 shows the parameters needed for specifying some of the swept type of volumes. A pocket can be represented as a rectangular profile swept along a linear path. The fillet between the pocket walls and the bottom face of the pocket can be modeled by an end blend condition.

Blend Representation Referring back to Figure 7.15, we see that there are two types of blending representations, *edge-blend-rep* and *corner-blend-rep*. These terms refer obviously to blend surfaces and edges, respectively. For both edge and corner blends two types of blends are supported: flat and round. Specification of edge-blend-rep requires the identification of the two surfaces whose intersection is to be blended (or the curve of intersection) and the dimension parameters shown in Figure 7.19. Corner blends are specified along the same lines.

Replicate-ff and ff-pattern Representation *Replicate-ff-rep* specifies a feature that is the same in all respects to another feature, except location. A replicate feature is defined by declaring it to be identical to another feature and then specifying the location where it is replicated. A special case of replicate-ff is a *reflection feature*, which is mirrored across some reflection plane.

A ff-pattern-rep is a replication of a feature in a geometric pattern such as a circular or an array pattern. Arrays may be either parametric or parallel. A parametric array is placed on a parametric surface at fixed Δu and Δv spacing. To specify a parallel array, such as the pattern of holes shown in Figure 7.20, we need to specify the base feature (which is replicated), number of rows and columns, row and column spacing, and row and column vectors. Circular patterns are represented by a center line, number of members, and angular spacing between adjacent members.

7.3.3 Final Remarks

Using Part 48, it is possible to describe the same part in terms of different sets of features, so no feature decomposition is forced upon the user. It is not necessary to have a complete part model in terms of features. It is not necessary to have any underlying geometric model. It is possible to express the same feature by many alternative representations. Indeed, multiple representations can pose serious

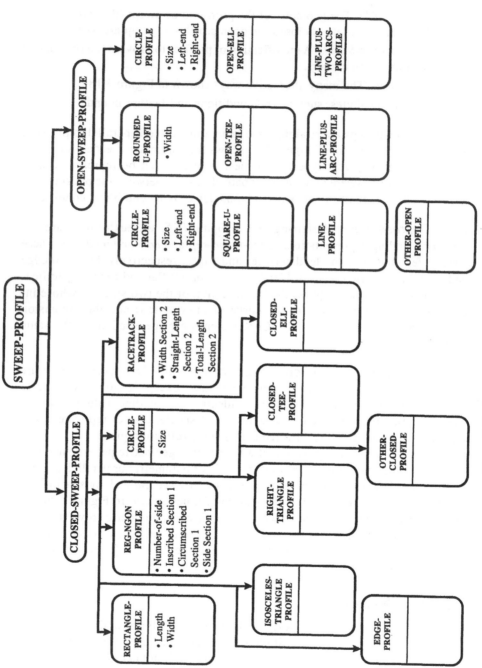

Figure 7.18 Feature sweep paths and profiles (courtesy of M. Rogers)

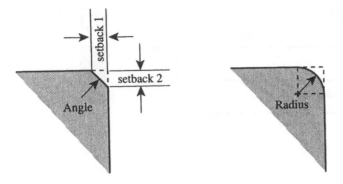

Figure 7.19 Edge-blend representation

data exchange problems. It is possible to have overlapping features (two features partially or fully using the same geometric entities).

In this overview of Part 48 draft proposal, we have concentrated only on some selected feature types. We have intentionally left out many details. It was not our intent to provide a comprehensive coverage, just to give a sense of what the draft standard is about. The reader should refer to the documents cited in the references (or later versions that may have appeared since the writing of this chapter available via SOLIS). Once again, we point out that Part 48 has yet to be accepted as an international standard. Despite its uncertain future, Part 48 provides an insight into the structure and contents of feature models, independent of domain and modeler type.

7.3.4 Case Study: STEP-Part 48 Representation

In this section we look at an example of generating a physical file representation of a part's features, using Part 48 information model. The example part is shown

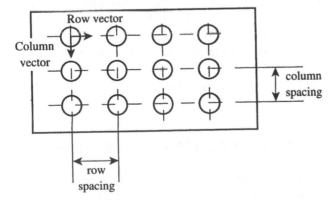

Figure 7.20 Parallel array pattern of holes

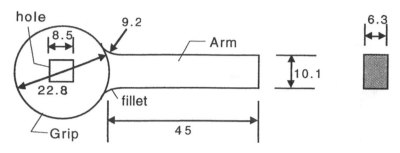

Figure 7.21 Sample part

in Figure 7.21. There are of course alternative feature decompositions of this part. We will consider the part to be made up of five features: a cylindrical grip, a square hole, a rectangular cross-sectional arm, and two fillets, as shown. The first three are volumetric features, while the fillets are transition features. All of the volumetric features in this case study can be represented as constant profile linear sweeps.

The physical file for this part, in EXPRESS, is given in Table 7.1 (Rogers 1994). The English-like syntax makes it easy to read, even if one is not familiar with EXPRESS. The order that must be followed in this file requires that any entity that is referenced by another entity must be defined before it is referenced. Therefore the dimension values are defined first, then their types, then the profiles, axes, and geometric model elements. The number preceded by the @ sign is the identifier for the entity defined on that line. One might find it easier to read this file in reverse order.

Line @32, the last line in the file (Table 7.1), defines the part in terms of its five features. The five features identified by lines @26 through @30 are grip, arm, square hole, and the two fillets, respectively. One can look at the definition of each of these features by locating the respective identifier in the file. For example, @26 is the cylindrical grip, which is a positive volume, defined by a constant profile linear sweep, which uses the circle profile @13, and the sweep length @6 (referred to by @12). The arm is similarly defined. The square hole @28 is defined as a negative (subtraction) volume. To understand how the fillets are defined, refer to Figure 7.13. It can be seen that to define an edge blend, one needs to define the elements: the two surfaces being blended, the removed edge, and the fillet radius. The comments in the file (enclosed by /* ... */) should make it easy for the reader to decipher the descriptions.

7.4 ISO10303-224: PRODUCT DEFINITION FOR PROCESS PLANNING

Part 224 is an Application Protocol developed for mechanical product definition for computerized process planning using form features. Part 224 and Part 48

Table 7.1 Part 48 physical file for sample part

```
STEP;
HEADER;
...
ENDSEC;

DATA;
...
/* The comment structure from C will be used */

/* In this example, we will use the
form_feature_representation_ schema (not the
form_features_schema). The necessary references to other
schemas are noted. Unless otherwise specified, an entity is
from the form_feature_representation_schema */

/* DEFINE THE LENGTHS */

/* length_measure entities from the specific_measures_schema
(Part 41) */

@1 = LENGTH_MEASURE(22.8, 'MM');                /* units are mm */
@2 = LENGTH_MEASURE(45.0, 'MM');
@3 = LENGTH_MEASURE(10.1, 'MM');
@4 = LENGTH_MEASURE(8.5, 'MM');
@5 = LENGTH_MEASURE(9.2, 'MM');
@6 = LENGTH_MEASURE(6.3, 'MM');

/* ff_rep_length_parameter entities */

@7 = FF_REP_LENGTH_PARAMETER(@1, 'FULL');   /* full indicates
                                               a diameter */
@8 = FF_REP_LENGTH_PARAMETER(@2, 'FULL');
@9 = FF_REP_LENGTH_PARAMETER(@3, 'FULL');
@10 = FF_REP_LENGTH_PARAMETER(@4, 'FULL');
@11 = FF_REP_LENGTH_PARAMETER(@5, 'HALF');   /* half indicates
                                                a radius */
@12 = FF_REP_LENGTH_PARAMETER(@6, 'FULL');

/* PROFILES */

/* subtypes of sweep_profile */
/* sample entity:
     circle_profile (users, size); */
@13 = CIRCLE_PROFILE((@26),@7);          /* the circle profile */
@14 = RECTANGLE_PROFILE((@27), @8, @9);   /* the arm profile */
@15 = RECTANGLE_PROFILE((@28), @10, @10); /* the square hole */
```

```
/* AXES */

/* axis2_placement from the geometry_schema */
@16 = AXIS2_PLACEMENT(...);
@17 = AXIS2_PLACEMENT(...);

/* REFERENCE GEOMETRIC SHAPE MODEL */

/* This reference is to a geometric_representation_item (from
Part 43, but sub-typed in other parts). */
@18 = GEOMETRIC_shape_model(...);

/* Some of the sweeps reference a geometric_representation_
items. For example, it might be used to reference the pre-
existing surface (initial_bound) for a linear sweep. */
@19 = REP_GROUP(a surface in the geometric_shape_model - the
top of the grip);
@20 = REP_GROUP(a surface in the geometric_shape_model - the
bottom of the grip);
@21 = REP_GROUP(a surface in the geometric_shape_model - the
outside of the grip);
@22 = REP_GROUP(a surface in the geometric_shape_model - the
left side of the arm);
@23 = REP_GROUP(a surface in the geometric_shape_model - the
right side of the arm);
@24 = REP_GROUP(a surface in the geometric_shape_model - the
left blend edge of the arm);
@25 = REP_GROUP(a surface in the geometric_shape_model - the
right blend edge of the arm);

/* VOLUME FEATURE REPS */

/* subtypes of volumetric_ff_rep */
/* sample entity:
    constant_profile_linear_sweep (model, sweep_sense,
profile, initial_bound, terminal_bound, interrupts, blend,
location, length, direction); */
/* the grip */
@26 = CONSTANT_PROFILE_LINEAR_SWEEP(@18, 'ADD', @13, NULL,
NULL, NULL, NULL, @16, @12, 'PLUS');

/* the arm */
@27 = CONSTANT_PROFILE_LINEAR_SWEEP(@18, 'ADD', @14, NULL,
NULL,
NULL, NULL, NULL, @17, @12, 'PLUS');

/* square hole */
@28 = CONSTANT_PROFILE_LINEAR_SWEEP(@18, 'SUBTRACT', @15, @19,
@20, NULL, NULL, @16, @12, 'PLUS');
```

```
/* FILLETS */

/* subtype of edge_blend_rep from form_feature_representation_
schema */
/* sample entity:
      edge_round_rep (surface1, surface1, edge, radius); */
@29 = EDGE_ROUND_REP(@21, @22, @24, @11);
@30 = EDGE_ROUND_REP(@21, @23, @25, @11);

/* ff_precedence: the square hole references the surfaces of
the grip, so the grip must exist first. The rules say if a
reference exists to a form_feature_rep, the precedence is
implicit. But here, the reference is to the surface that is
part of a form_feature_rep, not the entire ff_rep, so we'll
make the precedence explicit. */
@31 = FF_REP_PRECEDENCE(@26, @28);

/* THE FEATURE MODEL */

/* The easiest way to read this file is to begin here, and
read up - i.e., the feature_model is comprised of entities 26,
27, 28, 29, and 30 */
@32 = FEATURE_MODEL(@26,@27,@28,@29,@30);
```

Source: (Rogers 1994; by permission of the author)

differ in many aspects due to the difference in the function they are designed for. First of all, Part 224 is an AP for a specific application (process planning), while Part 48 is a Generic Resource, which must provide domain-independent definition of features. Second, Part 224 is limited in scope to features produced by turning and milling processes. Third, in Part 48 no unique representation of features is prescribed, while in Part 224 common features, such as slots, pockets, holes, fillets and grooves, are parametrized in a unique way. Fourth, Part 48 deals with nominal shape only, while Part 224 includes tolerances, material and surface properties, and administrative and production control data. The terminology is also not consistent between the two parts.

We will discuss some selected aspects of Part 224. Figure 7.22 shows the major portion of feature classes defined in Part 224. A manufacturing feature is defined as product information needed in automated process planning. There are three categories of manufacturing features: *transition, replicate*, and *machining features*. A machining feature is defined as a shape that represents volumes to be removed by machining. However, a boss is treated as a machining feature too. Therefore the above definition is not strictly true. A transition feature specifies a transition area between two surfaces; it differs from machining features in that no orientation for placement is needed. A replicate feature is

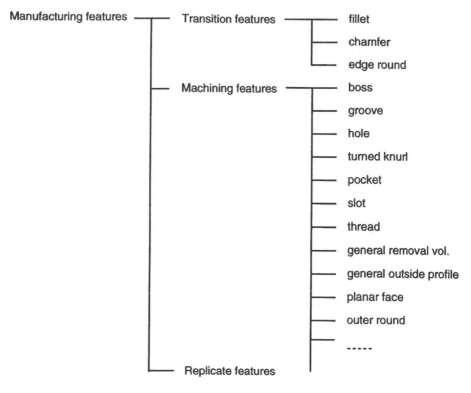

Figure 7.22   Feature classification in Part 224 (partial)

specified by a base feature and the geometric arrangement for copies of the base feature.

Machining features are defined in terms of *application objects*, which include feature type definition (boss, hole, etc.), profile, bottom/top/end conditions (open, radiused, etc.), location/orientation, dimensions, and tolerances. All ANSI Y14.5M tolerance classes are supported, in the manner specified by the standard (see Chapter 5). Holes are defined by orientation element, end condition (through, blind; flat, radiused, or "pointed", if blind), diameter, diameter taper, diameter tolerance, and other tolerances. Another example is that of slots; they are specified by end conditions open, radiused, flat end, and Woodruff. The slot shape is defined by an open profile and a (sweep) path.

Transition features apply only to edges, unlike Part 48. *Fillets* are blends applied to concave edges. *Chamfers* and *edge-rounds* are applied to convex edges, the difference between the two is that a chamfer is flat, while edge-round is curved. A look at Figure 7.9 will reveal that Part 224 supports only a subset of the transition elements in Part 48.

Replicate features can be in circular or rectangular patterns, similar to array patterns of Part 48. However, Part 224 provides some special cases of pattern

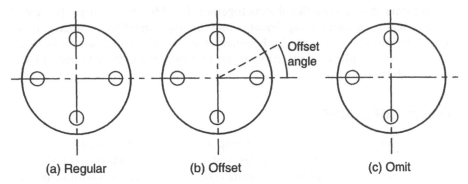

(a) Regular   (b) Offset   (c) Omit

Figure 7.23 Pattern deviations

deviations as well. These include *circular/rectangular offset*, and *circular/rect-angular omit patterns*. In the former, an additional replication of the base feature is made at a given offset from one of the features in the pattern, as shown in Figure 7.23(*b*). The other case involves omitting one of the replications (Figure 7.23*c*). In addition another deviation from the pattern is when each of the features is rotated about its own axes.

Composite features are defined as a union of one or more features in a specified sequence. For example, a counterbored hole consists of two holes, one of which is always blind bottomed, while the other can be through or blind. As in Part 48, Part 224 contains some common 2D profiles, open and closed. Examples are tee, vee, *n*-gon, circular, and rectangular.

Another entity unique to 224 is a *general removal volume*, which is an enclosed volume of arbitrary shape that needs to be removed from the part. Similarly, for turned parts, a *general outside profile* is provided. Apparently the usefulness of these general shapes is in the event that shapes cannot be represented by other operations. Examples of these are shown in Figure 7.24. Another specific machining need is fulfilled by features *catalog knurl* and *catalog thread*, which can be specified by reference to a document containing information on how to create the knurl or thread.

Application assertions specify the relationship between application objects, the cardinality of the relationships and the rules required for validity. These are

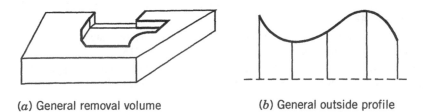

(*a*) General removal volume   (*b*) General outside profile

Figure 7.24 General features

the elements that bind all the objects together. In addition to being represented parametrically, manufacturing features may be augmented by geometric/topological definitions, which can be boundary models. The object *shape to B-rep shape rep* is an application assertion object that can bind a shape to one or more B-rep models.

REVIEW QUESTIONS

7.1 Consider a case of feature mapping where a model defined in terms of generic machining features (holes, slots, pockets, etc.) must be transformed to a model of more specific features (holes, slots, pockets with some particular dimensions and tolerances, etc.). What is the mapping class of this mapping?

7.2 Study the object in Figure 3.4. Code the feature relations between its features using the intermediate geometry scheme of (Srikantappa and Crawford 1992).

7.3 Study the part in Figure 6.1. Apply the idea of the Vandenbrande and Requicha's method (1993) to recognize the "required" and "optional" components of each feature of the part (see Figure 7.4). Using these, can you extract machining features not explicitly present in the original model?

7.4 Compare the scope and limitations of each of the mapping techniques described in Section 7.1.2. It will be useful if you keep in mind some context, such as design to machining feature mapping or machining to inspection feature mapping.

7.5 Describe (a) blind hole with conical bottom (b) keyway slot (c) relief with a corner blend using the STEP form feature schema concepts described in Section 7.3.2.

7.6 Describe the conrod features shown in Figures 5.7 and 5.8 in terms of STEP Part 48 representation schema.

BIBLIOGRAPHY

Feature Mapping

Bidarra, R., and Teixeria, J. C., 1993, Intelligent form feature interaction management in cellular modeling scheme, in J. Rossignac, J. Turner, and G. Allen, eds., *Proc. of Second ACM Symp. on Solid Modeling and Applications*, Montreal, 19–21 May, ACM Press, pp. 483–485.

Chamberlain, M. A., Joneja, A., and Chang, T.-C., 1993, Protrusion-features handling in design and manufacturing planning, *Computer-Aided Design* **25** (1): 19–28.

Falcidieno, B., Giannini, F., Porzia, C., and Spagnuolo, M., 1992, A uniform approach to represent features in different application contexts, *Computers in Industry* **19** (1992): 175–184.

Fu, Z., de Pennington, A., and Saia, A., 1993, Graph grammar approach to feature representation and transformation, *Int. J. of Comp. Integrated Manufacturing* **6** (1 & 2): 137–151.

Gadh, R., 1994, Feature mapping and recognition in geometric design generation, in J. J. Shah, M. Mäntylä, and D. Nau, eds., *Advances in Feature Based Manufacturing*, Elsevier Science Publishers, pp. 107–128.

Gomes, A. J., and Teixeria, J. C., 1991, Form feature modeling in a hybrid CSG/B-rep scheme, *Comp. & Gr.* **15** (2): 217–229.

Gupta, S. K., Nau, D. S., Regli, W. C., and Zhang, G., 1994, A methodology for systematic creation and evaluation of alternative operation plans, in J. J. Shah, M. Mäntylä, and D. Nau, eds., *Advances in Feature Based Manufacturing*, Elsevier Science Publishers, pp. 161–184.

Hsiao, D., 1990, Feature mapping and manufacturability evaluation, Ph.D. dissertation, Department of Mechanical Engineering, Arizona State University.

Karinthi, R., and Nau, D. S., 1992, An algebraic approach to feature interactions, *IEEE Trans. on Pattern Analysis and Machine Intelligence* **14** (4): 469–484.

Kramer, T. R., 1992, *A Library of Material Removal Shape Element Volumes (MRSEVs)*, Research Report NISTIR 4809, National Institute of Science and Technology, Gaithersburg, MD 29899.

Shah, J. J., 1989, Feature transformations between application specific feature spaces, *Computer Aided Engineering J.* **5** (6): 247–255

Shah, J. J., Bhatnagar, A., and Hsiao, D., 1988, Feature mapping and application shell, *ASME Computers in Engineering Conf.*, San Francisco, CA, July 31–August 4, ASME Press, pp. 489–495.

Shah, J. J., Shen, Y., and Shirur, A., 1994, Determination of machining volumes from extensible sets of design features, in J. J. Shah, M. Mäntylä, and D. Nau, *Advances in Feature Based Manufacturing*, Elsevier Science Publishers, pp. 129–157.

Shen, Y., 1994, Design to manufacturing feature mapping based on volume decomposition using half space partitioning, Ph.D. dissertation, Department of Mechanical Engineering, Arizona State University.

Srikantappa, A. B., and Crawford, R. H., 1992, Intermediate geometric and interfeature relationships for automatic GT part coding, *ASME Computers in Engineering Conf.*, San Francisco, ASME Press.

Vandenbrande, J. H., and Requicha, A. A. G., 1993, Spatial reasoning for the automatic recognition of machinable features in solid models, *IEEE Trans. on Pattern Analysis and Machine Intelligence* **15** (12): 1269–1285.

Vandenbrande, J. H., and Requicha, A. A. G., 1994, Geometric computation for the recognition of spatially interacting machining features, in J. J. Shah, M. Mäntylä, and D. Nau, eds., *Advances in Feature Based Manufacturing*, Elsevier Science Publishers, pp. 83–106.

Wang, M.-T., Chamberlain, M. A., Joneja, A., and Chang, T.-C., 1993, Manufacturing feature extraction and machined volume decomposition in a computer-integrated feature-based design and manufacturing planning environment, *Computers in Industry* **23**: 75–86.

Feature Standards

Dunn, M., 1988, *PDES Form Feature Information Model (FFIM)*, PDES Form Features Group.

Dunn, M., ed., 1992, *Industrial Automation Systems and Integration—Product Data Representation and Exchange—Part 48: Integrated Generic Resources: Form Features,* second edition, ISO/WD 10303-48.

Owen, J., 1993, *STEP—An Introduction,* Information Geometers Ltd., 47 Stockers Avenue, Winchester, England.

Rogers, M., 1994, Case study of feature representation in STEP, Part 48, Tech. Report, Design Automation Laboratory, Department of Mechanical Engineering, Arizona State University.

Sanford, D., 1994, *Introduction to STEP,* Workshop notes, ISO-STEP meeting, Mesa, AZ.

Schenck, D., and Wilson, P., 1994, *Information Modeling: The EXPRESS Way,* Oxford University Press.

Shah, J. J., and Mathew, A., 1991, An experimental investigation of the STEP form feature information model, *Computer-Aided Design* **23** (4): 282–296.

Slovensky, L., ed., 1994, *Industrial Automation Systems and Integration—Product Data Representation and Exchange—Part 224: Application Protocols: Mechanical Product Definition for Process Planning using Form Features,* working draft, ISO TC184/SC4/WG3_N333.

Spiby, P., 1991, *EXPRESS Language Reference Manual,* Document 14, ISO TC184/SC4/WG5.

IV

DESIGN AND IMPLEMENTATION

The chapters in this part focus on the major software techniques and components for implementing feature based systems. Tools and techniques for design-by-features systems are the topic of Chapter 8. The chapter investigates the main architectural approaches to design by features, including procedural and declarative approaches, and also takes an in-depth look at other related areas such as representation of constraints. Feature recognition and extraction techniques based on various kinds of geometric models are investigated in Chapter 9. Chapter 10 discusses a collection of software tools that are important for implementing feature-based systems, including tools for feature representation, geometric modeling, constraint management, and feature recognition. Application of features to process planning of machining operations is a major application of feature models, an application where the current state of the art of features can be said to be the most advanced. Therefore Chapter 11 is completely devoted to this topic.

8

DESIGN-BY-FEATURES
TECHNIQUES

When geometric model information is available either from ordinary CAD systems, or in neutral CAD data formats such as IGES or STEP, feature recognition may be the only attractive and possible method of creating features needed in manufacturing applications. On the other hand, designers might also want to take advantage of the improved environment created by features by constructing the part model directly in terms of its constituent features, and create a geometric model of the part (if needed at all) on the basis of the features. This approach is termed *design by features,* although the approach may be of interest also in other applications besides design.

Design by features was already discussed briefly in Chapters 4 and 5 from the user's perspective. This chapter will take a closer look at the basic issues of designing a design-by-features system from the developer's perspective by exploring the available approaches and techniques to system construction. First, we will study the main issues related to the overall software architecture of a design-by-features system. This will be followed by a detailed discussion on two main approaches to representing generic feature class information for design-by-features systems: the procedural approach and the declarative approach. The remaining sections discuss various other specific techniques for implementing a design environment on the basis of features; in most cases the techniques will be illustrated with the help of case studies of representative systems giving a better feel for the issues and their solutions.

8.1 ARCHITECTURAL FRAMEWORK

Before attempting to design and implement a complex piece of software such as a design-by-features system, it is vital to understand the issues and possible solutions related to its design. Besides the system designer, such knowledge is also useful to the advanced user, who must be capable of specifying the characteristics of a desired system for a developer or a supplier.

This section will look at the range of architectural alternatives of design-by-features systems by identifying a number of important system characteristics and studying the range of approaches for addressing the chosen characteristics. This will result in an architectural framework for classifying design-by-features systems in terms of certain fundamental design decisions that influence the overall system performance. Important characteristics to be studied are as follows:

- *Representation of feature definitions.* A design-by-features system is based on generic feature class definitions that are instantiated to create individual feature instances. The choice of a representation for feature definitions is the most significant design decision the implementer of a design-by-features system must face.

- *Level of support of user-defined features.* As noted in Chapter 3, no "complete" set of features can be defined. To support applications of features, some level of support of user-defined features is therefore usually desired. This characteristic ranges from "none" to "full" as explained later in this chapter.

- *Type of the linkage with a geometric modeling system.* Even though it may not be directly visible to the user, the type of the linkage of a design-by-features system with a geometry system determines to a great extent the capability of a system developer to support the desired system characteristics. This characteristic ranges from "static, one-way" to "dynamic, two-way." It is also possible to have no underlying geometric modeler at all.

- *Application context.* Not all design-by-features systems are intended for design applications proper; the application context may also be feature creation for analysis or manufacturing. Also the desired properties of a design-by-features system for innovative design may differ considerably from routine design.

- *Support for feature validation.* A critical property of any design-by-features system is the quality of the model produced. It is highly desirable that features be validated before they are placed into the model. The characteristic ranges from "none" to "full."

It appears that the functionality possible in a design-by-features system are mainly determined by the first three characteristics above. Therefore, we will treat the representation of feature definitions, the level of support of user-defined features, and the type of geometry system linkage as the major architectural dimensions of design-by-features systems and will discuss the other characteristics while exploring these three.

The three major architectural dimensions are by no means independent, even though we choose to discuss them separately. Instead, they are related to each other in interesting and important ways. It is precisely these interdependencies that a software engineer designing a design-by-features system, or a designer specifying desired characteristics of one, needs to understand in order to create a realizable and balanced end result.

8.1.1 Representation of Feature Definitions

The characteristic that sets design-by-features systems apart from other feature creation methods is that design-by-features systems are based on generic *feature definitions* that are used as templates for creating individual features. The existence of explicit feature definitions makes design by features the most general feature creation method: as long as a feature definition can be created for a feature, it can be used in design. This is in contrast to feature recognition, which is necessarily limited to those kinds of features that can be effectively recognized.

Feature definitions need to store several types of information. To serve as templates for feature instances, they must specify the attributes to be placed in instances, how the values of the attributes are determined (on the basis of user's input or other attributes), and the range of permissible attribute values. In particular, feature definitions must specify the feature instance geometry and how it is constructed on the basis of values of other attributes. A feature-based model of a part is created by organizing the feature instances in a suitable data structure encoding the required feature relationships; feature definitions must cater for these as well. A geometric model of the part is created by combining the feature instance geometries.

As one might expect, representation of feature definitions has fundamental significance to the overall architecture and performance of a design-by-features system. Two main issues related to feature definitions are outlined below; later sections of this chapter will discuss these in greater depth.

Procedural versus Declarative Feature Definition As already outlined in Chapter 4, we can choose between two approaches to feature definition representation:

- *Procedural feature definition.* Feature definitions are encoded in a procedural language that combines the definition of feature properties and relationships among the properties with procedures for computing the properties and relationships.
- *Declarative feature definition.* Feature definitions are encoded in a nonprocedural language where the declaration of properties and their relationships is decoupled from the computation of the same. Rules and constraints are two important methods for declarative feature definition.

In its simplest form a procedural feature definition consists of a collection of related procedures, coded in a programming language such as C, for the computation of dependent feature attributes, relationships, and geometry on the basis of independent attributes given by the user. If an object-oriented language such as C++ is used, the various procedures can be collected as methods related to a class definition of the feature. We will introduce methods for the procedural approach in Section 8.2.

A declarative feature definition consists of a collection of related declarations, coded as constraint specifications, rules, or predicate logic, specifying the desired dependencies between feature attributes, relationships, and geometry. The actual method for satisfying the declarations is operationally decoupled from the feature definitions. For rule-based declarations, an inference engine may be used; for constraints, a constraint satisfaction algorithm; for predicate logic, a unification algorithm. As a result, compared to the procedural method, more modularity is achieved by the separation of feature definitions and feature representations and a more flexible design environment can potentially be realized. Another advantage is that declarative definitions may more readily be transferred from one feature-based system to another. These benefits are balanced by more complex software architecture and potential overheads incurred by it. Declarative techniques are discussed more extensively in Section 8.3.

The two approaches can also be combined. In fact they should be seen as the extreme points of a continuum of alternative approaches where a "procedural" representation becomes increasingly "declarative." For instance, instead of using a conventional programming language such as C or C++ for feature definition, a procedural feature definition may be coded in a special definition language interpreted by the system. In this scenario the interpreter decouples the feature definitions from the actual feature definitions. The extent to which the resulting system can be regarded as "declarative" depends on the expressive power of the definition language and the interpreter.

Implementation Strategy An issue closely related to the previous one is the overall *implementation strategy* of feature definitions. While not as fundamental as the procedural versus declarative issue, the choice of the implementation strategy defines limits to how flexible and responsive a design-by-features system can be made.

Among the more important alternatives are the following:

- *Hard-coded feature definitions.* Feature definitions are encoded in an ordinary programming language notation. New or altered definitions must be compiled and linked with the rest of the system using programming tools not ordinarily available to an end user.
- *Interpreted feature definitions.* Feature definitions are encoded in an interpreted language, either a general-purpose programming language supporting dynamic loading of procedures, such as LISP or Smalltalk, or a special-purpose feature definition language. In this scenario feature definitions can be more readily edited by the end users.

- *Prototype-based feature definitions.* In this approach the strict separation of feature definitions and feature instances is relaxed, and all feature instances serve as templates ("prototypes") for creating additional feature instances. It is not necessary to create feature definitions separately; instead, feature definitions are created automatically and dynamically as needed.

Hard-coded feature definitions lead most naturally to procedural methods for feature definition. Generation of hard-coded definitions is greatly simplified if an object-oriented language can be used to benefit from inheritance of attributes and procedures.

To support interpreted feature definitions, declarative techniques have several advantages. In particular, the higher level of semantics made possible by a declarative technique allows the details of feature instance generation to be hidden from the user, hence simplifying the definition of new feature classes. Also in this case an object-oriented implementation is attractive.

The main challenge of prototype-based feature definitions is that a semantic mapping from the low-level prototype feature instances to high-level feature definitions must be performed automatically. For instance, some (but not necessarily all) constraints between attributes of the prototype must be preserved in the instances created. We will discuss a sample research system following this approach in Section 8.8. The system discussed in Section 8.7 also uses a kind of prototype-based approach combined with an object-oriented technique.

8.1.2 Support for User-Defined Features

The level to which a design-by-features system supports user-defined features has profound significance on the usefulness of the system for design. As noted in Chapter 3, the number of feature classes potentially needed in design cannot be limited. Therefore a system that restricts the user to a fixed set of predefined features is not likely to be useful for all design applications.

User Features and Model Features To start our discussion, it is first important to realize that the collection of features available to a designer at the level of the user interface of a design-by-features system, and the collection of features actually preserved in a resulting model may and often are different. Therefore both the extendibility of the user interface level feature collection and the internally used feature collection are of interest. This means that the characteristic "dimension" of the level of support of user-defined features actually breaks into two distinct axes as shown in Figure 8.1.

In some systems, features only exist at the level of the user interface, and the actually recorded model only contains the evaluated geometric primitives. It may be argued that such systems are not full-fledged feature modelers at all; however, even in these systems the original definition entered by the user may

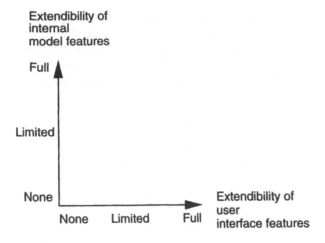

Figure 8.1   Levels of support to user-defined features

be interpreted as a feature model in its own right, provided that it is preserved and made available to applications.

At the other extreme, features are only used to represent the internal model, and the user sees no features at all. Instead, he or she manipulates the model on the basis of entirely different entities, and these actions are interpreted as features. This situation may apply to function-based design environments discussed in Chapter 12.

Ordinarily features would appear both in the user interface and in the internal model. In this case a possible scenario is that the internally recorded feature collection is larger than those available to the user. If so, the user-level features must be transformed to model features using a feature mapping approach based on some type of geometric reasoning. In feature mapping terms introduced in Chapter 7, this is a case of specialization mapping. Clearly a system that can use some feature mapping from user-level to system-level features has the advantage that different feature models may be produced from the same definition. Moreover, if and when the underlying feature collection is changed, the user does not have to learn the new feature collection, as long as the feature mapping rules can be changed to cover the conversion from the generic user-interface features to the specific internally used ones. We will discuss a sample system using feature mapping to decouple user level and model level features in Section 8.5.

Alternative Approaches to Supporting User-Defined Features   Simple design-by-features systems have a fixed set of features embedded in the implementation of the system; therefore the collection of features cannot be extended at all by an external user. Such systems in general are too restrictive to be useful in innovative design. In routine design, however, a fixed set of features may sometimes be actually desirable to make sure that routine designs stay within the permissible limits of product variations. For nondesign applications the same situation may apply.

To support design applications properly, an extendible set of features is preferred. Some systems provide for an extendible collection of user-interface level features, while the internal set of features recorded in the model representation remains fixed. For instance, a user interface level feature may be defined as a macro that is "evaluated" into a collection of internal features. The implementation of such a system requires a macro language that can be interpreted at run time to decide which internal features need to be created. However, the various internal procedures of the system related to instantiating internal features, assigning values to their parameters, and so on, can remain hard-coded. While still being too restrictive for innovative design, these systems may be quite appropriate for routine design because they support the inclusion of reusable macros corresponding to preferred design solutions, while making sure that the macros evaluate into known basic features determined, for example, by manufacturability viewpoint.

Both of the above approaches can be implemented on the basis of hard-coded feature definitions. If also the internal features must be made extendible, a more functional interpreted definition language for feature classes is needed. Clearly the definition language must be powerful enough to handle all types of feature characteristics discussed in Chapter 3, such as defining and computing feature attributes, coding feature relationships, and defining feature geometry.

Complete support of user-defined features in a design-by-features system requires that feature classes created by the user become full-privileged members of the feature collection of the system. That is, they can be created, deleted, and manipulated; they can have relationships to other features (and these relationships themselves can be defined too); they can be validated by validation constraints or rules (and new validation constraints and rules can be defined); their geometry can be anything that can be described in the underlying geometric modeling system. Clearly, to create a feature definition mechanism that covers all these facilities completely is a challenging task of software engineering that necessarily introduces certain complexity and overhead to the resulting system.

Some systems seek to avoid the possibly large cost of full-fledged user-definable features by accepting some limitations in the functionality of user-defined features. Functional limitations may apply to all feature characteristics mentioned in the previous paragraph. For instance, user-defined features may not be validated; they can only have predefined relationships to other features; their geometry must be expressible using a fixed, hard-coded set of geometric primitives. In fact, most present design-by-features systems stay in the "limited" level of support of user-defined features of Figure 8.1.

The actual methods of adding new feature classes vary, to some extent, according to the type of the geometric modeler linkage to be explained in the next section. Some systems are based on extendible software libraries that allow a new modeler version including the added feature classes to be created. This approach requires that users have the system available in the form of object module libraries, a rare case. Some others include a special feature definition language that can be dynamically interpreted by a feature modeler. A few modelers include a facility for adding features directly in the user interface. Examples of various approaches are described in more detail later in this chapter.

In the final analysis, the choice of the level of support of user-defined features in a system must depend on the particular external requirements of the system, particularly the intended application domain. The most general system may not be the most useful one.

8.1.3 Types of Linkages with a Geometric Modeling System

The third important characteristic of a design-by-features system describes the type of the linkage the system has with a geometric modeling system or the geometry facilities of an ordinary CAD system. In the rest of this section, we will use the expression "geometry system" to cover both geometric modelers and geometry facilities of CAD systems.

Again there are several subcharacteristics of the geometry linkage type that we choose to discuss simultaneously in this section:

- *Closeness of the linkage.* The linkage may be *static* (i.e., realized off-line through an intermediate file), or *dynamic* (i.e., realized on-line through procedure calls).
- *Information flow.* The information flow between the features system and the geometry system can be *one-way* (i.e., from the features system to the geometry system or vice versa), or *two-way* (i.e., the features system can access and utilize information computed by the geometric system, and vice versa).
- *Incremental/nonincremental operation.* In the incremental arrangement, changes to the features can be propagated incrementally to the geometry representation by inserting, deleting, and modifying geometric elements. In the nonincremental arrangement, the whole geometric model must be regenerated from scratch after each change of the feature model.
- *Locus of control.* This characteristic determines which of the two interacting systems is considered the "main program."

Some possible arrangements of these subcharacteristics are illustrated in Figure 8.2. Of course the subcharacteristics are not at all independent from each other; indeed, two-way information flow requires a dynamic linkage between the features system and the geometry system. Similarly incremental operation typically also requires a dynamic link.

As we saw earlier, the level to which user-defined features can be supported partially depends how the geometry of new feature classes can be defined. In a static, one-way system the system designer must be content with whatever facili-

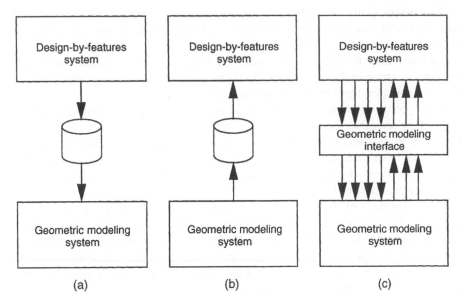

Figure 8.2 Types of linkages with a geometric modeling system: (*a*) Static, one-way interface, locus of control in the features system; (*b*) static, one-way linkage, locus of control in the geometry system; (*c*) dynamic, two-way interface, locus of control in either system.

ties the static geometry interface provides. Typically parametric variations of features' shapes expressible in a static interface are limited. The following sections show that the choice of the geometry linkage type influences heavily the design choices related to the other important characteristics as well. The remainder of this section discusses some typical arrangements.

Static, One-Way Linkage, Features to Geometry In the static features-to-geometry arrangement, the designer operates the features system, and this generates input for the geometry system (see Figure 8.2a). A typical scenario is that the geometry system provides a command language interface that allows geometric models to be created, but no direct programming interface; this scenario is typical for "closed-architecture" CAD software. The user operates by using the features system to edit the feature model; the features system generates command language statements for the geometry system corresponding to the changes of the feature model.

The problem of this arrangement is that changes to the feature model typically require complete reevaluation of the geometric model. That is, the geometric model cannot be updated incrementally according to the changes in the feature model. Also the user must typically operate the geometry system directly to evaluate the generated command files, leading to a complex user interface of the overall system.

The functionality of design by features in this arrangement is necessarily limited. For instance, feature validation cannot use the facilities of the geometric modeler as predicates in validation rules. This makes it difficult to include, for instance, rules that determine whether the feature is manufacturable by checking the free space in the tool access direction, since this would require the use of Boolean set operations or like to perform interference testing.

This type of a system is also limited in its facility to handle feature relationships. It is desirable that a design-by-features system can deduce feature relationships autonomously; for instance, a system should be capable of deducing that a hole must penetrate though a block and of using it as a constraint. Such a facility is severely limited in this architecture because the required geometric reasoning cannot use the facilities of the geometry system.

The advantages of this scenario include the possibility of using a neutral file format such as IGES to realize the communication between the features system and the geometry system. This makes the features system quite independent of the particular geometry system being used. At any rate, this architecture effectively separates the two systems from each other, making the features system more portable from one geometry system to another.

Static, One-Way Linkage, Geometry to Features

In static geometry-to-features arrangement, the user interacts with the geometry system, and this generates input for the features system (see Figure 8.2*b*). Although rarely used in practice, this arrangement is a viable architecture in the scenario where the geometry system provides a good command language facility or can be extended by using a direct programming interface such as provided by "open-architecture" CAD systems.

Using such a tool, it may be possible to extend the geometry system with commands that, as a side effect, generate information that is sufficient to create features. In other words, the feature system is embedded with the geometry system. For instance, the geometry system might be extended with a "Make hole" command that not only creates a graphical representation of the hole in the geometry system but also a block of information that is sufficient for the embedded features system to create a more complete representation of the hole feature.

The level to which user-defined features actually can be supported depends on the facilities available in the extension language of the geometry system. For instance, feature validation requires a fairly complete facility of performing geometric computations, and using the results as predicates in control structures. Then, to implement the reasonable validation rule that a hole must be placed orthogonally with its starting surface, access to surface normals and some vector algebra is required. Not all geometry systems provide a command language with this level of expressiveness.

The problem of this architecture is that users may decide to use geometry operations that have no features counterpart. If so, the feature representation becomes incomplete. The advantage is that users can continue using the familiar user interface of the geometry system.

Dynamic, Two-Way Linkage, Features to Geometry In the dynamic features-to-geometry arrangement, the user operates the features system that runs the geometry system directly by means of procedure calls or some form of interprocess communication (e.g., remote procedure calls or mailboxes; see Figure 8.2c).

In the typical scenario the geometry system has a direct procedure call interface that provides a fairly complete collection of geometry-creating procedures. The features system can call the procedures to create feature geometries. More important, the resulting geometric model data structures can be investigated by the features system either through special procedure calls or directly in a single-process implementation.

This scheme is quite attractive for user-defined features. Definition of feature geometries can be supported by including an interpreted interface to the geometry system procedures in the features system. Feature validation is facilitated by the possibility of running "geometric queries," creating geometric objects corresponding to interesting spatial characteristics of the model, letting the geometry system evaluate the query by Boolean set operations or the like, and investigating the result. Typical cases include noninterference tests, where a Boolean set operation is executed to determine whether a prohibited intersection exists. For a valuable exposition of using such operations for the validation of incremental changes to a feature model, see (Rossignac 1990).

Similar considerations apply to other interesting facilities, such as the determination of feature relationships. Extracting and enforcing feature relationships, in general, requires the capability of performing geometric queries on the underlying geometric representation of the features. For instance, if a hole feature is determined to be "through," then the entry and exit faces must be retrieved from the geometric model to create the required relationships.

The dynamic two-way linkage scheme requires very close access to the geometry system. It is becoming increasingly attractive as "open" geometry systems are becoming available to developers, such as CAD systems with an extensive programming interface, or solid modeling libraries, such as the ACIS system of Spatial Technology, Inc. (Spatial 1993). The problem with this approach is the inherent overhead in the case where some form of interprocess communication must be used (Magleby and Gunn 1992, Hummel and Wolf 1990). Geometric model data structures are large, and a high communication bandwidth is required to implement typical geometric queries.

Dynamic, Two-Way Linkage, Geometry to Features Also in the dynamic geometry-to-features arrangement, the user interacts with the geometry system, and this generates the input for the features system (see Figure 8.2c). Information located in the feature representation must be accessible and useful in the geometric system.

This scenario is possible in geometry systems that support an open, extendible architecture that covers all facilities required by feature modeling. Presently these characteristics are possessed only by some knowledge-based geometry shells such as the ICAD modeler or some generic knowledge-based system shells such as KEE. Some more common systems such as CATIA or AutoCAD are approaching a level of tailorability that can support the scenario.[1]

In the scenario a design-by-features system becomes embedded in a more general geometry system. Full support of design by features requires the capability of changing the user interface of the system, and defining and using feature validation and manipulation procedures.

The advantage of this approach is a uniform user interface that covers both geometric modeling and feature-based modeling. This may be of great advantage in defining, say, feature relationships or dimensioning and tolerancing of features, both of which may be much simplified by the uniform availability of geometric information. For instance, the center line of a keyway may be associated to a line entity in a geometric model that allows the use of the geometry system facilities for defining the positioning and orientation of the keyway through positioning and orienting the center line.

8.2 PROCEDURAL TECHNIQUES

In the procedural approach generic features are predefined in terms of a collection of related procedures. Procedures may include methods for instancing, modifying, copying, and deleting features, generating feature geometry, deriving certain parameters, and validating feature operations. The procedures may be encoded in an ordinary programming language notation or using a special-purpose feature definition language.

The distinctive characteristic of procedural techniques that separates them from declarative techniques is that feature definitions are expressed directly in terms of one-directional computation specifications. For instance, a procedural feature definition of a prismatic feature is likely to include the following definition of the attribute volume:

```
volume := width * length * height
```

The operational interpretation of the definition is that during feature instantiation, the value of the attribute is computed on the basis of the feature dimensions. If the feature dimensions are changed later, the procedure must be re-executed by the user or the procedure responsible of changing the dimension. In contrast, a declarative system interprets the definition as a constraint that must be maintained; such a system will use a general algorithm for deducing which values must be updated after a change has been performed.

---

[1]ICAD® is a registered trademark of ICAD, Inc. KEE® is a registered trademark of Intellicorp, Inc. CATIA® is a registered trademark of Dassault Informatique; AutoCAD is a registered trademark of AutoDesk.

The following subsections introduce briefly procedural techniques through examples from existing systems. A more thorough example of a procedural feature definition method will be discussed in Chapter 10.

8.2.1 Definition by General-Purpose Programming Language

The simplest approach to procedural feature definition is to use a general-purpose programming language for feature definition. An example of such a system is the HutCAPP feature modeler constructed in the Helsinki University of Technology in 1987–1988 (Mäntylä et al. 1987).

HutCAPP was based on a hybrid software architecture where a LISP-based feature definition language was interfaced to a C-based geometric modeling system GWB, the Geometric WorkBench (Mäntylä 1988). The LISP-based definitions supported a simple form of object-orientation by means of frames, LISP data structures roughly comparable to objects of a regular object-oriented language. On the other hand, access to the solid modeler was available strictly in terms of a library of C procedures.

The interfacing problem was solved by interfacing the geometric modeler to the LISP core by means of the foreign function interface capability of the LISP environment used. In the resulting system the feature definitions include a reference to GWB procedures to be called in order to construct the geometric model corresponding to the feature model.

The mechanism is illustrated in Figure 8.3. In the figure, the groove feature instance of the sample part is represented by means of the LISP frame data structure GROOVE1 shown in the bottom left. As expressed by the attribute is-a, GROOVE1 is an instance of the feature class EXTERNAL-SLOT shown in the bottom right. The attribute make-geom of the feature class stores a reference to the C function ext-slot-geometry, which is used to insert the feature into the solid model. As a result a dynamic one-way linkage between features and geometry was realized.

The solid model of the whole part is created by going through the feature hierarchy, generating all feature geometries and combining them with Boolean set operations deduced on the basis of the feature type (depression or protrusion). Hence the method is nonincremental: After each change to the feature model, the whole geometric model must be regenerated. The connection between feature model and the geometric elements in the solid model is established by an index table. The table makes it possible, for instance, to support selecting features by pointing at them in the geometric model.

8.2.2 Special-Purpose Feature Definition Languages

The problem of using a programming language notation directly for feature definition is lack of modularity: If the solid modeling system is changed, large parts of the definitions will have to be changed. An improved design-by-features system architecture can be realized using a special-purpose language for feature

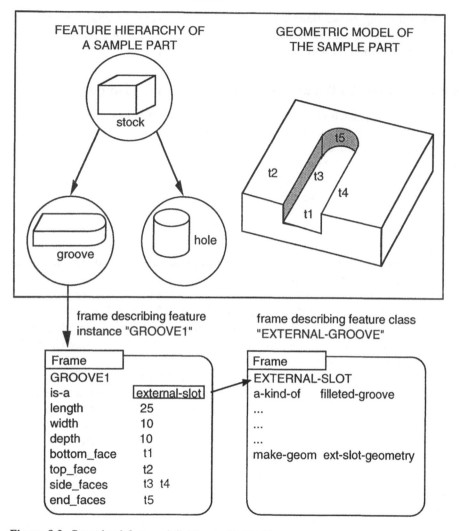

Figure 8.3 Procedural feature definition in HutCAPP

definition. In this architecture the particular idiosyncrasies of a certain modeling system are effectively hidden by the interpreter of the language. In fact the EXPRESS language of the STEP standard can be viewed as an example of a procedural feature definition language.

An example of the definition language approach is the IMPPACT feature modeler developed at Technical University of Berlin in the context of the ESPRIT Project 2165 *Integrated Modelling of Products and Processes using Advanced Computer Technologies* (IMPPACT) (Krause et al. 1991).

IMPPACT uses a textual feature definition language called PDGL (*Part Design Graph Language*). In PDGL, feature definitions are loaded dynamically as needed by the system for feature instantiation. Different aspects of feature definition covered by the language include geometry of form features, derivable attributes, relations to other features, constraints, rules, and technology definitions for process planning application. The language is intended to be readable to support adding new feature classes.

A sample feature definition written in PDGL for a stepped thru hole feature is given in Figure 8.4. The language supports a variant of object-oriented notation

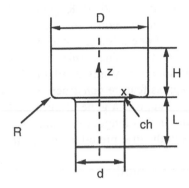

```
SCHEMA IWF_Example_3
ENTITY stepped-thru-hole SUBTYPE OF(feature)
    D: distance := 1.0 - Diameter of first step
    L: distance := 1.0;- Length of inner hole
    d: distance := 1.0;   - Diameter of inner hole
    DERIVE
        H: distance := z_master();      - Length of first step
    WHERE
        d =< D; H =< L;
END_ENTITY;
FUNCTION stepped_thru_hole(
        position: transformation_matrix,
        D, L, d, radius_thickness, chamfer_thickness: distance):
        stepped_thru_hole;
    LOCAL
        a, b: geometric;
        object: stepped_thru_hole;
    END_LOCAL;
    object := stepped_thru_hole(position, D, L, d, H);
    a := cylinder(NULL, H, D);
    b := cylinder(set_z_translation(-L), L, d);
    object.chamfer := implicit_edge_flat(cartesian_point(d/2,0,0),
            cartesian_point(-D/2,0,0), chamfer_thickness, 45.0);
    object.radius := implicit_edge_round(cartesian_point(D/2,0,0),
            cartesian_point(-D/2,0,0), radius_thickness);
    object.form_feature := a + b;
    object.solidity := negative;
    RETURN(object);
END_FUNCTION;
END_SCHEMA;
```

Figure 8.4 IMPPACT definition of a stepped thru-hole (Krause et al. 1991; reprinted by permission of the authors)

where the feature class `stepped_thru_hole` is declared to be a subtype of feature class `feature`. By virtue of this, it inherits information from the supertype.

The definition consists of two "sections." The ENTITY section defines the independent and dependent feature attributes and validity constraints among them; observe that default values for the independent variables can be given. The FUNCTION section defines the function `stepped_thru_hole` which gives an instantiation procedure for the feature. Its statements compute a geometric representation for the feature by using various canned procedures and Boolean operations (the Boolean union is expressed as "+").

The first generation of the ASU Features Testbed (Rogers 1987) gives another example of a system based on procedural feature definitions. The feature descriptions of library features consist of operation sequences that define features, and a set of inheritance and validation rules. These rules are used while creating feature based part models by instancing features available in the library. An interpreted language is used to express feature construction, parameter inheritance, and validation. The language supports a general-purpose C parser, which converts feature definitions written in this language to standard C. This allows features to be defined as data files in the interpreted language, thus avoiding the need for recompiling the source code.

Feature producing volumes can be defined by sets of procedures, such as

```
CYL(attach_face, diameter, length, pos_vector,
    orientation_vector)
EXT(attach_face, curve, depth, sweep_vector)
```

where CYL is a procedure for creating a cylinder primitive and EXT is for creating a linear sweep. Simple inheritance is achieved by expressions of the form

```
#(s1,b1)(p1,a1)
```

which defines that parameter b1 of feature s1 is equal parameter a1 of feature p1, thus implying an equality constraint. Such inheritance may sometimes be specified as conditional

```
#((if_attach_face=1 or 6)(s1,b1)(p1,a1))
```

Validation rules are also specified in a similar syntax:

```
#((s1,a1)<(s3,a2))
```

This specifies that parameter a1 of feature s1 must always be less than parameter a2 of feature s3. Capabilities to do arithmetic computations, logical operations, and specify simple functions are also supported. Implementation details of the modeler are covered in Chapter 10.

8.3 DECLARATIVE TECHNIQUES

The essential characteristic of the declarative approach is that the system uses a nonprocedural method to describe features and their properties. On the basis of this description, some type of a general algorithm constructs the actual detailed feature model. Hence declarative methods separate feature definition from the implementation. This is in contrast to the procedural approach, where the two are intertwined in the procedure definitions.

This arrangement simplifies the task of defining new feature classes considerably: unlike the procedural method, where detailed algorithms for creating feature attributes, computing their values, and constructing feature geometry must be provided, declarative definitions can hide many of these details in the general evaluation algorithm. This lets the user concentrate on the essential aspects of the feature, while the evaluation algorithm "fills in the details."

To achieve the separation, the geometry and other properties of features is defined in a "neutral" (implementation independent) form. The definition may be in terms of relationships between primitive volumes (blocks, cylinders, etc.) or in terms of relationships between boundary-based modeling entities faces, edges, half-spaces, etc. Therefore the main capabilities needed for declarative modeling are

- Constraint specification
- Constraint based feature definition
- Constraint solution and validation

Facilities for supporting these functions are discussed in the following sections. Again examples of actual systems are used to illustrate the various techniques.

8.3.1 Constraint Specification

As discussed in Chapter 2, a *constraint* is a declared property of some entities that must hold. A constraint-based model of some objects describes the objects as abstract entities with certain properties, and it describes their properties by means of predicates that must be true. The operation of a constraint-based system is based on a sufficiently general constraint satisfaction algorithm that can construct a detailed model such that all required constraints are satisfied. If the model is edited by changing the values of some properties, the constraint satisfaction algorithm must be able to update values of other properties so that the declared constraints remain satisfied.

In declarative feature representation, constraints can be used to represent several characteristics of features:

- *Intra-feature dependencies* Dependencies between instance parameters within a single feature

- *Composite dependencies* Dependencies between features forming composite features such as stepped holes
- *Inter-feature dependencies* Dependencies between geometric attributes of several features within a part
- *Assembly dependencies* Mating and other dependencies between several parts expressed by means of dependencies between mating features.

In the following, we will introduce a set of generic constraints for use in orienting and positioning geometric entities belonging to features, parts, and subassemblies relative to each other. Various generic constraint sets have been proposed in the literature, but there are, as yet, no standards for specifying or representing constraints. Therefore we will use the set proposed by (Balakrishnan 1993 and Ali 1994) as representative examples. This collection was customized for features on the basis of Kramer's kinematic constraints (Kramer 1991, 1992).

The classification is shown in Figure 8.5. The constraints are organized into two main groups: *orientation* and *position*. Orientation constraints are further classified into five sets: *parallel, perpendicular, angle, coplanar,* and *coaxial.* The definition of each member of the sets is given later in this section. Position constraints also have four types explained later.

Each of the constraints relates two geometric or feature entities, a *reference entity* and a *target entity*. Observe that this does not imply that the constraints

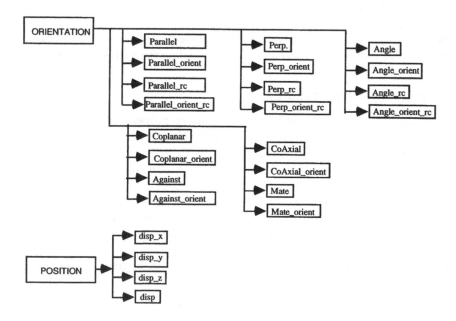

Figure 8.5 Generic constraint set example (Ali 1994; reprinted by permission of the author)

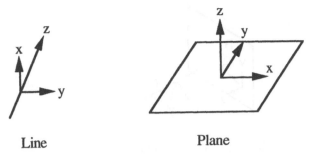

Figure 8.6 Co-ordinate system

are applied from the reference to the target; a constraint satisfaction algorithm may well choose to use the constraint specification for computing parameters of the reference entity on the basis of the target entity.

A reference entity is a constituent element of a feature whose position and orientation are known, while a target entity is considered fixed to the feature or part whose position/orientation are to be determined. In the constraint set chosen for discussion here, only points, planar faces, and straight edges are used as references and targets. The assumption is that either the feature itself is composed of such bounding entities, or that reference planes, axes, and center/corner points can be computed from its composing entities for the purpose of constraint specification.

The coordinate system selected is such that the z-axes of planes point outward (normal) and the z-axes of lines are along the line, as shown in Figure 8.6. Therefore the constraints are defined with respect to the z-axes of both the reference and target entities. Figure 8.7 shows the Parallel(R, T) constraint applied to different reference and target entity combinations. Note that in all cases the z-axes are parallel. In all subsequent figures, R and T signify the reference and target entities, respectively. The Perpendicular(R, T) and Angle(R, T, Ø) constraints are defined similarly; they specify that the z-axis of the target is perpendicular or at a specified angle to the reference z-axis, respectively. All angles specified are measured in the clockwise direction, from the reference entity to the target entity.

The Coplanar(R, T) constraint is applied between two planes. The target entity T is constrained to lie in the plane through the reference entity R; the x- and y-axes of the target must lie in the plane of the reference, as illustrated in Figure 8.8. The Co-axial(R, T) constraint is applied between two lines. The z-axes of both the target T and reference R entities are specified to be coaxial as illustrated in Figure 8.9.

For each of the five basic orientation constraints, a more restrictive "oriented" constraint is defined by specifying the angle between the x-axes of R and T, in addition to the relation between the z-axes. The "oriented" suffix is used to designate these constraints in Figure 8.5. For example, Perpendicular_

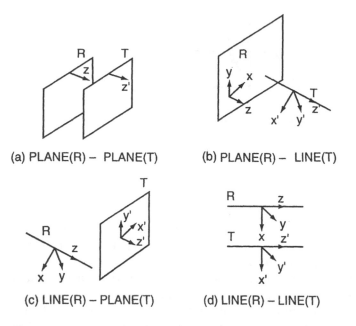

(a) PLANE(R) – PLANE(T)　　　(b) PLANE(R) – LINE(T)

(c) LINE(R) – PLANE(T)　　　(d) LINE(R) – LINE(T)

Figure 8.7 The `Parallel` constraint (Balakrishnan 1993; reprinted by permission of the author)

`oriented(R, T, Ø)` specifies that in addition to the z-axes of R and T being perpendicular, the angle between the x-axes must be Ø, measured in the clockwise direction. Other oriented constraints, `Parallel_oriented(R, T, Ø)`, `Angle_oriented(R, T, β, axis, Ø)`, `Co-axial_oriented(R, T, Ø)`, and `Coplanar_oriented(R, T, Ø)` are defined similarly.

There are two complementary constraints for each type of orientation constraint we have discussed. This happens when the z-axes are pointing in opposite directions, that is, rotated 180 degrees to each other. We designate these constraints as *reverse complements* of the above types, indicated by the rc suffix in Figure 8.5.

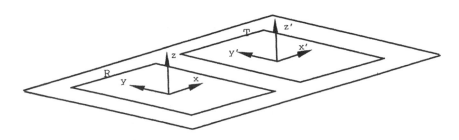

Figure 8.8 The `Coplanar` constraint (Balakrishnan 1993; reprinted by permission of the author)

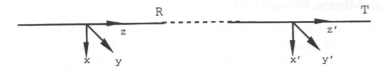

Figure 8.9 The Co-axial constraint

In addition to the orientation constraints above, we need *position constraints*. This set consists of displacement constraints between two points in the *x*-, *y*-, or *z*-directions, or in terms of the distance between the two points. The four subclasses of these constraints, disp_x, disp_y, disp_z, and disp, are based on displacement measured along *x*-, *y*-, and *z*-directions or along a general direction, respectively, as shown in Figure 8.10. The position constraints can be applied on any combination of planes and lines. For example, disp_x(R, T, A) specifies the distance measure *a* from the reference entity R to the target entity T measured along the positive *x*-axis of T as shown in Figure 8.10*a*. Similarly, Figures 8.10*b–d* show constraints disp_y(R, T, B), disp_z(R, T, C), and disp(R, T, D), respectively. A special case of the last constraint, of course, is the useful constraint coincident(R, T) = disp(R, T, 0).

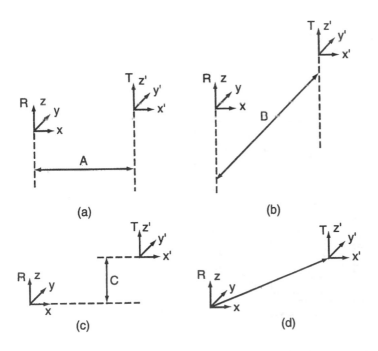

Figure 8.10 Position constraints (Balakrishnan 1993; reprinted by permission of the author)

8.3.2 Constraint-Based Feature Definition

Combinations of orientation and position constraints can be used to describe spatial relations between geometric entities within features, between features, and even between parts in sub-assemblies. Combinations of constraints are sometimes represented as *constraint graphs* because the methods for constraint solution/validation usually requires input in the form of a graph. A constraint graph consists of *nodes* and *links* between the nodes. The nodes are geometric entities (faces, axes, edges, and mid-planes), and the links are constraints.

A simple example of a stepped hole feature and its dimensioning is given in Figure 8.11; the corresponding constraint graph composed of the generic constraints from Figure 8.5 is shown in Figure 8.12. The sample part has two simple features (holes) that form a composite feature (stepped hole), which is placed inside another feature (block). We can see three sets of constraints: intrafeature (within the holes and the block individually), compound constraints (between the two holes), and interfeature (between the stepped hole and the block). These are indicated by the shaded areas in Figure 8.12.

In interpreting these constraints, the following points need to be kept in mind:

- The reference or target entities for cylindrical faces are the center axes, with the origin at the one of the extremal bounds of the cylinder.
- Face normals for real faces point away from the material; face normal for removed faces point toward removed material.

In the example, we have avoided specifying redundant constraints. Therefore the graph only contains those constraints which are required to fully determine the part.

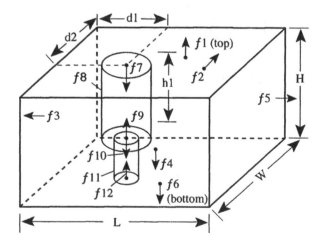

Figure 8.11   Stepped hole on block

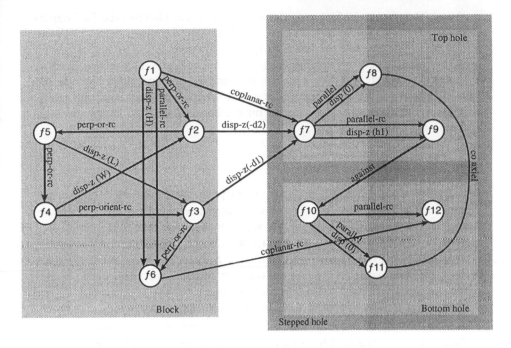

Figure 8.12 Constraint graph for a stepped hole on a block

Constraint-based feature modeling and constraint satisfaction can both be facilitated if a group of related constraints is considered a *compound constraint*. For instance, certain combinations of positioning and orienting constraints arise frequently in feature-based models. The constraint graph notation can accommodate compound constraints easily by allowing *hierarchical constraint graphs* where a group of nodes may be treated as one single node and links may be formed from this composite node to other nodes. Thus a finite and definite set of nodes representing primitive geometric entities may be grouped together to define a new composite node for a form feature.

Figure 8.12 can also be interpreted as a hierarchical constraint graph; the compound nodes of the hierarchical graph are presented as shaded outlines. In the hierarchical graph the group of nodes forming the block may be thought of as one single node and referred to as "block." Similarly the nodes for the stepped hole may be grouped together to form the two cylinders first, which may then be combined to form the stepped hole node.

Representation of feature geometry in terms of composite nodes helps in utilizing inferencing techniques for analyzing a complex part. A complex constraint graph for a part may be broken down into several simpler subgraphs which are analyzed separately. Such an approach may also be used in recognizing features from a complex constraint graph.

Apart from design by features, constraint graphs can also be used for interactive definition of new feature classes. For instance, (Salomons et al. 1994 and Salomons 1995) describe the FROOM system where features can be defined by drawing interactively a "conceptual graph" that includes face nodes (planar, cylindrical, conical) and their constraints (parallel, perpendicular, etc.). In the system, degrees-of-freedom analysis is used to derive and draw a sample geometry for the new feature class directly on the basis of the face nodes and their constraints.

8.3.3 Constraint Satisfaction

Declarative modeling requires a general purpose constraint satisfaction algorithm. Such an algorithm does not care about the semantics of the constraints (i.e., features, in our case); one simply supplies the algorithm with a set of geometric constraints, expressed in a generic way, and it will determine if it is possible to satisfy the set of constraints and, if so, construct an assignment of values to variables appearing in the constraints that satisfies the constraints. Sometimes the procedure may yield multiple solutions.

Constraint satisfaction algorithms can be split into several types:

Sequential constraint satisfaction	These algorithms solve constraints by applying sequentially assignments to variables, where each assigned value is computed as a function of the previously assigned values. The sequence of assignments may be *fixed*, determined by the user of the system, or *flexible*, determined by a constraint propagation algorithm.
Numerical constraint satisfaction	These algorithms satisfy constraints by constructing a system of equations representing the constraints, and solving the system on the basis of a numerical equation-solving procedure or some other method.
Symbolic constraint satisfaction	These algorithms satisfy constraints by applying a sufficiently general inferencing scheme for finding simultaneously a set of assignments to model variables that satisfies the given constraints. Examples include symbolic algebra and predicate logic.
Truth maintenance	Truth maintenance systems provide a data structure for maintaining the dependencies between assumptions and other information that is deduced on the basis of the assumptions.

Also hybrid methods that combine characteristics of several of the above approaches have been developed. Representative examples of these techniques are described in the following subsections.

Sequential Constraint Satisfaction Sequential constraint satisfaction algorithms solve a system of constraints by a sequence of assignments to entities appearing in constraint specifications. The assigned values are computed on the basis of the already computed entities or constants. Applying all constraints in sequence amounts to completely re-evaluating the model. If just a few constraints have been changed, an *incremental* algorithm that can detect those constraints which must be evaluated is preferred.

In simplest form the order in which the assignments are applied is *fixed* and determined by the user of a system. The associative representation of graphical primitives briefly mentioned in Section 2.2.1 can be regarded as an example of this approach. In this case the evaluation order of the "constraints" is determined by the associative representation of the graphical primitives in terms of already constructed ones. Many systems that can capture a log of the operations applied to the construction of a model can also be considered cases of fixed sequence approach. We may observe that these systems do not really qualify as declarative models: No real separation from the constraint specification and constraint solution is achieved, and they might better be considered procedural methods.

From the viewpoint of declarative feature modeling, *flexible* sequential constraint satisfaction methods are of much more interest. These methods work by deciding algorithmically a suitable order in which the assignments can be performed. That is, constraints are treated as *multidirectional*: A constraint such as coincident(T, R) may be used to position T with respect to R, and vice versa, as determined by the algorithm. The logic-based method used in Geomap-III described in Chapter 2 belongs to this class; the following subsections give further examples.

Serrano's Method Many constraint propagation algorithms are based on viewing a constraint network such as that shown in Figure 8.12 as a graph, and using graph algorithms to decide on the order in which the constraints must be sequentially satisfied. (See Appendix A for an introduction to graph terminology.)

An example of a graph-theoretic approach is given by (Serrano 1987). His method is best explained using the example of Figure 8.13a, which shows a simple welding problem and its geometric parameters. The constraints binding the parameters in this case are

$$f1: I = 0.707h \frac{bd^2}{2}$$

$$f2: \sigma = \frac{Mc}{I}$$

$$f3: c = \frac{d}{2}$$

$$f4: M = FI$$

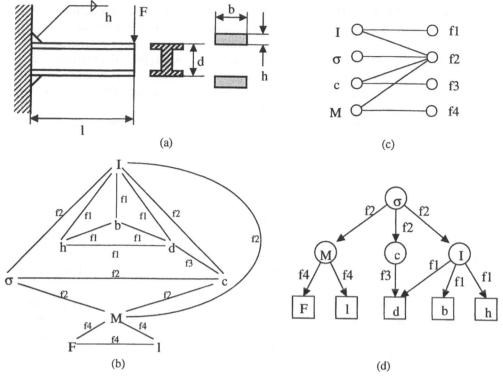

Figure 8.13 A constraint network example (Serrano 1987; reprinted by permission of the author)

leading to the constraint graph shown in (*b*), where the vertices correspond to the variables and edges with constraints so that if two variables appear in the same constraint, they are joined with an edge of the graph.

The graph (*b*) is initially treated as undirected; that is, no particular direction for the flow of computation is assumed. To obtain a particular solution from the graph, the user must specify which variables are input and which output. In this case we assume that the set of input nodes $K = \{F, l, d, b, h\}$ and the set of output nodes $U = \{I, \sigma, c, M\}$.

The basic idea of the method is to construct a *bipartite matching* for the output nodes U (Even 1979). A graph $G = \{V, E\}$ is bipartite when its set of vertices V is the union of two distinct subsets N and F such that every edge of E connects uniquely one vertex in N with one vertex in F. The method computes a bipartite matching for $N =$ the set of output nodes U and $F =$ the set of constraints $\{f1, f2, f3, f4\}$. The resulting matching is given in Figure 8.13*c*. Observe that each arc in the graph matches one output parameter with a constraint.

Given the bipartite match (*c*), the original graph (*b*) can be converted to a directed graph of the form (*d*), where only those edges are kept which are labeled with the correct matching. When the resulting directed graph is a tree (such as in this case), the unknown parameters may be computed on the basis of a topological sort. In the general case the directed graph may have cycles. These are handled by "collapsing" each cycle to a "supernode," which must be solved using a numerical method in the order defined by the tree formed of the supernodes. See (Serrano and Gossard 1992) for a more extensive description of the method.

DeltaBlue When a constraint system is overdetermined, a constraint propagation algorithm specifically designed to handle such a situation must be used. *DeltaBlue* (Freeman-Benson et al. 1990) is a simple constraint satisfaction algorithm based on graph propagation that fits this requirement.

DeltaBlue is based on constructing an explicit representation of the numerical equations corresponding to the constraints. The internal representation is a *multigraph*, whose vertices represent the constrained values and edges constraints. (A multigraph is a graph where edges may associate more than two vertices.)

For instance, let us consider the simple case of the block with a through-hole, shown in Figure 8.14. (Observe that a left-handed coordinate system is used due to the idiosyncrasies of the experimental system to be discussed.) Using the nomenclature of the figure, the requirements that the through hole h must reside at the center of the rectangular block b, and extend all the way through it, can be translated to the following collection of constraints:

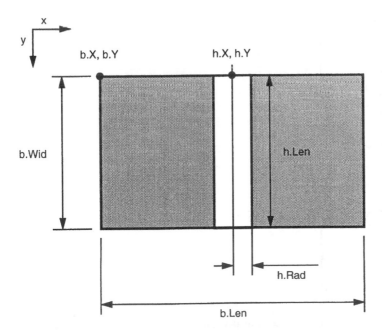

Figure 8.14 A block and a through-hole (Mäntylä 1990, © 1990 by International Business Machines Corporation; reprinted with permission)

$$h.Y = b.Y$$
$$h.X = b.X + b.Len / 2$$
$$h.Len = b.Wid$$

where b.X, b.Y are the coordinates of the upper left corner of the 2D block b, and h.X, h.Y are coordinates of the top center of the hole. Actual assignments of dimensions and positions can be modeled as further constraints:

$$b.X = 0$$
$$b.Y = 15$$
$$b.Len = 50$$
$$b.Wid = 20$$
$$h.Rad = 10$$

The multigraph representation of constraints is shown in Figure 8.15. For constraint propagation, every arc of the multigraph is associated with alternative procedures that can satisfy the corresponding constraint when executed. For instance, the constraint

$$a = b + c$$

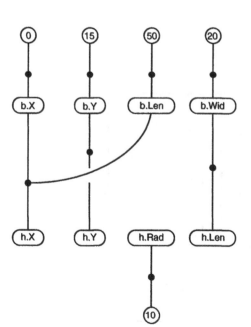

Figure 8.15 The multigraph representation of the constraints of Figure 8.14 (Mäntylä 1990, © 1990 by International Business Machines Corporation; reprinted with permission)

is associated with the three procedures

$$a := b + c$$
$$b := a - c$$
$$c := a - b.$$

where ":=" denotes assignment, in contrast to "=" denoting equality constraint. Given the multigraph, DeltaBlue will find a sequence of procedure applications that, when executed sequentially, will result in a state where as many constraints as possible are met.

The operation of the algorithm is based on the concept of "strength." All constraints have a strength attribute given by the creator of the constraint. The strengths of constraints are used to compute a strength for each variable during the propagation as follows. The strength of a variable whose value is (yet) undetermined by constraints is the absolute minimum 0; otherwise, the strength of the variable is the minimum of the strength of the constraint that determines the value of the variable and the strengths of the input variables of the corresponding procedure.

DeltaBlue works incrementally, by considering one constraint at a time and constructing an intermediate solution at each step. When a new constraint is added to the multigraph, the algorithm selects the weakest variable associated with it as the potential output. If the constraint is stronger than the variable, the constraint can be satisfied by assigning a value to the variable by means of the corresponding procedure. Other variables act as input variables for the procedure. If a previously satisfied constraint is overridden by the new constraint, the algorithm will try to satisfy it recursively. If the new constraint is weaker than the weakest associated variable, the constraint cannot be satisfied. A detailed description of the algorithm is given in (Freeman-Benson and Maloney 1988).

A solution to the constraint graph of Figure 8.15 is shown in Figure 8.16. In the figure, arrowheads are used to indicate the chosen procedure of each constraint, and numbers indicate the evaluation order of the procedures.

The procedure outlined above can be shown to find a best possible solution to the constraint graph in the sense the constraints are satisfied in decreasing order of their strength. Hence, DeltaBlue behaves properly also in overconstrained situations. Because of fully incremental operation, DeltaBlue is also fast enough for interactive use. On the negative side, it cannot deal with coupled sets of constraints, which would lead to cycles in the graph. DeltaBlue can neither support inequality constraints. For instance, in the above example the following additional useful constraint cannot be handled:

$$b.Len > 2 * h.Rad$$

DeltaBlue is used in the feature-based top-down assembly modeler *Why-Are-You-There?* (WAYT) (Mäntylä 1990, 1991). WAYT capitalizes on several properties of DeltaBlue. One useful application of constraints is the relaxation of the

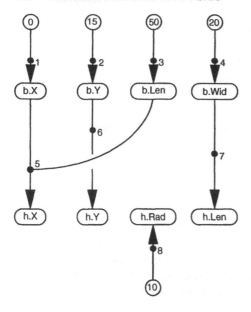

Figure 8.16 The solution of the constraints of Figure 8.15 (Mäntylä 1990, © 1990 by International Business Machines Corporation; reprinted with permission)

fixed parametrization of geometric features implied by its parameters. For instance, instead of the top left point, it might sometimes be more convenient to use the center point of a rectangular block for specifying its position. With the help of the constraints, it is straightforward to state that

$$\texttt{b.Xcenter = b.X + b.Len / 2}$$
$$\texttt{b.Ycenter = b.Y + b.Wid / 2}$$

and then let the user assign values to `Xcenter` and `Ycenter` instead of X and Y.

Another example is given by the cone sink feature of WAYT, which has a redundant set of "natural" parameters (see Figure 8.17), bound by the following constraint:

```
length = (topRadius - bottomRadius) / tan (sinkAngle / 2)
```

By including this expression as a constraint, WAYT can let the user select any three of the four parameters that may be convenient. Hence the separation between "independent" and "derived" parameters introduced in Chapter 3 is unnecessary in WAYT.

Most important for its intended application, WAYT also makes use of the strength of constraints to model the degree of commitment the designer has on the geometry of features. In particular, weak constraints are used to model interim aspects of a model, whereas strong constraints model important aspects. At any time a weak constraint can be incrementally overridden by a strong con-

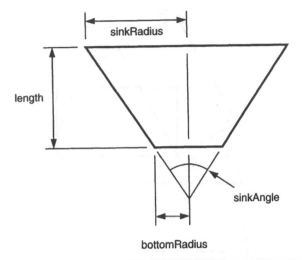

Figure 8.17 Natural parametrization of a `ConeSink` (Mäntylä 1990, © 1990 by International Business Machines Corporation; reprinted with permission)

straint; the unsatisfied weak constraint can still be kept in the graph. If the strong constraint is later revoked, the propagation algorithm will satisfy the weak constraint again.

Propagation of Degrees of Freedom Both of the above methods have difficulty to deal with coupled constraints. A popular approach to constraint propagation that can deal also with some types of coupled constraint systems is the *propagation of degrees of freedom* method (Kramer 1991, 1992). The basic idea of the method is to generate a *plan* consisting of *actions* (e.g., translations and rotations) that solve constraints of the type in Figure 8.5 defined for a set of geometric objects. The plan is generated incrementally; at each step the satisfaction algorithm chooses an action that will satisfy one of the remaining unsatisfied constraints, while not violating any of the constraints satisfied by the already chosen actions.

To choose such an action, the algorithm keeps track of the remaining degrees of freedom (dof) for moving the geometric objects. Initially, all objects have full freedom of motion; they have three translational and three rotational dof. A chosen action will reduce the dof of the objects it deals with. When all dof of some object have been eliminated, it cannot be moved by any further actions.

Let us visualize the method with help of the simple two-dimensional problem depicted in Figure 8.18(*a*); the actual method works in three dimensions. It shows a brick of material with two unsatisfied constraints:

$$\text{coincident}(b1, g1)$$
$$\text{coincident}(b2, g2)$$

stating that points *b1, g1* and points *b2, g2* should be made coincident.

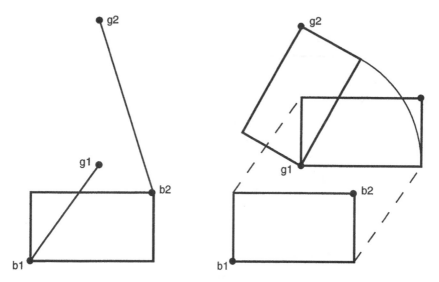

Figure 8.18 Brick problem.

The algorithm will solve the system by generating a plan of movements for the brick that will satisfy incrementally the constraints. Initially the block is completely free to move in the two-dimensional space. In terms of the degrees of freedom (dof) of motion, it has two translational dofs (translations along x- and y-axes) and one rotational dof (rotation around z). To satisfy the constraint coincident(b1, g1), the algorithm translates the brick to a position where the constraint is satisfied (see Figure 8.18b).

To ensure that coincident(b1, g1) remains valid, all further actions that move the brick must be rotations because the brick only has its rotational dof left. To satisfy the other constraint, the algorithm therefore chooses to rotate the brick so that b2 and g2 become coincident. At this stage the brick loses its only remaining dof, and the algorithm terminates. The resulting plan can be simply implemented with homogeneous coordinate transformations. Observe that the plan is independent on the actual geometric positions of the points and remains valid for all nondegenerate configurations of the points.

The actual planning procedure can be implemented by means of a *plan fragment table* indexed with information on the present available dof and the constraint type. For instance, the plan fragment for the first constraint above would be fetched with the index "(2, 1, coincident)," indicating that initial state of the planning action has two translational and one rotational dof, and that the constraint type "coincident" is being handled. Kramer reports that a total of 112 plan fragments are needed to handle a set of constraint types that covers most mechanism types. He also shows that the action analysis is complete (there are no dead ends in the algorithm) and canonical (the constraints may be satisfied in any order).

Another type of a constraint propagation scheme is proposed by (Owen 1991), who describes a graph-based method for solving an interesting subset of constraint systems. He shows that the class of constraints that results from using the conventional drafting methods as implemented in most CAD systems (basically constructions that can be made with ruler and compass) can be solved using purely algebraic methods. The basic idea is to split a constraint graph in triconnected components and to solve the components by canned solutions methods in a sequence. Special "virtual links" are inserted during the decomposition of the graph to propagate intermediate results from a component to the next ones. The method is commercially available as the Dimensional Constraint Manager offered by D-Cubed, Ltd. (1992).

Numerical Constraint Satisfaction Numerical constraint satisfaction is based on converting constraint specifications to a system of equations that is then solved using standard methods of numerical mathematics. An extremely valuable source of readily useful numerical algorithms is provided by (Press et al. 1992); the methods described below can be implemented with the programs given in the reference with relatively ease.

Consider, for instance, the constraint `disp(R, T, D)` of Figure 8.10. The constraint states that the distance between two points R and T must be D. Using the constraint and equality constraints for specifying constants, a two-dimensional triangle can be defined with the following constraints:

$$\text{disp}(p_1, p_2, 5)$$
$$\text{disp}(p_2, p_3, 4)$$
$$\text{disp}(p_3, p_1, 3)$$
$$p_1 = (1, 1)$$
$$p_{2x} = 4.$$

These constraints can be transformed to the following system of six nonlinear equations

$$\begin{cases} (p_{1x} - p_{2x})^2 + (p_{1y} - p_{2y})^2 = 25 \\ (p_{2x} - p_{3x})^2 + (p_{2y} - p_{3y})^2 = 16 \\ (p_{3x} - p_{1x})^2 + (p_{3y} - p_{1y})^2 = 9 \\ p_{1x} = 1 \\ p_{1y} = 1 \\ p_{2x} = 4 \end{cases}$$

Given a set of n nonlinear equations in n variables such as the system generated from the triangle example, a popular solution method is the *Newton-Raphson iteration*. Let x denote the entire vector of variables x_i, $i = 1, 2, ..., n$, and $\mathbf{F}$ be the vector of equations

$$F_i(x_1, x_2, ..., x_n) = 0, \quad i = 1, 2, ..., n$$

In the neighborhood of **x**, each of functions F_i can be expanded in Taylor series

$$F_i(x + \delta x) = F_i(x) + \sum_{j=1}^{n} \frac{\partial F_i}{\partial x_j} \delta x_j + O(\delta x^2).$$

The matrix of partial derivatives in the series is termed the *Jacobian matrix* **J**:

$$J_{ij} = \frac{\partial F_i}{\partial x_j}$$

By neglecting the higher-order terms and setting $F_i(x + \delta x) = 0$, a linear system of equations for the corrections δx that move each function towards zero is obtained as

$$\mathbf{J} \cdot \delta x = -\mathbf{F}$$

The vector $-\mathbf{F}$ is sometimes termed the *residual* of the iteration; when it becomes (effectively) zero, the iteration has converged. The resulting linear system can be solved for δx by Gaussian elimination, by which the new solution vector is obtained:

$$\mathbf{x}_{k+1} = \mathbf{x}_k + [\mathbf{J}(\mathbf{x}_k)]^{-1}\mathbf{F}$$

where $\mathbf{x}_k$ is the vector of the variables in kth iteration.

The triangle problem resulted in a system of six equations in terms of six variables. Commonly, however, a constraint-based definition results in an overconstrained system, where the number of equations is larger than the number of variables. If such a system is nonredundant, it has no solutions. In many cases, however, an overconstrained system simply has redundant equations that can be eliminated without changing the solution.

If the original system is overdetermined, its Jacobian matrix will have more rows than columns, and also contain mutually dependent vectors. In their seminal work on variational geometry, (Light and Gossard 1982) developed a method for detecting groups of mutually dependent equations in the Jacobian using Gaussian elimination. By eliminating one dependent equation from each group, they were able to eliminate the mutual dependencies. Lee and Andrews (1985) solve the same problem by picking arbitrarily n from the remaining set of m equations, and observing the convergence of all m residuals. If some of the equations not chosen for the Newton-Raphson iteration fail to converge along with the chosen ones, then another set of equations is chosen, until all equations converge.

While the above method is simple to implement, it suffers from some problems. First, an initial guess must be supplied to get the iteration started. If multiple solutions are present, it may be difficult to give an initial guess that converges to the expected solution. There is no satisfactory way to handle underconstrained systems. Some types of systems may converge to completely spurious solutions; see the discussion on symbolic methods below.

The above method is applicable to equality constraints only. Sometimes also inequalities need to be included in the system of equations, for instance, to describe parameter restrictions and interference. These types constraint systems can be handled by *optimization methods*.

One such example is the work of (Kim and Gossard 1989), who use a physics-based model for studying *packaging problems*. Packaging is defined as the process of locating components in an available space while satisfying given spatial relationships among the components. Some of the given relationships are equality constraints on the relative location of the components corresponding with rigid joints between the components. Some others are inequalities, specifying that certain components must be placed "close" or "far" from each other. Noninterference is also treated as an inequality constraint.

The central idea of the method is to transform the inequality constraints into an *energy function*. Specifically, an inequality constraint on the distance of two components $P1$ and $P2$ is transformed into an energy form by conceptualizing the required spatial relationship ("near" or "far") as a spring attached to the components as shown in Figure 8.19. The potential energy of a spring is given by

$$E_{12} = \tfrac{1}{2} K (L - L_0)^2$$

where K is the spring constant, L is the distance between the two components, and L_0 is the free length of the spring.

Similarly the interference of two components can be converted into an energy function by approximating the size of the interference volume. Referring to the

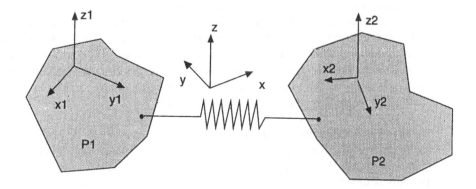

Figure 8.19 Spatial relation represented as a spring constraint

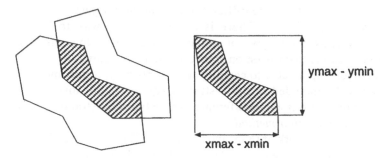

Figure 8.20 Example of interference

two-dimensional case in Figure 8.20, the energy generated from an interference can be expressed as

$$E_{12} = \tfrac{1}{2}\, KL_C{}^2,$$

where L_C is the "characteristic length" of the interference volume:

$$L_C = [(x_{max} - x_{min})(y_{max} - y_{min})(z_{max} - z_{min})]^{1/3}$$

These formulations lead to an optimization problem, where the total "energy" of the assembly must be minimized subject to the equality constraints. The optimization problem is solved iteratively by using a *gradient method* which basically works by determining the most promising search direction for minimizing the energy in the space defined by the equality constraints. See (Press et al. 1992) for details of gradient methods.

An interesting different type of a numerical approach to solving constraints is presented by (Kin et al. 1992). They use a neural network based method to solve a set of nonlinear geometric constraints. In particular, the constraint satisfaction problem is converted into a energy minimization problem which is solved using a *Boltzmann machine*. Other similar novel methods that have successfully applied include *generic algorithms* and *simulated annealing*. In particular, simulated annealing has proved to be attractive for solving nonlinear, highly coupled systems of inequality constraints (Thornton 1993).

Symbolic Constraint Satisfaction Numerical techniques do not work well for overconstrained nonlinear sets of constraints. Buchanan and de Pennington (1993) point out that using a least-squares method to deal with overconstrained systems is unsatisfactory because the system may converge at a spurious solution. As an alternative to numerical techniques, they propose an evaluation method based on *symbolic algebra*, where possible redundancies can be automatically pruned.

In their method, the computer algebra system REDUCE is used to convert the implicit equations derived from the constraints to *Gröbner basis* form. The Gröbner basis of a system of *n* polynomials in *n* unknowns can be considered a canonical form where the resulting polynomials are arranged in the order of "simplicity" in the sense that the result is a triangular system that can be solved by univariate equation solving and backsubstitution. The procedure is analogous to Gaussian elimination for the case of a linear system; indeed, for linear polynomials, a Gaussian triangulation is obtained.

For instance, (Buchanan and de Pennington 1993) give the following example: Consider again the triangle example in the previous section. After assigning the constants and rearranging the polynomials (something which REDUCE is good at), we get the equations

$$9 + (1 - p_{2y})^2 - 25 = 0$$

$$(4 - p_{3x})^2 + (p_{2y} - p_{3y})^2 - 16 = 0$$

$$(p_{3x} - 1)^2 + (p_{3y} - 1)^2 - 9 = 0$$

For this system, the Gröbner basis (using the ordering $p_{3y} > p_{2y} > p_{3x}$) is found to be

$$16p_{3y} + 3p_{2y}p_{3x} - 12p_{2y} - 3p_{3x} - 4 = 0$$

$$p_{2y}^2 - 2p_{2y} - 15 = 0$$

$$25p_{3x}^2 - 104p_{3x} + 16 = 0$$

The result is in triangular form, where the last equation is univariate, and it can be solved for p_{3x}. In this case the second equation also happens to be univariate. The solved values of p_{3x} and p_{2y} can be substituted in the first equation, which then can be solved for p_{3y}.

There are a number of benefits to the Gröbner basis technique. The Gröbner basis is independent of possible overdetermining redundant (consistent) equations; these get eliminated by the basis construction algorithm. An inconsistent system can be determined as such. A basis can also be computed for an underdetermined system, in which case possible fully determined variables can be detected.

Overdetermined nonredundant systems can also be treated. Consider the system

$$(x - 1)(x - 2) = 0$$

$$(x - 1)(x - 3) = 0$$

which is overdetermined because we have two equations in one variable. The system is, however, not inconsistent because it has the solution $x = 1$. The Gröbner basis of the system turns out to be

$$x - 1 = 0$$

which leads to the correct root. In this case a Newton-Raphson iteration would produce completely spurious results.

Another interesting example of algebraic methods in constraint manipulation is given by (Kondo 1992) who describes a method for editing a parametric two-dimensional CAD model. The model is given in terms of polynomials that express the relationships between independent and dependent variables. The polynomials are created simultaneously with the modeling operations creating the geometry. The dependencies between the modeling operations are encoded in a dependency graph.

The proposed method uses Gröbner bases to update the polynomials after a change in the declared parametric scheme. For instance, assume that a constraint that used to determine a dependent variable x is replaced with a new constraint that determines a new dependent variable y. Now a new polynomial is needed that expresses the relation of x (which becomes a independent variable) from y, and other independent variables preceding the added constraint in the dependency graph. Such a polynomial is constructed by computing the Gröbner basis of the set of polynomials that binds x and y and the other independent variables "higher" than x and y. The lexicographic ordering of the basis computation is arranged in such a way that a basis polynomial that expresses the desired relationship is created.

Algebraic methods can deal with situations where numerical methods fail. The downside of the method is the high computational cost of the symbolic algebra manipulations required for the basis construction. Moreover exact arithmetic must be used throughout the computation, and this precludes the use of variables with irrational values.

Truth Maintenance A popular approach for maintaining knowledge on dependencies between various types of entities in knowledge-based systems is _truth maintenance._ Several types of truth maintenance systems have been constructed; of these, let us concentrate on the _assumption-based truth maintenance_ (ATMS) approach (de Kleer 1986).

An ATMS is a data structure representing the relationship between various types of _assumptions_ presently believed to be true, and other pieces of information whose truth values are determined from the assumptions on the basis of some type of deduction. In truth maintenance parlance, information presently deduced to be true is labeled _in_ and information deduced to be false _out._ Furthermore each piece of _in_ information is labeled with the assumptions that justify its truth status. Using the labels, the ATMS can maintain the _in_ and _out_ labels of deduced information if the truth values of assumptions change. Mutually inconsistent sets of assumptions can also be detected and labeled as such.

Suzuki et al. (1990) use an ATMS to deal with default constraints in their logic-based constraint system. Default constraints are deduced from user input; for instance, if two lines are drawn at a straight angle, but no explicit constraint stating that the angle between them must be 90 degrees is given, a default constraint is created and labeled as an assumption of an ATMS. This makes the ATMS able to keep track of the relation between the constraint and its consequences. If a contradiction occurs, the ATMS can detect it, and the default constraint can be labeled *out*.

Truth maintenance systems separate the maintenance of relationships among pieces of related data from the actual method used to generate the relationships; therefore any type of constraint satisfaction method, including rule-based deduction, can be supported. An ATMS, in particular, can deal with inconsistent sets of assumptions without backtracking. The bad news is the inherent overhead caused by the maintenance of the complex data representation.

8.4 FEATURE REFINEMENT

One of the possible problems of a design by features environment is that features to be inserted in the design must be selected from a large feature library. Imagine searching a desired feature from a menu with several hundred entries! As already mentioned in Section 8.1, this problem can be avoided by making a distinction between user-level and model-level features. In this approach the user designs the part in terms of a simple set of user-level features; these are converted to more detailed model-level features by means of a special feature mapping method. The quick turnaround cell (QTC) system (Anderson and Chang 1989, 1990) introduces such a mapping method, known as *feature refinement*. Therefore we will discuss the concept by describing the feature refinement method of QTC.

The main goal of the QTC design system is to provide input to a generative process planning system. The feature-based design environment is based on high-level features such as hole, slot, or counterbore that correspond loosely to manufacturing operations. The designer is not restricted to use these features in a strictly predetermined fashion. For instance, a slot feature can carry several meanings; as shown in Figure 8.21, it can be blind, through, or degenerate to a pocket, depending on its location and orientation with respect to the part it occurs in.

The mapping from high-level features to low-level features corresponding more directly with manufacturing operations is implemented by means of a feature refinement procedure. Feature refinement is based on inspecting the actual geometry caused by the design feature. This is implemented by marking the faces appearing in the boundary representation solid model representation of the feature model with feature information, a technique frequently called *tagging*.

The basic idea of feature tagging can be expressed with reference to Figure 8.22, showing a slot feature (*a*) and a part where a slot has been inserted (*b*). All design features of QTC have a native boundary model representation. In these representations, the faces are marked with tags indicating the position of the

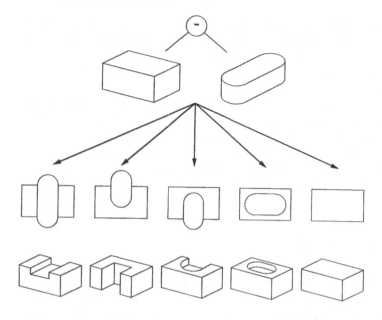

Figure 8.21 Example of feature refinement (Anderson and Chang 1990; reprinted by permission of Elsevier Science Ltd.)

face in the feature (top, bottom, side, etc.). A boundary representation model corresponding with a feature model is created as Boolean combination of the features; in the case of the slot feature, the slot shape is created through a Boolean difference operation. The difference operation can be implemented in a fashion that transfers the tags of the slot boundary model into the boundary model modeling the result of the operation; therefore, in the example of Figure 8.22, the slot faces inserted into the block carry the tags shown.

Using the tags, the refinement procedure can be implemented. First, all faces that belong to the same feature are collected. Next, classification rules are applied to the set. For instance, for the slot feature typical rules would be as follows:

- If the slot has a missing end face and a missing top face, then the slot is blind.
- If two end faces and a top face of the slot are missing, then the slot is through.
- If both the top and the bottom faces of a slot are missing, then the slot is hollow.
- If only the top face of a slot is missing, then the slot is a pocket.
- If no faces are missing, then the slot is a cavity.

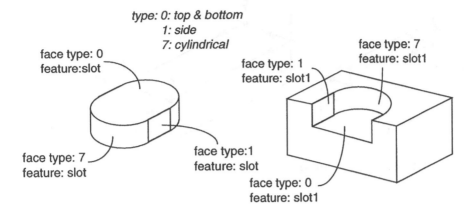

Figure 8.22 Example of feature tagging (Anderson and Chang 1990; reprinted by permission of Elsevier Science Ltd.)

After applying the rules, feature parameters are computed on the basis of the faces present in the model. For instance, in the case of Figure 8.22*b*, the actual length of the blind slot is computed.

Observe that a feature can degenerate into another feature after several Boolean operations. For instance, a pocket will degenerate into a slot if two of its sides are removed. Similarly a slot with one side and both ends missing becomes a step.

During the refinement process, feature interactions are also found by means of a procedure that compares each pair of found features and determines whether their geometries interact. For use by the process planning application, information such as approach and feed direction is also extracted.

8.5 FEATURE RELATIONS

In a design-by-features system a major portion of user's input is related to positioning and dimensioning features of a part with respect to each other. Clearly a user interface that can help in this process is very attractive. This section will discuss two sample systems with attractive methods for positioning and dimensioning features.

8.5.1 Handles in QTC

The QTC system mentioned in Section 8.4 uses object-oriented techniques to implement the feature-based model and its components. Therefore features are "objects" that "know about'" their instantiation and dimensioning properties;

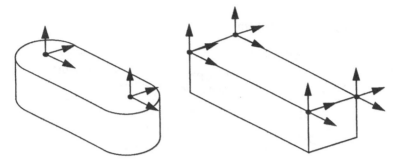

Figure 8.23 Features with handles

some of these are described on a general level so that they apply to all features, while other more specialized characteristics can be described "locally." For instance, all features must be capable of being drawn or having their parameters changed interactively; in the object-oriented approach these operations can be treated as methods defined for an abstract feature class.

To assist the designer in interacting with the three-dimensional geometry of the features and in overall construction of a feature model, graphical entities called "handles" are used in QTC. Handles are characteristic elements of feature geometries, corresponding to points and lines of interest. For instance, point handles are used to give access to the endpoints of the axis of a hole, and line handles are used to give access to geometric characteristics of features, such as the length of a slot or the depth of a pocket. Some examples of handles are shown in Figure 8.23. Observe that for the slot feature, handles are placed at the intersection points of the cylindrical ends and the top surface; this makes sense because these points are often of interest for dimensioning. Hence handles need not be placed at real vertices of the feature.

Positioning, dimensioning, and tolerancing of features takes place in terms of the handles. The relative position of two features can be expressed by a relation between appropriately chosen handles in the two features. Tolerances can be associated to the relative positions. Figure 8.24 shows a simple example of feature relations expressed in terms of handles. Observe that the step feature is positioned with respect to the block, and the slot with respect to the step. Hence certain types of dimension chains can be modeled.

8.5.2 Geometric Trees in Geonode

A very attractive user interface for feature modeling is described by van Emmerik and Jansen (van Emmerik and Jansen 1989, van Emmerik 1990). Their system, Geonode, is based on a procedural definition of features. These definitions are coded in a CSG-oriented definition language providing a variety of useful operations such as various expressions, functions, and variables. Repetition and

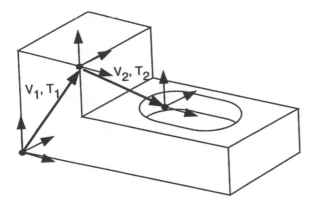

Figure 8.24 Example of feature relations expressed with handles

conditionals are included. Feature descriptions can be encapsulated into procedures and functions that can be stored into a library for usage in other models.
Further progress of this research has been reported in (van Emmerik et al. 1994).

The basic modeling entities in the Geonode system are primitive volumes
and local coordinate systems (lcs). Local coordinate systems are used as reference structure for dimensioning, positioning, and orientation of primitive volumes or assemblies. Each object is positioned and oriented in the three-dimensional space by one lcs; one or several other lcs's are used to specify the
dimensions of the objects. For instance, a cylinder primitive is defined by two
lcs's, one located at the center of the bottom circle of the cylinder, and the other
at the edge of the top circle (see Figure 8.25). The translation transformation
between the two lcs's defines the height and the radius of the cylinder.

Geometric and topological relations between lcs's are captured in a *geometric tree* data structure. Each node in the tree represents a lcs defined with respect
to another lcs. The user can manipulate the geometric tree directly. New lcs's can
be defined with respect to the existing ones, and moved, rotated, or scaled by
direct graphical manipulation of an isometric view of the tree. The implemented
system exploits very cleverly hardware-supported dynamic three-dimensional
graphics in its user interface.

A simple example of a geometric tree is shown in Figure 8.25. In (*a*), a geometric design and its dimensioning scheme is shown. A geometric tree that captures the dimensioning scheme of (*a*) is shown in (*b*). The "root" of this tree is the
coordinate system lcs_0; lcs_0 and lcs_2 define the size and orientation of the rectangular block of material. Observe that lcs_2 is defined in terms of three translations
with respect to lcs_0; these translations define the height, width, and length of the
block. Coordinate system lcs_3 is defined in terms of lcs_1, which in turn is defined
in terms of lcs_0; it determines the position and orientation of the circular hole.
Finally, lcs_4 defines the height and radius of the hole. The final design is shown
in (*c*).

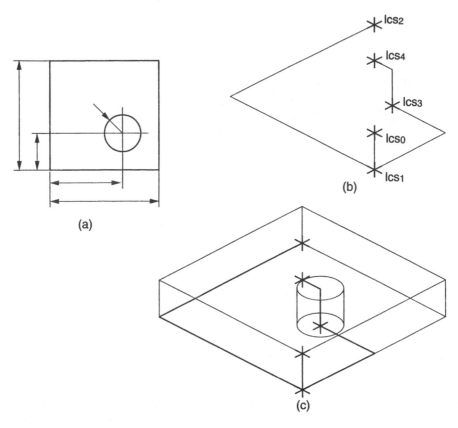

Figure 8.25 Example of a geometric tree (van Emmerik and Jansen 1989; reprinted by permission of Elsevier Science)

An example of a feature definition is shown in Figure 8.26. The feature is composed of two primitive volumes, a block (*par*) and a cylinder (*cyl*). Geometric relations between the primitives are defined by means of three coordinate systems *root*, *n1*, and *n2*. Initially the *root* lcs is presented to the user. This coordinate system serves as a basis for the position and orientation of the feature. The block is positioned at the root lcs and the cylinder at *n1*. Dimensions of both primitives are determined by the lcs *n2*. Observe that the whole feature can be positioned by referring to the *root* coordinate system.

Objects such as the one shown in Figure 8.26 can be defined in terms of direct manipulation. For instance, to define a new node, variables into the modeling language template "*newnode* = lcs(*parent*)" can be substituted by selecting the parent node graphically. Object naming is performed by the system. Positioning, orientation, and scaling of objects is defined by modifying the internal fields *tx*, *ty*, *tz* (translations), *rx*, *ry*, *rz* (rotations), and *sx*, *sy*, *sz* (scalings) of the coordinate systems. Assignments to these fields are created automatically by the system on the basis of interactive menu selections. After the object has been defined, it can be stored in a database for later retrieval.

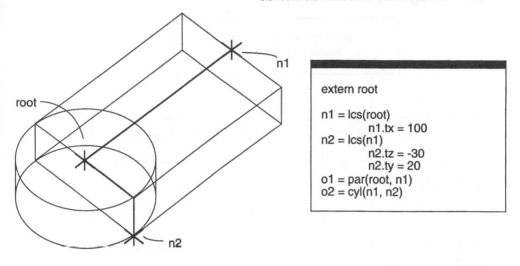

The diagram panel contains:

extern root

n1 = lcs(root)
        n1.tx = 100
n2 = lcs(n1)
        n2.tz = -30
        n2.ty = 20
o1 = par(root, n1)
o2 = cyl(n1, n2)

Figure 8.26 Example of partially rounded slot feature (van Emmerik and Jansen 1989; reprinted by permission of Elsevier Science)

8.6 PART AND PRODUCT FAMILY MODELING

The procedural methods discussed in Section 8.2 covered only single features. Similar concepts can also be applied on the level of whole parts and assemblies of parts, leading to the concept of *part and product family modeling*.

A part family model, in brief, represents a collection of parts exhibiting some variation in dimensions, tolerances, and overall shape that nevertheless are considered "similar" from the viewpoint of a certain application. For design, a part family may correspond to a "standard part," a parametric collection of parts that may be included as a component in a design. For manufacturing, a part family may be a collection of parts with similar process planning requirements (routing, tool selection, process parameters). Many such applications of features benefit from explicit models of part families. For instance, process planning applications can use part family descriptions to store part specific routing and process selection information.

Parametric part family modeling was already introduced from user's viewpoint in Chapter 5. Here we will take a closer look at part families from system designer's viewpoint by investigating the design of the EXTDesign feature modeling system (Laakko 1993).

EXTDesign puts a special emphasis on computer-aided generation of part family models to support the transition from novel to parametric design. For this end, EXTDesign introduces methods for creating feature and part family classes on the basis of a previously designed feature model. A part family model created in this fashion becomes a permanent part of the part taxonomy, and it can be

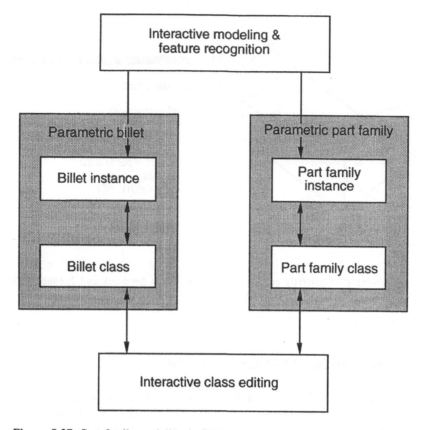

Figure 8.27 Part family modeling in EXTDesign

used as a basis of parametric design. A combination of interactive and algorithmic modeling is used to implement the approach.

The part family modeling methods are illustrated in the diagram of Figure 8.27. In brief, part family modeling consists of two tasks, namely (1) modeling the initial part (billet) and (2) modeling the features of the part. The first task is handled mainly through interactive modeling with the help of a *history log* mechanism that stores a trace of the solid modeling operations performed on the part. The trace can be retrieved and edited to make it a parametric solid representation that can be associated with a billet-type feature.

A typical history log would contain entries such as the following:

```
LAMINA obj-1 0.0 0.0 0.0 20.0 0.0 0.0 ...
SWEEP obj-2 obj-1 15.0
TRANSF obj-2 obj-3 40.0 30.0 0.0 0.0 0.0 0.0
```

After compilation, these would be turned into a billet class description of the following outline:

```
(new-billet
 (is-a billet)
 (instance-slots
  (length) (width) (height))
 (geometry
  (solid-id-1 (geom-lamina 0.0 0.0 0.0 20.0 0.0 0.0 ...))
  (solid-id-2 (geom-sweep solid-id-1 15.0))
  (geom-transf solid-id-2 40.0 30.0 0.0 0.0 0.0 0.0)))
```

The definition can be edited with a frame editor to add parameters, expressions, and so on. Presently, work is being done to use a constraint-based mechanism for recording parametric dependencies of various geometric objects automatically.

The second task, that is modeling of a part family consisting of an initial part and several detail features, is also accomplished by a combination of interactive design and class editing. The basic idea of the approach chosen is illustrated in Figure 8.28. As the figure indicates, the designer first uses the incremental fea-

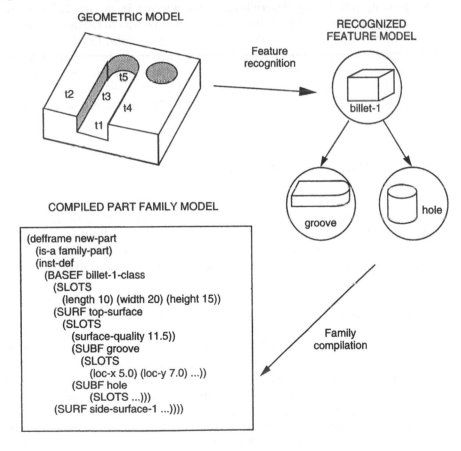

Figure 8.28   Translation of a feature structure to a part family model

ture modeling approach to create an instance of the desired feature structure. This may involve feature recognition from a solid model. Once the desired structure has been created, the user can invoke an algorithm that traverses the feature structure and creates automatically a procedural description of the part family. The description is stored into a LISP frame. A specialized editor is provided for editing the part family description part of the feature definition frame. The editor provides facilities for defining parameters, writing expressions, and so on.

It is also possible to instantiate an existing part family, perform incremental changes to it, and generate a new part family on the basis of the result. Any feature properties, constraints, and other characteristics unaffected by the incremental changes are preserved. For details, see (Laakko and Mäntylä 1994).

Figure 8.29 shows the part family editing process in operation. In the figure the user has created a simple object with a rectangular depression and a large circular hole. These geometric elements are recognized as rectangular slot and through-hole features. After the user selects the operation "new part family" from a menu, EXTDesign will translate the recognized instance structure into a corresponding part family description, which appears in the top left window. Then the user will proceed by defining the parametrization of the new family. To do this, he chooses the menu selection "edit instance definition," upon which the structure editor for the part definition is opened in the bottom left window. The editor provides facilities for defining parameters and entering parametric formulas for computing the size and position of the features on the basis of the parameters. The implementation methods of EXTDesign are discussed more in Chapter 10.

8.7 CUTTING AND PASTING FEATURES

Most of the sample systems discussed earlier in this chapter are based on a more or less strict separation between feature definitions and feature instances. The emphasis of these systems is on using predefined feature definitions to support feature-based design. The (silent) assumption behind this approach is that the feature library containing the definitions changes slowly if at all compared to the designs.

The validity of this assumption clearly depends on the type of design work being performed. In a variant design, the designed parts are simple variants of previous parts. In this scenario we can expect that the feature library identified for the earlier designs is still valid. For a creative or innovative design, on the other hand, the assumption is debatable. Since novel solutions must be found to design problems, it is reasonable to expect new feature classes to emerge during the design. Clearly then a feature-based design environment where creation of new features is a complex operation cannot be attractive for innovative design.

An interesting approach to feature-based design intended particularly for innovative design is presented by (Ranta et al. 1993). They consider a system where new features can be defined interactively during a regular design process

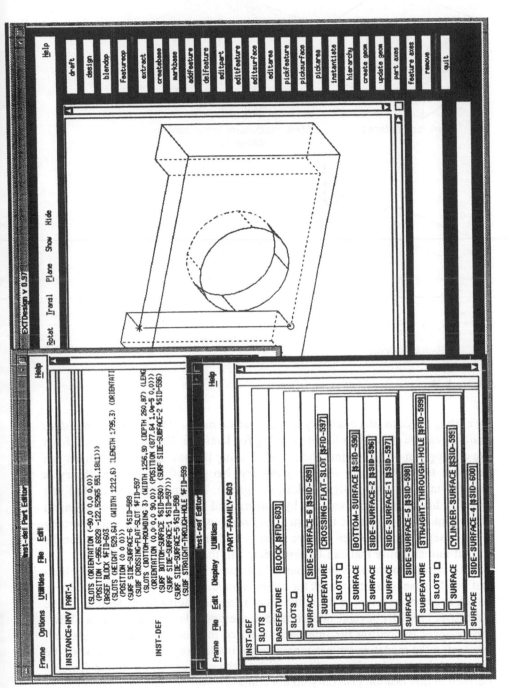

Figure 8.29 Part family modeling with EXTDesign

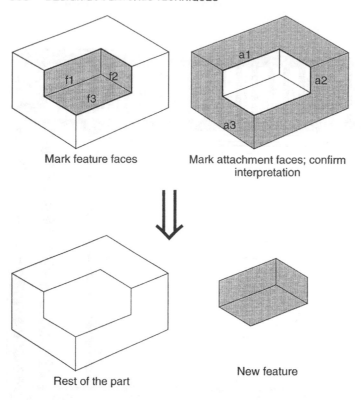

Mark feature faces

Mark attachment faces; confirm
interpretation

Rest of the part

New feature

Figure 8.30 Example of cutting operation

by *cutting* portions of a boundary representation model. The resulting *boundary features* can be stored in a feature catalog for later use. Features retrieved from the catalog can be *pasted* into the model. During the pasting, local changes can be made to the boundary feature geometry. No predefined feature library is needed; instead, each designer (designer group, design department, etc.) can develop his or her local catalog by cutting and pasting. From the technical viewpoint, we characterize the system as *prototype based*; instead of enforcing a strict separation between feature classes and instances, any feature can be turned into an entity that can be instantiated in the model.

The cutting operation is implemented interactively; see Figure 8.30 for illustration. The user can either mark the *attachment faces* of the portion of boundary which becomes a feature or select the set of faces belonging to the feature. In the first case, typically several interpretations are possible, and the system allows the designer to confirm the intended subset of the boundary will be selected. Thereafter the modeling system separates the marked region from the rest of the part, and the new feature can be stored into the catalog. Observe that features defined in this fashion generally do not contain a volume and are incomplete as geometric models. For instance, the resulting feature consisting of exactly three faces in Figure 8.30 does not define a closed volume.

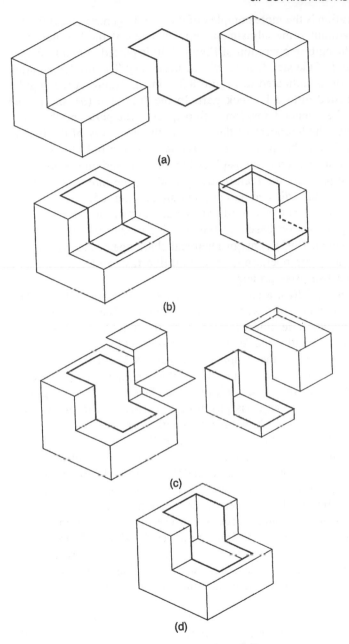

Figure 8.31 Implementation of the paste operation

The pasting operation is the more complex of the two. In general, a cut feature cannot be pasted without some adjustment. For instance, if the "corner step" feature defined in the cutting operation of Figure 8.30 is pasted onto a L-shaped part, some adjustment of the step feature will be necessary. The implementation of the paste operation is indicated in Figure 8.31. In the figure, a rectangular pocket feature is pasted onto a L-block part. In the first step (*a*), the pasted feature is placed in the intended position with respect to the part, and the intersection curve between the boundary of the part and the boundary of the feature is calculated. In the figure the intersection curve is shown in bold lines. In the second step (*b*), the intersection curve is placed on the part and on the boundary feature, and both the part and the feature are split along the intersection curve (*c*). In the final step (*d*), the adjusted part and feature are merged.

The geometric elements cut or pasted can include constraints implemented using a constraint propagation based system similar to the one discussed in Section 8.3.3 (Ranta et al. 1995). A major technical challenge of the system is to implement the cut and paste operations in an intuitive fashion from the user's viewpoint ("the lowest surprise principle").

As shown in Figure 8.32(*b*), a cut operation yields a constrained boundary feature that is an incomplete solid with broken constraints. The open edges and broken constraints maintain default information on the neighbor and reference faces, and this allows an unattached feature to be modified by changing its size dimensions such as the width of the sample slot. Figures 8.32 (*c*) and (*d*) demonstrate the pasting of a constrained feature. First, the designer repairs the positioning constraints by replacing the default reference faces with those appropriate to the new environment, and assigns proper values to the positioning dimensions. Figure 8.32(*c*) shows how the slot length is set to refer to the front face of the part, the slot depth to the top face, and finally the position to the right-hand side face of the part. After the designer accepts the positioning, the system adjusts the boundary and constraint models together. As Figure 8.32(*d*) shows, the border edges of the feature are replaced by new ones calculated according to the intersection of the surfaces of the meeting faces.

Figure 8.33 shows how a feature structure is useful in maintaining a constrained boundary model. When the designer removes the slot in Figure 8.33(*a*) the hole becomes a "floating" entity, with its position constraints referring to the faces of the removed slot. The designer may now either delete the hole or repair the positioning by attaching the constraints to the remaining faces of the

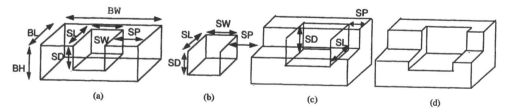

(a)   (b)   (c)   (d)

Figure 8.32 Cutting and pasting a constrained boundary feature (Ranta et al. 1995; reprinted by permission of the author)

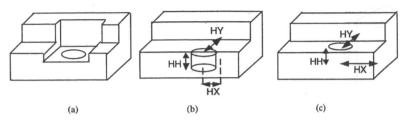

Figure 8.33 Repairing constraints after removing a feature (Ranta et al. 1995; reprinted by permission of the author)

part as shown in Figure 8.33(*c*). Observe in the figure that the dimension *HX* of the hole is now measured from the right edge of the part instead of the right edge of the recess feature.

The cut and paste design process explained here has been greatly simplified in order to give an overview of the technique. In practice boundary features are more complicated and larger entities. The attractiveness of the approach is in the way it enables new products to be created from just a few large design and function-oriented features.

REVIEW QUESTIONS

8.1 Discuss the possible use of design-by-features methods for applications other than design.

8.2 Analyze some feature-based system known to you in light of the characteristics discussed in Section 8.1. Are feature definitions static or dynamic? Are user-defined features supported, and if yes, to what extent? How is the geometry linkage realized? (Answers to some of these questions may be difficult to extract from outside of the system!)

8.3 Discuss the benefits of declarative feature definitions for feature data exchange.

8.4 Discuss the benefits of decoupling user-level and model-level features from the viewpoint of the user interface of a feature-based system. Analyze each of the axes of Figure 8.1.

8.5 Analyze the characteristics of a geometry system that you know well in light of the discussion of Section 8.1. Can feature geometry definitions be implemented? How about feature validation rules? Is it possible to implement geometric reasoning operations?

8.6 Can you think of a reason for separating the ENTITY and FUNCTION sections of the PDGL feature definition language (see Figure 8.4)?

8.7 Prepare a constraint-based model in the style of Figure 8.12 for the part shown below. (Create a convenient dimensioning scheme. Assume that the hole is centered in the relief feature.)

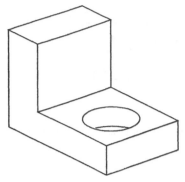

8.8   Draw the constraint graph of the "triangle problem" discussed in Section 8.3.3. Can the solution be computed with sequential constraint satisfaction?

8.9   Repeat question 8.7 using WAYT-style constraint equations as described in Section 8.3.3. Draw a constraint multigraph for the system. Can you find a sequential order for satisfying the constraints?

8.10 Apply Kramer's method (Section 8.3.3) for the triangle problem. (Consider each corner an entity initially with two translational and one rotational degrees of freedom. Contrive some actions. Observe that after a distance constraint between two points has been satisfied, they both still have the rotational dof left, and both can rotate around the other.)

8.11 Can you identify other features with a redundant set of "natural" parameters in addition to the ConeSink feature of Figure 8.19? If yes, identify constraint(s) that bind the parameters.

8.12 Consider feature refinement of a generic hole feature in the style of Figure 8.21. What more specialized kinds of holes may be produced? Can you outline the refinement rules?

8.13 Critique the feature handles approach to representing dimension chains in light of the discussion in Chapter 5. What types of dimensioning schemes can be represented? Cannot be represented?

8.14 Repeat question 8.13 for the geometric trees outlined in Section 8.5.2.

BIBLIOGRAPHY

Ali, A., 1994, Declarative approach to form feature definition, M.S. thesis, Department of Mechanical Engineering, Arizona State University.

Anderson, D. C., and Chang, T. C., 1989, Automated process planning using object-oriented feature based design, *Proc. of International Symposium on Advanced Geometric Modeling for Engineering Applications,* November 8–10, Berlin, FRG, North-Holland.

Anderson, D. C., and Chang, T. C., 1990, Geometric reasoning in feature-based design and process planning, *Comp. & Gr.* **14** (2): 225–235.

Balakrishnan, G., 1993, Constraint based approach to product modeling, M.S. thesis, Department of Mechanical Engineering, Arizona State University.

Buchanan, S. A., and de Pennington, A., 1993, Constraint Definition System: A computer-algebra based approach to solving geometric-constraint problems, *Computer-Aided Design* **25** (12): 741–750.

D-Cubed Ltd., 1992, *The Dimensional Constraint Manager, the 2 Dimensional DCM Technical Overview*, Cambridge, England.

de Kleer, J., 1986, An assumption-based truth maintenance system, *Artificial Intelligence* **28**: 127–162.

Even, S., 1979, *Graph Algorithms*, Computer Science Press.

Freeman-Benson, B. N., and Maloney, J., 1988, The DeltaBlue algorithm: an incremental constraint hierarchy solver, Technical Report 88-11-09, Department of Computer Science, University of Washington, Seattle, Washington.

Freeman-Benson, B. N., Maloney, J., and Borning, A., 1990, An incremental constraint solver, *Comm. ACM* **33** (1): 54–63.

Hummel, K., and Wolf, M., 1990, Integrating expert systems with solid modeling through interprocess communications and application interface specification, *ASME Computers in Engineering Conf.*, Boston, ASME Press, New York.

Kim, J. J., and Gossard, D., 1989, Reasoning on the location of components for assembly packaging, in B. Ravani, ed., *Advances in Design Automation—1989, Vol. 1, Computer-Aided and Computational Automation*, ASME Press, New York., pp. 251–257, Proc. of 15th ASME Design Automation Conf.

Kin, N., Takai, Y., and Kunii, T. L., 1992, Geometrical constraint solving based on the extended Boltzmann machine, *Computers in Industry* **19**: 239–250.

Kondo, K., 1992, Algebraic method for manipulation of dimensional relationships in geometric models, *Computer-Aided Design* **24** (3): 141–147.

Kramer, G. A., 1991, Using degrees of freedom analysis to solve geometric constraint systems, in J. Rossignac and J. Turner, eds., *Proc. of Symposium on Solid Modeling Foundations and CAD/CAM Applications*, ACM, New York, pp. 371–378.

Kramer, G. A., 1992, *Solving Geometric Constraint Problems*, MIT Press.

Krause, F.-L., Ulbrich, A., and Vosgerau, F. H., 1991, Feature based approach for the integration of design and process planning systems, presented at the *IFIP 5.2 Workshop on Geometric Modelling*, Rensselaerville, NY, June 17–21, 1990, North-Holland.

Laakko, T., 1993, Incremental feature modelling: methodology for integrating features and solid models, Dr. Tech. dissertation, Helsinki University of Technology, Laboratory of Information Processing Science.

Laakko, T., and Mäntylä, M., 1994, Feature-based modeling of product families, in K. Ishii et al., eds., *ASME Computers in Engineering Conference*, Vol. 1, Minneapolis, September 11–14, ASME Press, New York, pp. 45–54.

Lee, K., and Andrews, G., 1985, Inference of positions of components in an assembly: Part 2, *Computer-Aided Design* **17** (1): 20–24.

Light, R., and Gossard, D., 1982, Modification of geometric models through variational geometry, *Computer-Aided Design* **14** (4): 209–214.

Magleby, S., and Gunn, K., 1992, Flexible integration of CAD/CAM modelers and application programs, Tech. Report, Brigham Young University.

Mäntylä, M., 1988, *An Introduction to Solid Modelling*, Computer Science Press.

Mäntylä, M., 1990, A modeling system for top-down design of assembled products, *IBM Journal of Research and Development* **24** (5): 636–659.

Mäntylä, M., 1991, WAYT: Towards a modeling environment for assembled products, in H. Yoshikawa, F. Arbab, and T. Tomiyama, eds., *Intelligent CAD III*, North-Holland, pp. 187–204 (Proc. of Third IFIP W.G. 5.2 Workshop on Intelligent CAD, Osaka, Japan, 26–29 September 1989).

Mäntylä, M., Opas, J., and Puhakka, J., 1987, A prototype system for generative process planning of prismatic parts, in A. Kusiak, ed., *Modern Production Management Systems—Proc. of IFIP TC 5/WG 5.7 Working Conference on Advances in Production Management Systems (APMS '87)*, Winnipeg, Manitoba, Canada, 1987, North-Holland, pp. 599–611.

Owen, J. C., 1991, Algebraic solution for geometry from dimensional constraints, in J. Rossignac and J. Turner, eds., *Proc. of Symposium on Solid Modeling Foundations and CAD/CAM Applications*, ACM, New York, pp. 397–407.

Press, W. H., Flannery, B. P., Teukolsky, S. A., and Vetterling, W. T., 1992, *Numerical Recipes in C, 2nd edition*, Cambridge University Press.

Ranta, M., Inui, M., Kimura, F., and Mäntylä, M., 1993, Cut and paste based modeling with boundary features, in J. Rossignac, J. Turner and G. Allen, eds., *Proc. of Second ACM Solid Modeling Symposium*, ACM Press, pp. 303–312.

Ranta, M., Inui, M., Kimura, F., and Mäntylä, M., 1995, Cutting and pasting constrained boundary features, To be presented at CAPE '95, Beijing, May 1995.

Rogers, M., 1987, Form feature modeling shell for design of mechanical parts, M.S. thesis, Department of Mechanical Engineering, Arizona State University.

Rossignac, J. R., 1990, Issues on feature-based editing and interrogation of solid models, *Comp. & Gr.* **14** (2): 149–172.

Salomons, O. W., 1995, Computer support in the design of mechanical products. Constraint specification and satisfaction in mechanical feature based design and manufacturing, Ph.D. dissertation, University of Twente.

Salomons, O. W., van Slooten, F., Jonker, H. G., van Houten, F. J. A. M., and Kals, H. J. J., 1994, Interactive feature definition, *Proc. of IFIP W.G. 5.3 Working Conference on Feature Modeling and Recognition in Advanced CAD/CAM Systems*, Valenciennes, France, pp. 181–202.

Serrano, D., 1987, Constraint management in conceptual design, Ph.D. dissertation, Department of Electrical Engineering, MIT.

Serrano, D., and Gossard, D., 1992, Tools and techniques for conceptual design, in C. Tong and D. Sriram, eds., *Artificial Intelligence in Engineering Design Vol. I: Design Representation and Models of Routine Design*, Academic Press, pp. 71–116.

Spatial Technology Inc., 1993, *ACIS Reference Manual,* Boulder, CO.

Suzuki, H., Ando, H., and Kimura, F., 1990, Synthesizing product shapes with geometric design constraints and reasoning, *Intelligent CAD II*, North-Holland, pp. 309–324 (Proc. of Second IFIP W.G. 5.2 Workshop on Intelligent CAD, Cambridge, UK, 19–22 September 1988).

Thornton, A. C., 1993, Constraint specification and satisfaction in embodiment design, Ph. D. dissertation, University of Cambridge.

van Emmerik, M., 1990, Interactive design of parameterized 3d models by direct manipulation, Ph.D. dissertation, Technical University of Delft.

van Emmerik, M., and F. Jansen, 1989, User interface for feature modelling, in F. Kimura and A. Rolstadås, eds., *Computer Applications in Production and Engineering (CAPE '89)*, North-Holland, pp. 625–632.

van Emmerik, M., Rappoport, A., and Rossignac, J., 1994, ABCSG: A hypertext approach for the interactive design of solid models, assemblies, and patterns, *Visual Computer,* in press.

9

FEATURE RECOGNITION
TECHNIQUES

Several feature creation techniques were introduced in Chapter 4. Of these, the design-by-features approach was the topic of the preceding chapter. In this chapter we will discuss another important feature creation method—*automatic feature recognition*. In automatic feature recognition, portions of a geometric model are compared to predefined generic features in order to identify feature instances that match the predefined feature patterns. Typical subtasks in feature recognition introduced in Chapter 4 are the following:

- Constructing an auxiliary data structure, from the geometric model, to facilitate the search for features.
- Searching the geometric model to match topological and geometric patterns.
- Extracting recognized features from the geometric model.
- Determining feature parameters.
- Completing the feature geometric model (edge and face growing, closure, etc.).
- Combining simple features to get composite features.

In Section 9.1 we start by investigating some of the key issues in the design of a feature recognition system. As we will see, the most important issue is the type of the interface the feature recognizer has with the geometry system. In Section 9.2, we discuss some key aspects of boundary-based feature recognition methods. Feature recognition methods working on CSG type input are briefly presented in Section 9.3. Another important family of recognition techniques is based on some kind of volume decomposition; these algorithms are discussed in Section 9.4. Section 9.5 looks at the problem of recognizing features from two-dimensional drawings, which is of practical importance to companies. Section 9.6 provides a summary of the current state of the art. Finally, some interesting research directions are described in Sections 9.7 and 9.8. These include hybrid systems, incremental feature recognition, use of neural nets, and differential depth filters to aid feature recognition.

9.1 ARCHITECTURAL FRAMEWORK

Ideally a feature recognizer is designed on the basis of the expected scope and use of the features system, and a good match between the characteristics of the recognition algorithm and the desired characteristics of the application is achieved. Therefore, before inspecting particular feature recognition techniques in detail, we will first have a look at the requirements space for a feature recognizer and develop an architectural framework for different feature recognition subsystems.

Any feature recognizer is expected to find and report feature instances in a geometric model on the basis of predefined generic feature templates. This general functional requirement, however, leaves room for several more detailed characteristics that may be needed to satisfy the needs of a particular application:

- Can the whole part be recognized as consisting of features, or only some portions thereof?
- Can the recognized features be extracted, namely can the recognizer "remove" them from the model or not?[1]
- What validity checking can be performed on the recognized features?
- Are volume features or surface features required?
- How can feature interactions or overlapping features be handled?

Choosing among the potentially desirable characteristics of a feature recognizer turns out to depend mainly on the application of the feature system that the recognizer is servicing. In the following discussion we will briefly touch on the requirements of the main application elements of feature recognition:

- Design
- Engineering analysis

---

[1]This use of "recognition" and "extraction" is nonstandard, and some words on how they are to be distinguished may be necessary here. "Feature recognition" is required to report the existence of a feature in the part, including its attributes and relationships. "Feature extraction" is a process whereby a recognized feature is removed from the rest of the part generally with the remainder of the part somehow "patched" to eliminate any trace of the feature. Hence a sequence of feature extraction operations reduces a part to a "basic shape" with detail features removed. The reader is cautioned that many authors use the two terms interchangeably.

- Group technology coding
- Manufacturing.

9.1.1 Design

Feature recognition is typically thought of as a process that is performed on a geometric model of a finished part. Therefore feature recognition is not commonly applied in a design process. However, as we will see later in this chapter when discussing the incremental feature modeling approach, it is possible to use feature recognition successfully on geometry given to the recognizer that does not yet constitute a finished design.

The particular requirements on the characteristics of the feature recognizer depend on how the recognized features are expected to be handled during design. In the incremental feature modeling scenario, once a feature has been recognized, it can be preserved in future applications of the recognizer as long as a valid subset of the recognized feature remains in the model. In another scenario, recognized features are only temporary entities that are used to support a particular design task (e.g., resizing or repositioning a collection of related geometric entities), and they are discarded after the task has been accomplished.

We can also look at some of the possible requirements listed in the above to illuminate the use of feature recognition in design further:

Can the whole part be recognized as features, or only some portions thereof? Design activities do not necessarily require that the whole shape of the part is treated as features. Typically most of the attention of the designer is pointed at some functional portions of the part, while the other portions of the geometry are secondary to the desired function of the part and hence to the designer.

Will the features be recognized or extracted? A typical application of features during design is to support operations such as repositioning and removing related geometric elements or adjusting their dimensions. This requires the capability of recognizing an interesting subset of the geometry as a feature, removing the feature from the model, "patching up" the part, and reinserting the geometry in a new location in the case of repositioning. Hence true feature extraction capability is strongly preferable. If the whole part is recognized as features, it may also be possible to regenerate completely the part geometry after an incremental change; in this case extraction is not required.

What types of validity checking will be performed on the recognized features? An evolving design may not satisfy physical validity criteria at all times. A shape may initially be described in terms of disconnected main surfaces (features) that are combined as a physical whole only at a late stage of the design. A feature recognizer should therefore also work for "invalid" instances of features.

9.1.2 Engineering Analysis

A typical scenario for using features to aid engineering analysis is the generation of input data for the finite element method (FEM). In most cases the full details of the designed object are not of interest for the analysis; instead, an idealized model that only contains the subset of the geometry essential to the analysis is used (Korngold et al. 1989, Shepard 1990). While using feature recognition to drive this application still is an area for research, features may have potential for supporting the generation of idealized models for engineering analysis.

In terms of application we can characterize the requirements of the feature recognizer as follows:

Can the whole part be recognized as features, or only some portions thereof? Only some subsets of the whole geometry are significant for the analysis; many geometric details can be ignored and should be removed.

Will the features be recognized or extracted? Automatic idealization seems to require the capability of recognizing insignificant details and removing them from the model; generation of the idealized result requires true feature extraction. For instance, for stress analysis, small holes in the part away from the expected center of the stress should be recognized and removed.

9.1.3 Group Technology Coding

Group technology (GT) coding is used to analyze the shape of a part according to classification criteria. The result is reported in a multiple digit group technology code. As we saw in Chapter 6, the first digit in the GT code may note whether, for instance, the part is prismatic, rotational, or of sheet metal; the second digit might note the overall dimensions of the part, and so on.

GT coding is historically an important application of features: the achievement of seminal work by (Kyprianou 1980) was to support GT coding. We can again analyze the particular requirements of feature recognition as follows:

Can the whole part be recognized as features, or only some portions thereof? Feature recognition can be regarded as a bottom-up approach to understanding a designed object: On the basis of the low-level details of the part, higher-level semantic entities are created. GT coding, in contrast, requires a top-down view of the part. The overall choice between rotational, prismatic, or sheet metal types requires the capability of analyzing the part as a whole (Ames 1991). Therefore it is vital that a model somehow capture the whole part.

What types of validity checking will be performed on the recognized features? The result of GT coding is not a complete description of the part but a condensed summary of the part's main characteristics as required by the chosen coding system. As long as the coding decisions can be performed correctly and systematically, validity of the recognized features is not vital.

Are volume features or surface features required? GT coding decisions typically require inspecting the characteristics of both volumes and surfaces of the part. Therefore both types of features should be recognizable.

How will feature interactions or overlapping features be handled? Feature interactions are not typically a major issue for GT coding.

9.1.4 Manufacturing

Using feature recognition to drive manufacturing applications is probably the most important application of feature recognition systems. In this scenario a finished design description must be converted to features useful for various tasks in manufacture planning, such as setup and fixturing design, machining operation planning and NC generation, inspection planning, or assembly planning.

The requirements for each of these manufacturing applications vary considerably, making the design of a feature recognizer for manufacturing applications a very challenging task:

Can the whole part be recognized as features, or only some portions thereof? For each of the manufacturing applications listed, only a subset of the whole part is really of interest. For instance, machining operation planning and NC generation concentrates on the machined features of the part, while assembly planning concentrates on the mating surfaces of the parts to be assembled. A special problem arising in machining applications is that feature recognition must be performed with a certain stock. As we saw in Chapter 6, stock shapes should not be recognized as features if they are not going to be machined. Stock selection for machining planning requires the capability of classifying the overall shape of the machined part as one of the available stock types, requiring a holistic view to the part.

Will the features be recognized or extracted? Manufacturing applications such as fixture planning may require the capability of representing "intermediate stages" of the part after some but not all machined features have been created. This concerns at least the capability of deducing the stock shape, which in the general case involves feature extraction.

What types of validity checking will be performed on the recognized features? As we will show in Chapter 11, the capability of checking various types of technical validity criteria is critical for using features in manufacturing planning.

Are volume features or surface features required? Both volume and surface features are required. Applications such as fixture planning do most of their reasoning on the basis of surfaces; also operation planning for turning and face milling generally requires surface features. The recognition of surface features should ideally be based on inspection of surface quality information of the faces of the solid model. Unfortunately, such attributes are rarely available.

How will feature interactions or overlapping features be handled? Recognition and explicit representation of interacting or overlapping features is important for applications such as operation sequencing and inspection planning. In general, overlapping features can be recognized in several different ways, corresponding with different sequences of machining operations. Ideally a feature recognizer is capable of generating all relevant interpretations of the part in terms of manufacturing features in order to provide the planning application with the full freedom of selecting the best plan.

9.2 RECOGNITION FROM BOUNDARY MODELS

A solid model described as a boundary representation is by far the most common starting point for feature recognition. Therefore we will look at the recognition algorithms aimed at dealing with boundary model data structures in relatively close detail.

Since boundary representation data structures can be viewed as graph structures, *graph matching* has been a popular method for feature recognition. Pure graph matching done on unaugmented solid models amounts to topological matching: The searched feature characteristics are based on the number of boundary representation entities (faces, edges, vertices) and their topological type, connectivity, and adjacency. If matching were done this way features of very different semantics would be classified as being the same, as we have demonstrated in Chapter 4. Therefore some subclassification using geometric relationships between adjacent boundary entities (usually faces) is necessary. In the following sections we describe some of the principal methods for matching, entity classification, and restructuring of the geometric model to prepare it for recognition.

Other methodologies that take advantage of the graph view of boundary data structures are syntactic approaches, such as *graph grammars* for feature recognition. This approach provides a very powerful formalization of features as *graph productions*, which can be extended to deal also with feature attributes.

9.2.1 Graph Matching

A boundary representation of a part can be regarded as a graph structure, where, for instance, faces are considered nodes of the graph and face-face relationships form the arcs of the graph. The advantage of the graph view is that the well-established techniques of graph algorithms can be readily adapted to feature-based modeling. See Appendix A for basic definitions of graphs and some discussion of graph algorithms.

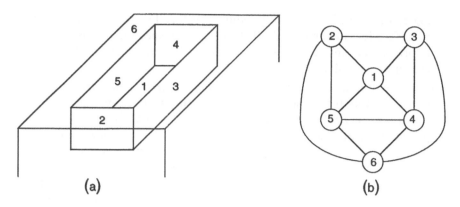

Figure 9.1 Topological relations of pocket surfaces

To understand the graph notation, let us study the surfaces of the rectangular pocket in Figure 9.1(*a*). The pocket starts off planar face 6; its sides are faces 2 to 5, and the bottom is face 1. The neighborhood relationships of the faces can be modeled by means of a *face adjacency graph* (FAG) in Figure 9.1(*b*). Nodes of the graph represent the faces, and arcs between the nodes the neighborhood relationships between the faces. See also Figures 4.6 and 4.7 for another example of how attributed graphs are used to define and recognize features.

An example of a "pure" graph-based feature recognition method based on FAG's is given by (De Floriani and Bruzzone 1989) for recognizing protrusions or depressions on a face and through-holes or handles from a relational boundary model, called *symmetric boundary graph*. The proposed feature extraction method is based purely on topologic information. The feature extraction process produces an object decomposition graph, which provides an unambiguous description of the global shape of the object.

Entity Classification The FAG shown in Figure 9.1 contains only topological information in that it indicates which face is adjacent to which other faces. As mentioned in Chapter 4, this is usually insufficient for feature recognition. In addition to topological adjacency information, it is necessary for the graph to capture also the type of geometric relation between adjacent faces. This is called *entity classification* whereby the arcs are flagged with an entity type. A feature recognizer can then use entity flags to distinguish between topologically similar features.

Observe that arcs of a FAG correspond to the edges separating faces. Consequently arcs of the FAG can be flagged by attribute information that describes more closely the type of the edge. On the basis of edge attributes, other entities such as vertices and loops of edges (in graph parlance, circuits) can be classified. This type of structure is known as an *attributed face adjacency graph* (AFAG) discussed in Chapter 4.

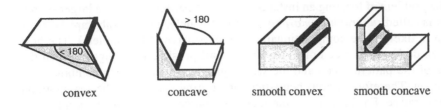

convex   concave   smooth convex   smooth concave

Figure 9.2 Kyprianou's edge classification criteria

An entity classification method devised by (Kyprianou 1980) has been used widely. The method is based on the magnitude of the angle of intersection. Edges are classified as convex, concave, smooth convex, or smooth concave, as shown in Figure 9.2. For edges at which planar faces meet, the angle between those faces on the solid side must be less than 180 degrees for the edge to be classified as convex; otherwise, it is concave. For nonplanar faces, smooth edges are reclassified as concave or convex on the basis of local curvature.

On the basis of edge classification, other boundary model elements can also be classified (Jared 1984). Vertex classification is based on its incident edges. If two or more incident edges are concave, the vertex is deemed to be concave; otherwise, it is classified as convex. Similarly loops are classified as convex (all edges convex), concave (all concave), or hybrid (mixture). Finally, faces of the object are marked "primary" if they contain a concave edge or an inner loop, and primary faces are ordered on the basis of the number of concave edge sets. A hierarchical face-set data structure is built by processing the geometric model which now contains entities tagged by the above classification.

Most published works on graph-based feature recognition are related to recognition of relatively simple prismatic features (holes, slots, bosses, pockets), reflecting the fact that most work on feature recognition has been done in the context of machining-type applications. An exception is the feature recognizer by (Lentz and Sowerby 1993) that is capable of recognizing sheet metal features. The algorithm applies a face-adjacency hypergraph representation of the various convex and concave regions, and the intersections thereof, of a sheet metal object. In this case the regions are separated by changes in the local curvature rather than sharp edges. Consequently entity classification is based on curvature rather than sharp angles.

Subgraph Matching The notation of attributed FAG's directly leads to consider using graph matching as a means of feature recognition. In this technique the whole boundary model is first converted to a FAG such as in Figure 9.1(*b*). Edges are classified and edge attributes added to the arcs of the graph. For example we may use the attribute "0" to signify a concave edge and "1" for a convex edge. Then graph-processing techniques can be used to locate instances of predefined patterns in the intermediate representation.

The problem of locating an instance of a given pattern graph in a larger search graph is called *subgraph isomorphism*. Unfortunately, general subgraph isomorphism is likely to be computationally very expensive (NP complete). The best one can do involves a complete search over all possible mappings between the nodes of the pattern graph and the search graph, which leads to combinatorial explosion. Therefore various heuristics for limiting the size of the search graph are imperative. For instance, if the search graph can be split in subgraphs, and the search limited to these, considerable savings can be achieved.

After a pattern has been located, the actual faces identified with the pattern nodes can be used to compute the required parameters of the recognized feature. Examples of graph-matching-based feature recognition algorithms are numerous. Several notable ones are mentioned in the following subsection.

Feature Interaction   A major problem that must be addressed in graph matching based feature recognition algorithms is *feature interaction*. Consider the two cases shown in Figure 9.3 (Joshi and Chang 1988). In the above case, a

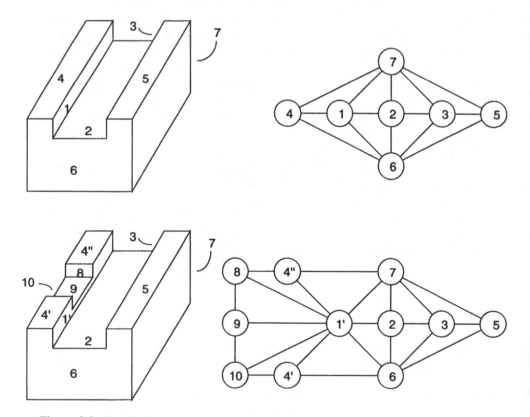

Figure 9.3   Type I feature interaction (Joshi and Chang 1988; reprinted with permission from *Computer-Aided Design*, Butterworth Heinemann, Oxford, England)

regular "open slot" feature and its FAG are shown. Typically a graph-matching recognition algorithm would include this (or similar) graph in its library of patterns; upon recognition of a subgraph of this form with matching arc attributes, a slot feature consisting of faces 1, 2, and 3 would be recognized.

Observe, however, that other features may well be present that penetrate in the faces belonging to the slot feature. In the lower part of Figure 9.3, another slot feature (faces 8, 9, and 10) has been added to the model. Face 4 of the original model has been split into faces 4' and 4", and face 1 has also been altered in shape into face 1'. Although the graph-matching algorithm will have no difficulty in recognizing that faces 8, 9, and 10 form an open slot feature, it is not immediately clear how faces 1', 2, and 3 could be recognized.

Joshi and Chang (1988) investigate this phenomenon what they call the "type I feature interaction", and they propose heuristic rules that can be used to overcome certain instances of it. Consider now the case of two overlapping slots shown in Figure 9.4(*a*). In this case another slot has been added on the bottom of a slot, hence causing the bottom face to split in two parts (faces 2 and 6).

To deal with the situation, Joshi and Chang use the heuristic

remove the arcs having the connection type "convex" from the graph

that leads to the situation of *b*. Next, they apply the heuristic

if the rule (b) has been used, then join split faces

that finally leads to situation (*c*). In the modified graph the two features have now been separated, and they can be individually recognized. Observe that the

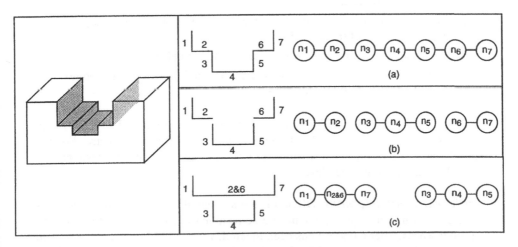

Figure 9.4 Splitting and merging heuristics (Laakko and Mäntylä 1991; reprinted with permission from *Computer-Aided Design*, Butterworth Heinemann, Oxford, England)

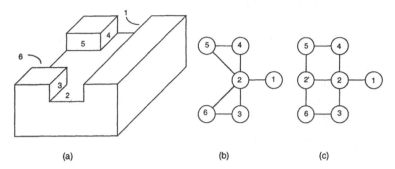

Figure 9.5 Type II feature interaction (Joshi and Chang 1988; reprinted with permission from *Computer-Aided Design*, Butterworth Heinemann, Oxford, England)

second heuristic requires some method for determining whether two faces can be considered as results of splitting an original face. In general, this is quite difficult to show.

A single face may be also "shared" by several interacting features. A sample case of this "type II interaction" in the parlance of Joshi and Chang is shown in Figure 9.5(*a*). Here the situation is similar to that of the lower half of Figure 9.3, except that the second slot now extends all the way to the bottom of the first slot. As a result the two bottom faces coincide and appear as a single face in the model (*b*).

To solve this situation, Joshi and Chang propose a procedure with the following outline:

1. Determine the split faces of the situation (in Figure 9.5(*a*) these are faces 3 and 4). Call these the set A.
2. Find face(s) that are incident to faces of set A at a concave edge (in this case, face 2). Call these set B.
3. Find nodes "causing the split" (faces 5 and 6); call these set C.
4. The "shared" face is now identified as the one having concave edges with faces in A $\cup$ C (in this case, face 2).

After this, the procedure will create a new node in the graph and will rearrange the arcs so that faces in set C will become incident with the new arc. For the sample case, the result is shown in Figure 9.5(*c*). Again geometric tests are required to execute the procedure.

Entity-Growing Problem Often it is not sufficient just to recognize the presence of a feature in a model; one must also be able to *extract* it out of the model. In other words, after a feature has been located, we would like to remove it from the model, leaving us a model where the effects of the feature presence have been eliminated.

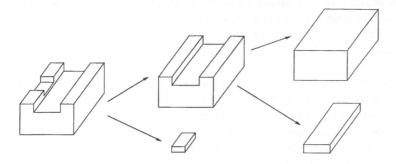

Figure 9.6 Feature extraction problem

The need for feature extraction arises most often in manufacturing applications, where features correspond to areas that must be machined from a blank piece. This case is depicted in Figure 9.6 for the sample part of Figure 9.3. As shown, the feature extraction results in a *volume decomposition* of the original model, which is directly useful for manufacturing planning applications.

The basic problem encountered in feature extraction is *entity growing*. Recall that a feature recognizer is only capable of locating some of the surfaces of a volumetric feature. For instance, when we recognize a slot in the first step of the case in Figure 9.6, we find three of the six faces of the slot volume. Somehow the three missing ones must be found as well. Moreover, after the three slot faces have been removed from the model, the remaining gaps must be filled. See Figure 9.7 for illustration.

The entity growing can affect the recognized feature as well. From the geometric model, we have extracted three faces of the slot feature. If a volumet-

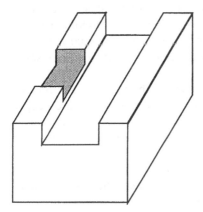

Figure 9.7 Entity-growing problem

ric feature is desired, the remaining faces must somehow be computed. This information may be required, for instance, for finding the attributes of the recognized feature. For the case of the slot, the depth of the slot is the distance between its bottom face and its top face; however, only the bottom face can be explicitly recognized.

Entity growing is considered by, among others, (Falcidieno and Giannini 1987). Their approach is based on extending the edges appearing to be cut by the gaps. The intersection points of the extended edges are used to construct potentially missing vertices and finally the mended faces.

Sakurai and Gossard (1990) developed another graph-based method that defines a shape feature as a single face or set of contiguous faces possessing certain characteristic facts in topology and geometry. The system searches the solid model for boundary representation subgraphs with the same characteristic facts as the feature to be recognized and removes the geometry associated with a recognized feature from the original solid model. The entity-growing (creating feature volumes) problem is handled by adding half-spaces corresponding to feature faces. The process is repeated until no more features are found. A candidate set of new edges is formed by intersecting all surfaces appearing at the gaps with each other. The candidate edges are combined in edge loops by means of the "wire frame fleshing" algorithm of (Markowsky and Wesley 1980). Next faces are assembled from edge loops, and blocks of material from faces. The process creates a block of material that may be added to the original model (which still has the feature present) to completely fill the space of the gap.

Dong and Wozny (1991) consider the entity-growing problem in the form of converting surface features to volumetric features. Their algorithm is based on extending the feature faces and/or the neighboring faces, and performing a case analysis on the intersections of the face extensions.

9.2.2 Syntactic Recognition

General subgraph matching can be regarded suboptimal in the sense that it does not take advantage of the fact that a boundary graph is a very special case of a graph. Indeed, a valid boundary graph must satisfy a number of topological and geometric consistency criteria. It is built using a sequence of special modeling operations and apart from purely topological relationships other relationships such as geometric constraints may be also available.

Syntactic feature recognition methods try to use the characteristics of boundary graphs to gain more expressiveness and speed. These methods are deeply rooted in pattern recognition. Even the term "feature" is extensively used in pattern recognition to denote a high-level property of a signal that is of interest for some analysis or application.

Syntactic pattern recognition *Syntactic pattern recognition* is a classical method for recognizing shapes from raster images. In the original context the basic ideas of syntactic pattern recognition can be outlined as follows:

1. Extract the contours of the shapes from the raster image by means of image-processing techniques. This results in a intermediate representation that consists of elements such as line and arc segments.

2. Match patterns of adjacent elements against predefined patterns. The patterns are described in terms of primitive elements corresponding to lines and arcs in various orientations. Compound patterns consisting of simpler ones can also be defined. A symbolic encoding of the pattern is used; hence pattern definition and matching can be performed by syntactic means.

3. When a matching pattern is recognized, application-dependent action is taken. For instance, a symbolic model of the overall scene may be created for further image understanding.

This approach has also been widely used for feature recognition on the basis of graphical and boundary models. Step 1 above is of course unnecessary because the model is already expressed in suitable primitives.

A simple example of the technique is presented in Figure 9.8. In the top part a collection of eight primitives corresponding with line segments of varying orientations is introduced. The bottom part shows a particular matching rule that recognizes a flat-bottomed hole shape. Symbolically this matching rule can be expressed as

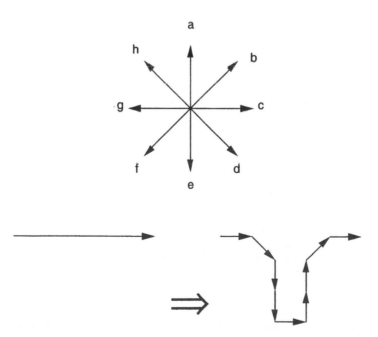

Figure 9.8 Syntactic recognition of a 2D hole shape

$$c \quad ::= \quad cd\{e\}^n c\{a\}^n bc$$

where $\{x\}^n$ denotes the repetition of x n times. Examples on the use of "classical" pattern recognition techniques include (Jakubowski 1982) and (Staley et al. 1983), who used strings of straight lines and curve segments to recognize 2D profiles of holes.

Ideas of syntactic pattern recognition can also be applied in three dimensions on the basis of higher-dimensional primitives. An example of this is given by (Choi et al. 1984) in the recognizer of the STOPP process planning system. Their technique was based on surface primitives that were extracted from a boundary model by a preprocessor.

Figure 9.9 (Choi et al. 1984) displays several syntactic elements useful for recognizing holes. Element HSS (hole-starting surface) is described as a planar surface with an internal circular list of edges. Similarly various subtypes of element HES (hole-element-surface) correspond with a cylindrical surface bound by two circular edge lists, a conical surface bound by circles, or a circular planar area with a concentric circular hole. Elements HBS (hole-bottom surface) are a planar circle, a cone, or another planar surface similar to HSS.

With these syntactic elements, the general concept of a hole is easily described:

<hole> ::= HSS {HES}* HBS

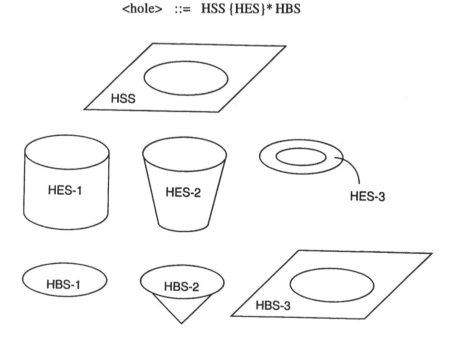

Figure 9.9 Syntactic elements for recognizing holes (Choi et al. 1984; reprinted with permission from *Computer-Aided Design*, Butterworth Heinemann, Oxford, England)

<HES> ::= HES-1 | HES-2 | HES-3

<HBS> ::= HBS-1 | HBS-2 | HBS-3

Here {X}* stands for the repetition of X 1 ... n times, and "|" for "or". Alternatively, the same elements could be used to model more refined kinds of holes:

<straight hole> ::= HSS HES-1 HBS-1

<countersink> ::= HSS HES-2 HES-1 HBS-2

<step hole> ::= HSS HES-1 {HES-3 HES-1}* HBS-2

Similar rules can be developed for slots; see (Choi et al. 1984) for details.

Graph Grammars   A *graph grammar* is a formal description of a class of graphs that can be created by applying a sequence of *graph productions* defined in the grammar. Given a graph and a graph grammar, a *graph-parsing algorithm* can determine whether the graph belongs to the class of graphs corresponding to the grammar and, if so, which productions are needed to create the graph.

Because boundary models can be viewed as graphs, feature recognition can be regarded as a graph-parsing problem. In this view feature descriptions are given in the form of graph productions, and the graph-parsing algorithm is used to extract instances of the given features in the part. The result is a sequence of graph productions that, when applied in sequence, generates the part. Therefore the graph grammar approach can be also regarded as a kind of declarative feature modeling mechanism: given the graph productions corresponding to the features, the actual creation of feature instances and feature geometry can, in principle, be left to the system.

One of the originators of graph grammars in geometric modeling was (Fitzhorn 1987), who observed that both CSG and boundary representations can be fit into the graph grammar formalism. The graph grammar approach was adopted for feature modeling by (Pinilla et al. 1989), who present a simple feature description and recognition system based on graph grammars. A designed object is an element in the language generated by the grammar, and hence the features can be recognized by parsing the feature against the graph of the object.

Let us take a closer look at the graph grammar technique as used by (Fu et al. 1993), who use a combination of graph grammars and constraint satisfaction techniques to deal with declarative feature definition and recognition and also feature mapping. In brief, they combine constraint propagation with graph grammar parsing by associating constraint propagation operations with graph productions. Feature mapping is accomplished by bottom-up parsing of the feature graph created by top-down productions.

The basis of the approach is a representation of a geometric design in terms of a set of geometric constraints. These include both topological constraints specifying relationships between surfaces for geometric reasoning (`side-of`, `top-of`, etc.) and geometric constraints (`distance`, `coplanar`, `angle`, etc.). The

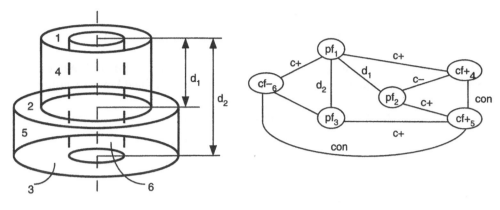

Nomenclature:

pf$_i$	planar surface i	c+	convex circle constraint
cf+$_i$	external cylindrical surface i	c-	concave circle constraint
cf-$_i$	internal cylindrical surface i	con	concentricity constraint
		d$_i$	distance constraint

Figure 9.10   A component and its constraint graph representation (Fu et al. 1993; reprinted with permission from *Int. J. of Comp. Integrated Manufacturing*)

whole part is represented as a graph, where nodes correspond with various kinds of geometric objects (solid primitives or surfaces) and arcs with various types of constraints. In Figure 9.10 (Fu et al. 1993) a simple component with its constraint graph is shown; the nodes of the graph are indicated by labeled ovals, and the constraints by labeled arcs.

A feature is seen as a subset of the nodes and constraints in the graph. As such, it can be represented as a subgraph of a whole design. The subgraph contains the geometric primitives that make the feature, plus a set of relationships between these entities. Thus the feature thru-hole in Figure 9.11 (Fu et al. 1993) corresponds with the subgraph on the left that contains the two planar faces and an internal cylindrical surface.

Features can also be introduced as abstract entities on the graph representing the whole part. When the feature thru-hole is introduced in the graph of Figure 9.10, we get the modified graph on the right side of Figure 9.11. Hence a purely constraint-based description can be transformed to a feature-oriented description. The manipulations of the constraint graph needed in feature recognition is formalized as a graph production, which defines a correspondence of two subgraphs, the *left-hand side* (LHS) and the *right-hand side* (RHS) of the production. In Figure 9.11 the two graphs form the RHS and LHS of a graph production.

Graph productions are understood as replacement operations that can be applied in either direction. In the feature recognition scenario, one starts from a complete graph representing a part and applies productions "backward" (bottom-up parsing). In the design-by-features scenario, one starts from an initial graph corresponding with a blank part, and applies graph productions that cor-

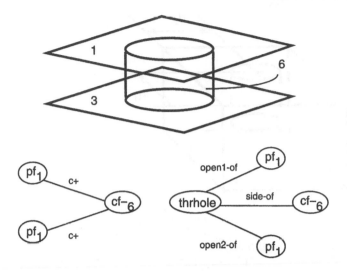

Figure 9.11 Graph representation with feature `thru-hole` abstraction (Fu et al. 1993; reprinted with permission from *Int. J. of Comp. Integrated Manufacturing*)

respond to adding features or constraints to it (top-down parsing). In grammar parlance, blank parts are termed *starting symbols* of the grammar.

Another example of a graph production is given in Figure 9.12 (Fu et al. 1993). This production adds a hole feature to a block (which might appear as a blank in the system). The link OF in the LHS of the production is a generalized link that matches any topological link (`top-of`, `side-of`, etc.). The RHS inserts the hole and also the relations to the starting surface of the hole and the surfaces with reference to which the hole is dimensioned.

Top-down and bottom up graph parsing can be combined to convert a model expressed with one feature set to another. Initially a top-down process is used to create a detail constraint graph on the basis of, say, design features. This model is then parsed in a bottom-up process to derive a manufacturing feature model of the same design. In the work of Fu et al., the above approach is implemented by associating graph productions with a procedure that is executed if the production is fired. The procedure consists of operations that manipulate a geometric model corresponding to the design in a fashion that guarantees that the constraints involved with the graph production get satisfied. A very simple example of this is given in Figure 9.13 (Fu et al. 1993) showing a graph production that creates a hole feature on the top surface of a cylinder. The constraint specified by the graph production, `top-of`, requires that the hole be placed on the top surface of the cylinder. This constraint is satisfied by the construction procedure described in terms of the operations to be performed when the production is fired.

The actual process of feature transformation by graph productions is illustrated in Figure 9.14 (Fu et al. 1993). In (*a*), the constituents of the design feature

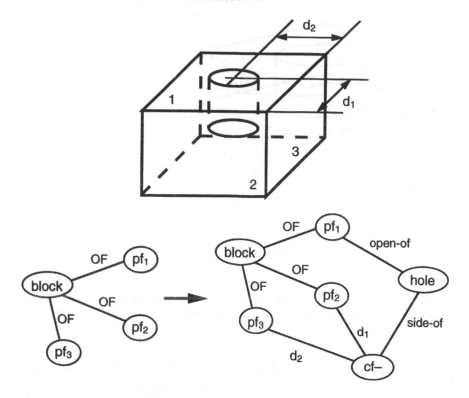

Figure 9.12 Graph production for adding a hole in a block (Fu et al. 1993; reprinted with permission from *Int. J. of Comp. Integrated Manufacturing*)

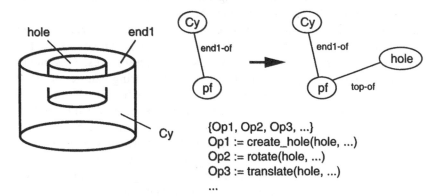

Figure 9.13 A graph production and its related operations (Fu et al. 1993; reprinted with permission from *Int. J. of Comp. Integrated Manufacturing*)

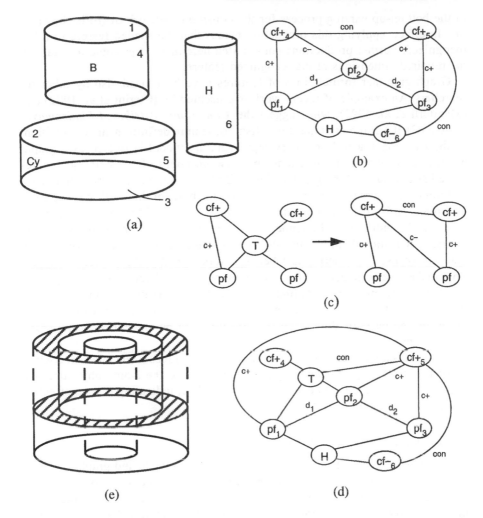

Figure 9.14 An example of feature transformation (Fu et al. 1993; reprinted with permission from *Int. J. of Comp. Integrated Manufacturing*)

model are shown—a cylinder, a boss, and a through-hole. They can be combined as a model by means of a top-down graph production process that ultimately creates the constraint network shown in (*b*).

Our desire is to construct another feature model for the part that makes it possible to consider it a turned part. For this purpose we apply bottom-up graph parsing to the model shown in (*b*) using graph productions that recognize manufacturing features for turning. One of these is shown in (*c*); this graph production is capable of creating a "step end" in a turned part (when read from LHS to RHS) or recognizing one in a model (RHS to LHS). The result of firing this production in the bottom-up parsing process for the constraint network of (*b*) is shown in (*d*). In effect, applying this production means that the shaded feature in (*e*) is recognized. Further productions not detailed here make it possible to establish the required dimensions of the recognized feature.

Graph grammar formulations of features have been used also by other researchers. An example of recent work is presented by (Cugini et al. 1992) and (Mandorli et al. 1993), who suggest the *Conditional Attributed Lindenmayer System* (CAIL) graph grammar formalism for feature definition and recognition. In their approach a full boundary representation model is treated as a graph; geometric properties and relationships between nodes of the graph are represented as attributes of the graph nodes. A CAIL interpreter can create, maintain, and interrogate a boundary data structure on the basis of the CAIL descriptions. The main utility of a strong graph formalism such as CAIL is that it permits procedural conditions to be embedded in graph grammar productions; in particular, CAIL formalism has the ability to capture various kinds of knowledge that can be used to discriminate between topologically similar feature types. This makes the formalism considerably more powerful for feature recognition and feature mapping than a "blind" graph-matching method. For instance, conditions for distinguishing between "pockets" and "slots" during feature recognition on the basis of dimension relationships can be embedded in the graph productions.

A main disadvantage of the graph grammar techniques is the inherent computational cost of graph parsing. Again this reduces to the isomorphic subgraph search problem which is known to be NP-complete, indicating that no effective algorithms are likely to be found for it.

9.2.3 Rule-Based Algorithms

The previous techniques have used face adjacency graphs and graph matching for the analysis of topological relationships among model entities. Alternatively, the analysis can also be done on the basis of rules that inspect directly the underlying model. In this approach, features are formalized by templates that consist of pattern rules. Templates are defined for both general features (like holes) and specific features (e.g., flat bottomed, constant diameter hole). A general rule for a hole, for example, would look like this:

> The hole begins with an entrance face. All subsequent faces of the hole share a common axis. All faces of the hole are sequentially adjacent. The hole terminates with a valid hole bottom (Henderson 1984).

The geometric and topological conditions of such rules have to be tested separately; all conditions have to be satisfied in order for a rule to be satisfied. Typically the procedure is to recognize general features (depression, protrusion, passage), classify general features into specific features (T-slot, round hole, rectangular pocket, etc.), create and subtract the volume corresponding to each feature from the cavity, and repeat all the preceding steps until there are no residual entities.

```
get list of all circular edges;
feature_count = 0;
for(count = 0; count < number of circular edges; count = count + 1)
{
    e = next edge from list of circular edges;
    f1 = the planar parent face of e;              /* f1 is the entry face */
    f2 = the cylindrical parent face of e;
    if (number of loops of f1 ≥ 2 and
        f1 and f2 share a convex edge and
        normal of f1 and axis of f2 are parallel)
    {
        f3 = the planar adjacent face of f2 that is not f1; /* exit face */
        if (number of loops of f3 ≥ 2)
        {
            /* a hole feature is recognized */
            diameter of hole = diameter of f2;
            depth of hole = distance between f1 and f3;
            feature_count = feature_count + 1;
            save the recognized hole feature
        }
    }
}
```

Figure 9.15 Feature recognition procedure for a hole (Sreevalsan 1990; reprinted by permission of the author)

9.2.4 Procedural Feature Recognition

The preceding techniques all have used some formalism of feature definition as a basis for recognition. Of course it is also possible to use purely procedural representations. In this approach, the recognition is performed by a specialized procedure that can recognize features of a particular type.

A sample recognizer for through-holes is shown in pseudocode in Figure 9.15. As shown, the procedure scans the boundary model directly, gathering references to relevant model entities during the traversal. After all entities forming a feature have been found, feature attributes are computed. A higher-level scheduler procedure must be included that executes the recognition procedures in proper sequence. If feature extraction is desired, another procedure would be used to implement it on a case by case basis.

9.3 RECOGNITION BY VOLUME DECOMPOSITION ALGORITHMS

Feature recognition techniques utilizing a boundary representation data structure work by investigating the faces, edges, and vertices of a geometric model—

that is, 2-, 1-, and 0-dimensional entities. In contrast, volume decomposition algorithms operate more directly on three-dimensional volumes. There are essentially two different approaches: alternating sum of volumes (also known as convex hull decomposition) and delta volume decomposition. Each of these is discussed in the following sections.

9.3.1 Alternating Sum of Volumes Decomposition

The convex decomposition process was utilized in a fundamental work on feature recognition by Woo (1982). He developed a method called the *alternating sum of volumes* (ASV) *decomposition*, where a nonconvex object is represented by a hierarchical structure of convex components. The principle of the ASV decomposition is illustrated in Figure 9.16.

First, the convex hull H_0 of the original object S_0 is computed. The convex hull can be thought of as a volume obtained by stretching an elastic membrane over a body; it is the minimal convex volume that encloses the body. By subtracting S_0 from H_0, the object S_1 is obtained. When S_1 is subtracted from its convex hull H_1, the object S_2 is obtained, and similarly S_3. Since S_3 is its own convex hull, the algorithm terminates. A feature decomposition of the part can be obtained from the resulting volumes.

Unfortunately, the ASV decomposition in its original form does not always converge, and this limits the domain of objects the method can handle. An example of a nonconvergent situation is shown in Figure 9.17. In this case the convex hull $CH(D^2(B))$ is the same as $CH(D^1(B))$, and an endless loop is entered. Tang and Woo (1991a; b) consider algorithmic aspects of the nonconvergence detection.

The ASV approach has been developed further to solve these problems. By combining ASV decomposition with cutting operations, a new variant called the *alternating sum of volumes with partitioning* (ASVP) decomposition method has been developed and its convergence proved by (Kim 1992).

The method is based on analyzing the vertices of a nonconvergent (ASV-irreducible) object. If a vertex is located such that it has at least two noncollinear concave incident edges, then a *remedial partitioning* operation where the object is partitioned with the plane spanned by the edges is performed. In the case of Figure 9.17, the object $D^1(B)$ can be partitioned with the result shown in Figure 9.18. The resulting two parts $D^1_1(B)$ and $D^1_2(B)$ are now convergent.

The benefit of the ASV/ASVP decomposition is its generality (at least within the domain of polyhedral objects; for a generalization of the method to limited cases of cylindrical surfaces, see [Menon and Kim 1994]). The decomposition is also unique; hence the shapes recognized constitute a kind of "canonical" decomposition of the original solid.

The problem of the method for practical purposes is that objects extracted during the usual ASV decomposition may be shapes that are not directly useful for some applications of features, such as feature-based manufacturing. In particular, the decomposition includes both positive and negative features. Waco

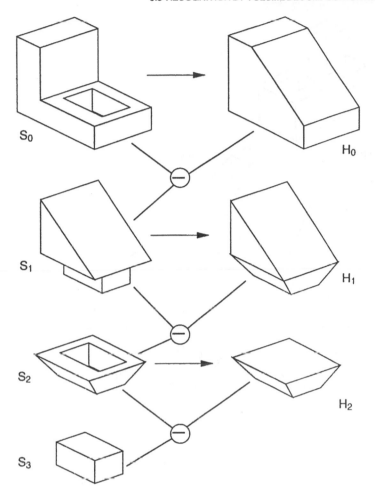

Figure 9.16 Convex decomposition by alternating sum of volumes

and Kim (1993) present a technique that can convert positive features to negative machining features. The technique is based on combining positive features with a suitably chosen negative feature; as a result equivalent negative components are formed.

9.3.2 Delta Volume Decomposition

Another approach to volume decomposition is the *delta volume decomposition*, which was introduced in Chapter 4. The objective of delta volume decomposition is to decompose a volume to be machined, to identify material to be removed from a base stock and to break down this volume into nonoverlapping units corresponding to distinct machining operations. Generally, the total mate-

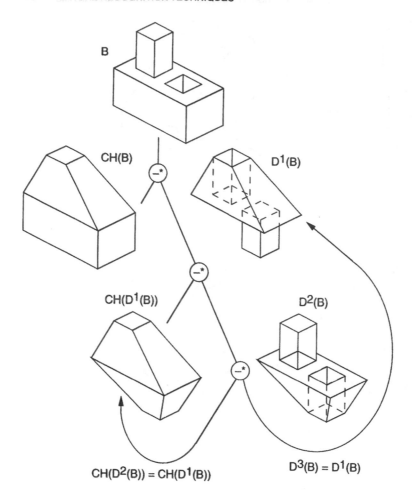

Figure 9.17 A non-convergent ASV decomposition (Kim 1992; reprinted with permission from *Computer-Aided Design*, Butterworth Heinemann, Oxford, England)

rial volume to be removed by machining is found by a Boolean difference between the stock and the finished part. This volume must then be decomposed into units that correspond to practical machining operations.

The earliest work on volume decomposition was performed by (General Dynamics 1985) for CAM-I. The purpose of the project was to achieve a high degree of automation for generating NC programs for parts defined by "noncomplex" surfaces (planar and quadric). An algorithm was developed for operating on a boundary model of the total volume to be removed augmented with tool accessibility codes for each face. A library of generic delta volumes existed in the system; new delta volumes could be added by users.

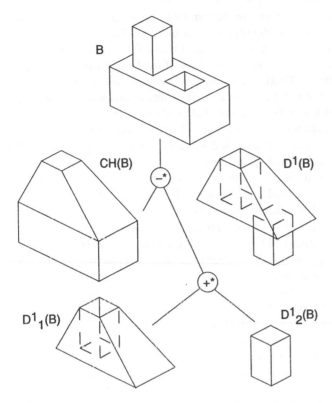

Figure 9.18 Remedial partitioning of an ASV irreducible object (Kim 1992; reprinted with permission from *Computer-Aided Design*, Butterworth Heinemann, Oxford, England)

The set of generic delta volumes was required to meet the criteria for *completeness* and *richness* as specified below:

- For every milled part the material to be removed can be decomposed into the union of disjoint delta volumes (*completeness*)
- For any volume of material to be removed there exists a delta volume contained in it (*richness*).

These two criteria guaranteed that any machining volume could be decomposed into a set of generic delta volumes.

Decomposition was carried out in two major stages. First, the primitive (parametrizable) volumes were recognized and extracted by surface extension. Because surface extension could be done by interrogating the boundary model, considerable computations were saved. Complex depressions (2½D pockets) were recognized by sectioning. A set of cross-sections was constructed by using a set of planes perpendicular to the cutter axis. Then relationships between adjacent cross-sections were determined to decompose the volume into disjoint "superdelta volumes," which were decomposed further based on tool accessibility. All delta volumes had to have at least one accessible face. A face on a delta volume was inaccessible if it coincided with a face of the finished part. If a face was partly coincident with the finished part, then it was assigned connectivity to another delta volume with which the rest of the face was coincident. Finally, all deltas were compared with generic delta volumes and classified.

Delta volume classification is the crucial step from the viewpoint of feature recognition. This step could be implemented by rule-based recognition applied to the topology and geometry of delta volumes. An alternative approach is to classify delta volumes on the basis of their degrees of freedom (dof), which roughly correspond to cutting tool motion needed to produce the volume defined. For instance, dof is 1 for plunging motions (e.g., drill motion for producing a hole), 2 for plunging and linear sweeping (tool motion for producing a thru-slot), and 2.5 for plunging and sweeping along a planar curve (producing a pocket). Additional criteria needed for recognition may include tool access direction, dimensions, and tolerances.

Yet another way to classify volumes is to look at the relative dof of the delta volume and the rest of the part. Any volume in space has three translational (TDOF) and three rotational (RDOF) dof. If we want to remove a volume that has been magically separated from the workpiece at the boundaries, the directions in which the volume can move is the relative TDOF or RDOF. For example, a thru-hole feature can rotate 360 degrees about its own axis and also translate along its axis in both directions. Therefore its RDOF is 2π, 0, 0 and TDOF is 1, 0, 0. A blind hole can only translate out in one direction, so its dof is 1/2 in the axial direction.

Figure 9.19 (Shah et al. 1994) shows a delta volume classification scheme based on relative dof. The delta volume generation method is discussed in the next section; Chapter 11 will discuss an extension of this method that takes tool kinematics into account in order to map recognized shapes to machinable features.

9.3.3 Recognition of Multiple Feature Models

Recently several new techniques utilizing volume decomposition have been introduced that aim at recognizing not just one particular way of representing a given design in terms of features. Instead, the objective is to recognize a redundant set of features that covers all features that may be found in the part. This redundant set can be used to create a set of different feature interpretations of the part, and these interpretations are all reported. Such a facility is important for many applications, notably machining planning, where the choice among the possible interpretations depends on manufacturability criteria not normally available to a feature recognition algorithm.

Cell Decomposition Algorithms An important group of algorithms that can recognize several interpretations of a given part is based on the idea of *cell*

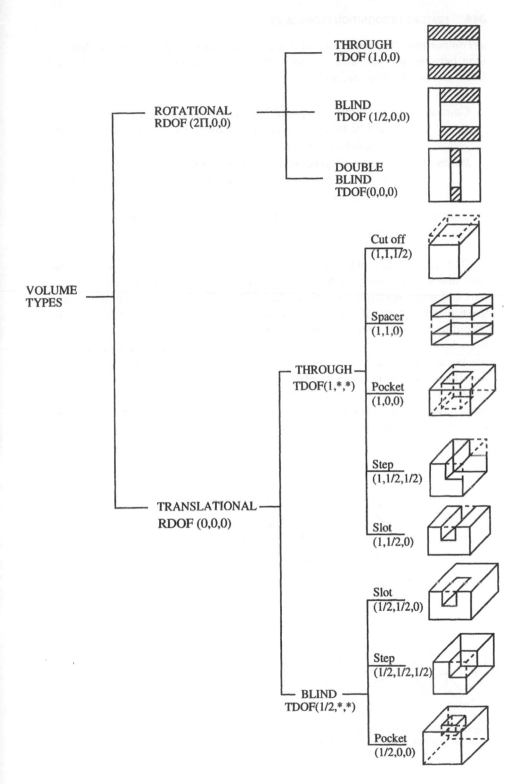

Figure 9.19 Delta volume classification by degrees of freedom

decomposition. The basic idea of these algorithms is to subdivide the delta volume between the part and the stock uniquely in elementary volumes or *cells*. Cells are usually required to be

Convex   To decouple any possible interacting features, the shared space should be treated as a cell of its own. This is achieved if all cells are required to be convex.

Minimal To allow the generation of all possible interpretations of the volume, cells should be elementary enough to allow all possible features to be composed of them.

Unique   The cells should be independent of the particular decomposition procedure used.

One such cell decomposition method is described by (Sakurai and Chin 1994), who aim at generating all possible machinable features corresponding a given part and stock. A simple example of their idea method is given in Figure 9.20. In the top left, a part with two crossing slots is shown. Assuming that the part is manufactured off a rectangular block of material, a cross-shape delta volume must be recognized as features. In the top right of the figure, the delta volume has been partitioned in five convex cells. The partitioning is performed by splitting the delta volume with the extended surfaces contained in it; in this case the volume is split with the "side" surfaces of the cells. In the bottom, various features have been generated by combining the cells; these include an open pocket, two long slots, and four smaller slots.

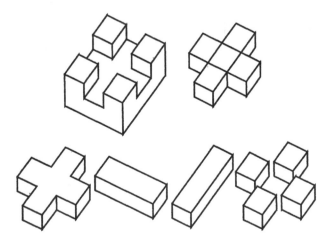

Figure 9.20 Feature recognition by cell decomposition (Sakurai and Chin 1994; reprinted with permission from the publisher)

To generate machinable features, two conditions for cell combination are used: Cells must be connected in order to be combined, and the first cell must share at least one face with the part. In addition the composed subvolumes are matched with the topological and geometric characteristics of a set of predefined features. Observe that the recognized features can be combined in several ways as a full feature model; for instance, one may choose to view the object as having two intersecting long slots, or as having one long and two small slots. The actual algorithm organizes the different interpretations as a feature graph. The method can be combined with a conventional feature recognizer by using the conventional recognizer to extract noninterfering features as the first step of feature recognition, and then using the decomposition method to handle the remaining interfering features.

The problem of this method is that generating all intermediate geometric entities can be computationally expensive, especially if curved surfaces are included; many of the cells are eventually discarded. As a result the number of composed subvolumes may grow formidably, while many of these may be invalid features that are afterward thrown away. The generality is also limited by the set of predefined features.

Shah et al. (1994) describe a cell decomposition method that also is intended for the recognition of machinable features but that is designed to handle also undocumented features. Moreover the combinatorial explosion of candidate cells is avoided by using an incremental method for decomposing the solid that can also exploit some geometric optimizations. First, design features are separated into documented and undocumented features by a feature filter. Documented features can be mapped directly to machinable shapes; therefore volume decomposition is only used on the undocumented features. These volumes are decomposed into minimum convex cells by a method called *half space partitioning*. After partitioning, cells are reconstituted into larger volumes based on a maximum convex volume criterion. These latter volumes are classified with respect to machining attributes by degree of freedom analysis discussed in Section 9.3.2.

To gain a feel of cell decomposition algorithms, let us take a closer look at the half-space partitioning method. Cell decomposition is equivalent to generating a *partition* of a nonempty set S. A partition is defined as a set $\pi = \{F_1, F_2, ..., F_K\}$ of non-empty subsets of S, called *blocks*, such that the following conditions are satisfied:

$$F_i \cap F_j = \varnothing \quad (i \neq j) \tag{9.1}$$

$$\bigcup_{i=1}^{K} F_i = S \tag{9.2}$$

Here $\cap$ and $\cup$ stand for Boolean intersection and union operations, and $\varnothing$ stands for the empty set. In the following, we also use $\cap^*$ and $\cup^*$ denoting the corresponding regularized operations (see Chapter 2).

Consider a set of half spaces H: $\{H_1, H_2, ..., H_p\}$. A *minterm* of H is defined as an intersection of the form $X_1 \cap^* ... \cap^* X_i ... \cap^* X_p$, where X_i is H_i or its complement. There are 2^p possible minterms of H. The table below shows the 8 minterms for 3 half-spaces; 1 versus 0 stands for the positive versus negative half of the space divided by the half-space. For instance, $F_2 = H'_1 \cap^* H'_2 \cap^* H_3$, where H'_1 means the complement of H_1 and so on. It can be shown (Brown 1990) that the set of minterms F: $\{F_1, F_2, ..., F_k\}$, $k = 2^p$, is a partition of the universe.

	H_1	H_2	H_3
F_1	0	0	0
F_2	0	0	1
F_3	0	1	0
F_4	0	1	1
F_5	1	0	0
F_6	1	0	1
F_7	1	1	0
F_8	1	1	1

Denote $V_i = V \cap^* F_i$ where V is a volume to be decomposed. From Equations (9.1) and (9.2) and Boolean algebra, we obtain

$$V_i \cap^* V_j = (V \cap^* F_i) \cap^* (V \cap^* F_j) = V \cap^* (F_i \cap^* F_j) = \varnothing \quad (i \neq j) \quad (9.3)$$

$$\cup^* V_i = \cup^* (V \cap^* F_i) = V \cap^* (\cup^* F_i) = V \quad (9.4)$$

Therefore, the set $\{V_1, V_2, ..., V_K\}$ is a partition of the volume V. We may conclude that a partition of a volume can be obtained using its constituent half-spaces; moreover the resulting partition satisfies the conditions of convexity, minimality, and uniqueness stated above.

Unfortunately, if there are n half-spaces, the number of possible minterms is 2^n, and we have a combinatorial explosion. However, many of the minterms obtained correspond to empty cells. For example, in Figure 9.21 (Shah et al. 1994) the U-shaped volume is decomposed into five cells by the three half-spaces of the depression. In this case three of the eight minterms are null.

To avoid constructing minterms corresponding to empty cells, the implemented method works incrementally by considering the half-spaces one at a time. Suppose that we have m half spaces $H_1, H_2, ..., H_m$. To every cell produced by half space partitioning we assign a m-dimensional vector called a *half-space vector* HSV $= (a_1, a_2, a_3, ..., a_m)$, where the component a_1 corresponds to H_1, a_2 to H_2 and so on; each a_i is 1 or 0, indicating whether the cell lies in the positive or the negative side of the corresponding half space. For instance, HSV $= (0, 1, ...)$ indicates that the cell is produced by the Boolean intersection $V \cap^* H'_1 \cap^* H_2 \cap^* ...$.

The algorithm starts by considering the whole volume V as the initial cell. First, half-space H_1 is chosen and the algorithm intersects V with H_1 and its comple-

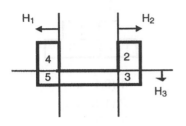

cell	H_1	H_2	H_3
$\emptyset$	0	0	0
1	0	0	1
2	0	1	0
3	0	1	1
4	1	0	0
5	1	0	1
$\emptyset$	1	1	0
$\emptyset$	1	1	1

Figure 9.21 Example of half-space partitioning (Shen 1994; reprinted with permission from the author)

ment H_1'. HSVs associated to the resulting intermediate cells are (1, ...) and (0, ...), respectively. Components from the second to the last in these HSVs are left undetermined. Next, each intermediate cell is intersected with H_2 and H_2'. Similarly to the above, the HSVs associated with the cells generated from intersection with H_2 are (1, 1, ...) and (0, 1, ...), and with H_2' (1, 0, ...) and (0, 0, ...). This process continues until the last half-space H_m is chosen. In the end the ultimate cells with their HSVs result; null cells are never generated.

Special relationships between half-spaces are exploited to cut down the computational load. Given two planar half-spaces H_1 and H_2, there are three special kinds of relationships between them as shown in Figure 9.22 (Shah et al. 1994).

For any arrangement that applies, one can avoid computing the set operations that otherwise would be needed. For instance, in the case of Figure 9.22(a), $H_1 \subseteq H_2$ and the following applies:

$$H_1 \cap^* H_2 = H_1$$
$$H_1' \cap^* H_2' = H_2'$$
$$H_1 \cap^* H_2' = \emptyset$$

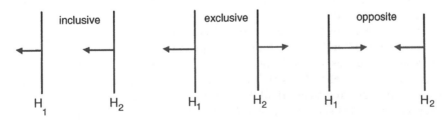

Figure 9.22 Special relationships between half-spaces (Shen 1994; reprinted with permission from the author)

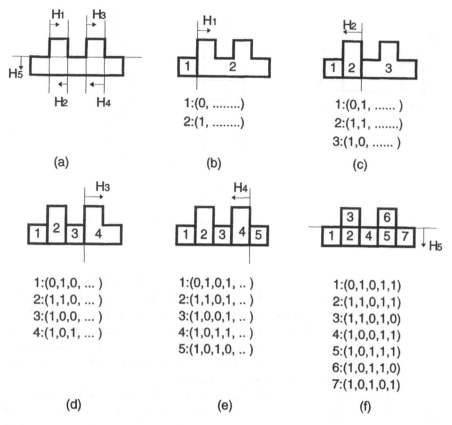

Figure 9.23 Cells and HSVs at each partitioning step (Shen 1994; reprinted with permission from the author)

Similar equations apply to the other cases (b, c). To exploit this, any groups of parallel planar half-spaces are ordered before partitioning, and the partitioning is done in the sorted order. Hence only the relationship to the next half-space in order needs to be considered.

Figure 9.23 (Shah et al. 1994) gives an example of the method for a volume consisting of a block with two ribs on it. The intermediate cells and their HSVs corresponding to each decomposition step are shown. Half-space relationships have been used to simplify the decomposition; for example, in (d), H_3 and its nearest half space H_2 in (c) are exclusive of each other, so there is no need to intersect cells 1 and 2 in (c) with H_3 or its complement.

It is also obvious, as shown in (e), that Boolean intersection with H_5 is not necessary for all the cells. To exploit this, one can investigate the relationship between a half-space and a cell. If all the vertices of a cell lie *in* or *on* one side of a half-space, the cell is said to be *one-sided* with respect to the half-space; if the vertices of a cell distribute over the *both* sides of the half-space, the cell is said to be *two-sided*. In *e*, cells 1, 3 and 5 are one-sided, and cells 2 and 4 are two-sided with respect to H_s. No Boolean intersections are needed for one-sided cells.

Geometric Reasoning by Volumes Another feature recognition algorithm that is capable of recognizing several interpretations of a part is described by (Regli and Nau 1993), who give a feature recognition technique for MRSEVs, a library of form features defined in STEP and EXPRESS. Their main contribution is a formalization of the feature search on the basis of an algebraic view of features and geometric reasoning on the basis of volume information. The method is currently restricted to holes and (general) pockets. The basic assumption of the technique is that for a given part and stock, a "manufacturable" feature model consisting of holes and pockets exists. This assumption means, for instance, that a cylindrical surface in the delta volume (the difference between the stock and the part) always indicates the presence of a hole feature.

The basic idea of the method is to first extract the faces of the part *P* not present in the stock *S*. Letting b(*X*) denote the boundary of *X* and –* the regularized set difference (see Chapter 2), this can be written simply as

$$U = \mathrm{b}(P) -^* \mathrm{b}(S).$$

The extraction algorithm can then be expressed as follows (Gupta et al. 1994):

1. Let the set of recognized features *F* be initially empty.
2. For each face *u* of *U*, add to *F* the features *f* that have the following properties:
   - *f* can create *u* (i.e., *u* is a subset of some face of *f*), and *f* does not intersect the part (i.e., $P \cap^* \mathrm{rem}(f) = \emptyset$, where rem(*f*) is the removal volume of *f*)
   - for every feature *g* that satisfies the above condition and contains *f*, *f* and *g* have the same effective removal volume
   - for every feature *g* that satisfies the above condition and is contained by *f*, *g* has a smaller effective removal volume.

The recognizer that implements the above abstract algorithm is based on a geometric reasoning technique that requires the use of a solid modeling subsystem. The basic geometric queries used by the recognizer are (1) searching a maximum enclosing cylinder for a cylindrical surface, (2) projecting an object (or a subset thereof) onto a plane, and (3) finding the closest point of an object to a plane. An intersection test is also needed. Given these geometric reasoning tools, as long as a piece of the surface of a feature exists in the delta volume, the full feature can be extracted. For instance, given a cylindrical surface, the technique fits a maximum enclosing cylinder around the surface such that the end surfaces of the cylinder extend outside the part. If the cylinder does not intersect the part, a thru-hole is found. Otherwise, an intersection must exist along one direction of the hole axis for the hole to be machinable. The hole bottom is located in this direction by means of a closest point search. The main restriction

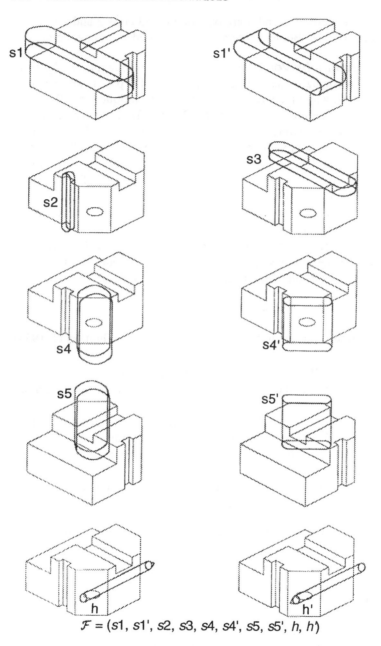

$$\mathcal{F} = (s1, s1', s2, s3, s4, s4', s5, s5', h, h')$$

Figure 9.24 Features extracted by Regli et al.'s method (Gupta et al. 1994; reprinted with permission from Elsevier Science)

of this method is that all features must be linear sweeps (holes, slots, pockets, etc.).

On the basis of the techniques presented, the authors prove that the recognition method is complete in the sense that if a feature model in terms of holes and pockets is known to exist for a given part and stock, the algorithm will find a feature model. They also show that the method can handle arbitrarily complex feature interactions between holes and pockets. Moreover the technique can identify all features that can generate the machined surfaces. For instance, a sample part and the various features extracted by the algorithm are shown in Figure 9.24 (Gupta et al. 1994). The resulting redundant set of features forms a basis for constructing all possible feature models of the part.

Because the different feature interpretations typically correspond with alternative ways of manufacturing the part from the stock, the availability of all feature models is very valuable for applications such as process planning and setup planning. One example is the system presented by (Das et al. 1994), where the alternative features are considered from the viewpoint of setup planning in a scheme for representing functional requirements by tags associated with geometric elements of a model. For instance, a face may have a minimal area tag. Another tag may mark a face or volume unchangeable. Using the changed features, a better setup solution may be found than in the original part, making it possible to suggest a redesign. A similar system for machining operation planning is described by (Gupta et al. 1994). Both works exploit heavily the techniques presented by (Karinthi and Nau 1992) and (Regli and Nau 1993).

9.4 RECOGNITION FROM CSG MODELS

CSG-based algorithms concentrate on feature recognition from CSG representation solid models. Generally the goal of these algorithms is to rearrange the CSG tree to a form where CSG expressions of each of the features have been separated. The fact that the CSG representation scheme is unambiguous but not unique has posed many difficulties in the development of recognition algorithms: The same model can be represented in terms of many different CSG trees, all of which should be mapped to a unique result where the features are made explicit. Rearranging a large set theoretic expression as required is a hard problem for which efficient solutions may not exist.

Lee and Fu (1987) propose an approach, based on principal axis and tree reconstruction, that extracts and unifies feature representations while retaining the simplicity and conciseness of CSG. The principal axes are collected and clustered according to their spatial relationships. The features are unified in two steps: First, the tree is reconstructed, with all participating nodes of the feature relocated and grouped together to form a subtree, and then the tree is transformed, with the resulting subtree replaced by an equivalent subtree.

Shpitalni and Fischer (1994) consider the problem of machining region extraction on the basis of a CSG model, a problem closely related to feature extrac-

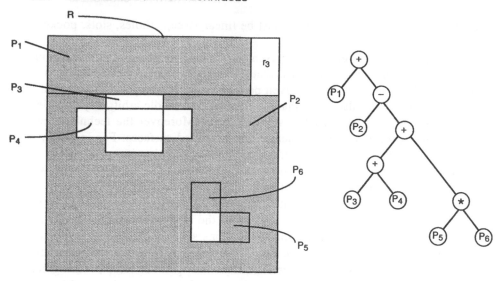

Figure 9.25 An object and its CSG tree (Shpitalni and Fischer 1994; reprinted with permission from *Computer-Aided Design*, Butterworth Heinemann, Oxford, England)

tion. They use octrees for intermediate evaluation of the machining regions and CSG tree pruning. In the result the machining regions are represented by small CSG trees that form a good basis of machining feature extraction. To give a sense of the CSG manipulation methods, let us review this method to some extent. For simplicity, we will examine the method in two dimensions.

Consider the sample object and its CSG tree depicted in Figure 9.25 (Shpitalni and Fischer 1994). The objective is to represent the part as a rawstock R minus a set of connected machining regions $region_i$, each represented in terms of an independent CSG tree. Here R is the whole square; the three unshaded subsets are the machining regions.

As the first step, the algorithm forms the CSG tree CSG(*Cavity*) representing the total space to be machined. This is simply the set difference of R and the object, and it is shown in Figure 9.26(*a*) (Shpitalni and Fischer 1994). As the second step, CSG(*Cavity*) is converted into *positive form* where only Boolean union and intersection operations are present. The conversion works by scanning the CSG tree, and (1) replacing each subtraction operator with a combination of intersection and negation, (2) pushing all negation and transformation operators to the level of leaves, and (3) eliminating the transformation operators by applying the transformation directly to the (copied) primitives. The positive form of CSG(*Cavity*), Positive-CSG(*Cavity*), is given in Figure 9.26(*b*). Observe that primitives P_1 and P_2 have been negated, and appear in complemented forms CP_1 and CP_2.

As the third step, the algorithm computes a quadtree Quad(*Cavity*) that describes the cavity. The algorithms for converting a CSG tree to a quadtree-type representation were outlined in Chapter 2, where we saw that the algorithm can

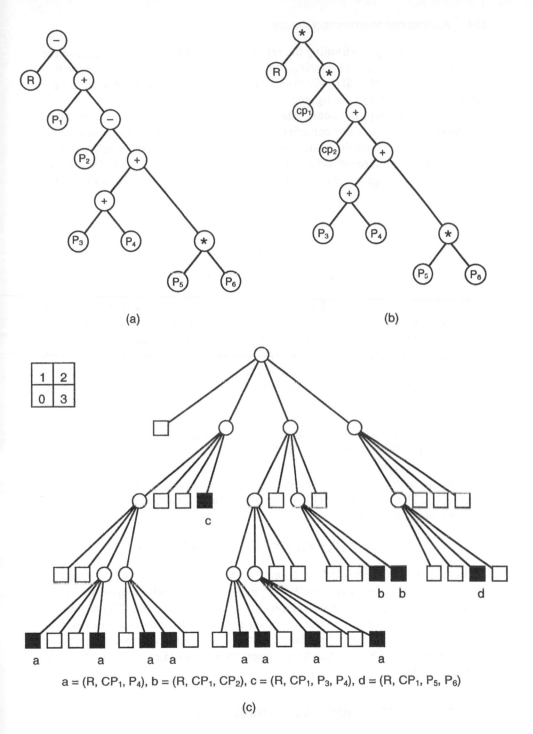

(a)

(b)

$a = (R, CP_1, P_4)$, $b = (R, CP_1, CP_2)$, $c = (R, CP_1, P_3, P_4)$, $d = (R, CP_1, P_5, P_6)$

(c)

Figure 9.26 CSG tree for the cavity and its positive form; quadtree for the cavity (Shpitalni and Fischer 1994; reprinted with permission from *Computer-Aided Design*, Butterworth Heinemann, Oxford, England)

work by recursively subdividing the region of interest R. The resulting quadtree is given in Figure 9.26(c). During the creation of the quadtree, the algorithm keeps track of which CSG primitives are active in each black node; these are labeled a, b, c, and d in the figure.

As the fourth step, the connected components in the cavity are recognized and labeled; they will be identified as machining regions. This operation is simply implemented on the basis of the explicitly recorded spatial relationships encoded in the quadtree structure. For each region so formed, the CSG primitives active in the region are formed by inspecting the labels of the black quadtree nodes:

$$region_1 = \{R, CP_1, P_3, P_4\}$$
$$region_2 = \{R, CP_1, P_5, P_6\}$$
$$region_3 = \{R, CP_1, CP_2\}$$

As the fifth and final step, the CSG trees for each of the regions are formed by a pruning procedure applied to the original CSG tree. To see how this is achieved, observe that the active CSG primitives in $region_1$ do not include primitives CP_2, P_5, or P_6. Hence, these primitives do not contribute to the shape of $region_1$. This has the consequence that a CSG tree for $region_1$ can be formed from the CSG tree of the whole cavity by replacing the leaves for CP_2, P_5, and P_6 by the null set. The resulting tree CSG ($region_1$) is shown in top left of Figure 9.27 (Shpitalni and Fischer 1994).

The pruning algorithm works by scanning the tree and executing some tree manipulations. First, a "+" node with one null set input in its left subtree is replaced by its right subtree. Next, a "*" node with at least one null set input is itself replaced with a null set. Thereafter the "+" node compaction rule is applicable again. The resulting CSG tree can be compacted further by first writing it into sum-of-products form:

$$R * CP_1 * (P_3 + P_4) = R * CP_1 * P_3 + R * CP_1 * P_4$$

It is easy to establish that $P_3 \supset R$ and $P_3 \supset CP_1$; therefore $R * CP_1 * P_3$ evaluates simply to P_3. Similarly $R * CP_1 * P_4$ evaluates to P_4, which gives the result CSG($region_1$) $= P_3 + P_4$. Other regions are extracted similarly. The technique must be elaborated to some extent to cover the case where there are nested machining regions (e.g., nested pockets). For details, see the original publication. Other advances in CSG approach have been reported by (Lee and Jea 1988) and (Perng et al. 1990).

9.5 RECOGNITION FROM TWO-DIMENSIONAL DRAWINGS

Many companies have accumulated through years of engineering practice vast amounts of two-dimensional engineering drawings that may constitute the bulk

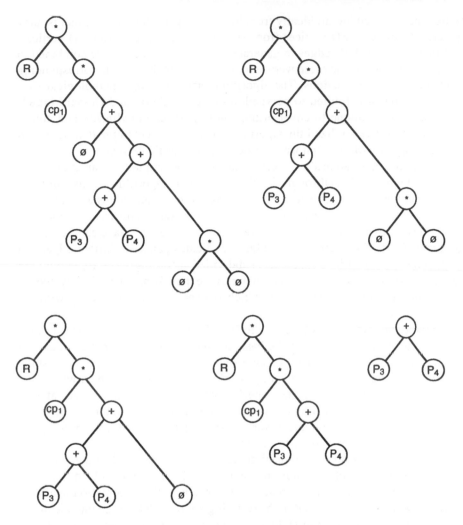

Figure 9.27 Stages of the pruning algorithm (Shpitalni and Fischer 1994; reprinted with permission from *Computer-Aided Design*, Butterworth Heinemann, Oxford, England)

of the information on past designs. A method that could recognize these data as three-dimensional feature models would be of obvious economic interest to these companies and would certainly make the transition to feature-based design and manufacturing much smoother.

In solid modeling the analogous problem is present. The problem of interpreting a collection of orthographic drawings as a three-dimensional solid has been studied since solid modeling technologies were introduced in the 1970s. An early algorithm was presented by (Wesley and Markowsky 1981), who extended their "fleshing out wire frames" algorithm to recognize orthographic projections. They worked hierarchically from lower to higher dimensions; that is, they generated candidate 3D vertices from 2D vertices, 3D edges from 3D vertices, and then assembled 3D edges to generate 3D faces. 3D faces were combined to form 3D subobjects, and these were assembled to form the objects corresponding with the original projections. The algorithm handled various pathological situations well but was limited to polyhedral objects. Sakurai and Gossard (1983) extended this technique to cover orthogonally positioned cylinders and cones. Gu et al. (1986) generalized the algorithm further by a technique that permitted the handling of cylinders whose axes lie on any coordinate plane.

To see how these algorithms work, consider the example by (Yan et al. 1992) shown in Figure 9.28(*a*) through (*h*). The input to the algorithm consists of three orthogonal views of an object *a*. First, the 3D vertices and edges are generated by "intersecting" the three original views to generate a wire frame model (*b*). Next, closed edge cycles of the wire frame are retrieved and face candidates are generated (*c, d*). By intersecting the face candidates pairwise, further edges can be generated (*e*), and face candidates subdivided accordingly (*f*). By combining candidate faces, candidate blocks of material are then formed (*g*). Finally, blocks are combined into the final object, which is checked for consistency with the original drawing.

Observe that many objects can be formed from the blocks; the correct interpretation usually is selected on the basis of line hatches and other attributes in the original drawing. Of course, without such auxiliary information, the best the algorithm can do is to enumerate all possible interpretations of the drawing and let a human user choose the correct one. To handle more realistic models, at least cylinders, cones, and tori should also be supported. However, their introduction could considerably complicate several stages of the algorithm; no complete solutions have been published to our knowledge.

The previously discussed algorithms can of course be used to generate features by having a standard feature recognizer work on the recognized boundary model. A problem with this approach is that much of the information available in the drawing is not preserved in the resulting solid model. These include drawing conventions such as line style and standard representations of certain mechanical joints. This information cannot be used during feature recognition.

A recognition technique that tries to map drawings directly to somewhat higher-level structures than mere geometry is described by (Vaxiviere and Tombre 1992). They describe the CELESSTIN system that can interpret (certain types of) scanned mechanical drawings into CATIA form, including interpreting the significance of various linetypes and recognizing some standard mechanical elements such as bearings.

Figure 9.29 (Vaxiviere and Tombre 1992) gives an example of the type of drawings that CELESSTIN would be able to recognize. The recognition algorithm works by first dividing the drawing into "blocks," minimal sized polygons surrounded by thick lines. Line styles and hatching are taken into account; here the hatching denotes an imaginary section plane. Next, the "technical attributes" of blocks are determined by analyzing the neighborhood relationships of adjacent

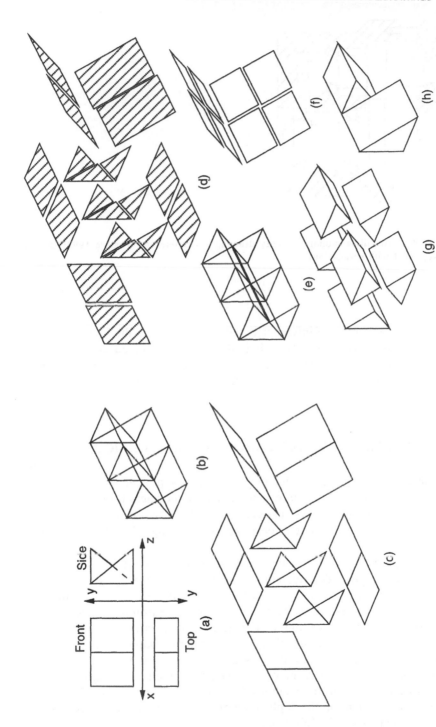

Figure 9.28 Recognition of a solid from orthogonal projections

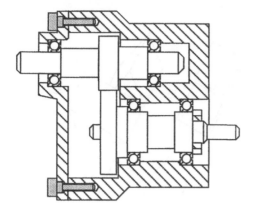

Figure 9.29 A two-dimensional assembly drawing (Vaxiviere and Tombre 1992; ©1992 IEEE. Reprinted with permission)

blocks using certain rules of inference based, in this case, on the French drafting standards. Higher-level elements such as shafts are recognized by propagation rules. In the figure the system would correctly recognize two shafts (including gear segments), several ball bearings, threaded holes, fasteners, a casing, and a cover.

9.6 COMPARISON OF FEATURE RECOGNITION TECHNIQUES

The principal advantages of the feature recognition approach are the possibilities of using current CAD databases and geometric modelers for design, and of making the recognition process application specific whereby separate applications are given their own recognition programs working with domain-specific recognition rules.

The principal problems of feature recognition include the limited domain of recognition techniques. The domain of early techniques, for instance, is not general enough to capture the complexity of real parts. Rule-based techniques are unattractive in cases where extensive geometric reasoning is needed, and graph-based techniques have high computational complexity and require additional heuristic procedures to handle all cases. Other weaknesses fall in the area of recognizing complex cases such as interacting features and the loss of nongeometric information that may have been available in the original model.

Comparison of the various methods for feature recognition is difficult and depends to some extent on the application domain as discussed in Section 9.1. However, we may make the following observations:

Rule-based feature recognition: A main disadvantage is the ad hoc nature of rules: A rule written for a particular configuration of a feature cannot be generalized to cover a similar feature in a different configuration (e.g., due to feature interaction). Also the exhaustive searches needed to match rules against the solid model data representation make the method quite slow.

Graph-based feature recognition: Graph matching is capable of locating directly a "canonical" instance of a feature. If feature interactions are present, costly and potentially dangerous heuristics are needed. Moreover, since graph algorithms rely primarily on graph topology, they have difficulties in distinguishing between features that differ only geometrically.

Graph-based methods also must perform exhaustive searches of feature patterns in a (potentially large) boundary representation data structure. Because the computational complexity of general subgraph matching is exponential, graph-based methods are inherently slow. Graph grammar based methods suffer from the same problems but to somewhat lesser extent.

Volume decomposition based feature recognition: The main advantage of volume decomposition methods (including the CSG-based region identification method explained in Section 9.4) is that several candidate models can be generated to suit the requirements of an application. Another benefit is that they can deal with incomplete instances of features (e.g., interacting features). In fact the initial stages of a volume decomposition algorithm (subdivision of the part in elementary volumes, accessibility computation) are independent of the feature types being searched, and this makes these steps quite general. While the computational cost of these methods is high, they can benefit from rapidly advancing nonmanifold solid modeling techniques.

On the negative side, the volume decomposition methods are still at an early stage of development, as is reflected in the lack of generality in implemented systems. Many of these examples concentrate on simple prismatic objects with nice orthogonal features, whereas real parts involve smoothly blended curved surfaces and features in general orientation.

9.7 HYBRID SYSTEMS

From the preceding sections we can conclude that a general method for feature recognition that would cover all practically important cases has not yet been found. Graph matching suffers from lack of generality in dealing with interacting features. Worse yet, application demands may require recognition criteria that lie outside of the realm of "pure" techniques described in the preceding sections. Consider machining planning. The same geometric shape may be classified as a "slot" or a "pocket" depending on its general dimensions and tolerances and on the availability of milling tools of different types and sizes.

These considerations have led several researchers to consider *hybrid* feature recognition algorithms that combine several basic techniques. For instance, (Laakko and Mäntylä 1991) present an algorithm for machining feature recognition that combines a graph-matching algorithm similar to Joshi and Chang's method with a rule- and constraint-based system. The basic idea is to extract candidate face sets by a graph-matching technique and to use constraints and rules to determine more closely the recognized feature type. The algorithm also gets extra mileage from a global analysis performed in the initial stage on the basis of its knowledge of the possible blank shapes. This technique is discussed further in Chapter 10. Other hybrid methods are described in the following sections.

9.7.1 Hybrid Methods for Interacting Features

One of the weaknesses of graph-based methods discussed in Section 9.2 is their inadequacy to handle feature interaction. Several hybrid methods have especially emphasized this issue.

For instance, Vandenbrande and Requicha (Vandenbrande 1990; Vandenbrande and Requicha 1993, 1994) use a hybrid technique to overcome problems with feature interaction. Their algorithm uses face patterns as clues to the existence of a feature, and then attempts to create the largest volumetric features consistent with the data available in the original model. It takes into account machinability conditions such as accessibility and nonintrusion. Complex geometric relations, such as tolerances between surfaces, can also be considered. Their method relies heavily on artificial intelligence techniques, mainly a partitioned blackboard architecture supporting hybrid reasoning methods. Geometric reasoning is performed with the PADL-2 modeler.

The goal of the algorithm is to produce valid machining features for a part. A central concept for the algorithm is a *feature hint*, a specific pattern in the boundary of a part, characterized by some geometric and topological relationships. Feature hints are based on feature existence rules that specify how much of the boundary of a feature must remain in the part after interaction with other features. For instance, a linear slot feature must have some subset of its both lateral faces remaining. Once a feature hint has been found, the algorithm will *complete* the feature by extending it to one or more directions without intruding the part; hence the goal is to produce the largest volumetric feature that is compatible with the other information in the part model. In the completion process, portions of a feature that were separated by feature interactions may be reunited. Portions of the completed feature are marked as "optional" and "required" to represent the feature interactions.

The required portions of a feature represent the minimal volume that a feature-shape cutting tool must sweep to generate the surface of the feature. The optional portions correspond to regions that the feature shares with other interacting features; these areas may be removed by machining the feature itself, or as a side effect of machining the interacting features. For instance, in Figure 9.30

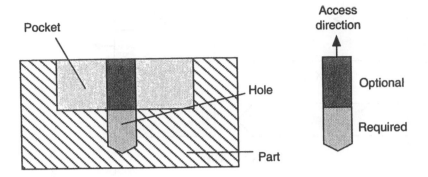

Figure 9.30 Optional and required parts of a feature (Vandenbrande and Requicha 1994; reprinted with permission from Elsevier Science)

(Vandenbrande and Requicha 1994) the required part of the hole feature corresponds to the surfaces present in the part; the optional part is shared with the interfering pocket feature. As shown in Figure 9.31 (Vandenbrande and Requicha 1994), the completer may combine two matching hints. Here the optional part spans the cavity between the two required portions.

The principle of operation of the feature completion algorithm is illustrated in Figure 9.32 (Vandenbrande and Requicha 1994) for a case of one-dimensional completion. The method is generally geared toward using CSG type operations. In this case a feature hint S_1 is first generated by a cylindrical face. Then a cylindrical half-space V^∞ is generated as a maximal extension of the cross section of the cylindrical face related to S_1 along the cylinder axis. As the next step, V^∞ is intersected with the stock to create a finite solid. The solid is enclosed within a minimal cylinder, and the part is subtracted from the minimal cylinder to eliminate all portions of the cylinder that would intrude the part. For each

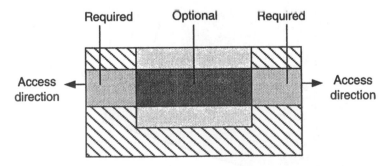

Figure 9.31 Hole-pocket interference (Vandenbrande and Requicha 1994; reprinted with permission from Elsevier Science)

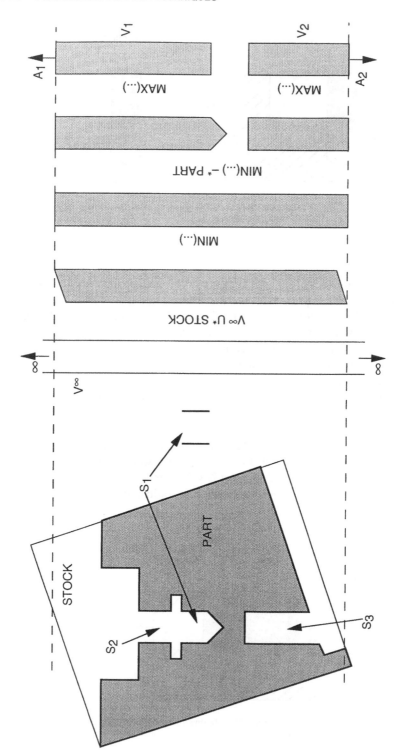

Figure 9.32 One-dimensional feature completion (Vandenbrande and Requicha 1994; reprinted with permission from Elsevier Science)

connected component in the result, a maximal cylinder totally enclosed within the component is finally produced. Observe that the original hint S_1 produces two disjoint primitive volumes V_1 and V_2. V_1 is related to the original hint, whereas V_2 is related to another hint S_3. Moreover, hint S_2 leads to the same volume as S_1, although the two hints are separated by an interfering groove.

A similar hybrid technique is described by (Ames 1991), whose feature recognition algorithm is intended for group technology classification. Similar to the method of Vandenbrande, the method is based on using "hints" of features, termed by Ames "featurettes." For instance, a pair of parallel edges is a featurette that suggests the existence of a slot feature and possibly a hole feature. The featurettes are organized as a hierarchy; hence, if a "pair of parallel edges" featurette is found, the adjacent faces are inspected to find further hints of either slots or holes.

The featurette tests are further organized by means of feature precedences that resolve some ambiguous situations. Those features that determine the overall shape of the part for group technology coding are given higher precedence. For instance, if a part is already determined to be extruded, the recognition of "slot" features along its profile is suppressed, while slots still may appear elsewhere in the part. Problems of feature interaction are avoided by allowing faces to belong in several features; for group technology coding this seems to be appropriate.

9.7.2 Real-Time Feature Recognition

Most automatic feature recognition systems scan the whole geometric model in an effort to identify all the features that they have been programmed to find. Feature recognition has been traditionally used in the batch mode after a geometric model has been created. This approach is not suitable as a design environment. Recognition can be made a lot easier if the user can tell the program what to look for and also pick one of the entities of the feature to get the process started on the right track. This is easy to do when a graphical image of the part is before the designer. However, picking all the entities belonging to a feature is cumbersome and unnecessary. Instead, one can automate the process of finding any features that a selected entity is part of.

A hybrid system combining interactive and automatic feature recognition was developed by Sreevalsan (Sreevalsan 1990; Sreevalsan and Shah 1992) to provide real-time feature recognition. The user creates a solid model first, which is converted to a data structure suitable for feature recognition. A wire frame image of the part is displayed by traversing and drawing all the edges. Predefined generic features are stored in feature libraries as lists of topological and geometric conditions such as number of faces, adjacency, and face types. Since the user can see the part model, the assumption is that he or she knows what features exist in the model. Therefore the features of interest can be recognized and extracted in one of three ways:

1. The user tells the system to recognize all features of type X (dovetail slot, obround pocket, etc.). Since the system is looking for a specific type of

features, exhaustive searches are not necessary. For example, if a hole feature is specified, the system will ignore all noncircular edges during its search.

2. The user picks an edge and asks the system to recognize any feature(s) of which it is a constituent. The search is limited to entities in the immediate vicinity of the selected edge.

3. The user tells the system to recognize a feature of type X. The system prompts for a starting entity (edge or face of a certain type). The user picks an edge, and the system finds the rest of the entities that belong to the feature of type X. This is the most efficient of the three methods, provided that the user knows the type of feature of which the entity is part.

The advantage of this hybrid system is that a small amount of user interaction saves a lot of the time spent in searching through the model.

Some recent experiments have been done to identify the problems in combining feature recognition and design by features. The user may mix and match the modes by combining direct feature definition with postrecognition from a geometric model. If jumping back and forth between these two modes is to be supported, a controlled interface to solid modeling is needed to ensure that one does not inadvertently destroy or alter features, when working directly with solids. Also there has to be some means of making incremental changes without having to regenerate the entire model. This requires control over tagging of geometric entities, retention of entity attributes after Boolean operations, and two-way (dynamic) communication between the feature and geometric modelers.

In such a system, feature recognition or interactive definition can identify the entities in the geometric model that correspond to a feature. In some cases it is also possible to extract the dimensional parameters of the features and their values, such as the diameter of a hole or the depth of a slot. Thus recognition amounts to making explicit what is implicit in the model. However, features defined by the design by feature approach usually contain richer information not even implicitly represented in the geometric model. All the additional information associated with features which is not available from the geometric model has to be incorporated somehow if there is to be no difference between features defined by different modes. This may include the feature hierarchy, adjacency and the attribute information, tolerance, surface finish and material properties.

9.8 RESEARCH TRENDS

Feature recognition is a research area where considerable effort is needed to develop more robust and less computationally expensive systems. This situation is likely to remain unchanged for a number of years into the future. Therefore we conclude this chapter by looking at some present research trends. However, research is also likely to continue along the lines of the methods already discussed.

9.8.1 Neural Network Based Recognition

Recently artificial neural networks have been used for feature recognition from 2D drawings (Peters 1994) and from solid models (Prabahkar and Henderson 1992; Henderson et al. 1994). A neural net consists of nodes and connections. Nodes are input, output, or intermediate. Each node receives inputs from other nodes (or externally), transforms the data received in some way, and outputs the result to other nodes. Weighting factors are also attached to each node. The outputs of certain nodes can be sampled to determine the reaction of the net to a set of inputs.

Prabhakar's method provides parallel inputs to the neural net by splitting the boundary model into a five layers, as follows: The B-rep geometry to be recognized is coded as a face adjacency matrix, containing eight-digit codes for each face. Each code indicates the face type (planar, cylindrical, etc.), convexity of the edge separating the faces, number of loops, and so on. A feature is recognized if the presence of a sequence of codes characteristic of that feature is detected in any row of the adjacency matrix. For each type of feature to be recognized, a neural network is created by training, using a feature definition language. The adjacency matrix is fed row at a time to each net; hence the resulting algorithm essentially performs pattern recognition on each row of the matrix. Outputs from the nets denote recognized features. Examples of feature types that can be recognized include flat-bottomed hole, through-slot, and through-hole. The advantage of neural net based recognition is that partial features can be recognized, since the method is not just pass/fail. Among the limitations are the fact that dimensions cannot be taken into account, and that only features consisting of a single "primary face" and several "secondary faces" can be considered. Included in the second restriction is the fact that recognition depending on the relations of "secondary faces" is not possible.

9.8.2 Differential Depth Filter

Many of the methods discussed above are quite sensitive to the size of the geometric model from which features are to be recognized. Given a large model consisting of hundreds of thousands of faces, feature recognition on the basis of the "raw" model is close to impossible, unless the model can be preprocessed in some fashion before recognition.

Gadh and Prinz (1992) have introduced an approach for feature recognition using a *differential depth filter*. The idea is to handle substantial geometric and topologic variations by defining features in terms of loops. Both the filtering and the looping assist in the reduction of the large search space of topological entities.

The basic aim of the method is to construct a geometric model that facilitates feature recognition but does not contain irrelevant entities in feature recognition. This is done by first extracting silhouette edge information from a polyhedral boundary representation solid model by means of a filtering procedure that

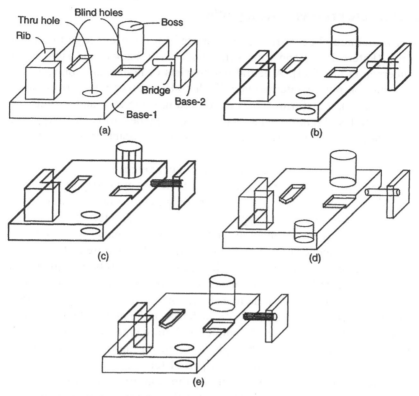

Figure 9.33 Differential depth filter concepts (Gadh and Prinz 1992; reprinted with permission from *Computer-Aided Design*, Butterworth Heinemann, Oxford, England)

considers each edge of the model in turn. An edge is considered a silhouette if one of its faces has a normal pointing toward the viewing direction, while the other face's normal points away from the viewing direction. Consider the sample part containing a number of features shown in Figure 9.33(*a*). Using the viewing direction normal to the page, the silhouettes extracted are those shown in dark lines in (*b*). This is termed the *unidirectional positive filter*.

If the filtering process is repeated from several viewpoints spaced evenly in 3D space (3–14 directions suffice for most features), and the results are united, the *multidirectional positive filter* is constructed as shown in Figure 9.33(*c*). The *negative differential depth filter* is defined as a positive filter operating on the complement of the object. The result of applying the negative filter to the sample object from the viewing direction normal to the page is shown in (*d*); filtered edges in the figure are shown in gray. Analogously to the above, the *multidirectional negative filter* consists of the union of several applications of the negative filter. Finally, the results of multidirectional positive and negative filters can be combined in a single result, shown in (*e*).

A filtered model such as (*e*) can be used for feature recognition by extracting positive and negative cycles of filtered edges. The various arrangements of cycles immediately lead to a characterization of the following basic types of features:

- Projection features
- Blind depression features
- Through depression features
- Bridges

For instance, the boss and the rib are characterized as projection features because both enclose material and contain a negative cycle. Further classifications can be made on the basis of that they also contain a positive cycle, which separates them from single-ended projection features such as a cone.

The loop-based characterization of feature types has several advantages. First, thin two-ended projection features can be recognized as ribs independently on the detailed shape of the feature, whereas a graph-based method should consider each and every rib topology separately. Such feature characterization is much more natural for many applications. Second, by eliminating from consideration all edges that are not filtered by the positive or the negative filters, the method can handle effectively also large models. The authors have analyzed injection molded parts having several hundred edges and noticed that as much as 90% of the edges are removed by filtering and loop construction.

The main difficulty of the method is choosing an appropriate number of viewing directions to be included in the filters. If too many directions are included, little filtering is achieved; if too few, some features are not recognized properly. In practice, 3–14 viewing directions were found to be sufficient for the recognition of "most of the 120 test parts" investigated.

9.8.3 Incremental Recognition

Most feature recognition algorithms view feature recognition as a one-time process with is applied to an essentially complete geometric model to generate features. The geometric model is assumed not to be changed afterward. While this assumption is relatively reasonable for applications such as generating machining features from a geometric model representing the final result of a design process, it may be oversimplistic for actual design. During the design process, geometry is used not only to express a final result but also as a working medium for expressing intermediate stages of the design.

Feature-based design techniques discussed in Chapter 8 are traditionally viewed as the best approach to provide the benefits of features for design proper. Nevertheless, this approach may sometimes limit the designer unnecessarily to express his or her design intentions with a vocabulary that does not fit the purpose. Therefore an *incremental recognition* approach to feature-based design that gives the designer the freedom of choosing whether to work on a design through its geometry or through its features becomes attractive. To work, the incremental feature modeling approach requires an *incremental feature recognition algorithm* that can create features on the basis of a geometric model where some features already have been recognized during previous applications of the recognizer. This section will review an incremental feature recognition algorithm. More detail of the method will be presented in Chapter 10.

The EXTDesign feature modeler (Laakko and Mäntylä 1993) aims at creating a feature modeling system that can combine both the design-by-features and feature recognition methods into a single framework. In the feature modeling approach implemented in EXTDesign, solid and feature-based modeling operations can be utilized in parallel during the design process of a part. With this approach a part can be modeled by design-with-features operations, by regular solid modeling operations combined with feature recognition, or by mixing these two approaches as may be convenient. The implementation of EXTDesign is based on a feature definition mechanism (to be explained in Chapter 10) that provides a good foundation for an integrated approach to feature-based modeling.

The incremental design process is illustrated in Figure 9.34 (Laakko and Mäntylä 1993). Note that geometric modeling and feature-based modeling operations have a symmetric status in the system. The process typically starts by first instantiating a feature class that will become the root (i.e., the *base feature*) of the instance hierarchy of the part. Alternatively, a solid model can be declared the root feature, or a known base feature type can be recognized from a solid

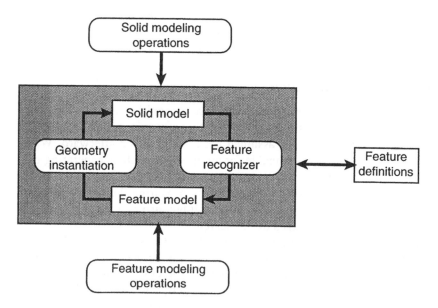

Figure 9.34 Design process using incremental feature recognition (Laakko and Mäntylä 1993; reprinted with permission from *Computer-Aided Design*, Butterworth Heinemann, Oxford, England)

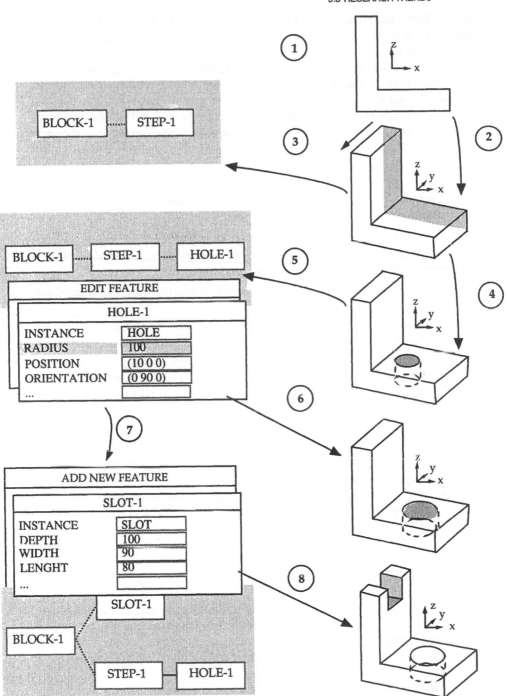

Figure 9.35 An example of incremental feature modeling (Laakko and Mäntylä 1993; reprinted with permission from *Computer-Aided Design*, Butterworth Heinemann, Oxford, England)

model. With a feature editor and its feature-based modeling commands, feature instances can be added to or deleted from the model. Feature attribute values can also be edited.

New features can also be added by utilizing the conventional geometric modeling operations (Boolean set operations, sweeps, etc.) provided by the system, followed by the execution of an incremental feature recognition algorithm that preserves already recognized features and interprets changed or new geometry as changed or new features. An example of the incremental operation is shown in Figure 9.35 (Laakko and Mäntylä 1993). The flow of operations in the figure is as follows:

1. First, the user creates a two-dimensional outline of the shape using the drafting-type operations of the modeler.
2. The outline is swept linearly to create an L-block.
3. The model is recognized using the incremental recognition algorithm. A feature model consisting of a block and a step is recognized.
4. The user creates a hole by using a Boolean difference operation subtracting a cylinder off the L-block.
5. The incremental recognizer is invoked again and the feature model is updated with a hole feature.
6. The hole feature is edited using the feature editor to change the radius and position of the hole; an updated geometric model is created.
7. A slot feature is added to the model by invoking the "add new feature" operation of the feature editor.
8. A new geometric model incorporating the slot is created.

The incremental technique is particularly effective in combination with the other techniques provided by EXTDesign, particularly the part family modeling methods discussed in Chapter 8. These techniques make it possible to introduce new feature types during the design process, if necessary, and to convert a finished model to a parametric part model.

REVIEW QUESTIONS

9.1 Identify interactive modeling operations that can be supported by dynamic feature recognition, whereby a feature is recognized for the purpose of supporting the operation.

9.2 Complete the graphs in Figure 9.3 by adding arc labels (1 = convex, 0 = concave).

9.3 Draw an attributed FAG for the part shown below:

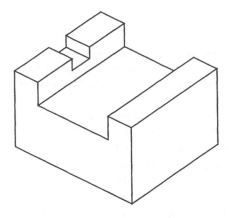

9.4   Draw a constraint graph representation for the part shown below using the notation of Figure 9.10 (invent a convenient dimensioning scheme):

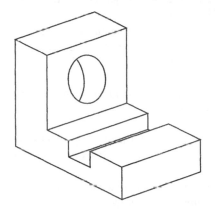

9.5   Give the graph production for adding the slot feature in the part of Question 9.4. (See Figure 9.12 for an example of the notation.)

9.6   What are the features of the solid in Figure 9.16? Which of them can be formed as Boolean combinations of an ASV decomposition?

9.7   Give the delta volumes of the part in Question 9.4.

9.8   Perform degrees of freedom analyses to the delta volumes identified in Question 9.6, using the classification scheme of Figure 9.19.

9.9   Apply the spatial decomposition method of Sakurai and Chin (Figure 9.20) to the part in Question 9.3. Give all features that may be extracted from the part.

9.10   Form all possible subsets of the redundant set of features in Figure 9.24 that are complete feature models of the part.

9.11   Identify the optional and required parts of the features appearing in the part in Question 9.3. (See Figure 9.30.)

BIBLIOGRAPHY

Ames, A. L., 1991, Production ready feature recognition based automatic group technology part coding, in J. Rossignac and J. Turner, eds., *Proc. of First ACM Symp. on Solid Modelling Foundations and CAD/CAM Applications,* June 5–7, ACM Press, pp. 161–169.

Brown, F. M., 1990, *Boolean Reasoning: The Logic of Boolean Equations,* Kluwer.

Choi, B. K., Barash, M. M., and Anderson, D. C., 1984, Automatic recognition of machined surfaces from a 3D solid model, *Computer-Aided Design* **16** (2): 81–86.

Cugini, U., Mandorli, F., and Vicini, I., 1992, Using features as knowledge formalization for simultaneous engineering, in G. J. Olling and F. Kimura, eds., *Human Aspects in Computer Integrated Manufacturing,* Elsevier Science Publishers, pp. 337–349.

Das, D., Gupta, S. K., and Nau, D. S., 1994, Reducing setup cost by automated generation of redesign suggestions, *ASME Computers in Engineering Conf.,* Minneapolis, September 11–14, ASME Press, pp. 159–170.

De Floriani, L., and Bruzzone, E., 1989, Building a feature-based object description from a boundary model, *Computer-Aided Design,* **21** (10): 602–610.

Dong, X., and Wozny, M., 1991, A method for generating volumetric features from surface features, in J. Rossignac and J. Turner, eds., *Proc. of First ACM Symp. on Solid Modelling Foundations and CAD/CAM Applications,* June 5–7, ACM Press, pp. 185–194.

Falcidieno, B., and Giannini, F., 1987, Extraction and organization of form features into a structured boundary model, in G. Maréchal, ed., *Proc. of Eurographics '87,* North-Holland, pp. 249–259.

Fitzhorn, P., 1987, A linguistic formalism for engineering solid modelling, in *Graph-Grammars and their Applications to Computer Science,* Lecture Notes in Computer Science, Springer Verlag, New York.

Fu, Z., de Pennington, A., and Saia, A., 1993, Graph grammar approach to feature representation and transformation, *Int. J. of Comp. Integrated Manufacturing* **6** (1 & 2): 137–151.

Gadh, R., and Prinz, F. B., 1992, Recognition of geometric forms using the differential depth filter, *Computer-Aided Design* **24** (11): 41–49.

General Dynamics Corporation, 1985, Volume decomposition algorithm—Final report, Technical Report R-82-ANC-01, CAM-I, Inc., Arlington, Texas.

Gu, T., Tang, Z., and Sun, J., 1986, Reconstruction of 3D objects from orthographic projections, *Comp. Gr. Forum* **5** (4): 317–323.

Gupta, S. K., Nau, D. S., Regli, W. C., and Zhang, G., 1994, A methodology for systematic creation and evaluation of alternative operation plans, in J. J. Shah, M. Mäntylä, and D. Nau, eds., *Advances in Feature Based Manufacturing,* Elsevier Science Publishers, pp. 161–184.

Henderson, M. R., 1984, Extraction of feature information from three dimensional CAD data, Ph.D. dissertation, Purdue University.

Henderson, M. R., Srinath, G., Stage, R., Walker, K., and Regli, W., 1994, Boundary based feature identification, in J. J. Shah, M. Mäntylä, and D. Nau, eds., *Advances in Feature Based Manufacturing,* Elsevier Science Publishers, pp. 15–38.

Jakubowski, R., 1982, Syntactic characterization of machine parts shapes, *Cybernetics and Systems: An Int. J.* **3** (1): 1–24.

Jared, G. E. M., 1984, Shape features in geometric modelling, in M. S. Pickett and J. W. Boyse, eds., *Solid Modelling by Computers: From Theory to Applications*, Plenum Press, pp. 121–137.

Joshi, S., and Chang, T.-C. 1988, Graph-based heuristics for recognition of machined features from a 3-D solid model, *Computer-Aided Design* **20** (2): 58–66.

Karinthi, R., and D. S. Nau, 1992, An algebraic approach to feature interactions, *IEEE Trans. on Pattern Analysis and Machine Intelligence* **14** (4): 469–484.

Kim, Y. S., 1992, Recognition of form features using convex decomposition, *Computer-Aided Design* **24** (9): 461–476.

Korngold, E. V., Shephard, M. S., Wentorf, E., and Spooner, D. L., 1989, Architecture of a design system for engineering idealizations, in B. Ravani, ed., *Proc. of 15th ASME Design Automation Conf.*, Montreal, September 17–21, ASME Press, pp. 259–265.

Kyprianou, L., 1980, Shape classification in computer aided design, Ph.D. dissertation, University of Cambridge.

Laakko, T., and Mäntylä, M., 1991, A new form feature recognition algorithm, G. Doumeingts, J. Browne, and M. Tomljanovich, eds., *Computer Applications in Production and Engineering: Integration Aspects (Proc. CAPE 91)*, North-Holland, pp. 369–376.

Laakko, T., and Mäntylä, M., 1993, Feature modelling by incremental feature recognition, *Computer-Aided Design* **25** (8): 479–492, August 1993.

Lee, Y. C., and Fu, K. S., 1987, Machine understanding of CSG: Extraction and unification of manufacturing features, *IEEE Comp. Gr. & Appl.* **7** (1): 20–32.

Lee, Y. C., and Jea, K.-F. J., 1988, A new CSG tree reconstruction algorithm for feature representation, *ASME Computers in Engineering Conf.*, San Fransisco, July 31–August 4, ASME Press, pp. 521–528.

Lentz, D. H., and Sowerby, R., 1993, Feature extraction of concave and convex regions and their intersections, *Computer-Aided Design* **25** (7): 421–437.

Mandorli, F., Otto, H. E., and Kimura, F., 1993, A reference kernel model for feature-based CAD systems supported by conditional attributed rewrite systems, in J. Rossignac, J. Turner, and G. Allen, eds., *Proc. of Second Symp. on Solid Modelling and Applications*, Montreal, May 19–21, ACM Press, pp. 343–354.

Markowsky, G., and Wesley, M. A., 1980, Fleshing out wire frames, *IBM J. of Res. and Dev.* **24** (5): 582–594.

Menon, S., and Kim, Y. S., 1994, Cylindrical features in form feature recognition using convex decomposition, *Proc. IFIP W.G. 5.2 Working Conference on Feature Modelling & Recognition in Advanced CAD/CAM Systems*, Valenciennes, May 24–26, North-Holland, pp. 295–314.

Perng, D. B., Chen, C. and Li, R. K., 1990, Automatic 3D machining feature extraction from 3D CSG solid input, *Computer-Aided Design* **22** (5): 285–295.

Peters, T., Rosen, D. W., and Shapiro, V., 1994, A topological model of limitations in design for manufacturing, *Res. in Eng. Design* **6** (4): 223–233.

Pinilla, J. M., Finger, S. and Prinz, F. B., 1989, Shape feature description and recognition using an augmented topology graph grammar, *Preprints of the NSF Engineering Design Research Conference*, University of Massachusetts, Amherst, MA, June 11–14, pp. 285–300.

Prabhakar, S., and Henderson, M. R., 1992, Automatic form-feature recognition using neural-network-based techniques on boundary representations of solid models, *Computer-Aided Design* **24** (7): 381–393.

Regli, W. C., and Nau, D. S., 1993, Building a general approach to feature recognition of material removal shape element volumes (MRSEVs), in J. Rossignac, J. Turner, and G. Allen, eds., *Proc. of Second ACM Symp. on Solid Modeling and Applications,* Montreal, May 19–21, ACM Press, pp. 293–302.

Sakurai, H., and Chin, C., 1994, Definition and recognition of volume features for process planning, in J. J. Shah, M. Mäntylä, and D. Nau, eds., *Advances in Feature Based Manufacturing,* Elsevier Science Publishers, pp. 65–80.

Sakurai, H., and Gossard, D. C., 1983, Solid model input through orthographic views, *Computer Graphics* **17** (3): 243–252.

Sakurai, H., and Gossard, D. C., 1990, Recognizing shape features in solid models, *IEEE Comp. Gr. & Appl.* **10** (5): 22–32.

Shah, J. J., Shen, Y., and Shirur, A., 1994, Determination of machining volumes from extensible sets of design features, in J. J. Shah, M. Mäntylä, and D. Nau, *Advances in Feature Based Manufacturing,* Elsevier Science Publishers, pp. 129–157.

Shen, Y., 1994, Design to manufacturing feature mapping based on volume decomposition using half space partitioning, Ph.D. dissertation, Dept. of Mech. Eng., Arizona State University.

Shephard, M. S., 1990, Idealization in engineering modeling and design, *Res. in Eng. Design* **1**: 229–238.

Shpitalni, M., and Fischer, A., 1994, Separation of disconnected machining regions on the basis of a CSG model, *Computer-Aided Design* **26** (1): 46–58.

Sreevalsan, P., 1990, An investigation into the unification of form feature definition methods, M.S. thesis, Department of Mechanical Engineering, Arizona State University.

Sreevalsan, P., and Shah, J. J., 1992, Unification of feature definition methods, in D. Brown, M. Waldron, and H. Yoshikawa, eds., *Intelligent Computer Aided Design,* Elsevier Science Publishers, pp. 83–100.

Staley, S. M., Henderson, M. R., and Anderson, D. C., 1983, Using syntactic pattern recognition to extract feature information from a solid geometric data base, *Comp. in Mech. Eng.* **2** (2): 61–66.

Tang, K., and Woo, T., 1991a, Algorithmic aspects of alternating sum of volumes. Part 1: Data structure and difference operation, *Computer-Aided Design* **23** (5).

Tang, K., and Woo, T., 1991b, Algorithmic aspects of alternating sum of volumes. Part 2: Nonconvergence and its remedy, *Computer-Aided Design* **23**(6).

Vandenbrande, J. H., 1990, Automatic recognition of machinable features in solid models, Ph.D. dissertation, Electrical Engineering Department, University of Rochester, New York.

Vandenbrande, J. H., and Requicha, A. A. G., 1993, Spatial reasoning for the automatic recognition of machinable features in solid models, *IEEE Trans. on Pattern Analysis and Machine Intelligence* **15** (12): 1269–1285.

Vandenbrande, J. H., and Requicha, A. A. G., 1994, Geometric computation for the recognition of spatially interacting machining features, in J. J. Shah, M. Mäntylä, and D. Nau, eds., *Advances in Feature Based Manufacturing,* Elsevier Science Publishers, pp. 83–106.

Vaxiviere, P., and Tombre, K., 1992, Celestin: CAD conversion of mechanical drawings, *IEEE Comp.* **25** (7): 46–54.

Waco, D. L., and Kim, Y. S., 1993, Geometric reasoning for machining features using convex decomposition, in J. Rossignac, J. Turner, and G. Allen, eds., *Proc. of Second ACM Symp. on Solid Modeling and Applications,* Montreal, May 19–21, ACM Press, pp. 323–332.

Wesley, M. A., and Markowsky, G., 1981, Fleshing out projections, *IBM J. of Res. and Dev.* **25** (6): 934–954.

Woo, T., 1982, Feature extraction by volume decomposition, *Proc. Conference on CAD/ CAM Technology in Mechanical Engineering,* MIT, Cambridge, MA, pp. 76–94.

Yan, Q.-W., Chen, C. L. P., and Tang, Z., 1992, A complete algorithm for automatic reconstruction of objects from orthographic projections, manuscript.

10

IMPLEMENTATION TOOLS

The previous chapters have discussed various techniques for feature-based systems at a relatively abstract level. This chapter will take a more detailed look at the design and implementation of feature-based modeling systems. Our aim is to describe a collection of implementation tools for feature-based systems that might be applied by the developer of a feature-based system either directly or as a framework for related implementation.

10.1 OVERVIEW

A feature modeling system is a nontrivial piece of software. The design and implementation of such a system is a challenging task even for experts in computer-aided design and manufacturing systems. Any effort at realizing a feature-based system must be grounded in a thorough understanding of the overall issues relating to features, proficiency in software engineering, and good basic programming tools.

Earlier chapters of this book aimed at providing an overview of the concepts, issues, and main techniques related to features. This chapter gives a more practice-oriented outline of tools and software methods for feature-based systems. It is mainly derived from the authors' own experience in developing feature-based CAD software. These include the EXTDesign feature-based modeling system (Laakko 1993, Laakko and Mäntylä 1991, 1993a, b, c, 1994), which builds on experience from earlier systems developed at HUT (Mäntylä et al. 1987, 1989; Nieminen and Tuomi 1991). The ASU Features Testbed II, based on a dynamic, two-way interface with the popular ACIS modeling kernel (Spatial 1993), also provides an interesting case study (Rogers 1987, Bhatnagar 1988, Shah and Rogers 1988, Shah et al. 1990, Shah and Rogers 1994). Selected aspects of this system's implementation discussed in this chapter are interpretive language and procedural feature recognition (Sreevalsan 1990, Sreevalsan and Shah 1992), procedural user-defined features for design-by-feature systems (Rogers 1987), and dynamic interfacing with solid modeling (Pherwani 1993, Rogers 1994).

We include this chapter with some hesitation, and advise our readers to take it with a grain of salt. We are fully aware that many of our solutions could well be replaced by others, perhaps better ones. If we had the opportunity to start all over again, we might ourselves do some things differently. Nevertheless, the whole of any complex system is more than its separate parts. Providing a vision of a "whole" feature-based system, therefore, must be a vital part of this book. We draw this material from our own systems more because we are familiar with all the details than because we regard our systems to be superior to other systems.

Sections 10.2 to 10.6 will present Lisp implementation ideas modeled after EXTDesign. Sections 10.7 to 10.9 will present C, C++, and Acis implementation ideas modeled after the ASU Testbed I and II. The feature modeling tools will be presented in a bottom-up fashion, starting from the most basic levels and ending in the higher levels based on the lower ones. It will cover the following areas:

Basic representation methods	Feature representation facilities and conventions using an object-oriented technique.
Feature definition	Feature definition facilities needed for realizing design-by-features and feature recognition
Feature geometry definition	Various methods needed for feature geometry definition and communication with geometric modelers
Constraint definition	A simple method for algebraic constraint definition and satisfaction
Feature recognition	An incremental feature recognition algorithm and a procedural framework for supporting feature recognition and interactive feature creation
User interface design	Selected aspects of creating user interfaces for design-by-feature systems

Even within the scope of a full chapter, it is not possible to describe fully everything that is needed to put together a working feature-based system. Nevertheless, by using the described tools and techniques as a framework for specifying and implementing the various software tools required, we believe a simple feature-based system can be realized much more rapidly than starting from scratch.

10.2 TECHNIQUES AND NOTATION

The design-by-features system was characterized in Chapter 8 as a feature modeling approach based on a predefined library of generic feature classes. The designer can invoke the templates corresponding to these classes, fill in the needed geometric and other attributes, and place the instantiated template directly in a model. A geometric model, if needed at all, is created from the feature description, and contrary to the feature recognition approach no preexisting geometry needs to be assumed.

It was also argued that the capability of adding new feature templates is essential in this scheme. Any collection of feature templates is necessarily incomplete: Analysis of new design tasks will always reveal a need for new types of features with new feature properties. Therefore for most practical purposes the feature library must be extendible by the user.

In Chapter 9 feature recognition was characterized as an approach where instances of previously defined feature patterns are recognized in a geometric models. On the basis of these patterns, a feature model including parameter values and feature relationships can be built. In addition to topological and geometric criteria, recognition may also need to consider application-specific recognition criteria. Therefore the capability of extending the collection of predefined patterns, and augmenting them with application-specific rules and constraints, is essential for the feature recognition scheme.

The feature definition techniques used for building a feature library must be quite general to support the above requirements and the implementation of all types of feature properties discussed in Chapter 3. Therefore, as noted in Chapter 8, a popular approach to implementing feature libraries is to use a general interpretable programming language notation for expressing feature types. We will follow this approach in this section and use LISP as the basis of feature definition.

While not popular to the same extent as C or C++, LISP has the advantage that it supports *dynamic interpretation*. All LISP systems include an interpreter that can execute dynamically new procedures. With this capability it is straightforward to implement systems that can load new procedural components from external files and hence extend and modify themselves at run time. It is also straightforward to store procedures in data structures, and evaluate such embedded code as needed. Such dynamic modifiability can be implemented in other programming languages, but, for example, the resistance of C to it is much larger. Sections 10.7 and 10.8 will investigate feature recognition and definition in a C-based environment.

Another advantage of LISP is that popular and powerful programming techniques such as object orientation can be implemented in a straightforward manner. In particular, we will use as the basis of our exposition a popular LISP technique, *frames*, that can be regarded a generalized approach to object-oriented programming. The following paragraphs will provide an overview of the frame system used in the later discussion. It is hoped that readers with little previous exposure to LISP will be able to follow the exposition.

10.2.1 Frames and Object-Oriented Programming

Frames are a popular LISP programming technique for knowledge representation. Although they can be used quite generally for creating complex data structures, we will be content to use frames for *object-oriented programming*.

The recent years have witnessed a great increase of interest in the object-oriented programming paradigm for developing complex software systems. In brief, object orientation has been seen as a (partial) solution to defeat complexity in software design and implementation, to enhance reusability and maintainability of software, and to encourage software design on a higher level of semantics.

Object-oriented programming is based on two kinds of entities. *Classes* model the common properties of structurally similar instances. Typically they record a template of the instance structure. The template can be used as a basis of creating instances of the class. *Instances* record information on individual objects in terms of a data structure that contains values of some attributes. The values may be references to other objects. Therefore complex data structures (lists, trees, graphs, etc.) can be modeled. Classes can also record attributes whose values are shared by all instances of a class.

Classes are typically organized into a hierarchy that supports *inheritance* of information (attributes and methods). That is, information defined in a higher-level class is treated as if it were defined in the lower-level class. The simplest arrangement is *single inheritance*, where each class except for the most general root class has a single parent class. Therefore, each class inherits from all its parents up to the root. A class can also override some piece of inherited information by redefining it.

Objects not only encapsulate information but also procedures. Typically procedures can be associated to classes, and they are termed *methods* of the class. Methods can be invoked by sending *messages* to instances to the class. The same messages can be implemented by several classes, leading to a situation where the interpretation of a message is determined by the receiver of the message. This is termed *polymorphism*. Methods can be inherited from parent classes. In this fashion, parent classes can define a message protocol and default behavior for its children. By redefining an inherited method, a class can change the default behavior if needed.

Object-oriented languages differ in their treatment of classes. In some languages, such as C++, classes are not treated as objects themselves. In these languages new classes cannot easily be added at run time. Some other languages, such as Smalltalk and LISP, treat classes as fully privileged objects. In these languages new classes can be created dynamically if needed. Frames belong to the second category, although we will only use the dynamic class creation facility to support the creation of user-defined feature types.

Frame system implementation is not a standard part of the LISP language. Therefore individual frame systems differ to some extent in their implementation details. The frame system used in this section, BEEF (Lassila 1991), follows the notation of the Carnegie Representation Language (CRL) of the Knowledge Craft[1] system (Carnegie 1986).

---

[1]Knowledge Craft is a registered trademark of Carnegie Group, Inc.

10.2.2 Instance Frames

A frame is a data structure similar to C struct or Pascal record. Therefore a frame consists of a sequence of attributes and values. In frame parlance, the term *slot**
is used to denote an attribute; the value of the attribute is said to be "contained" in the slot. A difference between an ordinary record and a frame is that frames typically are self-explanatory in that the frame structure records both the name and the value of each slot. Frames as used here have a symbolic name (in LISP parlance, the frame is *bound* to the symbol) that can be used to refer to it and to get access to its slots and their values.

Let us start by looking at instance frames representing information on individual objects. A typical instance frame representing a feature is given below; see Figure 10.1 for illustration on the meaning of the slots of the frame.

```
(internal-keyway-slot-11
  (bottom-rounding 2)
  (bottom-surface internal-keyway-slot-11-bottom)
  (depth 10)
  (instance internal-keyway-slot)
  (length 100)
  (orientation (0 0 0))
  (position (0 0 0))
  (side-surface-1 internal-keyway-slot-11-side-1)
  (side-surface-2 internal-keyway-slot-11-side-2)
  (width 20))
```

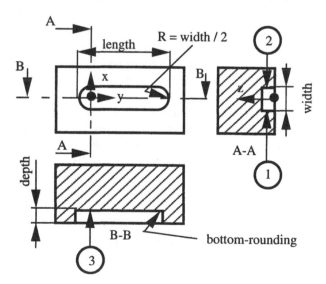

Figure 10.1   Internal keyway slot feature

Slot has two meanings in this section: it is the name of a geometric feature (as in keyway-slot) and the name of an item in the frame data structure.

The name of the frame is internal-keyway-slot-11. The other parts of the frame contain the slots of the frame; each slot is a pair consisting of an attribute name (a literal) and a value. The pairs are enclosed in matching brackets; so is the whole frame. Thus the value of the slot depth is an *atom*, the numerical constant 10. Values may be also *lists*, such as the value of the slot position, which is the list (0 0 0), indicating the *x*, *y*, and *z* coordinates of the reference point of the slot. Again braces are used to denote a list. A value can also be a *symbol*, such as the value of the slot side-surface-2, which is the symbol internal-keyway-slot-11-side-2. As we shall see, this symbol refers to another frame that contains information on the side surface of the feature.

In LISP programs manipulating the frame, values of the individual slots can be retrieved using the frame system function value. For instance, when evaluated by the LISP interpreter, the expression

```
(value 'internal-keyway-slot-11 'bottom-rounding)
```

will reply 2. Values can be assigned using the LISP function setf; thus, the expression

```
(setf (value 'internal-keyway-slot-11 'length) 50)
```

will change the value of slot length to 50.

10.2.3 Class Frames

In the previous example, the slot instance has a special role: It indicates the type of the frame, namely the class of which the frame is an instance. Classes are represented as frames as well; hence they are fully functional objects themselves. The following gives the frame representing the class internal-keyway-slot referred to by the slot instance:

```
(internal-keyway-slot
  (definition internal-keyway-slot_def)
  (instance+inv internal-keyway-slot-11)
  (instance-slots
    (length 100)
    (depth 10)
    (width 20)
    (bottom-rounding 2))
  (is-a internal-slot)
  (surface-slots
    (side-surface-1 basic-surface "-side-1")
    (side-surface-2 basic-surface "-side-2")
    (bottom-surface basic-surface "-bottom")))
```

As can be verified looking at the instance frame given in the previous section, the slot instance-slots contains a template for instance frame creation in the form of a sequence of slots and default values to be inserted into the instance. We discuss instance creation further in Section 10.2.5.

The class frame `internal-keyway-slot` gives examples of several useful facilities of frames beyond the ones we have encountered so far. The slot `instance-slots` contains not a single value, but instead a sequence of several values. In such a case the expression

```
(value 'internal-keyway-slot 'instance-slots)
```

would return `(length 100)`. To retrieve all values, one can use the expression

```
(all-values 'internal-keyway-slot 'instance-slots)
```

which will return all values in a list:

```
((length 100) (depth 10) (width 20) (bottom-rounding 2)).
```

The slot `instance+inv` is also special: It contains a reference back to the instance frame `internal-keyway-slot-11`. The purpose of the slot is to contain a sequence of all present instances of the class. Therefore it can be thought of as an inverse of the relation defined by the slot `instance` of the instance frame `internal-keyway-slot-11`. In fact, as we will see, the frame system supports the definition of such inverse relationships and automates the maintenance of back references such as `instance+inv`.

10.2.4 Class Hierarchy

The slot `is-a` has also a special purpose. It contains the name of the parent class of the class `internal-keyway-slot`. The parent class `internal-slot` is simply as follows:

```
(internal-slot
  (is-a slot-feature)
  (is-a+inv inner-cylindrical-slot internal-polygonal-slot
            internal-flat-slot internal-keyway-slot))
```

The slots of the frame `internal-slot` indicate that, in turn, the parent class of `internal-slot` is `slot-feature` and that the set of subclasses of `internal-slot` is the sequence given as the value of slot `is-a+inv`, the inverse relation of `is-a`. As expected, the sequence includes `internal-flat-slot`.

The relation `is-a` defines the class hierarchy of class frames. As we will see later, this leads to a taxonomical classification of feature classes. In the full taxonomy the full sequence of parent classes of `internal-flat-slot` is

```
(feature basic-feature prismatic-feature slot-feature
  internal-slot internal-keyway-slot)
```

which can be retrieved with the expression

```
(all-values 'internal-keyway-slot '(repeat is-a))
```

That is, the parent class internal-slot is slot-feature whose parent is prismatic-feature and so on until the root class feature. The form `(repeat is-a) in the above expression tells all-values that the reply should be fetched by following repeatedly is-a links and gathering all symbols found.

10.2.5 Instance Creation and Inheritance

Instances of a class are created using the frame system function make-inst. In commonly used LISP documentation notation, it is described as follows:

make-inst *frame &key name with*   [Function]

This statement indicates that make-inst is a function (instead of a macro) that takes a positional parameter frame and two key parameters name and with. Key parameters are optional and need not be given. When given, parameter name assigns a name for the instance; if it is missing, a unique default name is used. Parameter with can be used to override or extend the default values of slot instance-slot of the class (see below for further explanation).

Hence an instance of the class internal-keyway-slot will be created with each of the following three Lisp procedure calls:

```
(make-inst 'internal-keyway-slot)
(make-inst 'internal-keyway-slot
      :name 'internal-keyway-slot-11)
(make-inst 'internal-keyway-slot
      :name 'internal-keyway-slot-11
      :with '((length 50) (width 5)))
```

The last example would create an instance frame where the default values of length and width have been overridden. The operation of make-inst gives an example of inheritance of information. Recall the definition of the class internal-keyway-slot:

```
(internal-keyway-slot
  (definition internal-keyway-slot_def)
  (instance+inv internal-keyway-slot-11)
  (instance-slots
   (length 100)
   (depth 10)
   (width 20)
   (bottom-rounding 2))
```

```
(is-a internal-slot)
(surface-slots
(side-surface-1 basic-surface "-side-1")
(side-surface-2 basic-surface "-side-2")
(bottom-surface basic-surface "-bottom")))
```

As mentioned above, the purpose of the slot instance-slots is to contain a description of the structure of the instance frame. That is, when an instance is created, the slot names and default values contained in instance-slots will be inserted into the instance. However, several of the parent classes of internal-keyway-slot also contain instance-slot descriptions, including the root class feature:

```
(feature
(instance-slots
(position (0 0 0))
(orientation (0 0 0)))
(is-a+inv surface-feature surface container-feature billet
transition basic-feature))
```

What happens is that the instance-slots of the class feature are also inherited by all its subsequent subclasses, including internal-keyway-slot. As a result the full sequence of instance-slots applied during the instantiation is

```
((bottom-rounding 2) (width 20) (depth 10) (length 100)
(orientation (0 0 0)) (position (0 0 0)))
```

as can be seen by inspecting the instance internal-keyway-slot-11. A class definition mechanism similar to C++ class definitions is created, where each class can define additional instance slots to be inserted into the instances. A subclass can also override a default value given in a superclass by redefining it in its own instance-slots.

The advantage of LISP and frames is that also other types of inheritance and interpretation of inheritance can be implemented. This is exemplified by surface-slots of internal-keyway-slot:

```
(surface-slots
(side-surface-1 basic-surface "-side-1")
(side-surface-2 basic-surface "-side-2")
(bottom-surface basic-surface "-bottom"))
```

Just like instance-slots, the purpose of this definition is to specify the structure of the instance frames. The difference is in the interpretation. Instead of simply copying the contents of the definition to the instance, what happens for each form in the definition such as

```
(side-surface-1 basic-surface "-side-1")
```

is as follows:

- A slot named side-surface-1 is inserted into the instance frame.
- An instance of the frame basic-surface defined separately is created and inserted as the value of the slot.
- The name of the basic-surface instance is formed by appending the string "-side-1" to the name of the internal-keyway-slot instance; for instance, if the name of the internal-keyway-slot instance is internal-keyway-slot-5, the name of the basic-surface instance will be internal-keyway-slot-5-side-1.

This apparently complex inheritance behavior can be programmed for the frame system quite easily. This operation can be verified by inspecting the instance frame internal-keyway-slot-11. Indeed, the surface slots are bound to frames modeling the surfaces of the feature:

```
(internal-keyway-slot-11-side-1
  (instance basic-surface)
  (orientation (0 0 0))
  (parent-feature internal-keyway-slot-11)
  (position (0 0 0)))
```

Observe further that a back reference from the surface frame to its parent feature frame is stored in the slot parent-feature. This back reference is created automatically be means of a *relation definition* of the following form:

```
(defrelations
  (side-surface-1
    (is-a            slot)
    (inverse         parent-feature))
  (parent-feature
    (is-a            relation)
    (inverse         side-surface-1))
  )
```

The definition states that parent-feature is an inverse of the relation defined by the slot side-surface-1. Operationally this means that if a reference to surface frame is inserted to a side-surface-1 slot, the corresponding inverse relation is automatically created in the surface frame. Similar definitions can be made for all relations between features or surfaces.

Just like instance-slots, also surface-slots are inherited from parent classes. The treatment of surface-slots during the instantiation process exemplifies how the creation of complex frame structures can be described in LISP;

it would be cumbersome to do the same using the native C++ class definition mechanisms. While this interpretation of inheritance may not be of interest in a more general context, it does lead to a concise definition mechanism of feature information. We will see other examples of such capability of defining concise definition languages on the top of LISP later in this section.

The mechanisms introduced implement *single inheritance*: Each class has exactly one parent class and hence a single inheritance path. Some systems, notably the Common LISP Object System (CLOS), provide also *multiple inheritance* where classes can inherit information along several paths. Multiple inheritance may be a useful facility also for feature definition. Nevertheless, we will only consider single inheritance in this section.

10.2.6 Methods

To fully support object-oriented programming, methods and messages are also needed. For BEEF frames, methods are defined with the form defhandler:

```
(defhandler (addSubfeature feature) (theSurface theSubfeature)
  (add-value (value self theSurface) 'features theSubFeature))
```

This particular method defines a message called addSubFeature for the class feature; by inheritance, all subclasses of feature will inherit the message (but can redefine it, if needed). The method has two *formal parameters*, theSurface and theSubfeature. The *body* of the method consists of the single LISP form

```
(add-value (value self theSurface) 'features theSubFeature).
```

The method implements the important operation of making a feature instance a "subfeature" of another. Consider the situation depicted in Figure 10.2, show-

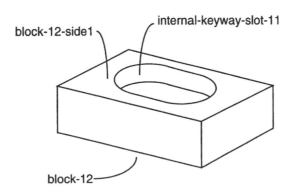

Figure 10.2 A keyway feature in a block feature

ing an instance of a block feature and a keyway feature appearing on the top surface of the block.

The block instance feature is as follows:

```
(block-12
  (height 100)
  (instance block)
  (length 500)
  (orientation (0 0 0))
  (position (0 0 0))
  (side-surface-1 block-12-side1)
  (side-surface-2 block-12-side2)
  (side-surface-3 block-12-side3)
  (side-surface-4 block-12-side4)
  (side-surface-5 block-12-side5)
  (side-surface-6 block-12-side6)
  (width 300))
```

Initially the surface block-12-side1 is as follows:

```
(block-12-side1
  (instance basic-surface)
  (orientation (0 0 0))
  (parent-feature block-12)
  (position (0 0 0)))
```

One of the purposes of surface frames is to record feature containment relationships. To record the useful fact that internal-keyway-slot-11 is located on the top surface of block-12, we can execute the method addSubFeature:

```
(addSubFeature 'block-12 'side-surface-1
              'internal-keyway-slot-11)
```

As a result the surface and keyway feature frames become as follows:

```
(block-12-side1
  (features internal-keyway-slot-11)
  (instance basic-surface)
  (orientation (0 0 0))
  (parent-feature block-12)
  (position (0 0 0)))

(internal-keyway-slot-11
  (bottom-rounding 2)
  (bottom-surface internal-keyway-slot-11-bottom)
```

```
(depth 10)
(instance internal-keyway-slot)
(length 100)
(orientation (0 0 0))
(parent-surface block-12-side1)
(position (0 0 0))
(side-surface-1 internal-keyway-slot-11-side-1)
(side-surface-2 internal-keyway-slot-11-side-2)
(width 20))
```

As can be seen, the containment relationship is recorded in the slot features of the surface and the slot parent-surface of the keyway. The parent feature is recorded in the slot parent-feature of the surface frame. The creation of the back reference in parent-surface is automated by the relation definition

```
(defrelations
  (features
    (is-a          slot)
    (inverse       parent-surface))
  (parent-surface
    (is-a          relation)
    (inverse       features)))
```

Methods form a powerful tool for defining access methods of feature information recorded in the frames. To give a somewhat more complex example, the following parameterless method replies a list containing all subfeatures of its receiver:

```
(defhandler (get-subfeatures feature) ( )
  (mapcan #'(lambda (surface-spec)
        (all-values (value self (first surface-spec))
                    'features))
     (all-values self
      '(sequence instance (repeat is-a) surface-slots)))))
```

The method works by retrieving a list of all surface-slots specifications from the class frame of the receiver and its superclasses with the form

```
(all-values self
  '(sequence instance (repeat is-a) surface-slots))
```

and applying the anonymous inline procedure

```
#'(lambda (surface-spec)
    (all-values (value self (first surface-spec))
                'features))
```

to each `surface-slots` entry in turn. The form (`value self (first sur-`
`face-spec)`) retrieves the surface slot name from the specification, so that
`all-values` can retrieve the contents of the slot `features` from the surface
frame referred to by that slot. The LISP form `mapcan` is a looping construct that
scans through a list and passes each element as a argument to a procedure, collecting the results in a list.

10.3 FEATURE DEFINITION AND FEATURE TAXONOMY

We have now introduced all basic facilities required for feature definition using
a frame system. In general, our feature definitions will have the following outline:

```
(defframe <feature class name>
  (is-a <parent class name>)
  (instance-slots <sequence of instance slot definitions:
    (<slot name> <default value>)>)
  (surface-slots <sequence of surface slot definitions:
    (<surface slot name> <surface class> <tail of name>)>)
  <misc. definitions: sign, constraints, geometry, ...>
)
```

The frame system macro `defframe` defines a new frame. Using the LISP documentation notation is described as follows:

defframe name {slot | (slot {value}*)}*   [Macro]

That is, the definition consists of a name and a sequence of either slot names
or slot-value pairs.

Except for `is-a`, none of the parts of the feature definition template is really
mandatory. Recall that all definitions are inherited. The inheritance of `instance-`
`slots` and `surface-slots` is *additive* in that lower-level definitions do not
override the higher levels but are concatenated to them. The inheritance of all
other information is *substitutive*: The lower-level definition replaces the higher-
level definitions. Miscellaneous definitions are discussed in their proper contexts.

10.3.1 Abstract Features

Many of the feature definitions in the feature taxonomy are *abstract* in the sense
that they do not designate classes intended to be instantiated. Instead, they are
present to give a clear structure to the feature taxonomy and to take benefit of
inheritance. Let us start by first outlining these higher levels of the feature taxonomy.

The goals of any feature taxonomy is to give a natural structure for the feature library and to simplify and encourage the extension of the library. A particular feature taxonomy also depends on the intended application area. The taxonomy to be discussed is somewhat oriented to feature-based manufacturing. The taxonomy also addresses the problems of parametric design on the basis of part family templates, and therefore includes special classes and related capabilities dealing with part family descriptions.

An outline of the feature taxonomy is shown in Figure 10.3. As shown, the direct subclasses of the root class `feature` are `basic-feature`, `transition`, `billet`, `container-feature`, and `surface`. These abstract classes form the roots of subtaxonomies of features for the following purposes:

`basic-feature`   This class consists of regular features appearing as detail features in feature models. It is further divided into several subclasses (as described in the below).

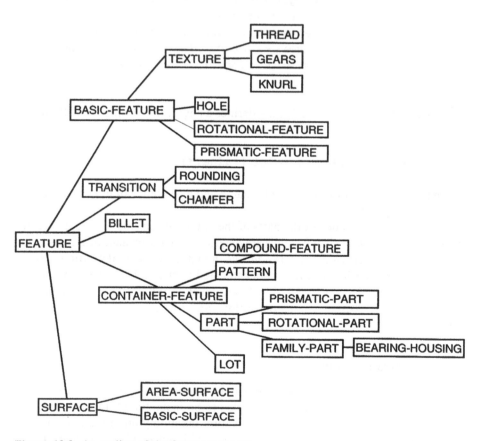

Figure 10.3 An outline of the feature taxonomy

transition	This class consists of features corresponding with various types of roundings and blends between two regular features.
billet	This class is the root of features representing various kinds of "base objects" that form the basis of feature-based design and also act as initial workpieces for machining applications. Typical billets include block, L-block, and more complex solids such as special castings.
container-feature	This class is the root of all feature types that are made of other simpler features, such as compounds, patterns, and also whole parts and assemblies.
surface	This class includes surface types. As we have seen, surfaces are used to denote areas of features for recording feature containment relationships. Surfaces are also useful to model certain manufacturing processes applied to a planar or cylindrical area.

The definitions of the above classes are shown in Figure 10.4. Observe that class feature does not have an is-a slot, indicating that it is the root of the class hierarchy. Also note that instance slots position and orientation are defined in it. Thus all features will contain instance slots position and orientation. These definitions give the x, y, and z translations and rotation angles about x-, y-, and z-axes of the feature with respect to the part coordinate system.

The class slot sign of the frame basic-feature states that by default, all basic features are considered negative in that they denote removal of material from a basic parts. (Those basic features for which this is not true can override the definition.) Similarly all billets are marked positive. The slot parent-surface-def states that by default, basic features are oriented along the normal direction of the surface they are contained in. This information can be used in feature recognition. Finally, all surfaces will contain a working allowance; observe that no default is given to this instance slot.

10.3.2 Basic Features

The subtaxonomy rooted by the class basic-feature contains all regular individual features. As already shown in Figure 10.3, basic-feature is further classified into more detailed abstract subclasses as follows:

texture	Textures denote geometric details such as threading and gear teeth. These can be considered modifier features that may be assigned to geometric features to describe further geometric details. No detail geometry is generated for these features; their purpose is simply to provide information for manufacturing analysis.

```
(defframe feature
  (instance-slots (position (0 0 0)) (orientation (0 0 0)))
)
(defframe basic-feature
  (is-a feature)
  (sign NEGATIVE)
  (parent-surface-def (constraints (axis_normal_c)))
)
(defframe transition
  (is-a feature)
  (instance-slots the-surfaces)
)
(defframe billet
  (is-a feature)
  (sign POSITIVE)
)
(defframe container-feature
  (is-a feature)
)
(defframe surface
  (is-a feature)
  (instance-slots working-allowance)
)
```

Figure 10.4 Definitions of abstract feature classes

`hole`	Holes include all types of drilled features. Holes can of course be treated as a kind of `rotational-feature` as well. However, since the main purpose of this taxonomy is to support process planning applications, it was decided that inheritance can be more readily utilized if holes are treated separately from rotational features.
`rotational-feature`	Rotational features denote various types of features that are generally made by turning-type processes.
`prismatic-feature`	Prismatic features denote various types of features that are made by milling-type processes.

The subtaxonomy of holes is shown in Figure 10.5. In the taxonomy the second level still denotes abstract features that are not intended to be instantiated directly. The third level contains typical basic features that may be instan-

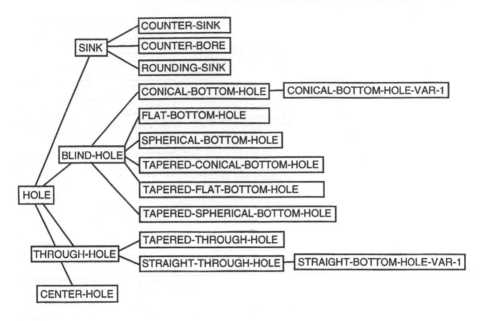

Figure 10.5 Subtaxonomy of hole features

tiated and included in a feature model. The taxonomy contains some still further refined features on the fourth level. These are termed *variant features* in the taxonomy. In general, variant features denote more constrained variants of the basic features. Typical constraints include certain limitations on dimensions, tolerances, or position. The purpose of variant features in the taxonomy is to act as containers of more specialized manufacturing information.

Prismatic features include various types of milled shapes such as slots, pockets, and steps. The subtaxonomy is shown in Figure 10.6. This subtaxonomy exhibits some more variety according to whether the features are through, extend to the edge of the parent object, and so on. A design-oriented taxonomy might do with less detail. Some typical prismatic features of the collection are depicted in Figure 10.7.

The subtaxonomy of rotational features consists of various types of segments (see Figures 11.10 and 11.11). In the chosen approach, complete rotational parts are modeled as a combination of segments; the class segment-sequence (a kind of container-feature) is used to represent the segment combination as a whole. Complete rotational parts typically also include detail features such as keyways and holes that may be located radially or at end surfaces of a rotational object (see Figure 11.26 for illustration of similar features).

10.3.3 Container Features

Basic features are atomic in that they do not consist of more primitive features (excluding surfaces). In contrast, container features denote features which con-

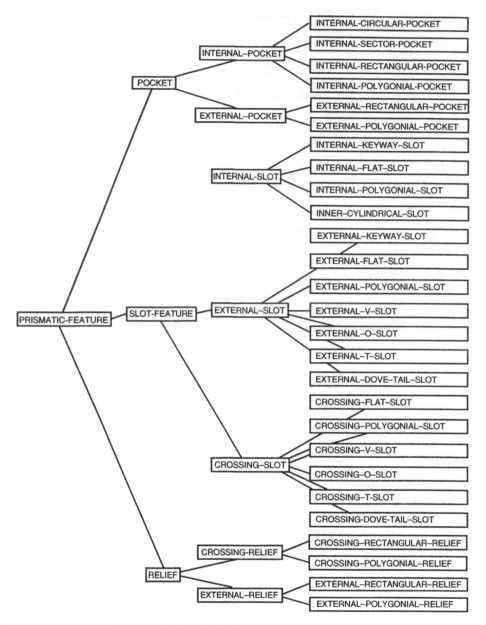

Figure 10.6 Subtaxonomy of prismatic features

sist of more primitive parts. As already shown in Figure 10.3, containers break into several abstract subclasses:

compound-feature   Compound features are made of several lower-level simpler features. Typical examples include step holes and rotational parts made of several rotational segments.

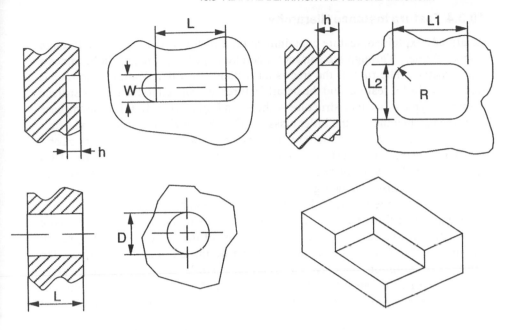

Figure 10.7 Examples of prismatic features

pattern	Patterns are made of several instances of similar features, typically arranged in some regular pattern.
part	The whole part is also treated as a special type of a container feature. In this taxonomy, parts consist of a billet feature and several detail features. Representation of part instances is outlined in the next section.
assembly	Several parts can be combined into an assembly. The abstract assembly class simply models a collection of parts; more refined models of assembly relations etc. are handled by the subclasses.
lot	For purposes of process planning, a collection of parts to be manufactured on a single pallet can be modeled as a lot feature.

All container features share the capability of containing a description of their internal structure in terms of simpler features. For this purpose the special class slot inst-def is used. The slot contains a description of the structure of the container feature instance that will be interpreted when instances of the container are created; that is, when a container feature is created, all constituent detail features will also be created automatically. The description language for inst-def definitions is outlined in the next section.

10.3.4 Feature Instance Hierarchy

As already explained, feature containment relationships are represented through surface frames. Through the surfaces a complete part representation becomes a tree structure. The root of the tree is an instance of a part feature. The root is related to a billet feature, and the detail features are related to the billet's surface frames. A typical instance structure is shown in Figure 10.8. In this case the base feature is an instance of the billet class L-block. Detail features straight-through-hole-17, straight-through-hole-18, and crossing-flat-slot-17 are related directly to surfaces of the L-block; crossing-flat-slot-18 is related as a child feature of crossing-flat-slot-17. For simplicity, surface frames are not shown in the figure.

The part instance structure shown in Figure 10.8 can be created as an instance of the part definition of class L-block-part shown in the upper part of Figure 10.9. The part definition is expressed by means of the macro defpart, which applies the defframe operation to a frame definition and also interprets the inst-def definition contained. The base of L-block-part is an instance of L-block (defined by means of the reserved word BASEF of the definition language). The instance of L-block has a local slot (reserved word SLOTS) named height and a subfeature (SUBF) which is an instance of crossing-flat-slot. The inclusion of this subfeature is based on the condition (COND) that the value of the local parameter neck-height is greater than 100. The definitions are inherited by subclasses of L-block-part to support the definition of variant parts. Assembly classes consisting of several parts can be defined similarly.

The part structure definition language is geared towards supporting parametric parts. Local parameter specifications (PARAMS) can be given in several nested levels so that a parameter defined at a lower level hides the definitions at upper levels; for instance, the parameter param2 has the value 30 inside the specification of the first crossing-flat-slot but the value 50 outside the scope of the

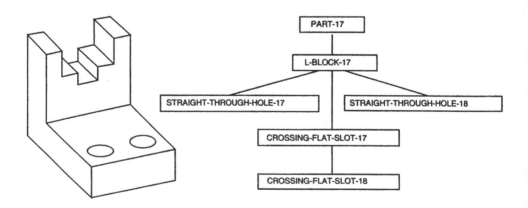

Figure 10.8 A sample part instance structure

```
(defpart L-block-part
   (is-a family-part)
   (param-list
      (param1 300)
      (param2 20))
   (inst-def
      (PARAMS
         (neck-height param1)
         (param2 50))
      (BASEF L-block $fid1
         (SLOTS (height (+ neck-height param2)) ...)
         (SURF side-surface-6 $sid1
            (COND ((> neck-height 100)
               (SUBF crossing-flat-slot $fid2
                  (PARAMS (param2 30) ...)
                  (SLOTS ...)
                  (SURF bottom-surface $sid10
                     (SUBF conical-hole $fid3
                        (PARAMS (dia (/ param1 2)) ...)
                        (SLOTS (width dia) ...)))))))))
         (SURF bottom-surface
            (SUBF crossing-flat-slot $fid3
               (SLOTS
                  (width param2)
                  (depth 30) ...)))
      ...)))
```

```
(defpart L-block-part-A
   (is-a L-block-part)
   (param-list)
      (param1 400)
      (param2 30)))
```

```
(defpart L-block-part-B
   (is-a L-block-part)
   (param-list
      (param1 80)
      (param2 40)))
```

Figure 10.9 Part family definitions

specification. A special slot `params-list` can be used to supply default values for the parameters. Feature and surface identifiers (`$sid1`, `$fid1`, `$fid2`, etc.) are included for cross-referencing purposes. For details of the part definition language, see Laakko and Mäntylä (1993a).

Part definitions are particularly powerful for the definition of parametric variants of a part type. The lower parts of Figure 10.9 show two parametric variants of the class `L-block-part`. Because the part structure definition in the `inst-def` slot is inherited, it suffices to redefine the default parameter values by including a `params-list` slot in the two variant definitions. A modeling system can also allow the parameters to be specified interactively.

10.4 FEATURE GEOMETRY TOOLS

So far we have only considered the definition of features in terms of their constituent attributes, taxonomic relations, and feature relationships. In doing so, we ignored the important aspect of defining the geometry corresponding to the features. This section will look at this problem.

A geometry definition facility for features depends on the desired type of linkage between a features system and a geometry system, which in turn depends on the design style supported by the system. A very simple feature-based design system that marks features interactively in geometric models may work without any geometry definition facilities. A true design-by-features system must, however, contain feature geometry definitions supporting the insertion of feature geometries in the part being modeled, and preferably supporting feature validation. Similarly a system based on feature recognition must store recognition templates.

The following subsections will outline the design of a geometry definition mechanism that can support both design by features and feature recognition. This design makes it possible to combine design-by-features and feature recognition in a single system that lets the designer choose the definition strategy best suited for the modeling of a given part. The feature recognizer itself is described in Section 10.6.

10.4.1 Geometry Definition Frame

We will follow the convention of storing feature geometry definitions separately in geometry definition frames. In this approach feature definitions only need to store a reference to the definition frame. The convention of separate geometry definitions has the benefit that several features of the taxonomy may share the same geometry definition frame. This is particularly advantageous for some cases of prismatic features that differ in intended semantics and manufacturability rules but not in nominal geometry.

As an example of feature geometry definition, let us consider the internal pocket feature shown in Figure 10.10(*a*):

```
(defframe internal-rectangular-pocket
  (is-a internal-pocket)
  (instance-slots (width 50) (length 90) (depth 45)
              (corner-rounding 5) (bottom-rounding 5))
  (surface-slots (side-surface-1 basic-surface "-SIDE-1")
              (side-surface-2 basic-surface "-SIDE-2")
              (side-surface-3 basic-surface "-SIDE-3")
              (side-surface-4 basic-surface "-SIDE-4")
              (bottom-surface basic-surface "-BOTTOM"))
  (definition internal-rectangular-pocket_def)
)
```

In this feature definition, the slot `definition` contains a reference to another frame, `internal-rectangular-pocket_def`, which contains the definition of the geometry of the pocket. This frame is given in Figure 10.10(*b*).

The slots of the frame can be explained as follows:

`type`	Specifies that this geometry definition applies to the feature type `internal-rectangular-pocket`.
`topology`	Specifies the topology of the feature's geometry in terms of a graph representation (as explained below).
`auxgeom`	Specifies auxiliary geometric entities that can be used for feature validation and the computation of feature attributes after recognition.
`rules`	Specifies predicates that must be true for a geometric pattern to be recognized as an instance of the feature type.
`attributes`	Specifies computation rules for feature attributes for use during feature recognition.
`geometry`	Specifies the construction of the feature geometry as a parametric procedure.

Further slots for geometric constraints and parametric surface descriptions may also be used. A scheme for representing constraints is explained in Section 10.5. The following sections will look in more detail into the various other aspects of feature geometry definitions.

10.4.2 Graph Representation of Geometry

The topology representation is based on a graph representation of solid model as a directed labeled graph that describes adjacency relationships between the entities of the model. The graph is a data structure consisting of nodes and links. Nodes correspond roughly with "surfaces" of the geometric model, and links represent surface-surface adjacency relations.

An instantiated node data structure of the graph contains the following information:

- Node identifier
- References to one or several adjacent solid model faces considered to belong to the same surface
- Connectivity information
- Reference to a shape data structure

The second item is useful for decoupling geometry definitions from possible conventions used in the underlying solid modeler. For instance, it can be used to eliminate the face meshes modeling a curved surface in a solid modeler that only supports polyhedral boundary representation models, or it can be used to unite several faces corresponding with a single surface as may appear after Boolean set operations.

The implementation is based on associating *surface* and *curve tags* to those faces and edges of the boundary representation that actually correspond with feature surfaces and curves. For instance, consider the case of the cylinder object represented in Figure 10.11. Assume that a polyhedral modeler is used; hence the cylinder surface is split into several planar facets, and the top and bottom circles into straight lines. When creating a cylinder, the solid modeler creates two surface tags representing the two half-cylinders, and four curve tags representing the half-circles (only the bottom curve tags are shown in the figure). Each face and edge contains a pointer to the appropriate tag. (Halves are used to simplify certain geometric computations in the modeler.)

All nodes that relate to a single feature are collected to a shape data structure that forms the main interface with the feature modeler. In particular, when a feature is created with a cylinder geometry (e.g., a hole), the feature modeler will create the shape data structure consisting of the nodes representing the full

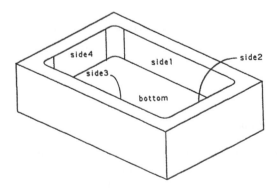

Figure 10.10(a) Geometry of internal-rectangular-pocket

```
(defframe internal-rectangular-pocket_def
   (type internal-rectangular-pocket)
   (topology
      (n        5)
      (surf   (1 PLANE) (2 PLANE) (3 PLANE) (4 PLANE) (5 PLANE))
      (adj    (1 (2 CONCAVE) (4 CONCAVE) (5 CONCAVE))
              (2 (1 CONCAVE) (3 CONCAVE) (5 CONCAVE))
              (3 (2 CONCAVE) (4 CONCAVE) (5 CONCAVE))
              (4 (1 CONCAVE) (3 CONCAVE) (5 CONCAVE))
              (5 (1 CONCAVE) (2 CONCAVE) (3 CONCAVE) (4 CONCAVE))))
   (auxgeom
      ((rotat_nodes  4 0 (- 5)))
      ((auxblock)))
   (rules
      (right_angle1 2)
      (right_angle2 3)
      (right_angle3 4)
      (right_angle1 4)
      (right_angle1 5))
   (attributes
      (length           (distpl2 plbl1 plbl2))
      (width            (distpl2 plbl3 plbl4))
      (depth            (distpl2 plbl5 plbl6))
      (orientation      rxryrz)
      (position         (int3pl plbl6
                            (midpl plbl1 plbl2) (midpl plbl3 plbl4))))
   (geometry
      (geom-block2
         length width depth
         (- (/ length 2.0)) (- (/ width 2.0)) 0.0
         (first 'orientation) (second 'orientation)
         (third 'orientation)
         (first 'position) (second 'position) (third 'position)))
```

Figure 10.10(b) Geometry definition frame for internal-rectangular-pocket

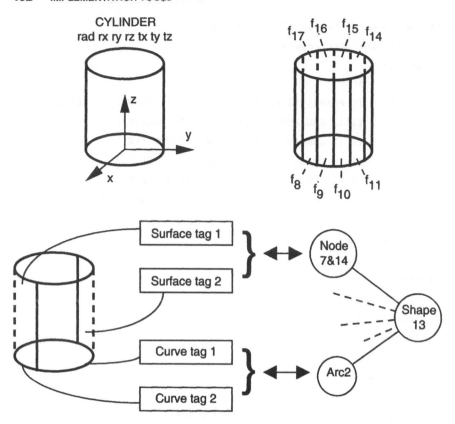

Figure 10.11 Relations between solid model faces, tags, and feature topology graph nodes

cylinder surface and the full circular arcs. These nodes contain pointers to the appropriate tag data structures, and vice versa.

Feature interaction can cause originally continuous feature surfaces to become disconnected. To deal with this situation, we allow nodes to be composed hierarchically so that a higher-level node can consist of several lower-level nodes. A high-level node contains the following information:

- Node identifier
- References to one or several lower-level nodes corresponding to disconnected pieces of a surface
- Connectivity information
- Reference to a shape data structure

The graph representation is mainly intended for feature recognition. As will be described in Section 10.6, a recognition algorithm can work by first creating a node data structure for each face of a geometric model, and then combining

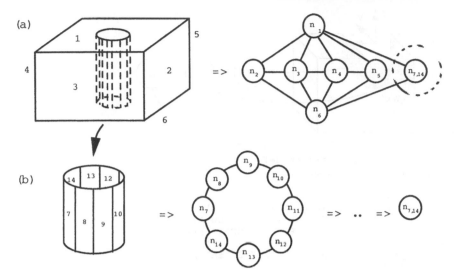

Figure 10.12 Using the graph representation for feature recognition (Laakko 1993; reprinted with permission)

nodes corresponding same feature surfaces by inspecting the tags. As Figure 10.12 shows, the combining of polyhedral meshes reduces the size of the feature search graph.

The definition of the feature topology is based on enumerating the nodes and arcs of the graph using a suitable syntax:

```
(topology
 (n     5)
 (surf  (1 PLANE) (2 PLANE) (3 PLANE) (4 PLANE) (5 PLANE))
 (adj   (1 (2 CONCAVE) (4 CONCAVE) (5 CONCAVE))
        (2 (1 CONCAVE) (3 CONCAVE) (5 CONCAVE))
        (3 (2 CONCAVE) (4 CONCAVE) (5 CONCAVE))
        (4 (1 CONCAVE) (3 CONCAVE) (5 CONCAVE))
        (5 (1 CONCAVE) (2 CONCAVE) (3 CONCAVE) (4 CONCAVE))))
```

This definition specifies a graph of $n = 5$ nodes, all of which are declared planar. Node relations are represented as an adjacency list, where the adjacent nodes and the connection types (CONVEX, CONCAVE, SMOOTH) are listed for each node.

10.4.3 Auxiliary Definitions

To express feature validation rules and to compute feature attribute values, auxiliary geometric entities are often useful. In the geometry definition frame, such auxiliary entities can be defined by using the node identifiers specified in the topology section as a collection of built-in functions. The defined auxiliary entities can be utilized in the other feature definition sections.

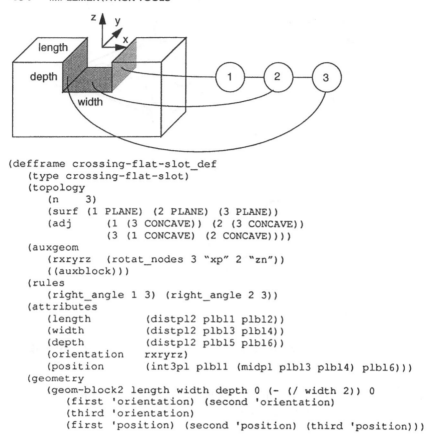

```
(defframe crossing-flat-slot_def
   (type crossing-flat-slot)
   (topology
      (n     3)
      (surf (1 PLANE) (2 PLANE) (3 PLANE))
      (adj     (1 (3 CONCAVE)) (2 (3 CONCAVE))
               (3 (1 CONCAVE) (2 CONCAVE))))
   (auxgeom
      (rxryrz   (rotat_nodes 3 "xp" 2 "zn"))
      ((auxblock)))
   (rules
      (right_angle 1 3) (right_angle 2 3))
   (attributes
      (length         (distpl2 plbl1 plbl2))
      (width          (distpl2 plbl3 plbl4))
      (depth          (distpl2 plbl5 plbl6))
      (orientation    rxryrz)
      (position       (int3pl plbl1 (midpl plbl3 plbl4) plbl6)))
   (geometry
      (geom-block2 length width depth 0 (- (/ width 2)) 0
         (first 'orientation) (second 'orientation)
         (third 'orientation)
         (first 'position) (second 'position) (third 'position))))
```

Figure 10.13 Geometry definition of `crossing-flat-slot`

For an example consider the feature geometry definition of the crossing flat slot feature shown in Figure 10.13. In the figure the auxiliary vector `rxryrz`, which contains local rotation angles around the *x*-, *y*-, and *z*-axis of the feature, is defined by relating the node 3 to the direction of the positive *x*-axis and 2 to the negative *z*-axis. The auxiliary function `auxblock` matches the whole geometry of the feature with an enclosing rectangular block and, as a side effect, defines the auxiliary variables `plbl1 ... plbl6` corresponding with the 6 planes bounding the block. The block is used to compute the dimensions of the feature after recognition, as discussed below.

10.4.4 Rules

Rules are useful for expressing feature validation conditions for feature recognition. In geometry definition frames, rules can be defined using a collection of built-in rule types referring to node identifiers or auxiliary geometries. In the example of Figure 10.13, two right-angle rules between the nodes 1 and 2 and the nodes 2 and 3 are specified.

10.4.5 Feature Attributes

In feature frames, feature geometry is represented only in terms of feature attributes such as length, depth, and diameter. The feature attributes section of geometry definitions can be used to specify computation rules for the attributes.

The computation rules can be expressed using built-in procedures that work on the basis of node identifiers and auxiliary entities. In the example of Figure 10.13, the attributes length, width, and depth are defined as distances between auxiliary planes by the built-in function dist2pl. The attribute rotation is directly related to the auxiliary geometry rxryrz. The attribute position is defined as the intersection of three planes (intpl3) which are given as functions of auxiliary planes; function midpl computes the center plane of two parallel planes.

10.4.6 Feature Geometry Definition

The geometry section is used to generate the geometry of the feature type. It stores a LISP form that will evaluate to the geometry of the feature. Essentially the form stores a parametric CSG expression, where primitives may include swept objects in addition to regular CSG primitives. An illustrative example is given below:

```
(geometry
   (height2 (/ height 2))    ; auxiliary variables   (solid1
      (geom-lamina (0 0 0)    (height2 100 0) ...)))
   (geom-union
      (def-schema             ; geometry definition schema
         (faces        (f1 (l1 l2) s1) ...)
         (vertices     (v1 0 0 auxvar2) ...) ...)
      (geom-sweep solid1 height2)))
```

In the above, def-schema, geom-lamina, geom-union, and geom-sweep are *geometry definition functions* that return a solid identifier that can be used to access the solid. The geometry definition functions provide a set of basic solid modeling operations that are either LISP functions, macros, or even C functions imported into LISP. As indicated in the example, feature slot values can be accessed by using slot names as variables in the geometry definition; hence parametric geometries can easily be implemented. Examples of geometry definition functions are given in Table 10.1.

Figure 10.14 contains a more realistic example of a parametric feature geometry definition. This definition specifies the geometry of an internal keyway slot. First, the slot shape is defined as a sequence of lines and arcs using the def-schema function; observe that the origin resides at the center point of the left semicircle. Feature dimensions are specified using the values of the feature slots width, depth, and length. Next, the resulting lamina object is swept by the value of the depth attribute of the feature using the geom-sweep function. Finally, the resulting solid is transformed with the geom-transf function to the desired position and orientation.

Table 10.1   Examples of geometry definition functions

`def_schema &rest def_form`	Evaluate the geometry definition schema given as argument. The argument `def_form` consists of a sequence of lists defining the faces, loops, edges, vertices, surfaces, and curves of the solid model.
`geom_lamina &rest sequence_of_vertices`	Create a lamina face (a "flat" solid consisting just of two faces, e.g., useful for sweeping operations). The macro takes as argument a sequence of vertices defining the boundary of the lamina face.
`geom_sweep s_id depth`	Perform a linear sweep of a lamina face.
`geom_swing s_id x1 y1 z1 x2 y2 z2 nfaces`	Transform a wire object into a true 3D solid model by "swinging" it around a axis. The axis goes through two points $(x1, y1, z1)$ and $(x2, y2, z2)$.
`geom_profop s_a_id s_b_id`	Combine two profiles defined by two laminas.
`geom_union s_a_id s_b_id`	Perform the set union of two solids. Similar functions exist also for set difference and intersection.
`geom_transf s_id rx ry rz tx ty tz`	Transform a solid with rotations rx, ry, and rz around the x-, y-, and z-axes, and translations tx, ty, tz along the x-, y-, and z-axes, respectively.
`geom_scale s_id sx sy sz`	Scale a solid along the x-, y-, and z-axes with scale factors sx, sy, and sz, respectively.

10.4.7   Evaluating Part Geometry

When the design-by-feature scenario is followed, the feature representation is considered the primary representation, and a solid model representation is generated algorithmically.

A geometric model of a whole part defined in terms of features is formed by combining the feature volumes defined by the feature instances using Boolean set operations. The geometry is evaluated by traversing the instance hierarchy tree in preorder, and interpreting the instance hierarchy as a CSG tree, where the internal nodes correspond to set operations and the leaves correspond to the feature instance volumes. The CSG operator is determined by inspecting the `sign` attribute of the feature instance.

To get the correct result, all feature volumes must be transformed to their correct positions. Each feature has a local coordinate system. The local transformations of feature instances are defined by the slots `orientation` and `position`. These define transformations about the part coordinate system. In turn the

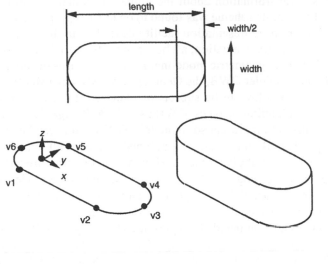

```
(geometry
    (geom-transf
        (geom-sweep
            (def_schema
                (faces (f1 l1) (f2 l2))
                (loops (l1 v6 v5 v4 v3 v2 v1)
                       (l2 v1 v2 v3 v4 v5 v6))
                (edges (e1 v1 v2) (e2 v2 v3 c1) (e3 v3 v4 c2)
                       (e4 v4 v5) (e5 v5 v6 c3) (e6 v6 v1 c4))
                (vertices (v1 0 (- (/ width 2)) (- depth))
                          (v2 (- length width) (- (/ width 2)) (- depth))
                          (v3 (- length (/ width 2)) 0 (- depth))
                          (v4 (- length width) (/ width 2) (- depth))
                          (v5 0 (/ width 2) (- depth))
                          (v6 (- (/ width 2)) 0 (- depth)))
                (curves (c1 ARC v2 v3 (- length width) 0 (- depth))
                        (c2 ARC v3 v4 (- length width) 0 (- depth))
                        (c3 ARC v5 v6 0 0 (- depth))
                        (c4 ARC v6 v1 0 0 (- depth))))
            depth)
        (first 'orientation) (second 'orientation)
        (third 'orientation)
        (first 'position) (second 'position) (third 'position)))
```

Figure 10.14 Geometry definition of internal keyway slot

part has a transformation about the global coordinate system of the modeling space. This simple scheme was found to be most appropriate from the viewpoint of the constraint representation facility described in the next section. As a side effect of geometry evaluation, a shape data structure is also formed.

For low-level geometric modeling, EXTDesign uses the boundary representation (B-rep) modeler GWB, the Geometric WorkBench (Mäntylä 1988). In GWB the faces of a solid can be subsets of planes, natural quadrics and tori, or of polynomial blending surfaces. GWB uses the *half-edge data structure* described in Appendix B to represent solid models. GWB solids can be represented in two ways: polyhedral and exact. In a polyhedral model all curved faces are represented via a mesh of planar facets. However, geometric information (tags) about the ideal shape of edges and facets is also stored in the model, which forms the basis of the feature linkage explained above. Tags also make it possible to support an automatic conversion to the exact model, where all surfaces and their intersections are computed and represented "exactly." GWB itself is implemented using the programming language C. Currently a new implementation of EXTDesign on top of the ACIS solid modeler (Spatial 1993) is being developed.

10.5 CONSTRAINT TOOLS

Pure procedural parametric modeling has its limitations. If more drastic changes to the part must be made to adapt it to new requirements, the procedural parametric approach may break down: the existing parameterization must be abandoned to adapt the model.

To cover these situations, EXTDesign also includes an incremental constraint facility ICONF for modeling parametric part families (Lagus et al. 1994). The facility allows constraint definitions to be stored in part family descriptions. When the part family is instantiated, the constraints are created and enforced. The constraint facility also supports interactive constraint manipulation where the designer can add further constraints in the part to adapt it to particular requirements. Moreover, because the concept of constraint "strength" is supported, it is possible to override predefined part family constraints.

10.5.1 SkyBlue

For constraint representation and satisfaction, EXTDesign uses the SkyBlue algorithm (Sannella 1993). SkyBlue is a derivative of the DeltaBlue algorithm described in Chapter 8. As in DeltaBlue, SkyBlue constraints are represented as groups of methods, each of which can be used to satisfy the respective constraint, whether numerical or some other type. When a constraint is satisfied, one of its methods is activated (chosen to satisfy the constraint). The active methods form a graph that is manipulated by using local propagation techniques. Strengths assigned to constraints enable hierarchical priorities.

10.5.2 Architecture of ICONF

ICONF consists of three main levels. The top level contains constraint manipulation functions (i.e., the procedures for a user interface). The middle level handles constraint parsing and interpreting, and translating the conceptual, high-level constraint definitions into groups of simple, atomic constraints. The lowest level is closely related to SkyBlue, and it handles the actual SkyBlue constraint, variable, and method creation for each type of atomic constraint.

Top Level   Constraints are always created for a frame. If the constraint is defined in a feature class or a part family, the definition will be *inherited* by all the subclasses and instances of the class. To activate an inherited constraint definition, it must be instantiated.

A constraint may refer to several features of a part or an assembly. Since a constraint cannot exist until all its references have been created, the instantiation of the definitions takes place only after the part (or assembly) and all its subfeatures have been created. Constraint creation as described above, and later the manipulation, is possible directly from the user interface of the system. For example, one can delete a single high-level constraint (a group), or all the constraints referring to a given frame, or all constraints dealing with a single attribute of a frame. Constraint browsing works similarly.

Parser Level   The parser processes a constraint expression, carrying out syntax checking, replacing slot references with variables and surfaces with plane equations, and interpreting the parsed expression into several simple, atomic constraints.

First, the parser replaces frame slot references with SkyBlue variables. The variables are connected with their owner slots so that each update of the variable causes the respective slot to be updated. Each surface reference encountered in an appropriate context (within a distance constraint) is substituted with its plane equation.

Next, the parser scans the result and creates the SkyBlue constraints that, as a group, arc equivalent to the expression. For instance, the constraint expression

```
(= (+ a b) (* c 3))
```

is simplified into the following two atomic constraints:

```
(= auxvar-1 (+ a b))
(= auxvar-1 (* c 3)).
```

Auxvar-1 is a new variable, which is used to mediate between the atomic constraints, propagating changes to both directions.

Finally, the appropriate SkyBlue data structure for each atomic constraint is created by calling low-level operations. Constraints are added to the SkyBlue

Table 10.2 Constraint types

Type	Description	Methods Used
Equality	a = b	a <= b b <= a
Additive	a = (oper b c ...) where oper is additive (e.g., + or *) and has an inverse	a <= (oper b c d) b <= (inv-oper a c d) c <= (inv-oper a b d) . . .
Subtractive	a = (oper b c ...) where oper is subtractive (e.g., / or -) and has inverse	b <= (inv-oper a c d) a <= (oper b c d) c <= (oper b d a) . . .
Unary	a = (oper b) where oper takes one argument and has inverse (e.g., sin b, $-180 \leq b \leq 180$)	a <= (oper b) b <= (inv-oper a)
Distance between two points, planes, or a point and a plane	d = (dist p1 p2) If p1 and p2 are planes, they must be parallel. Signed distance is used.	d <= (dist p1 p2) Move p1 to directly toward or away from p2 to distance d. Same for p2.

constraint graph only after the whole expression has been successfully interpreted.

Lowest Level At the lowest level, declarative atomic constraints are translated into appropriate procedural methods for satisfying them. Of all possible methods only those are created that would set a variable; obviously assigning a new value for a constant is not permissible. Different types of constraints with methods for satisfying them are presented in Table 10.2. In the table, <= denotes assignment, in contrast to = denoting equality constraint.

At the moment, only operators with a defined inverse operator are supported. One-way operators, however, might be desirable in cases where the user always wants one-way action.

10.5.3 Constraint Definition Language

ICONF uses a *constraint definition language* to express different kinds of conceptual constraints. This design separates the developer of feature descriptions from the actual constraint satisfaction algorithm used and also simplifies the definition of complex constraints by moving some of the complexities of constraint definition to the parser of the definition language. The language contains basic arithmetic and trigonometric operators and a special binary operator DIST to specify distances between planar surfaces and points.

We will use the following notation to express the language:

::= Denotes "may be replaced by"

| Denotes a choice

*   Denotes repetition zero or more times

+   Denotes repetition one or more times

<>   Denote a nonterminal symbol inside the braces

Other symbols are terminals that should be taken literally.

Using the notation above, we can define the constraint language as follows:

```
<constraint-def> ::=   { (CONSTRAINT
                           (NAME name-string)
                           (STRENGTH <str-value>)
                           (CODE <statement>)) }*
<str-value> ::=        Integer from 1 to 10 (1 = strong, 10 = weak)
<statement> ::=        (= <expr> <expr>) | (<statement>+)
```

The code of the constraint may consist of one or more equality constraints expressed as a Lisp form. Several examples of constraints are given in the following section.

```
<expr> ::=   number | <slot-ref> | (<oper> {<expr>}+)
             | (DIST (<surf> | <point>) (<surf> | <point>))
```

An expression may be a number, a reference to a slot, an operator applied to further expressions, or a distance between surfaces or points. All expressions evaluate to numbers.

```
<oper> ::=   + | - | * | / | sindeg | cosdeg | tandeg
```

The basic arithmetic operators, and trigonometric functions for degrees are included.

```
<slot-ref> ::=   (VARIABLE <frame> <slot>) | <slot>
                 | (VALUE <frame> <slot>) | (<coord> <point>)
```

A slot reference enables one to express that the value of a particular slot should participate in a constraint. If the slot itself needs to be constrained, the slot may be referred to with the keyword VARIABLE. If the value of the slot is treated as a constant in the expression, for example, to traverse to other frames via inheritance relations, the keyword VALUE is used. This only returns the current value of the slot without trying to constrain it. References may be recursive, since slots may contain references to other frames. The syntax of VALUE-references follows the BEEF syntax for recursively referencing frames and their slots.

> *<frame>* ::=   A name of a frame
> | *<slot-ref>* to a slot that contains the frame name
> | SELF | (FEATURE-ID *<fid>*+)

The keyword SELF provides a way for referencing the owner feature of the constraint (the one for which the constraint is instantiated). This is necessary in constraints embedded in feature class definitions. FEATURE-ID is a shorthand for referencing any feature within a part using the feature identifiers (see Section 10.3.4). Features within different parts of an assembly may be accessed by listing the feature identifiers of each part in the path.

10.5.4 Constraints in Use

The main purpose of ICONF is to support constraints embedded in feature class definitions. When a feature has some inherent conceptual constraints that should be exhibited in every subclass and instance of the feature, the constraint definition may be embedded in the feature class definition. This way the constraint definition will be inherited by all instances and subclasses of that feature. If one wants to activate the inherited constraint for a specific instance frame, the constraint must be instantiated, that is, parsed and added to the SkyBlue constraint graph.

Embedded constraints in feature class definitions allow the user to express highly abstract constraints that apply to a large variety of features. As an example, an abstract constraint could be: *"The feature should always stay on its parent surface."* The following example shows how constraints can be embedded in feature class definitions.

To describe the constraint facility, let us consider the sample part shown in Figure 10.15 (*a*), L-block-17 with two crossing-flat-slots. Some of the related frames are shown in Figure 10.16. Crossing-flat-slot-17 is the one positioned on top of the L-block. The other slot, crossing-flat-slot-18, starts from the bottom of crossing-flat-slot-17; therefore the z-coordinate of crossing-flat-slot-18 is equal to negated depth of crossing-flat-slot-17.

Since the positions of both the L-block and the crossing-slots are each expressed individually in the part coordinate system, moving the L-block without constraining it first will leave the two crossing-flat-slots behind (see Figure 10.15(*b*)). However, since the concept of a crossing-slot requires that the slot should always stay on the surface that was assigned as its parent, we would like this to be a generic constraint for all crossing-flat-slots, crossing-T-slots, crossing-V-slots, and so on. This can be achieved by including the following constraint in the definition of the class crossing-slot, the parent class of crossing-flat-slot:

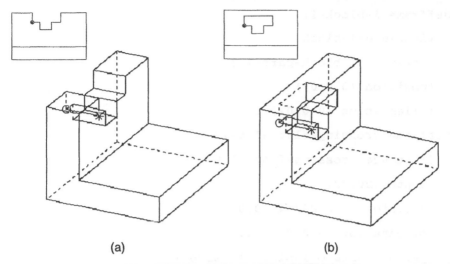

Figure 10.15 A part with `L-block` and two `crossing-slots`

```
(defframe crossing-slot
   (is-a slot-feature)
   (constraint-slots
      (constraint
         (name "Stay on parent surface")
         (strength 4)
         (code (= (DIST position
            (value SELF parent-surface)) 0)))))
```

The constraint states that a `crossing-slot` should always be positioned on its `parent-surface`. The first argument for the operator `DIST` is the `position` slot of the `crossing-slot` instance, and the second is its parent surface frame. `Crossing-flat-slot` is related to `crossing-slot` with an `is-a` relation and therefore we can instantiate the above constraint for the `crossing-flat-slot-17`:

```
(instantiate-constraints 'crossing-flat-slot-17)
```

In fact the call instantiates all the constraints that `crossing-flat-slot-17` owns or inherits, but so far only one has been defined. The result is shown in Figure 10.17(*a*). The upper slot has moved upward onto its parent surface. We observe that the lower slot was not affected, and was left behind. In Figure 10.17(*b*) the constraints for the lower slot have also been instantiated, which has caused the slot to find its correct place on the bottom surface of the upper slot. Here the slots happened to follow the block, although this was not strictly determined by the constraints. The user may control the selection of the solution by adding weak *stay constraints* to the values which preferably should stay as they are.

```
(defframe l-block-17
   (instance l-block)
   (the-part l-block-part-17)
   (position (0 0 0))
   (orientation (0 0 0)) ...)
(defframe crossing-flat-slot-17
   (instance crossing-flat-slot)
   (depth 220.33)
   (position (0.0 803.49 0.0))
   (orientation (0 0 0)) ...
   (parent-surface l-block-17-side6)
(defframe l-block-17-side6
   (instance basic-surface)
   (parent-feature l-block-17)
   (features crossing-flat-slot-17)
   (surface-type plane)
   (surface-eq (0 0 -1 0)))
(defframe crossing-flat-slot-18
   (position (0.0 781.17 -220.3))
   (orientation (0 0 0)) ...
   (parent-surface crossing-flat-slot-17-bottom).)
(defframe crossing-flat-slot-17-bottom
   (instance basic-surface)
   (parent-feature crossing-flat-slot-17)
   (surface-eq (0 0 1 depth))
   ...
   (features crossing-flat-slot-18))
```

Figure 10.16 Frames for the part family L-block-17 with two crossing-flat-slots

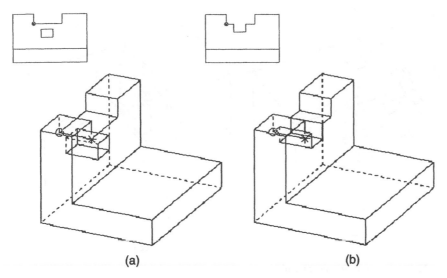

Figure 10.17 Constraining the slots

From here on, if the block is moved in the z-direction, the crossing-slots will either follow, or change their depth so that their positions stay on their parent surfaces. The actual behavior depends on other constraints. On the other hand, if one now moves the block in x- or y-direction, the slots will not follow the block because the same plane equation would still describe the parent surface of the upper slot. Additional constraints must be specified in order to achieve this behavior.

10.5.5 Dynamic Constraint Creation

During the design of a new part or an assembly one would often like to create and delete constraints dynamically, to achieve an optimal description of one's model. As an example, consider an assembly with a block having a T-shaped slot crossing one of its surfaces, and a T-shaped billet that fits in the T-slot. The initial assembly of two parts is depicted in Figure 10.18(a), and the corresponding assembly class definition in Figure 10.19.

In Figure 10.18(a) the two parts have been created, of which the smaller is called T-billet and the bigger T-part. Apparently their orientations are not as we wish, a rotation of 90 degrees is necessary. Since initially the T-billet is oriented 90 degrees away from what it should be, we decide to constrain the orientation so that this won't happen again. The following constraint which requires the two parts to have the same rotation around the assembly coordinate system is added:

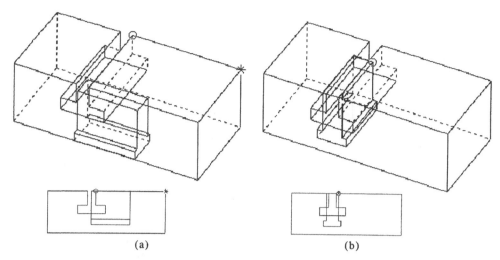

(a)   (b)

Figure 10.18 Constraining an assembly

```
(create-constraint 'example-assembly-20
 :name "orient correctly"
 :strength 5
 :code '(= (z-coord (variable crossing-t-slot-24 orienta-
      tion))
  (z-coord (variable t-part-23 orientation)))))
```

Figure 10.18(*b*) shows the situation after addition of the constraint. Now the billet has flipped 90 degrees but does not fit in the slot yet. To handle this, we have two choices: adding constraints between surfaces and points or between local dimensioning slots of the features. We choose the surface-distance approach, and add a constraint requiring that the distance between the bottom surfaces of T-billet and T-slot be 60:[1]

```
(create-constraint 'example-assembly-20
   :name "Distance between bottoms"
    :strength 4
    :code '(= (DIST crossing-t-slot-24-bottom t-billet-23-
bottom) 60))
```

The resulting assembly is shown in Figure 10.20(*a*) Now there is space between the billet and bottom of the slot, but the billet neck is still too thick, as is its bottom bar. To correct the model further, we add two scaling constraints between the neck-surfaces of the two T-shapes, and another between their bottom depths. Now we achieve our goal (in Figure 10.20*b*): The billet fits tightly in the slot.

---

[1]The order of the surfaces in the expression matters, since signed distances are used. A distance is positive, if the second surface is in the direction of the normal vector of the first surface.

```
(define-assembly example-assembly
   (is-a assembly)
   (inst-def
      (PART t-part $fid-1200 (SLOTS (position (800 0 0))))
      (PART example-part $fid-1500)))
(define-part t-part
   (is-a part)
   (inst-def
      (BASEF t-billet $fid-1260
         (SURF side-surface-4 $sid-1210)
         (SURF bottom-surface $sid-1211))))
(define-billet t-billet
   (is-a billet)
   (instance-slots (length 700) ... (neck-width 230))
   (surface-slots
      (side-surface-1 basic-surface "-SIDE-1" 1)
      (side-surface-2 basic-surface "-SIDE-2" 2) ...)
   (nodes(1 PLANE (0 -1 0 (/ bottom-width 2)))
           (2 PLANE (0 1 0 (/ bottom-width 2))) ...)))
(define-part example-part
   (is-a part)
   (inst-def
      (SLOTS (orientation (0 0 0)) (position (0 0 0)))
      (BASEF block $fid-1555
         (SLOTS(height 750) (width 996) (length 2160)
               (orientation (0 0 0)) (position (0 0 0)))
         (SURF side-surface-1 $sid-1555) ...
         (SURF side-surface-5 $sid-1559
            (SUBF crossing-t-slot $fid-1608
               (SLOTS(rounding 2) (neck-width 150) ...
                     (orientation (0 0 90))
                     (position (800 0 0)))
               (SURF side-surface-1 $sid-1608) ...)
         (SURF side-surface-6 $sid-1560))))
```

Figure 10.19 An example assembly definition

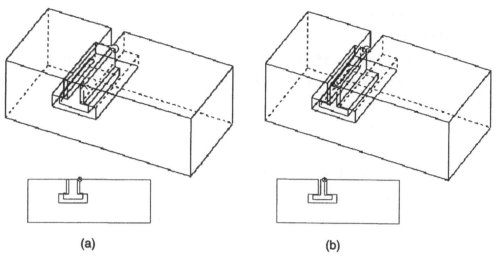

(a)   (b)

Figure 10.20   Assembly constraint example

10.5.6 Case Study

Figure 10.21(*a*) depicts a bearing-housing cover, which is an equipment found in paper mills. Its class frame, called `external-cover-dry`, was initially designed with parametric modeling techniques and is presented in Figure 10.22. We would like to dynamically change its dimensions without having to define a new parametric part class each time. However, the parametric equations that define the geometry of the object need to be maintained during the interactive design, or else the geometry of the part will fall apart. In addition we would like to define a new relationship that defines the position of the circular pattern of holes in relation to the outer diameter and the width of the plate that the holes

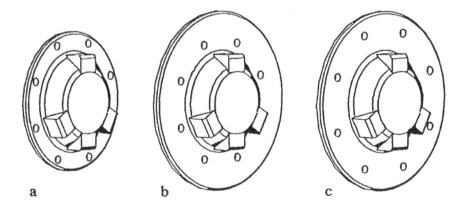

a   b   c

Figure 10.21 A bearing-housing cover: (*a*) initial model; (*b*) with coherence constraints; (*c*) with further positioning constraints

```
(define-part external-cover-dry
   (is-a external-covering)
   (instance-slots
      (drawing-no 276640)
      (material GRS250) ...)
   (inst-def
      (PARAMS
         (inner-diameter 158)
         (outer-diameter 250)
         (plate-width 30)
         (circular-pattern-radius 110)
         (circular-pattern-number 8)
         (hole-diameter 14.5) ... )
      (BASEF ext-cover-billet $fid-1
         (SLOTS (inner-diameter inner-diameter)
                (outer-diameter outer-diameter)
                (plate-width plate-width) ... )
      (SURF annulus-surface-1 $sid-1
         (SUBF annular-relief $fid-11
            (SLOTS (outer-diameter outer-diameter)
                   (position (0 0 length1)) ...)
            (SURF annulus-surface $sid-11
               (SUBF circular-pattern $fid-111
                  (SLOTS (n circular-pattern-number)
                         (radius circular-pattern-radius) ...)
                  (SUBF straight-through-hole $fid-1111
                     (PARAMS ...)
                     (SLOTS ...))))))
      (SURF annulus-surface-2 $sid-2
         (SUBF annular-area $fid-21 ...))))
```

Figure 10.22 Partial part class frame of bearing-housing cover

pierce as seen in Figure 10.21(*b*) and (*c*). As will be seen, this task is suitable for constraints.

After instantiating the initial part, the following constraint was added, along with two others to maintain geometric coherence of the parameters that we may want to change:[1]

```
(create-constraint
   'external-cover-dry-1338
   :name "outer-diam2"
   :strength 5
   :code '(= (- (/ (variable ext-cover-billet-1338
                    outer-diameter) 2)
             (variable ext-cover-billet-1338 plate-width))
         (variable annulus-surface-1339 smaller-radius)))
```

The coherence constraints were adopted directly from the parametric equations. Some weak stay constraints were added to set the initial values of some of the dimensions. The result, after adding the coherence and stay constraints and changing the outer diameter, is presented in Figure 10.21(*b*). The model is coherent, but the radius of the ring of holes did not behave as we had wished; therefore we decided to constrain it. We introduced a further constraint that determines the radius of the hole pattern in relation to the outer and inner diameters, stating that the radius is in between them at some point, and closer to the outer diameter:

```
(create-constraint 'external-cover-dry-1338
 :name "circular-pattern-radius"
 :strength 6
 :code '(= (variable straight-through-hole-1338 radius)
         (/ (+ (variable ext-cover-billet-1338 outer-diameter)
               (variable annulus-surface-1338 inner-diameter))
            3.82)))))
```

We observe that the ring of holes has grown along with the plate (Figure 10.21(*c*)).

The above mechanisms have been integrated with the incremental part family modeling approach of the EXTDesign modeler discussed in Chapter 8. True to the incremental part family modeling approach, after the design session has been concluded, the constraint definitions created interactively may be saved into a part class with the EXTDesign *create new part family* mechanism. Figure 10.23 gives a part of the resulting part family with some of the new constraints. From now on, whenever the part family is instantiated, the constraints will be automatically created and enforced.

---

[1]To fully define the geometrical dependencies of this part we would need several further constraints.

```
(defframe part-family-1672

  (is-a family-part) ...

  (inst-def

    (basef ext-cover-billet $fid-1 ...))

  (constraint-slots

    (constraint (name "outer-diam2") (strength 5)

    (code

      (= (- (/ (variable (feature-id $fid-1) outer-diameter) 2)

            (variable (feature-id $fid-1) plate-width))

        (variable (feature-id $fid-21) smaller-radius))))

    (constraint (name "circular-pattern-radius") (strength 6)

    (code

      (= (variable (feature-id $fid-111) radius)

        (/ (+ (variable (feature-id $fid-1) outer-diameter)

            (variable (feature-id $fid-11) inner-diameter))

        3.82))) ...))
```

Figure 10.23 New bearing-housing cover class with interactively created constraint definitions

10.6 FEATURE RECOGNITION TOOLS

A functionally complete feature modeling environment also requires feature recognition tools. This section outlines a feature recognition method that can work on the basis of the feature definitions explained in Sections 10.2 and 10.3 (Laakko and Mäntylä 1991). The algorithm also illustrates the use of various optimization tricks needed to speed up a recognizer to make it suited for practical use.

The basic method to be described is based on graph recognition. However, the method has been made incremental to support incremental feature modeling outlined in Chapter 9.

10.6.1 Basic Concepts

The feature recognizer is based on a hybrid technique where several recognition methods can be utilized simultaneously. In particular, the feature geometry definition frames provide tools for specifying which methods are used for recognition on a type-by-type basis. This supports the inclusion of new kinds of features more easily than similar techniques of single-paradigm systems. An adjacency graph representation of a solid model facilitates the feature recognition of more complex features including curved surfaces.

While basically a graph-match technique, another unusual characteristic of the algorithm is its feature-search procedure which reverses the usual order where single features are extracted first. To diminish the computation required, the algorithm first tries to determine the overall shape of the solid by recognizing a "base feature." This leads to splitting the complete search graph into several smaller partial graphs which are used for searching the detail features. Feature interactions are principally treated by heuristic rules that split combinations into their components, and hence the (potentially large) search graph is rapidly subdivided into more manageable partial graphs. This makes feature recognition a significantly fast process, which is essential for incremental feature modeling.

For the recognizer, a feature is a partial graph of the complete adjacency graph that satisfies the conditions specified in the feature geometry definition frame of some feature class. Features are classified as base, single (basic), container, and combination features from the viewpoint of feature recognition. A base feature corresponds to the overall shape of the part. Typically a base feature is a positive feature that corresponds to the stock for machined parts. A combination consists of several interacting single or container features that may intersect each other. Single and container features are regular features of the taxonomy.

The actual search of features is accomplished in four main steps: preprocessing, searching for a base feature, searching for single and container features, and interpreting feature combinations. The result of the recognition process is a feature model that consists of a base feature and several single or container features organized in a tree structure (i.e., a feature instance hierarchy), with proper feature relationships represented through surface frames.

10.6.2 Feature Topology Classification

One of the problems of graph-based recognition algorithms is the computational cost of subgraph matching. As discussed in Chapter 9, in the worst case, subgraph matching may take an exponential time as a function of the graph size. To counter the worst case, all practical feature recognition techniques must use special search structures that effectively decrease the constant factors of the worst-case complexity.

To speed up the search process in the incremental recognition algorithm, in the setup stage the recognizer organizes the feature types in an internal treelike structure shown in Figure 10.24, using the information of the definition frames. On the first level of the tree, features are classified according to the number of nodes, and on the second level according to the number of arcs. On the third level features are classified according to the local node topologies. The overall topology of each feature type is represented as a leaf (feature topology node) of the tree. Each leaf also has a reference to the corresponding feature definition frame. If a feature definition has no topology definition section, the corresponding node is connected to the first level of the tree. The topology classification needs to be performed only when the feature definition information of some feature type has been changed.

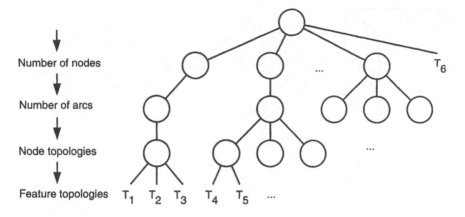

Number of nodes

Number of arcs

Node topologies

Feature topologies T_1 T_2 T_3 T_4 T_5 ...

Figure 10.24 Feature topology classification (Laakko 1993; reprinted by permission)

10.6.3 Preprocessing

First, in the preprocessing step, the graph representation (the shape data structure) of the solid model is generated. A temporary copy of the graph is used in
the search of features. Hence the original graph is not modified during the searching process.

In this step special transition surfaces of the solid model are handled separately. The surfaces include blending/rounding surfaces created using the blending facility of the underlying modeler. The information of the surfaces are marked
as attributes in the graph in this step. The attribute information is evaluated
afterward for feature frames representing the transitions.

Another type of preprocessing is performed with the aim of facilitating the
recognition of features with roundings and blendings. This operation is based
on a special implementation of rounding and blending operations in the underlying solid modeler, which leaves the resulting faces tagged with appropriate
information. Using these tags, the surfaces can be eliminated from the search
graph, as shown in Figure 10.25. Blend information is preserved as attributes
associated with the remaining edges of the graph; on the basis of these data, the
corresponding attributes of the recognized features can be computed. For those
blends that do not map to feature attributes, special blend features are inserted in
the final result of the recognition. For details, see (Laakko and Mäntylä 1993b).

10.6.4 Searching for a Base Feature

The input for searching a base feature is the whole graph which is matched
against base feature definitions. The conditions of a definition are checked in
the order of topology, geometric constraints, and rules. If the graph is found to
satisfy the conditions of a definition, nodes that correspond with the definition
are removed from the graph, as indicated in Figure 10.26. The removal divides

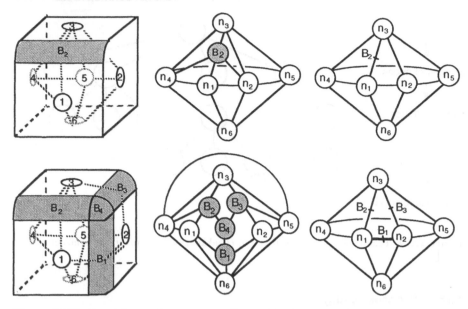

Figure 10.25 Removing nodes corresponding to blends and roundings from the search graph (Laakko et al. 1993; reprinted with permission from Blackwell Publishers)

the initial graph in several partial graphs. Each partial graph is then considered separately for finding single or combination features. The division reduces the required further computation significantly.

In the case of Figure 10.26 the nodes n_1 to n_6 are found to belong to the base feature type "block," and they are removed from the searching graph. The resulting graph will have only two nodes n_7 and n_8. In this situation the recognition is based on the following rule embedded with the feature definition for blocks: *If all the faces that are contained in a convex hull of the part belong to an arbitrary block, then the corresponding subgraph of graph represents a feature of*

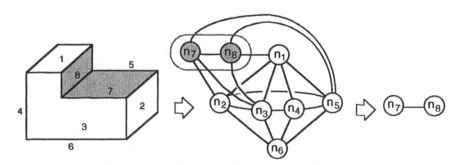

Figure 10.26 Removing nodes corresponding to a base feature from the search graph (Laakko 1993; reprinted by permission)

type "block." This recognition rule is implemented by means of the procedure
find-block embedded in the rules section of the block geometry definition
frame as shown below:

```
block-def
    type        block
    rules       (find-block)
    attributes
          (length       (dist-node2 1 2))
          (width        (dist-node2 3 4))
          (height       (dist-node2 5 6))
    geometry
          (geom-block length width height ...)
    nodes    ...
```

10.6.5 Searching for Single and Container Features

Single and container features are handled similarly, except that when instantiating a recognized container feature class, the contained features of the container
are also instantiated. The input for searching for single or container features is a
partial graph of the whole input graph. The partial graph is matched against
single and container feature definitions. If the whole partial graph is found to
satisfy the conditions of a feature definition, the recognition succeeds immediately. Otherwise, the partial graph is searched for feature combinations.

10.6.6 Interpreting Feature Combinations

Feature combinations arise in several situations. In some cases they correspond
to compound features that can be modeled as such in the feature taxonomy.
Sometimes they denote feature interaction. The algorithm described here takes
the very simple stance of first giving priority to compound definitions; this
allows also all "expected" types of feature interaction to be modeled in feature
geometry definitions. Compound definitions generally include rules that separate the component features of the compound so that they can recursively be
matched against single-feature descriptions. The division rules implement methods for dealing with "type I" and "type II" feature interactions discussed in
Chapter 9 (Joshi and Chang 1988). Recall, for instance, the following rule which
implements the "type I" heuristic (see Figure 9.4):

```
combination-27c-def
    type combination-27c
    rules (remove-convex-arcs)
           (joint-split-nodes)
```

The actual search algorithm is outlined in Figure 10.27. The input for searching for combinations is a partial graph that does not match any single- or con-

```
interpret-feature-combination:
    if match-the-input-graph-against-combination-definitions
        return true;
    if search-for-subgraphs-of-the-input-graph
        return true;

match-the-input-against-combination-definitions:
    while next combination definition exists
        if the conditions of the definition are satisfied
            if check-partial-graphs-for features
                return true;

search-for-subgraphs-of-the-input-graph:
    repeat for all subgraphs of the input graph
                in decreasing order of subgraph size i
        if a single or container feature with i nodes is found
            remove the subgraph from the input graph
                if check-partial-graphs-for features
                    return true;
```

Figure 10.27 Interpreting feature combinations

tainer feature definition. The partial graph is matched against combination definitions. If the whole partial graph matches the conditions of a combination type, it is further divided into smaller partial graphs by deleting and/or joining entities of the graph as specified in the rules of the combination definition. Then the resulting partial graphs are processed further by searching recursively single and container features. If a resulting partial graph does not match any feature, the next combination type (if any) is considered.

As the last resort, if a partial graph does not match any combination type, we perform a general graph-matching algorithm that tries to match subgraphs in the decreasing order of size of the subgraph with single- and container feature definitions. If a subgraph is found to match a feature type, it is removed from the partial graph, and the resulting smaller partial graphs are again recursively considered by searching for single features. If the recursion fails, the algorithm backtracks and considers the next candidate subgraph.

It should be noted that the use of heuristic rules neither decreases the generality of the algorithm nor makes the result less reliable. This is because the algorithm always backtracks when a partial graph is found not to satisfy the conditions of a feature type, whereby the next definition frame is considered for the parent graph. The result of successful feature recognition is that all nodes of the searching graph are associated with some feature types. In fact the use of heuristic rules makes the searching process considerably faster so that real interactive recognition becomes possible.

10.6.7 Instantiation of Feature Classes

The feature model is generated by first instantiating the feature types recognized and then building the feature instance hierarchy. Whenever the feature recognizer finds a partial graph or a subgraph that matches a feature type, it creates a shape data structure for that partial graph; see Figure 10.28. A shape relates the associated feature type with a portion of the solid model; it refers to the corresponding feature definition, and points at node data structures which, in turn, contain pointers to one or more surfaces in the feature searching graph of the part. A node may refer to several lower-level nodes in the case of split faces. Split faces are referred to by the same surface tags in the tagged solid model, and they will be referred to by one node data structure (e.g., nodes n_2 and n_6 in Figure 10.28). Some (if not all) nodes correspond to explicit surface frames of the feature representation.

After feature recognition has been completed, the feature classes related to the created shape data structures are instantiated, and feature slot values are evaluated by procedure calls embedded in the feature attributes section of the definition frame. As noted in the Section 10.2, a feature geometry definition may be associated with several feature classes. In this case the user can afterwards interactively change the class of an feature instance to another one having a reference to the same feature definition. This provides a restricted method for specialization mapping.

The feature instance hierarchy tree is generated level by level starting from the base feature instance. Hierarchical relations between feature instances are

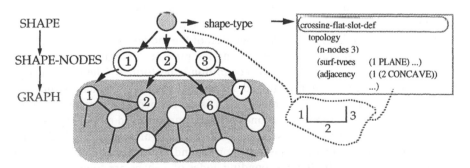

Figure 10.28 Relating shape data structures with the searching graph and feature definitions (Laakko and Mäntylä 1993; reprinted with permission from *Computer-Aided Design*, Butterworth Heinemann, Oxford, England)

created by inspecting the topological neighborhood relationships of the corresponding nodes. First, the algorithm finds all the surface-surface intersections between the current feature and all the unreferenced features (i.e., features not yet related to the hierarchy) of the model. Then, for all adjacent surfaces found of the current feature, the algorithm checks whether the feature may be related to that surface. This is accomplished by using the special conditions associated with the feature type as follows:

```
(parent-surf-def
    (surf-type      PLANE)
    (constraints    (constraint-1) (constraint-2))
    (adjacency      (1 CONCAVE) (3 CONCAVE)))
```

The conditions are specified in the slot `parent-surf-def` of the feature class frame, and may include the required surface type, geometric constraints, or adjacency requirements between the parent surface and the related feature. Finally, if a surface is found to satisfy the assigned conditions, a relation is created between the surface and the current feature, and the feature is removed from the list of unreferenced features.

10.6.8 Incremental Operation

Incremental operation requires that whenever the solid model representation of a part is modified, the corresponding feature model representation can be updated. Such a modification of the solid model representation might result from adding of one or more features to the model, or from direct manipulation of the model with solid modeling operations, in which case there are no direct feature counterparts with the modified parts of the solid model.

To support incremental operation, the previous feature model must be preserved. During an incremental update of the feature model, only those portions of the solid model that have changed after the previous update of the feature model are considered. That is, the algorithm works on new solid model entities that are not yet associated with any feature, or on solid model entities (faces, surface tags) related to a feature that have been modified or deleted. This is achieved on the basis of the `shape` data structure.

In the algorithm the incremental operation of the modeling process is accomplished by the feature recognizer by saving the previous recognition context so that it can be utilized when the next recognition is performed. The latest recognition context includes the recognized shapes and their `shape` data structures (search graph). When the next recognition is performed, the recognizer compares the new search graph corresponding to the current solid model representation of the part with the previous graph. First, the recognizer checks whether the new graph still contains the nodes that correspond to the nodes related to each saved shape structure. If all corresponding nodes of a shape are found, the shape will also be present in the new graph. Otherwise, the nodes related to the old shape must be reexamined by the recognizer.

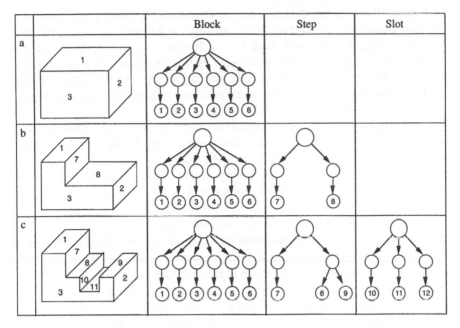

Figure 10.29 Operation of incremental feature recognition (Laakko and Mäntylä 1993; reprinted with permission from *Computer-Aided Design*, Butterworth Heinemann, Oxford, England)

When new entities are added to or removed from a solid model using solid modeling operations, one or more faces of the model are typically split into pieces. In such an event, however, the solid modeler used will make sure that split faces still contain the identical tag information, which simplifies the required geometric tests. The tags and other geometric tests allow the split faces to be detected by the recognizer.

Figure 10.29 gives a simple example of retaining search graphs during incremental feature recognition. First, a solid model representing a block is created by the designer and the feature recognition is performed. The recognizer finds the model to satisfy the conditions of a feature type "block" and creates a shape structure (Figure 10.29(a), the root of the tree) that has pointers to six nodes. Each node corresponds with one surface in the searching graph (the leaves in the tree). These in turn refer to surface tags in the underlying solid presentation.

As the next step, the designer uses solid modeling operations to remove a piece from the model (Figure 10.29(b)). Observe that even though the geometry of faces 1, 2, 3, and 5 (not visible in the figure) has been changed, the tags remain unchanged. Therefore, when the designer performs feature recognition once again, the recognizer can utilize the latest recognition context and find all the corresponding nodes of the saved shape structure in the geometry. Thereafter the recognizer removes the six unchanged nodes from the present searching graph (initially containing eight nodes) leaving just two nodes in the graph. The recognizer finds that they match the feature type "step."

In Figure 10.29(c), the designer has removed still another piece from the solid. This operation causes face 8 of the solid to be split in two parts, the remainder of face 8 and a new face 9. The Boolean set operation algorithm responsible for implementing the face splitting operation creates a new tag for face 9 by copying the information from the tag of face 8. By virtue of this implementation, the links from the corresponding node to the tags can be updated so that the node now refers to both tags.

When the feature recognition is performed once again, the latest recognition context includes two different shapes (a block and a step). For both of the shapes, all the corresponding nodes are found in the geometry. After removing these nodes from the searching graph (containing twelve nodes), there are four nodes left. By inspecting the tags, node 9 is found to be a split node which is merged with the shape node 8. This leaves us with three nodes 10, 11, and 12 in the graph, which are found to match the feature type "slot."

One of the advantages of incremental recognition over regular recognition is that a certain interpretation of otherwise vague situations can easily be enforced. For instance, consider the case shown in Figure 10.30. As shown in the right side of the picture, the part can be interpreted (at least) in two ways in terms of features. In the first view, it has two step features and one slot feature; in the other, there are two nested slot features. The preference of the two interpretations may ultimately depend on such criteria as dimensions and tolerances, materials, and characteristics of available machine tools. Therefore it is quite difficult to "teach" a feature recognizer to select the better alternative automatically.

Using the incremental approach, the issue can be avoided. If the designer creates and recognizes the part shown on the top left of Figure 10.30 first, then modifies the solid further and performs the feature recognition once again, the result is a model with two slots. If, on the other hand, the designer creates the geometry by means of solid modeling tools such as Boolean set operations, and

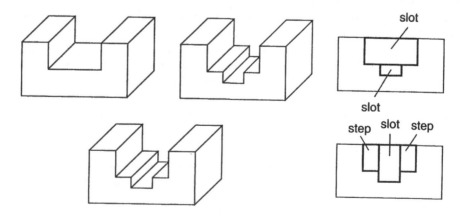

Figure 10.30 Enforcing a certain interpretation of a part by means of incremental operation (Laakko and Mäntylä 1993; reprinted with permission from *Computer-Aided Design*, Butterworth Heinemann, Oxford, England)

invokes feature recognition without a previous recognition context, the result of feature recognition for the solid shown is a model with two step features and one slot feature.

10.7 PROCEDURAL FEATURE RECOGNITION WITH C

In Section 9.2.4 procedural feature recognition was briefly discussed. In this section we give the implementation details of a feature recognition toolkit based on the procedural approach and implemented in the C language. It is assumed that the database of a commercial solid modeler is to be used, and features are to be recognized from a snapshot of the model, namely in batch mode after the design is complete, in some manner of judgment. Thus, for the time being, we do not need to worry about a dynamic interface with the solid modeler, nor about incremental changes; a text file produced by the solid modeler is used as the starting point for feature recognition. Two interesting aspects of this case study are:

- The solid modeler output is converted to a neutral, and more compact format that is more suitable for feature recognition. This also allows the recognition system to be independent of the particular solid modeler used, as long as programs can be written to convert its specific data format to the neutral format.
- A C interpretive language has been developed to make the system user-extendible; using this language, users can define recognition algorithms for new features, without the need to recompile. The language supports commonly needed functions for interactive and automatic feature recognition based on the procedural approach.

In the following sections we describe the design and implementation details.

10.7.1 Preprocessing

A solid model data format specifically designed to facilitate feature recognition was developed by (Hwang 1988). The general procedure for generating the format translated from CAD output file can be summarized into the following steps:

1. Collect the faces of the part in the solid model database.
2. Choose one of the faces.
3. Obtain the geometric and topological data of the face.
4. Collect the loops on the face.
5. Pick one of the loops.
6. Collect the edges on the loop.
7. Select one of the edges.

8. Obtain the geometric and topological data of the edge.

9. Get the two vertices of the edge.

10. Obtain the geometric locations of the two vertices.

11. Go to step 7 and repeat until all the edges in the loop are explored.

12. Go to step 5 and repeat until all the loops in the face are explored.

13. Go to step 2 and repeat until all the faces in the part are explored.

14. End.

The file format is shown in Figure 10.31. Although ComputerVision's CADDS system (Computervision 1987) was used for demonstration, the methodology is general enough to be applied to other modeler data files.

In the recognition system implemented by (Sreevalsan 1990), Hwang's model was converted to a modified half-edge data structure (see Appendix B). The contents of the modified model are as follows:

- The body node has the name of the body, the total number of faces, edges and vertices, pointers to doubly linked lists of all the faces, edges, and vertices and the bounds (the maximum and minimum x, y, and z coordinates). This forms the root node of the instance of the whole data structure.

- The face node contains the name of the face, the type of the face (plane, cylindrical, spherical, toroidal, conical), pointer to the body node, an integer indicating the direction of the normal (whether it is the same as or opposite to the direction given by the face equation), the total number of loops, the face equation, pointer to the list of the loops and pointers to the next and previous nodes in the list of the faces.

- The face_equation for the various types of faces contains geometric parameters for planes, cylinders, spheres, cones, and tori.

```
1.  (body (bodyname (face_list)))
2.  (face (facename type normal hatch (equation_list)))
3.  (face_loops (facename numloops))
4.  (loop_def (facename loopnum (pointname1 edgename1
                              pointname2 edgename2 ...)))
5.  (edge (edgename type (equation_list)))
6.  (edge_faces (edgename faceangle (coface_list)))
7.  (edge_direction (edgename facename reversed startpointname endpointname))
8.  (point pointname (x y z)))
9.  (point_edges (pointname (edge_list)))
10. (point_faces (pointname (face_list)))
```

Figure 10.31 Format of the processed solid model (Sreevalsan 1990; reprinted with permission)

- The loop node contains a pointer to the parent face, the loop number, a pointer to a list of edges that belong to the loop, a pointer to the list of vertices that belong to the loop and pointer to the next and previous loops.
- The halfedge associates two half-edges with each other. Each half-edge also has an associated orientation. The half-edge node contains a pointer to the parent face of the half-edge, pointers to the starting and ending vertices and a pointer to the mating half-edge.
- The edge node contains the name of the edge, the type of edge (straight line, circle, ellipse), the edge equation, pointers to the two half-edges, and pointers to the next and previous edges in the list of edges.
- The edge_equation contains the geometric parameters of: line segment, circular and elliptical arcs.
- The loopedge node contains a pointer to the edge, and pointers to the next and previous loopedges.
- The vertex node contains the name of the vertex, the coordinates of the vertex, a pointer to a half-edge with that vertex as its starting vertex, and pointers to the next and previous vertices in the list of vertices.
- The loopvertex node contains a pointer to the edge, and pointers to the next and previous loopvertices.

A wire frame display is required for interactive feature creation. It may also provide visual feedback and validation in automatic feature recognition. The wireframe picture is generated by traversing the data structure and drawing all the edges. The type of edge is determined and different routines are used depending on the nature of the edge's geometry. Common functions needed on the wireframe manipulation and display include rotation, translation, scaling, generation of orthographic views, multiple display of the three orthographic views and the isometric view on a partitioned screen, and zooming in or out. Since the user may have moved the model around in the geometric modeler, it needs to be centered in the world window. This is accomplished by translating the center of the bounding box of the model to the origin at the outset. The rotation, translation, and scaling is accomplished by straightforward application of viewing transformation matrices. Orthographic projections are generated by model rotation to generate the right view. To generate the multiple view, the display viewport is partitioned into four quadrants. Each quadrant is then treated as an independent viewport and a view is drawn in it. The manipulation functionality is accessed through menus. Mouse picking of menu items is implemented for additional user friendliness.

10.7.2 Interpreted Language

To support interactive and automatic feature recognition in a user-extendible system, an interpreted language was developed (Sreevalsan 1990). The language is C-like and interpreted into C. It supports a comprehensive list of variable

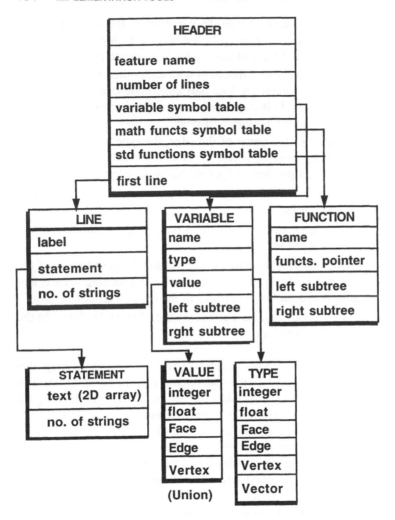

Figure 10.32 The interpreted language data structure (Sreevalsan 1990)

types and allows user defined types. Apart from providing general purpose capabilities, such as assignments, arithmetic, logic, and looping, higher level functionality is provided through special functions needed in searching the solid model, user interactions with wireframe displays, entity classification, and so on.

Figure 10.32 illustrates the data structures that were developed to support the language. The feature recognition procedure is stored as a doubly linked list of lines with a header. The header structure has the name of the feature, the number of lines in the template, a pointer to its first line, and pointers to the symbol tables of variables, standard functions, and math functions. The line structure contains the label (if present), the statement (which is a structure), and pointers to the next and previous lines. The statement structure has the template text (in a 2D array such that each row has one string) and the number of strings. The `variable` structure has the name of the variable, its type, a `union` that stores the value of the variable, and pointers to the left and right subtrees. Currently the value can be an integer, a float, a pointer to a face, edge, or vertex structure, or a vector.

The `function` structure contains the name of the function, the type of the function, pointer to the actual function, and pointers to the right and left subtree. Separating functions from actual calls like this serves many purposes. It makes it easy to change the front end name of the function; for instance, if `PrintLine` is a function provided by the language, its name can be changed to `Print` without any change to the actual function called.

The syntax of the language is similar to C in many respects. Every statement has to end with a semicolon `;`. Comments can be placed in the code between $ signs. Variable names may have numerals or special characters. All variables have to be declared using the reserved word VAR and by explicitly calling out the type, for example,

```
VAR circ_edge Edge;
```

Declarations may be made anywhere in the code. All variables have global scope. All the control blocks (if, `elseif`, `else`, `while`, `do-while`) must lie between independent curly bracket pairs (`{` and `}`). Nesting of structures is allowed. Function calls are made similar to C. Additional details can be found in Sreevalsan (1990).

10.7.3 Feature Recognition Functions

The built-in feature recognition functions of the interpreted language hide data structure traversals and other such details from the creator of the templates for interactive and automatic recognition. Both geometric reasoning and user interaction functions are included. For example, `ShareConvexEdge` is a geometric reasoning function, while `PickEdge` is a user interaction function.

The following is a description of the high-level functions for facilitating the definition of feature recognition procedures. This set has proved to be adequate for recognizing simple common features, such as holes, pockets, slots, bosses, and ribs, and for providing a simple user interface. In each description the expected argument types are indicated using ANSI C like notation.

`PickEdge(EdgeName e)`
    To process interactive picking of edges from display on screen.
`PickFace(FaceName f)`
    Processes interactive picking of faces from display on the screen. Returns error if attempt to assign to different variable type is made. Two edges belonging to the face have to be picked. Infinite loop until valid face is picked.

`PickVertex(VertexName v)`
Processes interactive picking of vertices from the screen. Converts picked point to world coordinates. To check if the picked point is valid, traverses vertex list, applies view transform and compares the coordinates.

`SetHighlight(Color c)`
Sets highlight color to given color.

`HighlightEdge(EdgeName e, Color c)`
Draws edge in the given color.

`HighlightFace(FaceName f, Color c)`
Draws the edges of the face in the given color.

`HighlightVertex(VertexName v, Color c)`
Marks the given vertex by drawing a box around it in the given color.

`RefreshEdge(EdgeName e)`
Draws the edge in white.

`RefreshFace(FaceName f)`
Draws all the edges of the given face in white.

`RefreshScreen( )`
Draws the whole wire frame in white.

`Print(String s)`
Echoes a string directly to screen. Useful to convey message to the user. Substitution of values of integer or float variables will be done if variable name is enclosed in quotes. Handles tab and newline characters.

`Read(VarName1 v1, VarName2 v2, ...)`
Reads values of the argument variables from the user.

`FaceType(FaceName f, FaceType ft, Boolean b)`
Checks if the face is of given type.

`AdjacentFaces(FaceName f1, FaceName f2, Boolean b)`
Checks if two faces are adjacent (i.e., share an edge).

`ParallelFaces(FaceName f1, FaceName f2, Boolean b)`
Checks if two faces are parallel.

`PerpendicularFaces(FaceName f1, FaceName f2, Boolean b)`
Checks if two faces are perpendicular.

`EdgeType(EdgeName e, EdgeType et, Boolean b)`
Checks if the edge is of given type.

`ParentFacesOfEdge(FaceName f1, FaceName f1, EdgeName e)`
Obtains the parent faces of the given edge.

`NumberOfLoops(FaceName f, Integer i)`
Returns the number of loops in a face.

`GetNormal(FaceName f, Vector v)`
Returns the normal vector of the given planar face.

`GetAxis(FaceName f, Vector v)`
Returns the axis of a cylindrical face.

`ParallelVectors(Vector v1, Vector v2)`
Checks to see if two vectors are parallel.

`PerpendicularVectors(Vector v1, Vector v2)`
Checks to see if two vectors are perpendicular.

`AllAdjacentFaces(FaceName f1, FaceName f2, Integer i)`
Returns all the adjacent faces of a given face (in the second argument) and their total number.

`GetFaceList(FaceType f1, FaceName f2, Integer i)`
Returns all the faces of the body that is of a specified type in a double linked list assigned to the second argument. If type is given as "all", then it gets all the faces of the body. The total number of faces in the output list is also returned.

`GetFromFaceList(FaceName f1, FaceName f2, Integer i, Boolean succ)`
Gets one face from a list of faces given its position in the list (head node of the list is at position 0). A Boolean value is returned to monitor the success of the operation.

`ShareConvexEdge(FaceName f1, FaceName f2, Integer i)`
Checks to see if two faces share a convex edge.

`ShareConcaveEdge(FaceName f1, FaceName f2, Integer i)`
Checks to see if two faces share a concave edge.

`ShareSmoothEdge(FaceName f1, FaceName f2, Integer i)`
Checks to see if two faces share a smooth edge.

`AllFacesSharingConvexEdge(FaceName f1, FaceName f2, Integer i)`
Gets all the faces that share a convex edge with a given face and their total number.

`AllFacesSharingConcaveEdge(FaceName f1, FaceName f2, Integer i)`
Gets all the faces that share a concave edge with a given face and their total number.

`AllFacesSharingSmoothEdge(FaceName f1, FaceName f2, Integer i)`
Gets all the faces that share a smooth edge with a given face and their total number.

`GetEdgeList(EdgeType f1, EdgeName f2, Integer i)`
Returns all the edges of the body that are of a specified type in a doubly linked list.

`GetFromEdgeList(EdgeName e1, EdgeName e2, Integer i, Boolean succ)`
Gets one edge from a list of edges given its position in the list (head node of the list is at position 0). A Boolean value is returned to monitor the success of the operation.

`VerticesOfEdge(EdgeName e, VertexName v)`
Returns the start and end vertices of an edge in a list.

`GetFromVertexList(VertexName v1, VertexName v2, Integer i, Boolean succ)`

Gets one vertex from a list of vertices given its position in the list (head node of the list is at position 0). A Boolean value is returned to monitor the success of the operation.

`AllIncidentEdges(VertexName v, EdgeName e)`

Gets all the edges that are incident on a given vertex in a doubly linked list.

`AllIncidentFaces(VertexName v, FaceName f)`

Gets all the faces that share a given vertex in a doubly linked list.

`AdjacentVertices(VertexName v1, VertexName v2)`

Gets all the vertices that are adjacent to a given vertex in a doubly linked list.

`DistanceBetweenParallelFaces(FaceName f1, FaceName f2, Float f, Boolean b)`

Computes and returns the distance between two given parallel, planar faces. Returns error if the faces are not parallel.

`DistanceBetweenPoints(Vector v1, Vector v2, Float f, Boolean b)`

Computes and returns the distance between two given points.

10.7.4 Examples

A user can write a template for interactive or automatic feature recognition using the interpreted language, predefined recognition functions, and (sometimes) additional user-defined functions. Before writing any code, the user needs to identify the geometric characteristics of the feature for which the code is to be written. For example, a through-hole can be found by looking for two circular convex edges that share a common cylindrical face. The actual details of the template may vary according to the nature of the geometric modeler used and the way it represents its entities. For example, a cylinder may have three faces in one modeler (the top and bottom planar faces and the cylindrical face) and four in another (the cylindrical face split into two). As discussed before, the database on which the recognition is based has been standardized. Different solid modelers can be used if we translate their database to this standard format so that the same templates will work for various solid modelers. The time to create and debug a new template is not very high if the geometric and topological properties are clear.

Two example templates, coded in the interpreted language, are given in this section. Both templates recognize through-hole features. Figure 10.33 gives the code for interactive recognition, while Figure 10.34 gives the code for automatic recognition. In interactive recognition the user picks a circular edge, which he or she suspects to be part of the hole to be recognized. The procedures in the template determine whether or not a hole exists at the picked edge. If the result is positive, the feature is highlighted; otherwise, an error message is displayed. In automatic feature recognition the entire model has to be searched to find all circular edges. Then each edge is investigated to determine if there is a hole there. All hole features found in the model are highlighted. Obviously there is much in common between the two templates.

```
VAR circ_edge Edge;
VAR face1 Face;
VAR face2 Face;
VAR entryFace Face;
VAR exitFace Face;
VAR cylFace1 Face;
VAR cylFace2 Face;
VAR true int;
VAR nl int;
pickedge: Print(\n Pick the circular edge on the entry face of the hole
\n);
do { $ The user will stay in this loop till a circular edge has been picked
$
    PickEdge(circ_edge); $ The picked edge is stored in circ_edge $
    EdgeType(circ_edge, Circle, true); $ Check the type of the edge geom-
etry $
    if(true != 1) {
        Print(\n The edge picked has to be circular. Try again \n);
        RefreshEdge(circ_edge); $ Redraws the highlighted edge in plain
color $
    }
} while(true != 1);
$ This template assumes that the entry face has to be a planar face. This
restriction is not necessary $
ParentFacesOfEdge(circ_edge, face1, face2); $ get the parent faces $
FaceType(face1, plane, true);
$ The following structure just assigns more readable names by identifying
the planar and cylindrical faces form the parent faces of circ_edge $
if(true != 1) {
    entryFace = face2; cylFace1 = face1;
}
else {
    entryFace = face1; cylFace1 = face2;
}
$ The entry face of a hole has to have at least two loops. The following
structure will validate the pick $
NumberOfLoops(entryFace, nl);
if(nl < 2) {
    RefreshScreen();
    Print(This cannot be an edge of a thru-hole. Do it again \n);
}
$ The circular edge of a thru-hole in its entry face is necessarily a con-
vex edge. If this is not true the edge picked cannot be right $
ShareConvexEdge(entryFace, cylFace1, true);
if(true != 1) {
    RefreshScreen();
    Print(This cannot be an edge of a thru-hole. Do it again \n);
    goto pickedge; $ The user is forced to repeat his pick $
}
VAR face_normal Vector;
VAR cyl_axis Vector;
$ The following check is to make sure that the thru-hole is straight. For
this to be true the normal of the entry face and the axis of the cylin-
drical face of the hole have to be parallel $
GetNormal(entryFace, face_normal); $ Stores the normal of entryFace in
face_normal $GetAxis(cylFace1, cyl_axis); $ Stores the axis of the cylin-
drical face in cyl_axis $
ParallelVectors(face_normal, cyl_axis, true);
if(true != 1) {
    RefreshScreen();
    Print(This cannot be an edge of a thru-hole. Do it again \n);
    goto pickedge; $ The user is forced to repeat his pick $
}
$ This is where the dependency on the solid modeler data structure is
encountered; if the cylindrical face does not have exactly three adjacent
```

Figure 10.33 Interactive recognition template for through-hole (Sreevalsan 1990; reprinted with permission)

```
faces (CADDS has four faces to a cylinder) the picked edge cannot belong
to a thru-hole $
VAR adj_face_list Face;
VAR index int;
VAR numf int;
AllAdjacentFaces(cylFace1, adj_face_list, numf);$ Gets all the adjacent
faces
of cylFace1 $
if(numf != 3) {
    RefreshScreen();
    Print(This cannot be an edge of a thru-hole. Do it again \n);
    goto pickedge; $ The user is forced to repeat his pick $
}
index = 0;
$ The following structure identifies from the adjacent faces of cylFace1
the exit face(the plane face that is not the entry face) and the other
cylindrical face. These are stored in exitFace and cylFace2 respectively $
do {
    GetFromFaceList(face1, adj_face_list, index, true);
    $ sample debug statement
    if(true != 1) { Print(ERROR in GetFromFaceList \n); stop; }
    if(face1 == entryFace) { index = index + 1; }
    else {
        FaceType(face3, plane, true);
        if(true == 1) exitFace = face1; index = index = 1; }
        else { cylFace2 = face1; index = index + 1; }
    }
} while(index < 3);
$ Another validation check is to ensure that the two cylindrical faces of
the hole share a smooth edge $
ShareSmoothEdge(cylFace2, cylFace1, true);
if(true != 1) {
    RefreshScreen();
    Print(This cannot be an edge of a thru-hole. Do it again \n);
    goto pickedge; $ The user is forced to repeat his pick $
}
$ At this point it is clear that the feature picked was indeed a thru-hole
Now the parameters of the feature can be extracted. Feed back to the user
regarding the positive identification is given $
RefreshScreen();
$ Highlighting of the two cylindrical faces will highlight the hole $
HighlightFace(cylFace1, RED);
HighlightFace(cylFace2, RED);
Print(\n THE THROUGH HOLE FEATURE IS HIGHLIGHTED IN RED \n);
VAR depth float;
VAR diameter float;
$ The depth of the thru-hole is the distance between the entry and exit
faces $
DistanceBetweenParallelFaces(entryFace, exitFace, depth);
$ The diameter of the cylindrical face is the diameter of the hole $
GetDiameter(cylFace1, diameter);
```

Figure 10.33 Interactive recognition template for through-hole (Sreevalsan 1990) (*cont.*)

10.8 PROCEDURAL DESIGN BY FEATURES

10.8.1 Feature Definition

An example of the implementation of design by features using the procedural approach and an interpretive language is provided by the first generation of the

```
VAR circ_edge Edge;
VAR circ_edge_list Edge;
VAR face1 Face;
VAR face2 Face;
VAR entryFace Face;
VAR exitFace Face;
VAR cylFace1 Face;
VAR cylFace2 Face;
VAR true int;
VAR nl int;
var index1 int;
VAR index2 int;
VAR num_circ_edges int;
VAR face_normal Vector;
VAR adj_face_list Face;
VAR numf int;
VAR features_found int;
features_found = 0;
pickedge: Print(\n Patience please. Recognition algorithm working ...\n);
$ Get all the circular edges in the model $
index1 = 0;
GetEdgeList(circle, circ_edge_list, num_circ_edges);
while(index1 < num_circ_edges) {
      $ Get the next edge from the list of circular edges in circ_edge $
      GetFromEdgeList(circ_edge, circ_edge_list, index1, true);
      ParentFacesOfEdge(circ_edge, face1, face2);
      $ This algorithm assumes that the entry face has to be a plane face. This
restriction is not necessary $
      FaceType(face1, plane, true);
      if(true != 1) {
          entryFace = face2; cylFace1 = face1;
      }
      else {
          entryFace = face1; cylFace1 = face2;
      }
$ Though at this point the plane parent face of the circular edge taken from
the list has been termed the entryFace, it is not clear if the edge is an
entity belonging to a thru-hole feature and the plane face qualifies to be
an entry face. The checks to confirm follow. If any of the checks fail then
another edge is taken from the list and the process repeated until the right
ones are found (in case of many features of the same type there will be many
qualifying entities) or none are found. $
$ The entry face of a hole has to have at least two loops. The following
structure will check for that$
      NumberOfLoops(entryFace, nl);
$ When the index is incremented and the continue statement is encountered the
loop is executed again. This is like C $
      if(nl < 2) { index1 = index1 + 1; continue; }
      $ The rest of the procedure is almost the same as that in Figure 10.33$
```

Figure 10.34 Template for automatic recognition of through-hole (Sreevalsan 1990; reprinted with permission)

ASU Features Testbed (Rogers 1987, Shah and Rogers 1994). The feature descriptions of library features consist of operation sequences that define the geometry of features, and a set of inheritance and validation rules. Another interpreted language allows users to define their own feature libraries, without modifying the code. This language was briefly discussed in Chapter 8; here we will look at the implementation in more detail.

A sample definition of a generic obround slot is shown in Figure 10.35. It is written as a text file in the interpreted language, which is translated into C, requiring no recompilation of the code. Each feature is defined by 15 properties generic to its class, labeled 1 through 15, as shown. The first five properties are feature identifier, name, type, compatible parents, and children (sub) features. The feature dimensions are divided into two types: independent/user-defined (listed in property 6) and dependent/derived (property 9). Independent dimensions are those that the user specifies at instance time. For the slot the independent parameters are `slot_width` and `slot_length`; these parameters are shown in property 6 (`User_Def_Param`). But `slot_depth` is specified as derived from something else, and as such it is listed under property 9 (`Derived_Param`). The procedure for deriving `slot_depth` is specified under property 14, inheritance rules. Before one can understand these rules, one needs to study the syntax.

To refer to parameters in a feature's definition, the following syntax is used:

```
(feature, parameter#)
```

where `feature` = `pi` refers to parent i and `feature` = `s1` to the feature itself, and `parameter#` = `aj` denotes the jth parameter in `User_Def_Param` list (property 6), `bk` to the kth parameter in the `Derived_Param` list (property 9), `lr` to the rth parameter in the `Local_Pos` list (property 7), and `os` to the sth parameter in the `Local_Orient` list (property 8).

For the feature shown, `(s1,a1)` = `slot_width`, `(s1,a2)` = `slot_length`, and `(s1,b1)` = `slot_depth`; also, `(p1,a1)` refers to the first `User_Def_Param` for the parent (block, in this case). Now the reader should be able to decipher the inheritance rules shown; for instance, the first rule says that if a certain condition is satisfied, then `(s1,b1)` = `(p1,a1)`. In other words, the `slot_width` is equal to the depth of the block (assuming that `depth` is the first parameter in the block's list).

The feature has some independent position and orientation parameters, namely the position of its center with respect to the parent center, `x-pos`, and `y-pos`, and the orientation in the parent face plane, γ. These parameters are shown in slot 7 (`Local_Pos`), and slot 8 (`Local_Orient`), respectively. The feature also must satisfy certain position and orientation constraints.

The *Feature-producing volume* (FPV) contains the implicit definition of the feature's shape in the form of a CSG tree. It is the procedure for creating the geometry corresponding to the feature. The CSG trees are constructed from a typical set of sweeps and primitives: box, cylinder, wedge frustum, solids of revolution, and linear sweeping. Combinations of these solids can be specified in the feature language along with Boolean operators. Positive volume features (blocks or bosses) result from unions or intersections and negative volume features (pockets or holes) are obtained by subtraction.

Within the FPV lies the mapping from parameters to shape. Instructions for the map from local coordinates to global coordinates and the degrees of freedom available when positioning a feature also hard-coded in the FPV. The requisite

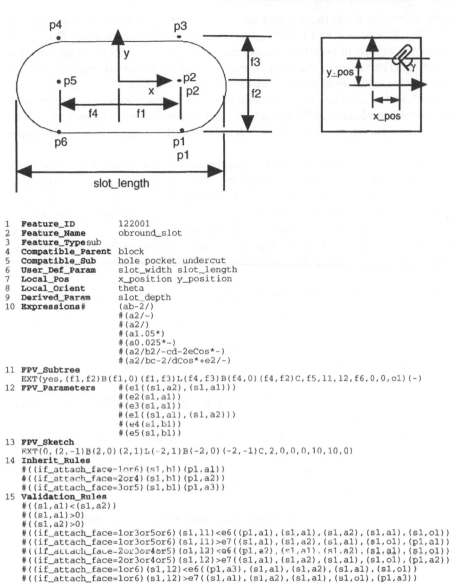

```
 1  Feature_ID        122001
 2  Feature_Name      obround_slot
 3  Feature_Type      sub
 4  Compatible_Parent block
 5  Compatible_Sub    hole pocket undercut
 6  User_Def_Param    slot_width slot_length
 7  Local_Pos         x_position y_position
 8  Local_Orient      theta
 9  Derived_Param     slot_depth
10  Expressions       # (ab-2/)
                      # (a2/~)
                      # (a2/)
                      # (a1.05*)
                      # (a0.025*~)
                      # (a2/b2/-cd-2eCos*-)
                      # (a2/bc-2/dCos*+e2/-)
11  FPV_Subtree
    EXT(yes,(f1,f2)B(f1,0)(f1,f3)L(f4,f3)B(f4,0)(f4,f2)C,f5,11,12,f6,0,0,o1)(-)
12  FPV_Parameters    # (e1((s1,a2),(s1,a1)))
                      # (e2(s1,a1))
                      # (e3(s1,a1))
                      # (e1((s1,a1),(s1,a2)))
                      # (e4(s1,b1))
                      # (e5(s1,b1))
13  FPV_Sketch
    EXT(0,(2,-1)B(2,0)(2,1)L(-2,1)B(-2,0)(-2,-1)C,2,0,0,0,10,10,0)
14  Inherit_Rules
    # ((if_attach_face=1or6)(s1,b1)(p1,a1))
    # ((if_attach_face=2or4)(s1,b1)(p1,a2))
    # ((if_attach_face=3or5)(s1,b1)(p1,a3))
15  Validation_Rules
    # ((s1,a1)<(s1,a2))
    # ((s1,a1)>0)
    # ((s1,a2)>0)
    # ((if_attach_face=1or3or5or6)(s1,11)<e6((p1,a1),(s1,a1),(s1,a2),(s1,a1),(s1,o1))
    # ((if_attach_face=1or3or5or6)(s1,11)>e7((s1,a1),(s1,a2),(s1,a1),(s1,o1),(p1,a1))
    # ((if_attach_face=2or3or4or5)(o1,12)<e6((p1,a2),(s1,a1),(s1,a2),(s1,a1),(s1,o1))
    # ((if_attach_face=2or3or4or5)(s1,12)>e7((s1,a1),(s1,a2),(s1,a1),(s1,o1),(p1,a2))
    # ((if_attach_face=1or6)(s1,12)<e6((p1,a3),(s1,a1),(s1,a2),(s1,a1),(s1,o1))
    # ((if_attach_face=1or6)(s1,12)>e7((s1,a1),(s1,a2),(s1,a1),(s1,o1),(p1,a3))
    # ((if_attach_face=2or4)(s1,11)<e6((p1,a3),(s1,a1),(s1,a2),(s1,a1),(s1,o1))
    # ((if_attach_face=2or4)(s1,11)>e7((s1,a1),(s1,a2),(s1,a1),(s1,o1),(p1,a3))
```

Figure 10.35 Sample generic feature file for an obround slot (Shah and Rogers 1994)

instructions for doing these operations are specified in slot 10 (Expressions), 11 (FPV_Subtree), and 12 (FPV_Parameters) of the feature file. The expressions are written in postfix notation. For example, (ab-2/) is interpreted as ((*a-b*)/2). The values of the expressions listed under 10 are assigned to variables ei, where i is the serial order of the expression. Therefore $e1$ = (ab-2/), $e2$ = (a2/), and so on. The FPV_Parameters (12) use these expressions to compute parameters needed for defining the FPV_Subtree. The value of each expression in 12 is assigned to fi, where i is the serial order of the expression. For example, f1 = (e1((s1,a2),(s1,a1))).

The reason for using these intermediate expressions is that the construction of the geometry of a feature can become complex, requiring computations involving user-defined parameters (a-list), derived parameters (b-list), local position parameters (l-list), the local orientation parameters (o-list), arithmetic, and trigonometric functions. To simplify this procedure, it is helpful to be able to define new variables. Each item in the expression list can be thought of as an arithmetic function that may take multiple variables as input but returns only one variable.

Returning now to the FPV for the slot, we determine that the geometry must satisfy the following constraints:

1. The opposite sides of the slot must be parallel.
2. The end radius must be half the width.
3. The sides must be planar and the ends cylindrical.
4. The depth of the slot must be inherited from it's parent block thickness (it is a through slot).
5. The slot's top face should be coplanar with one face from a block that the user selects (constrained DOF along z-axis).
6. The z-axis of the slot must be perpendicular to the selected block face (constrained DOF about x-axis and y-axis).

Constraints 1, 2, and 3 are hard-coded into the profile definition used for extruding the feature volume. Constraint 4 (i.e., slot-depth = depth-of-block) is specified by Inherit_Rules (slot 14). Constraints 5 and 6 are coded by FPV position and orientation parameters, which are derived in accordance with the procedure specified under FPV_Parameters (slot 12). In the example list, f1 = e1(s1,a2),(s1,a1) means to execute the first expression (e1) with a = (s1,a1) and b = (s1,a1). Since e1 is specified as (ab-2/), we interpret it as

f1 = (slot_length - slot_width)/2

The f-parameters are then used in the definition of the profile, or primitive dimensions and position under FPV_Subtree slot:

EXT(yes,(f1,f2)B(f1,0)(f1,f3)L(f4,f3)B(f4,0)(f4,f2)C,b1,11,12,0,0,0,o1)(-)

EXT stands for extrusion; it is followed by a string of parameters defining the profile curves, in a "standardized" order. The curve description is the second argument in the FPV. That is, (f1, f2) ... (f4, f2) C is a list of ordered points and curve instructions (lines, backward or counterclockwise arcs, forward arcs, and splines) for the profile. Position and orientation are the last six arguments in the FPV. The last six items within the FPV are the local position and local orientation of the feature in local coordinates. The local coordinates depend on the feature type and the attach face type.

10.8.2 Model Management

In design by features, the generic feature definitions, such as the one shown in Figure 10.35, are stored in a feature library. When modeling a part, the designer instances features from the library, which translates into specifying the independent dimensions and location parameters, and the attachment to another feature on the model. The instance data for an obround slot is shown in Figure 10.36. We need to read this data in conjunction with the generic definition given in Figure 10.35.

While positioning a new feature (other than the first feature) in local coordinates, the user must select an adjacent feature, a face on that feature, a face on the new feature, and then a local position and orientation on the face. The first feature is positioned in world coordinates. Subfeatures are positioned on faces of their parents, such as a hole on a block.

Thus there are two basic types of relationships that must be captured: parent-child and adjacency. These relationships are conveniently stored in feature relationship graphs of the type shown in Figure 10.37. The figure depicts the adjacency relations by a dashed line, and the child-parent links by full lines for a conrod using the features described in Chapter 5. The graph is needed when deleting or modifying features, or changing feature positions.

Default coordinate systems (LCS) are associated with features and their faces. The transformation matrices for such features are

$$[M_i] = \{[X_1][Y_1][Z_1][T_1]\}\{ [X_2][Y_2][Z_2][[T_2]]\}\{[X_3][Y_3][Z_3][[T_3]]\} [M_{i-1}]$$

```
1   Data_ID          004
2   Generic_type     122001
3   Parent_ID        002
4   Children_list     nil
5   User_Def_Param   0.25 1.00
6   Local_Pos        0.5.1.25
7   Local_Orient     90
8   FPV_ptr          27
```

Figure 10.36 Instance data example

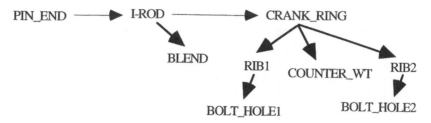

Figure 10.37 Feature relationship graph

M_{i-1} is the transformation matrix for the reference (adjacent) feature's local coordinate system, M_i is the matrix for the feature being positioned (target feature); X, Y, Z, and T are the rotation and translation matrices. There are three sets of coordinate transformations, designated by subscripts *1, 2* and *3*. The transformations take place in the following order: feature coordinate system to its entity cordinate system for the reference feature (subscript 3), reference entity coordinate system to target entity coordinate system (subscript 2), and target entity cordinate system to target feature coordinates (subscript 3). It must be noted that a reference feature can itself be positioned on another feature, which in turn can be positioned on another feature and so on. Hence transformation chains can be represented as

$$[M_i] = [M_{i-1}][M_{i-2}] \ldots [M_1][M_0]$$

where subscript 0 refers to the first feature which is positioned in world coordinates.

Constraints may be placed on how a feature is used through validation rules. These rules enhance the modeling environment through size and placement restrictions on features. The rule syntax is similar to the inheritance rules language, except that algebraic comparisons are supported. While the FPV can constrain the degrees of freedom for a feature, it cannot put a constraint on minimum or maximum values of size or position.

For example, the obround slot requires these additional constraints that the FPV cannot represent: the length must be greater than the width, the length and width must be positive, and the entire slot profile must fit within the block face. These constraints are all represented in the validation rules of Figure 10.35. The geometry construction commands are synthesized from all the FPVs of all the features and written out as a text file in a neutral format. Translators can be developed to transform the commands to specific commands required by various commercial systems; that is, program files can be generated to create or modify solid models through their proprietary programming interfaces. Further implementation details can be found in (Shah and Rogers 1991).

Thus the methodology described above accomplishes designing with user-defined features. The problem of modifying code and recompiling is avoided by means of procedures driven by data available in the various slots of the feature class. Inheritance rules also serve to facilitate change propagation even after the initial position is determined.

The procedural approach implemented via an interpreted language has been used by many other modelers. The advantages and disadvantages of the approach have been identified as follows:

- The methodology is quite general as users can define their own generic features without making changes to the code by virtue of the interpreted feature definition language.
- The inheritance rules/procedures defined create a unidirectional chain for change propagation and for initial derivation of derived parameters and entity local coordinate system.
- Conflicts in parameter values are avoided by using a parameter hierarchy.
- Special purpose rules are needed to specify how a feature or part needs to be attached/assembled to other features or parts. Unfortunately, this leads to a combinatorial explosion of possible combinations.
- Constraints cannot be applied mutually between two entities.

10.9 FEATURE-GEOMETRY PROTOCOL

In the previous section the system presented relies on static communication between itself and geometric modelers, which uses the latter's programming interface language. These languages are not well suited for use by application programs, because not only are they nonstandard, but they are sometimes too low level for feature applications. This section describes a dynamic interface between generic feature based applications and geometric modeling kernels, such as ACIS (Spatial 1993) and Parasolid (EDS 1994). This involves the creation of commonly needed geometric computation and interrogation functions, implemented in a modeler independent language. Since geometric modelers differ in the functionality that they provide and feature applications vary in the level of geometric operations that they can support internally, a multi layered communication architecture is required.

10.9.1 High-Level Functions

What are some common, generic functions needed by feature-based systems? Feature applications require interrogation of geometric data, computations involving interrelationships of geometric entities, and geometric reasoning. We can examine the needs of systems outlined in the previous chapters in order to derive functions listed in Table 10.3, which represent commonly used geometric construction, computation, graphic, and interrogation functions.

Table 10.3 Generic high level functions used in feature modeling

Construction Functions	Graphic Functions
Create feature volume	Pick feature (in order to do some operation)
Position feature on another feature, or geometric entity	Highlight selected features
Perform Boolean operations	Display feature parameters
Perform object co-ordinate transformations	Display feature hierarchy
Move feature	Show local coordinate system
Modify feature dimensions	Prompt the user
Delete feature	Confirm an operation
Copy feature	Perform viewing transformations

Computation Functions	Interrogation Functions
Select feature satisfying a condition (e.g., find holes of same diameter)	Get faces of body
Find distance or angle between features	Find all adjacent faces to a given face
Determine the face normal	Determine the face type (planar, cylindrical, etc.)
Determine if two faces are parallel or perpendicular	Find faces that lie on a common surface
Test for inadvertent intersections	Determine if faces/edges/vertices are adjacent
Determine overall shape (rotational, prismatic, aspect ratio, etc.)	Find principal feature axes
Determine relative orientations of feature axes	Find if faces belong to same surface
Find convex hull	List geometric entities of a type associated with a feature
Discover feature patterns (holes at regular intervals, etc.)	Find nested features
Determine axes of symmetry	List features associated with a geometric entity
Determine tool access	Give parametrized shape information
Decompose feature volumes into convex units	Determine if face is retained during Boolean operation
	Retrieve faces of intersection from Boolean operation

Applications must not only access the data of geometric modelers, but also their functions. For this reason, the interaction between the modelers must be dynamic, and must also allow two-way exchange of data. Further clarification of dynamic interfaces is given in the next section. We may choose to support many of the functions shown in Table 10.3 within the application. By providing a common geometric computation toolkit, we not only can save the application developer some effort, but we also can free him or her from the workings of the geometric modeler.

10.9.2 Communication Mode

In Chapter 8 we discussed static and dynamic interfaces between features and solid modelers. In dynamic interfacing, the solid modeler is used as a library of functions under the supervision of a controlling program (the feature modeler). This method provides complete access to solid modeling functions. Information is passed to the solid modeler as arguments by the feature modeler. Both programs run in parallel. All the control is held by the feature application. This is very desirable so that all the changes to the geometric model can be transferred upward and be monitored.

Standardizing dynamic communications with solid modelers would make feature applications independent of specific solid modelers. The CAM-I industry consortium recognized this need many years ago when it began its *Application Interface Specification*, or AIS effort (CAM-I 1990). AIS was originally developed as a library of procedural calls to solid modelers. Further work by CAM-I explored an object-oriented approach to an AIS. Variations in solid modelers were addressed by categorizing modeler functionality. An AIS entity class will only work when certain category requirements are met. Several research groups have implemented an AIS, and there are numerous commercial products that provide an AIS-type of interface. As of this writing, no commercial or research system has fully tested all aspects of the AIS approach, since the implementations have involved just one solid modeler (Magleby and Gunn 1992, Hummel and Wolf 1990).

Recently the need of dynamic communication has also been recognized by the international standards committees developing STEP. However, at this time the STEP initiative only involves development of low-level functions for reading and writing standardized data (PDES 1991); the initiative goes by the name of SDAI (*STEP Data Access Interface*). So far SDAI is too low-level to be useful in creating a standardized dynamic interface between feature applications and solid modelers.

The Application Procedural Interface (API) for ACIS provides a fairly generic set of procedures for creating and manipulating ACIS models. What is not generic in the API is that these routines have pointers to ACIS entities for arguments. The API is thus at a lower level of detail than an AIS layer. Pherwani (1993) implemented an AIS-like interface on top of ACIS API in such a way that it might be possible to replace ACIS with Parasolid, although the work to support Parasolid is still in progress. Both modelers have similar functionality and types of entities but are not identical. This feature-geometry toolkit is presented in the following sections.

10.9.3 System Architecture

Pherwani's geometric tools provide support for commonly needed functions through a standard dynamic interface with a core solid modeler. The layers of the interface are shown by the shaded regions in Figure 10.38. The system is organized into four layers between various feature applications on one side and various solid modelers on the other. At the lowest level is the *Procedural Interface*, a layer on top of the solid modeler designed to access the solid modeler's procedural or kernel interface (API for ACIS, KI for Parasolid) to create entities

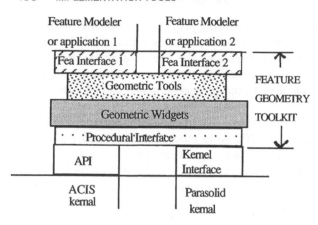

Figure 10.38 Architecture of feature-geometry system

or query the model. At the highest level are the *Feature Interfaces* which include routines that are specific to each application. The two middle layers, which are object-oriented, contain classes that are labeled *Geometric Tools* and the *Geometric Widgets*; the difference between them is the level of functionality—Widgets are lower level (more general) than Tools.

The Procedural Interface is built along the lines of CAMI-AIS philosophy. It consists of a set of solid modeling functions, which form a minimal set to suffice requirements of the supported applications. The procedures call functions of the underlying solid modeler. The difference in functionality between solid modelers restricts the universality of the interface tools. For accessing the object-oriented class instances, the Procedural Interface makes use of a pointer mapping system. The interface takes string identifiers from the application above it, and maps these identifiers to the class pointers. The mapping is done via a pointer mapping class, the instances of which define many-to-one mappings. That is, many string identifiers can map to one class pointer.

The Geometric Widgets form an intermediate object-oriented layer between the Geometric Tools and the low-level Procedural Interface functions. This library contains basic classes of objects needed by feature applications. Unlike the Procedural Interface, the functions of Widgets do not form a minimal set of functions but overlap in functionality. Knowledge of the structure of the underlying solid modeler is not required. Although the classes may call routines to process other topological entities present within the Tools, this is transparent to the application above. An example of a function at this level is edge-concavity, which tells the application if an edge is convex, concave, or flat. The function is required by feature recognition and process planning.

The Widget classes contain a character identifier for entities within the solid modeler. The geometric entities in the solid modeler are accessed via the solid modeler interface. Another instance of the data mapping class is used for accessing instances of an entity given the character identifier.

The Geometric Tools layer contains the high-level geometric reasoning, computation, construction, and interrogation functions needed by generic feature applications. However, this layer does not contain any explicit feature information, nor any geometric data. The classes have pointers to the Geometric Widgets of the widget library. All functionality of the Geometric Tools is derived from Widgets. An identifier mapping class is present as a part of the Geometric Tools. The identifier mapping class is similar to the pointer mapping class, and it is used to identify geometric entities within the Geometric Tools given the identifiers used by the feature application. This is done to permit the tools to organize the geometry independently of the feature application. It also allows different versions of the same application to interact with the tools.

10.9.4 ACIS Implementation

The conceptual design outlined above was first implemented for the ACIS solid modeler and several feature-based applications (Pherwani 1993, Rogers 1994). ACIS is an open architecture geometric modeler implemented in C++. It consists of various topological, mathematical, and geometric entities. Topological entities include BODY, FACE, EDGE, VERTEX; geometric entities include CURVE, SURFACE, PLANE; mathematical entities include VECTOR, POSITION, PARAMETER. All the entities are associated with functions, and each of the functions is accessible from within the environment. The environment is object oriented and allows development of multiple applications on it, object oriented or procedural. The entities within ACIS are at different levels, and the higher-level entity functions are built on the lower-level enity functions. ACIS also provides some high level functions built to provide an intuitive geometrical interface. The API from ACIS provides an extensible set of routines to create and manipulate data. Sample routines include

```
api_make_cuboid()  api_start_modeller()  api_mk_ed_line()
api_unite()        api_save_entity()     api_mk_ed_ellipse()
```

This discussion assumes that the reader is familiar with ACIS. The procedural interface code is mostly a one-to-one mapping from a new subroutine to an API subroutine. Arguments to the two types of subroutines are similar. The main difference between one of the procedural interface routines and an ACIS API routine is the BODY (or FACE, etc.) input argument. In a procedural interface routine, a string body_name (or face_name) is the input argument. Then, within the procedural interface routine, a directory is consulted that, given a body_name, will return a BODY pointer. The API routine is then called with the BODY pointer as an input argument.

The reason for using body_name as opposed to BODY pointers is to maintain the layers and intent of the code. By keeping the information about BODY (and other) pointers confined within the procedural interface layer, the rest of the code doesn't know that it is working with the ACIS kernel. Thus Parasolid or another kernel can be inserted, in theory, by replacing the procedural interface (api_routines.cxx, topology.cxx, create.cxx, and properties.cxx) with corresponding calls to Parasolid's procedural interface. Problems could arise in cases where a match in routines is unavailable.

Application programmers can add new API routines. For example, many topology inquiries of the sort body_lump (what lumps are in the given body) are not covered, and creation of auxiliary geometry (e.g., the "positions" needed to make an edge in api_mk_ed_line) is not supported via the existing API. Rather than adding new API routines, the implementation utilizes the direct interface to the kernel, using the methods associated with the topology, geometry, and other classes. The advantage of adding new API routines is that the rollback mechanism, journaling, and replay will all work with any new API routine, just as if it were defined by the ACIS developer, Spatial Technology. If, however, the direct interface to the ACIS kernel is used, the rollback functionality (and others) will not be available.

Procedural Interface   The Procedural Interface contains four basic types of functions: creation/deletion, topological, queries, and modifications; the complete list can be found in Appendix C. The first type of function involves the *creation and deletion* of entities. Each entity may have more than one way of being created and initialized. For example a vector may be initialized by supplying it three real values. Alternatively, it can be initialized as the difference between two positions. All entities that are created are not deleted automatically. Deletion functions delete it from the modeler and also remove it from the data-mapping directory. Create and delete functions exist for all classes in ACIS. Some of the derived classes can be deleted by deleting the parent class.

The *topological functions* are a set of functions by which the relationships between various topological entities can be queried. Examples of such functions are edge_start, which returns the character identifier of the starting vertex of the edge. The functions return the parent entities, first-child entities and the next-sibling entities of a list. Examples of function returning a parent entity is edge_face, which returns the face in which the edge lies. Face_edge returns the first edge in the data structure of the face. This is a child-returning function. Edge_next returns the next edge in the data structure of the face.

The *properties functions* returns evaluations of the topological entities. Example of such functions is face_normal, which returns the character identifier of the vector representing the face normal. Vector_x, Vector_y, Vector_z return the *x*, *y*, *z* components of the vector. The properties functions do not modify the class instances.

The *modification functions* perform operations on the topological entities and on the modeler. Examples of operations on topological entities are Boolean operations, sweeping face around axis. Examples of operations on the modeler are start_modeler, roll_back, note_modeler_state. Roll_back takes the modeler back to a previous state, and roll_forward returns it to its present state.

Each function returns a logical value that expresses the success of the operation. The operation may fail due to various reasons, such as an improper identifier or failure of the ACIS function. The functions of Procedural Interface have a one-to-one map with the ACIS functions. For substituting another modeler the functions may have to be modified. Also depending on the functionality of the modeler, some functions may have to be added or deleted if the entire functionality of that modeler needs to be used.

The procedural interface uses string identifiers to access that entities in the solid model. For example, in the function

```
body_lump(arg1(string), arg2(string))
```

arg1 and arg2 are string identifiers; arg1 is the identifier used to access the body within the solid modeler. After the lump of the body is accessed, arg2 is set as the identifier for it. The lump can then be accessed using the string argument arg2. The string arguments can be supplied by the user or the application.

Widgets In the popular X window system, "widgets" are pre-engineered user interface components such as menus and buttons that hide the intricacies of the lower levels of X. Complete user interfaces can be created as combinations of widget instances. By analogy, widgets in our work are C++ classes that use Procedural Interface functions. The goal of the widget classes is to represent the basic topology of the model in a separate layer from the geometric model. The classes implemented are shown in Figure 10.39 and summarized below:

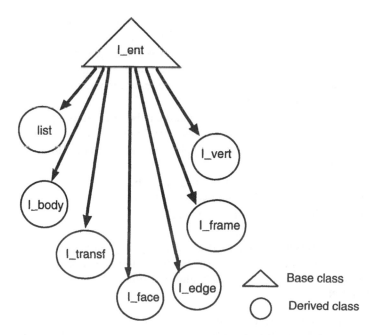

Figure 10.39 Widget class hierarchy (Pherwani 1993; reprinted with permission)

I_ent	This class is an abstract class and no direct instances of this class are used. It is used to manage the string identifiers for interacting with Procedural Interface.
I_body	This is a child of I_ent and represents the topological body. The body class is associated with various methods of construction. It is also associated with: various topological functions for accessing faces, edges, and vertices in the body; transformation routines such as move, rotate, rotate about a particular axis, and apply particular transformation created separately with the transformation entity routines; and various modifications such as Boolean operations unite, subtract, and intersect.
I_face	This entity represents a face. It is associated with construction routines as extracting it from a body, or creating it from a loop of edges. It contains topological functions such as parent_body() which returns the body of which it is a part, all_edges() which return all its edges, and all_adj_faces() which returns the adjacent faces of this face. Other functions return properties of a face. Face_type returns the type of face: planar, cylindrical, or conical. Face_normal returns the normal of a planar face. Face_center returns the geometric center of a face.
I_edge	I_edge represents an edge and can be constructed as a straight segment of a line joining two vertices or as a forward curve given the center or as a backward curve joining two vertices given a center.
I_vert	I_vert represents a vertex and can be constructed giving three real numbers representing its position. Topological functions include parent_edge which returns the edge the vertex belongs to, faces_at which returns all faces meeting at the vertex, and coords which returns three real numbers that give the position of the vertex.
I_transf	I_transf is a transformation and can be created as a translation or a rotation given appropriate real numbers as arguments. I_transf supports matrix algebra such as the matrix multiplication operation.
I_frame	I_frame is a coordinate frame and can be created by real numbers defining a position and two axes. The function ret_transf returns the transformation of a frame.

The classes do not represent an exhaustive set of topological classes. They are closer to the notion of a minimum set. For example, additional ACIS topological entities include LUMP, SHELL, LOOP, and additional Parasolid entities REGION, LOOP, and FIN.

Tools   The geometric toolkit layer consists of classes that are well suited to feature applications. The foundation of this layer is the tri_rep class. The

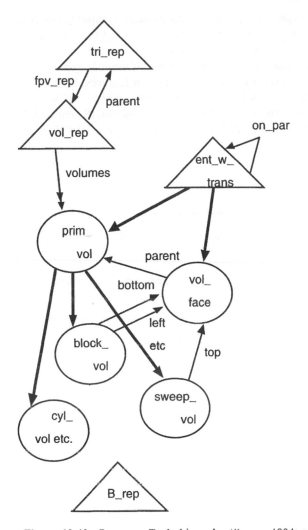

Figure 10.40 Geometry Tools hierarchy (Rogers 1994; reprinted with permission)

ent_w_trans base class supports relative positioning of faces and volumes on other entities. As shown in Figure 10.40, it is the superclass for vol_face and prim_vol; the latter entity is in turn a superclass for block_vol, cyl_vol, and sweep_vol, and of other common geometric construction primitives. The attribute on_par points to another instance of this same class.

Note that the B_rep class does not point to a set of tri_reps. The actual structure of the feature model is left to the feature modeler itself. The feature modeler controls the existence of a feature library; the Geometry Tools do not know anything about a feature library, nor about how the library parameters control the instance geometry, and how a feature is "added" into the feature model (as a child of one other feature volume, or perhaps attached to a face). The Geometry Tools layer only requires that an ent_w_trans be positioned on another ent_w_trans, and it expects the geometric parameters as input to create a tri_rep. In the constructor for each type of prim_vol (block_vol, cyl_vol, etc.), the link to the volume's vol_faces is established.

The Tools layer classes provide both an unevaluated volumetric representation and an evaluated, face-based representation suitable for features. It supports the relative positioning of entities, and the link from these entities to Widget layer entities, which in turn map to specific modeler entities (ACIS, Parasolid, etc.). The C++ header files for Geometry Tools are given in Table 10.4 (Rogers 1994).

Table 10.4 C++ headers geo_tools.hxx

```
class tri_rep   // represents a feature's geometry
{
public:
   tri_rep(tri_rep* on, int vol_no, int face_no, vol_struct&
all_volumes);
   tri_rep* copy();
   ~tri_rep();
   vol_rep* return_vol() { return fpv_rep; };
protected:
   vol_rep* fpv_rep;
   face_rep* eval_rep;
};


class vol_rep   // representation of the unevaluated volumes
{
public:
   vol_rep(tri_rep* of, vol_rep* on, int vol_no, int face_no,
           vol_struct& all_volumes);
   vol_rep* copy();
   ~vol_rep();
   tri_rep* ret_parent() { return parent; };
   gen_list_vol* return_list() { return volumes; };
   I_body* combine(logical*, char*, char*);
protected:
   tri_rep* parent;
   gen_list_vol* volumes;
};


class face_rep  // representation of tri_rep's faces in model
{
public:
   face_rep(tri_rep* of);
   face_rep* copy();
   ~face_rep();
```

```
   tri_rep* ret_parent() { return parent; };
   gen_list_face* return_list() { return faces; };
   vol_face* ret_face(int);
protected:
   tri_rep* parent;
   gen_list_face* faces;
};


class B_rep        // the current evaluated model
{
public:
   B_rep();
   void add(tri_rep*, char*, char*);
   I_body* return_body() { return obj_body; };
   void draw(int);
   void save(FILE*);
protected:
   I_body* obj_body;
};


class gen_item_vol    // a volume in a list
{
   friend class gen_list_vol;
public:
   gen_item_vol(prim_vol*);
   prim_vol& ret_el();
   gen_item_vol* get_next();
   void set_next(gen_item_vol*);
   char* save();
protected:
   prim_vol* item;
   gen_item_vol* next;
};


class gen_list_vol    // a list of volumes
{
public:
   gen_list_vol() { front = NULL; back = NULL; count = 0; };
   void add(prim_vol*);
   void replace(prim_vol*, int);
   int return_count() { return count; };
   prim_vol& operator [] (int);
   logical is_empty();
   char** save();
protected:
    int count;
   gen_item_vol* front;
   gen_item_vol* back;
   gen_item_vol*get_item(int);
};
```

Table 10.4 (continued)

```
class gen_item_face    // a face in a list
{
   friend class gen_list_face;
public:
   gen_item_face(vol_face*);
   vol_face& ret_el();
   gen_item_face* get_next();
   void set_next(gen_item_face*);
   char* save();
protected:
   vol_face* item;
   gen_item_face* next;
};


class gen_list_face    // a list of faces
{
public:
   gen_list_face() { front = NULL; back = NULL; };
   void add(vol_face*);
   void replace(vol_face*, int);
   vol_face& operator [] (int);
   logical is_empty();
   char** save();
protected:
   gen_item_face* front;
   gen_item_face* back;
   gen_item_face* get_item(int);
};


class ent_w_trans    // entity with associated transformation
{                    // an important parent class
public:
   ent_w_trans(ent_w_trans* parent);
   ent_w_trans* on() { return on_par; };
   void set_on(ent_w_trans* parent_ent) { on_par =
parent_ent; };
   virtual I_transf& ret_transf() = 0;
protected:
   ent_w_trans* on_par;
   virtual void globalize() = 0;
   virtual void in_on_coods() = 0;
};


class prim_vol: public ent_w_trans
// any type of primitive volume
{
```

```
      friend class tri_rep;
public:
   prim_vol(logical bool, char* given_name, ent_w_trans*
on_ent, double pos[], double orient[]);
      void set_body(I_body* abody) { prim_body = abody; };
      I_body* return_body() { return prim_body; };
      void in_on_coods();
      void globalize();
      virtual prim_vol* copy() = 0;
      I_transf& ret_transf();
      void transform(double orientation[], double position[]);
      logical bool_sign() { return sign; } ;
      char* is_a() { return name; };
      void unite_to(I_body* model_body){ prim_body->unite_with
(*model_body); };
      void sub_from(I_body* model_body){ prim_body-
>subtract_from (*model_body);};
protected:
      I_body* prim_body;
      logical sign;
      double position[3];
      double orientation[3];
      char name[10];
      void fix_trans();
};

class vol_face: public ent_w_trans      // any type of face
{
public:
      vol_face(prim_vol* par, I_face* the_face, int num, int
axis[]);
      void globalize();
      void in_on_coods();
      void create_transf();
      I_transf& ret_transf(){ return *face_transf; };
protected:
      face_rep* parent;
      I_face* prim_face;
      I_transf* face_transf;
      int no;
      int axis_pos_dir[4];
};

class block_vol: public prim_vol   // a block primitive
{
public:
      block_vol(ent_w_trans*parent_cood, double param[], double
position [], double orientation[], logical bool);
      double parameter(int);
```

Table 10.4 (continued)

```
    prim_vol* copy();
protected:
    double height;
    double depth;
    double width;
};


class wedge_vol: public prim_vol    // a wedge primitive
{
public:
    wedge_vol(ent_w_trans* parent_cood, double param[], double
position[], double orientation[], logical bool);
    double parameter(int);
    prim_vol* copy();
protected:
    double x_dist;
    double y_dist;
    double height;
};


class frustum_vol: public prim_vol    // a frustum primitive
{
public:
    frustum_vol(ent_w_trans* parent_cood, double param[],
double position[], double orientation[], logical bool);
    double parameter(int);
    prim_vol* copy();
protected:
    vol_face* bottom;
    vol_face* top;
    vol_face* bottom_in;
    vol_face* top_in;
    vol_face* curved;
    double bottom_dia;
    double top_dia;
    double height;
};


class cyl_vol: public prim_vol    // a cylinder primitive
{
public:
    cyl_vol(ent_w_trans* parent_cood, double param[], double
position [], double orientation[], logical bool);
    double parameter(int);
    vol_face* ret_face(int);
```

```
      prim_vol* copy();
protected:
    vol_face* bottom;
    vol_face* top;
    vol_face* bottom_in;
    vol_face* top_in;
    vol_face* curved;
    double diameter;
    double height;
};


class sweep_vol: public prim_vol
// a swept volume with profile definition
{
public:
    sweep_vol(ent_w_trans* parent_cood, int no_points, double
    pointsx [], double pointsy[], char edge_type[], double
    param, double draft, double position[], double orienta-
    tion[], logical bool, int typ);
    double parameter(int);
    int ret_num_pts() { return num_pts;};
    int ret_sweep_typ() { return sweep_typ;};
    prim_vol* copy();
protected:
    double cood_list[40][2];
    char command_list[40];
    double len_or_ang;
    double draft_ang;
    int num_pts;
    int sweep_typ;
};


class vol_struct        // input from a feature modeler
{
public:
    vol_struct(int no_volumes, int n_pts);
    int no_of_volumes;
    int_array* types;
    int_array* booleans;
    doubp_array* parameters;
    doubp_array* positions;
    doubp_array* orientation;
    int_array* no_points;
    doubp_array* points[2];
    arr_char_array* type_of_curve;
};
```

Several feature-based systems have been implemented using the dynamic interface of the geometry toolkit. These include design-by-features system, feature recognition using volume decomposition, and feature-based process planning. For the design-by-features system the following are the routines defined in the Feature Interface for this application:

void view_model(char* Brep_name)

Given a name of a B_rep model, it looks up the B_rep pointer and calls the B_rep member function draw(), which then will call an I_body member function draw(), which will call a procedural interface function to draw(), which will call a 3DVisualization function to draw a BODY. This routine is a good example of the layered code approach.

void save_model(FILE* file, char* Brep_name)

Calls the B_rep member function save(), which will call an I_body member function save(), which will call a procedural interface function to save(), which will call ACIS to save a BODY to file.

void inst_feature(Feat* i_feat)

The main feature interface routine. The Feat struct holds all of the instance attributes from the feature modeler. This routine calls to create a tri_rep in the Geo_Tools layer.

void add_to_Brep(int data_id, char* part, char* fea_typename,
                 char* Brep_name)

Calls the B_rep member function add() to add the newly created tri_rep (accessed via data_id) to the B_rep.

logical create_Brep(char* Brep_name)

Calls the B_rep constructor in the Geo_Tools.

Communications between Layers Figure 10.41 shows how the Widget constructor methods call the subroutines in the procedural interface layer. For example, create_vertex() is called by the I_vert constructor. Query functions in the procedural interface are also called by Geo_Widget methods. The existence of a method does not, of course, establish a lasting relationship between two entities. The relationship between I_ents and ACIS entities is established within the procedural interface subroutines and Widget methods via the DIR structure which provides the map between these layers. This mapping class provides a link between a string and a pointer. The current implementation uses three instances of the DIR class, with each instance containing a large directory of pointers and strings. These three instances provide the links from ACIS pointers to strings (dir1), from I_ent (Widget library) pointers to strings (dir2), and from Geometric Tool pointers to strings (dir3), as shown in Table 10.5. Each directory can operate in either direction.

The directory structure was designed to maintain the separation of the Widget layer from the Procedural Interface layer, and the Feature Interface layer from the Geometric Toolkit layer. Without such separation provided by dir1 and dir2,

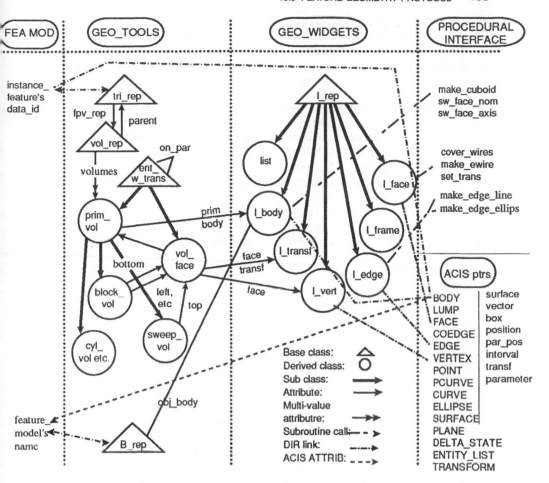

Figure 10.41 Overall structure of the system

the widget library would certainly need to be customized for each solid modeler. The separation provided by dir3 ensures that the Geometric Toolkit objects are not tightly bound to a particular feature modeler.

The ACIS ATTRIB class was used to add functionality not present in the dynamic interface (Khan 1994). Several classes were derived from the ATTRIB base class for such purposes as adding face tags to each face of the solid model in order to identify the feature to which it belongs. Figure 10.42 shows the class hierarchy derived from ATTRIB. The class level containing ATTRIB_ASU and ATTRIB_DECOMP is the suggested level for developer's classes derived from ATTRIB to maintain uniqueness among the derived classes. At this level no user data or function members are comprised in these classes except the members defined by ACIS macro expansions. ATTRIB_FEA is used to extend the function-

Table 10.5 DIR **pointer/string mapping class instances**

dir1 ACIS pointers to strings		dir2 strings to I_ent pointers (Widget Library objects)		dir3 Geometric Tool objects B_reps and tri_reps to strings.	
BODY*	aaabc	(The following objects are		tri_rep*	1
FACE*	aaadg	all derived from I_ent)		tri_rep*	2
EDGE*	abccc	I_body*	aaabc	B_rep*	Part3
ENTITY_LIST*	dfser	I_face*	aaadg		
position*	aswqe	I_vertex*	asdfg		
vector*	...	list*	adfhj		
unit_vector*		I_frame*	bdfgd		
matrix*		I_edge*	abccc		
transf*		I_transf*	dfggh		
parameter*					
TRANSFORM*					
SHELL*					
LUMP*					
SUBSHELL*					
COEDGE*					
VERTEX*					
CURVE*					
POINT*					

ality of the dynamic interface to ACIS from the feature modeler. ATTRIB_COEDGE, ATTRIB_FACE, and ATTRIB_VOL are used to identify elements of the solid model during volume decomposition done in a feature recognition system.

The ATTRIB_FEA class can be used for various purposes; for example, associating a feature with each face of the ACIS solid model, or a face with tolerance

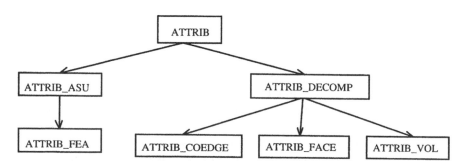

Figure 10.42 Classes derived from ATTRIB

Table 10.6 Data members of `ATTRIB_FEA` **class**

Data Type	Member Name	Member Description
character string (`char *`)	`fea_data_id`	Two-digit "number" assigned from feature model
character string (`char *`)	`fea_type`	Character string assigned from feature model
character string (`char *`)	`face_id`	Two-digit "number" identifying face in feature model
character string (`char *`)	`face_type`	String: PLANAR, CYLINDRICAL, SPLINE
character string (`char *`)	`datum_id`	Two-digit "number" assigned by tolerance class
character string (`char *`)	`datum_type`	String: PRIMARY, SECONDARY
character string (`char *`)	`partnum`	String (part name) assigned by feature model

data and toleranced frames. Table 10.6 shows the data members of the `ATTRIB_FEA` class. The `ATTRIB_COEDGE` class is used to identify the type of ACIS coedge during volume decomposition. This simple class has only one data member: a character named `coedge_type`.

The attribute classes were also needed for graphical picking, as seen by the procedure outlined below:

- The 3D visualization code steps through the BODY by nested loops for all lumps, then all shells, then all faces (which need to be faceted), and so on. The 3D visualization code calls attribute class functions to name drawn graphical primitives according to parts and facets they represent.
- An ACIS attribute structure tags each face with the instance name of the feature, plus additional information.
- The graphical interface implements the picking operation by first mapping the picked graphical primitives to faces, and then the faces to features or parts.
- To control picking, the graphical user interface can make only those graphical primitives pickable that correspond to certain parts or features.

10.10 USER INTERFACE DESIGN

The functionality needed to support feature-based operations in a uniform interface is described by (Bliznakov et al. 1995). A summary of the discussion in that paper is presented here. Apart from the usual facilities needed by other CAD systems, such as menus, display and viewing options, prompts and error messages, and textual and graphical user interactions, there are some additional requirements specific to feature-based modeling, as described below.

Selecting features and feature libraries. The UI should support menus to browse and select feature libraries and features. Sketches and parameterization of each feature should be available to users to help determine the proper feature to select.

Building feature libraries. If the system supports user-defined features, facilities for defining generic features in terms of their properties are needed. This also involves definition of geometry construction procedure, in which case, all the normal construction methods are needed. This includes primitive instancing, Booleans, profile definition by points, lines, arcs, and splines, and sweep definition. Also we need to specify constraints between the entities. Definition of feature coordinates is needed. Once an individual feature has been defined, putting the feature into a library, or moving features between libraries is required.

Instancing features. When instancing a feature, the significance of each parameter must be apparent. The means for positioning and orientation must be clear. These may include the instancing of a base feature with respect to a global coordinate system, and subsequent feature instances with respect to another feature's coordinate system or a face or an edge coordinate system.

Picking features. The UI must support graphical picking of features and constituent entities in order to facilitate positioning and orienting a feature relative to another feature and for various modification operations. The UI could place restrictions on what is pickable at any given time, based on the operation context. This can be implemented through an entity type filter such that only context-valid entities are picked. A sub-type filter may also be necessary in some contexts. For example, if a feature being instanced can only have web features as its parent, only web features must be pickable.

Multiple model support. Many applications operate on more than one model. For example, assembly modeling needs multiple part models. For such applications, support is needed to select the model or models on which to operate. Additionally, means to toggle the view (workpiece/part) is needed, as is picking of features when more than one model is on the screen.

Figure 10.43 illustrates the components used in the implementation of the ASU Features Testbed II. The main components are the Graphical User Interface (GUI), the Features component, the 3D Visualization Component that uses ACIS, the 2D Graphical Interface (G2D), and X-Window. OSF/Motif Widgets were used to construct the GUI components, while G2D, the 2D drawing system, was written completely in ANSI C, the UI exploited C++ classes as OSF/Motif Widget wrappers.

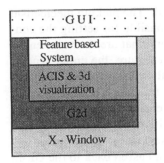

Figure 10.43 ASU Features Testbed II Architecture

Since ACIS is the current underlying kernel for the feature modeler and applications, it was evaluated for use in the 3D visualization. The advantage of using the facetting and hidden line husk (fhl husk) provided by Spatial Technology was the ease of writing this component. An ACIS body pointer is passed to the facetter, which facets the body and returns a list of edges to draw. This component then interacts with the G2D component, which performs the actual drawing. Several alternatives were considered for input in the form of graphical picking.

1. *3D picking*. Ray-firing upon user location; querying the solid modeler for valid type entities.
2. *Direct 2D picking*. Associating entity types with 2D drawing primitives explicitly.
3. *Indirect 2D picking*. Attaching user-defined attributes to entity types to identify 2D drawing primitives.

The 3D picking alternative makes the UI dependent on the solid modeler. Associating entity types with 2D drawing primitives explicitly is memory-inefficient and may result in poor performance if the feature model becomes large. Attaching user-defined attributes to entity types may provide functionality other than just picking. New applications can define their own attributes and attach them to entities. This provides a mechanism for new applications to supply a context for existing geometric entities. For example, a tolerance modeler could define datums as attributes and attach them to existing geometry (faces) in a feature model.

The 2D drawing system uses segment primitives to draw on the UI drawing area following the segment hierarchy from the relationships of the feature model as : Part → Feature → Face → Edge → Vertex. For each entity, a segment identifier is attached as an attribute to the entity and used as a segment name in the 2D drawing system. The 2D drawing system passes along the segment identifier to the UI which can now determine what has been picked. The picking mechanism provides the filtering capabilities, but the UI is responsible for setting the context for filtering. That is, the UI must specify a priori what are the valid entity types and identifiers for picking. Thus for picking a feature, the entity type of feature must be the only type passed to the picking filter. If only flange features can be picked, the additional identifier parameter for a flange feature must be passed to the picking filter. If the user approaches a segment in the drawing area with the pointing device, the segment is highlighted and becomes a candidate for a pick. If a mouse button is depressed while the segment is highlighted, it is selected and filtered. After passing the filter, it is then passed back to the UI. In case of ambiguous picks, resolving ambiguity can be left up to the UI or handled by the picking mechanism. The picking mechanism can "scroll" through possible selections by allowing the user to click a mouse button several times. The following sections describe the main components of the ASU Testbed UI.

Only one application can be "active" at any given time. The GUI Manager sets the context for a given application and updates all presentation components of the UI such as menus and dialogs. Application context is specified by data files. Menu hierarchy, dialog structure and context, control flow, and application-specific semantic data are described in the data files. The upper area of Figure 10.44 shows the active modeler (FormFeaModeler), the current library (USCARnonub), the current part file (File5), and the current view (ISOM [metric]).

When a feature is instanced, its parameterization must be apparent. Figure 10.44 illustrates the dialog box for feature parameter input. The parameters show a default value of 0. At the bottom of the dialog box, note the four buttons "sketch," "cancel," "check," and "ok." If "sketch" is selected, the sketch of the feature is popped up in another window, as shown. In addition to the parameterization, the sketch window also lists any constraints associated with this class of feature. The "check" button will tentatively instance the feature into the model, and the "ok" button confirms the instance.

Since the picking mechanism for features was implemented as part of the 2D drawing system, the UI notifies the drawing system of valid entity types and identifiers via function calls. This is done prior to the picking itself. The picking mechanism identifies the segment picked by the following convention:

[Part_id].[#-Fea_id].[Face_id].[Edge_id].[Vertex_id]

is a feature instance number for multiple instance of a feature.

The segment is then filtered for the appropriate type and identifier, then passed back to the UI. More than one valid entity type can be specified for filtering. For example, to position a feature relative to its parent, the parent's edge or face can be picked. Figure 10.45 shows a highlighted face of a Crank_end, just before a Crank_ring is instanced onto that face. (Refer to Chapter 5 for feature library of connecting rods). Figure 10.46 shows the just-instanced Crank_ring.

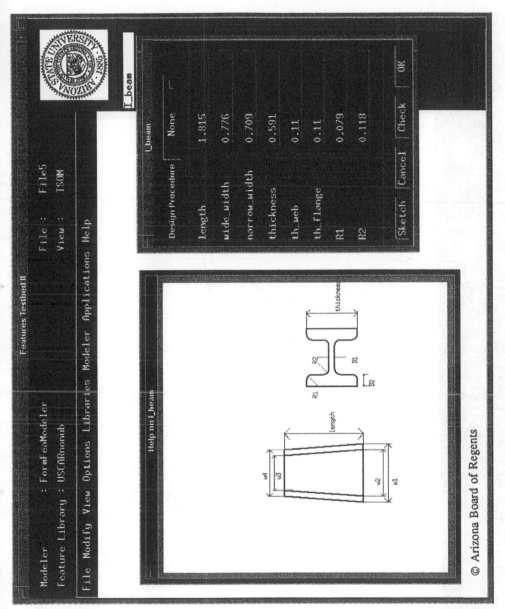

Figure 10.44 Feature sketch and instance template

© Arizona Board of Regents

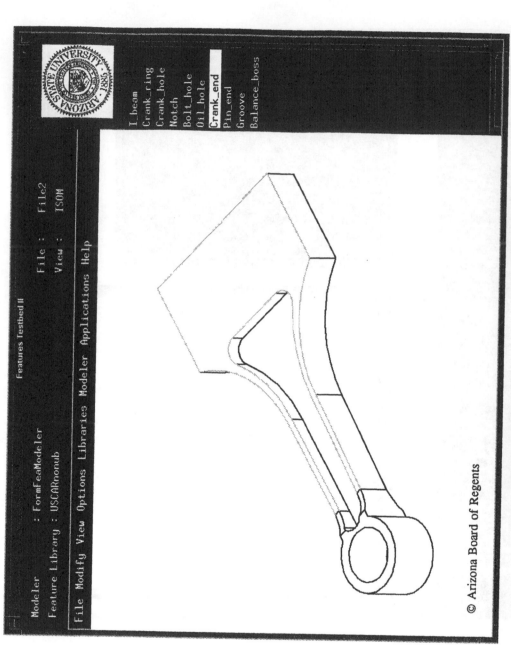

© Arizona Board of Regents

Figure 10.45 Dynamic-selective entity picking to attach the crank-ring

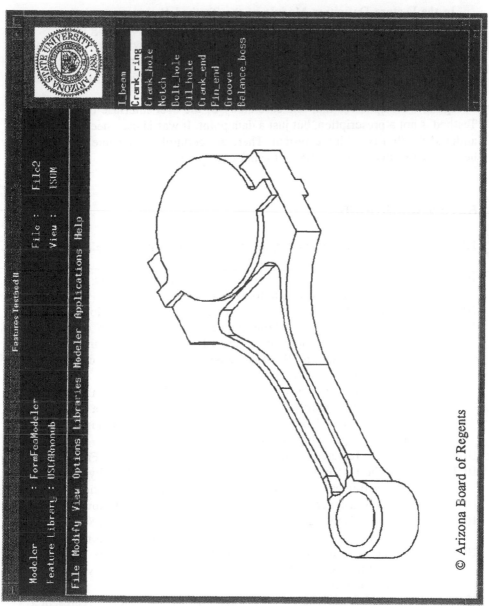

Figure 10.46 Model after crank-ring attachment

Once highlighted and picked, a segment remains highlighted until the UI releases the pick. This is typically done just after the pick input is received by the UI.

In the Feature Definition Module of the Testbed II, users can define new generic features and store them in libraries. To aid users in defining features, a toolbox is provided as a separate X-window to the main window. Users can instance primitives, define sweep profiles using planar geometry, and specify geometric constraints between constituent geometry. Further details of the implementation are omitted here.

Again, we emphasize that this case study of the user interface of the ASU Testbed is not a prescription, but just a data point. It was chosen because of the authors' familiarity with the system. There are certainly better interfaces, and better systems than the one chosen for our case study.

REVIEW QUESTIONS

10.1 Discuss how dynamic interpretation could be implemented on top of a programming language such as C.

10.2 Write a description of a blind hole instance feature using the notation of Figure 10.1 and the example following it.

10.3 Write a class definition for the blind-hole feature of Question 10.2.

10.4 The decision to include whole parts and even collections of parts as "features" in the taxonomy of Figure 10.3 is unusual. Discuss the pros and cons of this design. What is the benefit of the abstract class con-tainer-feature in the taxonomy?

10.5 In later versions of the taxonomy of Figure 10.3, the class area-sur-face has been renamed as area-feature and moved as a direct subclass of feature. Discuss the pros and cons of this design in comparison to the design in Figure 10.3.

10.6 Classify the features of Figure 10.7 using the taxonomy of Figure 10.6.

10.7 Redraw the part instance structure graph of Figure 10.8 by including the surface frames representing feature relationships (see Section 10.2.6).

10.8 Draw a part instance graph for the part at the top of the following page.

10.9 Write a part family definition for the part in Question 10.8 using the notation of Figure 10.9. (Invent a convenient parametrization scheme.)

10.10 Using the notation of Figure 10.10(b), outline a geometry definition frame for the keyway slot in Figure 10.2. (Don't worry if you cannot complete the definition—an outline is fine.)

10.11 Can you think of reasons why boundary modelers typically represent a full cylinder surface as two halves?

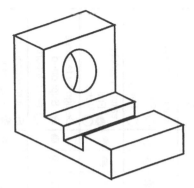

10.12   Draw a graph representing the shape data structure corresponding with the part shown below. Assume that the holes are made after the slot and that they are represented as two half-cylinders in the geometric model.

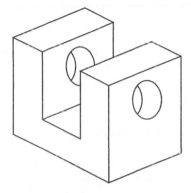

10.13   An alternative coordinate scheme is based on viewing the feature model as a tree structure, where each feature has a unique parent feature. In this scheme the local coordinate system would be represented through transformation relative to its parent. Discuss the pros and cons of this approach with respect to the actually implemented scheme.

10.14   Using the notation of Section 10.5, write a constraint specifying that the slot in the part of Question 10.8 remains on the top surface of the block.

10.15   Using the notation of Section 10.5, write a constraint that assures that the two cylinders of the part in Question 10.12 remain coaxial. (Use feature identifiers; see Figure 10.23.)

10.16   The constraint scheme represented in Section 10.5 is based on representing constraints on a fairly low level (i.e., between coordinate values and rotation angles). In contrast, the constraint facility described in

Attribute / Modeler	Definition Method — Declarative ● / Procedural ○	User defined features — Full support ● / None ○	Solid Model linkage — Dynamic ● / Static ○	Information flow — 2-way ● / 1-way ○	Feature validation — Full ● / None ○	Design by features — Supported ● / Not supported ○	Feature recognition — supported ● / not supported ○
ASU Testbed I	○	●	○	○	◐	●	◐
ASU Testbed II	◐	●	●	●	◐	●	○
EXT Design	◐	●	●	●	◐	●	●
IMPACTT	○	●	○	○	◐	●	○

Figure 10.47 Comparison of prototype feature modelers

Section 8.3.1 was based on vectors and points. Discuss the pros and cons of these two approaches.

10.17 Can you outline an algorithm for implementing the base feature recognition rule for a block base feature? (See Figure 10.25 and the text immediately following it.)

10.18 Discuss the pros and cons of the approach described in Section 10.6.6 for handling feature interactions.

10.19 Simulate by hand the feature recognition of the part in Question 10.8. First, draw the full search graph (assume the cylinder is represented as two half-cylinders). Match the graph against a block base feature. Use "type I" heuristic to deal with the remaining features. As a result, give the final shape data structures and the feature instance graph. (Did you get the same instance graph as in Question 10.8? Why?)

10.20 Review Figure 3.9. Which cases of feature interaction presented in the figure can be handled with the incremental recognition mechanism of Section 10.6?

10.21 Discuss the pros and cons of the approach depicted in Figure 10.30 to handling parts with multiple interpretations as features.

10.22 Write a C function for converting a solid represented by a half-edge data structure (Appendix B) to the intermediate format of Hwang (1988); see Section 10.7.1.

10.23 Interpret the validation rules of the obround slot in Figure 10.35. Do these rules capture all validity criteria that you can think of?

10.24 Rewrite the definition of the obround slot using the C++ functions of the Procedural Interface of Section 10.9.4 (see also Appendix C). Can you implement all validation rules?

10.25 Use the format of Figure 10.47 to compare commercial feature based systems that are available to you.

BIBLIOGRAPHY

Bhatnagar, A., 1988, Implementation of feature mapping and reasoning shell with application to GT coding, M.S. thesis, Department of Mechanical and Aerospace Engineering, Arizona State University.

Bliznakov, P., Rogers M., Khan N., Ali A., Shirur A., Shah J., 1995, User interface design for feature modelers and feature based applications, ASME Computers in Engineering Conference, Boston, September.

CAM-I, 1990, Application interface specification AIS 2.0 revision 2.0 B, Technical Report R-90-PM-03, CAM-I, Inc., Arlington, TX.

Carnegie Group, 1986, *KnowledgeCraft User's Manual*, Carnegie Group, Pittsburgh, PA.

Computervision Corporation, 1987, *CADDS Programmers CADDS 4X Database Reference*, Computervision Corporation, Cambridge, MA.

EDS, 1994, *Parasolid Programming Manuals*, EDS Corporation.

Hummel, K., and Wolf, M., 1990, Integrating expert systems with solid modeling through interprocess communications and application interface specification, in C. A. Born et al., eds., *ASME Computers in Engineering Conf.*, Boston, ASME Press.

Hwang, 1988, Feature extraction, M.S. thesis, Department of Mechanical Engineering, Arizona State University.

Joshi, S., and Chang, T.-C. 1988, Graph-based heuristics for recognition of machined features from a 3-D solid model, *Computer-Aided Design* **20** (2): 58–66.

Khan, N., 1994, ACIS extensibility for Testbed II, Tech. Report, Design Automation Laboratory, Department of Mechanical Engineering, Arizona State University, Tempe.

Laakko, T., 1993, Incremental feature modelling: methodology for integrating features and solid models, Dr. Tech. dissertation, Helsinki University of Technology, Laboratory of Information Processing Science.

Laakko, T., and Mäntylä, M., 1991, A new form feature recognition algorithm, G. Doumeingts, J. Browne, and M. Tomljanovich, eds., *Computer Applications in Production and Engineering: Integration Aspects (Proc. CAPE 91)*, North-Holland, pp. 369–376.

Laakko, T., and Mäntylä, M., 1993a, A feature definition language for bridging solids and features, in J. Rossignac, J. Turner, and G. Allen, eds., *Proc. of Second ACM Symp. on Solid Modeling and Applications*, Montreal, 19–21 May, pp. 333–342.

Laakko, T., and Mäntylä, M., 1993b, Introducing blending operations in feature models, Proc. of Eurographics '93, *Comp. Gr. Forum* **12** (3): 165–175.

Laakko, T., and Mäntylä, M., 1993c, Feature modelling by incremental feature recognition, *Computer-Aided Design* **25** (8): 479–492, August 1993.

Laakko, T., and Mäntylä, M., 1994, Feature-based modeling of product familics, in K. Ishii et al., eds., *ASME Computers in Engineering Conf.*, Vol. 1, Minneapolis, September 11–14, ASME Press, pp. 45–54.

Lagus, K., Laakko, T., and Mäntylä, M., 1994, ICONF—An incremental constraint facility in a feature modelling system, *Proc. IFIP W.G. 5.2 Working Conference on Feature Modelling & Recognition in Advanced CAD/CAM Systems*, Valenciennes, May 24–26, North-Holland, pp. 161–177.

Lassila, O., 1991, *BEEF Reference Manual: A Programmer's Guide to the BEEF Frame System, Second Version*, Technical Report no. HTKK-TKO-C46, Laboratory of Information Processing Science, Helsinki University of Technology.

Magleby, S., and Gunn, K., 1992, Flexible integration of CAD/CAM modelers and application programs, Tech. Report, Brigham Young University.

Mäntylä, M., 1988, *An Introduction to Solid Modelling*, Computer Science Press.

Mäntylä, M., Opas, J., and Puhakka, J., 1987, A prototype system for generative process planning of prismatic parts, in A. Kusiak, ed., *Modern Production Management Systems - Proc. of IFIP TC 5/WG 5.7 Working Conf. on Advances in Production Management Systems (APMS '87)*, Winnipeg, 1987, North-Holland, pp. 599–611.

Mäntylä, M., Opas, J., and Puhakka, J., 1989, Generative process planning of prismatic parts by feature relaxation, in B. Ravani, ed., *Proc. of 15th ASME Design Automation Conf.*, Montreal, September 17–21, ASME Press, pp. 49–60.

Nieminen, J., and Tuomi, J., 1991, Design with features for manufacturing cost analysis, in J. Turner, J. Pegna, and M. Wozny, eds., *Product Modeling for Computer-Aided Design and Manufacturing*, North-Holland, pp. 317–330.

PDES, 1991, Functional requirements for STEP data access interface, Technical Report ISO TC184/SC4/WG7, N23.

Pherwani, P., 1993, Dynamic binding of features and solid modelers, M.S. thesis, Department of Mechanical and Aerospace Engineering, Arizona State University.

Rogers, M., 1986, Form feature modeling shell for design of mechanical parts, M.S. thesis, Department of Mechanical Engineering, Arizona State University.

Rogers, M., 1994, Programmer's manual for the geometric toolkit interface to ACIS, Tech. Report, Design Automation Laboratory, Mechanical Engineering Department, Arizona State University, Tempe, AZ.

Sannella, M., 1993, The SkyBlue constraint solver, Technical Report 92-07-02, Department of Computer Science and Engineering, University of Washington, Seattle, WA.

Shah, J. J., and Pherwani, V., 1993, Dynamic binding of features and solid modelers, *Proc. of 19th ASME Design Automation Conf.*, Vol. 2, Albuquerque, ASME Press, pp. 284–292.

Shah, J. J., and Rogers, M. T., 1988, Expert form feature modeling shell, *Computer-Aided Design* **20** (9): 515–524.

Shah, J. J., and Rogers, M. T., 1991, ASU Features Testbed V1.2- User Manual, Dept. of Mechanical Engineering, Arizona State, Tempe.

Shah, J. J., and Rogers, M. T., 1994, A testbed for rapid prototyping of feature based applications, in J. J. Shah, M. Mäntylä, and D. Nau, *Advances in Feature Based Manufacturing*, Elsevier Science Publishers, pp. 423–453.

Shah, J. J., Rogers, M., Sreevalsan, P., Hsiao, D., Mathew, A., Bhatnagar, A., Liou, B., and Miller, D., 1990, The ASU features testbed: An overview, *ASME Computers in Engineering Conf.*, Vol. 1, Boston, ASME Press, pp. 233–242.

Spatial Technology Inc., 1993, *ACIS Reference Manual*, Spatial Technology, Boulder, CO.

Sreevalsan, P., 1990, An investigation into the unification of form feature definition methods, M.S. thesis, Department of Mechanical Engineering, Arizona State University.

Sreevalsan, P., and Shah, J. J., 1992, Unification of feature definition methods, in D. Brown, M. Waldron, and H. Yoshikawa, eds., *Intelligent Computer Aided Design*, Elsevier Science Publishers, pp. 83–100.

11

FEATURE-BASED PROCESS PLANNING

Process planning of machining operations is the application where features at present have found their most widespread use. As indicated in Chapter 1, process planning is also historically important for the development of feature-based systems, and it has influenced the overall progress of features and their related concepts. Therefore process planning is an attractive benchmark for applications of features, and this chapter is devoted to the study of feature-based process planning.

Process planning is a complex subject well worth a book of its own. Indeed, several have been written, and the reader interested in more detail than is possible to include in this chapter is referred to (Chang and Wysk 1985, Chang 1990, and Wang and Li 1991). Details of process planning algorithms are also discussed in many more general CAD/CAM books, such as (Kusiak 1990). Process planning in the wider context of production engineering is well presented in (Rembold et al. 1993). Instead of trying to give a complete exposition to the problems, issues, and methods of computer-aided process planning, our goal is to illuminate the role features play in process planning, and also how the overall design of a feature-based system is influenced by the requirements posed by process planning.

First, we will look at the architectural framework of process planning. The functional requirements for the development of a process planning system depend not only on the type of products and processes being considered but also on the type of enterprise in question. A general capability toolmaking machine shop requires a different type of a process planning system than a limited-function shop producing a limited range of parts belonging to well-defined part families. These and other dimensions of process planning are investigated in Section 11.1.

To work at all, a process planner requires a representation of the part to be manufactured. Among the several theoretically possible representations, we concentrate on a feature-based product model. Section 11.2 investigates the definition and implementation of process planning features on the basis of the more general discussion of Chapter 6 on manufacturing features.

To produce process plans, a process planning system requires knowledge of the processes available in the factory in question and their characteristics. Section 11.3 looks at the problems of machining process representation for process planning, including *process capability, process constraints,* and *process economics.* A process plan generated by a process planning system consists not only of the processes chosen but also of data representing *process sequencing*; problems related to this and other similar process plan data are also investigated.

The remaining sections describe various subtasks of process planning, such as *operation planning* (selection of elementary machining processes capable of creating a feature), *setup planning* (grouping of operations in sets performed in a certain fixed orientation of the part on a certain machine), *fixture planning* (selection of workholding fixtures for a certain setup to be performed on a given machine), and *NC program generation.* Each subtask is highlighted in the discussion by a description of selected feature-based process planning systems.

11.1 ARCHITECTURAL FRAMEWORK

11.1.1 Goals of Computer-Aided Process Planning

The sequence of technical planning and decision-making steps related to a product's manufacturing are called *process planning.* Process planning therefore includes tasks such as the determination of the manufacturing technologies to be used, breakdown of the product into a sequence of individual manufacturing or assembly tasks, design and selection of tools and fixtures for each manufacturing step, and derivation of control programs for driving various types of manufacturing machinery, such as CNC machines, robots, and automatic transportation and storage equipment. All together, these planning tasks may consume more human effort and time than the actual design itself. Therefore, to fully realize the benefits of computer-aided design and manufacturing, computer support for process planning activities should also be available in addition to more conventional CAD and CAM processes.

The input to process planning consists of finished design information. Traditionally design sketches or engineering drawings such as Figure 11.1 are given to an experienced human process planner, who is knowledgeable both about the products and about the manufacturing facilities of the factory. Unfortunately, even when this level of expertise is available, the cost of manual planning may be prohibitive in small batch or one-of-a-kind parts production.

As noted in Chapter 1, changes in the competitive environment is currently favoring small batch production over mass production in many important areas of mechanical production. As a result computer-aided process planning systems (CAPP) whose objective is to automate various aspects of process planning are becoming increasingly important for industrial companies. From the practical viewpoint, the goal of CAPP is to reduce the cost of process planning to an acceptable level for medium- or short-batch production while still achieving adequate plan quality in terms of throughput, lead time, product quality, and cost-effective utilization of various manufacturing resources.

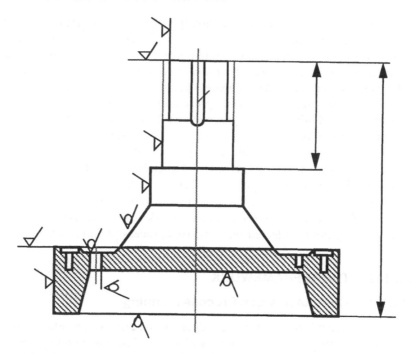

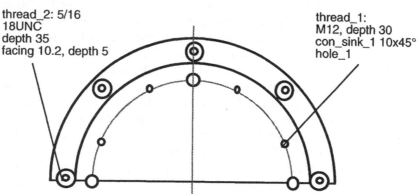

thread_2: 5/16
18UNC
depth 35
facing 10.2, depth 5

thread_1:
M12, depth 30
con_sink_1 10x45°
hole_1

Figure 11.1 Engineering drawing

The focus of this chapter is on discrete part manufacturing in machine shops; in this environment, process planning can be defined as an *act of preparing detailed processing documentation for the manufacture of a piece part or an assembly*. Hence it includes detailed tasks such as the following:

- Selection of machining operations
- Sequencing of machining operations

- Selection of cutting tools
- Selection of machine tools
- Calculations of cutting parameters
- Tool path planning and generation of NC part programs
- Determining setup requirements
- Design of jigs and fixtures
- Planning of auxiliary steps (material transfer, manual processing)

A complete process planning system for discrete manufacturing should also include inspection planning and assembly planning. However, we will not consider these tasks in detail, their importance notwithstanding.

The result of process planning for discrete manufacturing may be a rough process plan that only lists the major manufacturing steps required. Rough plans are useful to determine the overall technological requirements of a product, and may be used to assess the producibility and rough cost of a product. Skilled operators may be capable to execute such plans on the basis of technical drawings and their own experience.

Alternatively, more detailed plans may be preferred, such as the plan shown in Figure 11.2. Observe that the plan gives fairly detailed information on the processes, tools, and auxiliary materials needed. Detailed plans have the benefit that they can be utilized also by less experienced operators who may not understand the whole scope of the factory. Detailed plans are also needed to control automatic production systems such as flexible machining cells (FMC) and flexible manufacturing systems (FMS).

PROCESS PLAN					
Part No. HO345344 Part Name: Bearing housing Original: J.Puhakka 13/6/91 Checked: J. Opas 22/6/91 Approved: M. Mantyla 13/7/91				Material: Fe40400i	
No.	Operation descr.	Workstation	Setup	Tool	Time
10	Insert in fixture #1	Fixturing-14	See attach #1		2
20	Face mill bottom surface	Mill-12324		Face mill 4 teeth 100mm	2 6
30	End mill 4 holes on bottom surface	Mill-12324		End mill 40mm	5
40	Unmount and insert in fixture #2		See attached #2		3
50	Face mill annular area			Face mill 4 teeth 60mm	3
60	Finish mill bearing hole	Mill-12324		End mill 60mm	5
...					

Figure 11.2 A process plan

In a highly automated manufacturing environment, process plans generated by CAPP systems should form input to various shop-floor systems controlling the actual physical manufacture, such as production scheduling, material management, tool management, and FMS control. Therefore a process planning system should be capable of generating the attribute information as required by all these applications. Clearly a "neutral" process plan representation that can provide a vendor-independent linkage between planning and shop-floor control systems is very attractive. Consequently process plan representation is an important item for future standardization under the STEP umbrella (Paul 1994, Parker 1994).

11.1.2 Early Process Planning Systems

The progress of process planning technology reflects the general progress of production technology. Early process planning systems developed in the 1960s and 1970s addressed the needs of the factories of that time, characterized by relatively low level of automation and unspecialized machine tools. In this environment detailed plans were not practical because manual skills of operators were required for executing the manufacturing processes on the unsophisticated machinery. Instead, the focus was on standardization of work plans and the effective utilization of standard plans. Therefore, and also because of limitations of available computing methodology, early systems generally followed the *variant planning* approach.

The CAPP system developed for CAM-I, Inc. (Link 1976) is a typical example of early variant systems. The architecture of the system is shown in Figure 11.3.

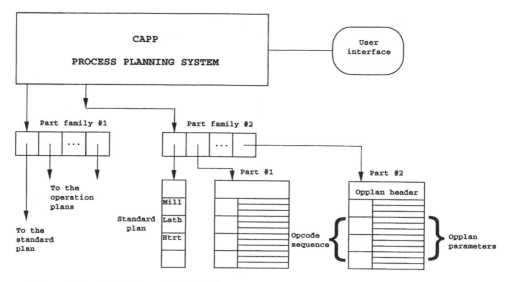

Figure 11.3 Architecture of the CAPP system

Its operation took the following outline which is shared by most variant planning systems:

- During a preparatory stage, production requirements of parts are analyzed, *part families* of parts with similar requirements are recognized, and *standard plans* are generated for the families. Standard plans consist of an operation sequence represented in terms of operation codes (*opcodes*). Opcodes correspond to complete machining cycles (e.g., select a tool, perform machining, return tool to home position).
- During the actual operation stage, the part family that best corresponds to the part is retrieved. The standard plan of the family is edited to yield the final plan for the part.

Part classification and part family organization in the early systems was generally based on Group Technology classification discussed in Chapter 6.

11.1.3 Current-Generation Process Planning Systems

During the last two decades production technology available to companies has changed very dramatically, mostly because programmable (computer controlled) tools were introduced to production. Highlights of this progress include CNC and DNC machines, robots, flexible manufacturing systems, programmable inspection machines, automatically guided vehicles, and automatic storage equipment. Instead of functional organization, production machines, cells, and lines are now organized according to the material flows. The focus is on quality, lead time, throughput, and low work-in-progress.

In this new production environment, variant process planning systems based on GT coding have various deficiencies that make them unattractive:

- The parts that can be handled are limited to the original part families known to the system, reducing the overall flexibility of the system
- Experienced human planners are required to edit the plans manually, increasing the lead time from production order to finished product
- Detailed plans required for controlling highly automated production equipment cannot be easily generated because the "opcodes" correspond to relatively rough level operations
- Existing plans cannot easily be updated as the manufacturing resources change

Current generation process planning systems try to address these problems on the basis of new tools and techniques from information technology, including features and other types of advanced product models. Armed with these weapons, developers and researchers on process planning systems can also explore a range of novel approaches to process planning. Many of these novel viewpoints

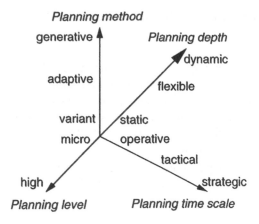

Figure 11.4 A four-dimensional framework for process planning systems

to CAPP can be inspected by means of a conceptual framework consisting of four "coordinate axes" shown in Figure 11.4.

Each of four coordinate axes has a strong influence on the architecture of a process planning system. The meaning of the various axes is as follows:

Planning level   Planning may be performed on a high level, where the focus is on overall selection of production technology (macro level), or on low levels increasingly concentrated on particular processes (micro level) (ElMaraghy 1993).

Planning time scale   The planning time scale can range from the short-term planning of a certain production run to long-term development of the whole production facility.

Planning method   The plan may be generated by varying existing plans (*variant planning*) or from scratch on the basis of available generic process knowledge (*generative planning*).

Planning depth   The generated plan can be treated as fixed or variable by the shop-floor scheduling system.

The effects of the various axes on process planning methodology and the significance of particular points along the axes are summarized in Table 11.1.

Of course the axes are not really independent. For instance, at a high level of planning a longer planning time scale is generally appropriate, and a generative approach is preferable to ensure that all feasible alternatives are taken into account. Conversely, low-level planning concerns itself with the immediate future, and it might be performed on-line by the shop-floor control system rather than by the off-line process planning system. In this case the focus is on effective utilization of existing production facilities rather than the theoretical optimal plan.

Table 11.1 Architectural dimensions of process planning

Axis	Alternatives	Planning Focus/Methodology
Planning level	Micro	Operation parameters, machining conditions, other parameters, NC code
	Detailed	Detailed process plans (operations, operation sequences, tools, other resources)
	Macro	Alternative routings (non-linear plans)
	High level	Overall manufacturing technology, materials
Planning time scale	Short scale (operative)	Processes, process steps, auxiliary steps, logistics, routing, capacity utilization
	Medium scale (tactical)	Cost, quality, process capability
	Long scale (strategic)	Materials, production technologies, plant, line, and cell layouts, production system capability
Planning method	Variant	Planning conducted on the basis of predefined process plans edited or parametrically modified to suit the new part
	Adaptive	Planning conducted on the basis of pre-defined skeletal plans as a rough plan that is automatically elaborated to a detailed plan
	Generative	A new plan is generated from scratch for the part
	Hybrid	A combination of approaches is used, such as high-volume parts with optimized variant plans and low-volume parts planned generatively
Planning depth	Static	Plan not modified after being generated
	Flexible	A rough plan without actual manufacturing resources created off-line; final detailed on-line planning and choice of resources by shop-floor scheduler
	Dynamic	Plan can be changed dynamically during manufacture of the part according to the dynamic state of the manufacturing system

The various approaches are not mutually exclusive, either. Process planning performed early in the life cycle of a product (e.g., for concurrent engineering or early producibility analysis) should concern itself with the overall production process alternatives, and therefore it is preferably carried out at a relatively high level by a generative approach. Later, when the product has entered the production stage, processes should not be altered unnecessarily, and a variant approach may be attractive to deal with predefined, limited variations in the product.

Various topics of modern process planning systems will be investigated in later sections of this chapter. Additional information on the development of process planning systems can be found in references (Eversheim and Schulz 1985; Alting and Zhang 1989; ElMaraghy 1993), which give good overviews of the progress of CAPP over the years.

11.2 PROCESS PLANNING FEATURES

Process planning, like most other computer-aided engineering applications, requires the definition of product geometry as input. But the geometric information alone is insufficient. Process planning needs additional data on the shapes, such as knowledge of the characteristic shapes producible by the various processes, and their dimensions, locations, tolerances, and surface finish. The information should also cover more specialized factors such as tool accessibility, fixturing possibilities, and inspectability. As already noted in Chapter 6, *manufacturing features* and their related *process models* are an attractive approach to realize such product definitions. Indeed, features have several advantages in process planning systems:

- Features are a convenient input data representation for the planning system.
- Process knowledge needed for planning can be associated with feature classes.
- Geometric reasoning for various tasks of process plans is facilitated by features.
- Downstream operations such as NC code generation can be supported.

It is not at all surprising that nearly all modern process planners utilize feature-modeling techniques. In this section we will look at some issues of process planning features, expanding on the general discussion of Chapter 6; the related discussion of process models is postponed to Section 11.3. We will also look at representative samples of process planning features coming from an implemented process planning system.

11.2.1 Process Planning Feature Issues

Various issues related to the identification and definition of manufacturing features were already discussed in Chapter 6. These include the following:

Level of abstraction	Are features identified as direct counterparts of processes, or are they abstracted away from the processes?
Level of specialization	Are features specifically related to certain processes available in a manufacturing environment, or are they generic?
Dimensionality	Do features relate to volumes, surfaces, or curves/profiles?
Completeness	Is the whole part modeled by features, or only some interesting subsets of it?
Temporal ordering	How is the sequencing information of manufacturing processes associated with features?

We refer the reader to Chapter 6 for a general discussion of these issues. Here we look at the resolution of these issues from the opposite perspective of the architectural dimensions of process planning systems identified in Section 11.1. For this discussion, let us consider three different scenarios of process planning, occupying different positions in the general framework of Figure 11.4:

- *Manufacturability evaluation* In this scenario the objective of process planning is to determine the manufacturability of a product being designed.
- *Capacity requirements planning and scheduling* In this scenario the objective is to determine the steps required for the manufacture of the product, their proper sequencing, and the resources required for the execution of each step. This information is required for production management (e.g., generation of the master production schedule of a plant).
- *Generation of numerical control programs* In this scenario the objective is to determine the detailed operating instructions for various types of numerically controlled manufacturing equipment, such as numerically controlled machine tools, robots, and automatically guided vehicles and storage equipment.

Manufacturability Evaluation The main issue for manufacturability evaluation is the determination of the feasibility and economics of manufacturing a product. With regard to the axes of Figure 11.4, this scenario would be characterized as *high level*, *medium to long scale*, *generative*, and *static*. For this application, features of relatively high level of abstraction and low level of specialization would be required. Emphasis is on judging the manufacturability of the features against generic knowledge of the capability of various types of manufacturing processes; rough cost modeling may also be required for comparing alternative designs. For instance, the manufacturability of a hole feature would be analyzed using generic manufacturing knowledge and geometric reasoning; specialized knowledge on the particular capabilities of certain machine tools and drills is not required or even relevant.

Capacity Requirements Planning and Scheduling The main issues for this scenario is to determine the production machines and their equipment, materials, auxiliary components, and the workforce required for the manufacture of the product. Using the axes of Figure 11.4, this scenario is characterized as *macro level*, *medium time scale*, *generative/adaptive*, and *flexible*. For this application, less abstract and more specialized features that make it possible to determine the manufacturing capability requirements are needed. The emphasis is on analyzing the features against available production facilities, with the aim of selecting appropriate facilities for production. Often the range of applicable resources is *a priori* limited on the basis of the overall production strategy of the company; for instance, certain types of products are always manufactured in a certain production facility. Features such as holes must be inspected from the viewpoint of tooling requirements to determine whether drills of requires sizes are available on candidate machining centers. Production cost and time are important aspects of the analysis.

Generation of Numerical Control Programs The main issues for this case are the correctness and efficiency of the programs generated. In terms of the architectural dimensions, the scenario is characterized as *micro level, short time scale, variant,* and (possibly) *dynamic.* Achieving these correctness and efficiency goals typically requires that fairly specialized features be used that can directly be mapped to processes. To generate NC instructions for drilling a hole feature, relatively detailed information on the machine tool, drill, material, and manufacturing parameters is required. Much of the information required is machine specific; hence the range of the analysis must be limited to a single machine or a group of machines with similar production capabilities.

Summary We may conclude that the identification and definition of process planning features must be based on the intended application. In particular, the choice of features must match the desired level of user control which in the above scenarios varies from very low (in manufacturability evaluation) to very high (in NC generation). For instance, using fine granularity features as input to a process planner effectively means that generating the input representation already specifies the processes to be used, and the process planner only needs to sequence the processes and select the resources to be used. In contrast, rough granularity features leave much more room for decision making in the process planner. Therefore fine granularity features seem ideal to provide detailed control of the processes to be selected (as required for NC generation), whereas low granularity features make it possible to explore a wide range of manufacturing options (as required for manufacturability analysis). It follows that if a range of applications must be supported, the feature model should support features of varying levels of abstraction and specialization.

11.2.2 Examples of Process Planning Features

This section clarifies the above by inspecting the collection of features of MCOES *(Manufacturing Cell Operator's Expert System)*, a process planning system constructed in the Brite-Euram project no. BE-3528 of the Commission of the European Communities (Mäntylä 1993, Laakko and Mäntylä 1992, 1993, Opas et al. 1994). Some other aspects of MCOES will be discussed later in this chapter.

MCOES was designed to cover both operative, short-term and tactical, medium-term process planning in a "workshop factory," a factory specializing on a limited range of known part families. In particular, MCOES aims at fully automatic generation of correct NC programs. Within this domain its feature definitions address most of the issues mentioned earlier in this section. In particular, it was considered important that the feature definitions support the notions of variant features and part families.

MCOES uses the feature-modeling system EXTDesign discussed in Chapter 10 for feature creation and manipulation. The technical issues related to feature definitions and taxonomy were covered already in Chapter 10; see Figure 10.3 and the subsequent figures for an overview. Here we will discuss the taxonomy in light of the issues identified earlier.

A major objective in the design of the feature collection was to provide a good basis for the representation of various type of processes, to offer variable levels of granularity and detail, and also to support user extendibility. To support these goals, MCOES adopts the variant feature approach discussed in Chapter 6. MCOES variant features make it possible to include quite specific features in the feature model as may be needed for recording the preferred production methods of a product. Alternatively, if the user of the system deems it not yet necessary to specify a process exactly, more generic features are also available. The level of specialization may also vary according to the process type. For instance, MCOES' prismatic features are generally more specialized than its rotational features, reflecting the relative complexity of machining planning in comparison with turning. Naturally both volume and surface area features are included to capture the required range of processes.

In addition to simple features, the taxonomy must also deal with more complex or high-level entities that should be included in the user-definable feature library of the system. The initial rough shape to which machining processes are applied is often a cast part that may have a complex shape of its own. In a machining process planner, one approach is to treat the whole casting as a "feature" in its own right. The machined part as a whole becomes a treelike structure consisting of the casting (a positive feature) at the root and a number of process planning features (generally, negative features for machining applications) as leaves. To implement the approach, a facility for maintaining a user-definable library of castings as a subset of the feature library is needed. A representation of casting geometry must be included in these features. For turned parts, the initial part may be produced by sawing a segment of a standard rod. The capturing of the sawing process requires a separate feature class with its related process models. The definition language of parts was described in Chapter 10.

The natural unit of work for a process planner is not necessarily a single part. In an FMS a collection of parts (similar or different) are often produced simultaneously by fixturing them on a single pallet. To produce valid plans, the concept of a setup of several parts on a pallet must be captured in the input representation of the process planner. One way to do this is to include a special user-definable compound feature class lot consisting of a collection of instances of parts into the feature library.

To clarify the above items, we give sample feature descriptions of the taxonomy in Figures 11.5, 11.6, 11.7, and 11.8 along with "typical" examples of the feature representations.

External-O-Slot Implicit surfaces: 1. side-surface-1, 2. side-surface-2, 3. end-surface, 4. bottom-surface.

```
     external-o-slot-1
 1   instance              external-o-slot
 2   length                100
 3   depth                 14
 4   width                 7
 5   bottom-radius         3.5
 6   end-radius            10
 7   position              (0 0 0)
 8   orientation           (0 0 0)
 9   side-surface-1        external-o-slot-1-side-1
10   side-surface-2        external-o-slot-1-side-2
11   end-surface           external-o-slot-1-end
12   bottom-surface        external-o-slot-1-bottom
```

The external-o-slot (Figure 11.5) is a typical prismatic feature. MCOES slot taxonomy is fairly fine-grained because of the emphasis of system on low-level planning and NC generation. Thus the system classifies slots in terms of the number of access directions, the types and orientations of roundings, whether the slots are linear or circular, and whether they are "through" or not.

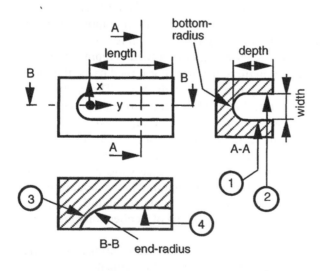

Figure 11.5 An external-o-slot feature

Internal-Flat-Slot Implicit surfaces: 1. side-surface-1, 2. side-surface-2, 3. bottom-surface.

```
      internal-flat-slot-1
1     instance                internal-flat-slot
2     length                  100
3     depth                   8
4     width                   20
5     bottom-rounding         2
6     end-radius              8
7     position                (0 0 0)
8     orientation             (0 0 0)
9     side-surface-1          internal-flat-slot-1-end-1
10    side-surface-2          internal-flat-slot-1-end-2
11    bottom-surface          internal-flat-slot-1-bottom
```

The `internal-flat-slot` (Figure 11.6) is another typical prismatic feature. "Internal" indicates that the feature does not extend to the edge of the part; hence plunging processes are required, unlike the case of "external" features.

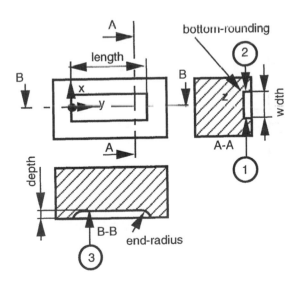

Figure 11.6 An internal-flat-slot feature

Counter-Sink

```
      counter-sink-1
  1   instance           counter-sink
  2   angle              90
  3   depth              7
  4   hole               through-hole-1
  5   position           (0 0 0)
  6   orientation        (0 0 0)
  7   cone-surface       counter-sink-1-cone
```

A counter-sink (Figure 11.7) is a typical "medium-granularity" prismatic feature. It is included in the taxonomy because countersinking is a fairly standard process that can be conveniently captured by knowledge associated with this feature. A nonstandard countersink (e.g., where the sink angle is other than the standard 90 or 135) can be modeled as a compound of a sink and a blind hole, if needed.

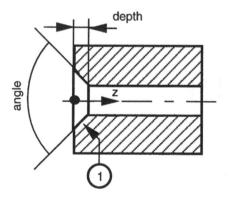

Figure 11.7   A counter-sink feature

Annular-Area

```
     annular-area-1
  1  instance              annular-area
  2  smaller-radius        30
  3  larger-radius         40
  4  working-allowance     50
  5  surface-quality       1.6
  6  position              (0 0 0)
  7  orientation           (0 0 0)
```

The annular-area (Figure 11.8) is a typical surface area feature that could appear in, say, bearing-type parts. Its purpose is to indicate that a certain subset (e.g., a sealing surface) of a face must be machined to higher surface finish than the rest of the face.

Surface features of MCOES do not have clear volumetric counterparts. Observe that the "volume" machined out of the workpiece for the annular-area feature is just the working allowance of the original surface. This also means that they cannot be recognized using the standard feature recognition techniques; currently MCOES supports only the recognition of rotational surface area features for grinding. Consequently surface area features are placed in the model using design-by-features techniques or procedural modeling.

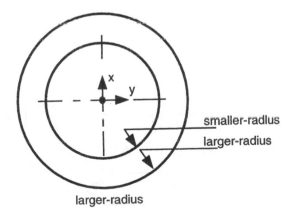

larger-radius

Figure 11.8 An annular-area feature

Rounding Rounding and chamfer are considered transitions. There are two cases in defining a transition, as shown in Figure 11.9. First is defining a transition between two surfaces of the same feature. The other case is defining a transition between two surfaces of two different features.

A rounding between two surfaces of the same feature is defined as an attribute of the feature. There is a slot for defining a transition (rounding or a chamfer) in the frame of each feature that can have one as we saw earlier in the descriptions of `external-o-slot` and `internal-flat-slot`. We handle roundings in rotational parts in this fashion. An example of such a rounding is presented in Figure 11.9*a*. Here the actual geometry of the rounding depends on the next segment. The slots that contain the definitions of the roundings in this case are `transition-end-1` and `transition-end-2`.

A rounding between two surfaces of two different features is a feature of its own and has a frame description. An example of a rounding as a feature is presented in Figure 11.9*b*.

```
    rounding-1
1   instance        rounding
2   radius          R
3   features        (relief1 bottom-surface)
                    (block1 side-surface-2)
```

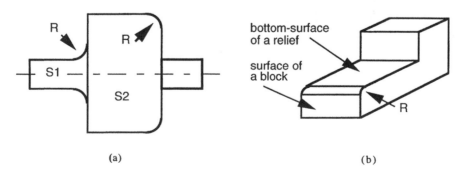

(a)   (b)

Figure 11.9 Two cases of a rounding

Segment-Sequence A segment-sequence is a compound feature that consists of a collection of cylindrical or tapered segments, as shown in Figure 11.10. The individual segments have the same center axis. The feature class is used to model shaft-like parts as a whole.

```
     segment-sequence-1
1  instance              segment-sequence
2  length                225
3  segments              (cylindrical-segment-1
                          cylindrical-segment-2
                          cylindrical-segment-3)
4  position              (0 0 0)
5  orientation           (0 0 0)
```

Shaft-like parts are somewhat problematic from the taxonomy point of view. On one hand, they should be treated as a single feature because they are manufactured as a single unit (a turning process works on the whole shaft). On the other hand, they appear in great variety of shapes. The MCOES approach is to treat the segment-sequence as the actual "feature," and the individual segments as the "modifiers" that indicate the overall shape of the feature. Detail features such as slots, grooves, and holes may be added to the segments. An example of such detail features is the `annular-slot` feature described in the sequel. As a result shafts in MCOES are modeled at a higher level of abstraction than prismatic parts.

Variant features may be used to model more specific types of shafts. For instance, "standard shafts" having well-established process planning requirements may be modeled as variants of the `segment-sequence` feature. Such variants would include a process plan template for the shaft family using the facilities to be explained in Section 11.3.

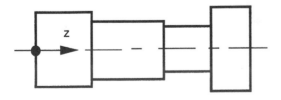

Figure 11.10 A segment-sequence feature

Tapered-Segment   Implicit surfaces: 1. end-surface-1, 2. end-surface-2, 3. cone-surface

```
        tapered-segment-1
  1  instance                tapered-segment
  2  diameter-1              90
  3  diameter-2              120
  4  length                 180
  5  transition-end-1        (chamfer 45 5)
  6  transition-end-2        (rounding 5)
  7  position                (0 0 0)
  8  orientation             (0 0 0)
  9  end-surface-1          tapered-segment-end-1
 10  end-surface-2          tapered-segment-end-2
 11  cone-surface           tapered-segment-cone
```

Tapered segments (Figure 11.11) appear in shaft-type parts. As observed in the discussion on the segment-sequence feature, the planner does not treat them as independent features. Instead, process planning logic mainly addresses the shaft as a whole to determine the turning operations needed in producing the shaft.

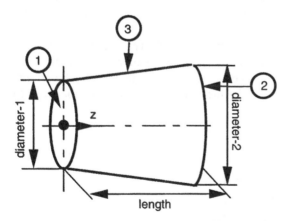

Figure 11.11 A tapered-segment feature

Annular-Flat-Slot Implicit-surfaces: 1. inner-cylinder-surface, 2. outer-cylinder-surface, 3. bottom-surface.

```
      annular-flat-slot-1
1   instance                  annular-flat-slot
2   inner-diameter            50
3   outer-diameter            60
4   depth                     12
5   bottom-rounding           5
6   position                  (0 0 0)
7   orientation               (0 0 0)
8   inner-cylinder-surface    annular-flat-slot-1-inner-cyl
9   outer-cylinder-surface    annular-flat-slot-1-outer-cyl
10  bottom-surface            annular-flat-slot-1-bottom
```

Annular slots may appear in shaftlike parts (in the end surface of a shaft or in a side face of a "step") as in Figure 11.12. The explicit surfaces (lines 8–10) exist mainly to record surface finish information.

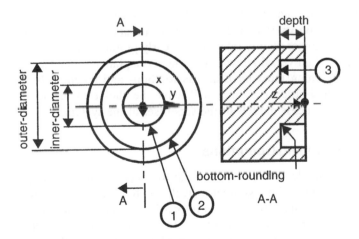

Figure 11.12 An annular-flat-slot feature

11.3 PROCESS MODELS

The capability of a process planning system to create useful process plans is largely determined by the available manufacturing process models. Various kinds of process knowledge needed in a process planning system include (Chang 1990):

1. The feature shapes and sizes a process can produce, or inversely, the processes that can produce a given feature.
2. The dimensions and tolerances that can be obtained by a process.
3. Geometric and technological process constraints that determine the conditions under which a process is applicable.
4. The economics of a process.

Process model information can be available on several levels of detail:

1. *Universal knowledge* Knowledge that is applicable to all processes of a certain type, independently of the details in a particular factory.
2. *Shop-level knowledge* Knowledge that is valid only in a particular factory or workshop.
3. *Machine-level knowledge* Knowledge that is valid only for a particular machine tool (or some particular instance of another resource).

The actual level of detail and specialization needed in a particular process planning system depends on its intended position in the architectural framework of Section 11.1. A planner mainly intended for early producibility analysis might work on the basis of universal knowledge, whereas a planner intended for short-term operative planning must have access to shop- and machine-level knowledge. Again an ideal process planner will leave the choice of the scope and level of detail of the process models to the superuser of the system.

11.3.1 A Model for Machining Operations

Ideally process models should be rigorous enough to support automatic algorithms for creating the mapping from geometry (features) to processes, to determine whether all constraints are satisfied, and to predict accurately enough the technical and economical performance of the feasible processes. However, these requirements are not easily satisfied and process modeling remains a challenging research topic. This and the following subsection will present a (semi-) formal model of simple machining processes and a mapping procedure from features to processes based on the work by (Shirur 1994). While the model is representative of current state of the art, further research is needed to generalize the models to a practical level of detail.

Once the volumes to be machined are found, we need to match them to machining operations that can produce them. In the past, "if-then" production rules were most commonly used; each feature was associated with the processes that may be used to produce it. In recent years, it has been recognized that the knowledge encoded in these rules is shallow, which cannot form the basis for robust systems that can deal with feature interactions and undocumented (user-defined) features. To capture the fundamental characteristics of a machining process, it is necessary to understand the tool-workpiece interaction (kinematics) to "generate" the removal volumes.

Metal cutting by any operation can be described as the successive removal of some characteristic shape. Successive passes of the tool on the workpiece is equivalent to the repeated instances of the characteristic volume. The total machined volume is the union of these volumes. In order to cut the material, the tool must spatially interfere with the workpiece with a relative motion normal to the interference. In addition, of course, the material and structural conditions must be met for fracture of the workpiece to take place. Only the geometric conditions will be discussed here.

Shirur's model represents the geometry and kinematics of machining operations by swept volumes, where the generator is the tool-workpiece interference, and the director is the tool-workpiece relative motion vector. There are two basic types of relative motions: the primary one causes the cutting action; the secondary one corresponds to feed. Therefore, two geometric operators are required. They are designated as "*" and "·" operators, to represent cutting and feed actions respectively. The operands are a closed profile, P and a bi-vector V_i defined as a set of two vectors, a direction vector v_e and a position vector p_e. The sweep operation is expressed algebraically as:

$$M_E = \{P * V_i(v_e, p_e)\} \tag{11.1}$$

The "*" operator signifies the sweep operation (translational or rotational) of the left operand using the attributes defined in the right operand and resulting in the elementary machinable volume M_E. The left operand must be a closed 2D profile, which defines the "imprint" of the process (i.e., tool-workpiece interference that results in cutting). The operand $V(v_e, p_e)$ specifies an ordered set of either sweep or transformation attributes. Because it is an ordered set of two vectors it is referred to as a bi-vector. With the selection of a proper bi-vector it is possible to represent both translational or rotational sweeps, sweep direction, and magnitude.

The "·" operator signifies the transformation operation of the left operand G using the attributes defined in the right operand, the bi-vector V:

$$\{G \cdot V(v, p)\} \tag{11.2}$$

G must be either a closed 2D profile or a 3D volume. The operation results in an object of the same manifold class as G. Repeated instances of any geometric entity with the same transformation attributes are modeled by using exponents to the transformation operands, symbolically written as $G \cdot \{V(v, p)\}^k$ that implies that the operator is used k times, operating on the result of the previous operation. Combining (11.1) and (11.2) gives us a means to represent machining processes by the following algebraic expression:

$$\mathbf{M_T} = \mathbf{M_E} \cdot \{ V_1(\mathbf{v_1}, \mathbf{p_1}) \}^{k1} \cdot \{ V_2(\mathbf{v_2}, \mathbf{p_2}) \}^{k2} \tag{11.3a}$$

$$= P * V_e(\mathbf{v_e}, \mathbf{p_e}) \cdot \{ V_1(\mathbf{v_1}, \mathbf{p_1}) \}^{k1} \cdot \{ V_2(\mathbf{v_2}, \mathbf{p_2}) \}^{k2} \tag{11.3b}$$

where $\mathbf{M_T}$ is the total volume removed by an operation, $\mathbf{M_E} = P * V_e(\mathbf{v_e}, \mathbf{p_e})$ represents the elementary machinable volume generated by the primary motion, and $\{ V_1(\mathbf{v_1}, \mathbf{p_1}) \}^{k1} \cdot \{ V_2(\mathbf{v_2}, \mathbf{p_2}) \}^{k2}$ represents further growth of this volume due to the feed (secondary) motion; k1 and k2 are scalars that could be computed from the dimensions of the volume to be machined and the dimensions of the profile P. Equation (11.3) provides a uniform mathematical representation of common machining processes: turning, 2 or 3-axis milling, shaping, planing, broaching, drilling, boring, EDM, etc. We will determine the conditions for representing each of these processes in this form. The algebra has several interesting properties, e.g., pseudo-commutative and identity relations:

$$P * V(\mathbf{v_1}, \mathbf{p_1}) \cdot V(\mathbf{v_2}, \mathbf{p_2})^k = P \cdot V(\mathbf{v_2}, \mathbf{p_2})^k * V(\mathbf{v_1}, \mathbf{p_1})$$

$$V(\mathbf{v}, \mathbf{p})^0 = V(\mathbf{0}, \mathbf{p})$$

11.3.2 Mapping Features to Processes Based on "Deep" Knowledge

The characteristic expression developed in the last section formulates a mathematical representation of the volume machinable by any process. For process planning the inverse mapping—namely the determination of the expression from a volume—is of high interest. This section outlines a model-based, "deep" mapping method from features to processes.

The sweep and dot operators of the machining algebra produce the geometric model of machining operations from the tool-workpiece kinematics. It can be shown that inverse operations produce non-unique results, which corresponds to different ways of machining the same volume. The elementary machining volume can be found by inverting (11.3a):

$$\mathbf{M_E} = \{ \{ \mathbf{M_T}^{-1} V1(\mathbf{v_1}, \mathbf{p_1}) \}^{k1 \cdot 1} V2(\mathbf{v_2}, \mathbf{p_2}) \}^{k2} \tag{11.4}$$

Here $^{-1}$ is the inverse dot operator. The profile can be found from $\mathbf{M_E}$ by inverting (11.1):

$$P = \{ \mathbf{M_E}^{*-1} V_e(\mathbf{v_e}, \mathbf{p_e}) \} \tag{11.5}$$

Here $*^{-1}$ is the inverse sweep operator. We could reverse the sequence in which the inverse sweep and dot operations are applied, which will result in a different profile and bi-vectors. In either case, there may be a choice of several V1 and V2.

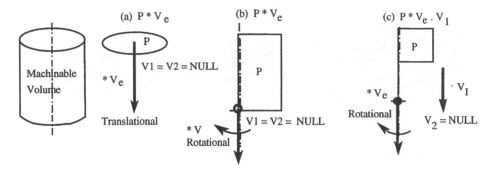

Figure 11.13 Alternative mapping of a cylindrical shaped machinable volume.

A third option is not to apply the dot operators at all, resulting in yet another mapping. These three options, when applied to a cylindrical volume, result in the three mappings shown in Figure 11.13.

For both translational and rotational directors, the inverse sweep operator involves slicing the volume using a plane to get a section profile. In the case of translational director, the sectioning plane is perpendicular to the director. On the other hand, in the case of rotational director, the sectioning plane is along the axis of the rotation (i.e., the plane contains the axis of rotation). Figure 11.14 illustrates an example inverse sweep operation on rotational volume. For the translational sweep director techniques for computing the sweep length need to be developed. In the specific case when the closing surfaces at the two ends of the translational volume are both planar and normal to the translational direction, the translational distance may be found as the distance between the two planar surfaces at the ends. However, the general case is still under investigation.

Two versions of the inverse dot operator have been developed; one for 2D entities, the other for 3D. Figure 11.15 shows an example in which a 3D entity E

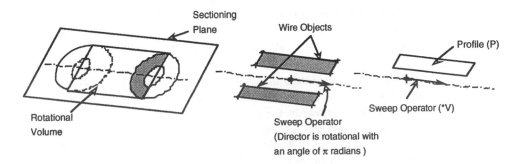

Figure 11.14 Inverse sweep operation on a rotational volume.

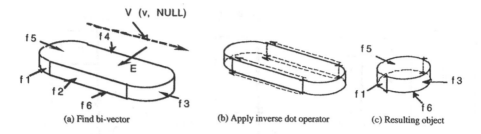

(a) Find bi-vector   (b) Apply inverse dot operator   (c) Resulting object

Figure 11.15 Inverse dot operation on a 3D entity.

is inverse dot operated using a bi-vector V. It is desirable to devise algorithms that will utilize topological and geometric operators already available in geometric modelers.

The volume classification strategy using degrees-of-freedom (DOF) analysis described in Chapter 9 (Figure 9.20) is especially conducive to extracting the possible machining axes from the fundamental axes of the volume. This is because the DOF of any volume along any axis determines the accessibility of that volume for machining along that axis. Second, the DOF of the tool with respect to the workpiece along or about the principal cutting direction or axis is a maximum (i.e., DOF = 1 for translationally swept volume or DOF = 2π for rotationally swept volume).

The selection of a machining process to machine a given volume is done in several steps, developed by Shirur (1994):

Step 1   Determine the kinematic feasibility of machining the volume by comparing its translational (TDOF) and rotational (RDOF) DOF to the TDOF and RDOF of the machinable volumes of each candidate machining process. A direct match signifies kinematic feasibility.

Step 2   Determine the direction in which the volume has a full DOF as the principal cutting direction. For example, the RDOF of a volume corresponding to a blind hole is $\{2\pi, 0, 0\}$. The full RDOF along the first component direction forms the principal cutting direction for the drilling operation. This hints that drilling is likely to machine the volume. Existence of more than one full DOF implies alternative machining processes or alternative machining setups.

Step 3   For each machining process find the specific relationships between different operands in the manufacturing expression. For example, in drilling one edge of the primary profile (*P*) must define the axis of rotation. In other words, the point $\mathbf{p}_e$ must lie on the straight line that contains one straight line segment of the profile. Also the vector $\mathbf{v}_e$ must be parallel to that edge of the profile. These process-specific constraints must be satisfied for a volume to be machinable by that process. The remaining steps are repeated for each feasible process passing these tests.

Step 4 Use the information on end conditions between two non-full TDOF directions of the volume to determine the constraints on the shape of the profile *P*. Since the principal axis of the volume (same as the principal cutting direction) is already known, the shape of the elementary machinable volume can be determined.

Step 5 Determine the values of the associated operands and also the exponents to the operands from the dimension of the machinable volume in the direction of the DOF specification and the process capabilities, such as material removal rate and cutting speed.

Step 6 Observe the range of possible values for each operand in the manufacturing expression that exists for the process. For example, the diameter of a hole machinable by drilling operation has both an upper and a lower bound. If the instanced value of the operands in the previous step doesn't conform to the range of feasible values of that operand, then the process can be rejected as geometrically not feasible.

From the values of the profile *P*, and operands that go to make the manufacturing expression, it is possible to determine the following about each feasible machining operation:

1. The machining operation.
2. The size and shape of the tool to be used.
3. The kinematics and geometry of the machining operation.
4. The cutting parameters such as depth of cut and feed.
5. The number of passes to machine a given volume, dimension of each pass, and so on.

For an example of the mapping process, consider a cylindrical machinable volume that corresponds to a blind hole with conical bottom face, shown in Figure 11.16. The DOF of the volume is

$\text{TDOF}\{\frac{1}{2}, 0, 0\}$

$\text{RDOF}\{2\pi, 0, 0\}$

The end conditions between two non-full TDOF of the volume are:

End condition between T_x and T_y, E_{xy} = angular (120 degrees)

End condition between T_x and T_z, E_{xz} = angular (120 degrees)

End condition between T_z and T_y, E_{yz} = round (90 degrees)

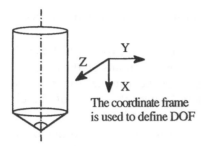

Figure 11.16 Machinable volume for the drilling operation

On the basis of these end conditions, the mapping of the example proceeds as follows:

Step 1   The machining operations that have the same DOF as the given volume are turning, reaming, drilling, boring, plunge end milling, and internal and external cylindrical grinding. Each of these machining operations allows enough degrees of freedom to the tool to machine the volume.

Step 2   The volume has only one full DOF, namely RDOF about the x-axis = $R_x = 2\pi$. Since this is a rotational DOF, the primary cutting direction is circular.

Step 3   Use attributes of the machinable volume (i.e., the DOF and end conditions with respect to the coordinate frame) to determine whether the constraints on operand relationships of each machining operation are satisfied. These relationships are defined for each machining operation, and they represent the geometric constraints specific to that process. In this case operations such as turning, boring, reaming, and cylindrical grinding have a common constraint on operand relationships. The constraint states that *the cutting edge must NOT be collinear to the axis of rotation*. The machining implication of this constraint is that *turning cannot reduce the diameter of the workpiece to zero*. For the sample volume the constraint is not satisfied for all radial values of the volume. After this step, only plunge end milling and drilling qualify as possible machining processes.

Step 4   The end conditions of the sample volume are achievable by the profiles of twist drilling operation but not by the profiles of plunge milling operation, which can produce only flat bottom faces. Since plunge end milling produces an angular (90 degrees) end condition along the x- and y- or z-directions of the local coordinate frame of the profile, it disqualifies for this volume which has end conditions $E_{xy} = E_{xz}$ = 120 degrees. This end condition is achievable only by drilling operation.

Step 5 Determine if the dimensions of the profile are obtainable with the process capability of the drilling operation (i.e., examine the sizes of the available drilling tools). Use the material removal rate to determine detailed process parameters such as feed and speed.

11.3.3 Mapping Features to Processes Based on "Shallow" Knowledge

The deep mapping method from features to processes is relatively complex. It does not generalize easily for all types of features and manufacturing processes. Therefore, for practical purposes, process planning systems mostly use shallow maps with symbolic representations of shapes for process representation. The shapes are classified in groups of similar shapes, and each group is associated with the processes that may be used to produce it. Features are primary candidates for such symbolic representations of shapes.

For process-modeling purposes, shapes of various dimensions may be used. Some processes may be characterized in terms of the kinds of edges (silhouette lines) that can be produced. Turning is a prime example of this situation. Processes can also be characterized by the surfaces and the surface characteristics they are able to generate. Such processes include, for instance, area milling. The problem with this approach is that if several surfaces are created by a single process, complex matching is required to associate the surfaces to the process.

For feature-based process planners, process modeling by volume (feature) is of course the preferred method. Sample characterizations of processes in association to features are listed in Table 11.2. Unfortunately, some processes are difficult or unnatural to model on the basis of volumes only. Turning, in particular, is cumbersome to handle if it must be modeled in terms of three-dimensional volumes removed from a three-dimensional stock. The rotational symmetry of turning planning strongly suggests a surface- or edge-based representation. Also hole-finishing operations (e.g., reaming and boring) do not match with well-defined volumes; the material removed from the workpiece is just a thin slice of material, the thickness of which is determined by the work allowance left by a previous operation (most likely, drilling). For these and other similar finishing operations, a surface-based representation seems more natural.

11.3.4 Process Capabilities

In addition to shape, each process has its intrinsic process capabilities in terms of dimensions, tolerances, and surface characteristics that can be produced by the process:

- Dimensions are determined by tool size and machine tool work envelope (e.g., drills are only available in some sizes).
- Many aspects (material, cutting conditions, machine-dependent parameters) determine the tolerances and surface characteristics attainable; in practice, experience-based values must be used.

Table 11.2 Process characterizations of some features

Feature Name	Process Name	Process Sequencing
Bevel (3 subtypes)	End-milling	1. Rough-end-mill 2. Finish-end-mill 3. Rough & finish-end-mill
Boss	End-milling	1. Rough-end-mill 2. Finish-end-mill 3. Rough & finish-end-mill
Centerhole	Centerdrill turning	1. Centerdrill 2. Rough-turn 3. Finish-turn 4. Rough & finish turn
Chamfer internal or external	Turning	1. Rough-turn 2. Finish-turn 3. Rough & finish turn
Counterbore	End-milling Counterbore Turning EDM Jig-grinding	1. Plunge-end-mill 2. Rough-profile-end-mill 3. Rough & finish profile-end-mill 4. Counterbore (with counterbore tool)
Countersink	Countersinking Jig-grinding Turning	1. Countersink 2. Countersink, jig-grind
Cutout 6 sub-types	Punching Laser End-milling EDM-wire EDM-electrod Broaching	1. Finish-punch 2. Finish-laser 3. Rough-end-mill 4. Rough & finish-end-mill 5. Rough-end-mill EDM 6. Rough & finish-end-mill EDM 7. Rough-end-mill finish broach
Fillet	End-milling	1. Rough-end-mill 2. Finish-end-mill 3. Rough & finish-end-mill
Flat (on cylinder)	End-milling	1. Rough-end-mill 2. Finish-end-mill 3. Rough & finish-end-mill
External cylinder	Turning	1. Rough-turn 2. Finish-turn 3. Cylindrical grinding 4. Centerless grinding

Some "textbook" surface characteristics that may be available about the reaming process are listed in Table 11.3. For process planning, such process capabilities form constraints to process selection. In practice, truly attainable values must be determined by experimentation on the basis of the actual materials, NC machines, cutting tools, cutting fluid, and so on, used in the process.

Table 11.3 Surface characteristics of the reaming process

Process Matrix for Reaming

Process = Reaming Number	Process Parameters	Feature types = holes Parameter Data
1	Diameter	Typical = (>= .0625 <= 1.500)
2	Diameter tolerance	Typical = (+/− .003 - +/− .001)
		Feasible = (+/− .001 - +/− .0005)
3	Depth range	Typical = (>= 1:1 <= 1:6)
4	Depth tolerance	Typical = (+/− .010)
5	Surface finish	Typical = (>= 32 <= 63)
		Feasible = (>= 16 <= 125)
6	True position	+/− .010
7	Roundness	+/− .0005
8	Straightness	+/− .001
9	Concentricity	+/− .001

11.3.5 Process Constraints

The applicability of a process to a particular manufacturing task is determined by various types of *process constraints:*

- *Interference constraints* The noncutting part of the tool cannot interfere with the workpiece (e.g., a reamer or a bore cannot be used without an initial hole; drills can be used to create holes of some maximal depth only.)
- *Physical constraints* For example, a hole cannot be drilled on a slanted surface.
- *Technological constraints* Constraints set by cutting forces applied by the processes, available power of the machine tool, and so on.

The representation of process constraint information is perhaps the biggest challenge in process planning systems. Clearly effective implementation of process constraint checking requires access to geometric representations of the part, the tool, the fixtures, and the machine, and advanced geometric reasoning capabilities. Examples of various interference and physical constraints are shown in Figure 11.17 (Chang 1990).

Analysis of technological constraints requires that properties such as cutting force and required power can be extracted on the basis of a process model. Exact physical models of cutting processes are a research subject of manufacturing science. Meanwhile simpler experience-based formulas can be used. To see the nature of these computations, let us consider the computation of some important parameters for drilling. The most important formulas relate the feed and speed of drilling to the available power of the machine tool. For instance, the cutting speed at point A of the figure is given by

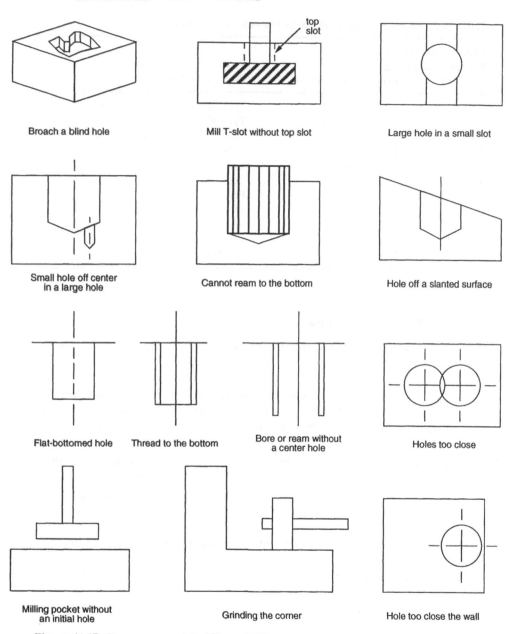

Broach a blind hole

Mill T-slot without top slot

Large hole in a small slot

Small hole off center
in a large hole

Cannot ream to the bottom

Hole off a slanted surface

Flat-bottomed hole   Thread to the bottom

Bore or ream without
a center hole

Holes too close

Milling pocket without
an initial hole

Grinding the corner

Hole too close the wall

Figure 11.17 Process constraints (Chang 1990)

$$V_c = \frac{dn\pi}{1000} \text{ m/min.}$$

where

V_c = cutting speed
n = drill rpm
d = drill diameter in mm.

The rate of metal removal is an important characteristic for power and time computations. It is given by

$$Qd = \frac{AnF}{1000} \text{ cm}^3/\text{min.}$$

where
Qd = volume of metal removed in cm³/min.
n = drill rpm
F = feed in mm per revolution of drill
A = area = $r^2 \cdot \pi = d^2 \cdot \pi / 4$ mm².

The required horsepower[1] at the tool spindle depends not only on process geometry but also on the material and the tool. The influence of the material can be represented in terms of a material constant k.

Using the material constant, the formula for power becomes simply

$$HP = kQd$$

where
HP = horsepower required for machining
k = material constant
Qd = volume of metal removed in cm³/min.

This formula assumes that the machine tool can be run at 100% efficiency and is hence theoretical. In practice, the feasible efficiency (E) depends on the condition of the machine tool and may vary in the range 0.7 to 0.85. Therefore the practical formula for calculating the horsepower becomes

$$HP = \frac{kQd}{E}$$

Similarly, the machining time T can be calculated as

$$T = \frac{L}{F}$$

where
L = depth of drilling in mm
F = feed in mm/min.

---

[1]Lamentably, horsepower is still the unit of choice for engineering use. 1 horsepower is defined 75 kg · m/sec.

In practice, the preceding formulas can be used to compute the possible feed and speed of drilling on the basis of required hole geometry, material, and the available machine tool characteristics, such as horsepower and efficiency. Other formulas for turning and milling processes can be found in (Sawa and Pusztai 1990).

11.3.6 Process Economics

An important goal of process planners is to produce cost-effective process plans. To achieve this goal, *cost models* can be associated with process representations. The contribution of features, then, is to provide simple access to cost models through process descriptions. A good reference for cost estimation is (Ostwald 1988).

A cost model should take into account the following items:

- Cost of the blank part and other materials
- Machining times of each machining step
- Cost of machines and fixtures per hour
- Tool and fixture wear
- Manual labor times of each step
- Cost of manual labor per hour
- Preparatory time
- Cost of preparatory work
- Fixed cost per batch

To apply this type of a model, fairly detailed process plan information is required, including information on the machining cycles and parameters, which are needed for estimating the machining times. Observe that the batch size also has an effect; this information may not be available at all at process planning time.

In practice, simplified models must be used, since often the final tool paths required for a detailed computation are not available at process planning time. Reasonable cost information can be obtained simply based on the material removal rates and machined feature volumes. A simple example of this approach is discussed in Section 1.4.2.

Cost can also be modeled qualitatively, *e.g.*, using a scale from 1 to 10. This may be good enough for process selection, but not for actual cost estimation.

11.3.7 Process Resources

Apart from product and process knowledge, information on the actual resources available in a factory is required for process planning. This information includes a wide range of data such as the shop and cell layouts, machine tools, tools, materials, fixtures, and even personnel. An important source of information for short-term process planning is the master schedule of the factory, which represents the tasks currently scheduled for execution in the factory, their timing, and the resources utilized. Much of the resource information is shared with shop-floor control systems and can be stored in shared files or databases.

11.3.8 Process Plan Representation

The representation of process plan information is another important issue of process planning systems. In addition to the final result of process planning, the representation must also cover intermediate process plan fragments generated during the planning process or given as input to the planner for variant planning. The importance of such representations has been recognized from standardization point of view, notably under the STEP umbrella (Paul 1994, Parker 1994). Therefore a brief discussion into the topic is included in this section.

A generic process plan representation must capture the full range of planning approaches indicated by the architectural dimensions as discussed in Section 11.1 For instance *nonlinear process plans* exhibiting some variability must be included. Moreover the plan representation must capture a natural hierarchy of plan detail to support various levels of planning depth.

The ALPS (A language process specification) representation (Ray and Catron 1991) is one such notation. ALPS defines a number of plan elements that can be divided in two main types. *Tasks* model the actual processes to be executed; tasks are further split in several subtypes according to whether they are considered atomic or whether they can be further decomposed into lower-level tasks. Hence ALPS supports plan hierarchies and variable levels of modeling detail. *Control structures* model sequencing constraints and selection criteria of their underlying processes. For instance, an `or` node models the choice of several alternative lower-level processes; hence nonlinear plans can be captured. Similar representations are also defined by (Krause and Altmann 1991).

ALPS was chosen as the basis of process plan representation in the MCOES process planner. In the MCOES implementation, ALPS becomes a hierarchy of classes that corresponds with various process plan task types and control structures, as shown in Figure 11.18. Class `work-element` is the root class of all primitive operations of the system. These represent a single machining cycles where a tool is applied to a feature. Other task classes (`ALPS-complex-task`) are defined in terms of a sequence of lower-level tasks. Class `method` models a sequence of work elements that produces a complete feature. Class `manufacturing-step` models a sequence of work elements or methods that are applied on a single machine in single part setup. The various subclasses of class `ALPS-split` correspond to various control structures. For instance, `ALPS-sequential-and` represents a set of tasks that must be executed in a given order, whereas `ALPS-serial-and` allows the tasks to be executed in any order. `ALPS-predicated-or` is used to express nonlinear plans.

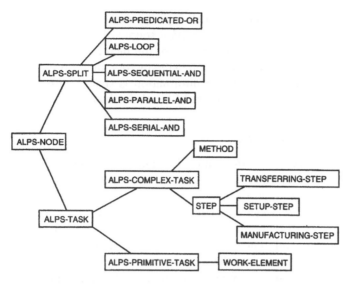

Figure 11.18 Taxonomy of ALPS entities

In the MCOES implementation, ALPS specifications are written in a special declaration language embedded in LISP. The specifications are associated with part family models to define a variant process plan template to each variant part family. The definition can be inherited; hence lower-level part variants can be defined simply by changing the inherited values of family parameters. The language provides a number of useful facilities such as parameter passing, local variables, arithmetic expressions, block structure, and conditional evaluation implemented through a rule interpreter. During the evaluation of the language, a number of auxiliary variables bound to the features and their attributes of a related part model can be used to facilitate accessing information from the feature representation.

A sample plan specification for a part family is shown in Figure 11.19. The presented plan specification states that the part is made in two steps, PART-STEP-1 and PART-STEP-2. The steps must be performed in the given sequence because they are bound with the sequential-and clause. The contents of each step is modeled by means of sequential-and and serial-and clauses, which ultimately refer to methods and work elements. The specifications of methods and work elements refer to feature instances by variable names such as $fid2 or $fid13. These variables are set in the part family model. Similarly datums for dimensioning are assigned to methods and work elements. Lot plans relating to a set of parts produced simultaneously on a single pallet are defined similarly. The language is also used to define feature-level process plan fragments (methods) in terms of the elementary processes.

```
(sequential-and
  (step-var-1 nil
    (sequential-and
      (sequential-and
        (serial-and
          (method-large-rectangular-area $fid2 ($datum 'datum-2))
          (method-large-annular-area $fid13 ($datum 'datum-1))
          (method-medium-rectangular-area $fid7 ($datum 'datum-0))
          (we-large-hole-si-milling $fid15 ($datum 'datum-1)))
        (serial-and
          (we-small-area-sre-milling $fid20 ($datum 'datum-1))
          (we-small-area-sre-milling $fid21 ($datum 'datum-1))
          (we-small-relief $fid3 ($datum 'datum-1))
          (we-small-relief $fid4 ($datum 'datum-1))))
      (serial-and
        ...))
    PART-STEP-1)
  (step-var-2 nil
    ...
    PART-STEP-2))
```

Figure 11.19 A sample part family plan specification

Observe that the plan specification does not define completely the sequencing of work elements and methods. For instance, the four subtasks contained in the first serial-and in Figure 11.19 can be executed in any order. However, the enclosing sequential-and states that they must all be completed before the subtasks in the second serial-and (which again can be executed in any order) can be started. In MCOES this freedom is utilized by a sequencing algorithm of the plan generation system that is intended to arrange the work elements into an optimal order in terms of tool changes and pallet rotations.

11.4 OPERATION PLANNING

To illustrate the issues and techniques of feature-based process planning further, this and the following sections will look at some specific tasks of process planning in light of several influential works in feature-based process planning. This section will consider the task of *operation planning,* which may be defined as the *task of choosing the most appropriate operations from an available collection for creating a feature*. Operation planning illuminates the relations between process models and features.

11.4.1 Operation Planning in SIPS

SIPS (*semi-intelligent process selector*) (Nau and Gray 1986, Nau 1987) is a generative process planner for machining process selection. SIPS illustrates the use of process knowledge for single-operation planning. It is somewhat less attractive for sequencing and global planning, where global optimization criteria for process selection must be considered.

SIPS is based on a machining feature representation of the original part. For each feature it generates a sequence of machining operations by reasoning about the capabilities of manufacturing operations. The feature structure is based on recording the surfaces of features explicitly: For example, a "hole" is known to contain an "internal cylinder surface."

The operation of the system is based on a frame representation of process knowledge. The representation can be explained on the basis of the sample frames of Figure 11.20. The figure displays a hierarchy of five frames; lines connecting frames indicate that the child frame describes an alternative method for realizing the goal represented by the parent. Leaf frames indicate completed searches. The information of the sample frames is as follows:

- The root frame `hole-process` is the starting point of planning when a hole must be made (slot `relevant` indicates that this frame is suited for producing holes).

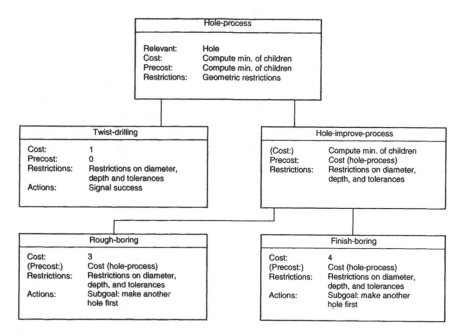

Figure 11.20 SIPS process model frames (Nau 1987; reprinted with permission of the author)

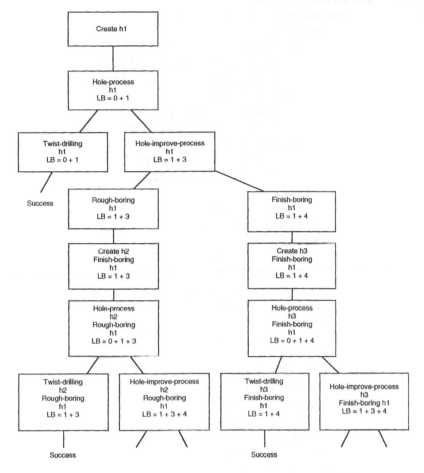

Figure 11.21 Search space corresponding with frames of Figure 11.20 (Nau 1987; reprinted with permission of the author))

- Slot cost stores the computed cost of the process. For the whole hole-making sequence, it is computed on the basis of the selected child processes.
- Slot precost is the cost of required preceding processes.
- Slot actions controls backward search from goal state.

A sample search space induced by these process frames is shown in Figure 11.21. Our initial goal is to create a hole h1. Since hole-process is relevant for making holes, we start the search from it. The children of hole-process provide two alternatives: twist-drilling produces immediate success, whereas hole-improve-process breaks into two additional alternatives, finish-boring and rough-boring. Both require that an initial hole h2 must first be produced. To produce h2, we start from hole-process once again.

```
process
    surface-process
        surface-create-process
            milling
                peripheral-milling
                    rough-peripheral-milling
                    finish-peripheral-milling
                face-milling
                    rough-face-milling
                    finish-face-milling
                end-milling
                    rough-end-milling
                    finish-end-milling
            turning
                rough-turning
                finish-turning
            facing
                rough-facing
                finish-facing
        surface-improve-process
            surface-grinding
            tapping
        surface-feature-process
            threading
    hole-process
        hole-create-process
            center-drilling
            twist-drilling
            small-hole-drilling
            spade-drilling
            gun-drilling
            end-milling-hole
                rough-end-milling-hole
                finish-end-milling-hole
        hole-improve-process
            boring
                rough-boring
                finish-boring
                finish-boring-2nd-pass
            reaming
                rough-reaming
                finish-reaming
            jig-grinding
            honing
        hole-feature-process
            chamfering
            counterboring
            countersinking
            tapping
```

Figure 11.22 SIPS process taxonomy

In principle, the search tree is infinite. However, because it is searched using a best-first branch and bound search algorithm that keeps track of the lowest-cost solution already found, the branches at the bottom will not be searched, and one of the three successful terminations will be chosen on the basis of technical constraints and cost. The actual width of SIPS process knowledge is indicated by its process frame hierarchy shown in Figure 11.22.

11.4.2 Operation Planning in RoCost

One of the desirable goals of process planning is to facilitate the design of cost-effective products by providing information on manufacturing cost back to the designers, who generally are not experts on manufacturing even though their decisions may determine as must as 90% of the manufacturing cost.

RoCost (Nieminen and Tuomi 1991) is a feature based system for cost evaluation of shaft-type parts. It consists of a simple feature-based modeling interface coupled with a process planner and technological information. The main goal of RoCost is to automate tender processing in a subcontracting factory. For this use, process planning operations are only carried out to the depth necessary for this application. Nevertheless, RoCost also includes fixturing planning and NC generation modules which are investigated later.

RoCost considers a fixed sequence of shaft-making processes:

1. Sawing
2. Center drilling
3. Turning
4. Drilling
5. Keyway milling
6. Generation
7. Slotting
8. Broaching
9. Cementation
10. Induction hardening
11. Tooth grinding
12. Circular grinding
13. Hole grinding
14. Grinding
15. Balancing

Each process is linked with the feature types for which the process is relevant and with process selection rules, tool information, machining parameter selection knowledge, and cost model information based on material removal rate. LISP frames representing machines, tools, and manufacturing processes are used

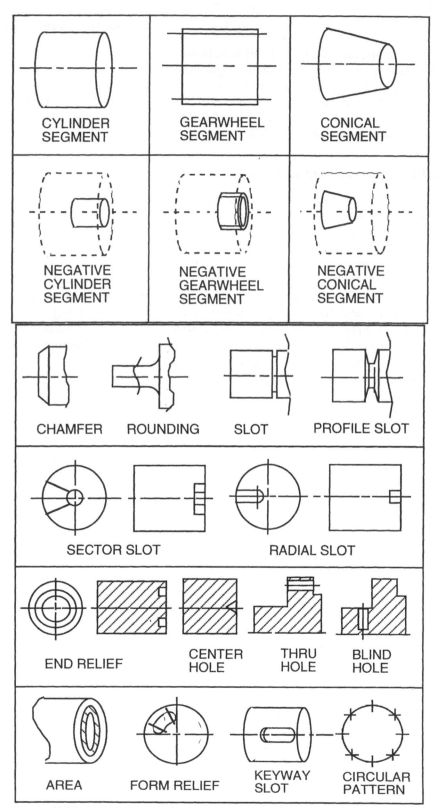

Figure 11.23 RoCost feature library (Nieminen and Tuomi 1991)

```
(circular-grinding-knowledge

    (type              (value    general-knowledge))

    (method            (value    circular-grinding))

    (factor-normal     (value    (* 8.5 (+ 1 (/ *num-of-segs* 10))))))

    (factor-hard       (value    (* 10.0 (+ 1 (/ *num-of-segs* 10))))))

    (time              (cutting  (* *grind-area* *factor*))

                       (prepar   30))

    (mantime-facts     (mass     1)

                       (time     2)

                       (area     2))

    (surface-finish    (ra       0.4)

                       (it       5))

    (tolerance         (value    0.5)))
```

Figure 11.24 A sample process knowledge frame of RoCost (Nieminen and Tuomi 1991; reprinted with permission of Elsevier Science)

for knowledge representation. In the main, LISP functions implement the planning logic. However, the operation sequence is represented as a frame that can be changed to fit the system for a difference sequence.

The feature model of RoCost is based on treating the whole rotational part a compound feature which consists of a number of cylindrical or conical segments. Detail features can be inserted into these. The feature library of RoCost is shown in Figure 11.23. The user interface of the system contains a simple feature-based modeler that supports the creation shaft-type parts on the basis of the a feature library as well as a knowledge editor for editing factory knowledge on machines, tools, materials, and processes, and access to the process planner.

In general, process frames contain parameters and equations used in process planning and cost analysis. A sample process knowledge frame is shown in Figure 11.24. This frame models the machining time of a grinding process as the product of the area and a factor computed on the basis of the overall shape of the part. The computation of the factor depends on whether a heat treatment has been performed on the part (factor-hard) or not (factor-normal). The preparation time for a batch is constant 30 minutes. Manual time is calculated on the basis of a formula (not shown here) that depends on the mass of the workpiece (mass), the grinding time (time), and the workpiece surface area (area). Other slots of the frame indicate the ISO surface tolerances that can be achieved by the process. These data are used to determine whether the process is required for some segments and to examine the manufacturability of the part.

LOPETA				LASKE UUDELLEEN								TULOSTA IKKUNA			
VAIHE	KONE	PIIRRE	s/[mm/r]	v/[m/min]	a/[mm]	r/[mm]	P/[kW]	N/[Nm]	w/[s/cm2]	T-LA/[min]	T-KA/[min]	T-VL/[min]	TUNT:H	MK/KPL	T/[h]
SAHAUS	SAH210538	AKSELI							2,0	2,7	0,0	18,0	100	34	0,35
SORVAUS	SOR210695									37,8	18,0	30,0	100	143	1,43
ROUHINTA		LOHK01	0,5	100	5	1,2	8,3	600		0,0					
		LIERIOULKOLOHK0934													
		LIERIOULKOLOHK0940													
		LIERIOULKOLOHK0941													
		LIERIOULKOLOHK0942													
		LIERIOULKOLOHK0943													
ROUHINTA		LIERIOULKOLOHK0934	0,5	100	5	1,2	8,3	475		12,7					
ROUHINTA		LIERIOULKOLOHK0943	0,5	100	5	1,2	8,3	550		5,4					
		LIERIOULKOLOHK0942													
		LIERIOULKOLOHK0941													
		LOHK01													
ROUHINTA		LIERIOULKOLOHK0943	0,5	100	5	1,2	8,3	475		2,4					
		LIERIOULKOLOHK0942													
ROUHINTA		LIERIOULKOLOHK0943	0,5	100	5	1,2	8,3	400		1,1					
VIIMEISTELY		LIERIOULKOLOHK0940	0,3	120	0,5	0,8	0,6	24		9,4		+08			
		LIERIOULKOLOHK0934													
		LIERIOULKOLOHK0941													
		LIERIOULKOLOHK0942													
		LOHK01													
		LIERIOULKOLOHK0943													
SORPORAUS															
SISAROU		SISAP_HAM_LOHK0944	0,2	100	5	1,2	3,3	90		0,1					
SISAROU		LIERIOSISALOHK0945	0,2	100	5	1,2	3,3	100		2,7					
SISAROU		SISAP_HAM_LOHK0947	0,2	100	5	1,2	3,3	90		0,8					
SISAVII		SISAP_HAM_LOHK0944	0,2	100	0,5	0,8	0,3	9		3,3					
		LIERIOSISALOHK0945													
		SISAP_HAM_LOHK0947								0,0					
K11-JYRS	KIJ210725	KIILAURA1075	0,3	20						1,5	5,6	30,0	140	87	0,62
PYOROHIONTA	P210544	LOHK01								60,0	4,0	30,0	125	196	1,57
		LIERIOULKOLOHK0941													
		LIERIOULKOLOHK0943											461		3,97

Figure 11.25 A RoCost process plan

The RoCost process planner interface is shown in Figure 11.25. Machining steps are listed on the left edge of the display; in each step a number of features are processed. In the middle, machining parameter information retrieved from the process knowledge base is shown, and on the right, cost information computed on the basis of the machining parameters and a simple cost model are shown. These data include the machining times, the manual times, the cost per hour of the machine tool, the cost per workpiece, and the phase time for a batch.

The user can work on the plan information similarly as on a spreadsheet. All parameters are editable entities, and the user can immediately recompute the cost after changing a value. The user can also go back to the feature modeler and, for example, change a surface finish, recompute the plan, and get a changed spreadsheet display. It is also possible to edit the knowledge frames and change the parameters of the equations used in the analysis. Such changes can be made permanent or just for a particular run.

11.5 SETUP PLANNING

Setup planning can be defined as *the task of grouping the required processes that can be executed on the same machine with the part clamped in the same position.* It involves the choice of part orientations and machining directions, and also the selection among possible several alternative methods for machining a feature. Hence the task requires a considerably more global view of the part and its manufacture than operation planning.

11.5.1 Setup Planning in HutCAPP

HutCAPP (Mäntylä and Opas 1988, Mäntylä et al. 1989) is an early feature-based CAPP system prototype constructed at HUT that demonstrates generative setup planning on the basis of a global optimization approach. HutCAPP includes a collection of prismatic features such as grooves, slots, and reliefs. A feature model is composed of instances of features organized as a tree. in Figure 11.26 displays the breakdown of a typical part into features.

The overall operation of the system is organized around the analysis of cutting directions of features in a part. To support the analysis, each feature is related to a collection of applicable *cutting strategies*. A cutting strategy is a combination of a machining direction and a tool that can be utilized to generate the feature. *Base strategies* are capable of producing exactly the shape of the feature, while *alternative strategies* are able to produce a relaxed shape where some roundings may have been altered. Figure 11.27 illustrates these concepts.

Cutting strategies are used to compute covering *cutting plans* for the whole part using global reasoning. For clarity let us consider the sample part with three relief features shown in Figure 11.28. First, all base strategies of each feature are enumerated. For the corner relief they would be the four alternatives indicated in

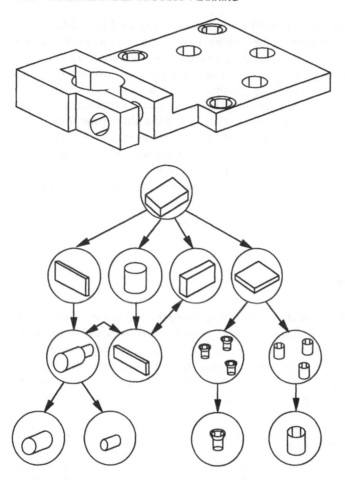

Figure 11.26 A HutCAPP feature model (Mäntylä and Opas 1988; reprinted by permission of ASME)

Figure 11.28. As a whole the reliefs of the sample part offer the work directions described in the table below, where 1 and 0 indicate whether the feature can be machined from the direction in that row.

	relief1	relief2	relief3
xp	1	0	0
xn	0	1	1
yp	1	0	0
yn	1	1	1
zp	1	0	1
zn	0	0	1

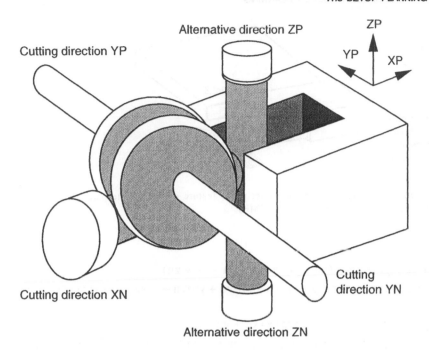

Figure 11.27 Cutting strategies of a three-way slot

The table is used to extract *covering cutting plans,* namely combinations of cutting directions that allow all features to be created. The computation can be expressed by means of lattice algebra. For instance, the first column indicates that to ensure that relief1 can be machined, at least one of the directions xp, yp, yn, zp, must be chosen. We will symbolize this requirement as

xp + yp + yn + zp,

where "+" reads "or." The whole table can be expressed as

(xp + yp + yn + zp) • (xn + yn) • (xn + yn + zp + zn)

where each multiplication • reads "and." When the resulting expression is evaluated, we will obtain the desired list of covering work directions. The necessary properties of the algebra are

1. x • x = x
2. x + x • y = x.

representing that each feature needs to be machined only once and that if a part can be machined from some direction, we may discard all plans involving that direction and something else. Hence the expression can be evaluated as follows:

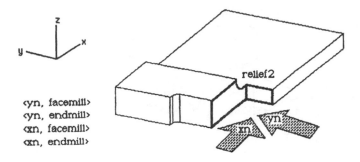

<yn, facemill>
<yn, endmill>
<xn, facemill>
<xn, endmill>

Figure 11.28 Base strategies for the corner relief feature of the sample part (Mäntylä and Opas 1988; reprinted by permission of ASME)

$(xp + yp + yn + zp) \bullet (xn + yn) \bullet (xn + yn + zp + zn)$

$= (xp \bullet xn + xp \bullet yn + xn \bullet yp + yp \bullet yn + xn \bullet yn + yn \bullet yn + xn \bullet zp + yn \bullet zp) \bullet (xn + yn + zp + zn)$

$= (xp \bullet xn + xn \bullet yp + yn + xn \bullet zp) \bullet (xn + yn + zp + zn)$

$= xp \bullet xn + xp \bullet xn \bullet yn + xp \bullet xn \bullet zp + xp \bullet xn \bullet zn + xn \bullet yp + xn \bullet yp \bullet yn + xn \bullet yp \bullet zp + xn \bullet yp \bullet zp + xn \bullet yn + yn \bullet yn + yn \bullet zp + yn \bullet zn + xn \bullet zp + xn \bullet yn \bullet zp + xn \bullet zp + xn \bullet zp \bullet zn$

$= xp \bullet xn + yn + xn \bullet yp$

The above computation works by applying rule 1 to the expression yn•yn and then rule 2 to all expressions involving yn.

The result of the above computation can be interpreted as follows:

yn is the best minimal cover cutting plan.

xp • xn is a second best minimal cover cutting plan.

xn • yp is a second best minimal cover cutting plan.

Hence in theory, just one direction might be sufficient. However, a more thorough analysis of the cutting strategies may reveal that these theoretical solutions are not feasible. Therefore also candidates other than minimal cutting plans need to be considered. A sequence of such plans can be simply formed by means of symbolic manipulation.

Observe that because yn is a covering plan, then plans xp•yn, xn•yn, yp•yn, yn•zp, and yn•zn formed by combining yn with all other directions are covering as well. Next, we can combine xp•xn with all other directions to form a sequence of covering plans consisting of three directions. For the sample part the sequence

<yn, xp•xn, xn•yp, yn•xp, yn•xn, yn•yp, yn•zp, yn•zn, xp•xn•yp, ...,
    xn•xp•yn•yp•zn•zp>

can be thus formed. It lists all covering plans in increasing order of complexity.

The best feasible plan is created by applying geometric and technological constraints represented as rules. The rules compute scores for each cutting strategy included in the plans. From this, overall scores are computed. Finally, all plans with low overall scores are rejected. Since plan candidates are inspected in increasing order of complexity, the first remaining candidate will be the best possible feasible plan.

The above computation considers only primary cutting strategies. When the alternative cutting strategies are also taken into account, the computation of minimal covering cutting plans will reveal plans that are "optimal" in the sense that all improvements possible through small geometrical variations of features have been exploited. For the sample case, the computation will lead to the following plans:

yn is a best cutting plan.

zp is a best cutting plan.

xp • xn is a second best cutting plan.

xp • zn is a second best cutting plan.

Hence both yn and zp are optimal plans of our sample part.

On the basis of the best feasible cutting plan and the optimal cutting plan, critique of the part design can be offered by comparing the two plans. In the case of Figure 11.29, the best feasible cutting plan is shown on the left and the optimal plan on the right. By incorporating some alternative cutting strategies (as indicated by slight geometry changes), the optimal plan can be implemented from one machining direction only (zp or zn). Hence, in this case, the planner can propose that these geometric changes are accepted. More generally the planner can produce several independent improvement proposals, if there are several different optimal plans. Critique is generated also on the basis of the scoring of the chosen alternatives.

11.5.2 Setup Planning in QTC

Setup planning in HutCAPP was based on a relatively simple part and process model. The Quick Turnaround Cell (QTC) system (Chang 1990) gives an illuminating example of a more complete environment for setup planning that can also reason with feature relationships.

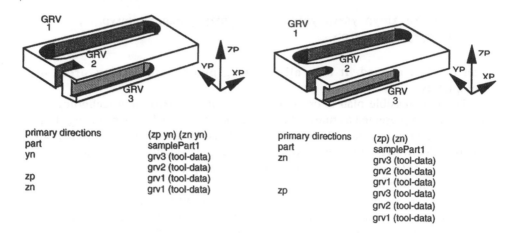

<table>
<tr><td>primary directions</td><td>(zp yn) (zn yn)</td></tr>
<tr><td>part</td><td>samplePart1</td></tr>
<tr><td>yn</td><td>grv3 (tool-data)</td></tr>
<tr><td></td><td>grv2 (tool-data)</td></tr>
<tr><td>zp</td><td>grv1 (tool-data)</td></tr>
<tr><td>zn</td><td>grv1 (tool-data)</td></tr>
</table>

primary directions	(zp) (zn)
part	samplePart1
zn	grv3 (tool-data)
	grv2 (tool-data)
	grv1 (tool-data)
zp	grv3 (tool-data)
	grv2 (tool-data)
	grv1 (tool-data)

Figure 11.29 Change proposal generation

Operation sequencing of QTC is based on constructing a *precedence diagram* on the basis of static geometric constraints available in the QTC feature-based part model. Four types of precedence constraints can be extracted:

- *Strict precedence* is due to process geometric constraint.
- *Loose precedence* is due to good manufacturing practice.
- *Location precedence* is due to location tolerance.
- *Reference precedence* is due to references to datum surface.

Precedences are created by means of rules. An example of precedences is shown in Figure 11.30. Observe that the resulting graph does not yet completely define the ordering of the operations; instead, it gives a partial order that still allows optimization in regard to tool changes.

To generate candidate setups, features are clustered on the basis of commonalty in tool approach directions or in tools. Figure 11.31 shows clusters constructed on the basis of the approach direction. Observe that some features appear in two clusters. Using the clusters, the actual setup generation algorithm can be expressed as follows:

1. Create clusters on the basis of tool approach direction.
2. Refine clusters using the preferences. This step may include splitting a cluster in two subclusters to avoid breaking required precedences.
3. Apply heuristics to remove duplicate features from clusters. (The present algorithms try to maximize the size of clusters.)

The remaining steps are performed after process selection and tool selection:

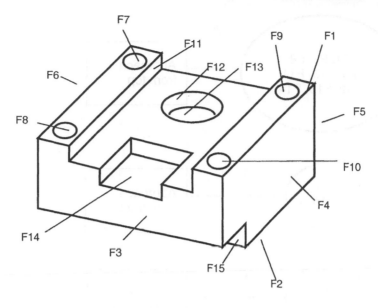

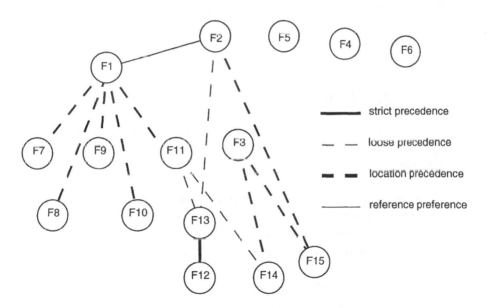

Figure 11.30 Precedence generation in QTC (Chang 1990; reprinted with permission of Addison-Wesley)

4. Create clusters on the basis of common tools.
5. Refine clusters to optimize tool changes.
6. Check precedences among clusters. In case of conflict, split and rearrange clusters.

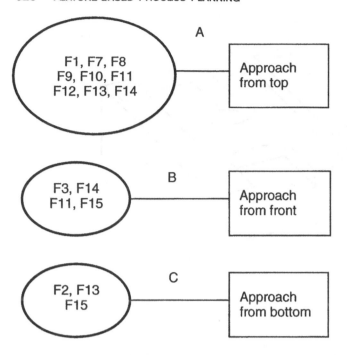

Figure 11.31 Feature clustering by approach direction (Chang 1990; reprinted with permission of Addison-Wesley))

11.6 FIXTURE PLANNING

Fixtures are required for positioning, clamping, and supporting of workpieces during manufacturing on a machine tool. The objectives of fixture planning are the following:

- Determination of clamping, positioning, and (if necessary) supporting fixturing features.
- Selection of fixturing elements.
- Calculation of the number of fixturing elements, their positions and orientations relative to the workpiece.
- Visualization of the fixturing layout.
- Documentation of the planning result for the shop floor.

11.6.1 Fixturing Principles

Let us first review briefly the principles of fixturing planning that have been used in manual fixturing design as well as a basis of computer-aided fixturing systems. We will follow the exposition of (Trappey and Liu 1990).

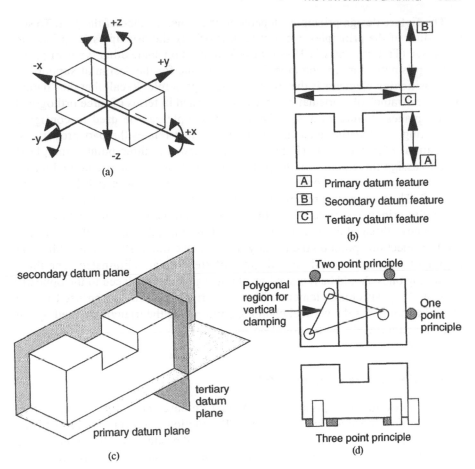

Figure 11.32 Fixturing principles (Trappey and Liu 1990; reprinted with permission)

The fixturing design principles can be divided in two categories—the *supporting and locating principles* and the *clamping principles*. As depicted in Figure 11.32(*a*), a rigid solid has a total of 12 directional degrees of freedom of motion: 6 translational degrees of freedom (positive and negative translations along the *x*-, *y*-, and *z*-axes), and 6 rotational degrees of freedom (positive and negative rotations around the axes). The goal of fixture design is to remove all these in a fashion that provides enough structural stability to withstand any cutting forces occurring during the machining operations to be applied. Usually *supporting* and *locating elements* are used to eliminate at least nine of these degrees of freedom of motion, while *clamping elements* are used to remove the remaining ones.

The fixture design principles depend on the general shape of the part. To see the nature of the principles, we will review briefly the principles for prismatic parts; see (Trappey and Liu 1990) for information on some other types of parts.

For prismatic parts, a common design principle for the design of supporting and positioning elements is the so-called 3-2-1 principle. Recall that the "datum reference frame" of a prismatic part can be defined in terms of three orthogonal datum planes (Figure 11.32b). The 3-2-1-principle can be used to configure supporting and locating elements in a fashion that relates the part properly to the datum reference frame (Figure 11.32c). First, the three-point principle is used to assign three points on the primary datum plane; these should be located as far apart as possible from each other to increase workpiece stability (Figure 11.32d). The three points remove five directional degrees of freedom. Next, the two-point principle is used to assign two points on the secondary datum plane; they remove three additional degrees of freedom. Last, the one-point principle is used to select one point on the tertiary datum plane that restricts one additional degree of freedom. In total, nine degrees of freedom are eliminated. The three remaining ones should be removed by clamping elements placed to the opposite side of the positioning elements. The most rigid area should be used as the clamping point; for the vertical clamp, a point inside the triangle defined by the three positioning elements should be selected.

11.6.2 Fixture Planning in PART

PART (van Houten 1990) is an integrated feature-based process planning system originally developed at the Laboratory of Production Engineering with the University of Twente and now offered as a commercial product by ICEM Gmbh. One of the strong aspects of PART is its fixture planning system, originally known as FIXES (Boerma and Kals 1988).

FIXES is a generative fixture planning system for prismatic parts. It can work without any user interaction. Since FIXES is an integrated component of the whole system, it can access a complete feature-based model of the workpiece, process information related to the features of the part, and various types of factory resource information available in PART.

The planning procedure of FIXES consists of two parts: the selection of setups and the design of a fixture for each setup. The automatic selection of setups is based on the comparison of the tolerances between the various features of the part. Another criteria that is used in setup planning is the orientation of the features. A *tolerance factor* is defined to enable comparison of different types of tolerance relations between features. A setup is composed of features carrying the smallest tolerance factors and having acceptable machining directions with respect to the axis configuration of the selected machine tool.

Figure 11.33 gives a sample part with some tolerances defined between the features. In the scheme a tolerance value specifies the admissible deviation from

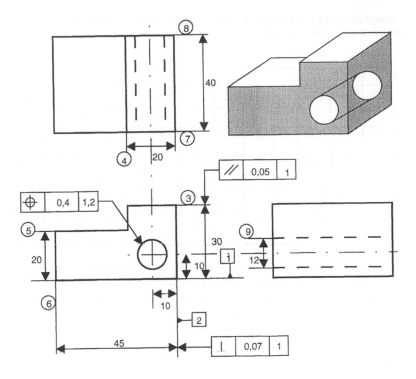

Figure 11.33 Example of tolerance factors (Boerma and Kals 1988; reprinted with permission)

an exactly defined relation between the two features. One of the two features is selected as the reference feature (REF), while the other is defined the tolerance feature (TOF). A tolerance specifies a type and a value, defined over a given length. Each tolerance can be related to fixturing misalignments in the three principal directions. Depending on the type of the tolerance, positioning errors can be composed of rotation and/or translation errors. However, errors caused by rotational misalignments are always dominant. Since translational errors can be compensated by the machine tool controller, only rotational errors are of importance in the planning phase.

A tolerance is converted to a tolerance factor (TF) by dividing the tolerance value by the respective length. The length depends on the tolerance type and part dimensions. Hence the tolerance factor represents the tangent of the maximum admissible angle of rotation of the part. In the case of the converted tolerance scheme shown in Table 11.4, the TF covering the relation between features 1 and 3 is the smallest; therefore these features must be machined in one setup. The next smallest TF suggests that feature 2 should also be assigned to the same setup, provided that the available machine tool orientations make it possible.

Table 11.4 Converted tolerance scheme of Figure 11.33 (Source: Boerma and Kals 1988; reprinted with permission)

TOF		REF		TOLERANCE		Length			Rotation			Translation			T.F.
No	F.O.	No	F.O.	Type	Value	LX	LY	LZ	RX	RY	RZ	TX	TY	TZ	
2	$-X$	1	Y	$\perp$	0.07	0	30	40	0	$\dfrac{0.07}{40}$	$\dfrac{0.07}{30}$	0	0	0	$\dfrac{0.07}{30}$
3	$-Y$	1	Y	$\parallel$	0.05	20	0	40	$\dfrac{0.05}{40}$	0	$\dfrac{0.05}{20}$	0	0	0	$\dfrac{0.05}{20\sqrt{5}}$
9	$-Z$	1	Y	$\oplus$	0.4	0	0	40	$\dfrac{0.4}{40}$	0	0	0	0	0	$\dfrac{0.4}{40}$
9	$-Z$	2	X	$\oplus$	0.4	0	0	40	0	$\dfrac{0.4}{40}$	0	0	0	0	$\dfrac{0.4}{40}$

The system automatically selects positioning surfaces according to the 3-2-1-principle and the tolerance factors. Supporting and clamping surfaces are determined following the same principles. First, the suitability of a vise is tested. If that is not possible, then fixture elements from a modular fixture kit are chosen. The generated fixture layout can be visualized using the geometric modular included in PART.

11.6.3 Fixture Planning in MCOES

One of the difficult practical problems of fixturing is the high relative cost of fixtures. It is typical that pallets and fixtures constitute 30 to 40% of the total investment of a FMS system. The high cost of pallets and fixtures actually limits the suitability of FMS systems for very short batch production because the high cost of special fixtures cannot be divided among many copies of a product.

The MCOES process planner stresses part family thinking in relation to fixturing planning. In addition to creating practically useful fixturing plans, the objective of the fixturing planning module of MCOES also include the development of adaptable family fixtures capable of being accommodated for many variants of the same part, and encouraging the reuse of existing fixturing elements created on the basis of a modular fixturing toolkit. The system does not attempt fully automatic solution to fixturing; instead, it tries to provide effective assistance to the human user.

Fixturing features are the kernel elements of the fixturing planning module of MCOES. Fixturing features are defined by a *fixturing function* and a point or area of a workpiece, where the fixture element and the workpiece are in contact. Fixturing features enlarge the MCOES product model with fixturing knowledge and facilitate fixture element selection.

A typical fixturing plan that can be created with the fixture planning module including a number of fixturing elements is shown in Figure 11.34 (Opas and

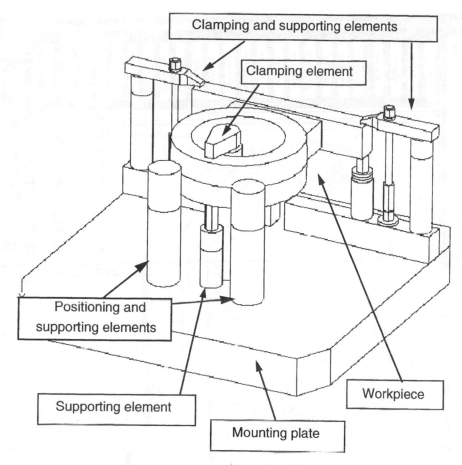

Figure 11.34 A fixturing layout (Opas and Mäntylä 1993)

Mäntylä 1993). The fixturing functions of the elements include supporting, positioning, and clamping, and also combinations of these (positioning/supporting, positioning/clamping).

Fixture planning in progress is shown in Figure 11.35. In a fixturing planning session as supported by MCOES, the following steps have to be performed:

1. The planner selects the type of fixturing system. Special fixturing elements or a modular fixturing tool kit can be chosen for part fixturing.

2. For every part setup the fixturing features are interactively defined. The user determines the fixturing function (positioning, supporting, clamping, combinations of these), a fixturing area (rectangular, one point, two points), and the position for the fixturing feature. Depending on the fixturing function and the area, the system provides a list of available fixturing elements from where the user selects a suitable element.

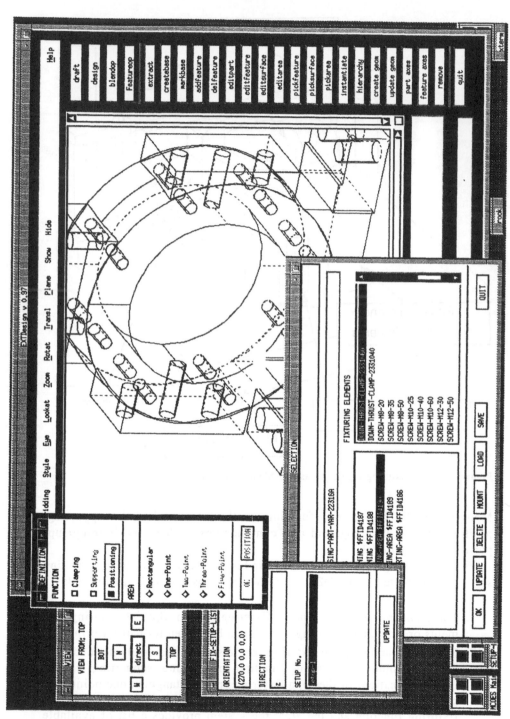

Figure 11.35 MCOES fixturing planning user interface

3. The number of suitable elements as well as the accurate arrangement of the fixture relative to the workpiece and the base element are automatically calculated by the system.

4. The calculated fixture will be displayed.

Fixture elements are modeled using an extension of the feature taxonomy containing primitive fixture elements and a fixture assembly modeling scheme. The modeling scheme uses the part family modeling facility to provide parametrically definable elements.

11.6.4 Fixture Planning in RoCost

Both of the previous examples relate to fixture planning for prismatic parts. For rotational parts, the planning logic is quite different. To illustrate fixture planning for turning, let us take a brief look at the planning strategy implemented in RoCost, a feature-based process planner for rotational parts constructed at HUT (Nieminen and Tuomi 1991) already encountered in Section 11.4.3.

For rotational parts, fixture planning is very closely related to setup planning. RoCost implements the two simultaneously on the basis of a variational technique. RoCost assumes that a set of available *variational setup planning strategies* is predefined. The set consists of a sequence of variational setups considered in turn. Planning according to a strategy automatically produces a sequence of setups in which all the required operations can be performed.

A sample set of five variational setup planning strategies applicable to turning is shown in Figure 11.36. Strategy 1 produces three setups, and all the others two. Obviously strategy 1 provides the most space for the cutting operations. Hence strategy 1 is applied whenever possible. When strategy 1 cannot be applied one of the others is selected.

The strategies of Figure 11.36 can only be applied when certain conditions are fulfilled. Consider, for example, the conditions of strategy 2:

- Strategy 1 cannot be applied (the fixturing elements are not available or the part is too long and thin).
- The part has a center hole on both ends.
- The part has no other feature than a center hole on either end.
- There is no negative segment (= axial hole) on either end.
- The part is long and thin (the proportion diameter / length is smaller than a limit).

Part classification is performed by procedures that examine the product model consisting of symbolic feature data and a machine tool database. Planning logic is implemented as procedural knowledge associated to the strategies. The following items of planning information are typical for a variational setup:

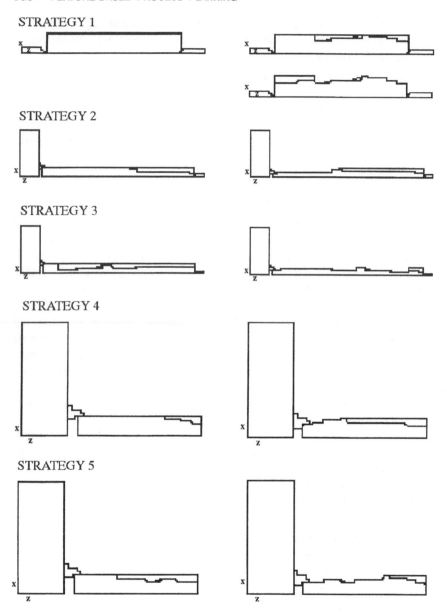

Figure 11.36 Fixturing strategies for rotational parts in RoCost

- Types of fixturing elements that must be used.
- Positioning method for the fixturing elements and the part.
- Selection and sequencing method for the operations to be performed in the setup.

For instance, the fixturing element types that must be available for the machine tool to implement strategy 2 are chuck, jaw, and tail stock. The logic for locating the part and the fixturing elements is the following:

- The chuck always resides in the global machine tool origin.
- The x-coordinate of the jaw position is equal to the chuck length.
- The z-coordinate of the part position is always zero.
- The x-coordinate of the part position and the z-coordinate of the jaw is calculated so that a surface of the jaw overlaps with a cylinder surface of the part by a length greater than a minimum limit (to guarantee adequate support of the part), and that no surfaces of the part and the fixturing elements (chuck, jaw) intersect.
- The tail stock is located at the bottom of the corresponding center hole of the part.

Operation planning is implemented on the basis of the selected setups. The first setup of strategy 2 corresponds to "turning from the right" and the second one to "turning from the left" (from the point of view of the original part orientation). Hence in setup 1 the first operation is turning, which produces a set of finished surfaces. Next operations of detail features that lie on these surfaces (for example holes, annular slots and keyway slots, assuming that the machine tool is a turning center with capabilities of turning, milling and drilling) are selected to the operation set of the setup. The following sequencing of operation types can be applied in most cases: turning, drilling, milling. Correspondingly the first operation of the second setup is "turning from the left" followed by the still unselected operations (drilling, milling).

11.7 NC PROGRAM GENERATION

Computer-aided process planning systems are mainly used in an advanced manufacturing environment that includes automated production machinery. Therefore code generation for CNC machines must be an important part of any process planning system for discrete parts manufacture. This section will look briefly at the main issues of feature-based NC generation. For simplicity and concreteness, we will concentrate on turning processes; see (Held 1991) and the general process planning literature for discussion of other types of processes.

NC generation for turning can be implemented by geometric reasoning on the two-dimensional profile of the part to be created; this in turn can easily be extracted from a feature-based representation. The nature of the logic is indicated in Figure 11.37. Typically several part setups are needed, consisting of turning from the left and from the right. In the figure roughing cuts 1–3 are from

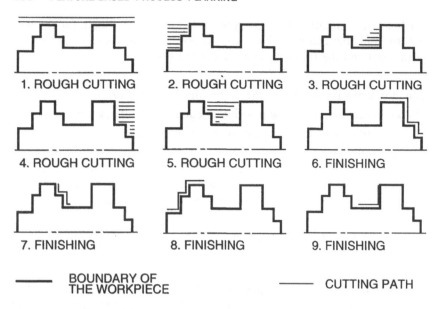

1. ROUGH CUTTING	2. ROUGH CUTTING	3. ROUGH CUTTING
4. ROUGH CUTTING	5. ROUGH CUTTING	6. FINISHING
7. FINISHING	8. FINISHING	9. FINISHING

——— BOUNDARY OF THE WORKPIECE ——— CUTTING PATH

Figure 11.37 Tool path generation logic for turning

the left, while cuts 4 and 5 are from the right. Generally, roughing and finishing cuts are implemented separately.

A key problem in turning is that a proper implementation of the turning planning logic requires the capability of modeling the *intermediate geometries* generated during the various operations. Figure 11.38 describes the modeling technique used in RoCost.

The initial feature-based representation of the body of the rotational part is based on the segment model discussed in Section 11.2. That is, the overall shape is regarded as a single compound feature, whose detailed shape is described as a sequence of cylindrical and conical segments (Figure 11.38a). A similar model of the stock is also required; typically a round rod is used. To support intermediate geometry, the segment-based representation of the part and the stock is first converted to an edge-based model (Figure 11.38b). Profiles for the selected fixturing elements are also generated and positioned according to the used fixturing strategy. The operations are determined by the setup strategy chosen for the part; this case uses strategy 2 of Figure 11.36. The goal geometry of the operation is determined through the four steps described below.

1. Determine the reference point. According to strategy 2, the part is first turned from the right until a *reference point.* Determining how far to turn from a direction is not a straightforward task and depends on the selected fixturing strategy and the overall shape of the part. However, the main principles is to avoid collisions with the fixturing elements and leave

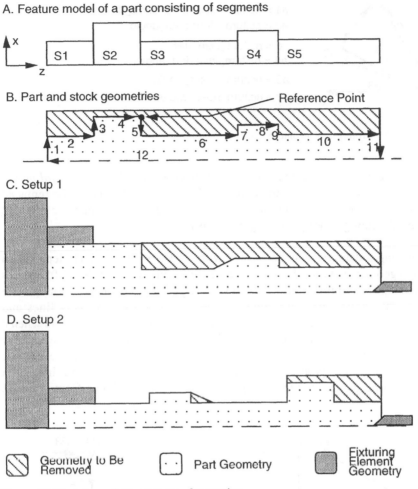

Figure 11.38 Intermediate geometry for turning

areas that can be manufactured better by the next operation untouched. In this case the reference point chosen as the starting point of the first encountered edge whose end point is nearer to the shaft center line than the starting point.

2. Generate the goal profile geometry from the right until the reference point. The goal profile is generated by scanning the edges from the right till the reference point; this creates right side of the intermediate profile of Figure 11.38(c).

3. Copy the rest of the spans to the left from the stock profile. This completes the intermediate geometry of Figure 11.38(c) left to the reference point.

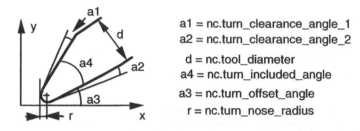

a1 = nc.turn_clearance_angle_1
a2 = nc.turn_clearance_angle_2
d = nc.tool_diameter
a4 = nc.turn_included_angle
a3 = nc.turn_offset_angle
r = nc.turn_nose_radius

Figure 11.39 Turning tool geometry

4. Sweep the depressions of the goal profile according to the tool movement capability. For example, line 7 of Figure 11.38(*b*) has to be replaced with a corresponding line seen in (*c*). The angle of this line is determined by the tool geometry (see Figure 11.39).

Sweeping a depression is performed with a case analysis which depends on the local geometry at the edge of the depression. Figure 11.40 shows four cases of sweeping from right to left. Black lines and points describe the initial profile to be swept, white points are points of the initial profile, and gray lines and points are new items created by the sweeping operation. Case (*a*) occurs when *e* the edge of the depression at point p2 is sharp. Because the area defined by points p1, p2, p3, and p4 can be cleared by the next operation from the left, the tool does not need to proceed downward immediately after point p2. Instead, a horizontal line p3–p2 is created to give the tool some distance from point p2

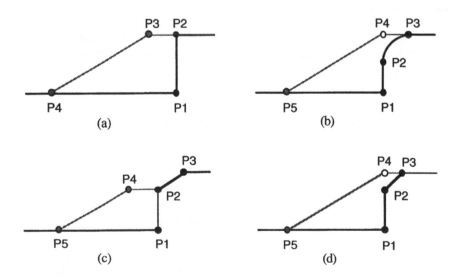

Figure 11.40 Four cases of sweeping a depression

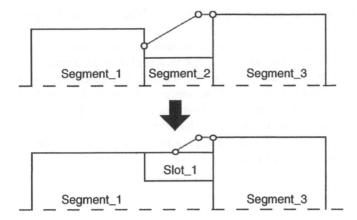

Figure 11.41 Automatic product model modification

before moving downward along line p4–p3; the distance is a parameter defined in the manufacturing knowledge of the system. As a result of the sweep, lines p4–p3 and p3–p2 are inserted to the profile, line p1–p2 is dropped, and p4 becomes the end of the line that used to end at point p1. The logic of the other cases is similar.

When all the depressions of the profile have been swept, the *goal profile* of the operation of setup 1 (Figure 11.38c) is ready. It becomes then the *stock profile* for the operation of setup 2 (Figure 11.38d).

If the resulting geometry of the last operation does not equal the desired final part geometry, the planning was not successful, and the product model must be changed. Corresponding feedback must be given, either to the designer so that he or she can modify the product or to the system so that the product model can be automatically modified to an alternative representation. In the example of Figure 11.41, the tool is not able to reach the bottom of a depression. A slot-turning method should be employed instead of a conventional turning method. Such a situation can be detected and the product model representation automatically modified. After the modification the segments are treated by conventional turning and a slot-turning method is applied to manufacture the slot.

REVIEW QUESTIONS

11.1   Discuss the requirements for process planning for the following types of products:

- Fully customized special products
- Modular products made of variant, repetitive modules and components
- Mass-produced products

Where would you place each of these scenarios along the axes of Figure 11.4?

11.2   Discuss the pros and cons of dynamic and static process plans. Can you identify cases where one or the other approach is clearly preferable?

11.3   For each of the sample features in Section 11.2.2, give an example of a more specialized and a more generic instance of the given feature. Can you indicate planning tasks for which features of some level of specification would be more appropriate than the others?

11.4   Apply the deep knowledge inverse mapping for selecting the machining process for the slot feature in the part shown below:

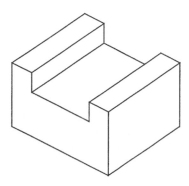

11.5   Discuss the pros and cons of deep and shallow features-to-processes mapping approach. Can you give a case where the first is preferable? the second?

11.6   Determine a complete set of constraints to describe the machining volume for turning. Outline a test for determining whether the constraint is violated. Which constraints can be performed "directly" on the basis of feature-level information? Which require geometric reasoning involving geometric models of the workpiece and the process?

11.7   The cutting strategy concept of HutCAPP actually defines groups of features that can be mapped to each other in order to minimize the setups required for the manufacture. Can you give an example of such a group?

11.8   Name the feature types of Figure 11.30. Give the reason for each of the various precedences displayed in the precedence graph.

11.9   Cluster the features of Figure 11.30 on the basis of tools required. (Invent feasible processes for making the part.)

11.10   Outline a geometric reasoning method for locating suitable surfaces for 3-2-1 fixturing. You can assume that tolerancing information such as that discussed in Chapter 5 is available in association with a feature model of the part.

11.11   Discuss the pros and cons of generative and variant approaches to fixture planning (the method of Section 11.6.2 as opposed to that of 11.6.3).

11.12   Draw the intermediate geometry remaining after each step of 11.37.

BIBLIOGRAPHY

Alting, L., and Zhang, H., 1989, Computer aided process planning: The state-of-the-art survey, *International J. of Production Research* **27** (4): 553–585.

Boerma, J. R., and Kals, H. J. J., 1988, FIXES, a system for automatic selection of setups and design of fixtures, *Ann. of CIRP* **37** (1).

Chang, T.-C., and Wysk, R. A., 1985, *An Introduction to Automated Process Planning Systems*, Prentice-Hall.

Chang, T.-C., 1990, *Expert Process Planning for Manufacturing*, Addison-Wesley.

ElMaraghy, H. A., 1993, Evolution and future perspectives of CAPP, *Ann. of CIRP* **42** (2).

Eversheim, W., and Schulz, J., 1985, Survey of computer-aided process planning systems, *Ann. of CIRP* **34** (2): 607–611.

Held, M., 1991, *On the Computational Geometry of Pocket Machining*, Lecture Notes in Computer Science, Springer Verlag.

Krause, F.-L., and Altmann, C., 1991, Integration of CAPP and scheduling for FMS, in G. Doumeingts, J. Browne, and M. Tomljanovich, eds., *Computer Applications in Production and Engineering: Integration Aspects (Proc. CAPE 91)*, North-Holland, pp. 535–541.

Kusiak, A., 1990, *Intelligent Manufacturing Systems*, Prentice-Hall.

Laakko, T., and Mäntylä, M., 1992, Feature-based modeling of families of machined parts, in G. J. Olling and F. Kimura, eds., *Man in CIM* (Proc. PROLAMAT 92), North-Holland, pp. 351–360.

Laakko, T., and Mäntylä, M., 1993, Feature modelling by incremental feature recognition, *Computer-Aided Design* **25** (8): 479–492.

Link, C. H., 1976, CAPP, CAM-I automated process planning system, *Proc. of 1976 NC Conf.*, CAM-I, Inc., Arlington, TX.

Mäntylä, M., 1993, MCOES overview, Report for the Commission of the European Communities, Brite-Euram Programme, Project BE-3528 MCOES.

Mäntylä, M., and Opas, J., 1988, HutCAPP—A machining operations planner, *Second International Symposium on Robotics and Manufacturing Research*, ASME Press, pp. 901–910.

Mäntylä, M., Opas, J., and Puhakka, J., 1989, Generative process planning of prismatic parts by feature relaxation, in B. Ravani, ed., *Proc. of 15th ASME Design Automation Conf.*, Montreal, September 17–21, ASME Press, pp. 49–60.

Nau, D. S., 1987, Automated process planning using hierarchical abstraction, *TI Technical J.* (Winter)

Nau, D. S., and Gray, M., 1986, SIPS: An application of hierarchical knowledge clustering to process planning, *Symp. on Integrated and Intelligent Manufacturing at ASME Winter Annual Meeting*, Anaheim, ASME Press, pp. 219–225.

Nieminen, J., and Tuomi, J., 1991, Design with features for manufacturing cost analysis, in J. Turner, J. Pegna, and M. Wozny, eds., *Product Modeling for Computer-Aided Design and Manufacturing*, North-Holland, pp. 317–330.

Opas, J., and Mäntylä, M., 1993, Parametric fixture layout models for operative process planning, in M. J. Wozny and G. Olling, eds., *Towards World-Class Manufacturing*, North-Holland, pp. 357–380.

Opas, J., Kanerva, J., and Mäntylä, M., 1994, Automatic process plan generation in an operative process planning system, *Int. J. of Production Research* **32** (6): 1347–1363.

Ostwald, P. F., 1988, *AM Cost Estimator*, McGraw-Hill.

Parker, L. O., ed., 1994, Industrial automation systems and integration—product data representation and exchange—Part 213: Application protocols: Numerical control (NC) process plans for machined parts, Project draft, ISO TC184/SC4/WG3_N303.

Paul, G., ed., 1994, Industrial automation systems and integration—Product data representation and exchange—Part 49: Integrated generic resources: Process structure and properties, Project draft, ISO/WD 10303-48.

Ray, S. R., and Catron, B. R., 1991, ALPS: A language for process specification, *Int. J. Computer Integrated Manufacturing* **4** (2): 105–113.

Rembold, U., Nnaji, B. O., and Storr, A., 1993, *Computer Integrated Manufacturing and Engineering*, Addison-Wesley.

Sawa, M., and Pusztai, J., 1990, *Computer Numerical Control Programming,* Prentice-Hall.

Shirur, A., 1994, Automatic generation of machining alternatives for machining volumes, M.S. thesis, Department of Mechanical Engineering, Arizona State University.

Trappey, J. C., and Liu, C. R., 1990, A literature survey of fixture-design automation, *Int. J. of Adv. Manufacturing Tech.* **5**: 240–255.

van Houten, F. J. A. M., 1990, PART: A computer aided process planning system, Ph. D. dissertation, University of Twente.

Wang, H.-P., and Li, J.-K., 1991, *Computer-Aided Process Planning,* Advances in Industrial Engineering **13**, Elsevier Science Publishers.

V

BEYOND FEATURES

The final part takes a brief look at current research on product modeling beyond features, including top-down assembly modeling, function-based modeling, and configuration modeling. Although these advanced modeling approaches will be based on concepts genuinely different from features, features are likely to play a role in their construction too.

12

FUTURE CAD/CAM TECHNOLOGIES

Basic premises of this book are that feature-based techniques can support a much more effective design environment, and that features are attractive in transferring product information between various tasks, such as design and process planning. Nevertheless, feature-based models have not been developed for all types of design or manufacturing tasks. Further research and development is necessary, and is being carried out, to cover these applications. An area where feature-based techniques need to be extended is in the early stages of design, the point where the designer is more concerned with the function and overall structure of the design than its detailed geometry.

This chapter will look at some research and development directions for product modeling that go beyond feature-based techniques. Some of these are being developed in conjunction with features, while others are being developed independently. It is not our intention to provide a full coverage of the field; indeed, that would require a book of its own. Instead, we merely want to put feature-based modeling concepts in perspective.

12.1 OBJECTIVES

In Chapter 1 the objectives of product modeling were discussed from the viewpoint of the integration between design, planning, and manufacturing functions of a company. In this view a main goal of product modeling was to communicate design information of a product to production planning and manufacturing. Product models were also related to other types of knowledge required, notably process models covering the design and customer order delivery activities, and factory models, covering the resources available to the company.

In later chapters features were introduced as recurring elements of designs that could be associated with significant engineering properties and behaviors.

These characteristics support capturing and reusing existing design and manufacturing solutions in feature libraries and developing methods for automating certain types of model manipulations. Features could be said to be based on an *extensional* view of design: We observe what designers do, and capture recurring aspects of their work in feature models.

Unfortunately, this view leaves out the *intensional* aspects of design, namely what designers really think and do when they design. Consequently it still remains questionable whether designers get the best possible support for their work, and whether their design intent is completely captured. A fundamental problem of product modeling is to find concepts and tools that would allow us to extend into the intensional realm of design. As many of the advanced lines of research to be discussed in this chapter aim to cover these deeper issues of design, let us start by a brief discussion of design processes and the requirements they pose to product models. For further discussion, see (Finger and Dixon 1989, Nevill 1988, VDI 1987, Mäntylä 1989).

12.1.1 Design Process

The design process of an industrial product typically consists of differentiable phases, each with somewhat distinct goals. During the early phases of design, decisions concerned with the desired characteristics and overall function of the product are made. In the later phases the specifications generated during the early phases are elaborated to make sure that the product indeed fulfills the specifications and that it can be manufactured efficiently. During the process the geometry and other information of the product are gradually elaborated from vague and fuzzy sketches to detailed descriptions. Finally, the detailed descriptions are transmitted to downstream phases of the design-manufacturing process, such as process and assembly planning.

Many decompositions of the design process have been proposed. For our discussion, the following five-stage division can be used:

1. *Functional design*, where the focus of design is on the function of the product: What must the product be good for? What are the numerical or qualitative functional requirements on its performance? What undesired behaviors must be prevented? For instance, we might choose as the target of design "a valve to unload powders from a blender, at a certain flow rate within some cost constraints".

2. *Conceptual design,* where a basic engineering structure is found that can deliver the desired functions and avoid the undesired functions determined during functional design. Ideas and concepts are generated and evaluated at an abstract level.

3. *Embodiment design,* where the result of conceptual design is mapped onto a realizable structure consisting of a number of submodules and compo-

nents, and interfaces between these. In the passenger vehicle example, these subsystems would include engine, drive train, rear and front axles, suspension, and body.

4. *Detail design,* where each submodule identified in embodiment design elaborated to a sufficient level of detail as determined by the manufacturing processes to be used for the production. Traditionally the results of this stage include detailed engineering drawings, part lists, and bills of materials.

5. *Engineering analysis,* where the results of design are investigated against the functional specifications. The characteristics studied typically include strength, heat transfer, vibration, and noise (acoustic and electrical). For more complex systems, simulation for predicting the performance of the product may be performed.

Naturally the different stages are not sequential but may involve iteration and mixing and matching the levels. Critical submodules may be designed long before less important ones. Some aspects of detail design may be postponed to production engineering, where the manufacturing constraints may be better taken into account.

In the discussion above, design was viewed as an activity whereby a person designs a product in relative isolation from other people in the company. Another, orthogonal view of design can be derived from the fact that design and manufacturing processes take place in human organizations as coordinated, collaborative efforts of many designers and planners. The subdivision of the design and manufacturing process into distinct phases is justified by the fact that this division also makes it possible to subdivide the design labor among various specialist designers. By this scenario, a "senior" designer first develops a global specification of the object to be designed. On the basis of this specification, he divides the design task into subproblems, which are allocated to a group of "junior" designers. The junior designers solve the subproblems independently and simultaneously; when combined, the partial solutions yield the solution of the whole problem.

Another typical subdivision is to separate functionally the design of new products from the engineering work required for satisfying the requirements of a particular customer order. This view leads to the separation of *innovative design,* a design task where the objective is to design a completely new product from *adaptive* or *variant design*, where an existing design is modified or varied to fit the new requirements. In variant design the breakdown of the design process may be represented as follows:

1. *Mapping of customer requirements to product specification* The customer requirements are analyzed and mapped to a product specification. For in-

stance, the customer may require a bulldozer that must have specified power and tooling characteristics.

2. *Configuration design* A product configuration is synthesized that satisfies the requirements and fulfills whatever technological criteria may apply. The bulldozer, for instance, is realized as a combination of variants of available modules; technological criteria determine which types of modules can be combined with each other. Also logistical criteria may need to be considered in order to synthesize a cost-effective design.

3. *Detail engineering* All submodules are designed to a required level of detail. Variant design can be typically implemented by varying, for instance, the dimensions and tolerances of existing modules. Some modules (e.g., operator controls of the bulldozer) may also require novel design.

12.2 TOOLS FOR PRELIMINARY DESIGN

In general, the early stages of the design process discussed above—functional, conceptual, and embodiment design—are not well supported by the present product modeling methods, including features. From the above list we see that they key aspects required for better coverage of design activities revolve around concepts such as *function*, *behavior*, and *structure* of a design, or in general the intensional aspects of design. This section will look at representative samples of work aiming at product models that can capture such aspects of designs.

12.2.1 Expert Systems

Expert systems are knowledge-based computer programs for solving specialized problems, mimicking the way human experts solve problems. The special characteristic of expert systems that sets them apart from algorithmic solutions is that they separate the domain knowledge from the inferencing mechanism. The advantages of this organization include the ability to maintain and update the knowledge base and the capability to follow the system's reasoning path (Hayes-Roth et al. 1983). Expert systems have demonstrated success in many areas, such as blood disease diagnosis [MYCIN (Buchanan and Mitchell 1984)], computer system configuration [R1 (McDermott 1982)], and spectrographic analysis [DENDRAL (Buchanan and Feigenbaum 1978)]. These early successes led to the rapid development of software tools for building expert systems in the form of knowledge-based system shells, which typically included some knowledge representation mechanism (e.g., the LISP frames in Chapter 10), a rule interpreter, and a graphical user interface for knowledge modeling and operative use of the system.

In the 1980s development of expert systems became a popular research subject in engineering. Applications included design, process planning, and finite element pre-processing. Many of the early systems were highly specialized. For example, (Dixon et al. 1984) created a system for the design of V-belts, (Brown and Chandrasekaran 1984) for air cylinder design, (Soni et al. 1986) for selection of mechanisms, (Zarefar et al. 1986) for gear drives, (Kulkarni et al. 1985) for the design of heat fins, and (Vaghul et al. 1985) for injection molding parts. Later research turned to more general systems that were domain independent. Of special interest is DOMINIC (Dixon et al. 1986), a system for iterative redesign in a domain-independent manner. The knowledge modeling and inferencing capabilities of expert system shells turned out to be suited for well-bounded domains, such as routine component sizing and matching, or variant design on the basis of predefined configurations. Configuration modeling is discussed in Section 12.3. However, system synthesis does not usually represent a well-bounded domain; therefore it has not been targeted successfully.

One of the original deficiencies of knowledge system shells was that they were not good at handling geometric information. When we think of the range of geometric reasoning needs that has been discussed in earlier chapters of this book, we can perceive the lack of expressiveness caused by this limitation. More recently expert system shells for engineering have been created with greatly improved geometric facilities, such as the ICAD[1] system, which combines a knowledge-based system with geometric modeling, and the Design++[2] system, which uses a dynamic link between a knowledge-based system shell and AutoCAD.

Nevertheless, the main problem of the expert system approach has been the relatively shallow level of knowledge that can readily be modeled. For instance, if only symbolic rules can be used, it is difficult to express reasoning which requires three-dimensional geometric computation. To bypass such limitations, fairly specialized rules are needed, and this makes the overall system brittle and difficult to maintain. On the basis of these experiences, most researchers in the field agree that the level of knowledge available in knowledge-intensive design and manufacturing systems must be enhanced considerably. To achieve this, good abstractions of the various entities and phenomena used in engineering design must be developed.

12.2.2 Top-Down Design

The top-down design approach is preferred by most designers for the conceptual design, since the design of assemblies starts at a high level of abstraction. Assembly design does not always require detailed design of constituent parts and subassemblies. Hence the design can be carried out in terms of abstract concepts, and this helps the designer in validating some of the design concepts prior to their implementation.

Ideally a top-down design environment should support transitions from high-level, conceptual assembly models stressing the function of the assembly to detailed models of the individual components. These transitions are illustrated

---

[1]ICAD ® is a registered trademark of ICAD corporation.
[2]Design++ ® is a registered trademark of Design Power, Inc.

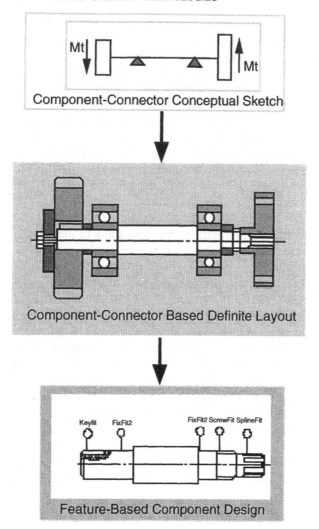

Figure 12.1 Levels and transitions of top-down assembly design (Gui 1993; reprinted by permission of the author)

in Figure 12.1. A number of requirements for modeling facilities for top-down design have been enumerated (Mäntylä 1990):

1. The model should provide support for representing the assembly information on *several levels of abstraction* (abstract structure, overall geometry, detail geometry). These levels should be retained even after more detailed modeling for later reference and modification.

2. The model structure should represent *design intent* by preserving the "reason" for the various model entities. The model should make it possible to

trace back from geometry to the assembly relationships and other specifications that the geometry implements.

3. The model should support *abstract geometry* that represents parts of the design where no commitment to a detailed solution has yet been made.

Starting in early and mid 1980s, significant research has been carried out to overcome the deficiencies of regular modelers and to build efficient and intelligent top-down modeling systems that can achieve these goals, and hence aid the designer in the design and analysis of mechanical assemblies. This section outlines some developments in the area of assembly design. For an overview of pre-1988 work, see (Libardi et al. 1988).

Struss (1987) developed a top-down design system that models the structure and function of devices for diagnosing malfunctions. As shown in Figure 12.2, products are represented in terms of *components* and *connections* joined at common *terminals*. The representation is hierarchic: A connection on one level (e.g., a passive wire) may be a structured object on another (e.g., a circuit with resistance and capacitance). Terminals have substructure according to the substructure of the corresponding components and connections. Components and connections are represented through variables. Terminals denote shared variables. The function of the design is described by equations and constraints. For instance, equations could represent Ohm's law for resistors. The constraints of an entity form a constraint network. Terminals hook networks of adjacent entities together for constraint propagation. Several views (e.g., electrical and mechanical) to the same basic data may be defined.

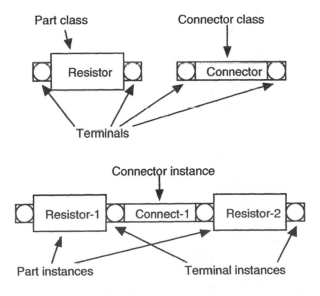

Figure 12.2 Concepts of Struss's assembly model

The system uses an assumption-based truth maintenance system (ATMS) (de Kleer 1987) to maintain the relations between model entities. This gives the system the capability of accommodating different parallel designs. The system cannot geometrically represent component shapes, since its main purpose is to support diagnostics. A major disadvantage of this system is its inability to relate the changes made in one viewpoint to the resulting changes in another viewpoint.

Model structures combining multiple viewpoints are also studied by (Schubert 1979), who introduced part graphs (P-graphs) for assembly modeling. P-graphs are graph structures of hierarchical assembly models where the nodes represent the objects or subassemblies, and the edges represent the nature of constraints and relationships. Capabilities to edit and retrieve the database, and propagate the changes made in different viewpoints, are improved considerably by using efficient methods to extract the knowledge about part relationships. Figure 12.3 shows an example P-graph of a lamp assembly. It can be seen that there are multiple ways of representing the same assembly using P-graphs depending on the type of viewpoint. The author proved that the implementation time for the

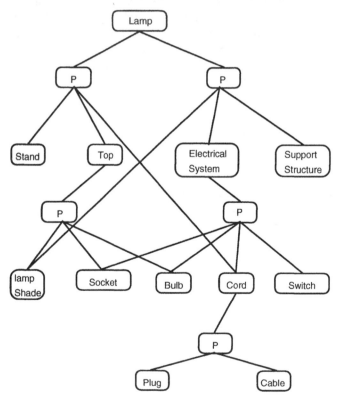

Figure 12.3 P-graph structure of lamp assembly (Schubert 1979; reprinted with permission of IJCAI)

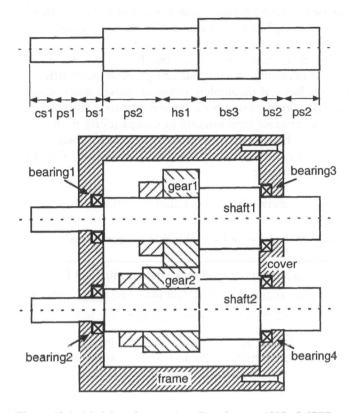

Figure 12.4 Modules of a gear box (Popplestone 1987; © IEEE; reprinted with permission)

procedures for answering queries is directly related to the number of edges of the
P-graph.

The Edinburgh Design System (EDS), developed by (Popplestone 1980, 1986,
1987), allows the user to define two types of modules, concrete modules and
interface modules; these in turn may have submodules or parts. Concrete modules contain parameters and variables whose values need to be explicitly specified at the time of design. These modules can be very abstract and are composed
of submodules in a hierarchical top-down structure. Interface modules specify
constraints between these parameters and variables. For instance, features may
be defined as concrete modules and their spatial relationships can be encoded as
interface modules. A computer program can be used to derive the relative position of the bodies from these modules. Figure 12.4 illustrates these concepts.

An important characteristic of a top-down design is that designers may work
with incomplete geometry, where only some important details are represented
exactly, while others are left vague or unspecified. Mäntylä (1990) describes a
system where part graphs and geometric features are linked with a constraint
scheme supporting the "strength" of constraints (see Chapter 8). In particular,

"weak" constraints were used to model default geometry to which the designer is not yet deeply committed. "Strong" constraints model important geometry that should not be changed in subsequent stages of the design process.

Using the logic-based mechanism outlined in Chapter 8, (Suzuki, Ando, and Kimura 1990) describe an interesting system that can generate geometries of sheet metal type parts on the basis of incomplete constraint-based descriptions. The system divides constraints in two categories. *Tight constraints* must strictly be satisfied to ensure proper product functionality or compatibility with other objects. *Loose constraints* specify properties that are considered attractive for manufacturability and product quality. For the sheet metal case, the following constraints would be considered tight:

1. The contour of the sheet metal object must contain certain prespecified segments.
2. Specified holes and cavities must be located inside the contour with some tolerance.
3. Interference with some other parts outside the contour must not happen.
4. The width of the narrowest region must be larger than a prespecified width.
5. The line segments must be horizontal, vertical, or mutually diagonal.

The fourth constraint is related to the physics of the stamping process. The fifth is desirable for the manufacturability of the part. Several of the constraints are indicated in Figure 12.5 illustrating the contour generation problem (Suzuki,

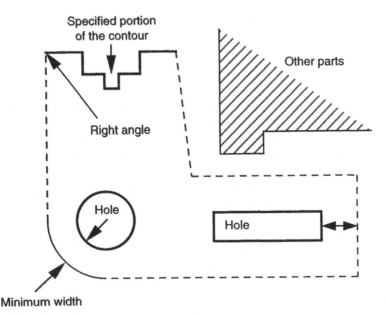

Figure 12.5 Contour generation problem (Suzuki, Ando, and Kimura 1990; reprinted with permission from Elsevier Science)

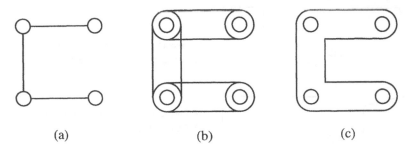

(a)   (b)   (c)

Figure 12.6 Contour generation on the basis of skeletons (Suzuki, Ando, and Kimura 1990; reprinted with permission from Elsevier Science)

Ando, and Kimura 1990). Observe that the detailed shape of the sheet metal part is unimportant except for a few specified portions. This characteristic is shared with many other geometric design problems.

The contour generation problem is solved in two stages. First, an initial contour is generated such that the contour satisfies all the tight constraints. In the second stage, loose constraints are satisfied to the maximum extent possible.

The initial contour is generated by either by an *envelope method*—with which the contour is created algorithmically such that it contains all the holes, excludes other parts, satisfies constraint 2 above, and follows the required contour segments—or by a *configuration method*—which allows the designer to specify the rough shape of the contour using a skeleton that connects the holes inside the contour. The principle of contour generation on the basis of the skeletons is shown in Figure 12.6. The initial skeleton is shown in (*a*). First, a primitive shape that satisfies the tight constraints is generated around each specified connection in the skeleton model (*b*). Then, the primitive shapes are combined into an overall contour (*c*). The resulting contour can be further improved by considering the loose constraints.

The second stage is implemented by a contour refinement process that modifies the initial shape so that it satisfies as many loose constraints as possible. Shape modification rules are used; they perform such actions as forcing "almost parallel" edges to be exactly parallel and removing very small line segments. Some shape modification rules are shown in Figure 12.7.

12.2.3 Function-Based Design

Design of assemblies on higher levels of abstraction is dominated by reasoning of the desired function and the actual behavior of devices. Modeling of function and behavior of mechanical devices is seen by many researchers as a major stumbling block on the path toward "intelligent CAD" systems that can support design on much higher levels than the traditional systems. The objective of function-based design is to support the early stages of design—functional design, conceptual design, and embodiment design. Some early work has been

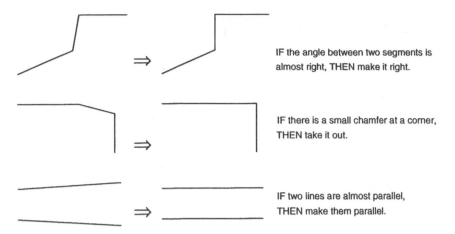

IF the angle between two segments is almost right, THEN make it right.

IF there is a small chamfer at a corner, THEN take it out.

IF two lines are almost parallel, THEN make them parallel.

Figure 12.7 Contour refinement rules (Suzuki, Ando, and Kimura 1990; reprinted with permission from Elsevier Science)

done in these areas. The major approach has been to develop methods for decomposing functions hierarchically into sub-functions at varying levels. Then, using catalogs of function-to-form mappings, a geometry is developed for the design. Nonuniqueness of such mappings, overlapping functions, and compatibility are some major obstacles to be overcome.

To illustrate the approach, let us consider the case of a contactor device for switching current on the basis of the discussion in (Ranta et al. 1995). In the early creative design stages a designer knows the required functionality of the device but has no idea about its implementation and appearance. First, the designer determines the functions that the design should perform (functional design). In the example, an electrical device which `switches current by signal` to start or stop a motor is desired. Figure 12.8 shows how the designer decomposes the basic function into subfunctions `generate signal`, `connect circuit`, and `switch mainCurrent on/off` and then continues to further particularize the last one. The result describes the function hierarchy of the target product. Of course this functional decomposition is just one way of implementing the top-level function.

At the next stage (embodiment design), the designer determines how the functional hierarchy can be realized by physical entities. For example, the embodiment of the function `generate electromagneticField` by `coil` requires entities `Coil`, `FixedIronCore`, `GapBetweenTwoEntities`, and `MovableIronCore` which have relations `Connection` and `GapBetween` illustrated in the sketch of the contactor in Figure 12.9. From the modeling viewpoint, the designer needs utilities for expressing that a function is associated to certain entities and relations, and collecting such information for later use. Furthermore the designer must be able to discover the phenomena that occur in the presence of the entities and relations in order to study the resulting behavior.

```
switch mainCurrent by signal
   generate signal
   connect circuit
   switch mainCurrent on/off
      connect electricalContactPoints
         generateForceTo electricalContactPoints
            generate electromagneticField
               generate electromagneticField by coil
         make electricalContactPoints contact
      maintain electricalContactPoints
         press electricalContactPoints
      disconnect electricalContactPoints
         returnPositionOf electricalContactPoints
            cut electromagneticField
            generateForceTo electricalContactPoints
               release spring
         remove arc
            move arc
            cooldown arc
```

Figure 12.8 Hierarchy of the functions of a contactor (Ranta et al. 1995; reprinted by permission of Elsevier Science)

Next, the designer should be able to evaluate the created model to check that all expected functions or phenomena occur and to observe possible unexpected side effects. For this, simulation of the behavior that results from the combined entities is needed. On the basis of the simulation, the designer can modify the model to enhance the product.

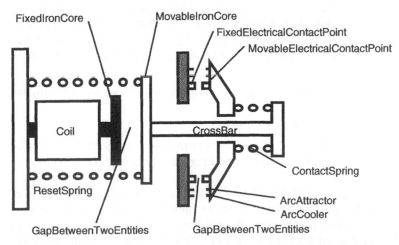

Figure 12.9 Structure of the contactor (Ranta et al. 1995; reprinted by permission of Elsevier Science)

After the designer is happy with the functional structure, he/she proceeds into the detailed definition of the product. Functional design produces a functional structure that consists of functional entities and functional relations. These should be realized in physical components and their geometry. Ideally the design system should assist the creation of a physical assembly, suggesting parts that may correspond with the functional entities, and include nonmaterial functional entities as constraints.

SYSFUND The SYSFUND system (*Systematization tool of FUNctional knowledge for Design*) created by Tomiyama et al. at the University of Tokyo is intended to support the designer in function-based design (Tomiyama 1993). The system gives a framework for representing functions and behaviors. When sufficient knowledge is described, it can support the designer in finding a solution to given functional requirements. At present, SYSFUND has a knowledge base dealing with machine functions, behaviors, and structures. SYSFUND also provides a qualitative simulation tool (Kiriyama et al. 1991) that allows the designer to construct a *function-behavior-structure* (FBS) model based on the *qualitative process theory* (Forbus 1984) for studying the qualitative behavior the design.

Figure 12.10 shows the functional model that designer has built for the contactor functions in Figure 12.8. The sample design has 30 function prototypes, 15 physical features, 32 physical phenomena, 27 entities, and 24 relations. These model concepts are explained below.

Function prototypes form the basis of the function-structure map as provided by the system. During functional design the design is decomposed until each subfunction corresponds to an available function prototype. The prototypes are used to instantiate *physical features* that embody the functions into a *behavior network*.

The upper part of Figure 12.10 provides an example for the functional decomposition of a contactor, while the lowest level corresponds to function prototypes. The lines crossing to the lower gray area show how prototypes are mapped into physical phenomena, entities, and relations. For example, the function prototype `generate(electromagneticField)by(coil)` on the left can be realized by the physical feature `magneticFieldGeneration` which consists of:

- Entities: `Coil`, `FixedIronCore`, `GapBetweenTwoEntities`, and `MovableIronCore`
- Relations: `Connection` and `GapBetween`
- Phenomena: `ElectricCurrent`, `StrongElectromagneticField Generation`, `MagneticForce`, and `IronCoreAttraction`.

A knowledge engineer must model in advance expected physical features of the intended application and attach them to function prototypes. The system assists this by revealing phenomena that are bound to occur in the presence of certain entities and relations (Ishii et al. 1993, Tomiyama and Umeda 1993). For

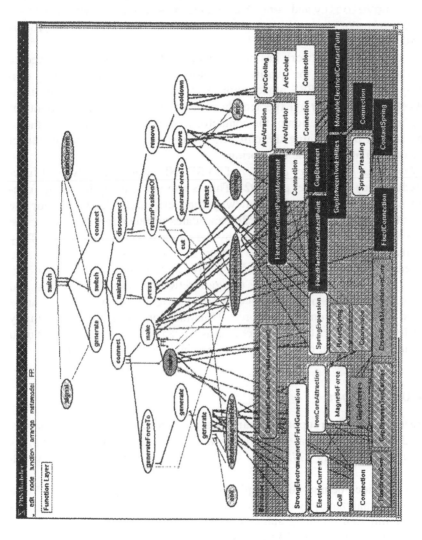

Figure 12.10 A FBS model of a contactor with functional redundancy (Ranta et al. 1995; reprinted by permission of Elsevier Science)

this, the knowledge engineer must have defined phenomena and their prerequisites and influences. For example, the physical phenomenon `IronCoreAttraction` is defined to occur in the presence of entities `FixedIronCore`, `GapBetweenTwoEntities`, and `FixedIronCore` having the relation `GapBetween`. It is also defined that if this phenomenon occurs, parameters `ClosingVelocity` and `length` are added to `GapBetweenTwoEntities`, and that `ClosingVelocity` is a positive constant and `length` is inverse-proportional to `ClosingVelocity`.

When the behavior network has been constructed, the designer may execute behavior simulation with the qualitative reasoning system. The reasoning system compares the initial FBS model with the result of the simulation and indicates whether expected or unexpected phenomena take place. For the contactor case the behavioral simulation of the contactor indicates that when the contactor cuts the current by switching the coil off, the contact points might reconnect because of oscillations of the two springs.

The *functional redundancy designer* of SYSFUND allows an analysis of functional redundancy (Umeda et al. 1992). This is a repair strategy for using functions of existing parts in a different way than originally designed. For the contactor case the system generated 26 candidates of redundant functions, one of which is highlighted in Figure 12.10 by the hatched rectangular nodes. They indicate that the target function make `electricalContactPoints contact` (presented by function node make and objective node `electricalContact Points`) can also be performed by the gap between `FixedIronCore` and `MovableIronCore`, since the iron cores are electrically conductive and can be connected by the electromagnetic force. Thus the iron cores, which originally have the function generate `electromagneticField` by `coil`, can be used for creating an electrical contact when the original contacts wear out.

12.2.4 Bond Graphs

Much recent research on supporting early design stages has centered on a behavioral modeling technique based on the *bond graph* theory of system dynamics (Karnopp and Rosenberg 1975). This section will take a brief look bond graph theory.

The central idea behind bond graphs is to use the concept of "energy" as a foundation in analyzing physical processes. Energy flow is modeled by a universal modeling tool, a bond graph composed of components bonded together at power exchange points much like atoms are bonded together to form molecules (Karnopp et al. 1979). These components are labeled (C, I, R, Se, Sf, TF, GY, 0, 1), representing different physical processes.

Bond graphs treat any kind of energy flow in terms of a force-like quantity and a flow-like quantity, referred to as *effort* (e) and *flow* (f). For a fluid they correspond with pressure and volumetric flow; for electricity, voltage and current; for mechanical movement, force/torque and velocity/angular rotation. Energy flows are influenced by *processes*. The processes are divided into the following basic types called "ports" in bond graph parlance:

Storage process. In an energy conserving process, energy is stored and released dynamically. Typical examples in the mechanical field are spring, flywheel, and moving mass. In bond graphs the storage process is represented by the generalized capacitor (C), effort like potential energy; the releasing process is represented by inertia (I), flow like kinetic energy.

Dissipative process. Because of resistive effects, energy is lost to the environment. This is symbolized by the resistor (R) in bond graphs. For example, friction in a bearing can be modeled as a resistor.

Source. Sources are the processes that supply effort (Se) or flow (Sf) directly; for example, a pump supplying pressurized oil to a hydraulic circuit.

Conversion process. The energy conversion law governs the conversion of types of energy. The generalized transformer (TF) transforms effort energy into flow energy, and vice versa, namely e_1 transforms to e_2 and f_1 transforms to f_2 so that $e_1 \cdot f_1 = e_2 \cdot f_2$. A typical TF process is a pair of gear meshes. Energy conversion may take place between different domains in terms of (GY), namely effort e_1 transforms to flow f_2 and flow f_1 transforms to effort e_2 so that $e_1 \cdot f_1 = e_2 \cdot f_2$. For example, a gear pump in a hydraulic system changes electrical energy into fluid power; electric motors of various types change electrical energy into mechanical energy.

Distribution process. An energy flow can be split and combined spatially much like electrical circuits are connected in parallel or series. The energy flow at a junction must be continuous in analogy to Kirchhoff's current law. There are two types of junctions: 0-junction, analogical to a parallel connection of electrical network, and 1-junction analogical to a series connection. Thus a 0-junction sums up the flow variables at the same effort e, $\Sigma f_i = 0$; A 1-junction sums up the effort variables at the same flow f, $\Sigma e_i = 0$.

All these components (C, I, R, Se, Sf, TF, GY, 0, 1) are linked with the power bond, symbolized by "—" in the graph notation. A half-arrow on one end of a bond indicates the power flow direction; the labels *e* and *f* mean that the power flow in the bond graph equals the product of *e* and *f*. The bond graph is also

TERM	SYMBOL	AS USED IN GRAPH	MEANING AND COMMENT
Power bond			
Effort	e	$\dfrac{e}{f}$	Power flow in bond equals e • f Potential, e.g., force, voltage, pressure
Flow	f		Flow, e.g., velocity, current, fluid flow
Inertive effect	I	⟶ I	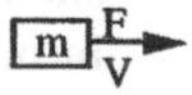 $\boxed{m}\;\dfrac{F}{V}$ $\qquad V = V_0 + \dfrac{1}{m}\int F dt$
Capacitative effect	C	⟶ C	 ►V1 ►V2 $\qquad F = F_0 + \dfrac{1}{m}\int V_{12}\, dt$
Resistive effect	R	⟶ R	 ►V1 ►V2 $\qquad F = R \cdot V_{12}$
Source	Se	Se ⟶	Effort is constant
	Sf	Sf ⟶	Flow is constant
Transformer	TF	— TF —	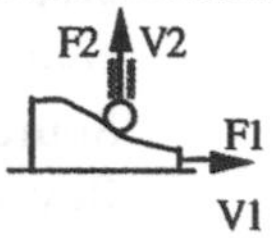 F2 ↑V2 $\qquad F_1 V_1 = F_2 V_2$ F1 V1
	GY	— GY —	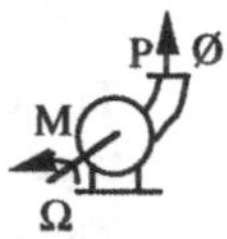 P↑∅ $\qquad P\emptyset = M\Omega$ M Ω
0-junction	0	—┤0 —	 f3 $\qquad f1 + f2 + f3 = 0$ f1 f2
1-junction	1	—┤1 —	 e1 e2 $\qquad e1 + e2 + e3 = 0$ e3
Power flow direction	►	⟶	Show dir. of power flow in each bond. Gives sign convention for equations to be formed for junctions.
Causality	|	├— ⟶ or ⟶ ┤	Shows which of the two variables on a bond is cause and which is effect.

Figure 12.11 Common bond graph terms and symbols (Gui 1993; reprinted by permission of the author)

augmented with causal strokes in addition to the convention of half-arrows signs. A causal stroke shows which of two variables (e or f) on a bond graph is regarded a cause or input and which is an effect or output. There are some rules to add causal strokes for types of 0- and 1-junction so that the possible causal conflicts and causal uncertainties can be automatically removed by programs (Karnopp 1983).

Figure 12.11 provides the standard bond graph terms and symbols developed by (Karnopp and Rosenberg 1975). Researchers such as (Dixhoorn 1977) and

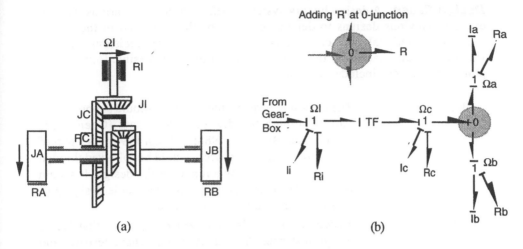

Figure 12.12 Bond graph model of a car's back axle (Gui 1993; reprinted by permission of the author)

(Breedveld 1985) have contributed much work to its extension. As an example of the notation, we give the bond graph model of a car back axle in Figure 12.12. As shown, we can capture power losses occurring at bearings as resistances in the graph notation.

So far bond graphs have mainly been used for computer simulation of dynamic systems because the behaviors of various types of systems (mechanical, hydraulic, thermodynamic) can be uniformly modeled. Recent research indicates that the bond graph method has potential also for qualitative reasoning and preliminary design (Rosenberg 1987, Finger and Rinderle 1989, Top and Akkermans 1990, Gui 1993; Gui and Mäntylä 1994).

12.3 COLLABORATIVE DESIGN TOOLS

To support collaborative design, the focus must be on the effective management of the engineering process to make it coordinated, dependable, and cost-effective. Hence the key issues for product modeling in this context include *standardization*, *modularity*, *quality*, *reuse*, *compatibility*, *constraints*, and *change management and propagation,* or in general the extensional aspects of design. Design systems aiming at supporting collaborative design will be discussed in this section.

12.3.1 Systems Based on Design History

An engineering design history is a step-by-step account of the events and the states through which a design artifact evolved. Some potential applications of design history models are (Shah and Urban 1994) the following:

Design Reuse A design history system (DHS) can provide various ways to examine previous designs to determine the steps that occurred in the design process, the rationale and constraints that affected design decisions, and the versions and alternatives of the design specification. The possible forms of exploring the history include the following:

Browsing.	The browsing form of interrogation should support navigation through the design history data (Chen 1991; Conklin and Begeman 1988; Ullman 1991). As a part of browsing, the design process would be followed through step by step, providing a replay of the design. It should be possible for the user to reuse the whole design process or to select portions of it for use.
Structural queries.	Structural queries include *process queries* that locate design instances that satisfy certain characteristics and *meta-data queries* that interrogate domain knowledge.
Advanced queries.	This type of query involves a deeper explanation of the design process. These queries may use domain knowledge to analyze a design history and recreate an intelligent explanation of the process. Advanced queries include *how queries* about design actions taken to produce specific designs, *why queries* about reasons for design actions and decisions, and *alternative design queries* that compare or explain different alternatives.

Analysis A design history can be reviewed and analyzed for many reasons. For example, to determine where time-consuming bottlenecks are, why the design failed, or why a certain alternative was chosen over others.

Design Learning Designs can be classified and maintained in a design library to provide a novice designer with design assistance.

Version and Configuration Management A DHS can provide the capability to maintain various versions and configurations of designs with their differing characteristics, design rationales, and justifications.

Design Maintenance A DHS may provide a way to backtrack to a previous design state and to iterate over some part of the design with changed parameter values.

To support these applications, a DHS needs to store both the evolving design object specification and information about specific occurrences of design steps. In addition the relationships between the object designed and processes must be represented. Given this need to capture artifact-to-process relationships, design history data elements can be classified as shown in Figure 12.13. The representation of design process instances needs to be combined with database models,

1. PRODUCT DATA

- specifications of attributes of the design (e.g., shape, size, material)
- assembly relations
- configurations of different versions
- bill of materials and parts list for each version

2. DESIGN STEPS

- classification of design steps into specific types (decomposing, analyzing, calculating, gathering data, etc.)
- relationship between design steps at different levels of abstraction
- temporal aspects of design steps (sequence, parallelism, iteration)
- information about who (or what entity) performed each design step and when it was performed

3. RELATIONSHIP OF DESIGN STEPS TO PRODUCT DATA

- what specifications provided input to the design step
- what specifications were modified as a result of the design step
- what specifications where created as a result of the design step

4. RATIONALE

- constraints, decisions, and reasons that affect design choices
- issues, alternatives, arguments, decisions

Figure 12.13 Design history data elements

versioning models, and knowledge representation techniques to provide expressive structures for the representation of all aspects of design histories. Object-oriented data bases are likely to be required for satisfying these requirements.

It is not clear how design histories can be captured in real time without unduly burdening the designer. If designers are burdened by having to provide too much explanation about what they are doing, their design productivity will deteriorate and the design environment will hinder rather than enhance their work. On the other hand, if historical information is too unstructured (e.g., textual representations), the system's ability to interpret the data will be severely limited.

Only a few experimental design history systems exist today (Brown 1989, Casotto 1990, Conklin and Begeman 1988, Fu et al.1990, McCall 1989, Potts and Bruns 1988, Shah 1995, Taylor and Henderson 1994, Thompson and Lu 1990, Ullman 1991). It is still too early to predict the direction that these systems will take and the level of success they might achieve. The existing systems are mostly design documentation tools (e.g., hypertext) that provide no real support in intelligently querying and interpreting design histories. In general, these systems provide tools for browsing design histories but do not intelligently assist in the browsing, searching, explaining processes, and in relating design steps to the product data they affect. The data for browsing must be "handcrafted," for instance from video recorded design sessions (Chen 1991).

12.3.2 Configuration Design

Product configuration models and configurators have been a subject for research since the 1970s. For a long time they were studied almost exclusively from the viewpoint of artificial intelligence. More recently, interest has shifted to link these methods to CAD systems. Hence, they qualify as a subject for this chapter.

Basic Concepts Complex products may consist of thousands of individual subparts and subassemblies that are designed, manufactured, and assembled during a time period of months or years. During the design and production process, several design offices and manufacturing plants may be involved, and transfer of information, materials, and finished parts from one location to another may be required. Subcontractors are often involved. A great deal of coordination and communication among the participating sites is required. Costly problems may emerge. Design or production facilities may become overcommitted, materials may not be available at proper times, or logistics may cause unexpected delays. In all such cases, replanning and re-engineering may be required, with high incurred costs and loss of profits.

Application of sound engineering principles in advance may reduce the possibility of problems. Product *design rules* may be enforced in order to guarantee that known solutions will be reused and that several manufacturing plants will be able to perform the manufacturing. Product *configuration rules* may be enforced that avoid costly and critical alternatives. Unfortunately, these rules, even if they have been identified, may be overlooked if they are only represented in manuals and directives. A *product configurator* is a tool intended to automate the product configuration process in such a fashion that all relevant design and configuration rules, expressed in a *product configuration model*, are satisfied. Hence problems should be avoided by construction.

Complex products are often built from predefined modules and components according to customer specifications. To fulfill the customer order, the designer must select appropriate components and determine suitable values for various parameters associated with the components. Usually the designer has a range of standard modules and components available as a basis for the product. A standard product typically defines some components and provides default values for some parameters. It can also limit the allowed choices for certain modules or components and their parameters. In many companies the configuration must be saved because various after-sales services require information on delivery to a customers. The resulting overall requirements for a configuration modeling system are represented in Figure 12.14.

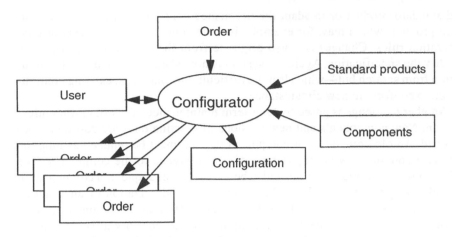

Figure 12.14 Configuration modeling environment

A configuration process can take a long time. The process usually begins with a standard product, which represents a "skeleton" of the final configuration. New components are gradually added as the configuration becomes more specific. The system must therefore store configurations of any detail between a standard product and a fully detailed configuration.

The use of components in configurations is governed by various rules. Rules can, for example, specify constraints on the permissible combinations of the values of the component parameters. "Global" rules of a component refer to other components in the configuration. For instance, a component rule can tell that this component cannot be used with a certain other component in the same configuration. Other rules describe how the configuration is affected by the specification. A rule can, for example, be of the form "if the specification has characteristic X, the configuration must include component Y."

The rules should allow the system to check the validity of a configuration created. They also should help the designer to create valid configurations. In an extreme case the rules may create a configuration automatically from the specification. Usually, however, the designer must make the decisions during the configuration process. The system will guide the designer interactively by displaying the possible choices at each step and warning against invalid component combinations.

Proper treatment of changes during and after the configuration process is a major challenge to configuration modelers. The specification, the standard products, and the components can all change while a configuration is being created. Suppose that a designer has picked a component for a configuration. A new, in some respect improved, version of the component is then introduced. The designer must now determine if the configuration should be changed to use the new version. Similarly a standard product may change during a configuration process based on that product. The designer must decide whether to continue using the old standard product or to adapt the unfinished configuration to the new standard product, which may, for example, include some new components or configuration rules. Changes can also originate from the customer, who wants to modify the specification. Again the system is not asked to create a new configuration from scratch but—which is more difficult—to change an existing configuration to conform to new circumstances.

Another challenge is posed by long-term maintenance of configuration information. New components and new versions of existing ones are constantly developed. An old component or component version must be retained as long the database contains any configurations with a reference to the component. The rules for the old components must also be saved. For example, if a component in an old configuration is to be replaced during a modernization of an installed product, the system must be able to check if the configuration remains valid with the new component. A saved configuration includes not only a list of components and their parameters but also the rules by which the configuration was created and validated—that is, its design history.

State of the Art and Current Work   The seminal configurator XCON at Digital (Barker and O'Connor 1989) was developed by the company itself without a universal model or a generic high-level modeling methodology. As a result the maintenance of configuration knowledge was difficult—after a few years of operation XCON was reported to involve more than 50 developers and maintainers. The same problems were shared by many other early developments. Therefore a key objective of product configuration research is to develop general models and methods for configuration modeling. In this section we take a look at current research following (Männistö 1995).

The most important concept in product configuration modeling is the *part-of relationship* (also known as component relationship, aggregation, composite object, complex object, and bill of material (BOM)). This concept has been studied in object-oriented spirit by (Kim et al. 1989). object-oriented data modeling owes much of its power to the concept of *inheritance*, or more generally, sharing of common properties (Chang and Katz 1991). Katz (1991) provides a survey on the third important concept of the area, namely *versions*. The three concepts—part-of relationship, inheritance, and versioning—form the core of configuration modeling.

Many of the current commercial configurators model product configuration data by extending bill of material (BOM) data of production management systems. Choice among alternative products is implemented by rules associated with BOM entities. Higher levels of abstraction, inheritance, or versioning are not supported. Each product variant needs its own BOM model, which makes the approach cumbersome for complex products. Validity checking beyond the selection rules is not available. Maintenance of configuration models is tedious.

The STEP standard discussed in Chapter 7 provides facilities for representing finished product configurations for manufacturing. Because the standards are based on extended BOMs, they are not well suited for describing configuration models or product families for a configurator.

Some researchers looking for an improved representation for the core concepts have recently turned their attention to an object-oriented modeling principle called *prototype object model*. The concept is not new (Lieberman 1986, Stein 1987), but its use for design (Zucker and Demaid 1992) and configuration modeling (Erens et al. 1994, Peltonen et al. 1994) seems attractive. PLAKON (Cunis et al. 1991) extends the object-oriented data model with part-of semantics and allows the construction of the configuration by stepwise refinements. Cunis et al. also consider different knowledge intensive techniques for finding a solution for a construction problem.

As an alternative to object-oriented methods, products can be modeled for configuration by extending the semantics of the BOM concept (van Veen 1991, Schönsleben and Oldenkott 1992). These approaches attack the need for a separate BOM for each product variant by describing a set of related variants by one generic BOM. This extension, however, has its limits and suffers from the same problems as traditional BOM-based models when the number of product variants increases considerably.

Artificial intelligence (AI) research plays a central role in configuration. As mentioned in Section 12.2.1, commercial expert systems (Nexpert Object, AION/ADS, ProKappa, etc.) have been used for configuration, but since these systems lack needed domain-specific expressive power, the implemented configurators become complex. As a result, product experts can no longer understand the rules of the configurator nor verify that the products are described correctly.

These deficiencies have led researchers to investigate more powerful AI methods. *Constraint satisfaction techniques* give a way of finding a valid configuration from a set of components when the dependencies between the components are given as constraints (Mittal and Frayman 1989, Mittal and Araya 1992). Another approach is *resource based configuration* (Heinrich and Jungst 1991). The activity of the field is shown by the Sisyphus competition, in which the vertical transportation (VT) configuration problem (Marcus et al. 1992) has been solved by several methods. The sample elevator used in VT is a simplified model from Schindler USA, who have since built a configurator for their own use (Businger 1993).

Product configurators have also been built with tools for intelligent CAD, such as ICAD and Design++ (Mishelevich et al. 1992). There are other configuration oriented systems, such as SalesBUILDER from Trilogy and TRITON. These tools are oriented towards configuration during the sales process, directly with a customer, a part of the configuration problem known as *specification mapping*.

12.4 QUALITATIVE REASONING METHODS

The motivation for developing qualitative reasoning methods came from the desire to support reasoning needed at the conceptual design level. This typically involves a common sense understanding of the behavior of devices at an abstract level. Conceptual design evaluations involve incomplete information, uncertainty, and contradictions. Qualitative models can also be used when quantitative models are too complex, too slow, or not available at all. We are going to touch upon this topic just briefly.

Bobrow (1984), Forbus (1984), and DeKleer (1984) have proposed qualitative reasoning (QR) approaches that have many similarities. The approaches also go by other names, such as Naive Physics and Qualitative Physics. Given a structural description of a device, QR methods try to predict its behavior under conditions of interest. QR models a system in terms of some key parameters which can assume only qualitative values. For example, real numbers between $+\infty$ and $-\infty$ can have values $[-]$, $[0]$, and $[+]$; that is, they can be negative, zero, or positive. Qualitative values of derivatives can be [inc], [0], [dec]; that is, increasing, zero, or decreasing. A few examples of qualitative operations are:

$[x] + [y]$ is $[+]$ if both are $[+]$ or one is $[0]$ and the other $[+]$; $[-]$ when both are negative or when one is $[0]$ and the other negative; $[0]$ when both are $[0]$. When x and y have opposite signs, the qualitative result is undetermined.

$[x] \equiv [y]$ means that both variables evaluate to the same qualitative values. Magnitudes are not considered.

Similarly other arithmetic operations can be defined. Another concept of QR is *landmark values*. These define boundaries of qualitative regions, such as the melting point being the boundary between a solid and liquid.

From these common concepts the proposed approaches diverge somewhat. Forbus (1984) uses *process based primitives* while (de Kleer 1984) and others use *device based confluences*. A confluence is a set of qualitative differential equations (QDE). Each device is divided into its components and the behavior of each is described by confluences. The parts of a device may not presume the functioning of the whole. State tables are constructed to show the different possible states in terms of the qualitative values of the state variables. Values are assigned to the independent variables and are propagated to the other variables by constraining equations. The procedure is analogous to solving simultaneous algebraic equations. An *envisionment graph* is a diagram that describes potential behaviors of a system.

Many electro-mechanical systems have been modeled with confluences and their static and dynamic behaviors correctly predicted. This exciting new branch of AI is still in formative stages. There is a potential that QR methods may be incorporated in conceptual design systems of the future.

12.5 EPILOGUE

We may conclude this last chapter by observing that advanced product modeling is a rich subject for research and development, and it is likely to remain so for a number of years to come. We hope we have given the impression of the richness and depth of features—even facing the danger of overwhelming the reader with information and detail. Yet we have seen in this chapter that features are just a part of a whole story that is still unfolding. Indeed, we have not touched upon many other areas where advanced product modeling methods are being developed. These include industrial design systems, rapid free form fabrication, and finite element modeling. Advanced product models are also closely linked with various types of methods of process modeling, ranging from informal CASE models to Petri nets.

Be it as it may, features are likely to play a role in the development of the more advanced modeling approaches discussed, just as features may be considered a next step beyond solid models. Therefore, in the future development of feature-based techniques, the advanced modeling requirements posed above must be taken into account.

REVIEW QUESTIONS

12.1 Discuss the usefulness of features for the various stages of innovative design and variant design (Section 12.1).

12.2 Consider the process constraints in Figure 11.19. Which of these could be implemented by symbolic rules? Which require some form of geometric reasoning?

12.3 Compare Struss's assembly model (Section 12.2.2) with assembly features discussed Chapter 5. Discuss similarities and differences.

12.4 Enumerate the different viewpoints of the lamp assembly included in the *P*-graph of Figure 12.3.

12.5 Discuss the justification of the sheet metal constraints used by Suzuki, Ando, and Kimura (Section 12.2.2).

12.6 Discuss the limitations of bond graphs for modeling mechanical devices. Can you indicate types of physical phenomena which cannot be modeled in the approach?

12.7 Discuss the usefulness of features for design history capture and manipulation. Refer to Figure 12.13.

12.8 Discuss the role of features for realizing various components for configuration models shown in Figure 12.14.

BIBLIOGRAPHY

Barker, V. E., and O'Connor, D. E., 1989, Expert systems for configuration at Digital: XCON and beyond, *Comm. of the ACM* **32** (3): 298–318.

Bobrow, D., 1984, Qualitative reasoning about physical systems, MIT Press, Cambridge.

Breedveld, P. C., 1985, Multibond graph elements in physical systems theory, *J. of The Franklin Institute* (special issue) **319** (1/2): 1–36.

Brown, D. C., 1989, Using design history systems for technology transfer, *Proc. of MIT-JSME Workshop on Cooperative Product Development*, pp. 545–559.

Brown, D. C., and Chandrasekaran, B., 1984, An approach to expert systems for mechanical design: a progress report, *ASME Computers in Engineering Conf.*, Las Vegas, ASME Press.

Buchanan, B. G., and Feigenbaum, E. A., 1978, DENDRAL and meta-DENDRAL, *Artificial Intelligence* **11**.

Buchanan, B. G., and Mitchell, T. M., 1984, *Rule Based Expert Systems: The Mycin Experiments*, Addison-Wesley.

Businger, A., 1993, Expertensysteme für die Konfiguration—Architektur und Implementierung, Ph.D. dissertation, Universität Zürich.

Casotto, A., Newton, A. R., and Sangiovanni-Vincentelli, A., 1990, Design management based on design traces, *27th ACM/IEEE Design Automation Conf.*, pp. 136–141.

Chang, E. E., and Katz, R. H., 1990, Inheritance in computer-aided design databases: Semantics and implementation issues, *Computer-Aided Design* **22** (8): 489–499.

Chen, A., 1991, A computer-based design history tool, Ph.D. dissertation, Mechanical Engineering Department, Oregon State University.

Conklin, J., and Begeman, M. L., 1988, gIBIS: A hypertext tool for exploratory policy discussion, *Proc. of Conf. on Computer-Supported Cooperative Work*, September 26-29, Portland, ACM Press, pp. 140–152.

Cunis, R., Günter, A., and Strecker, H., 1991, *Das PLAKON-Buch—Ein Expertensystemkern für Planungs- und Konfigurierungsaufgaben in technishen Domänen*, Springer-Verlag.

de Kleer, J., 1986, An assumption-based truth maintenance system, *Artificial Intelligence* **28**: 127–162.

de Kleer J., Brown J., 1984, A qualitative physics based on confluences, *Artificial Intelligence*, 24, pp 7–83.

Dixhoorn, J. J. V., 1977, Simulation of bond graphs on minicomputers, *J. of Dynamic Systems, Measurement and Control*, Trans. of ASME **99** (1): 9–15.

Dixon, J. R., and Simmons, M. K., 1984, Expert systems for engineering design: standard v-belt drive design as an example of the design-evaluate-redesign architecture, *ASME Computers in Engineering Conf.*, Las Vegas, August 12–16, ASME Press.

Dixon, J. R., Howe, A. E., Cohen, P. R., and Simmons, M. K., 1986, Dominic I: Progress toward domain independence in design by iterative redesign, *ASME Computers in Engineering Conf.*, Chicago, July 20–24, ASME Press, pp. 199–206.

Erens, F., McKay, A., and Bloor, S., 1994, Product modelling using multiple levels of abstraction-instances as types, *Computers in Industry* **24**: 17–28.

Finger, S., and Rinderle, J. R., 1989, A transformational approach to mechanical design using bond graph grammar, *Proc. of First ASME Design Theory and Methodology Conf.*, Montreal, ASME Press, pp. 107–116.

Finger, S., Dixon, J., 1989, A review of research in mechanical engineering design. Part I: Prescriptive, Descriptive, and Computer-based models of the design processes, *Research in Engineering Design*, V1, N1, pp 51–68.

Forbus , K., 1984, Qualitative process theory, *Artificial Intelligence*, **24**, pp 85–168.

Fu, H., Bansal, R., Haggerty, C. M., and Posco, P., 1990, Hyperinformation systems and technology transfer, in C. A. Born et al., eds., *ASME Computers in Engineering Conf.*, Boston, ASME Press, pp.121–129.

Gui, J. K., 1993, Methodology for modelling complete product assemblies, Dr. Tech. dissertation, Helsinki University of Technology, Laboratory of Information Processing Science.

Gui, J. K., and Mäntylä, M., 1994, Functional understanding of assembly modelling, *Computer-Aided Design* **26** (6): 435–451.

Hayes-Roth, F., Waterman, D., and Lenat, D., 1983, *Building Expert Systems*, Addison-Wesley.

Heinrich, M., and Jungst, E. W., 1991, A resource-based paradigm for the configuring of technical systems from modular components, *Proc. of 7th IEEE Conf. on Artificial Intelligence Applications*, pp. 257–264.

Ishii, M., Tomiyama, T., and Yoshikawa, H., 1993, A synthetic reasoning method for conceptual design, in M. J. Wozny and G. Olling, eds., *Proc. of Towards World Class Manufacturing*, North-Holland, pp. 3–16.

Karnopp, D., 1983, Alternative bond graph causal patterns and equation formulations for dynamic systems, *ASME J. of Dynamic Systems, Measurement and Control* **105**:58–63.

Karnopp, D., and Rosenberg, R. C., 1975, *System Dynamics—A Unified Approach,* 2nd ed., Wiley-Interscience.

Karnopp, D., Rosenberg, R. C., and Dixhoorn, J. J. V., 1979, Bond graph techniques for dynamic systems in engineering and biology, *J. of the Franklin Institute* (special issue) **308** (3).

Katz, R. H., 1991, Toward a unified framework for version modeling in engineering databases, *ACM Computing Surveys* **22** (4): 375–408.

Kim, W., Bertino, E., and Garza, J. F., 1989, Composite objects revisited, *Proc. of the Int. Conf. on Management of Data (SIGMOD)*, ACM Press, pp. 337–347.

Kiriyama, T., Tomiyama, T., and Yoshikawa, H., 1991, The use of qualitative physics for integrated design object modeling, in L. A. Stauffer, ed., *Proc. of Design Theory and Methodology—DTM'91*, ASME Press, pp. 53–60.

Kulkarni, V., Dixon, J. R., Sunderland, J. E., and Simmons, M. K., 1985, Expert systems for design: the design of heat fins as an example of conflicting subgoals, *ASME Computers in Engineering Conf.*, Boston, August 4–8, ASME Press.

Libardi, E. C., Dixon, J. R., and Simmons, M. K., 1988, Computer environments for the design of mechanical assemblies: A research review, *Engineering with Computers* **3**: 121–136.

Lieberman, L., 1986, Using prototype objects to implement shared behavior in object oriented systems, *Conf. on Object-Oriented Programming Systems and Languages (OOPSLA)*, ACM Press, pp. 214–223.

Männistö, T., 1995, State of the art of product configurator research, Unpublished Technical Report, Laboratory of Information Processing Science, Helsinki University of Technology.

Mäntylä, M., 1989, Directions for research in product modeling, in F. Kimura and A. Rolstadås, eds., *Computer Applications in Production and Engineering (CAPE '89)*, North-Holland, pp. 71–85.

Mäntylä, M., 1990, A modeling system for top-down design of assembled products, *IBM J. of Res. and Dev.* **24** (5): 636–659.

Marcus, S., Stout, J., and McDermott, J., 1992, VT: An expert elevator design that uses knowledge-based backtracking, in C. Tong and D. Sriram, eds., *Artificial Intelligence in Engineering Design Vol. I: Design Representation and Models of Routine Design*, Academic Press, pp. 317–355.

McCall, R. J., 1989, MIKROPOLIS: A hypertext system for design, *Design Studies* **10** (4): 228–238.

McDermott, J., 1982, R1: A rule based configurer of computer systems, *Artificial Intelligence* **19**.

Mishelevich, D. J., Katajamäki, M., Karras, T., Axworthy, A., Lehtimäki, H., Riitahuhta, A., and Levitt, R. E., 1992, An open-architecture approach to knowledge-based CAD, in C. Tong and D. Sriram, eds., *Artificial Intelligence in Engineering Design* **III**, Academic Press, pp. 125–178.

Mittal, S., and Araya, A., 1992, A knowledge-based framework for design, in C. Tong and D. Sriram, eds., *Artificial Intelligence in Engineering Design Vol. I: Design Representation and Models of Routine Design*, Academic Press, pp. 273–293.

Mittal, S., and Frayman, F., 1989, Towards a generic model of configuration tasks, *Proc. of IJCAI 89*, pp. 1395–1401.

Nevill, G., 1988, Computational models of design processes, in *Design Theory '88*, Newsome, S., Spillers, W., Finger, S. (eds), Springer-Verlag.

Peltonen, H., Männistö, T., Alho, K., and Sulonen, R., 1994, Product configurations—an application for prototype object approach, in M. Tokoro and R. Pareschi, eds., *Object Oriented Programming, 8th European Conf. (ECOOP '94)*, Springer-Verlag, pages 513–534.

Popplestone, R. J., 1986, An integrated design system for engineering, in O. D. Faugeras and G. Giralt, eds., *Robotics Research: The Third Int. Symp.*, MIT Press.

Popplestone, R. J., 1987, The Edinburgh designer system as a framework for robotics, *Proc. 1987 IEEE Int. Conf. on Robotics and Automation*, pp. 1972-1977.

Popplestone, R. J., Ambler, A. P., and Bellows, I., 1980, An interpreter for language for describing assemblies, *Artificial Intelligence* **14** (1): 79–107.

Potts, C., and Bruns, G., 1988, Recording the reasons for design decisions, *Proc. of 1988 IEEE Int. Conf. on Software Engineering*, pp. 418–427.

Ranta, M., Mäntylä, M., Umeda, Y., and Tomiyama, T., 1995, Integration of functional and feature-based product modelling—The IMS/GNOSIS experience, *Computer-Aided Design*, in press.

Rosenberg, R. C., 1987, Exploiting bond graph causality in physical system models, *ASME J. of Dynamic Systems, Measurement and Control* **109**: 378–383.

Schönsleben, P., and Oldenkott, H., 1992, Enlarging CAD and interfaces between PPC and CAD to respond to product configuration requirements, in H. J. Pels and J. C. Wortmann, eds., *Integration in Production Management Systems*, Elsevier Science Publishers, pp. 53–69.

Schubert, L. K., 1979, Problems with parts, *Proc. of Sixth IJCAI*, Tokyo, pp. 778–784.

Shah, J. J., 1990, The design of design environments, *ASME Computers in Engineering Conf.*, Boston, ASME Press.

Shah, J. J., and Urban S., 1994, Functional requirements for capturing design histories, *1994 NSF Grantees Workshop*, MIT.

Shah, J., Bliznakov, P., and Urban, S., 1995, Database infrastructure for supporting engineering design histories, *Computer Aided Design*, forthcoming.

Soni, A., et al., 1986, An intelligent mechanism selections consultant, *ASME Computers in Engineering Conf.*, Chicago, ASME Press.

Stein, L. A., 1987, Delegation is inheritance, *Conf. on Object-Oriented Programming Systems and Languages (OOPSLA)*, ACM Press, pp. 138–146.

Struss, P., 1987, Multiple representation of structure and function, in J. S. Gero, ed., *IFIP WG 5.2 Working Conference on Expert Systems in Computer-Aided Design*, North-Holland, pp. 57–85.

Suzuki, H., Ando, H., and Kimura, F., 1990, Geometric constraints and reasoning for geometrical CAD systems, *Comp. & Gr.* **14** (2).

Taylor, L. E., and Henderson, M. R., 1994, Validating a feature-based meta-model for mechanical products: a case study, *Proc. IFIP W.G. 5.2 Working Conference on Feature Modelling & Recognition in Advanced CAD/CAM Systems*, Valenciennes, France, 24–26.5.1994, North-Holland, pp. 21–40.

Thompson, J. B., and Lu, S. C., 1990, Design evolution management: a methodology for representing and utilizing design rationale, *Proc. of Second Int. Conf. on Design Theory and Methodology*, Chicago, IL, ASME Press, pp. 185–191.

Tomiyama Laboratory, 1993, SYSFUND manual, IMS/GNOSIS Report GNOSIS/U-TO-KYO/TW1/D/V1/July 9, 1993/C, University of Tokyo.

Tomiyama, T., and Umeda, Y., 1993, A CAD for functional design, *Ann. of CIRP '93*, pp. 143–146.

Top, J., and Akkermans, H., 1990, Processes as components: on the primitives of a qualitative scientific physics, *9th European Conf. on Artificial Intelligence*, pp. 643–648.

Ullman, D. G., 1991, Design histories: archiving the evolution of products, *Proc. of DARPA Workshop on Manufacturing*, February 5–6, 1991, Salt Lake City, Utah.

Umeda, Y., Tomiyama, T., and Yoshikawa, H., 1992, A design methodology for a self-maintenance machine based on functional redundancy, in D. L. Taylor and L. A. Stauffer, eds., *Design Theory and Methodology—DTM '92*, ASME Press, pp. 317–324.

Urban, S., Shah, J. J., and Rogers, M., 1993, Engineering data management: Achieving integration through database technology, *Computing and Control J.*

Vaghul, M., Zinsmeister, G. E., Dixon, J., and Simmons, M. K., 1985, Expert systems in a CAD environment: Injection modeling part design as an example, *ASME Computers in Engineering Conf.*, Boston, ASME Press.

van Veen, E. A., 1991, Modelling product structures by generic bills-of-material, Ph.D. dissertation, Technische Universiteit Eindhoven, 1991.

VDI Society for Product Development, 1987, Systematic approach to the design of technical systems and products, VDI Guidelines, VDI 2221.

Zarefar, Z., Lawley, T., and Etesami, F., 1986, PAGES: a parallel axis gear drive expert system, *ASME Computers in Engineering Conf.*, Chicago, ASME Press.

Zucker, J., and Demaid, A., 1992, Modelling heterogenous engineering knowledge as transactions between delegating objects, *Proc. Second International Conf. on Artificial Intelligence in Design*.

APPENDIXES

APPENDIXES

APPENDIX A

MATHEMATICAL ELEMENTS

A.1 GRAPH CONCEPTS

Several important algorithms related to features are based on the concept of a *graph*. Examples include constraint graphs discussed in Chapter 8 and graph-based feature recognition techniques presented in Chapter 9. The objective of this appendix is to provide basic concepts of graphs for the reader unfamiliar with the subject. For the purposes of this book, a very brief account is sufficient. For much more information, the reader should consult a basic text on graphs such as (Harary 1969).

A.1.1 Definitions

Many problems can be cast in a form where a computation is made on a collection of some entities and connections between them. A *graph* is an abstract structure that captures the essentials of such a collection.

A finite graph $G = (V, E)$ consists of a finite set of vertices $V = \{v_1, v_2, ...\}$ and a finite set of edges $E = \{e_1, e_2, ...\}$. Every edge e of the graph is related to a pair of vertices (v, w). If an edge e corresponds with a pair (v, w), then e is said to be *incident* to both v and w. A graph is *directed* if the pair of vertices (v, w) related to each edge is ordered; in such a case the edge is considered to be directed from v to w. $|V|$ and $|E|$ denote the number of vertices and edges of G.

An edge (v, v) that is incident to just one vertex is termed a *self-loop*. If two edges e_i and e_j are both incident to same pair of vertices (v, w) (and with the same direction for directed graphs), then e_i and e_j are said to be *parallel*. A graph with no self-loops and parallel edges is called *simple*.

A graph may be drawn by showing each vertex as a dot and each edge as a line segment connecting the dots. Note, however, that the drawing is merely an illustration of the structure; the basic definition of a graph does not associate any geometric information to vertices and edges. A simple example of an undirected graph of $|V| = 7$ vertices and $|E| = 11$ edges is shown in Figure A.1a. A directed graph is conventionally drawn by indicating the direction of edges with arrow-

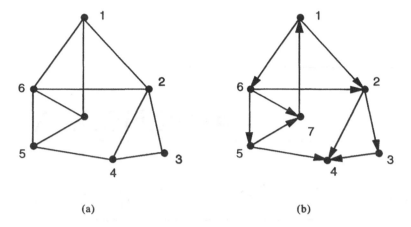

(a)   (b)

Figure A.1 An undirected graph and a directed graph

heads. A directed graph (*digraph*) is shown in Figure A.1*b*. Both graphs are simple.

A.1.2 Representations

Several types of computer representations of graphs have been devised, each with some advantages and disadvantages. The choice of a particular graph representation depends on the operations to be performed on the graph.

Adjacency Matrix   A common representation of graphs is the *adjacency matrix* representation. For a graph $G = (V, E)$, the adjacency matrix is a $|V| \times |V|$ matrix $A = \{a_{ij}\}$. If G has an edge e from vertex v_i to vertex v_j, then $a_{ij} = 1$; otherwise $a_{ij} = 0$. An adjacency matrix corresponding with the directed graph in Figure A.1*b* is as follows:

$$A = \begin{bmatrix} 0 & 1 & 0 & 0 & 0 & 1 & 0 \\ 0 & 0 & 1 & 1 & 0 & 0 & 0 \\ 0 & 0 & 0 & 1 & 0 & 0 & 0 \\ 0 & 0 & 0 & 0 & 0 & 0 & 0 \\ 0 & 0 & 0 & 1 & 0 & 0 & 1 \\ 0 & 1 & 0 & 0 & 1 & 0 & 1 \\ 0 & 0 & 0 & 0 & 0 & 0 & 1 \end{bmatrix}$$

Observe that self-loops can easily be represented by setting $a_{ii} = 1$. Parallel edges, however, cannot be represented unless other values than 0 and 1 are permitted for matrix entries.

At minimum, an adjacency matrix requires $|V|^2$ bits of storage. For undirected graphs, half of this can be saved because the matrix is symmetric.

List of Edges If a graph is *sparse*, that is, $|E|$ is much less than $|V|^2$, the size of an adjacency matrix can become prohibitive. A more efficient representation in this case represents the graph directly in terms a two arrays $g = (g_1, g_2, ..., g_{|E|})$ and $h = (h_1, h_2, ..., h_{|E|})$ where all array entries are vertex labels. The edge $e_i = (v, w)$ is then represented by setting $g_i = v$ and $h_i = w$. The directed graph of Figure A.1b is then represented by

$$g = (1, 7, 1, 6, 6, 6, 5, 5, 2, 2, 3)$$
$$h = (6, 1, 2, 2, 5, 7, 7, 4, 4, 3, 4)$$

In this representation, self-loops and parallel edges are simply represented. Analysis of the storage requirements of the representation must take into account storage needed for vertex labels; at minimum, ceil(lg $|V|$) bits are needed for each label. In practice, vertex labels might be represented as short (2-byte) integers, in which case the representation requires $4|E|$ bytes of storage.

Adjacency Structure In a directed graph, a vertex w is called the *successor* of vertex v if there is an edge from v to w. A directed graph can be represented by associating to each vertex a list of successors adj(v). For the sample graph, the adjacency representation is as follows:

v	adj(v)
1	2, 6
2	3, 4
3	4
4	
5	4, 7
6	2, 5, 7
7	1

If vertex labels occupy two bytes, then the representation takes $2(|V|+|E|)$ bytes of storage.

A.1.3 Terms and Properties

Two vertices v and w of a graph are said to be *adjacent* if there exists an edge (v, w) connecting them. Two edges are adjacent if they are incident to a common vertex.

A *path* is a sequence of adjacent edges $(v_1, v_2), (v_2, v_3), ..., (v_{k-1}, v_k)$, where all vertices v_i are distinct except possibly $v_1 = v_k$; if so, the path is a *cycle*. For instance, in the graph of Figure A.1b, the sequence (1, 2), (2, 3), (3, 4) is a path of length $k = 3$. The sequence $(1, 6)$, $(6, 7)$, $(7, 1)$ constitutes a cycle. A graph with no cycles is called *acyclic*.

A *subgraph* of a graph $G = (V, E)$ is a graph whose vertices and edges are all contained in G. The subgraph *induced* by a subset S of V is obtained by removing vertices $V - S$, and all edges incident to these from G.

An undirected graph is *connected* if there is a path between every pair of vertices of the graph. A directed graph is connected if the undirected graph obtained by ignoring the ordering of the edges is connected. A maximal connected subgraph of a graph G is called a *component* of G. A disconnected graph will have two or more components.

A directed graph is *strongly connected* if for every pair of vertices v_i and v_j at least one directed path from v_i to v_j and one from v_j to v_i exist. Analogously to the above, a maximal strongly connected subgraph is called a *strongly connected component*. A directed graph with its strongly connected components outlined in gray is shown in Figure A.2.

With the above terms, many other familiar structures can be characterized. For instance, a connected, undirected acyclic graph where one of the vertices has been selected a "root" is a *(rooted) tree*.

A connected graph may contain a vertex whose removal, along with its incident edges, would make the graph disconnected. Such a vertex is termed an *articulation point* of the graph. A graph that contains an articulation point is termed *separable*. A graph with no articulation points is called *biconnected*. A maximal biconnected subgraph of a graph is called a *biconnected component*. In Figure A.3, vertices *d*, *g*, and *i* are the only articulation points. Similarly a biconnected graph may contain a pair of vertices whose removal would make the graph disconnected; if so, the vertices form an *articulation pair*. Otherwise, the graph is *triconnected*.

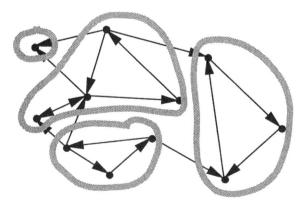

Figure A.2 A directed graph and its strongly connected components

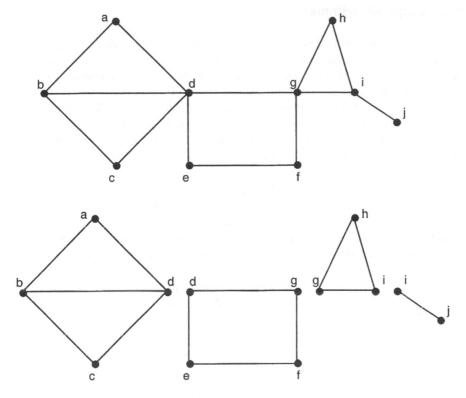

Figure A.3 A separable graph and its biconnected components

Two graphs $G_A = (V_A, E_A)$ and $G_B = (V_B, E_B)$ are said to be *isomorphic* if there is a one-to-one mapping $f: V_A \to V_B$ such that $(v, w) \in E_A$ only if $(f(v), f(w)) \in E_B$. That is, there must be a correspondence between the vertices that preserves all edge relationships. In practice, the related *subgraph isomorphism* is also often of interest: In this problem we wish to establish whether a given "to-be-searched" graph is isomorphic with a subgraph of a "search" graph.

A graph is said to be *planar* if there is a mapping of its vertices and edges into a plane such that (1) each vertex v is mapped to a point v' in the plane and (2) each edge (v, w) is mapped to a simple curve segment with endpoints v', w' so that (3) the curves only meet at common endpoints, i.e., they do not "cross" each other. All graphs in the Figures A.1 through A.3 are in fact planar, even though the graphs in Figure A.1 are not drawn so as to satisfy the above requirements.[1]

---

[1] The concept of planarity can be extended to mappings to other 2-manifold surfaces than planes. For the theory of boundary representation solid models, graphs that are planar on an n-holed torus but not on any m-holed torus, $m < n$, are of interest. See (Mäntylä 1988) for more detail.

A.1.4 Graph Algorithms

Graph algorithms seek to determine properties of graphs mentioned in the previous section. An algorithm may determine whether a graph is connected; if not, we may want to find its components. For two vertices in a component, we may want to find the shortest path joining them.

A typical method for processing a graph is *depth-first search*. The depth-first search process starts from a vertex v. After processing ("visiting") v, we follow one of its incident edges to another vertex w; if w has already been visited, we choose another edge. Otherwise, we visit w and continue recursively. If all incident edges of v have been traversed, we go back along the edge (u, v) that led to v and continue by exploring the edges incident to u. When we try to back off from the vertex where we originally started, the algorithm finishes. The depth-first search algorithm can be adapted for computing several of the properties discussed in the previous section, such as connected components, biconnected or triconnected components, strongly connected components, and cycles.

Another widely applicable algorithmic method is *breadth-first search*. The process starts from a vertex and traverses all edges incident to it, while storing the "end" vertices of those edges in a "first-in-first-out" queue data structure. Next, the edges incident to the vertices in the queue are traversed, and so on. Computation of shortest paths is a good example of the use of this method.

Determination of graph isomorphism is difficult because the most straightforward method is to use *backtracking* to examine all possible mappings between vertex labels of the two graphs. Backtracking, in general, constructs the solution of a problem by trying to expand a solution to a subset of the problem. In graph isomorphism, the process works by first mapping trivially a pair of vertices from the two graphs to each other, and then investigating all alternative ways to add other vertex pairs to the mapping in a fashion that preserves the constraints of isomorphism.

Unfortunately, for n vertices, there are $n!$ mappings, which renders the method computationally very expensive. Search tree pruning can speed up the computation, however, to the level of making it reasonable for modest-sized graphs. One such pruning method is to consider only those mappings where the number of incident edges in candidate corresponding vertices match. However, the worst-case complexity of the method still remains $O(n!)$, or worse than exponential.

Planarity testing is very complex. In can be based on first splitting the graph into its biconnected components, and then locating the cycles in each component. An algorithm can be devised that first maps the cycles onto the plane, and then tries to expand the mapping so that the remaining edges are consistently mapped.

A good and compact introduction to graph algorithms is given as Chapter 8 of (Reingold et al. 1977); a more extensive account is in (Even 1979).

A.2 SET ALGEBRA

Set algebra provides is a powerful notation for many uses in solid and feature-based modeling, such as the CSG models encountered in Chapter 2 and the CSG-based feature recognition algorithms in Chapter 9. This section provides briefly the basic concepts of set algebra, along with a list of useful properties. For much more information on sets and other mathematical concepts related to computer graphics, see (Hoggar 1992).

Set theory is a rich subject of pure mathematics. However, in this context the full generality is not needed. Instead, we will concentrate on the more intuitive notion of sets in a (three-dimensional) metric space, defined as follows:

A *metric space* is a pair (W, d) where W is a nonempty point set and d is a real *distance function* on points of W satisfying

$$d(x, y) > 0 \text{ if } x \neq y \text{ and } d(x, y) = 0 \text{ if } x = y \qquad (A.1)$$

$$d(x, y) = d(y, x) \qquad (A.2)$$

$$d(x, z) \leq d(x, y) + d(y, z) \qquad (A.3)$$

Property (A.2) is the *symmetry condition* and (A.3) is the *triangle inequality*. W denotes the "full set" (world).

Using the distance function, we define the *open ball* $B_a(r)$ of radius r around point a as

$$B_a(r) = \{x \in W: d(a, x) < r\}$$

On the basis of this definition, we call a subset A of W *open* if every point of A is in an open ball wholly contained in A. In particular, the empty set $\varnothing$ and the "whole" set W are both open sets.

The basic set operations *union* $\cup$, *intersection* $\cap$, and *set complement* $\bar{A}$ (Figure A.4) are simply defined as

$$A \cup B = \{x \in W: x \in A \text{ or } x \in B\}$$

$$A \cap B = \{x \in W: x \in A \text{ and } x \in B\}$$

$$\bar{A} = \{x \in W: x \notin B\}.$$

To these we often add the *set difference*, defined by

$$A - B = \{x \in W: x \in A \text{ and } x \notin B\}$$

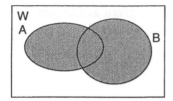
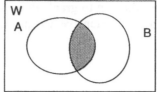
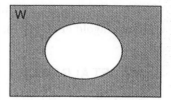

Figure A.4 Set operations: (a) $A \cup B$; (b) $A \cap B$; (c) $\bar{A}$

Expressions involving set operations can be manipulated using various laws of set algebra. A useful collection are listed in Table A.1.

A.3 GEOMETRIC TRANSFORMATIONS

Complex solid or feature models are typically composed from simpler predefined parts. Typically these parts are defined using some convenient local coordinate system. When a part thus defined is placed in a larger model, we need a *geometric transformation* to express the relationship between the local and the global coordinate systems.

This section provides a very brief introduction to geometric transformations. For more depth, consult any good text on computer graphics such as (Foley et al. 1994).

Table A.1 Properties and laws of set operations

$A \cup B = B \cup A$	Symmetry of union
$A \cap B = B \cap A$	Symmetry of intersection
$(A \cup B) \cup C = A \cup (B \cup C)$	Associativity of union
$(A \cap B) \cap C = A \cap (B \cap C)$	Associativity of union
$A \cap (B \cup C) = (A \cap B) \cup (A \cap C)$	Distribution of union
$A \cup (B \cap C) = (A \cup B) \cap (A \cup C)$	Distribution of intersection
$\overline{(A \cup B)} = (\bar{A} \cap \bar{B})$	De Morgan's laws
$\overline{(A \cap B)} = (\bar{A} \cup \bar{B})$	
$A \cup \varnothing = A$	Obvious properties
$A \cap \varnothing = \varnothing$	
$A \cup W = W$	
$A \cap W = A$	
$\overline{(\bar{A})} = A$	
$A \cup A = A$	
$A \cap A = A$	

A.3.1 Homogeneous Coordinates

Geometric transformations are most compactly represented in terms of *homogeneous coordinates*. Homogeneous coordinates represent three-dimensional points in terms of four-dimensional ones by adding one additional coordinate axis called *w*. Hence the three-dimensional point $(x\ y\ z)$ is represented by a four-dimensional point $(x'\ y'\ z'\ w)$ such that

$$x = x'/w$$
$$y = y'/w \qquad\qquad (A.4)$$
$$z = z'/w$$

The homogeneous coordinate representation offers many advantages. For instance, the four-dimensional representation can be scaled at will by multiplying all coordinates by the same factor, as this will not affect the correspondence given by the equations A.4. Observe also that points at infinity can be conveniently represented by choosing $w = 0$.

A.3.2 Coordinate Transformations

By far the most important property of homogeneous coordinates is that they allow all *coordinate transformations* needed in viewing and modeling to be represented compactly by 4-by-4 matrices. This means that the positioning of a feature (expressed in its own coordinate system) with respect to a global coordinate system can be represented compactly by a 4-by-4 matrix.

Translation The *translation transformation* that transforms a point $(x\ y\ z)$ to $(x+t_x\ y+t_y\ z+t_z)$ is represented by the matrix T constructed as

$$T(t_x,t_y,t_z) = \begin{bmatrix} 1 & 0 & 0 & 0 \\ 0 & 1 & 0 & 0 \\ 0 & 0 & 1 & 0 \\ t_x & t_y & t_z & 1 \end{bmatrix}$$

Given the matrix T, the translation can be calculated in the homogeneous coordinate representation as the vector-matrix product

$$[x'\ y'\ z'\ w] \cdot T = [x'+t_x w\ \ y'+t_y w\ \ z'+t_z w\ \ w]^T$$

The inverse translation is simply

$$T(-t_x,-t_y,-t_z) = \begin{bmatrix} 1 & 0 & 0 & 0 \\ 0 & 1 & 0 & 0 \\ 0 & 0 & 1 & 0 \\ -t_x & -t_y & -t_z & 1 \end{bmatrix}$$

Rotation The *rotation transformation* that rotates points around one of the coordinate axes has a similar simple structure. The rotation of ϕ degrees around the z-axis is represented by the matrix R_z as

$$R_z(\phi) = \begin{bmatrix} \cos(\phi) & \sin(\phi) & 0 & 0 \\ -\sin(\phi) & \cos(\phi) & 0 & 0 \\ 0 & 0 & 1 & 0 \\ 0 & 0 & 0 & 1 \end{bmatrix}$$

Angle ϕ represents a counterclockwise rotation; for instance, if $\phi = 90$ degrees, $R_z(\phi)$ maps the point (1 0 0 1) to the point (0 1 0 1). Rotation matrices $R_x(\phi)$ and $R_y(\phi)$ that represent corresponding rotations around x- and y-axes are given by similar matrices:

$$R_x(\phi) = \begin{bmatrix} 1 & 0 & 0 & 0 \\ 0 & \cos(\phi) & \sin(\phi) & 0 \\ 0 & -\sin(\phi) & \cos(\phi) & 0 \\ 0 & 0 & 0 & 1 \end{bmatrix}$$

$$R_y(\phi) = \begin{bmatrix} \cos(\phi) & 0 & -\sin(\phi) & 0 \\ 0 & 1 & 0 & 0 \\ \sin(\phi) & 0 & \cos(\phi) & 0 \\ 0 & 0 & 0 & 1 \end{bmatrix}$$

Scaling Finally, the *scaling transformation* $S(s_x, s_y, s_z)$ can also be expressed as a 4-by-4 matrix:

$$S(s_x, s_y, s_z) = \begin{bmatrix} s_x & 0 & 0 & 0 \\ 0 & 1 & 0 & 0 \\ 0 & 0 & s_z & 0 \\ 0 & 0 & 0 & 1 \end{bmatrix}$$

A.3.3 Combination of Transformations

A major advantage of homogeneous coordinate transformations is that they can be piled upon each other. Specifically, an arbitrary series of translations and rotations can be combined into a single transformation matrix simply by calculating the product of the corresponding translation or rotation matrices in the correct order.

For instance, the composite transformation matrix M consisting of a translation $T = T(t_x, t_y, t_z)$ followed by rotations $R_1 = R_x(\phi_1)$ and $R_2 = R_x(\phi_2)$ can be produced as the matrix product

$$M = T \times R_1 \times R_2$$

Combined, an arbitrary sequence of rotations will yield a general rotation matrix R of the form

$$R = \begin{bmatrix} r_{11} & r_{12} & r_{13} & 0 \\ r_{21} & r_{22} & r_{23} & 0 \\ r_{31} & r_{32} & r_{33} & 0 \\ 0 & 0 & 0 & 1 \end{bmatrix}$$

A useful observation is the fact that the 3-by-3 submatrix $[r_{ij}]$ is *orthogonal*; that is, its column vectors

$$v_i = [r_{1i}\, r_{2i}\, r_{3i}]^T, \quad i = 1, 2, 3$$

are mutually orthogonal unit vectors. Under R, they will be mapped to unit vectors on x-, y-, and z-axes, respectively.

A useful property of an orthogonal matrix is that its inverse is simply its transpose. Hence the inverse transformation matrix R^{-1} of R is simply

$$R^{-1} = \begin{bmatrix} r_{11} & r_{21} & r_{31} & 0 \\ r_{12} & r_{22} & r_{32} & 0 \\ r_{13} & r_{23} & r_{33} & 0 \\ 0 & 0 & 0 & 1 \end{bmatrix}$$

REVIEW QUESTIONS

A.1 Redraw the graph in Figure A.1 so that its edges do not cross each other.

A.2 Is the graph in Figure A.1b strongly connected?

A.3 Give and example of a triconnected graph.

A.4 Starting from vertex 1, apply (a) the depth-first search (b) the breadth-first search to the graph in Figure A.1b. You may choose any of the representations in Section A.1.2.

A.5 Using diagrams of the style shown in Figure A.4 (*Venn diagrams*), demonstrate De Morgan's laws in Table A.1.

A.6 Show how points at infinity behave under geometric transformation. Discuss your result.

A.7 Develop a transformation useful for viewing an object. As input, use two points in 3-space, the *eye* point and the *lookat* point, and a vector *up* determining the direction that will be "upward" in the final image.

BIBLIOGRAPHY

Even, S., 1979, *Graph Algorithms*, Computer Science Press.

Foley, J. D., van Dam, A., Feiner, S. K., Hughes, J. F., and Phillips, R. L., 1994, *Introduction to Computer Graphics,* Addison-Wesley.

Harary, F., 1969, *Graph Theory,* Addison-Wesley.

Hoggar, S. G., 1992, *Mathematics for Computer Graphics*, Cambridge University Press.

Reingold, E. M., Nievergelt, J., and Deo, N., 1977, *Combinatorial Algorithms: Theory and Practice,* Prentice Hall.

APPENDIX B

HALF-EDGE DATA STRUCTURE

Boundary representation solid modeling schemes were discussed in generic terms in Chapter 2. Because of their importance for feature modeling, notably for graph-based feature recognition, this appendix outlines for concreteness a sample boundary data structure, the *half-edge data structure*, in more detail. For still more information and many example algorithms working on the basis of the half-edge data structure, see (Mäntylä 1988).

B.1 ENTITY TYPES

All boundary data structures consist of a hierarchy of geometric entities of various dimensions. These entities are combined together through relationships to form a topologically and geometrically valid surface of a solid.

For representing the decomposition of the surface of a solid by geometric entities, the half-edge data structure uses a five-level hierarchic data structure consisting of entities of type Solid, Face, Loop, HalfEdge, and Vertex. The hierarchic features of the entity types are described below; the next section describes additional information that represents the relationship information.

Solid   Node Solid forms the root node of an instance of the half-edge data structure. At any point of time, several instances of the data structure may be in existence; to access any of them, a pointer to its solid node is needed. The solid node gives access to faces, edges, and vertices of the model through pointers to three doubly linked lists. (Edge nodes are presented in the next section.) All solids are linked into a doubly linked list realized by means of pointers to the next and the previous solid of the list.

Face   Node `Face` represents one planar face of the polyhedron represented by the half-edge data structure. Faces may have "holes" (i.e., multiple boundaries); hence each face is associated with a list of loops, each representing one polygonal boundary curve of the face. Since all faces represent planar polygons, one of the loops can be designated as the "outer" boundary, while the others represent the "holes" of a face. This is realized in terms of two pointers to a loop node, one that points to the "outer" boundary, and one that points to the first loop in the doubly linked list consisting of all loops of the face. Faces also have a vector of four floating-point numbers that represent its plane equation. To realize the doubly linked list of all faces of a solid, each face includes pointers to the previous and the next face in the list. Finally, each face has a pointer to its parent solid.

Loop   Node `Loop` describes one connected boundary as discussed above. It has a pointer to its parent face, a pointer to one of the half-edges that form the boundary, and pointers to the next loop and to the previous loop of the face.

HalfEdge   Node `HalfEdge` describes one line segment of a loop. It consists of a pointer to its parent loop and a pointer to the starting vertex of the line segment in the direction of the loop. Pointers to the previous and the next half-edge realize a doubly linked list of half-edges of a loop; hence the final vertex of the line segment is available as the starting vertex of the next half-edge.

Vertex   Node `Vertex` contains a vector of four floating-point numbers that represent a point of E^3 in the homogeneous coordinate representation explained in Appendix A. Two pointers to the next and the previous vertex realize a doubly linked list of vertices of a solid.

The hierarchy is depicted in Figure B.1, including the C identifiers of some of the pointers.

B.2 FACE RELATIONSHIPS

The strict hierarchy of Figure B.1 does not indicate directly how the individual faces are related to each other, except when several polygons refer to the same vertex node. We will add one additional node type that makes the face-to-face relationships more explicit.

Recall that every edge of a valid boundary representation model is associated with exactly two faces. Hence each half-edge should be associated with exactly

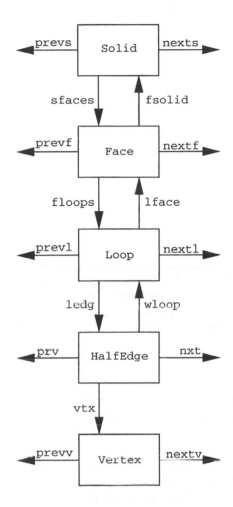

Figure B.1 Hierarchic view of the half-edge structure.

one other half-edge. We will use the additional node type `Edge` to record this information. As described below, we also add a few data items to certain nodes of the hierarchy.

Edge
: Node `Edge` associates two half-edges with each other; intuitively it combines the two halves of a full edge together. It consists of pointers to the "left" and to the "right" half-edge. The doubly linked list of edges is realized by means of pointers to the next and the previous edge.

HalfEdge
: Each half-edge includes an additional pointer to its parent edge.

Vertex
: Each vertex includes an additional pointer to one the half-edges

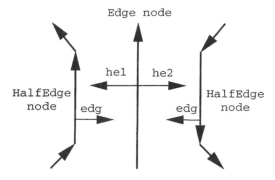

Figure B.2 Identification of half-edges

emanating from it. To represent the identification of vertices, all faces that have a corner at the some particular point must refer (through loops and half-edges) to a single vertex node corresponding with that point.

Observe that edges can be considered to define an orientation to its halves; that is, the "right" half is considered to be positively oriented, while the "left" half is negatively oriented. Representation of the face relationships is visualized in Figure B.2, which also gives the C identifiers of some of the required pointers.

Edge nodes of the data structure hold the key for more involved navigation in the data structure. In particular, from a half-edge that does not represent an empty loop, they allow the half-edge identified with it to be accessed. This task is so frequent that Figure B.3 defines a macro `mate` for accessing the "other" half-edge related to a given half-edge.

The special case of an *empty* loop with just one vertex but no edges is represented in terms of one half-edge whose vertex pointer points at the single vertex and whose edge pointer is nil. The pointers to the next and the previous half-edge refer to this half-edge itself.

B.3 IMPLEMENTATION DETAILS

The full C definition of the half-edge data structure is given in Figure B.3. In the definitions the `typedef` mechanism of C is used to define the nodes of the data structure as new types. The file also defines some general-purpose types such as the type `Id` for vertex and face identifiers and the types `vector` and `matrix` for 4-vectors and 4-by-4 matrices.

```
typedef float                vector[4];

typedef float                matrix[4][4];

typedef short                Id;

typedef struct solid         Solid;

typedef struct face          Face;

typedef struct loop          Loop;

typedef struct halfedge      HalfEdge;

typedef struct vertex        Vertex;

typedef struct edge          Edge;

struct solid
{
    Id          solidno;     /* solid identifier */

    Face        *sfaces;     /* pointer to list of faces */

    Edge        *sedges;     /* pointer to list of edges */

    Vertex      *sverts;     /* pointer to list of vertices */

    Solid       *nexts;      /* pointer to next solid */

    Solid       *prevs;      /* pointer to previous solid */
};

struct face
{
    Id          faceno;      /* face identifier */

    Solid       *fsolid;     /* back pointer to solid */

    Loop        *flout;      /* pointer to outer loop */

    Loop        *floops;     /* pointer to list of loops */

    vector      feq;         /* face equation */

    Face        *nextf;      /* pointer to next face */

    Face        *prevf;      /* pointer to previous face */
};
```

Figure B.3 C definition of the half-edge data structure

```
struct loop
{
    HalfEdge        *ledg;      /* pointer to ring of halfedges */
    Face            *lface;     /* back pointer to face */
    Loop            *nextl;     /* pointer to next loop */
    Loop            *prevl;     /* pointer to previous loop */
};
struct edge
{
    HalfEdge        *he1;       /* pointer to right halfedge */
    HalfEdge        *he2;       /* pointer to left halfedge */
    Edge            *nexte;     /* pointer to next edge */
    Edge            *preve;     /* pointer to previous edge */
};
struct halfedge
{
    Edge            *edg;       /* pointer to parent edge */
    Vertex          *vtx;       /* pointer to starting vertex */
    Loop            *wloop;     /* back pointer to loop */
    HalfEdge        *nxt;       /* pointer to next halfedge */
    HalfEdge        *prv;       /* pointer to previous halfedge */
};
struct vertex
{
    Id              vertexno;   /* vertex identifier */
    HalfEdge        *vedge;     /* pointer to a halfedge */
    vector          vcoord;     /* vertex coordinates */
    Vertex          *nextv;     /* pointer to next vertex */
    Vertex          *prevv;     /* pointer to previous vertex */
};
# define        mate(he)        (((he) == (he)->edg->he1) ? \
                                (he)->edg->he2 : (he)->edg->he1)
```

Figure B.3 C definition of the half-edge data structure (cont.)

REVIEW QUESTIONS

B.1   Sketch on paper the half-edge representation of a tetrahedron.

B.2   Devise an algorithm for traversing (a) all vertices in a loop (b) all vertices around a vertex. Hint: For (b), use the macro mate.

B.3   Devise an algorithm for converting a boundary representation to a face adjacency graph using some of the graph representations of Appendix A.

B.4   Devise an algorithm for determining the convex/concave status of an edge.

BIBLIOGRAPHY

Mäntylä, M., 1988, *An Introduction to Solid Modelling,* Computer Science Press.

APPENDIX C

LISTING OF PROCEDURAL INTERFACE FUNCTIONS

This appendix provides a complete listing of the procedural interface functions of the feature-geometry protocol described in Section 10.9 (Pherwani 1993).

C.1 CREATE AND DELETE FUNCTIONS

```
logical create_position(char* position_name=NULL, double x=0,
double y=0, double z=0);
// creates a position with given x, y, and z values

logical del_position(char* position_name);
// deletes the position

logical create_vector(char* vector_name, double x=0, double
y=0, double z=0);
// creates a vector

logical del_vector(char* vector_name);
// deletes the vector

logical create_unit_vector(char* unit_vector_name, double x,
double y, double z);
// creates unit vector and initializes coords to x, y, z

logical del_unit_vector(char* unit_vector_name);
// deletes the unit vector

logical create_matrix(char* matrix_name, char* vector1_name,
char* vector2_name, char* vector3_name);
// creates and initializes matrix to the three given rows

logical del_matrix(char* matrix_name);
// deletes a matrix
```

```
logical create_transf(char* transf_name, char* matrix_name,
char* translate_vec_name, double scale_factor);
```
// creates transformation and initializes rotational part to matrix,
// translational part to to the vector, and the scale part to the scale factor
```
logical del_transf(char* transf_name);
```
// deletes a transformation
```
logical create_vec_transf(char* transf_name, char* vec_name);
```
// creates translation transform using given vector
```
logical create_rot_transf(char* transf_name, char* vec_name,
double angle);
```
// creates transformation to rotate about given vector through given angle
```
logical create_param(char* param_name, double value);
```
// creates a parameter used in parametric equations
```
logical create_parpos(char* par_pos_name, double u, double
v);
```
// creates a two dimensional parameter
```
create_transform(char* TRANS_name, char* transf_name);
```
// creates a transformation of a body
```
logical create_entity_list(char* entity_list_name);
```
// creates an entity list
```
logical del_entity_list(char* entity_list_name);
```
// deletes an entity list
```
logical del_entity(char* ent_name);
```
// deletes any entity excepting ones above - body, lump, face, CURVE,
SURFACE
```
logical create_body(char* body_name);
```
// creates an empty body
```
logical create_lump(char* lump_name);
```
// creates an empty lump
```
logical create_shell(char* shell_name);
```
// creates an empty shell
```
logical create_subshell(char* subshell_name);
```
// creates an empty subshell
```
logical create_face(char* face_name);
```
// creates an empty face
```
logical create_loop(char* loop_name);
```
// creates an empty loop
```
logical create_coedge(char* coedge_name);
```
// creates an empty coedge
```
logical create_edge(char* edge_name);
```
// creates an empty edge
```
logical create_vertex(char* vertex_name);
```

```
// creates a vertex without a position and a parent edge
logical create_vertex(char* vertex_name, char* point_name);
// creates a vertex at the given point
logical create_point(char* point_name, double x=0, double
y=0, double z=0);
// creates a point at the given position
logical create_straight(char* curve_name, char*
position_name, char* vec_name);
// creates a straight line from a position along the given vector
logical return_ent(char* list_name, int number, char*
ent_name);
// returns entity from list
logical remove_ent(char* name);
// deletes a particular entity
logical count_in_list(char* name, int* int_val);
// returns count of entities in entity list
logical add_to_list(char* list_name, char* ent_name);
// adds entity to entity list
logical start_modeler(logical journal_on, char*
journal_name);
```
// starts ACIS, if `journal_on` is TRUE creates a journal file with `journal_name`

C.2 EVALUATION FUNCTIONS

```
logical make_cuboid(char* cuboid_name, double width, double
depth, double height);
```
// makes cuboid centred at origin with `width` in x, `depth` in y, and `height` in z
```
logical make_frustum(char* frustum_name, double height,
double rad1, double rad2, double top);
```
// makes frustum centred at origin with `height` in z, `rad1` is radius in x
// direction at base, `rad2` is radius in y direction at base and `top` is radius
// at top
```
logical make_edge_ellipse(char* edge_name, char*
center_pos_name, char* normal_unitvec_name, char*
major_vector_name, double radius_ratio, double start_angle,
double end_angle);
```
// makes ellipse edge given the position of the center, normal vector name,
// major x axis name, ratio of x to y radius; start and end angle give the
// elliptical arc angle
```
logical make_edge_line(char* edge_name, char* startpos_name,
char* endpos_name);
```
// makes a straght edge given two position names

```
logical make_ewire(char* body_name, int num_edges, char*
edge_names[]);
```
// makes a wire body given the edge names of the body

```
logical make_wire(char* body_name, int num_pos, char*
pos_names[]);
```

```
logical cover_wires(char* wire_body_name, char* surface_name,
char* faces_list_name);
```
// covers a wire body with faces of type surface and puts the face names in a
// list; for covering with plane surfaces use an empty string for surface name

```
logical cover_circuits(int num_circuits, char*
ent_list_names[], char* surface_name, char* FACE_name);
```
// covers edge circuits and returns faces, return NULL for surface name for
// a plain surface

```
logical list_no(char* list_name, int no, char* ent_name);
```
// returns given entity number from entity list

```
logical copy_body(char* orig_name, char* copy_name);
```
// copies body

```
logical sw_face_axis(char* body_name, char* face_name, char*
axis_point_name, char* axis_dir_name, double angle, int
steps, double draft_angle);
```
// sweeps the given face about the given axis through the given angle in
// specified no of steps; sweep is continous if steps = 0 and draft_angle = 0

```
logical sw_face_norm(char* body_name, char* face_name, double
dist, double draft_angle);
```
// sweeps face along its normal through given distance and returns body
// formed

```
logical boolean_unite(char* tool_name, char* orig_name);
```
// unites tool to given body and deletes tool

```
logical boolean_intersect(char* tool_name, char* orig_name);
```
// intersects the tool body with original body and modifies the original body
// returning the intersection; tool is deleted

```
logical boolean_subtract(char* tool_name, char* orig_name);
```
// subtracts the tool from the original body; deletes tool

```
logical apply_transf(char* body_name, char* transf_name);
```
// applies transformation to body

```
logical change_transf(char* body_name, char* transf_name);
```
// changes transformation to given transformation leaving body unaltered

```
logical remove_transf(char* body_name);
```
// removes all transformations applied to the body

```
logical q_edges_around_vertex(char* vertex_name, char*
entity_list_name);
```
// returns entity list containing all the edges adjacent to the vertex

```
logical save_body(char* body_name, char* file_name, logical
text_or_bin);
```
// saves the data structure of the body to the given file with text (TRUE) or
// binary (FALSE) option

```
logical restore_body(char* body_name, char* file_name,
logical text_or_bin);
```
// restore data structure in file to given body, specify text (TRUE) or
// binary (FALSE)

```
logical note_state(char* state_name);
```
// makes a record of the present state and the changes from the previous note

```
logical change_state(char* change_name);
```
// if this change applies to the present model it applies the rollback change
// to it

```
logical delete_change(char* change_name);
```
// deletes the record of a change made

C.3 GEOMETRIC INQUIRY FUNCTIONS

```
logical get_body_volume(char* body_name, double* voladd);
```
// gets the volume of a given body

```
logical body_bound(char* body_name, char* bound_name);
```
// returns box enveloping the body

```
logical box_lposition(char* box_name, char*
lowposition_name);
```
// returns lowermost vertex of the box

```
logical box_hposition(char* box_name, char*
highposition_name);
```
// returns highest position of the box

```
logical position_x(char* position_name, double* x);
```
// returns x value of given position

```
logical position_y(char* position_name, double* y);
```
// returns y value of given position

```
logical position_z(char* position_name, double* z);
```
// returns z value of given position

```
logical lump_bound(char* lump_name, char* bound_name);
```
// returns box surrounding lump

```
logical face_sense(char* face_name, int* sens);
```
// returns integer telling whether outward face normal is the same as the face
// equation normal or opposite direction (sens = 0 for forward 1 for reversed)

```
logical edge_CURVE(char* edge_name, char* CURVE_name);
```
// returns the CURVE associated with the edge

```
logical coedge_sense(char* coedge_name, int* sens);
logical coedge_curve(char* coedge_name, char* pcurve_name);
```
// returns parametric curve of coedge
```
logical pcurve_CURVE(char* pcurve_name, char* CURVE_name);
```
// returns the curve on which the parametric curve lies
```
logical CURVE_curve(char* CURVE_name, char* curve_name);
```
// returns the curve of the CURVE
// all three above functions have to be used in conjunction
```
logical pcurve_parpos(char* pcurve_name, char* parpos_name,
double at);
```
// returns the parameter range of the parametric curve
```
logical curve_position(char* curve_name, char* position_name,
double param);
```
// given parameter on curve returns position of point
```
logical curve_dir(char* curve_name, char* vector_name, double
param);
```
// returns the tangent vector on the curve at a particular parameter
```
logical curve_type(char* curve_name, int* typ);
```
// returns type of curve
```
logical vector_x(char* vector_name, double* x);
```
// returns x component of vector
```
logical vector_y(char* vector_name, double* y);
```
// returns y component of vector
```
logical vector_z(char* vector_name, double* z);
```
// returns z component of vector
```
logical vector_pos_add(char* vector_name, char* pos1_name,
char* pos2_name);
```
// adds a vector to a position and returns the final position
```
logical vec_negate(char* vector_name);
```
// negates a vector and returns it;
```
logical create_vector(char* vector_name, char* pos1_name,
char* pos2_name);
```
// defines a vector as a subtraction of two positions
```
logical curve_interval(char* curve_name, char*
interval_name);
```
// returns the parametric interval of the curve segment
```
logical interval_low(char* interval_name, double* low);
```
// returns the lower parameters of the interval
```
logical interval_high(char* interval_name, double* high);
```
// returns the higher parameter of the interval
```
logical edge_CURVE(char* coedge_name, char* CURVE_name);
```
// returns the curve on which the edge lies

```
logical vertex_point(char* vertex_name, char* point_name);
// returns the point on which the vertex lies
```
// returns the point on which the vertex lies

```
logical point_position(char* point_name, char*
position_name);
```
// return the position of the point

```
logical face_SURFACE(char* face_name, char* SURFACE_name);
```
// returns the surface on which the face lies

```
logical SURFACE_surface(char* SURFACE_name, char*
surface_name);
```
// return the surface of the surface

```
logical surf_type(char* surface_name, int* typ);
```
// returns integer giving type of surface 1 for plane, 2 for cylindrical

```
logical surf_pos_normal(char* surface_name, char*
position_name, char* normal_name);
```
// returns the normal to the surface from a particular position

```
logical surf_pos_point(char* surface_name, char*
position_name, char* returned_name);
```
// returns the position on a surface intersecting the normal from the given
// position to the surface

```
logical surf_pos_param(char* surface_name, char*
position_name, char* param_name);
```
// given position on surface returns its parameter value

```
logical param_u(char* param_name, char* u_param);
```
// returns u value of parameter

```
logical param_v(char* param_name, char* v_param);
```
// returns v value of parameter

```
logical param_double(char* param_name, double* value);
```
// returns value of parameter

```
logical surf_par_position(char* surface_name, char*
param_name, char* position_name);
```
// returns position of surface at given parameter

```
logical surf_par_normal(char* surface_name, char* param_name,
char* normal_name);
```
// returns the normal at a particular parameter

```
logical surf_test_point(char* surface_name, char*
position_name, logical* in_or_out);
```
// returns integer value telling if point lies in or out of the surface

```
logical plane_normal(char* plane_name, char* normal_name);
```
// returns the normal of a plane

```
logical plane_point(char* plane_name, char* point_name);
```
// returns the point on a plane

```
logical cone_point(char* cone_name, char* point_name);
```
// returns the center of the the cone or cylinder

```
logical cone_normal(char* cone_name, char* axis_name);
```
// returns the axis of the cone or the cylinder

```
logical cone_major_axis(char* cone_name, char*
major_axis_name);
```
// returns the axis of the major axis of the cone or cylinder

```
logical ellipse_center(char* ellipse_name, char* point_name);
```
// returns the center of the the ellipse

```
logical ell_major_axis(char* ellipse_name, char*
major_axis_name);
```
// returns the axis of the major axis of the ellipse

```
logical face_type(char* entity_name, int* ent_type);
```
// returns the type of entity

```
logical entity_num(char* ent_list_name, int num,char*
return_ent);
```
// returns the particular entity number in the list

```
logical return_cross(char* first_vec_name, char*
sec_vec_name, char* cross);
```
// creates and returns the cross product vector

```
logical return_len(char* vec_name, double* len);
```
// returns the length of the vector

```
logical return_dot(char* vec1_name, char* vec2_name, double*
dot);
```
// returns the dot product

```
logical return_unit(char* vec_name, char* unit_vec_name);
```
// returns unit_vector

```
logical body_trans(char* body_name, char* TRANS_name);
```
// returns transformation of body

```
logical TRANS_trans(char* TRANS_name, char* trans_name);
```
// returns the transformation of TRANS

```
logical TRANS_set(char* TRANS_name, char* trans_name);
```
// sets TRANS to transformation given

```
logical mult_trans(char* first_name, char* sec_name, char*
mult_name);
```
// creates a new transformation which is a product of given transformation

```
logical set_trans(char* body_name, char* transf_name);
```
// sets the body transformation given a transformation

```
logical vector_sub(char* first_vector, char* second_vec,
char* subtract_vec);
```
// creates a vector as a subtraction of two vectors

BIBLIOGRPAHY

Pherwani, P., 1993, Dynamic binding of features and solid modelers, M.S. thesis, Department of Mechanical and Aerospace Engineering, Arizona State University.

INDEX

609

Printed and bound by CPI Group (UK) Ltd, Croydon, CR0 4YY

27/10/2024

14580314-0005